The Children's
of Philade.

Book of
Pregnancy
and
Child Care

The Children's Hospital of Philadelphia

Book of Pregnancy and Child Care

PATRICK S. PASQUARIELLO, JR., M.D.

Senior Editor

Director, Diagnostic Center, The Children's Hospital of Philadelphia
Professor of Pediatrics, University of Pennsylvania School of Medicine

John Wiley & Sons, Inc.

New York • Chichester • Weinheim • Brisbane • Singapore • Toronto

Library of Congress Cataloging-in-Publication Data:
The Children's Hospital of Philadelphia book of pregnancy and child
   care / Patrick S. Pasquariello, senior editor.
       p.   cm.
   Rev. ed. of: The Great Ormond Street new baby and child care book
/ Tessa Hilton. London : Vermilion, 1997.
    ISBN 0-471-32012-9 (pbk. : alk. paper)
    1. Infants—Care—Popular works.   2. Child care—Popular works.
3. Child development—Popular works.   I. Pasquariello, Patrick S.
II. Hilton, Tessa. Great Ormond Street new baby and child care
book.   III. Children's Hospital of Philadelphia.   IV. Title: Book of
baby and child care.
RJ61.C5495 1998
649'.1—DC21   98-39009
                                        CIP

Printed in the United States of America.

10 9 8 7 6 5 4 3 2 1

Contents

8 Sleep, Wakefulness, and Crying 251

9 Your Baby and Child's Growth and Development 277

10 Your Baby's Developing Senses 295

11 Language 311

12 Play and Early Education 333

13 Toilet Training 363

16 Doctors and Medications 467

17 Common Health Problems 491

Foreword

Prior to my becoming surgeon general of the United States in 1981, I spent thirty-six years as surgeon-in-chief of The Children's Hospital of Philadelphia. During that period I visited the Hospital for Sick Children, Great Ormond Street, London, many times. Often I saw my fellow Children's Hospital staff members there on sabbatical leaves. Also, when I came home, it was not uncommon for me to bump into my British colleagues, who would spend time at Philadelphia's Children's Hospital.

The history of the two hospitals has been intertwined for 143 years. It goes back to the early 1850s, when Dr. Francis Lewis, a young Philadelphia physician, completed his residency at Pennsylvania Hospital, the nation's oldest. He then went to London on vacation and visited Great Ormond Street. Dr. Lewis was intrigued and impressed with the concept of a hospital that cared only for sick infants and children. The Hospital for Sick Children, which had opened its doors in 1852, was the first in the English-speaking world. Dr. Lewis, who had been appalled by the poverty, high infant mortality rate, squalor, and disease that afflicted Philadelphia's children, resolved to establish a similar hospital on his return.

Independently wealthy, Dr. Lewis persuaded two friends to join him in the endeavor. On November 23, 1855, an ad appeared in the *Philadelphia Ledger*, now known as the *Philadelphia Inquirer*.

> The Children's Hospital—located on Blight Street, running from Pine to Lombard, below Broad, is now open for the reception of Patients. Children suffering from Acute Diseases and Accidents will be received free of charge. A Dispensary for sick children is also attached to the Hospital and will be open every day (Sundays excepted) from 11 to 12 o'clock, when advice and medicines will be given free of charge.
>
> [signed]   T. Hewson Bache
>   Francis W. Lewis
>   R. A. F. Penrose
>   Attending Physicians

So began the specialty of pediatrics in the United States.

Children's Hospital has had the longest unbroken record of service devoted exclusively to children in the history of pediatric hospitals in the United States. Thus, too, began a relationship with Great Ormond Street that was reactivated shortly after the Philadelphia institution observed its Centennial in 1955. At that time, an annual year-long exchange of young physicians was established; it continued until the late 1980s, when new laws were enacted in Pennsylvania concerning all physicians educated abroad.

The Museum and Archives Service of what is now known as Great Ormond Street Hospital for Children NHS Trust and the historical exhibit of The Children's Hospital of Philadelphia contain letters, gifts, photos, and artifacts that have been presented over the years. In 1974, when the present building was dedicated in Philadelphia, Her Royal Highness Princess Margaret represented her sister, Queen Elizabeth, at the event because she was a patron of the London hospital. (I gave the dedication address.) The Children's Hospital's highest honor, its Gold Medal, was awarded to the London hospital during the U.S. Bicentennial in 1976. At that time the two institutions rededicated themselves to the well-being of children by signing the Charter for the Advancement of Children's Health. It was signed by the late Richard D. Wood, chairman of the Board of Managers of The Children's Hospital of Philadelphia, and Jean A. Cortner, M.D., then physician-in-chief. Great Ormond Street was represented by Mrs. Audrey Callahan, wife of the prime minister at that time, and J. Alastair Dudgeon, dean of the Institute of Child Health, the research arm of the hospital.

The *Book of Pregnancy and Child Care* prepared by The Children's Hospital of Philadelphia with Great Ormond Street Hospital for Children, London, is a logical collaboration between two institutions that maintain a relationship to this day with visits between executives and medical people. Both are world-renowned hospitals. Parents and other readers will find a comprehensive presentation that focuses on children ages zero to five. Its commonsense approach is reassuring to new parents and easily understood by everyone. The senior editor, Patrick S. Pasquariello, Jr., M.D., has been associated with the Philadelphia hospital for more than thirty-five years. He has been called the "pediatrician's pediatrician" for good reason. At one point, when we had young babies and children, almost all of the Children's Hospital medical staff used Dr. Pat, as he is known, as the physician for their children. His associate editors have also brought to the book skills usually used in speaking with parents so they understand everything with ease.

The book is comfortably organized so that parents can read it completely or can check the index for specific areas of health. The material covers day-to-day ways to keep babies and young children healthy as well as caring for them when they are ill. The material is based on documented pediatric practices and research.

Perhaps, most important, the subject matter is presented so that working parents and child care staff members can rapidly find what they need. The sections on illnesses and hospitalization are comprehensive.

In these harried times, parents want to know as much as possible. This book fills the bill.

C. Everett Koop, M.D., Sc.D.
Senior Scholar, C. Everett Koop Institute
@ Dartmouth College
Surgeon General of the United States
1981–1989

Introduction

This is an easy-to-read book for busy parents who want to have the healthiest children possible. The Children's Hospital of Philadelphia, together with the Great Ormond Street Children's Hospital, London, have made every effort to produce a book about babies and children under five that can help parents prepare themselves prior to each stage of their child's life or be used as a reference book when needed. It is organized so that grandparents or child-care workers can look up necessary information with ease.

Patient care is the cornerstone on which the Philadelphia institution has based its work. Its teaching and research are known worldwide. For instance, during a five-year period almost three hundred physicians from forty-seven countries came to the Children's Hospital under their own sponsorship or their countries' to learn how our pediatricians and pediatric subspecialists care for healthy children or those with special needs. During the same period dozens of members of the Children's Hospital's faculty traveled the world to teach physicians unable to come to this country. Research at The Children's Hospital of Philadelphia covers every aspect of child health. The program is the second largest in the United States, with emphasis on scientific investigation in the neurosciences, immunology, cancer, infectious diseases, and fetal development.

Great Ormond Street is a renowned hospital, as are its teaching and research programs, the latter through its link to the Institute of Child Health, which is said to conduct more research into child health and illness than any other institution in the United Kingdom. Its teaching is equally well known. These two organizations have combined their expertise to bring you the most complete guide available on pregnancy, birth, and caring for your child.

The book is organized into twenty chapters, beginning with pregnancy and progressing through each aspect of your child's development and health. There is a section on play and early education. A list of resources with their national addresses and telephone numbers is included at the back. It is divided so you can find general information or information for a child with special needs. Most of the organizations listed have local chapters or branches; your own area telephone book may be helpful.

I am very grateful to The Children's Hospital of Philadelphia's former surgeon-in-chief, C. Everett Koop, M.D., Sc.D., who spent his entire surgical career with us and left to become U.S. surgeon general (1981–1989), for his foreword to this book; to Shirley Bonnem, vice president, The Children's Hospital of Philadelphia, who was our interface with Ebury Press, London, and the American publisher, John Wiley and Sons, Inc.; to Christina Brown, director, Child Life Program, The

Children's Hospital of Philadelphia; to Fred Citron, director, Montgomery Early Learning Centers; to Ilene Rosen, child-care writer; to Kim Voight, who transcribed and corrected many of the chapters; to Zeb Haani, who assisted in research and transcription; and to Esha Bhatia, M.A., director, Partners for Child Passenger Safety and codirector, TraumaLink.

My particular appreciation is extended to those clinicians who completed this project under the pressure of their full clinical schedules and teaching or research responsibilities. All are members of the medical staff of The Children's Hospital of Philadelphia.

Judy C. Bernbaum, M.D., director, Neonatal Follow-up Program.

Nathan Blum, M.D., director, Center for Complex Medical Management, Children's Seashore House of The Children's Hospital of Philadelphia.

Deborah A. Driscoll, M.D., director, Adolescent Gynecology, Hospital of the University of Pennsylvania

Susan Friedman, M.D., director, Well Newborn Nursery.

Mark R. Magnusson, M.D., Ph.D., associate director, Diagnostic Center; medical director, Home Care, Case Management.

Donna Sammaritano, M.D., medical director, Primary Care Center at 34th Street.

Flaura Koplin Winston, M.D., Ph.D., director, TraumaLink.

Kathleen Zsolway, D.O., director, Faculty Practice.

Patrick S. Pasquariello, Jr., M.D.
director, Diagnostic Center
acting director, Division of General Pediatrics

CHAPTER 1

Before Pregnancy Begins

Why does preconceptual care matter? • Environmental factors
Genetic factors • Genetic counseling

Health is the best birthday present any parent could ask for their new baby. No wonder that from time immemorial the first question at the moment of birth, asked in a look, a touch, or in words, has always been: "Is my baby all right?" Most people know that good health begins before birth and that it's very important that the mother-to-be take care of herself and her unborn baby during pregnancy. But did you know that good health care can begin even before conception? It may seem strange to think that both men and women can help to give their baby a healthier start in life even before life begins for their baby, but it is true.

Once you start planning and looking forward to starting a family, you slowly begin to see the world around you in a different way. Pregnant women, babies in strollers, and even advertisements for products such as diapers and baby carriages, which you may previously not have noticed, suddenly come sharply into focus. But while the reality of a baby is still a daydream, your thoughts tend to turn inward and dwell most on how your lives will change. Women tend to think about how pregnancy will change their bodies, and what the birth will be like. Both men and women wonder how becoming parents may change their relationships and way of life. It takes a concerted effort as well as the right supply of information to realize that how you live and look after your body now can matter to this child who exists only in your imagination. If you are reading this book before pregnancy has begun, you have an extra opportunity to try to stack the odds in favor of a head start in health for your future family.

Preconceptual care means both partners cutting known risks before trying to conceive, to make it as likely as possible that the egg and sperm that will grow into an embryo are healthy and normal, and also to create the best environment for that embryo to grow and develop into a healthy and sound baby.

Why Does Preconceptual Care Matter?

Your baby's first twelve weeks of life in the uterus, or womb, are the most critical in many respects. During this time all of the essential organs are being formed, and by three months most are beginning to function. However, the majority of women do not even suspect they are pregnant until they miss a menstrual period, and even if they are very prompt in going to their physician and having their pregnancy confirmed, they are unlikely to have their first prenatal appointment much before they are eight or nine weeks pregnant—and often much later than that.

If this seems disconcerting, take comfort in the fact that the vast majority of babies develop and grow safely and healthily. But what doctors have now discovered is that there are easy measures every couple can take that will reduce risks even further. The idea of trying to minimize risks to a baby even before he is conceived is relatively new, but it makes sense to avoid environmental factors we now know can pose a hazard to the unborn baby and to follow simple guidelines we know to be beneficial.

That is not to say that every unborn baby who is exposed to such factors will be damaged in some way. Like adults, some unborn babies are more susceptible or more vulnerable at certain times and in certain ways than others. There are babies who seem to have incurred only slight risks before birth, yet, for reasons that may not be fully known, have sadly suffered some degree of damage. And there are babies who have been exposed to very many risks, sometimes considered serious, who have been born perfectly normal and healthy. In between babies born with a specific abnormality and babies born free of such damage there is a wide spectrum of varying shades of gray in terms of fitness and health. A baby who weighs less than 5 lb 8 oz (2,500 gm) at birth is classified as having a low birth weight. These small babies are more vulnerable in the early weeks and months of life and can take time to catch up with larger babies. We know that some environmental factors often can combine to prevent babies growing properly in the uterus and that some of these factors can be avoided.

Because there is no way of telling in advance which babies are likely to be vulnerable, it makes sense for all prospective parents to try to avoid risks within their control. Preconceptual care means weighting the odds in favor of a baby who is able to realize his full mental and physical genetic potential. If you plan to have a baby, here are some simple precautions you can take toward helping your child, even before you try to conceive. Six months ahead of conception is not too soon to start thinking about your health, but certainly try to consider these points at least three months before you hope to get pregnant.

Environmental Factors

Use Physical Methods of Contraception for Three Months Before

There has never been any suggestion that taking the Pill increases the risk of miscarriage or the possibility of any birth defects in later pregnancies. However, because it takes time for the effects of the Pill to disappear fully from a woman's system and for her normal hormonal pattern to reestablish itself, some doctors advise coming off the Pill three months before trying for a baby and using a physical method of contraception instead—that is, a condom or diaphragm.

What is the risk to a baby if the woman accidentally becomes pregnant and continues taking the Pill during pregnancy? The good news is that in most recent studies—and several of them have been large—the great majority of cases have not found any link between taking the Pill during pregnancy and birth defects in general or heart defects in particular.

Women who become pregnant accidentally when they have an intrauterine device (IUD) fitted are 40 percent more likely to miscarry, but those pregnancies that do continue appear to have just as good a chance of a normal outcome as any other. Pregnancy with an IUD in place, however, carries a greater risk that it may be ectopic—that is, the fertilized egg implants in some place other than the uterus, usually a Fallopian tube. However, as long as the pregnancy is in the right place, it is generally thought better to remove the coil early in pregnancy and risk miscarriage rather than leave it in the uterus.

The effect of taking the morning-after Pill (emergency contraception) if the pregnancy subsequently continues is not yet fully known because most women who try this go on to have a termination anyway if the Pill does not work. Most studies suggest that the baby has a good chance of remaining unharmed, however.

If you became pregnant accidentally, you may naturally worry more about risks you have unknowingly incurred and feel guilty. You may also feel very ambivalent about changing your lifestyle for the sake of an unplanned baby's health. If this is the case for you, be sure to seek extra support and an opportunity to talk about your feelings. Your physician is a good person to start with, although much depends on your relationship. A midwife, prenatal clinic staff, or friends also can be helpful. For more on mixed feelings during pregnancy see the section "Mixed Emotions—How You Feel During Pregnancy" in chapter 2.

Stop Smoking

I tried many times to give up smoking and actually stopped once or twice, but I felt it was really a positive reason to give up when we decided to have a baby. I carried a mental picture of a tiny fetus shriveling up in a smoke-filled womb— I know that sounds a bit morbid, but it did the trick.

It is now well documented that smoking can prevent babies from growing properly in the uterus, so that they are likely to be smaller and more vulnerable when they are born. Because smoking cuts the amount of oxygen that is being supplied to the baby through the placenta, it also puts the baby at risk before birth.

Giving up smoking, however, is very difficult because nicotine is highly addictive, and if you are a confirmed smoker you will need a lot of help and support to stop. It is important that your partner gives up as well—partly because it is unreasonable to expect you to try to give it up alone, which will make it twice as hard for you, and partly because you can inhale a lot of nicotine just by sitting in a smoky environment. Even women who do not smoke should avoid spending much time in places where people are smoking. Smoking may also make some men less fertile by affecting the numbers and mobility of their sperm.

Do not wait until you know you are pregnant before trying to give up smoking—your baby will already have spent his most vulnerable weeks suffering the effects. It also takes a few weeks, depending on how heavily you smoke, for the effects to clear from your system. If you or your partner feel unsure about making such an effort for a baby who does not exist yet, it may help to remember you are doing something that will be for your own benefit as well. You can find books and pamphlets on the subject at your local library, or your physician may be interested in trying to help you. Some people have found hypnosis or acupuncture helpful. Nicotine patches and other forms of medication are now available to assist you in discontinuing the smoking habit.

Cut Down on Drinking

It used to be thought that only heavy drinking could harm unborn babies, but research has now shown that even moderate drinking makes women more likely to miscarry and give birth to smaller, more vulnerable babies. These low-birth-weight babies can continue to be disadvantaged for some time. One study of babies born to moderate drinkers showed that at eight months old, the babies were still smaller and less developmentally and physically advanced than a similar age group whose mothers did not drink at all.

What is moderate drinking? Research has suggested that "moderate" means two drinks a day, meaning two glasses of wine or two ounces of alcohol. Six or more drinks a day puts the baby at risk of the fetal alcohol syndrome. These children are seriously damaged before birth and have abnormal and distinctive facial characteristics. They fail to thrive and can be delayed in their development. In addition, they have abnormal nails and can have heart defects. The best advice is to abstain or to drink very little from the time of the last period before you try for a baby until the end of the pregnancy. As with all hazards, the baby is most vulnerable in the early days and weeks of life, before you even know you are pregnant. If you find it hard to cut back, your partner should support you and abstain, too. If he drinks heavily, this could make him infertile—one estimate was that three to four bottles of beer a day could be enough to reduce the sperm count of some men to infertility level. Fertility should return after a few weeks of not drinking.

Women sometimes worry if they have been on a binge and drunk very heavily when they did not know they were pregnant. Unfortunately, as with many risks, there is no way of knowing if the unborn baby has been affected.

Illicit Drugs

There is increasing evidence that marijuana, Ecstasy, and so-called recreational drugs can harm the unborn child. It is best to avoid such drugs before conception and during pregnancy.

Eat Well

Eating a good, balanced diet with fresh food and not too much junk food is probably even more important before conceiving than during pregnancy. This is because the unborn baby is most vulnerable in the first three months, while the organs are still being formed. It is in these first fragile days and weeks of life, when many women do not even know they are pregnant, that nutritional reserves of vitamins and minerals probably matter most. Later, in the middle and last months of pregnancy, the unborn baby is able to become a far more effective parasite: The fetus will take what he needs from the mother, even if it is at her expense. So although, of course, a woman is better off if she is not on a poor diet or ill, the baby will usually still take what he needs to grow and thrive. Exceptions may be babies who are already vulnerable because of other factors, so all women should try to eat well during pregnancy.

What does eating well mean? In recent years we have been bombarded with theories about the best possible diet, but the basic rules are really very simple:

- Balance your diet by eating something from the five main food groups every day. These groups are milk and milk products; meat and high-protein foods; fruit and vegetables; cereal and grain products; and fats and oils.

- Eat fresh foods where possible, rather than prepackaged or convenience foods, and cut down on sugary foods.

- Follow your appetite and do not eat more than you need. For more discussion about weight gain see the section "Eating Well and Weight Gain" in chapter 2.

With the exception of iron and folic acid, it is not usually necessary to take any extra vitamins or mineral supplements unless prescribed by your doctor. Women planning to conceive should take a 400 mcg (micrograms) folic acid tablet daily, ideally for three months before conception and up to twelve weeks of pregnancy. This may help to reduce the risk of spina bifida and similar defects. The risk of having a baby with such a deficit is low, but it is thought to be even lower if this medication is taken. Mothers who already have a child with spina bifida should definitely take 5 mg daily, as this halves the risk of recurrence. These tablets are available from your local pharmacy but should be taken only under the supervision of your physician. Folic acid is usually included in vitamin preparations aimed at pregnant women. It is sensible to avoid certain foods that might be contaminated with salmonella or listeria. See the section "Eating Well and Weight Gain" in chapter 2 for more information on salmonella and listeria.

Regarding vegetarian and vegan diets, growing babies require a lot of protein. If you eat eggs, fish, and cheese, you can easily take in as much as required. But vegans, who avoid these foods as well as cutting out meat, need to take special care. If you do not drink milk or eat milk products, then substitute soy milk and soy foods. Eat a good supply of nuts and beans daily to get the protein you need. Vitamin B_{12} is found almost entirely in animal foods, so ask your doctor and nutritionist about supplements.

Do Not Diet Before Pregnancy
Do not go on any kind of diet in the three months before trying to become pregnant or during pregnancy, unless on medical advice. Fertility declines as women lose weight, and it has been found that some women become infertile at weights we used to think ideal. Studies also suggest that the babies of women who are very underweight before conception are possibly more at risk. With any kind of restrictive diet there is a danger of missing out on some nutrients because such diets are not balanced, but rely on excluding complete food groups entirely. At the other end of the scale, obesity can also lead to infertility—so if you have a weight problem, see your doctor to try to sort it out well before you begin to think about having children. For more on weight gain and pregnancy see "Eating Well and Weight Gain" in chapter 2.

Think About Pollutants
If you work with any kind of chemicals, find out what they are before getting pregnant—you can ask your doctors or possibly the human resources office at your workplace for advice. We still do not know a great deal about the unborn baby's vulnerability to many environmental factors, though studies suggest that people working with anaesthetic gases and other materials that have strong odors, or

indeed the wives of men working with them, may run a higher risk of miscarriage and possibly even some birth defects. There also has been concern about the safety of working with VDUs (visual display units) during pregnancy, but there is no good research showing that a higher risk of miscarriage exists from such exposure. More studies obviously need to be done in this field.

Sauna Baths and Hot Tubs
It is possible that prolonged very high body temperatures can affect the early development of the unborn baby, especially the brain. So if regular sauna baths are your habit, eliminate them when you start trying to get pregnant and during the pregnancy. However, there is no suggestion that ordinary hot baths, warm atmosphere, hot weather, low fever, or short spikes of high fever can be damaging.

Do Not Take Any Drugs Without Medical Supervision
The safest rule is not to take any drugs at all, whether over the counter, prescribed, or illicit drugs such as cannabis, heroin, or any other "street" drugs, either while trying to conceive or during pregnancy. Always tell a doctor who is prescribing drugs for you if there is a chance you may be pregnant. Having said that, there will be some women who need to take drugs to control illness during pregnancy. Those with an existing condition, such as epilepsy, heart disease, or diabetes, should always see their doctor before becoming pregnant to discuss how their condition can best be controlled and what drugs to take. It may be a good idea to ask the physician who normally supervises the control of your illness for a referral to a knowledgeable obstetrician for a consultation before becoming pregnant. Women who become ill during pregnancy should always make sure that whoever is treating them knows they are pregnant or, just as important, that they might be pregnant.

X Rays
X rays are best avoided in the first three months of pregnancy, and radiologists usually ask if there is any possibility of pregnancy. For this reason, many operators avoid giving X rays in the latter half of a woman's menstrual cycle. See the section "Avoid X Rays in Early Pregnancy" in chapter 2 for more on this.

Stay Healthy
Of course, we cannot always avoid illness, and there is no need to get neurotic about catching the odd cold or cough, but in general it makes sense to avoid contact with any infectious disease as far as possible.

Rubella (also known as German measles) is the most dangerous of these, and is dealt with in the following section. However, apart from rubella, there are a few other diseases that are known to pose possible risks—cytomegalovirus infection (CMV) is one such. The only symptoms of this virus may be vague aches and pains and possibly fever. It is thought that this virus may infect as many as 1 percent of unborn babies, and of these infected babies, about 10 percent may suffer permanent damage. As with rubella, the effect is likely to be most serious when a pregnant woman catches the disease in the first three months of pregnancy. It can cause various degrees of mental deficiency, blindness, and possibly deafness. At the moment there is no preventive vaccine, but research is still under way, and there may be one in the future.

A less common risk to the unborn baby is toxoplasmosis—a parasitic infection that causes fever and swollen glands. It is thought that a significant number of babies a year are born throughout the world seriously damaged as a result of their mothers being infected by toxoplasmosis. It is thought that this infection can occur from eating undercooked or raw meat. Another source of infection is from exposure to infected cats because there is a particularly resistant form of toxoplasma that is peculiar to members of the cat family. Do not get rid of the family cat, but it makes sense for a pregnant woman to avoid cleaning out a cat's litter tray; to wear gloves when handling raw meat or gardening; not to eat raw or undercooked meat; and to wash fruits well. She should see her doctor if she has enlarged glands, especially those in the neck, and has malaise and fever. When a diagnosis has been confirmed, specific medications are available to treat this infection.

Check your immunity against rubella, ideally before conceiving.

I had two perfectly normal children, but during my third pregnancy I had what my doctor thought was scarlet fever in the early weeks. My daughter was born deaf and has only partial sight in one eye. I was never tested to see if I was immune to rubella in my first pregnancies, and the third time I had a test later in pregnancy, which, of course, showed by then that I had had it.

If a woman has rubella in the first three months of pregnancy, it can cause devastating damage to her baby. This is easily preventable, because a simple blood test can show if a woman has immunity to the disease, and if not, she can have a vaccination to protect her. All children have been routinely vaccinated in schools since 1970, but sadly many still slip through the cracks for various reasons, with the result that infants are born deaf, blind, and mentally and physically handicapped because their mothers were never protected. All children should receive the vaccine after twelve months of age, which will give them temporary protection against rubella and reduce the chances of exposing pregnant women to the disease. A booster of the MMR (measles, mumps, rubella) should be administered between four and six years of age. It is not enough to rely on the fact that you think you had rubella, because there are at least twelve other viruses with similar symptoms. It is also possible to get rubella and not to be immune and even, in rare cases, to be vaccinated and still not have immunity. It is therefore prudent, if you are considering pregnancy, to ask your physician to arrange a blood test to check your immunity and for you to have a vaccination if this proves necessary. You must not get pregnant for three months following the vaccination.

Sexually Transmitted Diseases Should Be Treated
Syphilis, gonorrhea, hepatitis B, genital herpes, and human immunodeficiency virus (HIV) all represent serious risks to the unborn baby. If there is any chance you may be suffering from one or more of these diseases, or have had one or more in the past, you should be tested and get help by going to your doctor, or to physicians spe-

cially trained in infectious diseases; such specialists usually are associated with major hospitals.

Syphilis can cause a miscarriage or a stillbirth or, if the baby does survive, there may be growth retardation or the infant may develop abnormalities of other organs such as the brain, bones, liver, etc. Because it is possible to have syphilis and not know it, all pregnant women under care are routinely screened early in the first trimester of the pregnancy and then again late in the third trimester.

Gonorrhea is more common than syphilis and, again, can go undetected. Nine of ten women have no symptoms, but if they do occur, they can manifest as pain when urinating, a foul-smelling vaginal discharge, and sometimes abdominal pain if it has spread to cause internal pelvic infection. Gonorrhea increases the risk of miscarriage and prematurity, and the baby may be ill and not grow properly after the birth. There is also a serious risk that the baby's eyes may be infected during delivery, leading to serious inflammation and possibly scarring and blindness if untreated. During pregnancy a woman who has gonorrhea can usually be effectively treated with antibiotics.

Genital herpes usually only represents a risk to the baby if the virus is active during a vaginal delivery, though, like any virus during pregnancy, an initial attack can cause miscarriage. If the virus is active, the baby can become infected as it passes through the vagina during delivery, and though it is not known how many babies do get herpes this way, of those who do, more than half do not survive unless they are treated promptly and aggressively with specific medications. After delivery the baby may develop a rash and be quite ill. Of those who live, half are likely to suffer serious damage to the eyes and nervous system. Unfortunately, there is still no cure for genital herpes, which initially presents with fever and painful blisters around the entrance to the vagina or other exposed areas. Subsequent attacks are usually less severe, and it can only be passed to a partner by having sex while the blisters are present. The same applies to the risk of infecting a baby, so women who have a history of genital herpes will usually have their babies delivered by cesarean section. Symptoms can be controlled, though the disease cannot be cured, by taking a drug called acyclovir. If you have the condition, you need careful counseling from medical personnel familiar with treating infectious diseases. You can also get help from your local health center, local medical society, or the American Medical Association.

Human immunodeficiency virus infection (HIV) is becoming much more prevalent in the United States, and most hospitals advise that pregnant women get the appropriate blood test to check for this. It is important to have expert counselling before you decide to go ahead with the test so you are fully prepared for the implications if the test is positive. Up to 15 percent of babies born to HIV-positive women (those with HIV infection) will have caught the disease from their mothers while in the womb. Because of transfer of antibodies from mother to baby during pregnancy, doctors cannot always be sure if the baby has been infected in this way until the baby is about nine months of age. If you are at risk of being HIV-positive it is important to have the test, as drugs can be given during pregnancy to reduce the risk of your baby also becoming HIV-positive. In some cases having your baby by cesarean section may also reduce the risk. Bottle-feeding rather than breast-feeding is essential, as the HIV virus is carried in breast milk. HIV infection in babies and young children is a very serious condition, so it is important to know how to prevent it.

Hepatitis B virus (HBV) is transmitted through blood or body fluids such as wound drainage, semen, cervical secretions, and saliva. Transmission from mother to infant during the perinatal period occurs in infants born to mothers who have chronic HBV infection. As many as 90 percent of infants born of these mothers will develop chronic HBV infection. If not infected during the perinatal period, these infants remain at risk of acquiring chronic HBV infection by person-to-person transmission during the first five years of life. Infants born of mothers with chronic HBV infection should receive hepatitis B immune globulin as protection against the development of acute HBV infections. Active immunization with the hepatitis B vaccine should be carried out simultaneously to provide long-lasting protection.

Genetic Factors

Many people are understandably confused about the exact meaning of words describing disabilities. "Congenital" simply means "born with." Therefore, a congenital disability is one a child is born with. This can be because of genetic or environmental factors, or a combination of both. It is estimated that 25 percent of all congenital abnormalities are genetic, 10 percent are due to environmental causes (including drugs), and the remaining 65 percent are due to a combination of factors. As a general rule, the earlier the fault or error in development occurs (whether because of genetic or environmental factors), the more serious the damage. If that seems to be an upsetting thought, you might consider the reverse, that once an organ has been properly formed, it rarely suffers damage, regardless of what happens to the mother. If there is the possibility of a genetic risk, you will likely be referred to a geneticist for genetic counseling. See the section "Genetic Counseling" later in this chapter for more information.

How Some Genetic Mistakes Happen

Genetic abnormalities can be either inherited from one or both parents as they are passed on in the chromosomes carried by the egg from the mother or the sperm from the father. When genetic abnormalities occur for the first time in either the particular egg or sperm involved in the conception of the unborn baby, this produces a "fresh mutation." Why do such mistakes happen in the first place? Although some contributory factors are known (such as the mother's age in certain chromosomal abnormalities), a mutation is essentially an unlucky accident when, instead of genes being perfectly reproduced each time, there has been a copying error, so that an egg or sperm or one set of cells in the early embryo carries a small mistake, which goes on to be multiplied with each cell division. We may not always know *why* a genetic mistake happens, but we do know *how* it happens. Every individual is made up of billions of cells, each derived originally from the fertilized egg, and each cell has a center called a "nucleus." Inside the nucleus is the genetic material divided up into twenty-three pairs of chromosomes. Along each chromosome are arranged thousands of genes—these are the chemical instructions that are made up of something called "deoxyribonucleic acid," or DNA for short. Just before a cell divides, the chromosomes can be seen under a microscope—they look like irregular sausage shapes—but the genes are too small to be seen.

To study a person's chromosomes, geneticists need to be able to grow cells in the laboratory from a sample of blood, or less commonly skin or bone marrow. Just at the point when the cells divide and the chromosomes can be seen most clearly, the process is halted so a photograph can be taken of the preparation. The photographed chromosomes from a single cell are cut out and arranged in their pairs in what is called a "karyotype."

Every cell of the body has forty-six chromosomes (twenty-three pairs), except the eggs in a woman and sperm in a man. These are formed by a special cell division called "meiosis," which results in each egg or sperm having only a single set of twenty-three chromosomes. When these two single sets come together at fertilization, they become a complete set of forty-six again and the beginning of a new individual.

The Sex Chromosomes

Of the twenty-three pairs of chromosomes in a cell nucleus, chromosome pairs one to twenty-two are common to both males and females, but the twenty-third pair determines the sex of that individual. In a woman there is an XX pair, one coming from her father and the other from her mother, but a man has one X and one Y chromosome. As we explained, the special cell division called "meiosis" results in eggs and sperms having only a single set of chromosomes, twenty-three. Because a woman has only an XX pair, the egg always carries a single X chromosome, but the sperm from the man can carry either an X or a Y chromosome, and this will decide the baby's sex. If an X-carrying sperm gets to the egg first, then the twenty-third set will be XX—a girl. If a Y-carrying sperm wins the race and fertilizes the egg, then the twenty-third set will be XY—a boy.

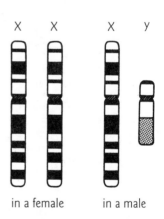

in a female   in a male

The twenty-third pair, or sex chromosomes

Mistakes in Chromosomes

On examining chromosomes, the first check is to count them—there should be forty-six. Sometimes a baby has one too many chromosomes, and where there should be a pair there are three—this happens in Down syndrome babies, who have an extra chromosome number twenty-one. Mistakes involving a whole chromosome usually happen when the egg or the sperm is being formed. If the chromosomes do not separate properly, the egg or the sperm may carry an extra one. This also can happen after fertilization during a cell division when the cells begin to divide and multiply to form the embryo. In this case some of the cells are normal and have the right number of chromosomes, but some carry an extra chromo-

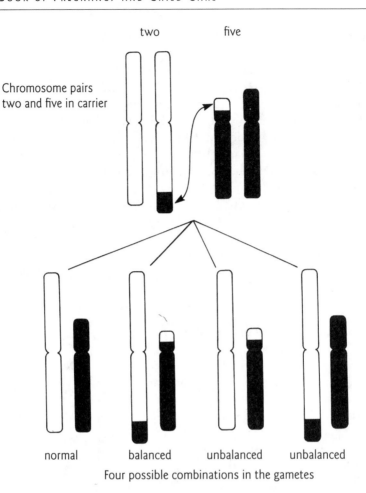

two   five

Chromosome pairs
two and five in carrier

normal   balanced   unbalanced   unbalanced

Four possible combinations in the gametes

One example of a person carrying a rearrangement of chromosome material between chromosomes two and five. While this person has no loss or gain of genetic material and is therefore healthy, his or her child has a high risk of ending up with genes missing from one of these chromosomes and extra copies of genes on the other. This causes the child to be born with brain and other malformations.

some—this will mean the individual will be less severely affected and the pattern is called a "mosaic," a mixture of two different cell types. More rarely there may be one too few chromosomes—an example of this is Turner's syndrome, where girls are missing one of the female X pair of chromosomes and fail to develop at puberty, though in recent times much can be done with hormone therapy to make the young lady have more of a normal life.

The second type of mistake in chromosome makeup occurs when a chromosome has a part missing or is rearranged. Sometimes the missing part has become attached to another chromosome. This is called a translocation. Most chromosomal abnormalities are "one-time" events that do not run in families, but parents or relatives should be checked if it is thought the problem may be due to the less common inherited forms that might mean future children would be affected.

Mistakes in Individual Genes

While mistakes in the chromosomes can be seen under a microscope, mistakes can also happen in individual genes, which are too tiny to be studied in this way. What causes these mistakes? Again, often we do not know *why* things go wrong, but we do know *how*. Imagine trying to photocopy thousands of tiny pictures hundreds of times so that each reprint is exactly the same as the original. That is what has to happen when the cells that contain a hundred thousand genes each divide to form eggs or sperm that are the starting point for a new person. A small mistake in just one reprint, or one gene, goes on to be multiplied, and may cause something to go wrong with the development of that baby. The existence of a single gene defect in an unborn baby would not be suspected if this was the first in the family. However, the original mutation—the photocopying mistake—may have occurred farther back in the family, and a history of the other family members having the condition can alert one to the risk of the baby having inherited the abnormal gene, too.

If a single faulty gene always showed its presence by causing something wrong in the person, then it would be easy to track its inheritance through the family. However, this is not always the case. Fortunately, geneticists are making great progress in detecting faulty genes by examining the genetic material, or DNA, directly.

Patterns of Inheritance

Genetic diseases due to a single gene defect can be passed on through families in several ways. In normal individuals chromosomes exist in pairs, as do the genes they carry. Each pair of genes is made up of one that comes from the egg and one that comes from the sperm.

- *Recessive inheritance.* In some gene pairs a person can carry one faulty gene, but the other, normal gene will be able to cope on its own. A person will only have disease when both genes are faulty, for example, when he has no "spare." In this situation, it means that both his parents must have passed on one copy of the faulty gene, although they themselves would have been healthy but be called "carriers." If two carriers of the same faulty gene marry and have children, they have a 25 percent chance of having an affected child. In this type of inheritance the genetic disease usually happens in one generation of a family only. An example of a recessively inherited disease is cystic fibrosis (CF)—an abnormality of the mucous glands and lungs in which digestive enzymes fail to flow from the pancreas into the intestine. It is thought that one in twenty people carry the CF gene, but it is only if two of these people marry that their child could inherit two CF genes and get the disease.

- *Dominant inheritance.* If a person inherits one faulty gene, the wrong programming in the faulty gene sometimes overrides the right programming in the healthy "spare," and he or she has a disease. When that person comes to have children, there is a 50 percent risk that the faulty gene will be passed on to any children. It is like flipping a coin: either the faulty gene or the normal gene is passed on purely by chance. This type of inheritance is called "dominant

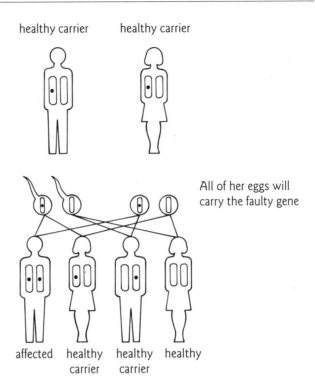

healthy carrier   healthy carrier

Half of his sperm will
carry the faulty gene

All of her eggs will
carry the faulty gene

Possible combinations
in the children: one
in four chance of
producing an affected
child

affected   healthy   healthy   healthy
            carrier   carrier

Recessive autosomal inheritance: those who are affected have the faulty gene present on both members of the chromosome pair. Those in whom the faulty gene affects only one chromosome are the only carriers and are not affected.

inheritance," and it can affect many generations of a family, both males and females. An example of such an inherited disease is Huntington's chorea. If a person inherits just one faulty gene of the pair responsible for this condition, he or she will have Huntington's chorea, which comes on in middle life and causes characteristic jerky movements that slowly get worse. Unfortunately, a person may already have passed on the gene to children before symptoms appear in the parent confirming the presence of the faulty gene.

- *X-linked recessive inheritance.*   A special type of inheritance happens when faulty genes occur on the X chromosome. Disease due to these faulty genes tends to occur in males. Females have two X chromosomes with two copies of all the genes on the X chromosome, so they have a backup. They will only have the disease if they inherit two X chromosomes that both carry the faulty gene, which is a very rare occurrence. If only one of their X chromosomes has a fault, they will remain healthy but are called "carriers."

- *Men have only one X chromosome.*   The Y chromosome is much smaller and carries fewer and different genes. Men therefore have no backup in the form of a spare, so if they inherit an X chromosome with a faulty gene they will get the disease. An example of this type of inheritance is seen with hemophilia, in

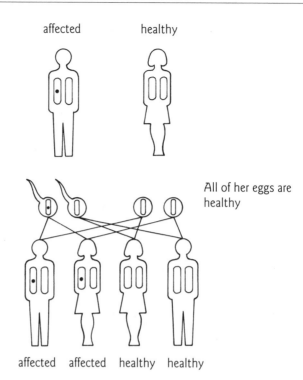

affected   healthy

Half of his sperm will
carry the faulty gene

All of her eggs are
healthy

Possible combinations
in the children: one
in two chance of
producing an affected
child

affected   affected   healthy   healthy

Dominant autosomal inheritance: only one chromosome has to save a faulty gene for a person to be affected

which the blood does not clot in the normal way. If a woman with the faulty gene (a carrier) marries a normal man, they can produce four types of children: a healthy daughter (normal X from mother and X from father); a healthy son (normal X from mother and Y from father); a daughter who is a carrier but is healthy herself (faulty X from mother but normal X from father); and a son who has the disease (faulty X from mother and Y from father). Another example of a well-known X-linked disease is Duchenne muscular dystrophy, which causes progressive muscle weakness.

Genetic Counseling

As you have read, unborn babies can be damaged by outside or environmental influences during pregnancy, such as disease, chemicals, drugs, or alcohol. Sometimes a baby can be damaged by the process of birth itself, although prenatal care can often predict and avoid or prevent that from happening. Unpredictable and unavoidable events can also occur within the uterus.

When a baby is born with an abnormality, at some point the parents will ask: "Why did it happen?" Unfortunately, there is not always a totally clear answer to this, but trying to discover the reason is at times part of the job of clinical geneticists.

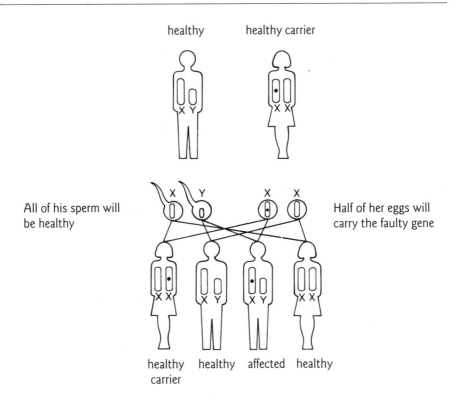

healthy   healthy carrier

All of his sperm will
be healthy

Half of her eggs will
carry the faulty gene

healthy   healthy   affected   healthy
carrier

X-linked genes: a woman who is a carrier for an X-linked faulty gene has a one in two chance that any son will be affected and a one in two chance that any daughter will be a healthy carrier. However, if an affected male has children, all his daughters (who receive his X chromosomes) will be carriers, but none of his sons (who receive his Y chromosomes) will be affected (see opposite)

Why Do People Go for Genetic Counseling?

- *Diagnosis.* A child with an abnormality may be referred to a geneticist, who will try to find out what caused the problem. An accurate diagnosis will enable other doctors to treat that child and avoid unnecessary tests. It will enable the geneticist to tell the parent what chance there is of the same thing happening with other children. Many parents also find it helpful to place a name on their child's problem.

- *The risk of passing on a genetic abnormality.* A couple who already have an affected child, or have a genetic disease themselves, or a relative with a genetic disease or abnormality, will want to know the risk of the same thing being passed on to their children.

  In X-linked diseases the answer to this question often depends on determining whether a female relative is a carrier of the faulty gene or not. If it can be shown that a woman is not a carrier, then she can be reassured about her future sons. There are rapid developments in carrier detection tests for X-linked diseases.

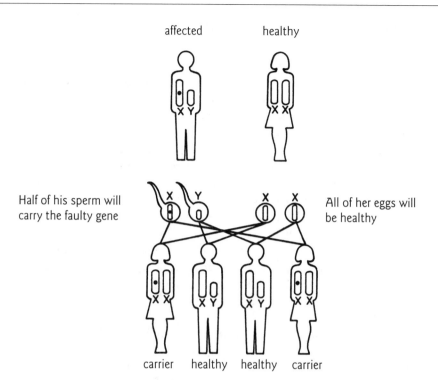

affected   healthy

Half of his sperm will   X   Y   X   X   All of her eggs will
carry the faulty gene   be healthy

carrier   healthy   healthy   carrier

- *Marriage of cousins.*   We all carry at least one harmful recessive gene but, as explained in the section on recessive inheritance, as long as we have one healthy "spare" it does us no harm. Only if we marry someone who carries the same harmful gene can we have a child with a double set of the same faulty gene and thus an inherited disease may occur.

  Relatives share some genes in common.   First cousins share an eighth of their genes in common, are therefore more likely to share the same faulty gene, and are at higher risk of having a child with a recessive disease. In general, marriage between first cousins or more distant relatives is not a major genetic risk for the couple concerned. A geneticist can put the genetic risks in perspective and sometimes help by telling if a fault is likely to exist in the family genes, making a marriage between cousins a concern.

- *Prenatal diagnosis.*   If there is a fairly high risk that a child may carry a genetic fault, a geneticist can sometimes make a diagnosis in the unborn child during pregnancy.

  If the geneticist wants to study the baby's chromosomes, the most usual way is to take a sample of the amniotic fluid containing some of the fetal cells by amniocentesis (as described in the section "Amniocentesis" in chapter 2). The drawback is that this usually cannot be done until fifteen to sixteen weeks gestation.

  An alternative way of obtaining a sample of the baby's cells is chorion villus sampling (CVS) (see the section "Chorion Biopsy" in chapter 2). This has the advantage of being able to be performed earlier, from ten weeks gestation, but carries a slightly higher risk of miscarriage and occasional limb malformation. It involves performing a biopsy on the placenta, which normally contains cells with the same genes as those in the developing baby. Tests can be done to identify gene defects for some genetic disorders, such as cystic fibrosis, Duchenne muscular dystrophy, and hemophilia if it is known that the disease is in the family.

Many congenital abnormalities can be identified by an ultrasound scan of the baby during the pregnancy. In experienced hands an ultrasound scan at eighteen to twenty weeks into the pregnancy can pick up problems such as spina bifida; brain problems such as hydrocephalus (when the head is enlarged by excessive fluid); some heart defects; and even smaller defects, such as cleft lip.

In a few cases, suspicion of an abnormality on ultrasound may mean that doctors suggest that the baby's chromosomes be tested by fetal blood sampling. This involves taking blood from the umbilical cord using a fine needle passed through your abdomen under ultrasound guidance. In rare cases of inherited diseases it may be necessary to take a skin biopsy from the baby—again under ultrasound control.

No medical procedure is without its risks; in doing such tests to try to make a prenatal diagnosis, the geneticist must weigh the possible risks involved against the likelihood of the baby proving to have some abnormality, and she will explain these very carefully to the couple when she gives her advice. But, as with all medical decisions, the final choice of whether to have the test rests with the couple. As part of her counseling the geneticist will also explain, as far as she is able, what the possible effects of the suspected abnormalities may be because these will weigh with the couple in making a decision to have the test. If, sadly, the baby does prove to be damaged, then the geneticist will give the couple all the information she can about the nature and extent of the damage, the baby's chance of survival, and life expectations. Most couples will want to know what sort of mental and physical capability their child could have, what sort of special care would be needed, and how much of the damage could be corrected. Unfortunately, these are often difficult questions to answer. Even when a geneticist is sure of the diagnosis and knows the baby is suffering from a recognized syndrome, it may be impossible to say whether he will be severely or mildly affected. Such couples need all the information, support, and counseling available to help them decide whether to continue with the pregnancy or to have a termination. Naturally, the medical staff will give them full backing whatever their decision.

How Do You Arrange to Have Genetic Counseling?

Your own physician or a specialist—for example, an obstetrician—will give you a referral. They may be able to offer you some genetic advice themselves, but a proper diagnosis, assessment, and advice on the probability of genetic risks is the job of a clinical geneticist working in a genetic clinic, usually in large hospitals. This may mean traveling some distance, but usually only one or a very few visits will be necessary. Genetic clinics usually do not supervise treatment but rather pass the information on to your own physician or any relevant specialists.

What Happens When You Go for Genetic Counseling?

Before you go for your first appointment at the genetic clinic, sit down with your partner and make notes of the details of your family tree. You do not need to draw it out in any way; just list the names, ages, and relation to yourself. Each time, ask yourself if there is anything relating to the health and condition of those relatives that is out of the ordinary. If there is, then try to find out if they have ever been for treatment; the list should include relatives who have since died, and, if applicable, at which hospital and under which consultant. If the geneticist thinks their condition may be relevant, this information will be very helpful because she will be able to write to the consultant to ask for confirmation or a diagnosis if one was made, and any other information. Start with your immediate brothers and sisters and their children, if any. Details about stillbirths or miscarriages also will be needed. Then go on to your parents, aunts, uncles, and cousins. If you know there are members of the family who were affected by some abnormality and a diagnosis was never made, then a photograph may sometimes help the geneticist. If this is the case, she will ask at your first visit to find out what sort of information needs to be gathered—for example, notes from other hospitals, results of postmortems, or tests to be arranged. Sometimes the geneticist may want to have a karyotype of both your chromosomes—this means taking a sample of blood, which will be sent to a laboratory for analysis.

The Assessment

Before giving you an assessment, the geneticist will have found out everything possible relating to your problem. You should expect the geneticist to take half an hour or even a full hour to explain the assessment and on what it is based. Don't be afraid to ask questions—it sometimes helps to note down anything you want to ask in advance. Understandably, there is often a great deal of anxiety and guilt about genetic abnormalities. One of you may feel it is your fault a child was born handicapped or that the problem stems from your side of the family. It is also very common to feel angry at the way things have worked out. "Why us?" is a very usual reaction.

In the majority of cases, couples want to know what their chances are of having a healthy or an affected child in the future. The geneticist will assess the risk in terms of probabilities and give you as accurate a figure as possible. For example, if a couple were given a one-in-two chance, it means that out of every two children born to that couple, one is likely to be affected, although, of course, both might be affected or both unaffected. The risk is the same every time for every pregnancy; chance has no memory. The probability of having an affected child can vary through lesser and lesser degrees of risk until you are talking about one in a hundred or smaller risks. Even if a geneticist cannot make a precise diagnosis, you should get some idea of what the risks might be, what is a bad risk, and what is a good risk.

The geneticist will also set the risk in some kind of context to help you assess what it means. Some geneticists estimate that any pregnancy has a one-in-thirty chance of producing a baby who will either be born with a serious abnormality, or will develop one in the early years. In broad terms it seems that genetic risks tend to fall into the risk category of either a one-in-ten chance or worse, or a one-in-twenty chance or better. Of course, in deciding whether to have children, every couple will need to know as much as possible about the disease or abnormality they risk passing on, just as couples who go for a prenatal diagnosis need to know. But again, the geneticist should never try to influence any couple's decision whether to have children. Indeed, in one study of couples attending a genetic clinic, it turned out that just over a third of those given a one-in-ten or worse risk decided to have children. If that is your decision, you can arrange to go back to the geneticist when the time comes for a prenatal diagnosis if you wish.

CHAPTER 2

Pregnancy

A new life begins • Fertility problems
How can you tell if you are pregnant? • Decisions, decisions
Your guide to prenatal care • Other tests during pregnancy
Eating well and weight gain • Avoid X rays in early pregnancy
Minor physical problems • More serious problems in pregnancy
Pregnancies needing the five-star treatment
Mixed emotions—how you feel during pregnancy
Shopping for the baby • Toward the end of pregnancy

A New Life Begins

Fertilization

From puberty onward a complex series of hormone signals and reactions stimulate one or another ovary to produce one egg a month until menopause. A woman's cycle runs from the first day of one period to the first day of the next and is about twenty-eight days. When the egg breaks free from the ovary, usually at about the fourteenth day of the cycle, this is called "ovulation." Filaments around the entrance to the Fallopian tube draw the egg into the tube, and the rhythmic contractions of the tube draw it along toward the uterus. It takes four to five days for the egg to travel from the ovary to the uterus. If it is not fertilized, it dies after one to two days and disappears, after which the lining of the womb, with its rich supply of blood vessels in preparation for a fertilized egg, begins to break down and is shed as a period at the end of the cycle. Although fertilization normally occurs about two weeks later, doctors date pregnancies from the first day of the last menstrual period (LMP).

Sperm have a longer life than eggs: it is usually thought to be about three to four days, and it takes them about an hour to swim the seven inches from the cervix (neck of the womb) through the uterus to meet the egg in the Fallopian tube. Usually the tiny canal through the cervix (the os) is blocked with a plug of mucus, and sperm cannot pass through. But when ovulation approaches, hormone changes make the mucus thin, opening the door to the sperm. Some women can recognize this change in vaginal fluid so they know when they are approaching a fertile period, while a few women actually experience some kind of pain at the time of ovulation itself. The egg is most easily fertilized twelve to twenty-four hours after ovulation, because changes in its structure make it easier for the sperm to penetrate. Although every ejaculation contains several hundred million sperm, only one can fertilize the egg. When the egg and the sperm merge at fertilization, the two halves of the chromosome set come together to form a complete set of forty-six, again—one-half from the mother and one-half from the father.

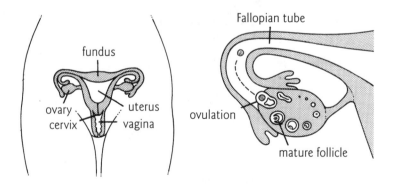

Female reproductive organs

Early Days of Life

Within about thirty hours of fertilization, the egg divides into two cells—the beginning of the complicated and amazing process of building a new person. By five days it has usually reached the sixteen-cell stage and has arrived in the uterus. It is now called a "blastocyst" and, if all goes well, it will implant itself in the wall of the uterus. Sometimes mistakes happen and it implants in the wrong place, such as in the Fallopian tube. When this happens it is called an "ectopic pregnancy." By about ten days the blastocyst has completely embedded itself in the lining of the uterus, but tremendous activity is going on within. The majority of the cells go on to form the placenta (called "chorionic villi" during early development) and the membranes, while an inner cell mass becomes the embryo proper. The embryonic cells are divided into three layers. The first layer is the ectoderm, which makes the outer layer of the baby, skin, hair, and nails, and will soon fold inward to make the nervous system as well. The second layer is the endoderm, which makes all the organs inside the baby. In week three a third layer of cells, the mesoderm, starts to make the beginnings of muscles, blood, heart, and bones.

Weeks 4–5. The unborn baby is technically known as an embryo now. Although only the size of a pea, it has a primitive heart, which begins to beat. Finger-shaped projections, the chorionic villi, have grown into the tissue of the uterine wall to anchor the embryo, and a string of blood vessels connecting mother and baby will form the umbilical cord.

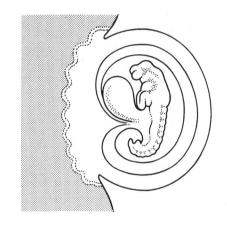

Weeks 6–7. Now about ¼ in (6 mm) long from crown to bottom, the unborn baby has limb buds that can move and will soon grow into arms and legs. The head is much larger than the body, with a bump where the brain is forming indentations will soon become ears. The eyes are still covered with skin that will be eyelids, and stay closed until about the twenty-sixth week.

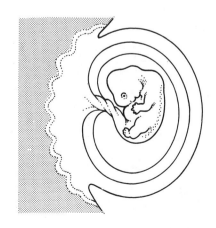

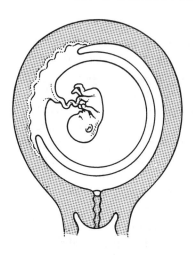

Weeks 8–9.   From nine weeks the unborn baby is called a "fetus" and, although you may not have had your first prenatal check yet, all the internal organs are forming fast. She has tripled her size to measure about ¾ in (2 cm). Although the head is still much larger than the body, she is beginning to look more like a baby, and toes and fingers are starting to form.

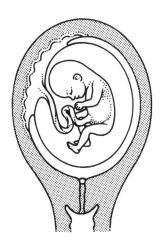

Weeks 10–14.   By twelve weeks your unborn baby is fully formed. All the organs are complete, and she needs only to grow and develop. Fingernails and toenails have begun to grow. She is about 2¾ in (7 cm) from head to bottom, and the top of the uterus, the fundus, can usually be felt beginning to rise out of the pelvis.

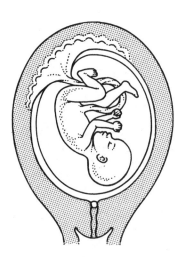

Weeks 15–22.   Although your unborn baby will have been moving spontaneously from about week twelve, she is usually not big enough for you to feel her movements until now. However, second-time mothers who recognize the fluttery sensations may notice them earlier. At twenty-two weeks the unborn baby is covered with a fine, downy hair called "lanugo," which is usually mostly shed before birth. A substance called "vernix," a greasy, white protective film that is often still covering the baby born prematurely, has begun to form. Sometimes the baby's sex can be detected at this stage with ultrasound scans.

Weeks 23–30.   With modern technology it is possible for a baby to survive outside the womb from twenty-three weeks, although babies born at such a premature age have a high chance of handicap later in life if they do not die from complications of prematurity first. Once twenty-six weeks have been reached, babies delivered prematurely have about an 80 percent chance of survival as long as they are in a special-care baby unit. Many will not have long-term health problems. With each additional week, the baby's chances improve considerably. The downy lanugo has usually disappeared, and the baby is covered in vernix. Her movements are very clear, and she still has plenty of room to maneuver, often turning complete somersaults. She may have regular patterns of activity and sleep, and some babies get hiccups that their mothers can feel. The baby may respond to sudden or loud noises by jumping or starting, and experiments seem to suggest that babies can respond to soothing sounds like singing or music. She probably begins to learn the rhythm and pitch of her mother's voice. At thirty weeks the unborn baby usually measures about 16½ in (42 cm).

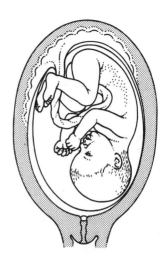

Weeks 31–40.   With every extra week that passes, your baby has a greater chance of surviving if she is born early. The baby begins to fill out and become plumper, and both the downy lanugo and vernix disappear. By about thirty-two weeks the baby has usually settled into the head-down position, ready to be born. If her head moves down into the pelvis it is said to be "engaged," but sometimes this does not happen until labor begins.

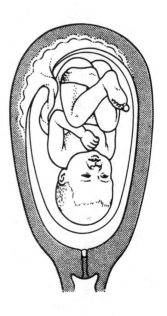

Fertility Problems

Becoming Pregnant

Pinpointing ovulation—that is, the time when an egg is released from the ovaries—has always been very difficult to determine. Ovulation is most commonly thought to occur fourteen days before the next period, but there can be very many variations, so even if you have a regular twenty-eight-day cycle, it is not enough just to count the days. If you are trying to conceive, regular sexual intercourse about three times a week should be enough to coincide with ovulation. It may help to increase the frequency to alternate days or even daily at about the time of ovulation.

A better but still very imprecise way of pinpointing ovulation is to take your temperature. To do this you need a fertility chart, and a special fertility thermometer, available from most pharmacies, makes things easier because the scale is bigger and easier to read. First thing in the morning your body is at its lowest temperature—called the "basal body temperature"—which is usually between 97.2°F and 97.4°F (36.2°C and 36.3°C). Leave the thermometer in for five minutes and record the temperature each morning on the chart before you get out of bed. When an egg has been released from the ovaries there is a sharp rise in the level of the hormone progesterone, which causes the body temperature to increase—usually to a level of about 98°F (36.7°C) or above. Sometimes there is a drop in temperature a few hours before this rise. But remember, the increase in temperature does not mark the time of ovulation itself—it only shows that ovulation has taken place. It is thought

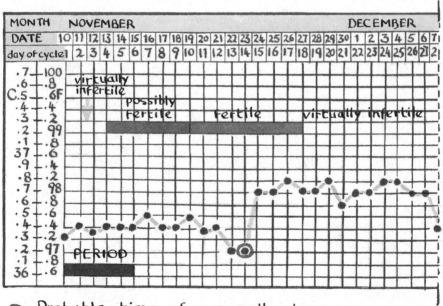

O   Probable time of egg cell release

that the day before this rise in temperature must be the time of ovulation, but obviously exact timing will vary with individuals, and in many women the rise in temperature itself is not easy to pinpoint. After ovulation the temperature stays raised until the start of the next period.

Another method is to test the urine for an increase in the level of a substance called "luteinizing hormone" (LH), which rises sharply and triggers ovulation about twenty-four hours later. A number of ovulation kits on the market use dipsticks to test the LH levels in urine as a means of predicting the most fertile time in a woman's cycle, but they are expensive, and it is possible to have an increased LH level without ovulating, perhaps because the ovary is not functioning properly. Remember that if you pinpoint ovulation successfully, this can be stressful for you and for your partner, who may feel he has to "perform" on command. If this causes problems, it is sensible to return to just making love two or three times a week.

Infertility

Problems relating to fertility are not uncommon—it is estimated that as many as one in seven couples has trouble trying to conceive. An average, fertile couple has a 15 percent chance of conceiving each month, which means that half the fertile population will take about four to five months to become pregnant and most normal couples will conceive within a year. Those who have not become pregnant after twelve months of regular intercourse probably have some problem, but in many cases this may be minor and easily treated. How soon you seek medical help depends slightly on individual circumstances, but there are some known indications of possible fertility problems. See your doctor if any of the following apply and you have had no luck after six months of trying to conceive:

- You are more than thirty-six years old. Fertility declines in women as they near forty, and a quarter of all normal women are subfertile by this age. Unfortunately, there is no way of knowing in advance which women are likely to belong to this group, so it is a good idea to get tests done if you are over thirty-six and do not conceive within about six months.

- You have infrequent periods. Usually this can be easily treated.

- You have increasingly painful periods or deep pain on intercourse. This may indicate a pelvic infection or a condition called endometriosis, requiring treatment.

- You've had a previous severe pelvic infection, a ruptured appendix, or a miscarriage. All of these can sometimes result in a problem with the Fallopian tubes or the inside of the womb, requiring treatment.

If none of these applies to you, your doctor may ask you to try for a year before doing tests.

It is estimated that in about 50 percent of all cases of infertility the problem lies with the woman, in about 35–40 percent of cases with the man, and in about 10–15 percent with both partners. By far the most common male problem is a low sperm count or sperm of poor quality.

It is most important in cases of infertility that proper tests and diagnoses are made without wasting too much time. However, no matter how thorough the tests, for many couples (10–15 percent) it is not possible to identify a cause. This is called "unexplained infertility." Today many infertility problems, including unexplained infertility, blocked Fallopian tubes, and low sperm counts, can be successfully treated by in vitro fertilization (IVF). However, problems conceiving can be very distressing, especially if your friends seem to be having babies at the drop of a hat. It is important not to let this interfere with your relationship with your partner. You should seek counseling if problems with infertility create strain in your relationship.

How Can You Tell If You Are Pregnant?

With my second baby, I knew even before I missed a period. My breasts starting aching and I couldn't tolerate coffee immediately—couldn't even stand the smell. Some of these signs might have been there with my first pregnancy but I just didn't recognize them.

Some women are so in tune with their bodies that they say they know within days when they are pregnant; but at the other end of the scale there have been reports of women who manage to ignore or suppress the signs of pregnancy so completely that they do not know they are expecting a baby until they actually go into labor. However, most women do suspect within a few weeks, because some or all of these signs are present:

- **Missed periods**   Light bleeding, like a period, can still happen during the early weeks of pregnancy, usually once or twice, but even, rarely, through the whole pregnancy. Apart from pregnancy, missed periods (amenorrhea) can also be due to emotional upset, illness, severe weight loss, overexercise, anxiety about getting pregnant, approaching menopause, or coming off the Pill.

- **Breast changes**   They may feel different immediately or not for three months, but at some point they will begin to feel heavier, fuller, and to ache or tingle.

- **Nausea**   This is very common in the first three months of pregnancy, sometimes first thing in the morning, but it can also happen at other times in the day. Some very unlucky women feel nauseated all the way through pregnancy.

- **Frequent urination**   It is very common to have to urinate more often in the first three months of pregnancy, which often means getting up in the night, too. This usually decreases slightly in the middle months and returns at the end, when the baby is bigger and physically pressing on the bladder.

- **Tiredness** This can be noticeable in the first three months, but usually resolves in the middle months, to return again when you are large and the baby has become heavy toward the end of pregnancy. Very early on, you can often feel heaviness in the lower abdomen.

Pregnancy Tests

I have used home pregnancy tests twice—once when I didn't want to be pregnant, and once eight years later, when I did. Both times I was really keyed up and nervous. Luckily, I got the result I wanted. My excitement the second time on being pregnant was just about as great as the relief I felt all those years ago when I got the negative result I was praying for!

All pregnant women start to produce a special hormone called human chorionic gonadotropin (HCG) within two days of the fertilized egg becoming embedded in the wall of the uterus. Pregnancy tests look for HCG in blood or urine. The most easily available and usual form of testing can be done within a day or so of missing a period by testing a sample of urine collected first thing in the morning. Wrong results do happen—false negatives are more common than false positives, usually the result of doing the test too early, before levels of HCG are high enough. Traces of detergent or something else in the container you use can also cause a false negative. False positives are rare but can occur because if you test at the time of ovulation or approaching menopause, another hormone, luteinizing hormone (LH), may be present. A recent pregnancy or miscarriage you are unaware of might cause traces of HCG to be present. Fertility drugs, some tranquilizers, and antihistamines can also affect the reading.

You can get a test done by your obstetrician, which is usually more accurate than the one you can buy at a pharmacy.

Earlier Tests

In rare cases some women may need to know if they are pregnant even before a period is missed, perhaps because of fertility problems where repeated early miscarriages are suspected, or in the case of a rape victim or someone with a suspected ectopic pregnancy. In these cases many hospitals are able to perform a blood test to look for the HCG in the bloodstream. This is not only very accurate but also can give an idea as to the chances of whether the pregnancy will be successful.

Ultrasound Scans

It is possible to detect a pregnancy sac inside the uterus as early as five weeks from your last period. This normally means having an internal or a transvaginal scan. A week after this, the specialist performing the scan may well be able to identify the fetal heart beating. By transabdominal (scan on the abdomen with a full bladder) scan, the pregnancy sac can be seen from about six to six and a half weeks, and the fetal heartbeat a week later.

Decisions, Decisions

As soon as you know that you are pregnant, you will probably select a caregiver (obstetrician, family doctor, or midwife), followed by where the birth will take place. This will depend on staff privileges your physician or midwife has.

Where Will You Have Your Baby?

Whether it is a first or a subsequent baby, most women have strong feelings about the circumstances they would like to give birth in, and some of the things they would or would not like to happen. In deciding on a place of birth, you are also choosing a set of options about who handles your prenatal care and about the style of the birth itself.

- **Home births**   It is generally accepted that the backup of hospital facilities gives a much better chance of survival if anything goes wrong with a birth. This is why most doctors do not agree with home births in any circumstances, although others are quite prepared to go along with the idea if everything seems normal and this is a second or subsequent baby, up to number four or five. Prenatal care will be with your obstetrician or a midwife.

- **Hospital births**   Find out about your local hospitals and birthing centers by asking other mothers. See our suggestions below for questions you may want to ask. A full stay in the hospital can mean two days and gives you a chance to learn about taking care of your baby. The disadvantages are separation from your partner and other children if you have them, and the drawbacks of hospital life. If you have a cesarean section, the normal hospital stay is two to four days.

Twenty-one Questions About Hospitals   If you live in a more rural area, you may have only one maternity hospital within reach of your home, but if you do have a choice, these are some of the questions you may wish to consider:

- What kind of atmosphere does the hospital have?

- How friendly and helpful are the staff when you make inquiries?

- Do they run parent education and prenatal classes?

- Can your partner and/or a relation or friend stay with you all the time during labor and birth?

- Will they really be welcome if they do?

- Are all mothers monitored continuously in labor, or only at intervals (called intermittent monitoring)?

- Is there a high rate of induced labor?

- Does the hospital have a high cesarean section rate? (In this case and in the previous case remember that some large hospitals get more problem cases referred to them, which may push up the rates.)

- Will you be able to move around freely during labor?

- Will they help you adopt any position you want during labor and birth?

- Are there any extra facilities—birthing beds, birth chairs or stools, or birthing rooms with mattresses on the floor? Is there a birthing pool?

- How freely available are epidurals? Is there an anesthesiologist or nurse anesthetist available twenty-four hours a day who can give an epidural anesthetic?

- Can they offer epidurals for suitably planned cesarean sections?

- Will you be able to make your own decision about what type of and how much pain relief you want in consultation with your doctor or midwife?

- Will they be happy for the second stage to continue as long as the mother or the baby is not distressed?

- Will the obstetrician or midwife attending the birth help you avoid an episiotomy?

- Can your partner visit you and the baby as often as he likes after the birth?

- Will you be able to keep your baby with you all the time after the birth?

- Does the hospital run well-planned and interesting postnatal classes for mothers to attend with their babies for either socializing or exercise sessions?

- Does the hospital have breastfeeding support services?

- Does your health care plan (HMO or other insurance) include your hospital choice on its list of approved facilities?

Choosing a Prenatal Class

- **Hospital classes**   These can vary enormously, and in the past, old-style classes often left much to be desired, but many hospitals have updated their approach

to offer really good advice. Classes may be held in the hospital or in the community, in the daytime or in the evening, be geared for mothers alone or for couples, or even provide facilities for mothers to go along with older children. A good class tries to be flexible and meet the needs of the people attending, but in general they aim to tell couples about the physical process of birth and what happens at each stage, and most teach some kind of breathing and relaxation techniques. Good prenatal classes also discuss all the other options for pain relief, and specifically what is available at that particular hospital. Even if you opt for another form of prenatal class, it is useful to attend some of the hospital classes as well, because they can tell you about that particular hospital's policy and approach on points that are dealt with differently in different hospitals.

It is useful to remember that in a given hospital two obstetricians can have very different attitudes, so talking to the other doctors from your obstetrician's practice group is useful. As well as discussing the physical side of birth, hospital classes, like all prenatal classes, can be valuable places for discussion with other parents-to-be about the emotional and psychological changes involved in becoming a parent. Other couples who are going through the same process can be invaluable sources of support to each other, and many long-lasting friendships stem from meetings in prenatal classes, clinics, and maternity wards.

- **Active birth classes**   At the beginning of the 1980s a number of birth educators began teaching women how they could be helped during labor by staying upright and mobile and also by using a variety of different positions, such as kneeling or squatting, during delivery. Their ideas were based on women's experiences and backed by medical research that showed that women who stayed upright and mobile during the first stage of labor, instead of lying on their backs on a delivery bed, needed less pain relief and had shorter labors. The idea of using the force of gravity to make contractions in the first stage of labor more effective and to help with delivery has largely become accepted practice, and most hospital teachers have incorporated it in their prenatal teaching.

- **Yoga classes**   Such classes are not strictly a prenatal course in that they do not teach specifically about hospital practice and other areas associated with birth, but in some areas there are yoga classes designed for pregnant women. These may be run by individual teachers or local community associations. Try your nearest library for contact addresses.

Working Through Pregnancy
After you have chosen your physician or midwife, where to have the baby and which prenatal class to attend, you may have to decide about your work. Most women expecting a first baby work through the early and middle months of their pregnancy, but many women are undecided about whether they will return to full- or part-time work after the birth.

From a purely practical point of view it is probably better not to announce your pregnancy at work too early, as miscarriages in the first three months of pregnancy can be quite common, and letting everybody know in the very first few weeks will make the pregnancy seem extra-long. Around the fourth month is probably a reasonable time: miscarriage is less likely by now, and you and your employer both need enough time to make decisions and plans for the future. At about this time you will also begin to look pregnant!

Your Rights   As far as your job goes, your rights are based on the American Disabilities Act and the Medical Leave Act, federal laws. They are based as well on the size of your company, how many hours you may work in a year, and the length of time you have worked for that organization. It is recommended that you discuss your rights with your employer or human resources department.

You have the right to

- Take paid time off during working hours to attend prenatal appointments.

- Not to be unfairly dismissed because you are pregnant.

- Return to the job after birth, if it can be held for you.

In addition to the rights listed above, some employers grant pregnant women extra rights. To find out if any special entitlements apply to your particular job, you must talk to your boss or, in a larger firm, the human resources department. Asking to hold a job and then not returning leaves a negative effect that could prevent returning at a later time.

Jobs That Are Dangerous in Pregnancy   If your job involves working with chemicals, toxic materials, or radiation, then obviously you need to think about this before becoming pregnant. Your obstetrician will be able to advise you if you think there may be some hazards attached to your work. In addition, most places will be able to let you know about recent research developments and about your right to a change of job during pregnancy. Most places of business will try to accommodate their workers in hazardous jobs.

Work that is simply physically unsuitable during pregnancy is obviously less of a problem. In general, standing for long hours, lifting heavy goods, or other manual labor becomes more difficult during the middle to later months; the problem may be exacerbated if you have a medical history of miscarriage or similar problems. However, depending on the individual circumstances of your employment, you could lose your job if being pregnant means you cannot do the work properly and if no suitable alternative can be provided. Again, your union, citizens' advice bureau, law center, and many maternity organizations can give advice.

Your Guide to Prenatal Care

The obstetricians and nurses couldn't have been better about discussing every-thing with me—the care was superb. My only criticism was the waiting involved—I had to take a complete morning off work for each visit.

Even doctors in the best practices sometimes seem to come across as having impersonal attitudes. And you may find that you're left to wait for a long time, often because some patients may take longer than others to see; it is not predictable. This combination can make prenatal appointments seem more of a chore than they're worth. Women who have become pregnant accidentally or who, for various reasons, feel unsure about whether they want to be pregnant may find prenatal appointments particularly annoying. Not understanding the point behind all those tests and questions can make prenatal care seem less important. If there is anything you are worried about or don't understand, always ask, but knowing something about the basics of prenatal care may help you to know *what* to ask.

Your first visit will probably take longer than most. The obstetrician will want to know about your own and your family's medical history, your normal state of health and menstrual cycle, and any previous pregnancies. This is to help him plan your care during pregnancy.

Clinical Tests

- **Height**   This is a guide to what your weight should be and can indicate frame size. Small women (under 5 ft) will be more carefully monitored in case their pelvis is too narrow for the baby's head to pass through. Shoe size used to be thought to be an indication of bone structure, but recent research does not confirm this.

- **Weight**   A record will be kept throughout pregnancy. Generally very slow gain or even weight loss is of more concern than gaining extra weight because it may be a sign that the baby is not growing steadily.

- **Blood pressure**   It is recorded like this: 120/80. The top figure is the pressure in the arteries while the heart is contracted, and the bottom figure is the pressure when it is relaxed. The lower figure is more important. Anything higher than 80 needs to be monitored to make sure it doesn't stay elevated or get any higher.

- **Urine**   At your first appointment you will be asked to perform a special trick well known to more experienced mothers—the collection of a midstream urine sample. This is not as difficult as it sounds, though even second-time mothers might remember it is a lot easier without a curious toddler in tow! The purpose is to check for infection, and it entails cleansing yourself with specially provided swabs and stopping in midstream to pass some urine into a sterile specimen container. Your urine is tested for:

    1. *Sugar*   Pregnant women do have sugar in their urine occasionally but if it persists you should be tested for diabetes.

    2. *Protein*   Traces can mean an infection or be a feature of pre-eclampsia, a special condition only associated with pregnancy where one of the main signs is high blood pressure.

    3. *Ketones*   A by-product when body fats are broken down. It can be a warn-

ing that the kidneys are not working properly or may be present if a woman is suffering from a great deal of morning sickness. Usually, though, the presence of ketones in the urine means you haven't eaten enough for a couple of hours.

*   **Blood** At your first visit a blood sample will be taken and screened for:

    1. *Your blood group* In case you ever need a transfusion. Everyone belongs to one of four groups: A, AB, B, or O. O is the most common.

    2. *Rhesus factor* Positive or negative.

    3. *Syphilis* Can damage the baby if left untreated.

    4. *Viral hepatitis B* A rare strain called Australian antigen can be a risk to nursing and medical staff.

    5. *Rubella immunity* If you are not immune you will be offered the vaccination after the birth to safeguard you in future pregnancies.

    6. *Other antibodies* Previous illnesses may be detected by the presence of antibodies in the blood.

    7. *Sickle-cell disease* A form of inherited anemia only affecting people of African American descent and some from Africa, the West Indies, and Asia.

    8. *Thalassemia* A similar condition affecting especially people from Mediterranean countries.

    9. *Hemoglobin levels* Will be checked at the beginning and at subsequent intervals throughout the pregnancy. Hemoglobin is the oxygen-carrying substance in the red blood cells, which have to increase in number to meet the demands of the expanding uterus and growing placenta and baby. Ideally the level of hemoglobin should not fall below 10 grams per deciliter of blood. Below 10 grams per deciliter usually indicates you are anemic and need to take iron supplements. However, in some cases a low hemoglobin level (even below 10 grams per deciliter of blood) is quite normal for pregnancy. Your doctor will check the size of the red blood cells to advise you if you need to take iron.

    10. *AIDS* The current screening test for the virus causing AIDS (HIV) infection is called an ELISA test. If your doctor offers you an HIV test, you should receive counseling to make you fully aware of the implications of a positive test.

Medical Examination

At your first appointment, your obstetrician will want to find out if you are in good general health. The examination entails listening to heart and lungs; examining breasts for any abnormal lumps; and to check for conditions such as inverted nipples, which may need special care to enable you to breastfeed, varicose veins, and any swelling of the legs or fingers. Later in pregnancy such swelling can be a feature of a condition called pre-eclampsia. If you do have an internal examination, it is usually for a pap (cervical) smear and cultures to exclude an infection (gonorrhea, Chlamydia). Feeling the size of your uterus, using two fingers inside the vagina and pressing down on the outside of your stomach, can enable the doctor to assess how far your pregnancy has progressed. Such an examination may also be done to exclude abnormalities of the pelvis, vagina, and cervix.

Prenatal Care in the Middle Months

If all is normal, you should see your obstetrician once a month to be weighed, and to have your urine tested and blood pressure checked. At each visit the doctor will feel your abdomen, especially the height of the top of the uterus, which is called the fundus and which usually rises at a steady rate as the baby grows. Your doctor will listen to the baby's heart through a special stethoscope, or by using a small, handheld Doppler ultrasound on your abdomen. It is possible to hear the fetal heart beginning at fourteen to sixteen weeks with this method. Although the doctor will note the baby's position, this is not important until later months, as the baby can move freely inside the uterus while she is still small.

Prenatal Care at the End of Pregnancy

In the last few weeks you should be seen at two-week intervals from twenty-eight weeks and then at weekly intervals from thirty-six weeks. If you have had any complications in your current pregnancy or in a previous pregnancy (including cesarean section), you will need to see your doctor more frequently. How often depends on your particular problems. Women over thirty-eight years having their first baby are often watched more closely. Prenatal care involves checking your blood pressure and urine for protein, checking that the baby is growing normally and is lying head down (cephalic) in these last few weeks, and performing a one-hour blood-glucose level at twenty-eight weeks to rule out gestational diabetes.

The Nuchal Translucency Scan Many doctors now offer an ultrasound scan when you make an appointment for between eleven and thirteen weeks. This checks that your baby is well and whether you are carrying more than one baby. It is possible to date your pregnancy very accurately at this point, and you may be given a new expected date of delivery. A discrepancy between your dates from calculating from your last period and from the ultrasound scan sometimes arises if you were unsure of your dates or did not ovulate when you thought.

At this scan some hospitals offer a nuchal translucency fold, or nuchal measurement. This is a measurement of the thickness of the back of the baby's neck. Babies with Down syndrome tend to have extra fluid at the back of the neck, which makes this measurement more than 3 mm. If this is found, you will be offered an amniocentesis or chorionic villus sampling. The nuchal fold measurement only indicates that the baby is at increased risk of Down syndrome and that further testing is indicated.

Other Tests During Pregnancy

Screening for Anencephaly and Spina Bifida

Many doctors encourage this test, although it is your choice whether to have it done. A blood sample taken in the sixteenth week is tested for a raised level of a protein called alpha-fetoprotein (AFP), which may be an indication of anencephaly (a defect in the skull in which the brain does not form and the baby dies) or spina bifida (where the bones in the spine are not properly joined together so that some of the spinal cord is exposed). Other very common reasons for raised AFP levels are a multiple pregnancy, the pregnancy being more advanced than was supposed, threat of miscarriage, or other birth defects especially involving the anterior abdominal wall. A positive test will be repeated and then followed up with an ultrasound and possibly amniocentesis. Hospitals with good scanning facilities avoid the blood test by offering careful detailed scanning to all their patients. If the baby appears to have a birth defect, the parents will be counseled about the likely outcome of the pregnancy and asked if they want a termination. A very low level of AFP can sometimes indicate Down syndrome, but this is not always the case.

Maternal Serum Screening Test

This blood test was developed in the late 1980s to identify women with an increased risk of carrying a baby with Down syndrome to help them to decide whether to have an amniocentesis or a chorionic villus sampling. The test measures levels of three substances in the woman's blood: alpha-fetoprotein (AFP), unconjugated estriol, and human chorionic gonadotrophin (HCG). The levels of the three substances are used in conjunction with the woman's age to estimate the risk of Down syndrome. When the risk of Down syndrome is 1 in 250 or more, the test result is said to be screen-positive. This result does not mean there is a birth defect, only that there is an increased risk and that further tests are indicated. If the risk of Down syndrome is found to be less than 1 in 250, then the result of the test will be screen-negative. More than nine of ten women will have a screen-negative result. It does not completely exclude the chance of Down syndrome, but does detect two of three cases of Down. In the future this test will probably be incorporated in routine screening of all pregnant women, to assist women in deciding whether to have an amniocentesis on the basis of maternal age alone.

Ultrasound

This is often called scanning or a scan. Most doctors do scans routinely at about sixteen to twenty weeks, and some do a scan at the end of pregnancy. The mother's abdomen is covered with a film of gel so the pickup head or transducer can slide easily backward and forward. Very-high-frequency sounds we cannot hear are directed into the uterus; the echoes bounce back off the tissue and bones of the unborn baby and are converted into a black-and-white picture, which builds up on a monitor screen. Real-time scanners produce moving pictures, while static scanners give a single, still picture. A scan can sometimes answer these questions:

- Are you pregnant? Is the baby alive? A skilled ultrasonographer can tell at as early as five to six weeks.

- How many weeks pregnant are you? Before twelve weeks the baby's age is calculated by measuring from crown to bottom, and later by measuring the diameter of the head. Then these measurements are compared to known average sizes of babies at particular stages in pregnancy.

- Are you expecting more than one baby? This can usually be answered after eight weeks.

- Is the pregnancy in the right place? Ectopic pregnancies where the fertilized egg implants in the Fallopian tube or elsewhere outside the uterus can be diagnosed by ultrasound.

- Where is the placenta? A low-lying placenta can cause problems. This is not so significant in the early stages of pregnancy, as the placenta may move upward of its own accord. However, in later months of pregnancy it needs careful monitoring to make sure it does not overlap the outlet of the uterus; this is called placenta previa.

- Is the baby developing normally? Not all abnormalities can be ruled out by a scan, but neural tube defects making the head extra large or the spine incompletely closed (hydrocephalus and spina bifida) can usually be detected. The eighteen-week scan is used to check the correct anatomy of the heart, the presence of kidneys, the normality of the gut, and that there are no severe skeletal abnormalities.

- Do you have ovarian cysts or fibroid tumors? These can be identified by ultrasound.

Amniocentesis

*I remember asking the nurse if it would hurt and she said "no" but held my
hand. It's true it didn't hurt, but it was a very odd sensation feeling the needle
going in so deep, and I worried in case the baby moved.*

The baby's position is checked with a scan, and then a fine, hollow needle is inserted through the abdomen to draw off a sample of amniotic fluid from inside the uterus. It is usually done at fifteen to sixteen weeks, when the uterus has risen out of the pelvis and there is enough amniotic fluid surrounding the baby. Some of the baby's cells present in the fluid can be grown in a laboratory and examined under a microscope, and the chromosomes can be examined. This test takes about three weeks, as the cells must be grown in cell culture so there are enough for analysis. Down syndrome shows as an extra copy of chromosome number 21, and other abnormalities include missing chromosomes or rearrangements between chromosomes. Amniocentesis may be offered routinely to mothers aged thirty-five or over, or when a combination of the mother's age and a low AFP result indicates a risk of

Down syndrome. Alternatively, your hospital may offer the nuchal translucency test. Other reasons for the test may be a history of an inherited abnormality, a fetal birth defect, or to check the progress of a baby with rhesus disease. Later in pregnancy amniocentesis can tell us how mature the baby's lungs are; this is important if a baby has to be delivered prematurely. There is a very small chance of miscarriage—about 0.5 percent—following this test.

Chorion Biopsy

This test carries a slightly higher risk of miscarriage, but has the advantage that it can be done at eleven to twelve weeks of pregnancy. If your doctor offers the nuchal translucency screening, you will be offered this if the measurements suggest you are at high risk for Down syndrome. A hollow needle is inserted through the cervix or the abdominal wall to draw off some cells from the chorionic villi—they are the projections that anchor the embryo to the wall of the uterus initially and are then incorporated as part of the placenta or disintegrate. The test gives the same sort of information as an amniocentesis test and can be used to detect genetic diseases such as cystic fibrosis, Duchenne muscular dystrophy, hemophilia, and thalassemia in families known to have those diseases, earlier than an amniocentesis could. The advantage of this earlier diagnosis is that the result is known early enough for a surgical termination if this is what you would like.

Cardiff Count-to-Ten Fetal Activity Chart

So called because it was a Cardiff, Wales, hospital that first devised it. Mothers are given the chart at twenty-eight weeks of pregnancy and are asked to note the first ten movements in a twelve-hour period starting from 9 A.M., and to fill in the time at which they feel the baby's tenth movement of the day. If they have not counted ten movements by the evening, they are advised to call the hospital and will often be asked to come in so the baby's heart can be monitored on a machine.

Monitoring

Cardiotography (CTG) is the proper name for this. The mother wears a belt with a sensor around her middle. The baby's heartbeat is picked up and recorded on graph paper, and the frequency and timing of the mother's contractions, if in labor, can also be recorded. Babies' hearts usually beat between 120 and 160 times a minute, and during a contraction, when the baby is under stress, the heartbeat slows a bit. It is also possible to monitor the baby's heart by connecting an electrode to her scalp during labor.

Fetal Blood Sampling

This is available in most secondary and tertiary care hospitals, and may be done if other tests indicate a high risk of abnormality in the baby. As with amniocentesis, the baby's position is checked with a scan, and a fine needle is introduced into the umbilical cord under ultrasound scan guidance. Samples of the baby's blood can be used to test for blood disease such as hemophilia, sickle-cell disease, and thalassemia, but these genetic diseases are now usually detected by chorion biopsy analysis. In cases of rhesus babies where their rhesus factor is incompatible with the mother's, blood transfusions can be given to the baby at as early as eighteen weeks of pregnancy to prevent her from becoming fatally anemic.

In Utero Surgery

Although this is very rarely done, it can occasionally be used to save a life. Sometimes unborn babies have a blockage in the tube leading from the bladder so that urine cannot drain and the bladder swells, eventually causing permanent damage to the kidneys due to back pressure. This can be detected by a scan, and under ultrasound control a shunt can be inserted that allows the urine to drain from the baby's bladder into the amniotic fluid and save the kidneys from permanent damage. Alternatively, if there is fluid on her lungs, a drain may be inserted to drain the fluid so the lungs can develop properly. In the future there will undoubtedly be many more ways to doctor the unborn baby. At the present time, fetal surgery has advanced to the point that many life-threatening conditions can be treated to prevent intrauterine deaths or severely debilitating handicaps.

Eating Well and Weight Gain

Because being weighed is a regular part of every prenatal check, it is hard not to become very conscious of how much you are gaining. Advice about weight gain in pregnancy has ranged over past years from "eating for two" to trying to limit gain to a pound a week. Present-day expert advice is against specific limits and encourages you just to eat sensibly and let your weight take care of itself. It is important to eat well during pregnancy, and this means a balanced diet, with something from each food group. It does not always have to be fresh food, but limit cakes, cookies and other sugary foods to avoid gaining too much weight.

Individuals vary tremendously in the amount they gain, but a very rough guide is that an average total gain tends to be between 22 and 28 lbs (10 and 12.5 kg). The rate at which you gain weight can also vary during pregnancy—you might put on a lot in a few weeks and then slow down. Because obstetricians are ever vigilant for any signs that may mean the baby is not growing at the expected rate, they are likely to be more concerned about slow weight gain or weight loss. It may be worth pointing out, though, that one off-the-cuff remark at a prenatal check is not a reason for sleepless nights—one prenatal teacher estimates that half of all her pupils had been told at some stage that they did not appear to be gaining enough weight. What matters is the weight gain over a prolonged period. If you are already overweight, consult your doctor about losing weight before you become pregnant, but it is not a good idea to go on a crash diet just before trying to conceive. You don't want to leave your body low in essential minerals and vitamins. If you have a weight problem, then pregnancy may be a time when it seems particularly hard to eat sensibly, but try not to use it as an excuse for binges of foods high in calories but not high in nutritional value. While it is estimated that pregnancy requires about four hundred extra calories a day, an average pregnant woman only takes in about two hundred extra calories; the other two hundred calories are "saved" by going about her ordinary life in a way that expends less energy. Most women feel hungrier, especially in early pregnancy, so it's easy to take in an extra two hundred calories in slightly larger portions at ordinary mealtimes. About half a pint of whole milk, or four apples, or a roast chicken leg weighing 4½ oz without skin or bone, or one ladleful (about 6 oz) of beef stew is roughly equivalent to two hundred calories. If you are on a vegetarian or vegan diet, you need to be particularly careful to get enough calories and all your nutrients.

- **Iron**   Iron is needed to make red blood cells, and more of these cells are required in pregnancy to supply the placenta, uterus, and unborn baby. At first the baby's needs are small, but they start to be more marked from about thirty weeks. It is rare for a baby to become anemic through lack of iron, because she will take what she needs from the mother at her expense, but most women need some extra iron toward the end of pregnancy. If they reach term with a barely adequate iron supply, even the moderate amount of blood lost in a normal delivery can be enough to necessitate a blood transfusion. This is why the levels of hemoglobin, the oxygen-carrying part of red blood cells, are measured in regular blood tests at prenatal visits. If the level of hemoglobin falls below 10 grams per deciliter of blood, the woman is said to be anemic. Some doctors routinely give iron and folic acid (see below) supplements, while others give iron only if blood tests show it is necessary. There can sometimes be side effects from taking extra iron—nausea, indigestion, and constipation are the most common—but they are rarely severe. Eating well before pregnancy will help to keep natural levels of iron high. Good natural sources of iron are liver and dark green leaf vegetables such as spinach.

- **Folic acid**   Ideally this vitamin should be taken before as well as during pregnancy. It is covered in chapter 1.

- **Listeria and salmonella**   Most bacteria are harmless, but some—especially those associated with food, such as listeria and salmonella—can be very harmful to the unborn baby. So general food safety and hygiene are very important. If you are pregnant or likely to be, it is best to avoid the following: soft cheeses such as Brie, Camembert, and similar varieties, or mold-ripened cheeses such as Danish blue and Stilton, because of the risk of listeria; raw or lightly cooked eggs because of the risk of salmonella—this includes foods containing raw eggs, such as homemade mayonnaise, and homemade ice creams, cheesecakes, and mousses; pâtés because of the risk of listeria unless they are marked as pasteurized; and raw or lightly cooked meat because of the risk of toxoplasmosis and other bacterial and parasitic infections.

Avoid X Rays in Early Pregnancy

Even though the level of radiation used in taking ordinary X rays is very low, radiologists always take care to protect the reproductive organs of men and women and try not to expose women inadvertently to radiation in early pregnancy. If you think you may be pregnant, tell the radiologist. If the X ray is for a serious purpose the doctors will exercise common sense in putting your general health first since the risk to the fetus is very slight. If you had an X ray without knowing you were pregnant, it is highly unlikely any harm could have resulted. In theory high levels of radiation could produce an abnormality in the genes of the mother's ova (eggs) that might be damaging to subsequent offspring; this has been shown to happen in experiments on animals. It is also possible that very high levels of radiation during early pregnancy could produce an abnormality in the baby—in the past, high levels were used to treat pregnant women who had cancer, and this did cause defects in some of their children. It is very unlikely that diagnostic X rays would do this, and before the development of ultrasound they were used routinely in early pregnancy.

Minor Physical Problems

Backache

The ligaments supporting your spine become looser. You have more weight to support, your center of gravity changes, and you may get into the habit of standing and sitting badly, all of which can contribute to backache. Avoid high heels, and learn to sit and stand correctly. Always bend your knees when lifting something from the

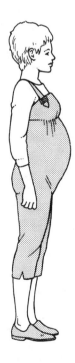

Correct posture   Bad posture

floor instead of bending your back, and keep heavy things close to your body. Do not stoop over a low work surface, and try a firmer mattress or board under your mattress to see if this makes a difference. Massage and relaxation exercises designed for pregnancy often help. If you have real problems with backache, ask your obstetrician for advice.

Bleeding Gums
The amount of blood circulating in your body increases during pregnancy, and this extra blood supply to the tissues makes gums more likely to bleed during pregnancy. Do not get into the habit of accepting it as normal—it is still caused by a buildup of plaque. Brush teeth extra-carefully with a soft brush, use dental floss, and take advantage of dental treatment in pregnancy.

Constipation
Hormone changes, relaxed muscle tone, and pressure of the womb on the bowel often cause constipation. Do not use laxatives, but instead drink plenty of water and eat whole-grain foods such as whole wheat or bran bread, rice, or pasta, plus plenty of fruits and vegetables. Iron supplements are likely to make constipation worse, so don't take them unless your blood tests show they are strictly necessary. Avoiding constipation can help avoid hemorrhoids and varicose veins. If it continues to be a problem, tell your doctor.

Cramps
The cause of muscle cramps is not known, though they are very common in pregnancy; one suggestion is that they may be caused by a lack of calcium. Rub the muscle very hard and, if the cramp is in your leg, bend your foot upward.

Faintness and Palpitations
These are due to changes in the heart and circulation system. Although such attacks can be worrying and unpleasant, they are not usually signs of anything abnormal, but are simply one of the side effects of pregnancy. Some people seem to be more prone than others. If you are at all worried, discuss this with your doctor, but generally the best tactics are to avoid certain situations as much as possible. This may mean altering your traveling arrangements so that you don't have to stand at rush hour, shopping out of peak times to avoid long waits at the checkout, and avoiding social events that entail hours of standing in hot or crowded situations. If you do feel faint, immediately find somewhere to sit down, even if it means asking someone to give up his chair or seat on the train. If the feeling persists, put your head down between your knees so the blood will flow more easily to the brain. Some women, especially in late pregnancy, find simply lying on their back is enough to make them feel faint because of the weight of the baby pressing on the large veins carrying blood back to the heart. If this is the case, simply turn on your side and make a point of explaining the problem to nurses at your next prenatal appointments to avoid having to lie on your back for longer than is absolutely necessary.

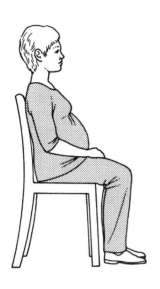

Make sure that the small of your back is supported

Try not to slump or cross your legs

Headaches

Taking an occasional acetaminophen (Tylenol) tablet is considered safe, but avoid aspirin. See your doctor if you have continuous, bad headaches. In later pregnancy these could be a warning of high blood pressure.

Heartburn and Indigestion

The valve at the entrance to the stomach relaxes in pregnancy, allowing stomach acids to filter back up the tube, causing that burning sensation we call heartburn. Pressure on the stomach from the growing baby also makes indigestion more common. Eat small amounts often and eat sitting upright, not slumping or lying back. Drinking milk can help, or try antacid medication.

Incontinence

Needing to urinate frequently is common in the first three months and also in the last three months because of the pressure of the growing baby against the bladder. Some women, especially if they have already had several children, can find themselves prone to stress incontinence, which means that laughing, coughing, or jumping up and down need to be undertaken with care and great concentration, because the extra stress can cause them to lose control and leak a small amount of urine. Stress incontinence usually disappears soon after the birth, though all women should do pelvic floor exercises during pregnancy and after the birth to prevent it from becoming a problem later in life. Continuing incontinence may indicate that nerve endings or muscles have been damaged during the birth, and you should consult your doctor.

Insomnia

Difficulty in sleeping is common as the baby gets very large. Many women often have vivid dreams in pregnancy about the birth and the baby. Try lying on your side with a pillow to support your abdomen, and take naps in the day if you can to make up for missed sleep. However, try not to attach significance to dreams or treat them as premonitions, even though for some months they may suggest some anxiety or mixed feelings about the baby.

Nosebleeds

These can be particularly common in pregnancy and, like bleeding gums, are due to the fact that an extra amount of blood is circulating around your body. The blood vessels lining the nose are more fragile and more likely to rupture at this stage. The best way of treating a nosebleed is to pinch your nostrils hard together to encourage clotting. A blocked or stuffy nose is also common and is due to increased production of nasal mucus.

Nausea

Usually this eases after twelve weeks, but for some unlucky women it can be a real problem that continues for much longer. Although commonly referred to as "morning" sickness, attacks of nausea or actual vomiting can occur at any time of day. It is thought that nausea may be caused by raised levels of female hormones circulating in the body, but despite the extent of the problem there has been surprisingly little research.

Traditional advice is to try eating something dry, such as plain crackers or a piece of toast, first thing in the morning, eat little and often, and avoid anything that makes you feel particularly bad. It seems that each person has to experiment to find the best methods or foods to alleviate the problem. Smells, such as fried food or even gasoline, can be enough to trigger an attack, but some women say certain smells—for example, that of sulfur when a match is struck—can help. Bland,

Use pillows to make yourself comfortable

starchy foods such as plain bread and cereals are usually safest, and it has been suggested that eliminating tea, coffee, and alcohol helps.

One age-old remedy is supposed to be ginger, but results are not guaranteed. The suggestion is to sip ginger tea—made with powdered ginger in boiling water or by steeping a small piece of fresh root ginger—first thing in the morning and half an hour before meals. However, since it has been suggested that a trigger for morning sickness can be swings in blood sugar levels, it is best not to seek a cure in ginger products that contain sugar, such as ginger ale. Some women crave sweet foods to relieve nausea temporarily, but eating sugary foods causes a sharp rise in blood sugar levels followed by a drop to an even lower level. Eating small but frequent snacks of wholesome foods rather than foods full of sugar and white flour can avoid this roller-coaster effect.

If you are feeling nauseated all the time or feel intolerably ill, see your doctor, but hard-learned lessons such as that of Thalidomide, given to prevent pregnancy loss, not nausea, and subsequently found to cause major birth defects, and more recently suspicions about Bendectin, have understandably made doctors wary of prescribing medications for a condition that, although extremely unpleasant, is not dangerous.

Very rarely, vomiting may lead to dehydration and even starvation. This is called hyperemesis gravidarum and needs treatment with intravenous fluids.

Skin
Stretch marks are red lines that fade into thin, silvery white lines. They occur when the elastic fiber under the skin breaks. Whether you get them depends on your inherited skin type, but using cream or oil to stop your skin from getting dry, eating well before and during pregnancy, and lightly pinching and massaging skin to stimulate circulation can sometimes help.

Some people suffer from itchy skin, especially late in pregnancy. This can affect just the abdomen or occur all over the body, and sometimes causes patches of red, flaky rash. If it is very bad, see your doctor, but otherwise loose clothing made from natural (not synthetic) fibers, oils, and creams may help, and some people suggest oatmeal in the bath does, too.

Pregnancy is also a time for changes in pigmentation—many women find that a dark line develops down the center of the abdomen from the navel from about the third month, but this has no significance and fades after the birth. Some people get patches of lighter or darker skin, which will also disappear. Freckles, moles, and scars can all become temporarily darker or more pronounced.

Sweating
Body temperature is higher during pregnancy. This is useful in winter, but if you have a summer pregnancy you may need cool showers and rest to avoid overheating.

Swelling
Legs, ankles, feet, and hands may all swell up during pregnancy because the body holds more water than usual. As long as your blood pressure stays normal, it does

not matter, but this should be checked because swelling (the medical name is edema) can sometimes be a forewarning of a condition called pre-eclampsia. Try to rest with your feet higher than your heart; wear flat, comfortable shoes; and take things easy.

Vaginal Discharge, Soreness, Itching, or Odor

Discharge is usually heavier during pregnancy anyway, but itching, soreness, or an offensive smell may mean an infection such as a yeast infection, so see your doctor.

Varicose Veins and Hemorrhoids

Hormonal changes and the pressure of the uterus on veins make varicose veins in the legs and vulva more likely in pregnancy. Wearing support pantyhose, putting your feet up, avoiding standing for long periods or sitting with crossed legs, and not getting constipated from the beginning of pregnancy can help to prevent or relieve them. Varicose veins around the rectum are called hemorrhoids and usually arise because of constipation. If they are troublesome and cause itching or soreness, see your doctor, but usually both hemorrhoids and varicose veins disappear after the birth.

More Serious Problems in Pregnancy

Ectopic Pregnancy

This occurs when the fertilized egg implants and begins to grow somewhere other than the womb, usually the Fallopian tube, but occasionally in the abdomen. The word "ectopic" simply means displaced. It usually happens because a blockage or kink in the Fallopian tube prevents the fertilized egg from reaching the womb. Signs are one—rarely two—missed periods, pain low down and to one side in the abdomen, often pain in the shoulder, faintness, and losing a slight amount of dark-ish blood. It is important that such pregnancies are diagnosed because they can cause internal bleeding and shock and can even be fatal. Since most ectopic pregnancies are in one of the Fallopian tubes, this usually means an operation on the tube. Sometimes this can be performed through surgery using a laparoscope. Alternatively, an open operation is needed and the tube may have to be removed. Further pregnancy is still possible, provided the other tube is undamaged.

Molar Pregnancy

This is a rare condition when the embryo usually fails to develop and the placenta grows abnormally and quickly. Signs are a large-for-date uterus but no sign of a fetal heartbeat and sometimes heavy bleeding. Although it has nothing to do with the kind of moles that grow on your skin, this "false embryo" is referred to as a mole and will be need to be removed with a dilation and curettage (D and C). In unusual cases the cells can show abnormalities that may lead to malignancy if untreated; therefore, continued and close surveillance by your obstetrician is recommended.

Bleeding in Early Pregnancy

Spotting sometimes happens at the time of a first missed period as the embryo implants in the wall of the uterus, but bleeding can also be a warning of threatened miscarriage or ectopic pregnancy.

Bleeding in Middle and Late Pregnancy

Incompetent Cervix   This usually occurs at about weeks eighteen to twenty-four, when the neck of a womb that is not able to stay tightly closed may begin to open. This could be because of damage during earlier pregnancies or during a gynecological operation. Treatment is a special stitch to draw the cervix tightly closed—rather like the neck of a purse. This is usually done at about week fourteen under general or epidural anesthetic, and the stitch can be taken out without anesthetic at week thirty-eight.

Placenta Previa   Painless bleeding from week twenty-eight is usually because of this. If the placenta attaches itself to the wall of the uterus low down, it partially or completely blocks the baby's exit by covering the cervix. If bleeding begins before the baby is due, then you will need to be admitted to the hospital for observation. In cases of very heavy bleeding a premature delivery by cesarean section will need to be undertaken. Once you reach thirty-eight to thirty-nine weeks a cesarean section is needed anyway if the placenta still covers the cervix, but sometimes vaginal delivery is possible with a placenta that only extends close to the cervix. Ultrasound can easily check the position of the placenta, and sometimes a low-lying placenta may move upward of its own accord as the pregnancy progresses. Rarely, placenta previa may not be evident until labor begins with heavy bleeding, and then an emergency cesarean and a blood transfusion are usually needed.

Placental Abruption.   Painful and heavy vaginal bleeding after twenty-eight weeks of pregnancy requires urgent admission to the hospital and investigation. It occurs when the placenta starts to shear away from the wall of the uterus. The bleeding can be very heavy and put both mother and baby in danger, so that the baby has to be delivered by emergency cesarean section. Such heavy bleeding is rare. More commonly, mothers complain of lower abdominal cramps and a small amount of vaginal bleeding, which settles after a few hours. Again, it is essential to go to the hospital, where you should expect to stay for observation and tests to check on the baby's well-being and your blood pressure. Normally if there has been no bleeding or pain for twenty-four to forty-eight hours you will be able to go home, but you may need to have more frequent prenatal appointments afterward. Your doctor may suggest that you be induced if your baby does not come on time. If bleeding occurs toward the end of pregnancy you may be induced to prevent any harm to the baby.

High Blood Pressure and Pre-Eclampsia

Some women already have high blood pressure; others develop it during pregnancy. A family history of high blood pressure, blood pressure problems while taking the Pill, smoking, or being overweight all increase the chance of this happening. High blood pressure is often the first sign of a condition called pre-eclampsia or toxemia, which occurs only in pregnancy. Although it may make the mother or the baby very sick, this condition always gets better after the baby is born. The other features of pre-eclampsia are swelling (edema) of the legs, fingers, and face, and protein in the urine. Poor growth of the placenta may occur, which makes it less efficient at giving oxygen and nourishment to the baby. Treatment is with rest initially, and medication may be needed to bring the blood pressure down. Early delivery by inducing labor or even by cesarean section is often necessary to prevent eclampsia (see below) or harm to the baby.

We do not know exactly why pre-eclampsia happens, but it is very much more likely in the first pregnancy and is also linked with a family history of the condition. Research suggests that an immune reaction in the mother may be involved.

Ten percent of women will get pre-eclampsia in their first pregnancy, and the risk is three times this if a woman's blood pressure was high before getting pregnant.

Eclampsia
If unchecked, pre-eclampsia can lead to eclampsia with convulsions. This condition can be dangerous but is fortunately very rare. The mother loses consciousness, may injure herself, and may have trouble breathing, which puts the baby at serious risk because the seizure drastically reduces the baby's oxygen supply. Prevention is nearly always possible, but very rarely such a seizure can happen without warning signs; if it does, treatment is anticonvulsant drugs and usually emergency delivery of the baby by cesarean section.

Unusual Birth Positions
Most babies are born head first, with the back of the baby's head toward the mother's abdomen. They usually settle into this head-down position at about the

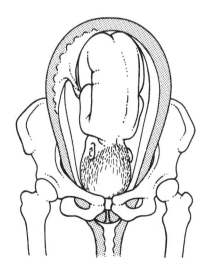

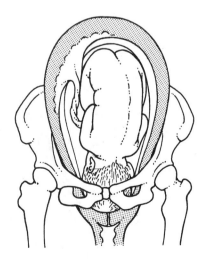

Unengaged   Engaged

seventh month, when they become too large to do those amazing somersaults and turns that make your stomach jump around. The reason why this is the preferred position for birth is that the head is the largest part of the baby and is also a hard, rounded surface, which works better to open up the birth canal slowly as the baby is born. It is also, conveniently, the end that takes in oxygen. The head is said to be engaged when it descends into the pelvis, and you will experience a noticeable easing as the bulge drops lower in your abdomen. Obstetricians will be concerned about the position of the baby, as more unusual positions sometimes need more care and attention at the birth.

Breech   This means that the baby is lying bottom or feet first. It is very common in the middle months, but only 6 percent of babies are still breech at thirty-four weeks and only 3 percent at term. Sometimes the doctor may try to turn the baby by gently manipulating her from the outside. Do not try to do this yourself, though, because it can cause the placenta to separate if not done properly. Breech babies can be delivered vaginally but will almost certainly need help with an episiotomy and perhaps forceps. Depending on your circumstances, a cesarean section may be suggested. Sometimes doctors suggest waiting for labor to begin naturally to see if a normal delivery looks possible.

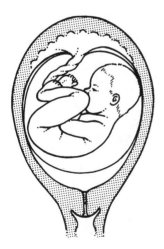

Transverse   This means the baby is lying crossways instead of vertically. This is more likely after several babies, when the muscles of the uterus have already been stretched. As in the case with breech babies, these positions can right themselves naturally, and sometimes a transverse baby turns head down only when labor begins. If not, the presenting part—the part of the baby that is born first—will usually be the shoulder, in which case a cesarean section is needed.

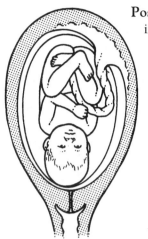

Posterior In this position the baby is head down, but instead of having the back of her head and backbone toward the mother's abdomen (anterior), the baby has her backbone to the mother's backbone, so face and limbs are all toward the mother's abdomen. The most likely effect during labor is that you will experience backache rather than pains across your abdomen. It can help to use different positions during labor, and medication may be recommended to help things along if labor is not progressing swiftly enough.

Unstable Lie An unstable lie means that the baby is sometimes transverse and sometimes head down or breech and is not fixed in one position.

Miscarriage

It is estimated that one in six of all pregnancies ends in miscarriage. The term applies to a fetus delivered dead before the twenty-fourth week of pregnancy—the stage at which, legally, a fetus is considered viable. The law used to state the twenty-eighth week, but this lagged behind medical skills in this respect because babies born as early as twenty-three weeks are now being saved in neonatal (new-born) intensive-care units. If a baby is delivered alive after the twenty-fourth week, this is described not as a miscarriage but as premature labor and delivery. A baby born dead after the twenty-fourth week is said to be stillborn. Thus the word "miscarriage" has a very precise meaning. The medical term for miscarriage is "spontaneous abortion," which can cause confusion because to many people the word "abortion" means only the deliberate termination of a pregnancy.

Why do miscarriages happen? Inevitably, as couples try to come to terms with the shock of a pregnancy that ends in miscarriage, they search for a reason. Sadly, in the vast majority of cases of miscarriage no cause is readily apparent, and because having even two miscarriages does not greatly alter the odds against success the third time around, doctors do not usually embark on a major investigation until a woman has experienced three or more repeated miscarriages, known as "recurrent miscarriage." In the absence of any medical explanation, couples may worry that they could have caused the miscarriage—perhaps by making love, by working too hard, by being under stress, by moving to a new house, or by having too many late nights. None of these factors has ever been shown to be linked with miscarriage, however, and when you consider the number of pregnancies that continue despite the most adverse conditions—war, famine, and emotional upheavals of all kinds—it is unlikely there would be a link.

There is still a great deal we do not know about why some pregnancies miscarry and why some others, especially when the baby has some kind of abnormal development, go on to term. However, some factors are known. The largest cause of early miscarriage is chromosomal abnormality. Studies of miscarriages where fetal tissue was examined—and this is only possible in 20 percent of miscarriages—show genetic mistakes in half of the cases. There appears to be some natural mechanism that operates to end such pregnancies, though this obviously does not always happen because of the numbers of children with physical problems who are born. In cases of repeated miscarriage, couples can have genetic counseling to make sure they do not carry a chromosomal abnormality, but in most cases of single miscarriage the couple's chromosome pattern is normal and any genetic abnormality in the fetus is a one-time mistake. Some malformations may be genetic but are not caused by chromosomal abnormalities—for example, spina bifida, in which the spinal cord does not form properly.

Other causes of miscarriage include:

- **Physical abnormalities**   During pregnancy the mother's uterus must expand as the baby and its surrounding bag of water grow. Occasionally the womb may be misshapen due to abnormal development when the mother herself was a fetus. The womb develops from two tubes that fuse together; failure to do this leads to a heart-shaped uterus or even to two separate, small uteruses, which may not expand so easily.

    Another cause of expansion failure is fibroids (noncancerous growths that are common particularly after age thirty) in the wall of the uterus. These rigid balls of fibrous tissue can misshape the womb and may need to be removed surgically before pregnancy.

- **Hormones**   These have long been blamed for miscarriage, and women thought to have a hormone deficiency can be treated with hormone therapy either by injection, suppositories, or orally. There is no clear evidence about the part hormone deficiencies play in miscarriages, and there is a good deal of disagreement about whether treatment with hormones has any effect. It is probably best to be cautious about taking hormones in early pregnancy. However, it is known that an over- or underactive thyroid can sometimes lead to repeated miscarriages. A blood test can be done to check that the thyroid is working normally.

- **Immunological**   This is a comparatively newly established cause of miscarriage and takes two forms. The first, which is thought to be responsible for a substantial number of all recurrent miscarriages, is when the mother's immune system reacts as though the cells of the fetus are foreign and rejects them—just as transplanted organs are often rejected. Of course, the baby's cells are made up of antigens (proteins) from both the mother and the father. Normally there is a mechanism that prevents the mother's body from reacting to the father's antigens—this is the production of antibodies by the mother that stop her immune system reacting to the baby's cells as foreign matter. Treatment is for the woman to be immunized with her husband's cells, by injecting blood lymphocytes, so her body makes the required antibodies that will protect subsequent pregnancies from being rejected, but this procedure has had limited success. The problem is not caused by any abnormality in either husband or wife; rather, it is a question of the choice of partner—with a different partner the woman may produce antibodies in the normal way.

In the second form it has now been recognized that certain women produce antibodies against fatty substances called phospholipids, which are found on the surface of all cells. This condition causes repeated miscarriages late in pregnancy, often after twenty weeks. Current treatment is with combinations of several drugs that may prevent miscarriage and allow the fetus to grow normally, but the risk of early labor remains.

* **Infection**   Rubella (German measles) is known to cause miscarriage as well as to cause abnormalities in surviving babies; so, too, may genital herpes during the initial infection. Uncertainty exists about the effects of other, more common infections, such as influenza; such effects are hard to prove or disprove. Infections that can exist without causing any noticeable illness in the mother may cause miscarriage—toxoplasmosis and mycoplasma are two. In the case of repeated miscarriages a woman should be screened for such conditions, which may show up in blood or cervical smear tests.

* **Age**   The risk of miscarriage does increase slightly with a woman's age, especially after age thirty, but, of course, most pregnancies in older women do not miscarry.

* **The IUD (intrauterine device)**   Pregnancies can happen with an IUD inside the womb, and if the IUD is left in place there is a 50 percent chance of miscarriage and also a high risk of infection. For this reason, IUDs are always removed once a pregnancy is confirmed if the IUD string is accessible.

Signs of a Miscarriage

> *I started bleeding and went to see my doctor. He advised bed rest, but after two days in bed I was still bleeding and I decided to get up. The miscarriage happened the next day. I had some abdominal cramps and felt sweaty and shivery. I kept going to the bathroom and eventually passed what I recognized as a tiny embryo. I was twelve weeks pregnant, but I was very shocked to find there was something there. I was terribly naive. I thought it would just be blood clots.*

Bleeding of some description is usually the first sign of a threatened miscarriage. It can be a slight discharge of a brownish color, a steady trickle of a bright red color, or blood clots. The good news is that about half of all pregnancies which have some bleeding in the first three months will actually settle down and continue normally with no harm at all to the fetus, any blood having come from the lining of the womb.

See your doctor as soon if you notice any bleeding during pregnancy. Generally if the neck of the womb (cervix) is open and the bleeding heavy, the woman will be referred to the hospital. An ultrasound scan can determine whether the pregnancy is still viable, that is, able to continue. If not, then a D and C under general anesthetic will be advised to remove any remaining clots or tissue. If the pregnancy is still viable, then she will be advised to take things easy. Depending on the situation, she may or may not be kept in the hospital. There is no evidence that staying in bed, either at the hospital or at home, actually helps to prevent miscarriage, but it is still commonly prescribed because it is something that is obviously hard to subject to scientific measurement. There are clearly many cases where a pregnancy continues after a woman has stayed in bed, but we do not know whether that would have happened if the same woman had continued her normal activities. Certainly it does no harm, and it seems to make sense. After the bleeding stops and the pregnancy settles down, doctors usually advise continuing to take things easy at home for two weeks or so before slowly resuming a normal pace of life.

Sometimes a fetus may die in the womb without any sign of bleeding. This is usually detected on an ultrasound scan. To feel well and to be told out of the blue that the pregnancy is not viable can be a great shock. This can occur when the embryo and surrounding membranes appear to develop normally for a short time and then the embryo dies while the membranes continue to function for a little longer. An ultrasound scan will reveal an "empty sac." Some obstetricians refer to this as a blighted ovum, an archaic term wrongly implying that the error is always with the egg. A "missed abortion" is the term used when the embryo dies but there is neither bleeding nor signs of miscarriage. The causes are not clear, but are thought to be due to some defect in the egg or sperm. The tissue is removed by a D and C under anesthetic, but this does not mean future pregnancies are more likely to run into problems.

Recurrent Miscarriage After having one miscarriage, women are naturally fearful and want reassurance about the chances of future pregnancies ending this way. Happily, one miscarriage does not alter the odds of the next pregnancy being successful, and even if a woman has had two miscarriages, there is still more than a 75 percent chance of success. But, statistically, having three recurrent miscarriages does affect the odds, which is why doctors only investigate once a woman falls into this category. It is important that the couple is properly examined, although they must still be prepared for disappointment, as a cause is often impossible to pinpoint even after thorough search.

It is thought that probably the most common cause of recurrent miscarriage is immunological. Genetic factors are common causes of a single miscarriage, but a much rarer cause of recurrent miscarriage. Women with a pattern of recurrent miscarriage also need to be screened to eliminate the possibility of infection, as well as any anatomical abnormality.

Coping with Miscarriage In addition to shock, guilt, and a sense of loss, women often feel thoroughly disoriented. The birth of a baby requires many decisions and much planning. It is only when the event is suddenly removed that we realize just how much, subconsciously, it has begun to dominate the horizon. It is often hard to go back to ordinary life with enthusiasm. Some women feel an overwhelming desire to become pregnant again as soon as possible to replace the familiar horizon. Others may wish to make changes in their lives to take a new direction. It helps to be able to talk to others who have experienced this common disappointment and for couples to talk to each other. Breaking the news to family, friends, and coworkers is sometimes hard, as they can occasionally be unintentionally brisk—"Never mind, you're young"—or add to guilt by making misplaced suggestions about the possible causes.

It is a good idea to allow the hormonal balance to settle and to wait several months before trying for another pregnancy and to discuss your understandable worries with your obstetrician first.

Pregnancies Needing the Five-Star Treatment

Age and Other Risks

Probably the best age to have a baby from a purely physical point of view is between twenty and twenty-four. Of course, that is not always the best time socially or emotionally, but women who have existing illnesses such as diabetes can help to reduce the risks if they have their children during their twenties. Pregnancies should be well spaced so the body can recover in between and so that the mother is not too exhausted with the demands of several very young children.

Younger Mothers   Under age sixteen there is a higher risk of having a small or premature baby, of becoming anemic, and of suffering from high blood pressure. Emotionally and socially such very young teenagers are likely to find pregnancy and motherhood much harder to cope with and to need a great deal of support.

Older First-Time Mothers   What is the greatest risk to the older mother? "Her doctor's anxiety, I would say," said one leading obstetrician. Certainly, feeling that this may be a woman's last chance of having a baby, especially if she has had years of fertility treatment to enable her to conceive, may make her doctor more likely to intervene at the first hint of trouble. With careful monitoring, however, there is no reason why older first-time mothers of thirty-five or over should not be just as able to have a normal, straightforward birth as a younger woman. The risk most associated with age is having a baby with some chromosomal abnormality, the most common being Down syndrome. A woman in her twenties has a chance of only 1 in several thousand of having such a baby, but by forty the risk is about 1 in every 110 births, and at forty-five the risk is about 1 in every 30. Amniocentesis can detect the extra chromosome that results in a Down baby. This may be offered routinely to women who are thirty-five or over or after positive serum screening or a nuchal translucency test. Fibroids, high blood pressure, and prematurity are all slightly more common among older first-time mothers.

Number of Children

A woman having her first pregnancy is called a "primigravida" and a woman who has already had one baby is called a "multiparous" by doctors. First babies represent a slightly higher risk because the "machinery" is untested and the mother inexperienced. Second and third pregnancies are more often straightforward, provided previous pregnancies have been free of complications. The risks begin to rise again with a fourth and successive pregnancies because the uterine muscles have less tone, are less efficient, and are worn thinner, though this also depends to an extent on age and natural health.

Heart Disease

Pregnancy puts an added strain on the heart anyway—it has to pump about a third more blood through the body, and at a faster rate. It is quite common to feel your heart beating more rapidly or to feel breathless in pregnancy, but existing heart disease is a different matter and relatively unusual. Sometimes a heart condition can be discovered for the first time during pregnancy just because this may be the first time a woman has had a complete medical examination. If it is mild, then taking things easy and staying calm may be enough. This could mean giving up work earlier in pregnancy, getting some help with housework or other children, and calling on friends and relatives to lend a hand. If your heart condition is more serious, it could involve much closer supervision by the physician and possibly admission to the hospital to monitor your condition. Heart patients should not eat too much, and should cut down on their salt intake to help keep their blood pressure down; also, their weight will be carefully monitored.

Unless there are other problems, a woman with a heart condition should be able to have a normal labor. An epidural may be suggested because it has the effect of lowering blood pressure and also reducing pain and therefore anxiety, and oxygen will be on hand to relieve breathlessness or chest pain. The effort of pushing as the baby moves down the birth canal is an extra strain on the heart, and forceps are often used to avoid a prolonged pushing stage. There is no reason why mothers with heart conditions should not breast-feed, but they generally have a longer stay in the hospital to make sure there are no complications. Again, pregnancies should be well spaced so the body has time to recover.

The Rhesus Factor

In addition to belonging to one of four different blood groups, your blood can be either rhesus (Rh)-positive or rhesus-negative. It is Rh-positive if it contains a particular antigen—a substance that stimulates the formation of antibodies—which happens also to be found on the red blood cells of rhesus monkeys. Eighty-five percent of people are Rh-positive. Your blood is Rh-negative if it does not have this antigen. Your baby is a mix of genetic information from both parents, and when an Rh-negative woman and an Rh-positive man have a baby, that baby could inherit the blood type of either parent. It is only a problem if the baby inherits her father's blood type and is Rh-positive—the opposite of her mother. During pregnancy, and particularly during the birth, some of the baby's blood cells may become mixed with the mother's and circulate in the mother's body. This also happens with unsuccessful pregnancies, which may be ectopic or end in miscarriage or termination. The mother's body reacts to these foreign blood cells by producing antibodies to fight them. These antibody molecules are small enough to cross the placenta and go back into the baby to start destroying the baby's red blood cells. If untreated, this could eventually make the baby so anemic that she will die. Usually the level of antibodies is not high enough to do serious damage in a first pregnancy, but they will remain in the mother's blood, and the problem becomes more serious with each successive pregnancy.

Fortunately, there is now a way to prevent this, and discovering a way to prevent rhesus babies has been one of the great success stories of obstetrics. If an injection of anti-D globulin (Rhogam) is given to the mother within seventy-two hours of the first delivery (and this applies to miscarriages and terminations at whatever stage of pregnancy), it stops her from becoming sensitized and making antibodies in future pregnancies.

However, if the woman has already become sensitized, perhaps because of an untreated earlier pregnancy or miscarriage, this injection cannot help. Instead, the level of antibodies in her blood will be monitored carefully through pregnancy, and the baby's condition may be checked by amniocentesis. The level of a yellowish pigment called "bilirubin" in the amniotic fluid is a rough guide to the degree of anemia in the baby, and several tests may be needed. If the baby is in danger of becoming anemic, she can have a blood transfusion while still in the womb. This may be done either by injecting blood into the baby's abdomen, from where it is absorbed into the bloodstream, or by transfusing it directly into the umbilical cord blood vessels. Both these procedures are done using expert ultrasound pictures showing where to pass the fine needles. This may have to be done several times during pregnancy until the baby is mature enough to be delivered by cesarean section, and it is a complicated procedure that can be done at most teaching hospitals. After birth the baby may need another transfusion, although this is a much simpler procedure.

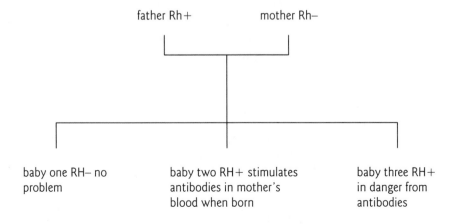

father Rh+   mother Rh−

baby one RH− no problem

baby two RH+ stimulates antibodies in mother's blood when born

baby three RH+ in danger from antibodies

Diabetes

Insulin is a hormone produced by the pancreas gland in the abdomen. Its job is to facilitate transfer of the glucose or sugar in the circulation into the cells, where it can be used as a source of energy. Diabetics either do not produce any insulin or not enough. When the body cannot use glucose for fuel it begins to use fat instead and, in the process, substances called ketones are produced. A buildup of ketones in the blood upsets the body's chemistry, making a diabetic feel nauseous or even pass out. The glucose is unused and makes the blood glucose level very high. Because of this high level, glucose begins to be passed out of the body in the urine. This is one of the first signs of diabetes. Diabetes carries a higher risk of miscarriage and some degree of fetal malformation—usually a single defect, such as a heart or lower spine abnormality—but provided the glucose levels are kept as normal as possible before and during pregnancy, the risk is very small. If the father is a diabetic his control before pregnancy does not make any difference to the risk.

Because the key factor in ensuring the successful outcome of a pregnancy is control of the diabetes, any woman with diabetes should see her doctor well before she plans to become pregnant. Getting very good control of diabetes may mean three to four injections of insulin a day, usually using a mixture of short- and long-acting insulins. Once pregnancy is confirmed, this good control must continue, and because urine tests are not reliable enough, frequent daily blood testing is necessary. During pregnancy the amount of insulin needed changes rapidly and can double in the second half. Diabetic women need to eat especially carefully.

A careful check will also be kept on the baby's size, for babies of diabetics have a tendency to grow very large. It used to be the practice to deliver the babies of diabetic women early, but this in turn led to problems of prematurity in some cases. When diabetes has been carefully monitored and controlled, it is now often possible to leave such babies until term when they can usually be delivered vaginally. During labor an intravenous drip will be set up, and insulin can either be added to the fluid being given through the drip or administered continuously with a special pump. Immediately after the birth the need for insulin will drop, and the day after the baby has been born the mother should go back to using the dosage and type of insulin she was on before she became pregnant.

Because the infants of diabetics are sometimes larger than average, such babies may lose a lot of weight in the first few days and seem sleepy, but after that they should develop normally. They will have tests in the first few days to check that their blood sugars are normal. Sometimes they may be immature if they have been delivered early and thus more likely to become hypoglycemic (very low blood sugar); for this reason they are usually nursed in a special-care baby unit for a few days.

Pregnancy Diabetes

Pregnancy predisposes the body chemistry toward diabetes, which can occur solely as a condition of pregnancy, disappearing again after the birth. If it happens in one pregnancy, it is more likely to recur in later pregnancies and may occur mildly in later life. It happens more often in older women, and the chance of it occurring increases slightly with the number of pregnancies. Treatment is just the same as for existing diabetes—diet and possibly insulin are needed to control the blood sugar levels.

Twins, Triplets, and More

Multiple pregnancies, where there is more than one baby, always require special care and monitoring. Identical twins are the result of one fertilized egg splitting in two. The babies share one placenta and are always the same sex. Anyone has a 1 in 250 chance of having identical twins, though there is often a family history. Nonidentical twins occur when two eggs are released and fertilized by two different sperm and have separate placentas, which may, however, fuse together. The babies are no more alike than any brothers and sisters. Nonidentical twins are more common than identical twins. A family history through the maternal line makes nonidentical twins more likely, and the chances are also slightly greater with taller women, older women, women who conceive easily, and with successive pregnancies. Triplets, quadruplets, quintuplets, and sextuplets can occur spontaneously and can be a mixture of identical and nonidentical fetuses. For example, triplets could have started as a nonidentical twin pregnancy, but then one twin split to become identical twins.

Today, many multiple births result from fertility treatment when drugs are used to stimulate ovulation and the ovary overreacts and produces several eggs at one time. The most common of these drugs, clomiphene, is capable of producing such a response. Test-tube treatments (IVF or in vitro fertilization), when a fertilized egg is implanted back into the uterus, are also likely to produce more than one baby because doctors usually put three embryos back—with the couple's agreement—in the hope that one will survive. Sometimes more than one can develop, resulting in a multiple birth.

Wider use of ultrasound has made undiagnosed multiple pregnancies rare. The uterus grows more quickly in size, weight gain is faster, and the mother often feels

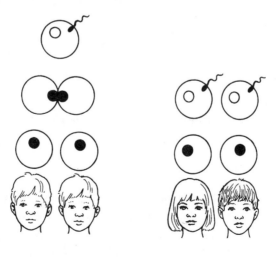

Identical twins   Fraternal twins

the side effects of pregnancy more strongly –nausea, tiredness, aching legs, varicose veins, plus a lot more movement and kicking inside. Occasionally, one embryo does not survive, and if this happens early in pregnancy it may be reabsorbed into the body with no ill effects to the remaining embryo or embryos. If it happens later in pregnancy, the dead fetus will usually remain in the uterus and be delivered at the time of the birth of the live baby or babies. The dead baby is usually much smaller than the surviving live baby or babies.

The main risk when there is more than one baby is that they will be born too early and be premature; this becomes a greater risk with a greater number of babies. Whether you stay at home or need to spend the last weeks in the hospital depends on your circumstances and health, but usually women expecting three or more babies will be admitted to the hospital. It is also most likely that in cases with three or more babies the delivery will be by cesarean section, but in the case of twins there is no reason—provided both twins are in the head-down position and every-thing else is normal—why they should not be delivered vaginally. The risk of hem-orrhage is greater with multiple births, but the medical staff will be well aware of this and take steps to prevent it.

There is no reason why mothers should not breast-feed twins completely or partly breast-feed any number of babies, though naturally this requires great moti-vation and extra help and support. There are national organizations for mothers of twins that any mother of more than one baby will find helpful.

Mixed Emotions—How You Feel During Pregnancy

During pregnancy most parents-to-be tend to think mainly of the birth ahead—it is hard to realize just how dramatically and permanently a baby alters your role in life forever. Not only are you and your partner becoming a father and a mother, but also your mother-in-law is becoming a grandmother, and your sisters and brothers are becoming aunts and uncles. And so it goes on, in ever-widening circles. Having a baby and becoming a parent is one of the greatest changes in anyone's life, and mixed emotions, including some anxieties, are natural, but recognizing some of the demands and problems that may arise makes it easier to cope.

Adjusting to Parenthood

"Involved" is the word of the moment to describe a modern father's role in parent-ing. Exactly what that means, most fathers are still trying to work out. But it is true that very many marriage problems in later life can be traced back to the arrival of children. Why should this happen?

A first baby does tend to turn life upside down for a while, and however much you both wanted one, there will be times when you both also resent the loss of free-dom and the tiredness that all new parents experience. It may seem old-fashioned in this age of equality and the "new man" to talk about fathers being left out, but very many men do report that they feel excluded, and a parting of the ways at this early stage can sometimes lead to more serious problems later.

On the woman's side, she is often totally submerged in the demands of her children; this is especially so if she has two or more children very close together. On the man's side, it may seem that after a day at work all that is expected of him when he gets home is more work. The arrival of a first baby may even coincide with a time when his job is particularly demanding, since the childbearing years often coincide with the career-building years. He may unconsciously begin to spend more time at work, which can lead to resentment when his wife feels she is being left to cope alone. She can feel under great pressure, not only with the practicalities of coping with a new baby (which can be very taxing) but also with coming to terms with a completely different role. Most women work until a few weeks or months before the birth of their first baby, and so may often know few people in the area where she lives and almost no other parents if this is her first child. Relatives often live some distance away. Suddenly her day has no shape except the one she feels inclined to impose on it, and she may often be lonely and feel lost in her new world. Because most couples find it hard to look beyond the birth, this sort of situation can creep up and surprise them before either has realized exactly what the problem is. It really does help during pregnancy to talk to each other about exactly what the other one expects life will be like after the birth. Men need to understand just how displaced a woman who has given up a job may feel when she begins to adjust to motherhood and staying home. Women need to understand how even the most involved father can sometimes feel a sense of loss when he sees his partner so completely submerged with the preoccupations and demands of parenthood.

One answer is to plan ways in which you can share each other's lives. Thinking about baby-sitting arrangements, which could work both in the day and evening to give you breaks to have time alone together and for the woman to have time away from her baby, is important. Finding a sitter need not be expensive—perhaps there are friends who would swap, or relatives who might help out. A man who is willing to take over the baby for a complete day so his wife can go out is much better able to understand the demands and problems of life with a small child. Most important, couples need to keep talking to each other as problems arise and as they feel difficulties are likely to crop up. Don't lose sight of the person in the parent—new fathers and mothers both need reassurance that they are still valued, loved, and needed for themselves.

Try cultivating friendships with other couples who have recently had children. You'll find they can be very supportive and will help you see that most of the problems you will be experiencing are very common. Prenatal classes that are designed for couples, or those that have several sessions for fathers to come along, too, are good places to meet other parents. There are now some organizations that, beginning in pregnancy, arrange groups to help couples promote positive early family and parent-infant relationships.

More importantly, learning together about how pregnancy is changing your body, how the baby is growing and developing, and what will happen at the birth means sharing the whole experience together. For men just to receive information secondhand from their wives who are attending prenatal classes on their own is not the same at all. Going to some classes together can often spark the kind of discussions that lead to looking to the future and imagining what sort of changes in both your lives the baby is going to mean. For example, how much will both of you be able to continue pursuing your interests, hobbies, or sports? Normal life does not have to stop after a baby arrives, though it may sometimes feel like it. But it is unrealistic to think you can continue exactly as you did before. Time is suddenly at a premium and if one partner expects or assumes that he or she will be able to keep up all the things that person enjoyed without making any changes or discussing how it can best be worked out with his or her partner, it will naturally lead to some resentment.

Women who hope to return to work, either part-time or full-time, also need to discuss the future with their partner—neither parent would want to feel that making arrangements for the child's care during working hours is entirely and solely his or her responsibility. It's important that you look at all the options together: deciding on day care or hired help in the home; interviewing potential caregivers together so you can both form a judgment; and making a decision together. For couples who are losing half or a portion of their joint income because the woman is giving up full-time work completely or moving to part-time work, managing on a much smaller income may also be a source of worry. Like all problems, it is better to discuss this before it happens.

Another source of stress in the future can be your changing relationship with your in-laws. Your relationship with them may have been somewhat distant in the past. Inevitably with the arrival of a grandchild it will become much closer. If you get along well together, sharing the excitement of the grandchild can be a great source of joy, but if you do not get along well with your in-laws it can be a difficult adjustment when the new grandmother and grandfather want to be on the scene more often. Again, it is not a problem to be ignored. Accept that all the grandparents will want to have far more contact with you after the arrival of the new grandchild. If relationships are difficult, work out how you can best manage the new situation. This is another area where tension may gradually mount without either of you being aware of it until it explodes. Looking ahead can sometimes help to avoid that.

Your Emotions During Pregnancy

All those hormones rushing around not only change your body, they also change the way you feel emotionally. Many women feel particularly sensitive, weepy, or otherwise emotional during pregnancy, especially in the first three months. It is very common to feel unusually sensitive as well as tired and possibly a bit nauseated at this time. It helps a great deal if your partner understands that this is something that happens to most pregnant women.

In addition to excitement and joy about the pregnancy, most women have moments of feeling uncertain and anxious as well. After all, you are saying goodbye to a certain stage of your life and lifestyle. For women who are on their own and without the support of a loving partner, or who have become pregnant by accident, these doubts and anxieties will probably be particularly powerful. It helps to voice your uncertainties to someone you trust who will understand that although you

useful to have a few cloth diapers as a standby in case you run out on some occasion. If you are going for cloth diapers alone, the minimum number is thought to be two dozen, and you also need diaper liners—thick squares of papery woven material that enable you to separate and flush any solid matter down the toilet before putting the cloth diaper to soak in diaper solution in a bucket. If you are using pins, be sure they are diaper safety pins with the protective hood over the sharp point, not ordinary safety pins. Some diapers have Velcro fasteners and do not require pins.

Plastic pants These are essential with cloth diapers. There are many different varieties on the market, some that snap up the front, some that are simply strips of plastic that tie at each side, and some with elastic at the legs. The best bet is to ask some experienced mothers what they recommend and look at what is available in the stores—you will need about six pants to begin with.

The design of disposable diapers has improved tremendously in the past few years, with elastic at the legs and a much better fit, but plastic pants can be useful at night or when traveling to make extra sure there are no leaks.

Clothes

The main thing to remember is that new babies need changing far more often than you can ever imagine, and many of them hate being undressed completely. This means that all clothes should have easy access for diaper changes without having to take everything off, and should also be easy to get on and off. Choose stretchy neck openings that go over heads without a struggle, and uncomplicated fasteners such as snaps in preference to ribbons, which have to be tied and which can easily become knotted or start to fray. Clothes also need to be machine-washable and not hand-washable only—an especially good point to remember when kind relatives or friends offer to knit clothes for you.

Undershirts New babies are not very good at keeping warm, and many of them hate to be undressed completely. For this reason undershirts are an essential item of wear both in winter and summer. There are three types—all-in-one stretch body suits, front-fastening undershirts with ribbons that tie, and the traditional style of undershirts with an envelope neck. Body suits give a nice, smooth outline, but diaper leaks can spread upward through the body suit, which can mean a complete change of clothes every time. Envelope-neck styles are probably cheapest and best—you will need half a dozen, and you can usually save money by buying them in bargain packs of three.

Stretch Suits These are the easiest garments to dress a new baby in and also very practical, with snaps around the crotch to allow for diaper changes without having to undress the baby completely, and they are also good at keeping her warm. You will need about half a dozen for a summer baby and a couple more for a winter one, but do not be tempted to get less than this because on a bad day you can get through an amazing number! Again, buying them in packs of three usually saves money.

Knitted Clothes Many people get great pleasure out of knitting for a new baby, but do steer them clear of very open, lacy patterns, which can easily get caught on a stroller or carriage and which small fingers can often get tangled up in. Also avoid tie necks. An undershirt, stretch suit, and knitted cardigan or pullover will keep a baby warm in winter.

New babies usually like being wrapped up and held securely, but it is up to you whether you prefer buying or knitting a shawl for your baby. If you want to avoid the expense, you can just as easily use receiving blankets. One advantage to these is that they they tend to be washable.

Other Clothes Dresses for girls make diaper changing easier, but hamper crawling babies. The easiest clothes for both sexes are sweat-suit-style tops and bottoms because you can remove the bottom half without interfering with the rest of the baby's clothes. A winter baby will need a pull-on woolly hat, but you do not need to dress her in an expensive snowsuit if you are taking her out in a carriage, because using a knitted cardigan and several layers of blankets and a quilt inside the carriage will keep her just as warm. But a snowsuit is necessary if you intend to forgo a closed-in carriage and put her straight into a stroller—there are several on the market that are designed for newborn babies. A summer baby needs a cotton sun hat with a brim. Shoes are not necessary until the baby actually begins to walk, and store-bought socks or quilted booties are fine to keep a newborn baby's feet warm.

Incidentals

A changing mat is a pretty essential piece of equipment, plus a good stock of cotton balls to use with water to clean your baby's bottom. Baby wipes are an easy way of cleaning the baby, but are more expensive than other methods. You may want to use a barrier cream to provide some protection from a wet cloth diaper, though today's disposables, which incorporate special granules to absorb the moisture, have largely made this unnecessary. Further, excessive use of cream may stop the diaper from absorbing. Cotton balls are also useful for cleaning your baby's face. In addition, you will need some mild soap and baby shampoo. Nail clippers are useful to trim tiny nails.

A good-quality diaper bag that converts to a changing mat is also a very good investment, or perhaps an item someone may like to give as a gift. Shop around and pick one that is large, wears well, and is preferably designed so that using the mat does not mean emptying out all the contents first. It will be useful for at least two years, and longer if you have a second baby.

Equipment

Cribs and bassinets Your baby will be fine sleeping in a bassinet for the first few months, or you can put her right in a crib. Bassinets can be bought as a separate piece of equipment. You may wish to consider buying a bassinet secondhand, since it has only short-term use. Always buy equipment that conforms to U.S. safety standards. No baby should ever be given a pillow, because there is a danger of suffocation. Instead, make sure the mattress is covered with a firmly stretched sheet—the stretchy, cloth, fitted variety is fine. A top sheet is not necessary, but your baby needs to be kept warm and secure by being tucked in snugly with two or three layers of receiving blankets or a comforter. If she is a restless sleeper, you may want to use a blanket sleeper, too, to be sure she stays warm. If your baby tends to vomit after feedings, try covering the head end of the mattress with a cloth diaper. It will save you from changing the sheets every time. In cold weather it may help your baby to settle if you warm a blanket over a radiator before wrapping her in it, or warm the crib with a hot water bottle before you put her in, but never leave a baby in a crib with a hot water bottle or electric blanket.

You can delay buying a crib until your baby has arrived, if you want to, because most babies are quite happy to spend the first few weeks in a bassinet. Again, the crib and mattress must conform to current safety standards, and it is important to check this if you are buying secondhand or borrowing. You will need a good supply of crib-size sheets and blankets, but again, no pillows. When your child is a young infant, it is recommended to use a crib bumper with several short ties (less than 6 inches in length) to keep it fastened in place. As soon as your child can pull to stand, you should remove the bumper and any large toys she may use to climb on to get out of the crib. Most recent research on crib death or sudden infant death syndrome (SIDS) shows that it is safest to place a baby on her back or side (and that becoming too hot is as much of a risk to a baby as being too cold).

Car Seat   The first journey your baby makes in a car when you bring her home should be as safe as every subsequent trip. Rear-facing car seats to be placed in the backseat of the car are often rented or loaned by the hospital itself, or by another agency acting through the hospital. They are very useful items of equipment in the first few months, as your baby can be carried from the car to the house without being awakened. They have largely replaced the older-style infant seats in the home, enabling your young baby to be supported and watch the life of the household.

Carriage or Stroller   This is usually a major item of expenditure and one you hope will do service for several years and for more than one child. The most important point when choosing this item is that it suits your lifestyle. Check how many functions you require from your carriage or stroller: some are very versatile, with a lift-out infant seat, and can double in function as a carriage or stroller.

If you have no car, and live where stores and other amenities are within walking distance, then the old-style built carriage may be a good answer, especially if you are expecting a winter baby. The advantage of a traditional carriage is that the baby can be put to sleep in it downstairs and wheeled out with very little disturbance just by adding a hat, extra layers of blankets, and a cover. The big wheels of an old-style carriage make them very easy to push, and later, if you have a second baby, toddler seats can be fitted across the top. The drawback of this type of carriage is that they do take up a lot of space in the house, although it can be very handy to have the baby downstairs, where you can easily rock her to sleep. They are also difficult to negotiate down flights of stairs or steps and so are not suitable if you live in an upstairs apartment without an elevator or have steps up to your front door. Most are pretty heavy and bulky to load in and out of cars. Bought new they also tend to be quite expensive. However, if you feel one of these may suit your needs, at least for the first three or four months while the baby is very tiny, a secondhand carriage can usually be bought at small cost and, if you take good care of it, you will be able to sell it without much loss.

If you use the car a lot, live in an apartment, or have older children who often have to go out in the car, you may find that a stroller with a tilting seat that is especially designed for a newborn baby may work better. Strollers generally cost less, take up very little space to store, and will probably work for your child until she is completely finished with the stroller stage. The disadvantage in the early days, and especially if you have a winter baby, is that you have to dress her very warmly in a snowsuit, as it is not so easy to tuck her underneath blankets, even in the most tilting seat. It also means a degree of disturbance having to get the baby in and out of the stroller. Strollers with small wheels and tires tend to be difficult to push across rough country, so if you live in the countryside or plan a lot of walks, go for a variety that has larger wheels and thicker tires.

There is such an enormous variety in the types of carriages and strollers now available that you should find the one that's best for you with a little shopping around. If you feel a little superstitious about investing in major items of baby equipment such as this before the baby is born, many big stores will deliver the carriage, or stroller, or furniture after the baby's birth.

Playpen   A playpen can be useful for putting a crawling baby in for a short period while you are cooking a meal, or answering the phone or the door, but do not leave a baby unattended in a playpen for long periods. In general, if you want to get your baby to accept being put into a playpen, it is best to start before she learns how to crawl by putting her in for two short sessions a day. Make sure it is stocked with a different variety of toys, and change them frequently so she does not get bored. Place the playpen in the room where you will be so she can still see you.

Baby Walkers   Many children do seem to enjoy baby walkers, but while parents may take care to watch them 99 percent of the time, there is a higher chance of accidents in the remaining moments. Danger arises especially as the baby goes across any uneven surface or anywhere near a step. There is no evidence that putting a baby in a walker benefits walking at all, and there may even be a disadvantage to using a walker before six months of age—before muscle development is mature enough. Because of the dangers, it is recommended NOT to use baby walkers.

Toward the End of Pregnancy

This is often quite a tedious time—most women have given up work, and there is a distinct sense of waiting. Being so large can make it difficult to get comfortable in any position, whether you are sitting on a chair or lying down trying to get some rest. However, at the other end of the spectrum, many women have a tremendous burst of energy toward the end of pregnancy and are frantically decorating nurseries or whole houses, or even, against all advice, moving. In theory this is not a good idea, but in practice there sometimes seems to be an unavoidable urge to get everything right and ready before the baby arrives.

Your Body

During the last months of pregnancy you might find that stimulating your breasts and nipples produces a few drops of colostrum. Obstetricians often recommend you do this if you are planning to breast-feed. If you doubt your ability to feed, it can have the effect of giving you some confidence, but if you dislike the feeling or feel uncomfortable, don't bother. It makes very little difference, and you can just as successfully breast-feed a baby if you have never expressed any colostrum during pregnancy. Whether you plan to breast-feed or not, it is important to wear a well-fitting bra day and night during the end of pregnancy and also after the birth when the milk comes in. This has more effect on whether your breasts retain their original shape than on whether you breast-feed or not. Eating large meals toward the end of pregnancy is not advised and is difficult to do anyway because your stomach is so squished by the size of the baby. Little and often is the rule when it comes to eating, and the same sometimes applies to sleep, unfortunately—your baby's movements and kicks can be enough to wake you at night, and getting comfortable is more difficult. If this is your first baby, take advantage of the chance to get plenty of rest, and take catnaps during the day to make up for lost hours at night.

Life becomes more comfortable if the baby's head "drops" during the last weeks of pregnancy—that is, the baby's head descends into the bony, pelvic girdle ready for the birth. Sometimes, however, the baby's head does not engage until labor begins—in a first pregnancy when the head does not engage, doctors may check with a scan to make sure there is nothing blocking the baby's path—for example, that the placenta is not low-lying or obstructing the baby's exit. It is more common that the head does not engage in second or subsequent pregnancies, and this may be because uterine muscles have already been stretched and are not providing so much pressure.

During early and middle pregnancy the muscles of the womb have been contracting very slightly, but you are unlikely to feel it. However, after about the twenty-fifth week you may feel this activity as a painless hardening of your abdomen as the muscles tense. It will go soft again as the muscles relax. This is the uterus limbering up for labor so that the muscles are in good trim. These contractions are called "Braxton-Hicks contractions" but are not the start of labor.

Packing a Bag

Do not leave it to the last month to collect the things you need to take to the hospital; babies sometimes come early. Cotton nightclothes are best, because hospitals tend to be very warm. Your clothes should be front-opening if you plan to breast-feed. In addition, you need sanitary pads, nursing bras or a good supporting bra, shampoo, toiletries, slippers, and a robe. Check what your hospital requires you to bring in the way of clothes and equipment for the baby.

You may also have comfort items you want to take in to use during labor, including extra pillows, a foam wedge, a hand-held fan, a natural sponge, and a CD or cassette player. Partners should think about taking some food supplies and money for the phone. Also, don't forget the camera, with fresh film and batteries!

Prepare your own and your baby's going-home clothes, too. Putting together your baby's first outfit is one of the nicest parts of pregnancy. You need undershirts, disposable diapers or cloth diapers plus plastic pants, a stretchy suit, a knitted cardigan plus a shawl or receiving blanket, and, depending on the weather, a hat. As you pack your own clothing, remember that you will not regain your figure immediately—bring maternity or very loose clothing.

Travel Arrangements and Phone Numbers

If you are having your baby in the hospital, plan who is to drive you there, and then make a second plan to fall back on in an emergency. If no transportation is available, make arrangements with an ambulance company to take you to the hospital. More careful planning is needed if this is your second or subsequent baby because obviously other children will have to be taken care of. Keep a list with phone numbers of friends who can help out with a lift, taxi services, and the hospital number, and have it on you when you go out or go away.

CHAPTER 3

Labor and Delivery

The start of labor • What happens during labor?
Birth—what will it be like? • The role of the father
The question of pain relief
Your birth checklist • You and your baby during labor
The first moments of life
Medical interventions—and why they may be needed
Problems in labor and delivery • Stillbirth

Hello Mummy!

The Start of Labor

I woke up early in the morning with a slight stomach ache and an attack of diarrhea and thought I must have a bug. It was only when the ache came back twice more that I realized it was happening every half an hour. It went on like that all day, gradually getting more often and a bit stronger. We went to the hospital in the early evening, and after five hours of strong contractions my baby was born at midnight.

I was bending down to pick up some laundry when I felt this uncontrollable trickle of warm water down the inside of my leg. At first I thought I had suddenly become incontinent! Then I realized it must be my water breaking. It didn't gush, just a steady trickle without any sensation of contractions. At the hospital they said I was three centimeters dilated, but I didn't begin to feel anything at all for another hour or so and then suddenly the contractions became very strong. My baby was born three hours later.

My labor stopped and started for two days. I went up to the hospital three times with contractions coming every ten minutes, only for everything to stop and I was sent home twice. But the third time when they examined me I was five centimeters dilated. I found walking around kept the contractions going, but lying or sitting stopped them. Only the last hour was difficult to cope with, but the actual birth went well.

The mechanism by which labor starts is not well understood, but it is thought that the baby triggers it in some way. A chemical or hormone message perhaps passes from the baby across the placenta into the mother's bloodstream, causing release of chemicals called prostaglandins, and a hormone called oxytocin from the pituitary gland. These cause the cervix to soften in preparation for dilation, and the uterus to contract. It is also known that the uterus becomes much more sensitive to oxytocin in the final few days of pregnancy. This has led to the theory that throughout pregnancy there is some sort of mechanism that prevents labor from starting. It is only when this inhibiting influence subsides that prostaglandins can be made by the body and labor can begin.

In the days before labor begins, some women find they are unusually active and have a tremendous burst of energy: they start decorating, cleaning out closets, and generally spring-clean—some call this "nesting." It is a dangerous old wives' tale that babies may become less active as labor approaches, so always tell your obstetrician if you notice a lack of movement over a period of twelve hours.

Some women find they have more frequent or loose bowel movements and increased hardening of the uterus called Braxton-Hicks or practice contractions. Women often worry that they will not recognize labor when it begins or that it will start with a dramatic flood as their water breaks when they are in a meeting at work or in line at the supermarket checkout. In fact, both occurrences are rare. False alarms, with women arriving at the hospital thinking they are in labor and being sent home, are much more common than missing the start of labor. Strong or regular Braxton-Hicks contractions are usually to blame for this, but don't worry—hospital staffs are happy to give advice and would rather you erred on the side of caution. Nor is it very common for a flood of amniotic fluid to be the first sign of labor—even if your water does break while you are out, it is likely to produce just dampness or a slight trickle.

Labor can begin in a variety of ways, but there are three basic signs to look for and that your obstetrician will want to know about to determine if labor is about to begin or has already started:

- **A "bloody show"**   This is the name given to the bloodstained, jellylike mucus you may notice coming from the vagina gradually over a day or so or all at once. During pregnancy the neck of the womb or cervix has remained tightly closed, sealed with this plug of mucus. As muscle contractions begin to pull the sides of the uterus upward, dilating the cervix, the plug is loosened and comes away. A show can occur several days or just a few hours before you actually go into labor.

- **Breaking or leaking of the amniotic fluid**   Pressure of the baby's head downward may cause the membrane sealing the amniotic fluid to rupture so that water either leaks in a slow trickle or gushes in a flood, although this is rarely the first sign of labor. It is not significant whether this happens at the start or much later in labor. Occasionally the water may break without contractions starting.

- **Contractions**   These are usually felt as low abdominal cramps or sometimes as backache. "The kind of pains you have when you get an attack of diarrhea," was one mother's graphic but accurate description. They usually begin as weak, erratic sensations but begin to occur with more regularity—once an hour, half an hour, and so on—and also with increasing severity. In this very early stage of labor, if your water is intact, it is best to stay active and carry on with ordinary life while alerting those who need to know, such as your partner and the person who will look after any other children.

  Time how often the contractions are coming and how long they last. With a first baby, aim to get to the hospital when they are coming about ten minutes apart. Do not go in too early because it makes labor seem so much longer, but on the other hand, do not be tempted to leave it to too late because both the car trip and the admissions procedures are harder to cope with when you're in strong labor. If your are unsure what to do, telephone your obstetrician or the hospital for advice. It may help you to time your arrival at the hospital if you remember that first babies are very rarely born in less than twelve hours. If labor is too slow or keeps starting and stopping, then try walking around and using various upright positions. Timing when to call the hospital or obstetrician with a second baby is harder because things can progress so much more unexpectedly.

When you call the doctor or hospital, tell them your name, the frequency and length of contractions, and any other signs. If your water has broken but you have no contractions, you should still call the hospital. It is best to stay upright and active, provided your pregnancy has reached term, in the hope that this may stimulate contractions. The amniotic fluid was the baby's protection from infection, and once the waters have drained away, doctors usually like labor to begin within 24 to 48 hours and will induce it if contractions do not begin naturally before then because of the risk of infection.

Your Arrival at the Hospital

When you arrive at the hospital, a nurse will go through the admissions procedure (lots of questions and form filling) and preparation for birth. The routine usually consists of checking blood pressure, taking temperature and pulse, and asking for a midstream urine sample to check for signs of protein, sugar, and infection. The obstetrician or midwife will also examine your abdomen to determine your baby's position and how far down his head has descended into the pelvis. Once the widest part of the head has moved down into the brim of the pelvis, it is said to be "engaged." The obstetrician will also examine you internally to find out how dilated the cervix has become. You have to lie on your back for some of these checks. Some women find this very uncomfortable in labor, so tell the obstetrician if this is the case so you do not have to spend more time in that position than is necessary. The obstetrician will usually listen to the baby's heart either by listening with a special stethoscope on your abdomen, or more commonly by using a Doppler ultrasound monitor—a small device or receiver that is held against your abdomen and that enables both you and your obstetrician to hear the fetal heartbeat. This is usually followed later by electronic fetal monitoring, a practice that prints out your baby's heartbeat or pattern of contractions to check your baby's well-being.

It used to be standard practice to give all women having a baby a full pubic shave in the belief that removing pubic hair cut the risk of infection. Enemas were also common, because it was thought that a full bowel would make the baby's passage through the birth canal more difficult and that the mother would be likely to defecate and soil the bed as she pushed the baby downward and outward. However, research has shown that leaving the pubic hair does not raise the incidence of infection and that most women empty their bowels naturally at the start of labor anyway. The majority of hospitals have stopped giving even a minishave and offer an enema or suppository only if the woman has not moved her bowels in the past twenty-four hours. Don't worry if you do defecate while pushing. The nurse will be prepared for this and will whisk it away quickly.

At some sites, you may be offered a warm bath or shower—the warmth of the water helps muscles relax. Some hospitals have bathrooms adjoining birthing rooms or delivery rooms, so you can take another dip later in labor if you wish. Alternatively, a few hospitals may have a birthing pool. You might want to consider using this in early labor even if you are not planning a water birth.

You will either be given a hospital gown or be able to use one of your own nightgowns. A large T-shirt will also do just as well—bring a few as you may need to change if, for instance, your water breaks during labor.

Some hospitals have a labor ward with several beds for women in early labor and then move them to a delivery room toward the end of the first stage, while others have individual labor and delivery rooms combined (also called birthing rooms) where you can stay until your baby is born. A few units offer extra facilities such as birthing beds—which are usually beds able to convert to different positions—as well as birth stools and chairs or mattresses on the floor to help mothers adopt a more upright position by squatting or kneeling if they wish. You will need to have checked in advance what your hospital has to offer. More and more hospitals are also able to give mothers the option of a water birth—that is, delivering your baby in a warm-water pool.

What Happens During Labor?

The First Stage: Dilation of the Cervix

This is when the muscles of the uterus contract, pulling the cervix outward and upward so it first thins and then begins to open out or dilate to let the baby come out. The cervix is said to be fully open when it is 10 cm dilated. This is when the first stage is complete. The early part of this first stage is less active. Contractions are usually irregular and weak and dilate the cervix to about 2 to 3 cm. Then an active phase occurs, when the contractions get more severe and dilate the cervix completely. The water may break naturally at some point during this stage or be broken by the obstetrician to check the color of the fluid around the baby and to speed up labor. Once the membranes have broken, contractions usually get more intense as the baby's head presses directly onto the cervix with each contraction without the bag of water to act as a buffer. Breaking the water also causes natural

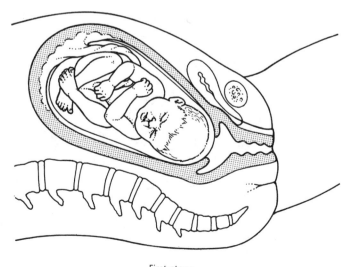

First stage

release of prostaglandins by the uterus, which act to speed up the labor. To begin with, contractions usually last about twenty to thirty seconds and come every thirty minutes, but gradually they increase until at the end of this stage they may last sixty to ninety seconds and come every two or three minutes. With a first baby this stage usually takes ten to twelve hours, but subsequent births may last half this time or less.

The Second Stage: Pushing and Birth

This begins when the cervix is fully dilated and the baby starts to move farther down the birth canal; it ends when the baby is born. Instead of being used to draw the cervix up, the contractions of the uterus are now being used to push the baby out and down the birth canal. You need to help, too, by taking a deep breath, holding it, and pushing with your diaphragm and abdominal muscles. Usually there is an overwhelming natural urge to push, but if you do not feel such an urge, then moving into a more upright position usually helps. If you have opted for an epidural, you may need your obstetrician to guide you as to when it is time to push.

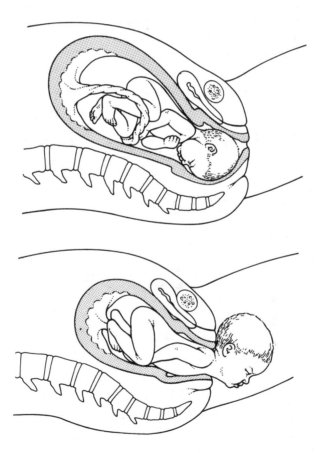

Second stage

At first the baby is moving directly downward, and as his head presses onto the pelvic floor, the pressure on the bowel makes it feel something like trying to pass a grapefruit. Then the baby's head turns a corner, and if he is face down—the easiest birth position—the back of his head passes underneath the front arch of the pelvis. Now his head begins to push against the perineum, making it bulge outward and producing a bursting, burning sensation, but with each push the entrance slowly widens and the tissues gradually stretch to allow the baby's head through.

The increasing stretching and the pressure of the baby's head have a deadening effect on the nerve endings in this area and act as a natural anesthetic. The obstetrician will be watching the tissues of the perineum very carefully all the time for any signs that it may begin to tear. Research shows that a small tear probably mends more quickly and is less painful than an episiotomy may be, but this is still controversial. An episiotomy is a small cut the doctor makes at the entrance to the vagina in the tissues of the perineum to enable the baby's head to be born more easily. You will not feel anything painful if an episiotomy does have to be made. You can feel your baby's head yourself with your hands or use a mirror to see. Although it slips back a little between each contraction, it gradually gains ground until it stays at the entrance to the vagina without disappearing—this is said to be when the baby's head is "crowning." The obstetrician will then tell you not to push but to pant with the next contractions so the head can be eased out very gently. A minute after the baby's head has been born it turns, with the help of the obstetrician, to the side: this is called "restitution," and it enables the shoulders to turn sideways so they can easily be slipped out of the vagina, followed by the rest of the baby's body. Usually the body follows easily, though it may need a second contraction. If you want your baby placed onto your abdomen after he is born, ask the obstetrician early in labor to do so; this is increasingly standard in many units. The warmth of your body will help to keep the baby warm, and you can enjoy the feel of your new baby against your skin as you feel and touch him for the first time. However, if you would rather your baby was cleaned up first, the obstetrician will be just as happy to do this and then hand him to you in a warm towel or blanket.

The Third Stage: Delivering the Placenta

If there is no intervention, then the placenta, or afterbirth, should normally separate and come down into the vagina within twenty minutes after the birth. Once this happens, the obstetrician pulls gently on the cord to ease it out.

If your obstetrician follows the traditional approach, she will clamp the cord at a point about four inches away from the baby and place a second clamp about another two inches away from the placenta. Using special scissors, she cuts the cord at a point between the two clamps. There is no sensation in the cord and it does not hurt the baby, nor is there any loss of blood. See chapter 4 for more about your newborn baby's first seconds of life.

A few obstetricians and mothers believe in the natural delivery of the placenta, but in general medical opinion supports the active management of the third stage of labor because it helps to prevent bleeding from the uterus. This means that the obstetrician gives an injection in your leg (or into your IV line) of a drug called oxytocin (Pitocin). This drug makes the uterus contract, causing the placenta to separate more quickly after the baby is born. The use of the injection makes the risk of bleeding after the birth far less likely because it causes the muscle fibers in the wall of the uterus to contract, preventing blood loss.

Bleeding after the birth—the medical term is "postpartum hemorrhage"—is rare, but it can be very serious, which is one of the main reasons in favor of active management. Timing of the injection is important. If the baby is born head first it is usually given into the mother's thigh once the baby's shoulders are out.

Birth—What Will It Be Like?

Contractions feel like that awful pain you get low down in your abdomen if you have an attack of diarrhea.

Male doctors tell you contractions feel like bad menstrual pains—how they should know what menstrual pains feel like or be able to compare them with contractions, I don't know. In fact my baby's backbone was pressing against mine and I just had continuous, dull backache.

You tend to forget what labor feels like until you start to feel contractions again, and then it all comes back. At first it was just a hardening of the abdominal muscles and a growing twinge that came and faded. But by the end of the first stage it was a really agonizing pain all across the lower part of my stomach—the contractions were going very fast together. They keep telling you to relax, but it is almost impossible. I had to concentrate and grit my teeth for all I was worth to cope with it.

Everybody's experience of labor is entirely different. This is one of the reasons why it is so hard to prepare people for what to expect. The experience of childbirth varies not only from person to person but also with each baby born to the same person. It is one of the unfair facts of life that some women seem to sail through labor and childbirth without needing much, or indeed any, pain relief and report there was one "uncomfortable" moment. There are also women who say that it was agony and who feel cheated that during prenatal classes people talked about "discomfort" without really telling them that it could be so painful.

Obviously we all wonder about the first experience, but what makes one woman find labor and birth easy while another finds it so painful? There are very many factors involved, and obviously a great many of them are outside our control. Our personal attitude toward our bodies, toward pain, and our pain "threshold," obviously have a great deal to do with the way we cope with labor. Another factor that is often out of our control is the position of the baby, for there are some birth positions that are likely to make labor more difficult and painful. Even in cases where the baby is in the right position to start with, complications can arise during labor—for example, the baby's head may fail to rotate as it moves into the birth canal, and this can mean that his backbone is pressing against yours. This may result in a slower descent, backache, and possibly a more difficult delivery.

However, there are some relatively simple things you can do to increase your chances of a good experience of labor and birth. The first is to find out as much as you can about the process: understanding what is happening makes it so much easier to cope. The second is to stay upright, active, and mobile for at least the early part of labor. This has definitely been shown to shorten length of labor, and women who stay upright and walk around during most of their labor need less pain relief. The third point may seem contradictory, but it is to follow your body's inclinations—if in your case you feel like curling up in a ball on your side on a bed and you find this helpful, then do that. Finally, it helps to know what different types of pain relief are available and to stay open-minded about the type of labor and delivery you will have and about the type of pain relief you will or will not consider using.

Experienced obstetricians can all quote examples of the woman who was very worried about the prospect of giving birth and determined that the only way she could cope was to have an epidural, and who then proceeded to have a short, easy labor, which she found she could cope with perfectly well without help. They have also seen many examples of women who have set their hearts on a "natural" birth without any pain relief at all, only to find it harder than they thought and then felt very disappointed and let down because they did not achieve the goal they had set themselves.

Obviously it is hard to prepare for what is essentially always going to be a unique and individual experience, but we can make some general points. First, most women manage to cope in the early part of labor with breathing and relaxation exercises and by walking around—this is when contractions are well spaced and fairly mild. It is also true that at the other end of the first stage—the point where the cervix is very nearly dilated to its full extent but before pushing can begin—most women experience a time that is very painful. This can vary between one or two very sharp contractions to an extended period when contractions are very strong and also come very frequently, with only short gaps in between. When you reach a point when you don't think you can cope anymore, it nearly always means that your baby is just about to be born. It will really help at the time if your partner also understands what is happening and reminds you that your baby will soon be there.

The Role of the Father

Sharing the experience of labor and birth together can be a good start to parenthood for very many couples, and most fathers are pleased that they were present at the birth of their child. It is also very common to feel some anxiety and apprehension beforehand: for the safety of their partner and the baby, about their own reactions to seeing their partner in labor and giving birth, and about the role they will play. Some women, too, may feel anxious about the effect that seeing the birth will have on their partners. Be honest with each other and talk about what you feel.

Going to prenatal classes together and finding out about pregnancy and birth by reading and talking to other couples together will help you decide what to do.

Most prenatal classes discuss the ways in which partners can be of practical help during labor. Keeping a check on the passage of time and encouraging their wives that they are making progress are helpful, for it is very easy for a woman to become disoriented during labor. Reminding the mother-to-be to go to the bathroom at regular intervals, and offering ice chips and small drinks, if allowed, also help, as does explaining her needs to the hospital staff without being overly aggressive. Women vary a great deal in whether back massage is a comfort or not; don't be offended if she suddenly can't bear you to touch her or says you do it all wrong. It is very common to find she may suddenly only be able to tolerate the obstetrician touching her—whether that has really to do with the difference in technique or with confidence in a professional is uncertain. Certainly there is a special relationship that develops between the obstetrician and the mother which is different from that between the father and the obstetrician.

Most maternity units now welcome fathers who are calm and understand what is happening because it frees the nursing staff for medical rather than purely supportive and supervisory work. But it would be wrong either for fathers to insist on staying or mothers to insist on the presence of their partners if there are serious worries on either side. Again, talking about things in advance helps.

If you are worried that your partner may not be able to be contacted when labor starts, there are several firms that offer pages or beepers for this purpose. See advertisements in the various parenting magazines.

The Question of Pain Relief

There are several ways of getting some relief from the discomfort and pain of labor, some of them very old methods indeed, but there are actually only two techniques that can completely take the pain away: a general or an epidural anesthetic. Because no two labors are the same and because no one can predict exactly how you will react in labor, it is best to know as much as possible about the kinds of pain relief available and to think about what you feel will suit you best, though it is essential to go into labor with an open mind.

Position and Movement
It is a natural reaction to ease pain of any kind by moving—rocking, rubbing, or massaging the area, or shifting to another position. If a child comes with a stomach ache we automatically try to soothe it by stroking or gently rubbing where it hurts, and we ease aching muscles in our own bodies by stretching and bending. The idea of "rubbing it better" is as old as the hills. To lie immobile during a contraction is to deny a natural source of pain relief, your own body. As well as shifting pressure, a rhythmic movement, such as rocking or rubbing, acts as a way of distracting the brain from the sensation of pain. Breathing exercises work in the same way.

Lying down has a number of disadvantages. It means the weight of the uterus is pressing on central arteries and veins, which reduces the blood flow both to your

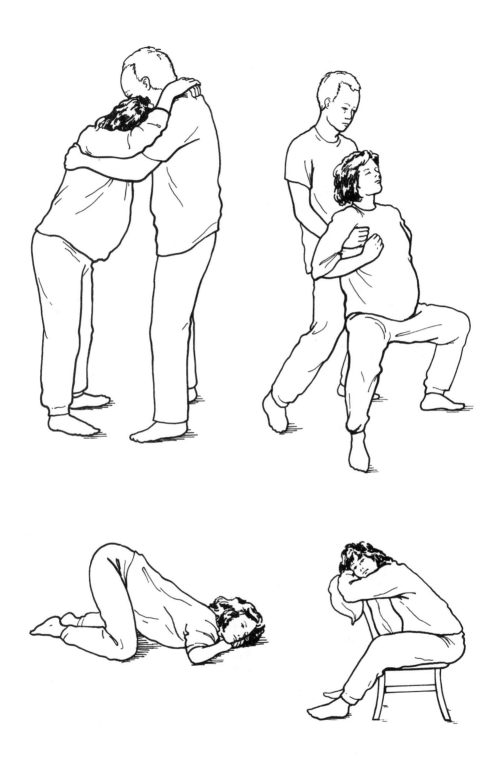

Alternative positions which may give pain relief during labor

own heart and also through the placenta to the baby. It can also cause backache. In addition, you are not making any use of a natural force that will make labor shorter and the baby's descent easier: gravity. Research has shown that more upright positions in labor make contractions more efficient and so shorten the time it takes for the cervix to dilate. Studies have also shown that women who stay active during labor need less pain relief.

Most prenatal courses now teach something about alternative positions in labor. The simplest approach is to do what feels best. Walking around and pausing during contractions to lean against a wall or the back of a chair is often sufficient in early labor. As contractions get stronger you may find that kneeling, kneeling leaning forward onto a pile of pillows or against your partner, or sitting on a back-to-front chair using the back as a support is helpful. During transition, a more upright posture or changing position can often help a baby in an unusual position shift into one that is easier for birth. In the second stage, the force of gravity can again help the baby's descent, and some positions open the joints of the pelvis wider to allow more room for the baby to pass through.

Massage during labor is very much a question of personal choice—some women cannot bear to be touched during a contraction, while others find that back rubbing helps, but only if their partner or birth attendant has the right technique. Some women want very firm, kneading massage, while others want a lighter touch.

Different Birth Positions

We have talked about how staying upright and moving around during labor usually make contractions more efficient and also easier to cope with; in general, research has shown that women seem to have shorter labors and need less pain relief if they stay upright and keep moving. However, toward the end of the first stage, when contractions become very intense and often close together, this does not suit everybody; if your inclination is to lie curled up on your side, then do so.

What about your position for the birth itself? Again, you do have a choice. Through the ages there have been different fashions in the most popular position to adopt for the birth of a baby—for example, birthing stools are not a new idea and were very popular in the Middle Ages. More recently, the most usual delivery position used to be for a woman to lie down, either on her back or on her side on a bed. Some obstetricians still favor the woman lying on her side today. Then the idea developed that a woman should be more propped up—although still basically lying on her back. It began to be usual for her to be supported by cushions or pillows, with her knees drawn up and open. This position is easy to adopt for the woman, and it does make it easy for the obstetrician to deliver the baby. A drawback is that sometimes the pressure of the baby is on the base of the spine. As the baby's head moves down out of the uterus into the vagina and begins to turn the corner so the head starts to press against the perineum, it means you are effectively pushing uphill. However, difficult deliveries, especially those needing forceps, usually require this position and often for a woman to be actually in the lithotomy position, which means lying back with your feet in stirrups.

What alternatives to the conventional positions are there, though, in the case

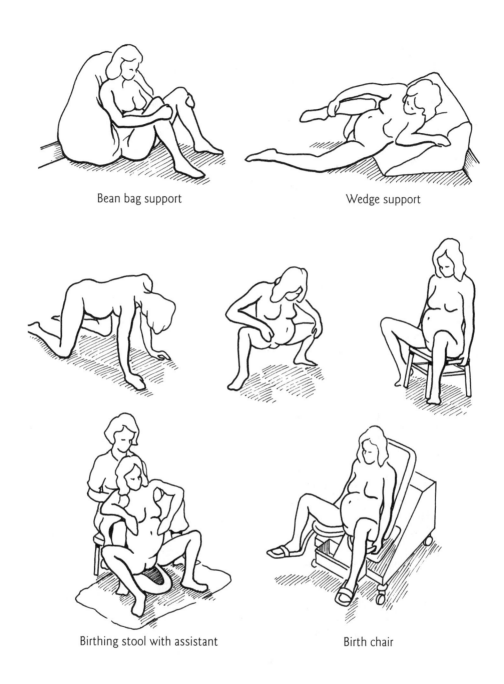

Bean bag support

Wedge support

Birthing stool with assistant

Birth chair

Different birth positions

of a normal delivery? Most obstetricians are increasingly willing to work with women to try to find the position that will be easiest for delivery. One alternative that is becoming more popular is kneeling on all fours. During contractions you either kneel on all fours or, more comfortably, lean forward against your partner, who can stand at the end of the bed, or against a large cushion for support. Between contractions you can rest back on your heels or kneel up. This has the advantage of taking the weight off the large blood vessels, and you can vary how upright you are to control the effect of gravity. This means that if the baby is being pushed downward too quickly and delivery looks like it will be too fast, then moving forward onto all fours or leaning down on to your forearms usually slows it down. If the second stage is very slow, you can kneel in a more upright position. The position is not difficult to adopt for the woman, but it does need the cooperation of the obstetrician, who needs to feel confident about delivering in this position, so talk about it during early labor with her.

Squatting and supported squatting are other alternatives. Not many women are supple enough to be able to squat right down on their heels during labor or delivery, and even if you have practiced this position, it can be more difficult for delivery. A supported semisquatting position is much easier to adopt and also makes the delivery easier. For this you need your partner or helper to stand behind you with his arms supporting your weight under your armpits. As you push with a contraction, you can relax your whole weight onto his arms and collapse your knees outward. This opens up the pelvic girdle as widely as possible and allows the full force of gravity to help the baby move downward. Again, you need the cooperation of your obstetrician, who needs to feel confident about this position. She will have to kneel, bend, or crouch down to deliver the baby.

A supported squatting position can also be achieved with birth chairs, birth stools, and some birthing beds. Birth chairs usually resemble a dentist's chair but with a semicircular cut-out seat and footrests at either side. Birth stools are also semicircular, but your feet are flat on the floor and they are much lower, which again requires the obstetrician to kneel on the floor. In a pinch almost anything—for example, an upturned bucket—can serve as a birth stool. Birthing beds can convert from flat delivery beds through various degrees of support into a chair that will support the mother in an upright squat. Not very many hospitals have them because they are very expensive. The advantage is that they can allow the mother to be upright while still making delivery easy for the obstetrician, who does not have to crouch or kneel on the floor.

Birthing Pools   Birthing pools, which allow a woman to stay in water during labor and for the baby to be delivered underwater, are occasionally available. Some women find the warm, buoyant effect of water helpful in coping with the pain of contractions. The pool is filled with warm water, which is constantly replenished to ensure that the water remains at the correct temperature. Normally the fetal heart is monitored intermittently using a waterproof, hand-held Doppler monitor. This is held against the mother's abdomen for a few minutes or so during and following a contraction every fifteen to thirty minutes. More and more obstetricians are developing the art of delivery underwater, and you may opt to try for this type of delivery.

Remember, though, that not all women who want to try for this type of labor find it beneficial, and if complications arise during labor your obstetrician may feel it would be safer for you and your baby to be on dry land.

Many hospitals have now invested in a purposely built pool—it looks like an enormous bath, complete with faucets and a plug hole. Alternatively, some privately practicing obstetricians will supervise home deliveries for couples who want an underwater delivery. There are several commercial firms that will hire out a pool that can be erected in your home—usually in a ground-floor room, as the weight of water in an upstairs room can be too much for your house's construction. There have been no studies yet as to whether labor is quicker or less painful, but women who have used pools during labor say that the freedom of movement and the support provided by the buoyancy of the water are very pleasant. The disadvantage from an obstetrician's point of view is that she cannot monitor the birth so easily, so only low-risk women, with no complications during pregnancy or labor, should use the pool.

When the baby is born into the water it is still receiving oxygen through the blood supply reaching it via the placenta and the umbilical cord. It does not take its first breath through the air passages and lungs until it is lifted out of the water.

Psychoprophylaxis

This is a long word to describe a method usually summed up as natural childbirth. There are two parts to the theory behind this approach. The first is that fear causes pain because it makes women tense up and fight against what is happening to their bodies instead of relaxing with the contractions. To stop women from being afraid, they need to understand what happens in labor and how they can help themselves. The second part of the theory is a way of distracting the brain from messages of pain by concentrating totally on another sensation—in this case a series of breathing exercises designed for all stages of labor and delivery. Most hospital prenatal classes include some kind of breathing techniques as well as explanation. You can benefit from learning these breathing exercises, even if you intend to have an epidural or know in advance you need a cesarean section, because you can use them to distract your mind and to relax you during any kind of difficult procedure—for example, during an internal examination, while an epidural is being administered, or for an epidural cesarean section.

Meperidine (Demerol)

This is an opiate drug, like morphine, given by injection, often together with a tranquilizer or antihistamine to counteract nausea. It produces a drowsy, detached state like a premedication before an operation or feeling mildly drunk. Some people hate to feel they cannot concentrate totally on what is happening and prefer to have all their wits about them, while others say it made all the difference and just took the edge off the pain. Meperidine has a relaxing effect on muscles. However, it also crosses the placenta into the baby's bloodstream and can make him drowsy, so ideally it should not be given close to the expected delivery because it could interfere with the baby's reflexes and make it more difficult for him to start breathing. If the baby is born sooner than expected and is very drowsy, an antidote can easily be given to counter the effect of the drug. Meperidine tends to act as a mood enhancer in the same way that alcohol does—if you are feeling happy and confident it will accentuate that feeling, but if you are feeling unhappy or frightened it can sometimes increase that emotion, too.

Nitrous Oxide

Nitrous oxide, an inhaled painkiller, is also known as laughing gas because of the light-headed, slightly high effect it produces. The mother holds a rubber mask over her mouth and nose or sucks on a mouthpiece and breathes in deeply—it is important that she hold the mask or mouthpiece rather than anybody else, because if she takes enough to make her lose consciousness, she will automatically drop the mask. Because it takes twenty seconds to have an effect, she should start to use it as soon as a contraction begins so the maximum effect is when a contraction is at its height. It does not affect the baby, and the mother can control just how much she uses. It is most useful at the difficult end of the first stage, during the transition from the first to the second stage, or for sewing up an episiotomy or tear.

Epidural Anesthetic

This is one of only two ways of giving total pain relief during birth (the other is general anesthesia) and is especially useful for deliveries that are likely to be difficult or that require intervention for an unusual birth position, a premature baby, or a multiple birth. A local anesthetic is injected near to the spinal cord and blocks the sensations in the nerves from about the waist down so the mother is awake and fully conscious but feels no pain. It works on the same principle the dentist uses when giving a local anesthetic to block nerves in your mouth during placement of a filling, but because having a baby takes longer than filling a tooth, more than one shot of anesthetic is needed. It would be impractical to keep injecting, so the procedure is to insert a hollow needle between the bones of the spine (vertebrae) into the space that surrounds the spinal cord called the "epidural space." A fine tube (catheter) is fed down the needle into the space, and the other end is secured up your back to your shoulder with adhesive tape. As the effect of the anesthetic begins to wear off, it can be added to by injecting more through the tube.

An epidural can be used for pain relief during the first stage of labor. It is best used when labor has been well established (pains occurring every five minutes) and with the cervix dilated 5 to 6 cm in a first-time mother and 3 to 4 cm in a woman who has previously given birth. The epidural can be extended for pain relief after the baby is born (second stage of labor).

In the past, having an epidural meant that you were fairly immobile during labor because although you might be able to move your legs, they felt numb or "odd." A more modern technique is to combine the local anesthetic that is used in a lower dose with a painkilling drug called Fentanyl. The result is that only the pain-carrying nerves in the lower part of your body are blocked, not the sensation-carrying nerves as well. This has been dubbed "the mobile" or "walking" epidural because it allows considerably more movement in labor, even to the extent that some women have been able to walk around with help. Sometimes this increased mobility means that pain relief is not as good as the old-style-type epidural. A significant number of women also experience itching during labor because of a side effect of the Fentanyl. Don't worry if this does occur, but do tell your anesthesiologist. It is always possible to inject local anesthetic into the epidural tube and convert the epidural back to the old-style type. There are new drugs being developed that promise to give both excellent pain relief and mobility, so if you are opting for an epidural, discuss the options with the doctor performing it.

An epidural also makes other interventions more likely. It tends to lower blood pressure and, although this can be useful when women suffer from high blood pressure, in ordinary circumstances care must be taken that it does not fall too low, and a drip will be set up as a safety measure. Very occasionally an epidural has the effect of weakening contractions, in which case a hormone may need to be dripped into your arm to stimulate the uterus. The anesthetic can be decreased for the second stage, with careful management, so that you can feel enough to push your baby out, but this does not always happen, and the rate of forceps deliveries is higher with epidurals. Because the mother cannot feel to empty her bladder, this usually has to be done with a catheter.

Epidurals cannot be guaranteed to work perfectly, and sometimes one side is numbed while sensation can still be felt on the other. Women have also been known to complain of backache afterward, but this is usually due to the position they were in rather than the epidural itself. Very rarely the needle can pierce the dura, which is the membrane surrounding the spinal cord, and this causes a bad headache afterward. A severe spinal headache that does not respond to bed rest, intravenous fluid, and pain relievers can be treated with a blood patch. In this procedure, a small amount of the patient's own blood is injected into the region of the previous spinal puncture. It seals the spinal fluid leak that is responsible for the headache.

Spinal Anesthetic

A spinal anesthetic is similar to an epidural in technique but involves injecting local anesthetic right beside the spinal nerves so that more profound or complete blockage in sensation of the lower part of the body is produced. A smaller quantity of local anesthetic drug is needed, and it has the advantage that it works within five minutes of carrying out the procedure. This makes it ideal for use in emergency situations and is often preferred to epidural for performing cesarean and forceps deliveries because it offers such excellent total pain relief. It is not suitable for pain relief in labor except in the final stages, because it only lasts for approximately one and a half hours and then wears off.

Transcutaneous Nerve Stimulation (TNS or TENS)

This is in widespread use in the United Kingdom and is becoming more common in the United States. It can be used at home in early labor after appropriate instruction from your obstetrician. Many hospitals rent TENS machines to prospective parents (either free or for a small charge), or advertisements in mother and baby magazines will inform you where you can obtain one.

A small control box called a "pulsar" uses a nine-volt battery, and four to six electrodes can be plugged into this power source. At the end of the wires leading from the box are flat rubber pads that are positioned at either side of the mother's spine. They are usually taped in place. The mother holds a control button, which she can press to produce an electrical pulse as the contraction begins. She can make this stronger and more frequent during the contraction or switch it off altogether in between. At the lowest levels there is a faint tickle that is barely noticeable, but as the power is turned up the sensation is more like a fizz and then a definite buzz, although it is never painful.

TNS is said to work in two ways to help kill the pain of labor. The first is that it stimulates the body to produce more of its own natural painkillers, which raise our pain tolerance threshold—these substances are called "endogenous opiates" or "endorphins." The second effect is that it interrupts the pain pathways from the womb to the brain. As the muscles of the uterus tense in a contraction, the nerve endings send messages to the brain. The brain converts or interprets the messages into the sensation we call pain and sends them back so that we feel this pain in our backs or stomachs during a contraction. The electrical pulse of TNS blocks those messages. Imagine that the nerve pathways are telephone lines and the brain is the telephone exchange that converts the messages into pain and sends them back again. When TNS is in use, messages or calls cannot get through because the line is already engaged or occupied by TNS.

The technique has no side effects, and mothers are free to move around during labor or adopt any position they want for delivery.

Acupuncture

This can be used quite successfully to ease pain during labor and delivery, but unless you go to a hospital doing research or where there is a member of staff with a special interest, it is normally a service you will have to arrange yourself. You either need a doctor who practices acupuncture or an acupuncture practitioner who is skilled in using it for childbirth, and you will also need the agreement of your obstetrician. There are various forms of acupuncture, but this is one mother's experience:

> The acupuncturist met me at the hospital, but she didn't put any needles in until contractions were quite strong and I needed help. I didn't feel them going in— one in my ear, one between my thumb and finger, and three at the end of one leg. They were all down one side, so if I had to move and they needed to be taken out she could put them in on the other side. She attached the end of the needles to a machine, which vibrated them. That felt like a very slight electric shock but nothing painful. After a while she turned this off, and although I couldn't see or feel anything, the needles kept on vibrating. Within half an hour I began to find the contractions easier to cope with—I used breathing exercises as well. The whole labor lasted six hours and I pushed the baby out without any problems—this was my second baby. The needles stayed in place all the time and didn't bother me at all. I was very pleased with the result.

Aromatherapy

This consists of the use of essential oils. It is important to have expert advice on which to use, especially if you are planning to use them in a birthing pool. You can get more information from a midwife, birthing center, or some obstetricians.

Hypnosis

Again, this is only available in special circumstances if there are staff who practice it at the hospital, but you can find someone to teach you during pregnancy. It is not, as many people think, a matter of going into a trance so you do not know what is happening, nor a way of becoming unconscious. In childbirth it is rather a question of teaching autohypnosis as a way of relaxation that mothers can use in labor. Ask your obstetrician or midwife for referrals. One mother recalls:

> I went to six classes in hypnosis as well as learning breathing techniques at the normal prenatal course. We learned the theory of hypnosis—it has nothing to do with being under someone else's control and having to obey that person. Instead we used to sit around and fix our gaze on a particular spot while the doctor talked us through until gradually we were unaware of everything around us. He'd asked us to imagine we were on a beach, to hear the waves, feel the sun and sand. My blood pressure dropped and I felt totally relaxed after, although I'd been aware of what was going on all the time. During the birth I found I was able to practice the same technique, to relax totally, and it helped during the first stage, although I also had some meperidine. But I couldn't use it in the second stage because too much was happening and I had to concentrate on breathing and pushing. I felt it was a help.

Your Birth Checklist

☑ Find out, from classes, books, and magazines, what will happen to your body during labor and delivery so you understand what is going on at each stage.

☑ Prepare for birth by learning and practicing breathing exercises, even if you intend to have an epidural.

☑ Stay relaxed and keep your muscles toned with exercises designed for pregnancy. Prenatal classes or birthing centers will give details or suggest books.

☑ Eat well and get plenty of rest at the end of pregnancy so you avoid going into labor in an already tired state.

☑ Talk to your partner about what will happen and how he can assist you. It really helps if you learn about the process together, and most prenatal courses include a fathers' session or are designed for couples together.

Early Labor

If it is nighttime or you are short of sleep, try to rest because you will need more energy later. Usually people cannot go to sleep because they are too excited!

Eat something light and easily digestible that will give you energy. Do not eat anything heavy, because digestion slows down during labor, and a full stomach makes nausea or vomiting more likely. In an emergency that requires a full anesthetic or a cesarean section, it also increases the risk of inhaling vomit.

Most women feel excited and elated at the start of labor. Continuing your normal activities and doing practical tasks are calming, while moving around and staying upright will encourage contractions.

A warm bath, if your water is intact, is often soothing and relaxing, or a shower if the water has broken.

Check that everything is ready to take to the hospital—prepare last-minute things such as sandwiches for your partner, a thermos of ice, drinks, etc. Having something practical to do is often helpful.

Established Labor

Try to listen to your body and be guided by what seems best. Most women find contractions in early labor are easy to cope with in an upright position, but experiment with different positions—try walking, kneeling, sitting on a chair, or even squatting if you are agile and have been practicing. Remember to go to the bathroom at regular intervals throughout labor.

Your partner can help by timing contractions and the gaps in between, by asking the medical staff to wait if they want to do something and you are in the middle of a contraction, by massaging the small of your back or your stomach if you find this soothing, and by reminding you to relax and breathe through contractions.

It is very easy to become disoriented or feel overwhelmed toward the end of the first stage of labor, especially if it has gone on a long time. This is when contractions are most intense and you are most tired. It is important to take each contraction one at a time, and remember that each one is a step nearer to the birth of your baby. Try to relax as fully as possible in between and concentrate on the present moment. Remember that if you have one or two contractions that are very hard to cope with, this is usually the signal that you are near the end of the first stage. If any medical intervention is needed, make sure you understand what it is and why it has to happen. Your partner can really help here by making your wishes known and also making sure you understand.

It is usual to limit intake by mouth to just small amounts of clear fluid during this stage, but many people find it helps to suck on ice chips or a moist, natural sponge, and to use Vaseline or lip salve on your lips to stop them and your mouth from getting dry, something that often happens with breathing exercises.

When You Reach the Second Stage

This is the big moment. Here are some tips:

- Get into the easiest and most comfortable position for pushing the baby out—again, listen to what your body is telling you.

- Try to relax your pelvic floor—keep your mouth and jaw relaxed because the two go together, and if you are clenching your teeth you are almost certainly contracting and tensing your pelvic floor muscles.

- Listen to what the obstetrician is telling you to do; if necessary your partner can often help by relaying information.

- Lots of people find it exciting or reassuring to realize that their baby is very nearly there; you can feel your baby's head crowning by reaching down with your hands, or use a mirror to watch.

- At the very moment of birth you do not need to push any more—the obstetrician will tell you to pant so that you stop pushing and the baby's head is eased out very slowly. It may take a second contraction for his body to be delivered. Don't worry, because during this time he is still receiving oxygen via the umbilical cord—he does not need to get oxygen by breathing air in through his lungs until the cord is cut.

Remember the Third Stage

That marvelous moment—your baby has arrived and the birth is over. In your excitement at greeting him, do not forget to help the obstetrician to deliver the placenta. She will probably ask you to push while she gently pulls on the umbilical cord to ease it out.

You and Your Baby During Labor

What's Happening to You

During labor the nurse will take your temperature and record your pulse and blood pressure at regular intervals, checking more frequently as labor progresses. She will also remind you to empty your bladder at intervals, because a full bladder can block the baby's descent. If your blood pressure is very high, an epidural anesthetic may be suggested because this always has the effect of reducing blood pressure. In women with normal blood pressure this can be a drawback because it may result in too low a blood pressure, but this is easily remedied.

What the obstetrician will be concerned with all the time is how far labor has progressed and how long it will be before the baby is born. The best guide to this is to time how often contractions are coming, how long they last, and how strong they are—you will probably have learned about this in prenatal classes. Apart from electronic monitoring (monitoring contractions and the fetal heartbeat by means of two devices held onto your abdomen by a belt), the obstetrician can also feel these things by putting a hand on your stomach and also by a vaginal examination to feel how far the cervix has dilated. Do remember that labor does not continue at the same even rate, so don't be depressed if you have been in labor for a long time but the cervix has only dilated a very small amount, because things can sometimes speed up very unexpectedly.

Early in labor the obstetrician will check for contractions every hour and then more frequently as labor progresses. Some hospitals do a vaginal examination every two to four hours routinely, while others may do only one when it is clear from the strength and frequency of contractions that the second stage is near. Again, practice among individual obstetricians varies considerably.

What's Happening to Your Baby

There are various ways of checking on what is happening to your baby, and one of these is for an obstetrician to feel (palpate) your abdomen to check what position the baby is in and how far down the head has moved. The most common and easiest way for a baby to be born is head first, facing backward, and with his head tucked tightly into his chest. However, the easiest way into the pelvic birth canal is looking sideways, so during the passage downward, the baby's head must rotate so that his face is toward your backbone. The head should remain tightly tucked in or "flexed" as it comes around the pelvic curve toward the perineum, so that the narrowest part of the head, the occiput, leads the way. The vast majority of babies—95%—follow this pattern at birth.

Some babies are not head down but instead are bottom or feet downward. This is called "breech presentation." A rarer variation is that a part of the head other than the occiput (back of the head)—for example, the face or the brow—is presenting first. If a baby is head down with the occiput leading the way but does not rotate so his backbone is toward your stomach, this is called an "occipito-posterior position."

Apart from checking what position the baby is in, the obstetrician will also listen very carefully to the baby's heartbeat—one of the most important indications of his condition. Normally a baby's heart beats 120 to 160 times a minute; girls' hearts beat slightly faster than boys'. The baby's heart may speed up slightly in response to the extra stress of a contraction and then go back to its normal rate in between. If it begins to fall below 110 beats or rise above 160 this may be a sign that his condition is not so healthy—the baby is then said to be distressed.

During labor the obstetrician will be continually deciding on the baby's well-being. The most accurate way of doing this is to monitor the baby's heartbeat and, in particular, watch his response to your uterine contractions. There are essentially two ways in which this can be done—intermittently or by continuous monitoring. If you are at low risk—that is, you have had no complications during pregnancy and your labor is straightforward—the obstetrician may decide to perform intermittent monitoring. She will listen to the baby's heartbeat every fifteen minutes throughout labor, using a hand-held receiver. It is normal practice to listen to the fetal heartbeat for up to a minute after a contraction. The aim is to establish that the baby's heart is beating at a normal rate, 120 to 160 beats a minute, and that it is not slowing down during or after contractions. If there is any concern, you will need to have continuous electronic fetal monitoring (EFM). EFM is offered to all women thought to be at high risk during labor—for instance, twin pregnancies, breech babies, or those who have had prenatal complications (diabetes, etc.). Many low-risk women will also be monitored continuously or this way for 20 minutes or so at the start of labor to ensure that all is well before going on to have intermittent monitoring.

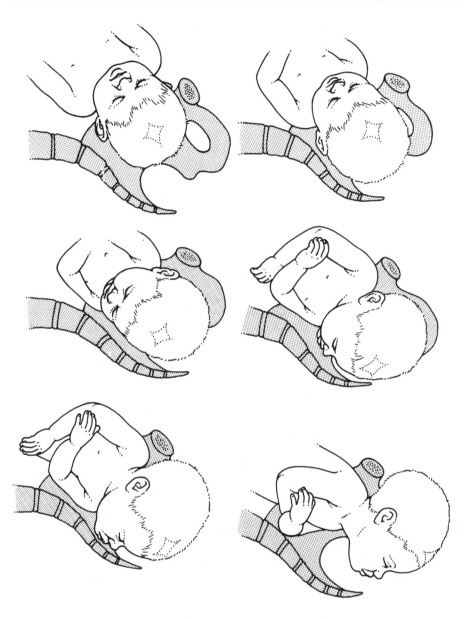

Rotation of the baby's head during a normal delivery

Continuous electronic monitoring involves placing two small devices on your abdomen, held in position by an elastic belt that fits around your abdomen. These act as receivers, one to pick up your baby's heartbeat and the other to act as a pressure gauge to record the strength and length of the contractions. The receivers are connected by long lengths of wire to a machine that produces a continuous printed record of the baby's heartbeat in relation to contractions throughout labor.

Occasionally it can be difficult to pick up the baby's heartbeat well using this method. If the water has broken, an alternative method is to place a small clip on the baby's head during a vaginal examination. In this case a wire leads from the clip out through the vagina to the monitor. Undoubtedly continuous electronic monitoring does restrict movement during labor, but you should still be able to be monitored while sitting in a chair rather than having to lie on the bed all the time. Some hospitals have "telemetry," a portable receiver that relies on radio frequency rather than wires to monitor the fetal heart rate. This allows women to walk freely around.

During labor the obstetrician will be checking for heart rate "decelerations"— that is, slowing of the baby's heart rate during or after your contractions. This could be a sign that your baby is in distress or short of oxygen in labor. It may be necessary to conduct further tests, such as checking the color of the amniotic fluid around your baby (if the water has not yet broken) or taking a small sample of blood from the baby (fetal blood sampling—see chapter 2). In some cases medical staff may feel your baby is safer being born by cesarean section or delivery speeded up by forceps delivery. One criticism of continuous EFM is that it has meant that the number of cesarean sections doctors carry out has increased. This is because only a small number of babies who show abnormalities of their heartbeat during labor are actually in danger. Unfortunately, doctors have to err on the side of caution, and if there are suspicions that your baby is distressed by labor, the doctor may well feel that cesarean section is the safest option for a healthy baby.

At some point before the baby is born the bag of membranes holding the amniotic fluid will either break naturally, or the obstetrician will rupture it. When the fluid leaks out this is another opportunity for the obstetrician to make an important check on the condition of the baby, because the amniotic fluid should be clear and colorless. If it is stained brown or green this may be a sign that the baby is becoming distressed, and other checks will immediately be made on his condition. The discoloration of the waters will come from meconium, which is the greenish-blackish, gluelike material inside the baby's bowel, normally expelled in the first few days of life. The intestines of a distressed baby may sometimes go into spasm, causing him to pass a bowel movement inside the uterus, which discolors the amniotic fluid. However, discolored amniotic fluid alone is not necessarily a reliable sign of distress in itself; it is simply a sign that other checks need to be made.

The First Moments of Life

While the baby is half in and half out of the vagina and when he is born he is usually a whitish, bluish color, which can be a shock if your partner or you expected the baby to come out looking pink immediately. Many babies are blue or purplish or pale as they have been squeezed through the final part of the birth canal and will turn pink after their first few breaths of air.

Some women feel very strongly about what they would like to happen after the birth—for example, they very much want the baby delivered onto their stomach, or may feel that they would like the cord to stop pulsing before it is cut. Others may feel neutral or be quite happy to put their faith in the obstetrician's decisions. Depending on what you and your obstetrician agree beforehand, the baby can be either propped against your thigh until the cord is cut, or the cord can be cut and the baby handed to you, or the baby can be placed on your stomach either before or after the cord has been cut. Many women simply need time to recover from the birth and are not ready to have the baby handed to them right away. It very much depends on the individual. There is always a worry that the baby will get cold after the birth, which is why the temperature in the delivery room should always be very high, but some hospitals also insist on the baby being wrapped in a clean, warm cloth before being handed to the mother.

The placenta is delivered into a pan, and the obstetrician will examine it carefully to make sure it is complete and that no parts have been left behind. If the placenta is not complete, bleeding is likely to occur. Mothers are usually surprised by the size of the placenta—although flatter, it is usually more than the width and length of the baby's head.

Once the placenta is safely delivered, the obstetrician will examine the mother's vagina and vulva to see if any tissues have been torn. If any stitches are needed to repair a tear or an episiotomy, it is usual for this to be done as soon as possible after the birth, while the tissues are still deadened. The areas will be carefully cleaned and anesthetized with an injection of local anesthetic. Depending on the repair to be made, some obstetricians prefer women to lie back with their feet in stirrups for the stitching procedure. It can help to use nitrous oxide if this is painful, although don't hesitate to ask for more local anesthetic if you need it. The nurse will also check the mother's blood pressure, temperature, and pulse.

Medical Interventions— and Why They May Be Needed

Sometimes some part of the pregnancy and labor is not entirely straightforward and an obstetrician may need to intervene, or to step in, and do something to make sure the baby is born safely. In nearly all cases the physician will consult you and explain what is happening and why, although in a real emergency this is more difficult. Nevertheless, you and your partner should never be afraid to ask if there is anything you are unsure about.

Induction of Labor

This means inducing or starting labor artificially. The most common reason for inducing labor is that the baby has stayed in the uterus beyond the date when he should have been born—this is called "postmaturity." The worry is that he may begin to suffer from lack of oxygen because the placenta may start to fail and no longer be able to work properly. Some hospitals do not like to leave babies longer than forty-one or forty-two weeks, while others will leave them longer provided that fetal heart rate testing and ultrasound exams show they are all right. Signs for concern may be fewer and weaker movements by the baby (although this is often hard for the mother to judge), any suggestion of an abnormal heartbeat, and poor growth, together with an overall weight loss in the mother for two or three weeks. Postmature babies will have begun to lose body fat and have saggy, wrinkly skin over their abdomen, longer fingernails, and often flaky, dry skin with very little vernix— that is the white, creamy substance that protects their skin while they are in the womb. It is very important that the expected date of birth is calculated carefully so a baby is not mistakenly induced and then proves to be premature. An ultrasound at about twelve weeks can tell the baby's age and due date of birth most accurately.

Other reasons for inducing labor may be that a problem exists or develops during pregnancy so that there comes a point when the baby may be safer outside than inside the womb, even though this means he will be born early. Examples of this are mothers who develop pre-eclampsia, or those who have heart conditions, kidney disease, or possibly diabetes. Babies who are not growing properly because the placenta is not working well enough to provide sufficient nutrients and vital oxygen supplies, babies showing signs of fetal distress, or babies with Rh disease may also fall into this group.

The oldest method of inducing or starting labor is castor oil, an enema, and a warm bath, and in fact if the cervix has begun to soften, this can still be very effective, but do not try dosing yourself with anything unsupervised. Modern methods, however, include breaking the water so the baby's head begins to press directly on the cervix, and local prostaglandins are released that stimulate contractions, or administering hormones either in the form of suppositories or by means of an intravenous drip that will stimulate the onset of labor. In deciding how to induce labor, obstetricians will try to determine how close the mother is to natural labor. An internal examination can tell how "ripe" the cervix is: this closed ring of fibrous tissue begins to soften and relax as the time for the baby to be born draws near. If the cervix is quite ripe; if the baby is already due; and if the mother has experienced erratic contractions, perhaps over a period of days, it may be sufficient simply to break the water. This is done by passing an instrument through the cervix during a vaginal examination to break the membranes or "bag" holding the fluid. It should not be more uncomfortable than an ordinary internal pelvic exam. After the first rush of water there will be more leaks with each contraction for a while. The condition of the water is an important guide to the baby's condition.

If the cervix is unripe, prostaglandin suppositories or gel are used to induce labor. These can be inserted high in the vagina to make the cervix soften and start to dilate. They take several hours to work and usually contractions begin gently and follow a natural pattern of buildup. Finally, an intravenous drip can be used to feed the hormone oxytocin directly into the bloodstream. This is the hormone produced naturally by the body to stimulate contractions. Instead of a slow buildup, contractions tend to start more strongly and to occur more frequently, but labor is usually shorter. Care must be taken that contractions do not come so fast that the baby becomes distressed.

Induced labor will be monitored, but you can sit in a chair if that is more comfortable than a bed, and there is a certain amount of leeway in being able to move around, albeit anchored to the intravenous drip.

Accelerated Labor

There are various reasons for wanting to accelerate labor. One of the most common ones is if the labor progresses very slowly, in which case it could become dangerously long. When this happens, the risk of either you or the baby becoming distressed or getting an infection increases, and careful checks will be made to make sure this does not happen. A long labor may be caused by an abnormal pattern of contractions, the baby's head lying in the pelvis in a difficult position, for example, occipito-posterior ("back to front"), or disproportion (where the baby's head is too large to fit into the pelvis). Any or all of these reasons may make a cesarean delivery advisable.

Sometimes other medical interventions can have the effect of making contractions diminish or become less effective; this can happen with an epidural anesthetic or sedatives. Other reasons for wanting to accelerate labor, usually with a hormone drip, may be a stop-start pattern of contractions that never gets properly established, although the baby is due, or a long period of weak contractions after the water has broken.

Episiotomy

This is a small cut in the skin of the perineum to enlarge the vaginal entrance just before the baby is born. There is a good deal of controversy surrounding this practice, which used to be almost routine for first-time mothers in some hospitals. The traditional view is that an episiotomy prevents serious tearing, which in a very few cases might even extend into the rectum. The thinking was that an episiotomy is easier to repair and mends better than a ragged tear and helps prevent rectal prolapse in later life. However, a more recent school of thought maintains that small tears mend and heal better and with less discomfort than an episiotomy, that many episiotomies extend into tears anyway, and that several episiotomies may actually make the risk of later rectal prolapse greater. Most obstetricians take great pride in trying to avoid an unnecessary episiotomy. The stretchability of the perineum and the skill of the obstetrician, coupled with the patience and perseverance of the mother, probably matter more than the size of the baby—very large babies have often been delivered without cuts or tears. However, sometimes there may be special reasons for an episiotomy to deliver the baby quickly and without great pressure on the head. A baby showing signs of distress or a premature or growth-retarded baby may need to be gotten out quickly, using forceps that form a protective cage around the baby's head so it is not subject to pressure during birth. Episiotomies and forceps generally go together, so an unusual position of the head, a multiple birth, or mothers who cannot push the baby out themselves—because they have had an epidural, lost their contractions, or are too exhausted after a very long labor—are more likely to require an episiotomy. Women with high blood pressure or a heart condition who should not exert themselves by excessive pushing may also be delivered by an episiotomy and forceps.

An episiotomy is made as the baby's head begins to crown. The obstetrician will be watching carefully to see how the perineum is stretching. If it seems very rigid and likely to tear badly, or if there is a special reason for the baby to be delivered quickly, or if the mother should not push, the obstetrician injects local anesthetic and makes the cut with a pair of surgical scissors at the height of the next contraction. The skin is already numbed by stretching, and the cut is usually painless. Although naturally this is a procedure that causes great concern in advance for first-time mothers, nearly all of them afterward say they did not notice when it was happening.

The cut should be sewn up as soon as possible after the baby is born and while the skin is still numb—the longer it is left, the more sensation returns to the area. Plenty of local anesthetic should be used and given time to take effect, so ask for more if you are in pain. It is usually necessary to put a woman's feet in stirrups for the repair—normally done by your obstetrician. The layers of the vagina, the muscles of the perineum, and the skin all have to be closed separately, but usually with thread that dissolves rather than having to be taken out.

Forceps

These are really tongs that fit around the baby's head and can be used to help lift the baby out or turn him if the head is in an unusual position. If the baby is very small, premature, or showing signs of distress and needs to be delivered quickly and without too much pressure on a delicate skull, forceps may be used. The blades of the forceps fit around the head like a cage, protecting it from pressure. They may also be used to protect the head in a breech delivery—that is when the bottom presents first. Other reasons for the use of forceps may be if the baby is very delayed in the second stage and if the mother seems unlikely to be able to push him out herself, or if an epidural anesthetic makes it more difficult for the mother to feel the contractions and push the baby out. Finally, forceps may be used when the mother has a condition such as heart disease or high blood pressure and should not overexert herself.

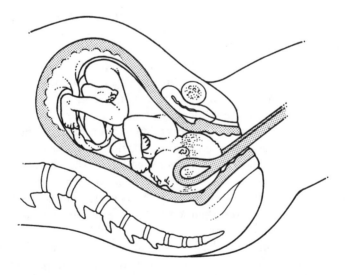

Forceps delivery

If you have not had an epidural anesthetic and there is no time to set one up, then a local anesthetic will be injected into the vulva and around the vagina to numb this area. This is called a "pudendal block." An episiotomy is usually carried out with a forceps delivery to avoid both tears to you and extra pressure on the baby's head. You will probably be asked to lie back and put your feet up in stirrups (the lithotomy position), and your thighs will be covered with sterile drapes. Don't be alarmed by all this surgical-seeming preparation—most forceps deliveries really are painless and will ensure the safety of your baby. The majority are "low forceps" when the baby has moved well down into the vagina and just needs help in the last stage. One blade of the forceps at a time is slid into the vagina, and once they are both safely tucked around the baby's head, the handles are locked into position. The doctor pulls very gently in time with the mother's contractions, stopping in between, until the head is low enough to be eased out.

Intervention is also required if the baby's head fails to rotate as it moves down into the birth canal, a condition known as "transverse arrest." Most babies' heads are turned to the side when they engage in the pelvis, known as "occipito-lateral position." Normally they rotate spontaneously so that the occiput, the bone at the back of the baby's head, is facing upward, toward the mother's stomach. This is the ideal birth position. However, the head may fail to rotate at all, or may rotate so the baby's face points forward—"occipito-posterior"; in both these situations the head is likely to get stuck and to need to be turned with forceps. Once the baby's head has turned, it will usually move farther down the birth canal to the entrance of the vagina quite easily. In general, difficult forceps deliveries with the head high up, which used to be common until the mid-1970s, are simply no longer attempted, having been replaced by cesarean section.

Marks may be left by the forceps on the baby's head, but they nearly always disappear within twenty-four hours. Occasionally a difficult delivery may leave longer-lasting bruises. As with all medical procedures, there is a slight risk of more permanent damage, but the risk of the procedure has to be weighed against the risk of doing nothing.

Vacuum Delivery

This is an alternative to forceps. It entails using a piece of equipment called a "vacuum extractor" which consists of a metal or rubber cup with a suction pump and chain attached. The reasons for doing a vacuum delivery are similar to the need for forceps, except that it is not suitable for a premature or breech delivery. It is also important that you are able to push well to help the vacuum delivery, or else forceps may be required. One major advantage over forceps is that vacuum delivery causes less perineal bruising and less likelihood of bad tearing in the mother. However, vacuum delivery babies are at a slightly higher risk of jaundice than those born by forceps. Occasionally they may suffer from bruising to the scalp, which in rare cases can be severe.

As with forceps, mothers usually have to lie back in the lithotomy position and be covered with sterile drapes. The cup is fitted over the back of the baby's head and a vacuum created with the suction pump so the baby's scalp is sucked up into the cup. The doctor pulls gently on the chain in time with the contractions, in the same way as with forceps, to ease the head downward. After the delivery, the baby will have a soft swelling on his head in the shape of a cup, which, although it looks odd, always goes down in a couple of days and causes no lasting effects. Often an episiotomy is not required.

Cesarean Section

This is an operation done under general, spinal, or epidural anesthetic in which a cut is made through the abdomen and the wall of the uterus and the baby is then lifted out. The need for a cesarean section may be recognized during pregnancy, in which case it is called a "planned" or "elective" cesarean section, or it may arise because of an emergency either during labor or before. A baby who is too large to pass through the mother's pelvis (disproportion), or when the placenta is covering the cervix (placenta previa), or in cases when the baby is lying transversely, will have to be delivered by cesarean section. It may be thought a safer way of birth for very vulnerable babies as well—these include babies who are premature, small, or lying in an unusual position. When the cord prolapses through the cervix into the vagina, a cesarean section is required. A prolapsed cord will require a cesarean delivery, and babies who become seriously distressed either during pregnancy or labor may also have to be delivered this way. Sometimes it may be done to protect the mother if she has a heart condition, very high blood pressure, pre-eclampsia, diabetes, or a detached retina. Cesarean section may also be the answer if all attempts to induce labor fail, or the cervix does not dilate, or if there was a previous very difficult birth, perhaps requiring high forceps, though doctors will often allow a trial labor to see if there is a chance of a normal delivery. In many cases, a combination of reasons can lead to the decision to do a cesarean section. A previous cesarean birth on its own is not a reason for a subsequent cesarean section, unless the same complications exist, but doctors will be monitoring the case more carefully to make sure the scarred uterus is working properly.

Like any operation, a cesarean section requires preoperative procedures. This means not eating for several hours beforehand, shaving pubic hair, possibly use of rectal suppositories the night before, and removal of false teeth, contact lenses, and jewelry, but no pre-medication injection, as this would affect the baby. In an emergency some or all of these procedures may be omitted. An intravenous drip will be set up and a catheter (hollow tube) inserted to drain the bladder, though if you are having a general anesthetic this may be done after you go to sleep.

The whole operation takes about thirty to forty minutes from start to finish. Cutting through the wall of the abdomen and uterus and lifting the baby out is the quickest part, and your baby will be born in about five minutes. Usually the cut is made horizontally very low down in the abdomen so it will not show above a bikini. Surgeons do a horizontal rather than a vertical cut unless there are exceptional circumstances, but ask beforehand. After the baby has been delivered you are given an injection of oxytocin, as in a normal labor, to help the placenta separate, and this is also delivered through the cut. The longest part of the operation is sewing together the layers of tissue. A dressing will be put on the wound, which will be inspected each day, and sometimes a tube to drain it will be in place for the first twelve to twenty-four hours. The stitches or staples usually come out on about the fourth day, depending on how the wound heals. The intravenous drip will be left in place until you are able to drink normally without feeling sick—again, this usually happens within the first twenty-four hours.

Under a general anesthetic the gases do not affect the baby, but because there is a high risk of vomiting with a pregnant woman, the anesthetic will be given by an experienced anesthetist or anesthesiologist. Today, obstetricians prefer to do cesarean sections under spinal or epidural anesthetic when possible because the risks to the mother are less and because it is very enjoyable to see your baby immediately after he is born, but you will have the choice unless it is an emergency, when there may only be time for a general anesthetic. A general anesthetic affects individuals differently, but it is common to feel nauseated afterward, and many women complain of a congested feeling where mucus has gathered in their lungs, and sometimes of a sore throat caused by the tube that was passed down it.

If you already have an epidural in and a cesarean section becomes necessary during labor, then extra care is taken to make sure it is fully effective, which usually means lying in all sorts of different positions, and having several tests, such as testing pinprick sensation before the operation. For elective or emergency cesarean

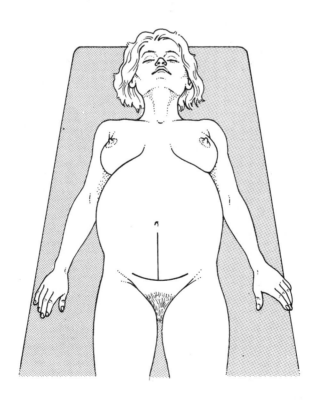

Alternative positions for Caesarean incision

sections where the mother does not have an epidural already in place, spinal anesthetic is being increasingly used. Although you can feel pressure during the operation, there is no sensation of pain. Most obstetricians will be happy for your husband to stay with you, and a sterile green cloth will be pinned up across your chest as a screen so you do not have to watch the procedure. Your blood pressure and pulse rate will be monitored, as with any surgical operation.

As long as there are no complications, the baby will usually be given to you to hold while the incision is repaired and, once this is done, you can put him to the breast if you plan to breast-feed.

Problems in Labor and Delivery

Premature Labor

This is a labor that starts after twenty-four weeks but before thirty-seven weeks; before twenty-four weeks it is, strictly speaking, said to be a miscarriage, but a very few babies have survived having been born before this. It is often hard to say why labor has started early; it is usually a combination of factors. Illness in the mother can sometimes be a reason—for example, diabetes, high blood pressure, preeclampsia, uncontrolled heart disease, anemia, urinary tract infection, or another infection with fever. Accidental hemorrhage when the placenta begins to separate early and causes bleeding can also cause premature labor. Mothers under twenty, smokers, and those suffering from poor nutrition and living standards may be more at risk, while an incompetent or damaged cervix, a failing placenta, or a malformation in the baby can also cause labor to begin prematurely. The most common fetal cause is a multiple pregnancy; the more babies, the earlier labor begins.

The baby's chance of survival in the case of premature labor and delivery depends on how mature the lungs are. Maturity is not necessarily related to size, and quite a large baby can be immature while a smaller one can have spent more time in the uterus and can be better developed to cope with life outside. As a rough guide, if the pregnancy is more than thirty-four weeks when labor begins, then it will usually be allowed to continue because by this stage the baby should be mature enough, if there are no other complications, to be taken care of in an ordinary hospital maternity unit.

Before thirty-four weeks doctors will take into account any known reasons for the start of labor—for example, illness in the mother or other complications that may make it more dangerous for the baby (or possibly for the mother) to stay in the uterus than to be born. If there is a chance that the baby may be delivered before twenty-two weeks, then two injections of a cortisone-like drug may be given twelve hours apart to help the baby's lungs mature more quickly. Before twenty-two weeks the baby's lungs are likely to lack a substance called "surfactant," which is secreted to line the mucous membranes inside the lungs and make them more flexible and less likely to stick together. Steroid injections boost surfactant production. If possible, labor will also be slowed down to allow time for the steroid injections to work (maximum benefit is after twenty-four hours) and to move the mother to a hospital with a neonatal intensive care unit, which will give the baby a better chance of survival. A first step in stopping labor is bed rest, but if labor threatens to become established, a drug can also be given, at first by an intravenous drip into a vein in the arm and then as pills. However, this treatment does not always work, and many doctors feel it is only of use as a means of delaying labor while the steroid injections are given time to work.

Water Breaking Prematurely

If the membrane containing the amniotic fluid ruptures, the water will either begin to leak slowly or to gush out. If it leaks slowly it can sometimes be mistaken for a vaginal discharge or urine, and you need to see a doctor, who can usually tell by an internal examination or tests whether it is amniotic fluid. Once the water has leaked out there is an increased risk of infection and, after thirty-four weeks of pregnancy, doctors will often decide to induce the labor if it does not follow naturally. Before thirty-four weeks doctors will normally try to give the baby extra valuable time in the womb, and resting in bed may be enough to delay labor. Cultures will be taken to check that there is no infection, and antibiotics may be given to reduce its risk.

Small Babies Who Are Not Premature

Some babies may be born at the right time but still be very small because they have failed to grow properly in the uterus. They are usually known as small-for-dates babies, which means they are smaller than the average-size baby would be at the same stage of pregnancy. Feeling the top of the uterus (the fundus) is a rough guide to enable doctors to see if the baby is growing at the right rate, but ultrasound scans can give far more accurate and detailed information. A special scan called a Doppler scan, looking at the pattern of blood flow through the placenta and in the baby's umbilical cord, may be performed.

These small or low-birthweight babies are more vulnerable than babies who have grown properly. Generally they are thought of as being babies who weigh less than 5 lb, 8 oz (2,500 gr). They are more likely to develop breathing or feeding problems and become ill, but given extra care in the early weeks, they still stand a good chance of developing quite normally, although at first perhaps a little more slowly. They will eventually catch up with other children of the same age both in size and development.

The most common cause for a baby failing to grow is that the placenta is not working properly and the baby is therefore being starved before birth—he is not getting enough nourishment. This might be because the mother herself is ill (e.g., because of high blood pressure or kidney disease), is a heavy smoker or a heavy drinker, or is suffering from poor nutrition herself. Women under eighteen or over thirty-five have also been shown to be slightly more at risk of having small babies.

Research is proceeding into the use of ultrasound scans to detect babies in the very early weeks of pregnancy who may be at risk—the scans can pick up which babies have a poor blood flow from the placenta. As yet these tests are in the research stage and not widely available. At the moment, therefore, doctors usually only pick up babies who are not growing properly later in pregnancy. What can be done to help them? If tests show that the placenta is still working, then resting in bed, eating well, and not drinking alcohol or smoking can give the baby a better chance. But if tests show that the placenta is beginning to fail altogether and the baby has stopped growing, he may have to be delivered—despite the risks because of his immaturity—because the chances of his survival in the uterus are so much less. Even if they are not premature, small babies are also less able to withstand the extra stress of labor, and there is a higher chance that they may have to be delivered by cesarean section or forceps, depending on their condition.

Bleeding

The loss of bright red blood without any pain, either at the start of labor or during pregnancy, is likely to be a warning sign of a condition called placenta previa. This means the placenta is lying low in the uterus, partially or completely covering the cervix and hence the baby's exit. A full placenta previa, where the placenta is directly across the cervix, always calls for a cesarean section, but there are degrees of this condition. Sometimes an ultrasound scan may reveal that the placenta seems rather low, but as the baby grows and the uterus expands, so the position of the placenta may improve and move farther from the cervix.

Blood loss accompanied by pain, however, is usually a symptom of a different condition, called abruptio placentae. In this case, the placenta is in the normal position in the upper third of the womb but begins to separate from the wall with bleeding, which can be of varying amounts and from any part of the placenta. Sometimes there may be no visible bleeding from the vagina, and diagnosis is often difficult. We do not yet know why this condition occurs—theories range from implicating high blood pressure, to abnormalities in the blood clotting factor, to accidental injury. The factors of each individual case need to be assessed to determine whether to deliver the baby by cesarean section—the baby's condition, the mother's blood loss, the maturity of the baby, and whether the cervix has dilated are some points that will be taken into account. It is more likely that the mother will need a blood transfusion following both these conditions.

Abnormal Positions of the Baby

Breech   In a normal birth the largest part of the baby, the head, slowly descends into the birth canal so the tissues are gently stretched. But with a breech birth the baby is lying head upward and the head is born last and more quickly, so there is an increased risk to the baby. Usually breech babies are born bottom first, but can also come out feet first. Doctors will assess the size of the mother's pelvis to be certain there is plenty of room and try to make sure delivery is slow and controlled. Mothers are usually offered an epidural, as the baby may need more manipulation or a forceps delivery. A cesarean section may be suggested, especially if the pelvis seems narrow or there are other complications, the baby is premature or very small, the baby becomes distressed at some point during labor, or the cervix does not dilate steadily during labor.

Transverse   This means the baby is lying crossways and cannot be delivered either head or bottom first. Attempts may be made near the end of pregnancy to turn him,

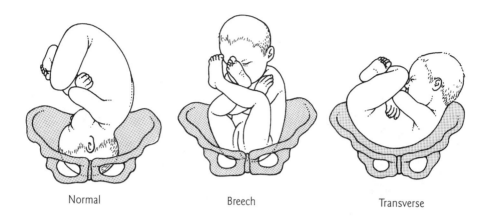

Normal   Breech   Transverse

but this should only be done by an obstetrician—do not try it yourself. If this fails, a cesarean section will be needed. This position is more common in women who have had several babies.

Unstable Lie   A few babies keep changing from breech or head first to transverse, even in the last weeks of pregnancy, and this may be because a low placenta or even a fibroid is blocking the cervix and the way out of the uterus. There is also a greater risk of a prolapsed cord when the membranes break. Examinations will be made to try to find the cause, which may mean a stay in the hospital, and delivery may be by cesarean section.

Different Head Presentations and Positions   Normally the narrowest part of the baby's head, the occiput, is born first, and this is the part that is presenting—or leading the way. The baby flexes his neck so his chin is tucked into his chest, and his head turns from facing to one or other side so his face is toward your backbone. His backbone lies uppermost, toward your stomach. Sometimes the head turns the other way so the baby's face is uppermost, and then the back of the baby's head and his spine are toward your spine—this is called "occipito-posterior position" and usually means a longer labor with backache. Occasionally a forceps or vacuum may be used to assist the delivery.

Deep transverse arrest occurs when the baby's head stays sideways and does not turn either toward your abdomen or toward your backbone. In this case, forceps or vacuum extraction are nearly always needed to turn the head and help the baby out, although a cesarean section may be a safer option in some cases.

If the baby's chin is not tucked tightly onto his chest, then a different part of the head will be born first, which can make the second stage slower and mold the baby's head into an odd shape, although this will correct itself after a few days.

Rarely, the baby's head is not flexed at all, and the face instead of the head is the presenting part—these babies can be delivered vaginally, but their faces are puffy and bruised for a few days from the pressure. Even more rarely, the brow can lead the way into the birth canal, leaving the head at such an angle that a cesarean section is almost always the only way of delivery.

Shoulder presentation

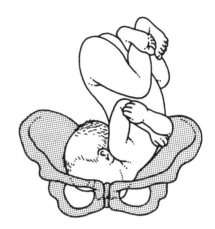

Face presentation

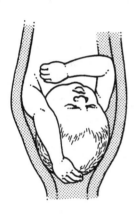

Compound

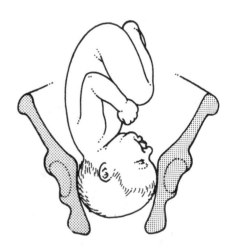

Deep transverse arrest

Twins and More

In nearly half of all twin pregnancies, both babies are lying head down by the end of the pregnancy, and in slightly fewer cases one baby is head down and the other is breech. It is rarer for both babies to be in the breech position and most uncommon of all for both babies to lie transversely. Identical twins develop from one large placenta and sometimes share one amniotic sac as well. Fraternal twins develop from two separate placentas and have two separate amniotic sacs.

Twins are more likely to be premature—about a quarter of all twins are born before the thirty-sixth week. This, coupled with an awkward position, can sometimes make a cesarean section more likely, but if the pregnancy is quite well advanced, the babies are not very small, and one or both of them are lying in the head-first position, then an ordinary delivery is usually possible, though an epidural

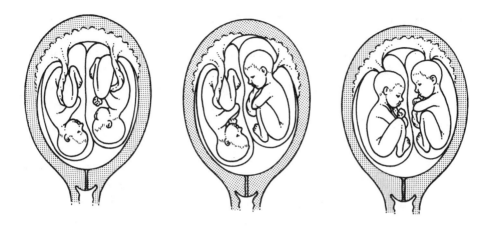

is normally suggested in case extra help is needed. In the case of fraternal twins, the cord of the first baby is cut after the birth and then the bag of water surrounding the second baby is broken—if it has not already done so. The second baby is usually born a few minutes later and much more easily, as the tissues have already been stretched. In both cases, whether identical or fraternal twins, the placenta or placentas are delivered last, as in a normal birth.

Prolapsed Cord

This occurs when the umbilical cord drops through the cervix into the vagina ahead of the baby when the membranes break. This can occur before or during labor. It is dangerous because the baby's head pressing onto the cord can cut off the oxygen supply to the baby. If the cervix has not fully dilated, a cesarean section will be performed to get the baby out quickly, but sometimes, if the cervix is fully dilated, the baby can be delivered quickly vaginally.

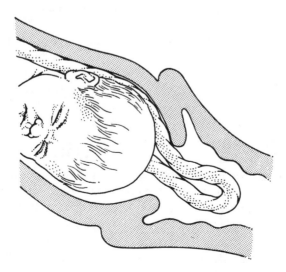

Cord Around the Neck

It is very common for the cord to be wound once or several times around the baby's neck. It is usually easy for the obstetrician to slip the cord over the baby's head after the head has been born, but very rarely the cord has become so short that it begins to pull tight, restricting the baby's supply of oxygen. If this happens, the cord can be clamped and cut after the head is born, allowing the body to be delivered easily and making the baby begin to breathe through his mouth and use his lungs.

Fetal Distress

This term usually indicates that the baby is not getting enough oxygen. Warning signs that the baby is distressed are that his heart begins to beat at more than 160 beats a minute or less than 110, and the baby may pass meconium, which produces a green or brownish staining of the amniotic fluid. Electronic monitoring will show how the baby is coping with the stress of contractions, and once the cervix is partly opened, this can be determined by taking a blood sample from the baby's scalp to measure the level of acidity in the blood. To take the sample the mother usually lies back on her left side on the edge of the bed and a cone-shaped tube is passed down the vagina and through the cervix so the baby's head can be seen. Then a small prick is made in the baby's scalp and a tiny amount of blood is collected in a capillary tube; if the cervix is not very dilated this can be painful for a moment, and you need to use breathing techniques or nitrous oxide if you have not already had any other pain relief. If labor is in the first stage and the cervix is only partly dilated, the baby may need to be delivered by cesarean section if he is in severe distress. But if the cervix is fully dilated, or if the baby becomes distressed during the second stage when he is moving down the birth canal, then usually forceps or vacuum extraction can be used to get the baby out quickly.

Disproportion

The baby's head may be either too large to fit into the pelvis, or the pelvis may be too small to accommodate the head. An internal examination can help a doctor to estimate the size of the pelvis, and occasionally an X ray will be taken. Apart from being simply too narrow, the bones of the pelvis can be shaped to make the passage of the baby's head very difficult. If there is doubt, a trial of labor may be allowed to see if the head will descend into the brim of the pelvis, when it is said to be engaged. Rarely, an abnormally shaped pelvis is not discovered until labor begins, and a cesarean section is necessary if the baby's head will not pass through easily.

Bleeding After the Birth

A small amount of bleeding will come from an episiotomy or tear in the perineum, but if there is a large amount of blood the doctor will check to determine whether there is a tear in the tissues of the vagina that may also need repairing. After the birth the uterus gradually decreases in size, and as it does, it sheds its lining. For the first few days, the discharge, called "lochia," is bright red, but gradually it turns reddish-brown and finally, after a few weeks, a pale browny-yellow color. Breast-feeding stimulates the release of hormones that cause the uterus to contract, so bleeding is usually heavier after feeding. This discharge should usually cease by about six weeks, but if it suddenly gets much heavier or if large blood clots appear, consult your obstetrician. The most common reason for heavier than normal bleeding or for bleeding not diminishing is that fragments of the placenta have broken off and are still attached to the wall of the uterus. Sometimes this is evident immediately after the birth because the obstetrician can see the placenta is not intact. A simple rule is that an empty, uninjured uterus does not bleed profusely, so very heavy blood loss after the birth is unusual. When the complete placenta fails to separate from the uterus at all, then it is said to be "retained." The first resort, whether it is the whole placenta or only parts that have been left inside, is to give an injection of Ergotrate and to rub the mother's abdomen gently to produce a contraction while the obstetrician gently tugs on the cord. If this does not work an anesthetic is needed, either to do a D&C (scraping operation) if there are only fragments, or for the doctor to remove the placenta by hand.

Stillbirth

Our first baby was stillborn. He died during labor, and although they did an emergency cesarean section, it was too late to save him. At the time you think you'll never see the world again except in colors of gray. But time does change things. Even though we have two school-age daughters now, I still think about our son, but with regret and not the terrible misery.

A stillbirth is a baby born without any sign of life after the 24th week of pregnancy. Both stillbirths and babies dying in the first week of life are considered perinatal deaths.

The main causes of stillbirth are congenital abnormalities, prematurity, and lack of oxygen either before or during labor. A baby who has not been growing properly during pregnancy may have been suffering from a gradual lack of oxygen, and this, in turn, may make him more at risk in the case of prolonged or complicated labor. A few stillbirths will be the result of a sudden lack of oxygen. Prolapse of the cord can cause this, as can abruptio placentae.

The Birth of a Stillborn
Even if it is known earlier in pregnancy that the baby has died, going into labor or continuing with labor will be a traumatic experience. Once it is known that a baby has died in the womb during a pregnancy, the medical staff will arrange for labor to be induced—suppositories are usually tried first and, if those are not successful, an intravenous drip with pitocin. Obviously, painkilling drugs can be given far more freely than in an ordinary labor.

A woman should always have someone with her—if not her husband or partner, then a close friend or relative. The experience of other couples shows that it usually helps for them to see and, if the mother wishes, to hold the baby in private. If the hospital staff does not offer to show parents their baby, they should never be afraid to ask. It is not a morbid request. It also helps to have a color photo of the baby to take home. This can go some way toward making the baby's existence and death a reality that can be shared later with relatives and sympathetic friends. As with a miscarriage, the couple is grieving for a child no one else but they knew.

Inevitably feelings of great shock, numbness, and often anger follow a stillbirth. Most women will want to be discharged from the hospital as soon as possible, but while they are there they should be able to choose whether to stay in a room by themselves or in a ward with mothers who have babies. If there is anyone else who has suffered a stillbirth, it may help to meet them. If a genetic problem or congenital abnormality is suspected, the hospital will probably ask permission to do a postmortem to discover the cause of death. As with miscarriage, it is vitally important that the parents are given the opportunity to ask and to receive honest answers to all their questions, when they are ready. Most couples do want answers, perhaps not immediately, but more especially when they think of having another baby and want to know if there is a chance the same thing might happen again.

Practicalities

In a shocked, confused state parents can be bewildered by having to cope with registration of death and arrangements for the burial of their baby. Experience shows that having a proper funeral and burial help considerably. Not having the baby buried in the way they would have wanted, because of misinformation or misunderstanding, can be a later source of pain and regret to parents.

One parent, usually the father, needs to go to the hospital administrative staff, who will explain how and where to go to register the birth and death and also to help with funeral arrangements. If parents want the hospital to arrange the funeral, they may choose between cremation or burial. The burial can usually be in a public grave that is shared with other babies, or the parents can pay for a private grave. Parents can ask any religious minister to hold a ceremony, or a service can be held in the hospital chapel. Of course, parents who wish to arrange a private funeral need only contact a funeral director—the hospital administration will help with telephone numbers if necessary, and provide the preliminary death certificate issued by the hospital.

The funeral is usually within ten days of the death. Although at the time going to the funeral may seem to be adding to misery, later most parents are glad they did attend.

It is one of the cruel ironies of late miscarriage and stillbirth that the mother's body continues to react as though a live, well baby had been born, so her breasts will start to become engorged with milk two to three days after the delivery. Stitches, flabby abdomens, and other aftereffects of birth can be so much harder to cope with in these circumstances. Some women may dread returning for a postnatal checkup to the hospital where their baby died; if so, their obstetrician should do this for them in a different office. Others may be reluctant to take this final step, the last acknowledgment of their baby's existence.

If the obstetrician is sympathetic, the postnatal visit can be a helpful time for questions. In many cases a full explanation as to why the baby died will not be possible, despite an autopsy. If a couple feels disappointed by lack of information, it often helps for them to say so and to put into words what they feel, even though this is not going to produce the answers they want.

Afterward

Everywhere I went I seemed to see nothing but pregnant women, tiny newborn babies in carriages, and couples with small children.

This is a very common feeling, and it helps to remember that grief can cause one's view of the world, at least temporarily, to be distorted. Talking to other couples with the same experience helps—not just immediately afterward but also months later, during a next pregnancy, and perhaps after the birth of a live baby, too.

Some couples react very differently and cannot accept comfort from each other or from other people. Sometimes there are difficulties in resuming sex after a still-birth, even though both partners may be very loving toward each other. In all cases it helps to take things at one's own pace—not to try to force oneself to "get over it" quickly or to rush at getting back to normal. If there are problems, couples should talk about them with each other and ask a trusted doctor, religious leader, or counselor for help or advice.

Your New Baby

First Reactions

You can never really believe, all through pregnancy, and even during labor, that you are actually going to end up with a baby. I remember the shock of seeing what seemed like this huge, healthy baby, and thinking that just a second ago it had been inside me. It really is a miracle.

I must admit I didn't feel anything special toward the baby right away. The birth had been so awful I was just thankful it was all over. I remember saying to my husband: "I guess I have to feed her now." It wasn't until about six hours later, when I'd been stitched up and moved to the regular floor, that I looked and saw her lying perfectly peacefully but awake, staring at me with little dark eyes. I fell in love with her.

I just felt a sense of wonder when I saw her for the first time. I still feel that often when I look at her now.

That moment, after the birth, when you first see, touch, and hold your new baby is very special and highly personal. Everyone reacts differently, and while many mothers feel an immediate rush of love and intense excitement, others may feel more detached and need time to adjust. Many women need time to recover from the labor and delivery, especially if they have had a difficult or a painful birth. Ambivalent feelings are perfectly normal, and can occur whether you desperately wanted a baby or if your pregnancy was unplanned. Take your time. There is no "right" or "wrong" way to feel. Such a major change in your life as becoming a parent will provoke very many different emotions in both of you at varying times.

Bonding

Much has been written and said about the importance of keeping mothers and babies together from birth and the way in which a bond begins to develop between them as they learn about each other by looking and touching. The baby is already familiar with the pattern and pitch of her mother's voice from her months in the womb. She soon learns to put a face, a smell, and a feel to the voice. A mother in turn begins to learn about her baby's needs from the baby's cries and how to soothe and comfort her.

Suggesting there is a need for parents and their baby to be alone together after the birth makes it sound as though during those first few minutes a magical process should take place that a woman will immediately recognize and that will equip her to cope with the many and varied demands of motherhood. In fact, of course, a relationship between parents and children evolves gradually, in a different way and at a different pace for everyone. However, it does seem true that in many cases we are especially sensitive to our newborns in the period immediately after birth—a period that often coincides with a particular awareness and alertness in the baby. Often animals whose babies are taken away at birth reject them if they are returned sometime later and, although our human reactions and emotions are far more complex and sophisticated, it is the most natural desire for a mother to want to keep her new baby close by her side. That is why medical staffs do all they can to keep them together as much as possible, even when the baby is ill and may need special care.

This idea of a sensitive period, when we are especially ready to learn something, seems to apply at other stages of development, too. Thus there is a certain stage when learning language is easier, and children who miss out at this time—perhaps because they are temporarily deaf, or are not spoken to enough—will find it harder to learn to talk later, while babies who are not introduced to solid food at the right stage may be very resistant to eating it later. It does seem certain that the beginning of a close relationship between parents and child is helped by time alone together after the birth, though it is also important to recognize that it is perfectly possible to form good relationships later if the mother and the baby do have to be separated, for example, because the baby has to be in intensive care, or because the mother is ill after a complicated delivery or a cesarean section. Also, adoptive parents often form extremely close bonds with their children.

First Contact with Your Baby

These days many physicians will ask if you want the baby placed onto your stomach after delivery. This immediate skin-to-skin contact can be very soothing and reassuring for both you and your baby. Many mothers, however, want time to recover from the birth itself and will enjoy having their baby in close contact with them a few minutes later. Some women may not like the idea of the baby being placed directly onto their stomach because they are concerned that the baby will be covered with mucus or blood. In fact there is not usually very much blood, although the baby will be wet from the amniotic fluid, but the physician or nurse can easily wipe her clean, dry her, and wrap her in a blanket before handing her to you or placing her on your stomach, if that is your preference. The important thing is not to feel pressured to behave in a certain way but to make your wishes known and do what comes naturally. In your own time you can enjoy a feeling of closeness by laying your newborn on your stomach or between your breasts with a blanket over her back to help keep her warm. Keeping a newborn baby warm is important because even though the room may feel very hot to you it is still about twenty degrees colder than the temperature the baby has been used to inside your womb. She will also lose heat more quickly at first because her skin will still be damp from the amniotic fluid.

Taking a Hold on Life—Your Baby's First Breath

Inside the womb your baby's lungs are filled with fluid, though she does practice breathing movements by moving amniotic fluid in and out in small amounts. After the birth the fluid is absorbed and the lungs can collapse inward if they are not filled with air. Imagine the difference between a balloon filled with air and then shriveled up after it is emptied. The sides of the shriveled lungs are stopped from actually sticking together by an important surface film called "surfactant," which begins to cover them from about the 22nd week of pregnancy. This also makes the lungs more elastic and better able to expand. The biggest problem for babies born too soon is that they often do not have enough surfactant to help the lungs work properly.

We do not know exactly what makes the baby take her first breath and draw air into her lungs—most probably it is a survival response, as oxygen-carrying blood no longer flows through the umbilical cord. As explained in chapter 3, this normally happens at a point before the cord is actually cut—usually as the placenta begins to separate from the uterus wall. Imagine the lungs like a bunch of grapes running off a central stem—the stems are the bronchial tubes and the grapes are the little air sacs, or alveoli. When your baby takes in her first breath, the air rushes down the tubes, filling out the alveoli. The remaining amniotic fluid that has not been squeezed out during the birth is absorbed into the bloodstream.

At the same moment as your baby begins to take in oxygen through her lungs, there is also a major change in the way her heart works. Inside the womb the two sides of the heart beat together, with oxygenated blood from the umbilical cord flowing into both sides, though the right side does most of the work. When the baby begins to breathe herself, the pressure in the lungs decreases, and the arteries that used to bring blood from the cord close down because there is no blood flowing through them any longer. These changes make ducts in the heart close so that the two sides are functioning separately, as in normal life. One side receives blood-carrying oxygen from the lungs and sends it around the body, and the other side receives the "used" blood that is coming back from the body with less oxygen in it and sends it on to the lungs. This is the ordinary pattern for the rest of life. For the vast majority of babies, this seemingly complicated process happens without any problems and they begin to breathe as soon as they are born. But a few, for various reasons, may need help, which can usually be given very easily.

Clearing the Airways

Your baby will still have some fluid in her nose and throat when she is born. Often it is enough to wipe her face gently and then lay her face down on your stomach or thigh so that it will drain naturally. If her airways seem blocked or if she does not start breathing, any fluid can be sucked out of her nose and throat gently with a soft suction tube or a "nasal bulb syringe." The doctor, nurse, or midwife just inserts one end into the baby's nose and throat and gently sucks so that fluid is cleared and caught inside the tube. This takes only a few seconds and can either be done as soon as the baby's head is born and while waiting for another contraction to deliver the body, or after the delivery itself.

Crying

A cry is proof that the baby is breathing, and the traditional way to ensure that this happened used to be to hold her up by her heels and gently smack her on the bottom. This rather traumatic introduction to life has since been shown to be unnecessary, and gentle stimulation and drying of the skin alone are usually enough to ensure that she will begin to breathe, with or without crying. If your baby doesn't cry, don't worry, because she is probably breathing perfectly well. Some babies come out crying right away and others begin to cry soon after the birth, both of which are entirely normal. Holding your baby close to your skin and stroking, cuddling, and soothing her will calm her down.

Is My Baby All Right?

This is the question that runs in and out of all parents' thoughts at times during the long nine months of pregnancy. It is the question they want answered first with the proof of their own eyes at birth. A full, detailed examination of your new baby will wait until a little later, usually the following day, because newborn babies can easily get cold, but the doctor or midwife will automatically check for any obvious problems at birth. This is the point at which any mistakes in the development of the baby, such as extra fingers or toes, club feet, extra earlobes, or hypospadias (a faulty position of the opening of the penis in boys), will be detected. Most of these can be corrected, some very simply by a small surgical operation. In addition, your caregiver will also look at the baby's overall condition, to see whether she is a vigorous, active baby with good color and able to suck well.

Doctors and midwives all use the same methods to check newborns and record what they find. This is called the "Apgar score" after pediatrician Dr. Virginia Apgar, who devised it as a method of assessing the condition of a new baby. At one minute after birth, and then again at five minutes, the doctor or midwife checks the baby's heartbeat, breathing, muscle tone, reflexes, and color and gives each a score of 0, 1, or 2. A total score of 10 means a baby is in the best possible condition, but 7 or over is normal. Between 5 and 7 means the baby is all right but will probably improve with some simple treatment such as clearing her airways, or she may be slightly sleepy from the effects of narcotics given late in labor. Babies with a score of less than 5 may need extra oxygen or possibly other assistance to help establish better breathing.

Heartbeat	Over 100	2
	Slow, below 100	1
	Absent	0
Breathing	Regular, crying	2
	Slow, irregular	1
	Absent	0
Muscle tone	Moving actively	2
	Moving extremities only	1
	Limp	0
Reflexes (usually response to catheter in nostril)	Cough or sneeze	2
	Grimace	1
	None	0
Color	Pink	2
	Body pink, extremities blue	1
	Blue, pale	0

The two other important statistics to be recorded about your child's delivery will be her birth weight and the circumference of her head.

Birth weight is an important indication of the baby's health. A baby is classified as of low birth weight if she weighs less than 5½ lb at birth. Very small babies may need extra care, and there are a number of ways of telling whether their size is because they are premature or have not grown enough in the uterus, or both. Obviously other factors influence the baby's size, such as the size of the parents and the mother's own birth weight, which often corresponds with her baby's. Ill health during pregnancy and other environmental factors such as smoking, drinking alcohol, or drugs can all retard the unborn baby's growth. At the other end of the scale, if a baby is very large, usually thought of as weighing 10 lb or more, this may indicate that her mother either has diabetes or has become temporarily diabetic during pregnancy. Recording a baby's weight at birth also helps doctors to see how she is progressing later. Newborn babies usually lose 5 to 10 percent of their weight during the first four days of life. This is mainly due to fluid loss until the mother's milk supply is established. Most babies have regained their birth weight by the tenth day and go on to gain about 5 to 7 oz a week, or approximately 1 oz per day.

Head circumference will usually be related to your baby's overall size; thus large babies will have large heads and vice versa. An unusually small head, out of proportion to the rest of the baby's body, may be a sign of developmental delay. An unusually large head can be a symptom of hydrocephalus, a condition where fluid that normally bathes the brain collects in the head because the pathways that drain it are blocked. In some families head size may be larger than average, but intellectual function is entirely normal. An average head circumference for a baby weighing 7½ lb would be around 14 in. As with the baby's birth weight, one of the important aspects of this single statistic is to follow the way the baby develops so that subsequent measurements can show if the head is growing at the expected rate.

The actual shape of your baby's head will be influenced by the kind of birth as much as by her inherited features at first. Babies born by cesarean section may have perfectly formed heads, while babies who have had a long second stage of labor or were a tight fit through the mother's pelvis will often have had their heads molded into rather odd-looking shapes. Don't be alarmed. This will correct itself fairly quickly. At the same time as measuring your baby's head, the doctor or midwife will feel the fontanelles, or "soft spots" (see the section "Your Baby's First Checkup" later in this chapter for more on this).

Many hospitals also measure the baby's length, either at birth or on the second day of life. The average length for a normal-weight baby is 20 in.

Sucking

In the period soon after birth, your baby has a strong sucking reflex. If you touch her cheek with your nipple she will turn her head toward it—this is called "rooting." She will probably need help to latch on properly. Your partner or the nurse can help you to get comfortable so that your arm is supporting the baby's head at the right level, or he can support the baby's head himself. The baby's head needs to be very close to the breast to enable her to take the nipple fully into her mouth so that, as she sucks, the pressure of her mouth and gums is on the areola (the darker skin around the protruding nipple), not just the nipple itself (see "Breasts and

Breast-Feeding" in chapter 6 for more on this). Some babies suck strongly right away; others may just lick and nuzzle. If she does not seem interested at once this may be because she has either swallowed a lot of mucus or still has some mucus in her throat, or she may be sleepy because of narcotics given to you during labor. Try expressing a drop of colostrum—the extra-rich creamy substance that is present before the milk comes in—and putting it onto her lips to encourage her. At this first session the baby will probably suck for only two or three minutes; if she does not release her hold on the nipple, or if you want to transfer her to the other breast, break the suction by gently inserting your little finger into the corner of her mouth and twisting. Latching the baby properly onto the breast, and taking her off properly, are important safeguards against sore nipples.

Early sucking is important for three reasons. First, it stimulates your body to produce the hormone oxytocin, which helps the womb contract to the size it was before pregnancy and causes the placenta to separate. Second, it is a good start to establishing breast-feeding. Although the baby is getting protein-rich colostrum, not milk at this stage, the more she sucks, the sooner an ample supply of milk is established, and while she has a strong sucking reflex, it is easier to get her to feed. Studies show that feeding within an hour of birth is an important stimulus to successful breast-feeding. Lastly, it helps to establish a closeness between you and your baby that you can both enjoy. (For a full discussion of breast-feeding, see chapter 6.)

Fathers

I had agreed to stay for the first stage of labor but didn't want to stay for the birth. I am not good at dealing with anything medical. But in the end it all happened much more quickly than anyone thought, and I ended up staying, even though I kept at the head end of the bed. I was surprised by how peaceful and unmessy it all was. In seconds the doctor was handing our daughter to us wrapped in green cloth. I was high for days afterward.

At the very beginning of the pregnancy I felt a bit apprehensive when my wife said she wanted me to be at the birth. But we went together to a course of good prenatal classes, and by the end of the pregnancy it would have been unthinkable for me not to be there. I felt my presence was very necessary. I was able to massage her back, support her in different positions, and encourage her when she began to get exhausted. After the birth the midwife, whom we got to know really well, told me to unbutton my shirt, and I held our daughter, loosely wrapped in a cloth, against my chest.

It was terrifying, but amazing, too. More so the second time because you know what to expect. There was this wrinkled skull, the color of blue plastic, emerging and then suddenly the rest of the baby sort of sprang out and she began to breathe and turn pink. The absolute miracle of the life force grips you. I admit I had to wipe away the tears.

Early contact with their newborn baby is just as important for fathers as for mothers. It is one of the drawbacks of a traditional hospital birth that, although it may be safer for high-risk pregnancies, it often means fathers do not have the same involvement in the first few days. Many hospitals now discharge mothers and babies after forty-eight hours, and allow very free visiting by fathers. Certainly that time after the birth is one to be savored together. Skin-to-skin contact is just as pleasant for fathers as for mothers—if you feel a bit self-conscious about this, wait until the doctor and nurses have left you alone together, then unbutton your shirt so that you can hold your new baby against your chest. Warming young ones by holding them against our own bodies is a very natural reaction, and by keeping a cloth or blanket loosely wrapped around the outside of your baby she will be well protected from getting cold. If the mother needs medical attention because of any complications or stitches, the doctor may hand the baby to the father first. Otherwise you can hold her after the cord has been cut, perhaps while your partner is being cleaned up and made comfortable. If your partner is going to breast-feed the baby, you can help her to get into a comfortable position and to latch the baby onto the nipple by supporting the baby's head very close to the breast—lots of babies do need help at first. Don't worry about doing the right or the wrong thing—in time it will all come naturally.

Sharing Caring—Looking Ahead

New parents take time to gain confidence in their abilities to look after their new baby. Even if one of you has more experience with babies than the other, remember that at the beginning neither of you knows more than the other about this unique new baby. It will help you both to adjust to parenthood more easily if you learn together. Of course, trying to change a diaper or wet baby clothes is more difficult at hospital visiting times than in the privacy of your own home, but it can be an important gesture. It can make you feel closer as a couple, and it will also encourage your partner, who may be feeling slightly overwhelmed by the enormous responsibility that caring for a baby can represent. It is a responsibility you are going to share together. If you are sharing a room and feel self-conscious, remember that the other couples in the room will have eyes only for their own baby, and if any of the other mothers notice that you are doing more than just cuddling your baby, you can be sure they will soon be suggesting the same thing to their own partners!

Initial Impressions

What Do Newborn Babies Look Like?

> *New-born of course. She looked already a centenarian, tottering on the brink of an old crone's grave, exhausted, shrunken, bald as Voltaire, moping, mewing and twisting wrinkled claws in speechless spasms of querulous doom.*
>
> Laurie Lee, from his essay "The Firstborn"

It is true that babies look their least lovely in the moments after birth—except perhaps to their adoring parents. "Purple and dented like a little bruised plum" was writer Laurie Lee's graphic description of his daughter immediately after she was born. Strangely, newborn babies do often look old—they may have very wrinkled brows, and their limbs may seem almost shriveled. The skin may be relatively translucent so that veins can be seen underneath. Despite this apparently fragile appearance, though, your new baby is tougher than you think. Remember that the smooth-skinned, plump picture of babyhood that beams back from so many magazine and television pictures is usually weeks or months old. In just a few days your baby, too, will begin to look quite different and start to fill out and unfold. But at the very beginning, expect a first encounter with a rather different sort of being— one whose arms and legs have yet to learn to adjust to the freedom of movement possible outside the womb, one who is used to existing in water and in darkness and who has just undergone the exhausting and terrifying process of birth.

Your baby will be wet from the amniotic fluid, which is colorless, and may have some blood picked up from the site of an episiotomy or tear as she passed through the lower end of the birth canal. There may also be quite a lot of vernix, especially in the folds of skin—this is the greasy, white substance that protects and lubricates the baby's skin inside the womb. Generally, babies born at term are more likely to have some vernix, whereas babies born after term may have rather drier, or even cracked or peeling skin. Sometimes patches of the fine, downy hair which covered her inside the womb—lanugo—may still be present. This is more noticeable in dark-haired babies and is seen most often on the shoulders, back, and sometimes ears and forehead, but it will rub off in a couple of weeks and does not mean your baby will be hairy later in life.

Before the baby begins to breathe, she is a bluish color, like the umbilical cord. As she takes her first breath, the color changes to a normal flesh tone, which can be reddish rather than pink.

The head is large in relation to the rest of the body, a quarter of the overall length, and is often oddly shaped at first because it has been molded by the passage through the birth canal. It may be long and pointed, flattened, or even lopsided, but this will disappear after about two weeks or even earlier. Your baby may have a fine head of hair or may be completely bald—color and quantity at this stage are not necessarily indications of future growth. The pressure of birth may make the baby's eyelids red and puffy. Purple or reddish marks on the eyelids and back of the neck ("stork marks") are very common and will soon fade.

A new baby's genitals are often large in relation to the rest of his body—the effect of hormones from the mother that have crossed the placenta—and this can also make the breasts of both boys and girls swollen, something that will disappear in a week or two.

What Is the World Like for Your Baby?

She lay perfectly calmly in the bed beside me afterward while I was being stitched, looking around so knowingly and intelligently with little dark eyes that seemed to have the wisdom of a hundred years, not just a few minutes, shining from them.

The unborn baby becomes sensitive to sound, light, touch, and pain quite early in pregnancy, so she is able to experience the sensations of birth in various ways. Pressure is the most obvious sensation she will experience, at first from the rhythmic squeezing of the uterus as it contracts to open the cervix; then she feels pressure from all sides, particularly on the head, as she is pushed down into the birth canal. Changes in the heartbeat and the amount of movement suggest that procedures such as blood transfusions done before birth are uncomfortable for the unborn baby. Having a scalp electrode implanted in the skin or a sample of blood taken from the scalp during birth, therefore, must be no less so. Some babies who have had difficult deliveries may act as though they have a significant headache afterward.

Your Baby's Senses

Don't think your new baby is unable to take in much of her newfound world—her senses are already finely tuned to pick up messages from all around.

Sight   One of the most common misconceptions is that babies are born blind or see only very hazily. In fact, the newborn baby can see very well and can focus clearly on objects about eight to ten inches away. This is about the distance between the mother's face and the baby during feeding, and parents often automatically position themselves at this distance when they talk to or do anything with their baby. New babies are sensitive to light and shut their eyes to avoid bright lights. They can tell the difference among shapes and patterns, and prefer patterns to solid colors, and stripes and angles to circular designs. They will follow their mother's face or an object that has caught their interest with their eyes, although in the early weeks they may have difficulty coordinating their eye movements. This can give them the appearance of a wandering eye or even of a squint; this, however, is not permanent and quickly improves as coordination increases.

Sound   The new baby has already learned to recognize her mother's voice from its pitch and speech patterns while inside the womb. Analysis of films has shown that newborn babies respond to the rhythm of the speaker addressing them by making movements with their own bodies or faces in response to a stressed word or pause. They very soon begin to copy the movements of the speaker's mouth—opening their own, putting their tongue forward, and so on. New babies are also startled by loud, sudden noises, such as the bang of a door. Inside the womb they have been used to the rhythmic pulse of their mother's heart pumping blood around her body—mothers usually hold their babies to their left side and probably the sensation of heartbeat is reassuring in its familiarity. Recordings of "womb music"—the sort of noises we think the baby heard inside the womb—sometimes have a calming effect on new babies.

Smell   New babies also have a good sense of smell. They quickly learn to recognize the smell of their mother's body and her milk. At three days, studies have shown that babies can already tell the difference between their own mother's and another mother's milk on breast pads placed near the nose.

Taste   Three-day-old babies can also distinguish among tastes and prefer sweet to bitter flavors, although the taste of breast milk is the best of all.

Minor Problems After Delivery

Occasionally babies need extra medical attention or care after delivery. One of the most common reasons is that the baby does not start breathing spontaneously. Premature and small babies may have special problems, both immediately and for a longer period. For more details, see chapter 5.

Breathing

It is very common for babies to need a little help to start breathing after the birth but does not necessarily mean they will need any further special care. A survey of sixteen thousand babies showed that nearly 5 percent had not breathed by three minutes after the birth. It may also be reassuring to know that newborn babies are better able to survive for a period without oxygen than adults because their metabolism is different. However, the doctor or midwife will be quick to give your baby some help if breathing does not begin naturally. Babies who have an abnormal delivery—for example, breech or cesarean section—are more likely to need help to begin breathing. If complications are expected a pediatrician may be on hand, or the mother may give birth in a unit that has intensive care facilities for such babies if needed.

Often simply clearing the baby's airways by more thoroughly using a nasal bulb syringe is enough to stimulate her into taking a breath. If not, oxygen can be blown lightly over the face, or the baby can be given oxygen by holding over the nose and mouth a rubber mask that is attached to a bag that is gently squeezed to pump air into the lungs. A more skilled procedure involves putting a small tube down the baby's throat into the windpipe so oxygen can be pumped directly into the lungs; this is called "intubation." This may be necessary if the baby has been deprived of oxygenated blood during the birth, perhaps because the cord became compressed, although, again, this does not necessarily mean the baby will need extra care or have other problems once breathing has been established.

Babies Affected by Narcotics

Narcotics (usually Demerol-meperidine) cross the placenta and can therefore make the baby as well as the mother sleepy. If a narcotic was given close to the time of delivery, and if the baby still has breathing difficulties after oxygen has been given, then an antidote in the form of a drug called Naloxone may be injected into one of the baby's veins; this reverses the effect of the narcotic very quickly.

Naloxone is safe, eliminates the effect of the narcotic, and decreases the respiratory depressant action of the narcotic.

More Serious Problems After Delivery

Lack of oxygen

Babies who have been deprived of a supply of oxygenated blood for some time before birth and who do not breathe naturally after the birth may be at greater risk than those who simply fail to begin breathing by themselves. The baby will usually be intubated so oxygen can be given directly into the lungs, and if the heartbeat is slow or stops (which is very unusual), then heart massage can be given. Babies who show signs of having been seriously deprived of oxygen before or after birth will need extra care in an intensive-care unit (see chapter 5 for more). Permanent damage can result from this, but each case is different, and the doctor will always explain what has happened and discuss with the parents how it may affect the individual baby.

Meconium Aspiration

Babies who have been stressed before birth may move their bowels in the amniotic fluid. This substance, meconium, can mix with the amniotic fluid and may be taken into the baby's lungs if she tries to breathe before the birth itself. This can clog up the lungs and make it difficult for the baby to breathe; there is also a risk of developing a type of pneumonia caused by irritation from the meconium or from bacteria.

Babies who have passed meconium before birth need to be very carefully sucked out to prevent any meconium in their throat or nose from being drawn down into the lungs. If the pediatrician is in the delivery room he may intubate the baby before she takes her first breath to stop this from happening. A baby who does inhale meconium needs careful monitoring, possibly extra oxygen to make sure she continues to breathe properly, and antibiotics to prevent her developing pneumonia. There is also a slight risk of inhaled meconium leading to a punctured lung.

Babies who develop symptoms related to meconium aspiration will require admission to special or intensive-care units for close observation and possibly help, such as mechanical ventilation, for a few days until their breathing is established.

Pneumonia

In addition to meconium inhalation, the unborn baby can get pneumonia if the amniotic fluid becomes infected and if that infected fluid is drawn into the baby's lungs. This is more likely to happen if the water breaks more than twenty- four hours before delivery, and if this does happen the mother may be given antibiotics to prevent infection. For this reason it is now very rare for a baby to be born with pneumonia. Treatment after birth is with antibiotics, possibly oxygen to help breathing, and careful monitoring.

Puncture of the Lung (Pneumothorax)

A hole in one of the baby's lungs (pneumothorax) can result from too much pressure when the baby is given oxygen through a mask or a tube.

It can also occur when meconium is inhaled, or it can happen naturally when the baby is making strenuous efforts to breathe herself. If the hole is very small and just a little air leaks out, it will heal naturally without any further treatment, though the baby will need to be watched more carefully for a period. Less than 1 percent of babies have this condition.

A larger hole may cause the lung to collapse completely. This is fortunately quite rare but needs immediate emergency treatment. Under local anesthetic, a tube is inserted through the baby's chest to draw off the air that now fills the chest cavity on the side where the lung has collapsed. As the air is drawn off, the pressure on the lung is relieved so it reexpands as the baby draws in breath. The tube will be left in for a few days and the baby cared for in an intensive-care unit.

Your Baby's First Checkup

At some point in your baby's first twenty-four hours of life she will be given a complete examination by a pediatrician. This usually happens the morning after the birth when you have both had time to rest and recover. The doctor may do the examination in your presence, near the bed if you are unable to get up yet, or in the newborn nursery. He will welcome any questions you may have. Don't be shy about asking anything that may be bothering you, however trivial you may think it is.

Your Baby's Head

The four main bone plates of the skull have not yet fused together, thus allowing the head to mold to the shape of the birth canal. This can lead to odd-shaped heads and even ridges on the side of the head where the plates have overlapped at some

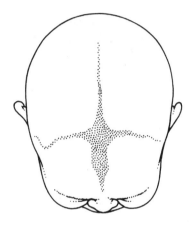

point. This is only temporary and will readjust in a week or two. The doctor will be concerned about the size of the baby's head in relation to her body, about a quarter of her overall length, and will also feel the fontanelles or soft spots where the skull bones have not yet grown across. The two main ones are near the crown and above the brow. You can often see the baby's pulse beating under the skin, but in fact these areas are covered by very tough membrane and there is no danger of hurting the baby with normal handling. If the fontanelles are sunken or depressed it may be a sign that the baby is dehydrated. The doctor will usually also measure the circumference of the head for the baby's records.

Your Baby's Eyes

Your baby's eyelids may be puffy and red from the pressure of birth. There can also be red or purple patches called "stork marks." A burst blood vessel in the eye ("scleral hemorrhage"), also caused by pressure, will show as a red spot, which may enlarge in the white of the eye. This may look alarming but is actually quite harmless and does not hurt the baby. It will fade within ten days or so. Because new babies cannot focus both eyes together for very long, one may begin to wander. This does not mean the baby has a permanent squint—an inability to focus both eyes together. Often folds of skin at the inner corner of the eye or close-set eyes can make new babies look as if they are squinting even more. Usually any apparent squinting has gone by four months, but if you have any worries about this ask your doctor. If a squint persists beyond four months it should be checked by a doctor.

Eye Discharge   This is very common in new babies and may be an infection of the eyes that appears as a yellowish discharge or crusting on the eye or lids. It may be associated with a blocked tear duct so that the fluid that normally lubricates the eye cannot drain away from the eye into the nasal cavity. It is important to contact the baby's doctor, who will determine if there is infection that requires medication. Treatment is to wipe the eyes with clear, warm water on a cotton ball and possibly to apply drops or ointment. The eyes should be cleaned with separate cotton balls for each eye, wiping the eye outward. Because eye infections spread easily, both eyes may be treated at the same time.

In the first week or two of life, an eye discharge may represent a very serious infection. Always contact your pediatrician about this. A simple culture of the eye discharge can be done to check for infection.

Your Baby's Nose
A baby's nose is usually broad and flat at this stage, which makes it easier for her to feed at the breast. Sneezing is very common and quite normal and does not mean the baby has a cold.

Your Baby's Mouth
The doctor will feel inside the baby's mouth to make sure the palate is fully formed. Rarely, babies are born with one or more teeth present—these may have to be taken out because they can cause ulcers on the tongue, or can become loose and pose a choking hazard. The teeth that are present at birth may be extra ones or may represent the first (primary) teeth. In the latter instance there may be a gap in the area of the missing tooth that will be present until the second set of (permanent) teeth erupt. Tiny white cysts that may appear on the gums or palate are harmless and will disappear. Blisters may appear on the baby's upper and lower lips from sucking. Again, they do not need treatment and will fade.

Your Baby's Ears
A new baby's ears may produce wax, but a discharge is not normal and you should ask advice if this happens. It is possible to test the hearing of a new baby, and babies who are considered to be at high risk for hearing loss are currently being screened in the newborn period. Universal screening of all newborns has been proposed and may become routine in the future. Parents can usually be fairly sure within a few weeks that their child can hear by watching her reactions. If there is any doubt, ask your pediatrician. It is very important that hearing loss be identified as early as possible.

Your Baby's Heart
After the birth the baby's pattern of circulation changes and the heart has to work hard, which may mean that for the first few days it is slightly enlarged. It also has to beat faster than normal to meet the baby's needs, which are greater as she adjusts to life outside the womb. Your baby's heartbeat will be above a hundred beats a minute. Because of the extra work, it is not uncommon for babies to have a heart murmur at the first examination. Nearly all these are harmless and are associated with the normal flow of blood. They will disappear as the heart settles down, although this will be checked at future examinations.

A baby born with something structurally or functionally wrong with her heart—congenital heart disease—is rarer. Just under one baby in a hundred has something significantly wrong with her heart, but only a third of these need any treatment; the rest resolve naturally as the baby grows. Causes of heart disease are still largely unknown, although one known cause is rubella (German measles) in the first three months of pregnancy, which can stop the heart from developing properly. There is only a very slight tendency for heart disease to run in families and mostly it seems to be an unlucky fault in development. Conventional tests, such as X rays and an electrocardiogram (EKG), when wires are attached to the chest with stickers to give a recording on paper, can be easily done on newborn babies and, if needed, echocardiography can be done as well. In this test, a probe about the size of a small flashlight is run over the chest, and the messages or echoes it picks up can be shown on a television screen in the same way as an ultrasound scan. It is painless and harmless.

The most common heart problem is a small hole between the two main chambers of the heart, which should normally be kept separate. This is called a ventricular septal defect (VSD). In more than 90 percent of babies who have this problem the hole closes, usually before they reach school age.

Other common problems include narrowing of a heart valve or the failure of fetal blood vessels to close at birth. A few babies with congenital heart disease will need an operation in the first year of life. Sometimes the defect will be definitively corrected, but in others surgery can improve the condition so the child can grow until she is big enough for a larger operation, when the risk is much less. Some conditions do not need to be corrected until the child is older.

Babies and children with heart conditions and who are waiting for operations are very unlikely to have a sudden serious collapse, which is usually what parents fear. If their condition worsens it usually is gradual, but parents will be advised by a heart specialist on what to look for and how to care for their child. Babies who have heart conditions are often more prone to chest infections, and these need to be treated more seriously than in a normal baby.

Your Baby's Lungs
During his or her routine examination the doctor will watch the baby's breathing pattern and listen to her lungs. Before birth these are filled with fluid that is rapidly cleared in the first few minutes or hours of life. If the baby has any difficulty breathing, the doctor will discuss this with you. Many babies, especially those who are premature, do have rapid breathing after birth. This usually recovers quite quickly and the lungs are entirely normal afterward.

Your Baby's Abdomen
The doctor will gently feel your baby's tummy to check the position and size of her liver, kidneys, and spleen.

Your Baby's Genitals and Anus
The genitals will also be checked. They may look large in proportion to the rest of the body at birth in both boys and girls, but this is quite normal, and it readjusts after a short period. The breasts may also be slightly enlarged and in a few cases

even produce drops of milk—known as "witches' milk." All this is caused by hormones from the mother that have crossed the placenta and will soon disappear from the baby's system. For the same reason there may even be a very slight bleeding from a baby girl's vagina, like a mini-menstrual period. The doctor will check to see that a baby boy's testicles can be felt in the scrotum; they are usually easy to feel at birth. If one of the testicles is undescended, the doctor will allow nature to correct this condition. If by one year of age the testicle has not descended into the scrotum, a surgical procedure is performed that will correct the situation.

The doctor will also check that the anus is normal and check whether the baby has passed meconium. In a very few babies, the gut or gastrointestinal tract is not properly formed, and there may be a narrowing (stenosis) or even a complete block (atresia), so fecal matter cannot get through. This will show up by the baby's vomiting or not passing meconium, but the problem may even be discovered before this during the doctor's initial examination. This can usually be corrected by a surgical operation shortly after it has been diagnosed.

Your Baby's Umbilical Cord and Groin

After the cord has been cut, a stump about one inch long is left with a clamp attached. This quickly begins to shrivel and dry up and within twenty-four hours usually turns almost black. The doctor or nurse will show you how to care for it, keeping the diaper below the cord and not covering it, as this will help it to stay dry. It should be cleaned at each diaper change with a cotton ball soaked with alcohol. The clamp will be removed on the second or third day and the rest of the cord will drop off about a week or two later and may leave a small raw or bloodstained spot, which can be cleaned and kept dry in the same way; it will soon heal.

Infection of the cord is unusual but can be serious or even life-threatening. If the cord seems infected (foul odor, puslike discharge, red surrounding skin), see your pediatrician immediately. Cord infections are readily treated when caught early, usually with intravenous antibiotics.

The shape of your baby's navel depends on the way the muscles lie around the base of the cord, not on the way the cord has been cut or clamped. Some children soon have flat navels ("innies"), while others protrude for some time ("outies"). An umbilical hernia is present when there is a weakness or gap in the muscles around the base of the cord so that the abdominal contents bulge through under the skin, making a soft lump. This may be present at birth or appear a day or so after and become larger when the baby coughs, cries, or strains, though there is no need to stop her doing any of these things. Umbilical hernias usually get smaller as the baby grows and do not need to be operated on in infancy. An operation will only be considered if the gap in the muscles gets larger after the first year, or shows no signs of closing by three to four years of life.

The groin is another site where hernias are sometimes seen and are more common in boy than girl babies. In the case of a hernia in the groin, a pediatrician will usually refer the baby to a surgeon promptly because there is a risk that some of the intestine can protrude and not go back in again easily, which may cut off blood flow to that portion of the intestines.

Your Baby's Hips

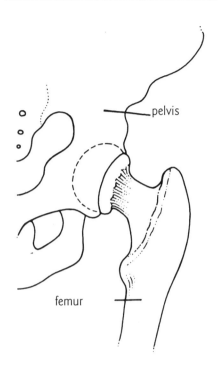

pelvis

femur

Congenital dislocation of the hips means that when the baby is born the head of the thighbone (femur) does not fit properly into the socket of the pelvis; thus it can easily come out or be dislocated. If this is untreated it means the child will walk with a limp and one leg will be shorter than the other. Fortunately, when detected early, treatment is both simple and successful, and this is why doctors are careful to examine the hips of all new babies.

We do not know exactly what causes the problem, but it may be related to hormonal changes before birth or to the position of the baby in the uterus. It is more common in breech babies, in girls, and when there is a family history of other babies having been affected. Between one and two babies per thousand are affected each year.

To test the hips, the doctor lays the baby on her back and gently bends both knees upward. Then, holding the top part of the thighbone between his thumb and finger, he gently pushes the baby's legs out to each side. Normally the legs should fall away easily until the baby's knees are almost flat against the table on each side of her body. The "ball" of the femur, if dislocated, will come into the socket of the pelvis and will not rotate smoothly. If the joint is dislocated, the doctor will feel a definite clunk as the ball slips in—this does not make a noise that can be heard and is different from normal clicking of hips, with which it is often confused. Parents should never try this procedure themselves.

Commonly, the examination produces a slight clicking, grating, or snapping noise; this can happen with any joint and is due to slight temporary looseness or laxity in the ligaments around it. If this is happening, the joint is normal and cannot be dislocated, so no treatment is needed. About 10 percent of babies have ligamental laxity of the hips on the newborn exam. It has generally resolved by the first well-child checkup.

A baby who has dislocated or dislocatable hips on the newborn exam should be referred to an orthopedist. An ultrasound of the hips will be done, usually at two weeks of age, to determine if the hips are truly abnormal. To treat dislocated hips, the baby's legs are placed in a froglike position, with her legs going out at right angles to her body. The bones of the pelvis will then develop to form a well-molded socket into which the head of the thighbone will fit without coming out. The legs are held in this position by a harness called a Pavlik harness, or by casting. Regular checks will be made to adjust it to allow for growth. It is perfectly possible to breast-feed a baby in a harness, though obviously caring for such a baby does have its problems. All babies with dislocatable or dislocated hips will need close follow-up by the orthopedist to check that the hips are forming normally.

Your Baby's Skin

The skin of newborn babies may be quite mottled or reddish, and sometimes the hands and feet may be pale or bluish. This is because of her changing circulation, which will quickly settle down. After a few days, the skin often becomes quite dry and flakes and peels slightly. Do not mistake flaky skin on the scalp for dandruff. Sometimes a thick circle of dead skin will form on the scalp. This is called "cradle cap," but it does not need any special treatment and will disappear with gentle treatment. You can soften these scales with baby oil applied twenty minutes before bathtime. Gently loosen them off with a soft toothbrush during shampooing. Stubborn cases can be treated with a small amount of dandruff shampoo, taking care not to get any in the baby's eyes.

Harmless Spots   Tiny white spots on the nose, called "milia," are just enlarged oily glands and will disappear by themselves. Also harmless are red blotchy spots around a tiny white or yellow bump. Called "erythema toxicum" or "newborn rash," these usually appear from about day two and resolve within forty-eight hours, often to be replaced by others elsewhere. They are quite common at any time in the first two weeks. They are harmless to the baby.

Pustules   These are the kind that need treatment because they result from infection. They are red and come to a white head filled with pus. Treatment is either a course of oral antibiotics, antibiotic ointment applied directly to the spots, or both.

Birthmarks   "Stork marks" are reddish or purple flat marks on the back of the neck, so called because they look like the marks the legendary stork would leave when carrying the baby. They are a form of birthmark but are harmless and do not need treatment. These marks usually fade, but if they stay, they will be covered with hair.

Strawberry marks are raised red areas and are so called because they look like a strawberry. They are the result of an overgrowth of blood vessels and usually start as tiny red spots, which then grow quickly for several weeks and, rarely, can become quite large. Most of these marks will disappear by themselves and usually begin to show white patches within the mark or around the edges and grow smaller between two and three years. Most are gone before the child's fifth birthday. If they remain after this time and are on the face, plastic surgery may be a possibility. Treatment will strongly be considered earlier if one occurs on an eyelid and prevents the eye from opening completely.

Mongolian Blue Spots   These have nothing to do with mongolism, but refer to patches of darker pigment that sometimes occur in babies with dark skin. They can be mistaken for bruises and are mostly seen over the baby's bottom and lower back. They are harmless and will fade as the baby grows.

Port-Wine Stains   As the name suggests, these are marks that look like a wine stain—irregular patches of reddish-purple skin that are flat and are of normal skin texture. These are rare, but unfortunately do not fade or diminish with time. They are most common on the face and very rarely, if they are large and on the forehead or scalp, the brain underlying the stain may also be affected. Laser treatment may help to eliminate them or make them smaller. No one knows why they occur.

Moles   Most adults have thirty or more moles, and occasionally babies are born with a few. They can be flat, smooth, raised, or hairy. Babies with large or unsightly moles on the face can be referred to a plastic surgeon, who may consider operating between the age of about eight years and puberty. The moles should be watched carefully for any change in color, size, or shape. If you have a question about a mole, consult your physician or a dermatologist.

Jaundice   A degree of jaundice is very common, and one survey showed that about one in five newborn babies developed jaundice. The condition shows as a yellowish tinge to the skin, usually making the baby look as though she has a suntan, although in severe cases the skin has an obviously yellow color. This change in skin color is caused by the presence of too much bilirubin in the body, a yellow chemical that is produced in the process of breaking down the hemoglobin contained in red blood cells at the end of their life cycle. The most essential job of hemoglobin is to carry oxygen to the tissues of the body, but before birth the placenta is not as efficient at keeping the blood oxygenated as the lungs are after birth. This means that the unborn baby has to have higher levels of red blood cells to provide more hemoglobin to give sufficient oxygen. After birth, when the baby begins to breathe, the lungs are much better at oxygenating the blood, so the baby's spleen has to work to break down a higher than normal number of red blood cells; a by-product of this process is a large amount of bilirubin. The liver is not very efficient at first in removing bilirubin from the blood so it often accumulates, making the skin yellowish. Usually this appears after the first twenty-four hours of life and is most marked between three and five days, disappearing after this time. In many babies the condition does not need any treatment.

However, a few babies will need treatment because blood cells are being broken down too rapidly and the liver cannot cope with the excess bilirubin. In general, jaundice that appears in the first twenty-four hours of life and continues after the seventh day, or that is producing a very high level of bilirubin in the blood or jaundice in a sick or premature baby, needs treatment. The color of the baby's skin alone is not a guide to the degree of jaundice, but a simple blood test will be done to check bilirubin levels. Before effective treatments were devised, serious jaundice could lead to deafness or brain damage, which is why it is always carefully checked and treated.

Apart from an immature liver, a different Rh factor and/or blood type in the mother compared with the baby can cause jaundice; so, too, can infection. Some mothers' milk contains a harmless substance that makes their babies jaundiced. It is not usually necessary to stop breast-feeding; the jaundice usually resolves naturally or can be treated by phototherapy. Some rare causes of jaundice include abnormal thyroid gland activity, genetic abnormalities, and hepatitis. It is important that jaundice persisting for more than a week is investigated.

It was quite by chance that the nursery staff of a hospital in the 1950s discovered that giving jaundiced babies a sunbath proved very successful in reducing the jaundice. They then found that jaundiced serum left in the sunlight was also paler. Bilirubin is broken down if it is exposed to bright light from several fluorescent tubes—this is called "phototherapy" and is now a standard treatment. The baby is placed under the light wearing only a diaper so the light can reach as much of the skin as possible; the baby is turned at intervals so the light reaches both front and back. Pads are put over the baby's eyes to protect them from the light. Side effects of phototherapy are transient skin rashes because the lights cause sweating, and also greenish, loose bowel motions because the substance formed by the breakdown of bilirubin is green. Babies under phototherapy often have greater fluid losses and may need extra fluids. Parents should feed, cuddle, and care for the baby as normal.

The time of phototherapy varies and depends on how rapidly the bilirubin level falls. There are now new techniques that allow phototherapy to be done at home. However, if the baby is ill or has a very high bilirubin level, treatment is done in the hospital.

If phototherapy alone is not enough, then some of the baby's jaundiced blood has to be drawn off—usually by inserting a tiny tube into the vein in the baby's navel—and fresh blood of the same group and Rh factor is infused. This will be repeated several times until her blood is exchanged, and is done in the intensive-care unit. This is called an exchange transfusion.

Your Baby's Reflex Actions

A reflex action is one we make automatically, without needing a conscious message from the brain, such as swallowing, blinking, or sneezing. At birth the baby has a number of primitive reflex actions that doctors can test to check that the central nervous system, muscles, and nerves are all working properly. They can also be a guide to maturity. About seventy or more primitive reflexes have been described in the newborn, but for purposes of checking your baby's health at her first general examination, doctors will probably only test a few. For your own understanding of some of your baby's behavior, it may be interesting to know about the most obvious and best-known reflexes.

Oral Reflexes   Newborn babies already have a very strong sucking reflex. If you put your little finger into her mouth, you can feel the suction. The "rooting" reflex means that when the baby's cheek comes into contact with something she turns her head toward that object—you can make her root by touching your nipple against her cheek. If he does not do this he is probably not hungry. Only the most premature babies lack these reflexes.

Eye Reflexes   Your new baby automatically blinks in response to light, sound, or touch. In the first ten days of life you may notice that if her head turns to one side, there is a delay before the eyes follow the same movement, so they stay fixed for a second; this is called the "doll's-eye response."

The Grasp Reflex   If you put your finger into your new baby's palm she will grasp it tightly, and if you pull away she will hold on and tense her arm muscles until her body begins to lift. This usually disappears in about two or three months. Touching the sole of her foot behind the toes gets the same reaction, with the toes clenching to grasp the object.

Moro (or Startle) Reflex   This is the most famous primitive response, but it is a frightened reaction, so when the doctor tests it he will do it gently. In response to the head or bottom being allowed to fall backward toward the bed, or if the bed is slapped on either side of the baby, she flings her arms sideways with her fingers spread and stretches out her legs, and then brings her arms in again, as if hugging or embracing something. She often cries and looks surprised. Do not try to prompt your baby into this reflex yourself, as it will upset her. It usually disappears by about three to four months.

Walking Reflex   When a new baby is held upright so the sole of her foot presses on to the table, she will automatically lift her leg and place the other down, as though walking. She also "steps" up onto the table if the front of her lower leg is touched against it. This reflex is strongest at about two weeks of age and disappears by about five to six weeks.

Tests and Immunizations

Vitamin K
Most hospitals routinely give all newborn babies vitamin K by injection immediately after the birth. This increases the clotting ability of their blood and protects against a serious form of spontaneous bleeding that can occur in newborn babies.

Hepatitis B Vaccine
The hepatitis B vaccine is now recommended for all newborns by the American Academy of Pediatrics. It protects against the hepatitis B virus, which can cause severe liver disease. The recommended schedule of vaccination is at birth, one month, and six months. Your physician should discuss the benefits and risks (minimal) with you. Most hospitals require that you sign a consent form before they administer the vaccine.

Newborn Screening Tests
A simple blood test is done on about the second day (before discharge from the hospital, but after twenty-four hours of life), when a small sample of blood is taken from the baby's heel and collected on absorbent paper to be analyzed for high levels of an amino acid called phenylalanine. Babies with high levels may have an inherited condition called phenylketonuria (PKU), which is rare, affecting about one in fourteen thousand babies, but which causes brain damage if not treated. Treatment with a special diet results in normal brain function. The condition is inherited as a recessive gene and so parents of an affected baby have a one in four chance of

another child having PKU. A variety of other metabolic disorders are also screened for; the specific disorders vary from state to state.

The newborn screen is also used to check the baby's thyroid function. Those who have a thyroid gland that is not working properly will also require treatment as early as possible to ensure normal development.

Taking Care of Your New Baby

I'd never even held a baby until I had one of my own. I felt very strongly that I knew better than anyone what she needed, but I just didn't have the confidence to say so to all the people who offered advice. Relatives were harder to handle than doctors and nurses. The second time it was so different. I was established as a mother and I didn't get the feeling everyone else was trying to take over.

Trust your instincts and don't worry about following some mythical rule book. It often takes time to gain confidence in your own abilities as a mother, perhaps especially in the hospital, where you are surrounded by many people who seem possessed of great expertise and knowledge. But no one else will have studied your own baby as closely as you, which gives you an expert knowledge of a particularly exclusive nature. You are an expert in your own baby's needs.

Whether at home or in the hospital, be relaxed about those early days after the birth. Don't worry about routines. Taking care of your baby at this stage is largely a matter of following her rhythms and supplying needs as they arise. Both of you need to get to know each other, to enjoy the comfort of each other's bodies, and to rest. Mothers with other children will also need to balance this with their desire to be with them and to satisfy their needs for contact, too.

Feeding Your Newborn

All babies are born with a set of reflex actions, and one of these is to suck. This instinct is very strong soon after birth, and allowing your baby to suckle at the breast as soon as possible after delivery is one of the most important first steps in establishing successful breast-feeding. It also gives a new baby great pleasure and comfort as well as giving her the best nutritional start in life—the colostrum, which is the creamy substance present in the breasts before mature milk is made. It is very high in protein and provides important antibodies that protect your baby's health. Suckling at the breast also stimulates the hormones in your body that are responsible for producing milk. A surge in the hormone oxytocin, which occurs each time you feed your baby, also helps the uterus to contract and shrink down to its prepregnant size; this is important both for your health and for your morale.

Your baby may be more sleepy in the few days following birth than she will later, a fact that often causes new mothers to feel they were doing it "right" while in the hospital, but that everything has gone all "wrong" since they got home! In fact, it is just a question of the baby gradually becoming more aware and alert. If you are breast-feeding, milk will not usually appear until about the third day after the birth, but allowing your baby to suck at the breast when he wants to will stimulate milk production, comfort your baby, and give her an all-important supply of colostrum. Newborns should nurse approximately ten to twelve times per twenty-four hours.

Bottle-feeding mothers should follow the same supply-and-demand pattern, offering a bottle whenever their baby seems hungry. Remember that hunger is the most common reason for crying. A new baby should not go more than three to five hours without food and may often want feeding far more frequently. If you offer food, whether breast or bottle, whenever she seems hungry, and do not try to force food on her if she is not interested, nor regiment feeding to an every-four-hours routine, you will be doing fine. (For a discussion of breast versus bottle and details of both types of feeding, see chapter 6.)

Asleep and Awake

Even newborn babies can spend six to eight hours of every twenty-four awake, so do not expect her to be either feeding or asleep all the time. Your baby may have periods when she is awake and calm, looking around and enjoying being talked to and played with. She may also have periods of wakefulness when she is less receptive and more inclined to be fretful. At the beginning, the new baby can only sleep for stretches of three to five hours and usually wakes from hunger. The length of time she can stay asleep increases as the brain matures, so by four months she will be sleeping two to ten hours at a stretch and staying awake for two to four hours. Like adults, babies vary in the amount of sleep they need, although their patterns can change. Place your baby on her back or side with the lower elbow slightly in front of her to prevent her from rolling onto her front. Keep her room at a constant temperature at night and do not allow her to become too hot or too cold.

"Is she a good baby?" new parents are regularly asked, usually meaning does she sleep a lot at night. Most parents naturally long for the time when their baby sleeps through the night. Although in the early days it is very much a matter of following her natural rhythm of sleeping and waking, there are some things you can think about that may help your child to avoid sleep problems later (see chapter 8).

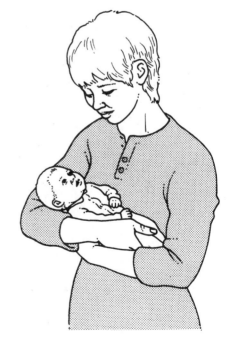

Handling Your Baby

Even if you have never held a new baby before, you will quickly become adept at this and able to handle your own. Diaper changes, which seem to take ages at the beginning, soon become quick routines; you will develop your own style of handling and holding your baby. This is one of the ways in which she recognizes and distinguishes you from other people.

Parents instinctively support the baby's head, which is too heavy for the strength of her neck for several months. Don't be afraid to remind other people who want to hold her who may not realize this or who are unaccustomed to handling new babies. Nor should you be afraid to take your baby back if you think she has had enough of being passed around among admiring friends and relatives, or is just unsettled and needs the reassurance of being held by you for the time being. The same goes for the baby's brothers and sisters. By all means let them hold the baby; the easiest way with little ones is sitting on a sofa or on the floor with the bulk of the baby's weight and head resting on a cushion, but even the youngest children can be told there are times when the baby is too tired, hungry, or upset to be held by them. It is better to encourage them to think about how the baby feels than to view her as a doll to be played with at any time.

New babies enjoy looking at mobiles and leaves waving in the wind when they are in the right mood, but the sight of a human face talking, smiling, and responding to the imitative facial movements they begin to make is still their main amusement. Look at your baby's face as you feed her, and talk and play with her while you are changing, washing, or dressing her. Talking and playing with your baby does not have to be confined to a special time. With so much emphasis on the importance of a child's experiences in the first five years of life, it is easy to feel guilty if you don't spend every spare minute stimulating, encouraging, and educating your baby from day one! In fact, of course, new babies have a limited tolerance for attention, and

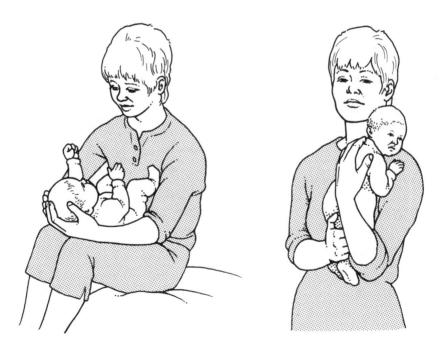

the amount of time you spend in contact with your baby will depend on both your personalities and needs as well as other demands on your time. Just be natural, be yourself with her. Taking your baby into bed with you and carrying her around most of the time in a sling is only right if it is right for the two of you. At the other end of the scale, of course, no baby will thrive on emotional neglect, even if her physical needs are catered for. Don't worry if at first your love for your baby is mixed with many other reactions, because adjusting to parenthood is often a longer, slower process and not just an immediate burst of unqualified devotion. For more about postpartum depression see the section "After the Birth—You and Your New Baby" later in this chapter.

Diapers and Diaper Changing

Meconium is the greenish-black substance that has filled your baby's bowels before birth and is usually passed in several bowel movements within twenty-four to forty-eight hours of birth. If this does not happen, your doctor needs to examine the baby to make sure there is no blockage in her intestine. Occasionally a baby may have passed meconium during delivery and it was not noted. After the meconium, breast-fed babies have watery, yellow, or mustard-colored stools that do not smell unpleasant. They may be passed frequently, contain mucus, or be green—all of which is normal. When your milk comes in at about day two or three, your baby's bowel movements may be very frequent but later decrease. It is quite normal for a breast-fed baby to have a dirty diaper at each feeding. By one month of age, however, these may decrease to only once every two to three days, or even more infrequently. A bottle-fed baby will pass stools that are mushy and may smell slightly. They do not contain mucus or fluid, but some formulas can make them dark green; this is also normal.

Even if your baby has not had a bowel movement, you will still find her diaper needs changing often; this is because new babies pass urine very frequently. A baby who does not pass urine within twenty-four hours of birth needs to be examined to make sure there is no blockage or other reason. If your baby subsequently stays dry for five or more hours, mention this to your doctor for the same reason. Occasionally it can be a sign that a baby may be starting to run a fever or is dehydrated.

Diaper changing, although a chore and not nearly as pleasurable as feeding a baby, does have a dual function. The first is the purely practical business of keeping your baby's bottom clean and as dry as possible; the second is that, just like feeding time, diaper changing is a time of intimacy and social interchange between the baby and the parent or carer. Obviously some diaper changes have to be much more hurried than others, but however quick the routine, the adult inevitably leans over the baby, establishing eye contact, and talking to her to distract and calm her while working.

Sometimes your baby will be in a wide-awake, playful mood, and provided you are not in a hurry, diaper-changing time will be a highly sociable opportunity, allowing your baby to play and kick. At other times your baby will be tired, hungry, or generally fretful, and diaper changing needs to be carried out as swiftly as possible. Remember, small babies are not good at maintaining body temperature, so

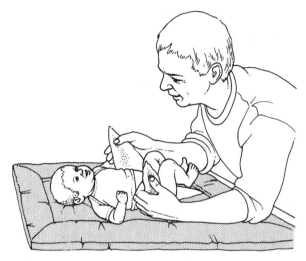

Remove the dirty diaper

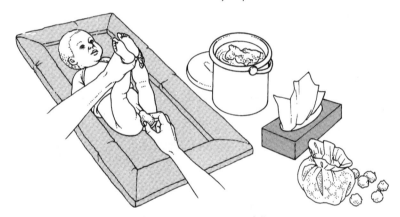

Clean the diaper area carefully

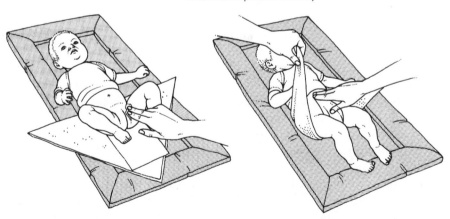

Apply the barrier cream

Redress the baby in a clean diaper

clothes that allow easy diaper-changing access with snaps around the crotch are preferable; if you do have to remove most of your baby's clothes, an undershirt or blanket will help to prevent her getting too cold.

Equipment Needed for Diaper Changing   You will need a changing pad or towel, preferably with waterproof backing, to lay the baby on. You also need cotton balls, soft paper towels, or soft washcloths and warm water (preferable) or baby wipes (be sure they are alcohol-free); some kind of protective cream such as Desitin, Balmex, Aquaphor, or other form of barrier cream; a clean diaper (plus pins and clean waterproof pants if you're using cloth diapers); a diaper pail for disposable diapers, and a diaper bucket if using cloth diapers. Talcum powder should never be used, for if inhaled, it can cause a serious pneumonia in the infant. Cornstarch powder may be useful in the creases to prevent chafing. Diaper liners are optional. They are convenient to allow solids to be flushed down the toilet instead of being disposed of with the diaper in the household garbage. If you are using reusable fabric liners, they need to be soaked, rinsed, and washed in the same way as the cloth diapers themselves. There is no need to invest in a specially designed changing table unless you want to, but because diapers need changing about every four hours, usually when you feed your baby, it makes sense to allocate an area where all the gear can be set up instead of having to make a space and get everything out each time. As your baby grows and you become a more experienced parent you will discover that diapers can and do have to be changed in all sorts of unlikely and not tremendously convenient places, but you may as well make it easy for yourself in your own home. If you have a lot of stairs in your house or have another young toddler you do not want to take up and down stairs at every diaper change, it makes it easier if you can have a second diaper-changing station, on the ground floor. The requirements of a diaper-changing station are pretty basic—enough flat space to lay the baby on the changing pad with room to work and space for materials alongside, a convenient height that does not necessitate too much bending, and somewhere that is warm and not too drafty. Never leave a baby unattended on a raised surface, though, even if she has not yet learned to roll over. You may find that the floor is the best place to change a very active baby.

Cloth Versus Disposable Diapers   Cloth diapers are either basic squares or else shaped to fit. The latter are easier for beginners to put on and give a neater fit, but the folding of the square gives a greater number of thicknesses at strategic points and consequently possibly more absorbency. Cloth diapers come in different quality and thickness, which is reflected in their price, but it is false economy to buy the thin, cheaper variety for a first baby if you plan to have more children, as the better quality will easily last for two children and probably a third. You will need at least two to three dozen cloth diapers. It is helpful to have an additional dozen to use as burp cloths. Cloth diapers also usually require pins or clips, and plastic pants. Alternatively, special diaper covers are available at specialty stores or by mail order. These cloth covers (often with attractive print designs) are waterproof but still "breathable." They encase the diaper and close with Velcro or snaps, eliminating the need for pins and plastic pants. They are also less likely to cause chafing around the legs. Plastic pants are usually the pull-on variety and come in any assortment of different types of plastic. The important point is that they fit well without causing any red marks due to tightness, but do an efficient job of enclosing the diaper completely—stray folds poking through at leg or waist will mean changing damp clothes as well as diapers. In addition, you will need two diaper buckets with lids on (one for the previous day's soaking diapers, one for the diaper just removed), and a washing machine. A clothes dryer is a boon to solve the problem of drying six-plus diapers a day. Diaper services are also available in some areas. The soiled diapers are picked up and clean diapers delivered, usually twice per week. The cost is usually well worth the savings in time and labor. When weighing the cost of cloth diapers versus disposables, the ongoing laundry costs of electricity, detergent, and wear and tear on the washing machine and dryer, or the cost of a diaper service, all have to be considered along with the basic outlay for the diapers and plastic pants or diaper covers, but generally they work out to be less expensive than disposables over a long period.

Disposable diapers have waterproof backing, elasticized legs, and sticky tape fasteners, or Velcro, dispensing with the need for pants, pins, and liners. The primary advantage of disposable diapers is that they are labor-saving, and a second consideration is that materials have improved so much that they now keep a baby's skin drier than cloth and decrease the incidence of diaper rashes. The disadvantages are cost and environmental concerns. They are not flushable—don't even try it.

Deciding whether to invest in cloth diapers or disposables depends on your lifestyle and personal preference as well as your finances and your concern for the environment. Some mothers combine the two, using cloth when they are home and using disposables when they are going to be out all day and once the baby becomes more active, as they tend to give greater freedom of movement than cloth.

Changing a Diaper

- Check to be sure that you have everything on hand before starting, as it is dangerous to leave a baby unattended on a high surface even if she has not yet begun to roll over by herself. Remove the dirty diaper and use baby wipes or cotton balls and water to carefully clean the diaper area. Always wipe from front to back when cleaning a girl's bottom—that is, toward and not away from her anus, because bacteria from the bowel can very easily be transmitted to the vagina, causing an infection. Clean between the folds of the groin and thighs of both sexes thoroughly.

- Pat dry using a cloth diaper or a towel even if you have used baby wipes, as moisture left on the skin can lead to diaper rash. You can sprinkle a small amount of cornstarch powder in the creases if you wish. If needed (with the first sign of irritation), apply a protective layer of baby cream, zinc oxide, or other barrier cream all around the diaper area to help protect the skin.

- Place the diaper underneath your baby's bottom, lifting her by her feet to do so. If you use diaper pins, place them horizontally, not vertically, so if they come undone there is less chance of the baby being hurt. Always use diaper pins with a safety catch rather than ordinary safety pins, and slide your hand down inside the diaper to form a protective layer between pin and skin as you fasten to avoid accidentally jabbing your baby. Disposable diapers simply need to be fastened securely with the sticky tabs, but make sure you have no baby cream, petroleum jelly, or powder on your fingers, as this will prevent the tabs' adhesive from working. Angle the tabs downward (toward the groin) so that the top corner of the tab cannot chafe the baby's abdomen.

- Put waterproof pants over the diaper if it's cloth, checking that no stray ends of diaper protrude and that the undershirt is not tucked into the top of the diaper at any point so that moisture spreads to the baby's clothing.

- Dispose of any solid contents of cloth diapers by flushing them down the toilet. Place cloth diapers in a bucket and used disposables in a diaper pail with a tight-fitting lid. If you use deodorizing tablets, be sure that they are not accessible to older babies and toddlers. If you're not using a diaper service, cloth diapers need to be washed with soap and hot water, rinsed well, and dried. Avoid fabric softeners and perfumes that can irritate a baby's skin.

Folding a Cloth Diaper

The kite method   Place the diaper so it lies in a diamond pattern in front of you and bring the two outer sides in to the center to make a kite shape. Fold down the top corner and bring the bottom corner up toward the center. This last fold can be adjusted to fit your baby. This shape is easy to fasten with two pins (see below).

Traditional triangle   Fold the diaper in two to make a triangle shape and place it before you with the center point toward you. When putting it on the baby bring a single thickness from the lowest point of the triangle up between the baby's legs first, bring the two sides in, and complete by bringing the lower thickness of the center point up last. Be sure to secure all thicknesses with the pin (see page 146).

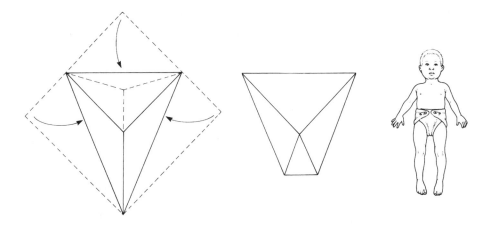

Kite Method

Triple fold   Fold the diaper in four by folding it in half and then in half again, giving four thicknesses. Place the square in front of you with the fold down the right-hand side and the unfolded edges at the top and left-hand side. Take the top left-hand corner of the first layer and open it out to the right. Keeping everything in place, carefully turn the whole diaper over so the point now lies to the left. Take the two layers that still form a fold down the right-hand side and turn them over twice so you end up with a triangle shape with an extra thickness pleat down the center. To fasten, bring all three corners in, as for a triangular diaper, and secure through all thicknesses with the pin (see below).

Bathing Your Baby

A new baby often does not like being undressed or generally disturbed, so keep such procedures to a minimum, doing everything very gently and soothingly and talking reassuringly to distract her from any unpleasant sensations. However, once undressed, many babies enjoy the freedom of movement lying naked on a towel gives, and often enjoy bathtime as well.

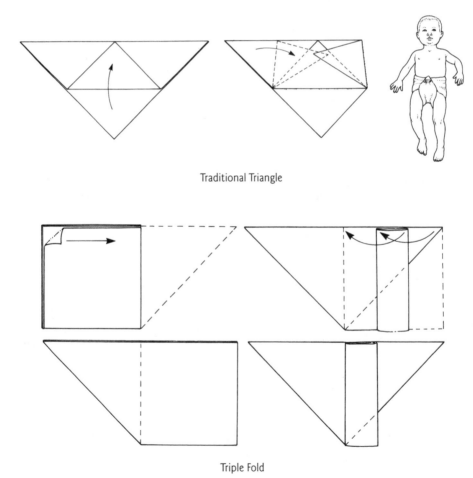

Traditional Triangle

Triple Fold

New mothers often worry about how frequently they should bathe their baby. The answer is not at all in the first few days unless you want to. Young babies do not have to be bathed every day. A couple of times a week is fine, as long as areas where the skin is soiled or where skin rubs against skin are cared for every day.

"Topping and tailing" is the name midwives give to the routine of cleaning parts of your baby's body, and you may be taught this in the hospital. You need warm water, cotton balls or soft washcloths, a mild cream soap such as Dove, preferably perfume-free, and soft towels. Begin with the face.

Use two separate cotton balls squeezed in the water to wipe the baby's eyes gently from the inner corner outward. This is the natural way the eyes drain and prevents infection. The reason you should not do both eyes with the same cotton is that an infection in one eye will be transmitted to the other. Because of this risk of infection do not use cotton that has already been used on any other part of the body.

Babies who are not yet eating solid food do not usually get dirty faces, but gently wipe all around the face and behind the ears. Lift her chin up or place her in a position where it is easy to reach the folds of skin under the chin, and gently wipe here as well. Dry each area thoroughly by patting with a soft towel.

Raise each arm separately and wipe the armpit carefully, as folds of skin rub together here and can become sore. Again, dry thoroughly.

Until the cord has dropped off, it needs to be kept as clean and as dry as possible. Wipe the cord gently with an alcohol pad or cotton ball wet with alcohol, especially around the base, where it meets the skin. Make sure the diaper stays below and does not make the cord stump wet. No tub baths are allowed until the cord falls off (usually by a week or two).

To avoid soreness, a baby's bottom needs to be kept as clean and as dry as possible, which means frequent diaper changes, cleaning, and drying the skin and, if necessary, applying a cream that will act as a barrier to protect the skin (for more on diaper rash, see the section "Skin Problems" in chapter 17).

Some babies take to water immediately and enjoy bathtime; others need a more gradual introduction. If yours is a baby who does not enjoy early bathing

experiences and you find it difficult, a thorough top-and-tail routine each day is fine and you can limit baths to once or twice a week. Probably the secret to helping your baby enjoy bathing is to be relaxed and unhurried yourself.

Babies tend to get cold quickly, so make sure the room you choose to bathe her in is warm. A portable baby bath means you can use the bathroom sink counter, bedroom, or kitchen if you wish, or put the baby bath inside the ordinary bath (although this is hard on your back). Always test the water temperature with your elbow or wrist, not your hands, which are often exposed to higher temperatures and are less sensitive. The water should feel warm but not hot. Put only about two inches of water in the tub for safety reasons.

Gather everything you will need before you start undressing your baby: two soft towels, clean diaper and clothes, soap or baby bath liquid, cotton balls, and wash-cloths. You do not have to bathe your baby at the same time on each occasion. Pick a time in the day when she is not too hungry or tired, which will make her fretful, and when she has not just been fed, which might make her spit up.

Undress your baby except for her diaper and wrap her in a towel so she does not get cold. Clean her face with cotton balls and water or a clean washcloth, as you usually do in the topping-and-tailing routine.

Wash her hair before putting her in the water so that you use clean water. Supporting her head and neck with one hand, tucked under your arm and against your hip like a football, hold her over the bath and wash her hair with baby sham-poo and water. Rinse thoroughly and gently pat her head dry with the second towel. Never hold the baby directly under running water, as the temperature may change suddenly. Instead, use a cup to rinse, and hold your finger in the stream of water as you fill it each time to monitor the temperature.

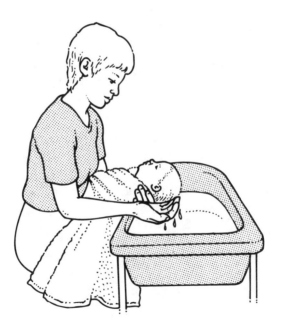

Unwrap the baby and gently lower her into the water feet first, holding her with one arm around the back of her neck and shoulders and encircling the far arm with your fingers to stop her from slipping. **Never let go, even if she is strapped into a molded infant bath seat.** Wet babies are extremely slippery and can slide under the water and drown in seconds, even in only a few inches of water. With your free hand, gently wash her body from the top down. Do the front first, then lean her forward to do her back. Talk to your baby to reassure her, and if she cries, always check that the water is not too hot or too cold. Generally, given time, most babies learn to enjoy the sensation of the water.

Lift her out of the bath with your arm still behind her back and your hand encircling her arm. Your other hand should be under her bottom, with the hand encircling her thigh. Lay her on a thick, soft towel and wrap her up. Dry her thoroughly in all the areas where skin rubs on skin by gently patting rather than rubbing. Routine use of powders or creams is not recommended, but a light dusting of cornstarch powder in creases during hot weather may be helpful to prevent chafing. If you do use cornstarch powder, make absolutely sure she is completely dry first; otherwise it will clog into irritating lumps. Put the powder in your hand first rather than shaking directly on her. Take care not to shake it around her nose and mouth so she doesn't inhale it. Close it immediately and place it out of reach. Do not, of course, mix cream and powder, and avoid powder in a girl's vaginal area, as it may cause irritation. Always use cornstarch, never talc, as talc cannot be degraded by the body and can do serious damage to the lungs if the child accidentally inhales it.

Dress your baby in clean diaper and clothes. New babies often find all the sensations involved in bathtime quite exhausting and may be ready for a feeding and sleep afterward.

Dressing Your Baby

At first you may feel that dressing and undressing your baby are difficult, but most baby clothes are designed to make this task as easy as possible, and you will quickly become very adept at such tasks with the minimum of upset to your baby. When you have to undress your baby, for diaper changing, bathing, or to change her clothes, choose a place where you can lay her down on a flat, warm surface. Before you begin, make sure you have everything you need at hand, remembering you may find you need a fresh diaper.

In general, babies and young children do not like the fuss entailed in dressing and undressing, so be very gentle as well as quick, and talk to distract her while you work. Taking clothes over her face and head is something she will especially dislike, so choose clothes that can be stretched wide and quickly lifted over without having to drag things across her face. The same goes for cuffs and sleeves—stretch the cuff wide open and fold the rest of the arm down so the whole thing can be easily fitted over the hand and fingers instead of trying to feed her hand and arm through the whole length of the sleeve. Most baby clothes are designed for easy diaper changing with snaps at the crotch or elastic waists, but if you always put an undershirt on your baby, this one layer of clothing will help her to stay warm, even if you do have to change the rest of the outfit. Because a baby's circulation is not very efficient in the early days, her hands and feet can get cold—in winter you may need to put socks over the toes of stretch suits. By the time your baby is about four months old (or earlier) she will almost certainly have grown out of newborn undershirts and stretch suits—do not try to cram her into stretch suits that are too short, as the pressure on her feet can have the same effect as badly fitting shoes later and can hinder the correct development of the still pliable bones in the foot or interfere with the circulation of blood to the area.

Crying and Comforting

Crying is the only way a baby has of telling you she needs something, and it is a distress signal ingeniously designed by nature to be one that parents cannot ignore. Most mothers at some times experience the awful distress of having their baby crying when they cannot comfort her—perhaps because they are driving a car, trying to get through the checkout at the supermarket, or seeing to another young child. The sound of crying will often stimulate the let-down reflex in breast-feeding mothers if it is near feeding time.

Finding out why your baby is crying is a process of elimination at which you will become increasingly skilled (see "Crying in Young Babies" in chapter 8). Like adults, babies have highly individual temperaments and personalities from the start, and therefore different things bother each baby to a different degree. Parents tend to automatically stroke, rock, jiggle, pat, or sing to their babies to find the best way to calm them. **Never shake your baby, as this can cause brain damage.** Some babies cry far more than others and may have set times of being fussy and crying when they are very hard to console, which can be extremely stressful (see also "If Your Baby Won't Stop Crying" in chapter 8). In general, do not think you will be spoiling your baby or encouraging bad habits if you pick her up when she is upset and crying—in fact, by responding to her cries, you are giving her a sense of confidence and security that will make her less fussy.

Warmth

From birth, babies have a working temperature-control mechanism, like adults, which enables them to generate body warmth when they get cold. But unlike adults they cannot conserve that warmth and can become very cold very quickly if the surrounding air is at a lower temperature than normal. This risk increases when they are undressed for any reason because they have a relatively large surface area compared to body weight, which means they lose heat quickly. That is why maternity wards are always such hot places. A room temperature of 80°F is about right for those times when you have to take baby's clothes off for changing or bathing. For the first month babies need to be warmly dressed with an undershirt, stretch suit, and sweater or receiving blanket. After the first four weeks if they are indoors, they do not need more clothes than their parents, although they need protection from drafts. Outdoors they do need more clothes than adults. Most recent research on crib death (SIDS) shows that becoming too hot is as much of a risk to a baby as becoming too cold. The ideal room temperature is 70°F during the day, 60°F at night. A simple wall thermometer will tell you if the room is the right temperature. You should never put your baby to sleep in front of a fire, by a radiator or heater, or by a very sunny window. Keep your baby's room at an even temperature so you can put on the right number of blankets at the start of the night and know that your baby will not get cold later. It can be dangerous to put on extra blankets when the room is warm for fear that the temperature will drop later. If you find that she kicks off the blanket, a blanket sleeper suit can be helpful in winter.

Do not use comforters or baby sleeping bags for babies under a year. You may want to use a blanket sleeper in cold weather, but diaper, undershirt, and stretch suit are all a baby needs to sleep in most of the time. In hot weather she may need less. To check how warm your baby is, feel her tummy. Hands and feet can often feel cool, but this is normal. If your baby's tummy feels hot, though, or if she is sweating anywhere, she is too hot.

What are the signs that your baby may be too cold? If she is having to work hard to keep herself warm she may become fretful and cry, her breathing will be faster than normal, and though her body is still warm, her hands and feet are cold. As she becomes chilled she will not be able to spare the energy for crying and becomes very quiet and still, and now her body, as well as her hands and feet, feel cold. In the most extreme stage, which is rare, the baby becomes very lethargic and almost unable to feed, and her hands and feet may become swollen and bright pink. Such babies need urgent medical attention and have to be carefully rewarmed to avoid seizures. If you think your baby has begun to get cold, do not just pile on extra coverings because this will keep the cold in—she does not have the energy to make more warmth herself. Instead, take her into a warm room and remove some of the layers so the warmth can reach her. Holding her next to your own body under a blanket helps, and so may a warm drink or feeding.

After the Birth—You and Your New Baby

Your Body

Two days after I had had the baby my stomach was flabby and hanging in folds of flesh, my stitches hurt like hell, and my breasts were rock hard and engorged. Nobody warned me I would feel like this!

Perhaps very few women leave the hospital with wonderfully flat stomachs and absolutely no problems from any of the less pleasant aspects of motherhood such as leaky, engorged breasts, hemorrhoids, or painful episiotomy stitches. Very many wonder at some point after the birth if their body will ever be the same again. Perhaps it is because so much attention is focused on the birth and the baby that few prenatal teachers or even obstetricians seem to pay much attention to what women feel like after they have given birth.

Many women are rather unprepared and feel a bit depressed when they find that their stomach is saggy and flabby afterward. However, a flat stomach is attainable eventually after having a baby and the skin does recover its elasticity, although you need to persevere at exercises. In general, the more weight you put on and possibly the older you are (because your skin is less elastic), the more work is needed to get back into shape. Some hospitals give mothers a series of postnatal exercises to do, and it is important that you follow these carefully and do them every day to get maximum benefit. In addition, breast-feeding certainly helps the uterus shrink back to its prepregnancy size more quickly—this is because every time the baby suckles at the breast the hormone oxytocin is released, which stimulates the womb to contract. Breast-feeding also uses up a certain extra number of calories, but the way it affects weight loss can be very variable. Some women find that weight just drops off while they are nursing, while others find they cannot lose all of the weight until they wean the baby. Stretch marks that may have occurred during pregnancy can also be distressing afterward—but they really do shrink to thin, silvery lines, given time.

Bruising, stitches, or even small tears from delivery that do not need to be stitched cause discomfort, and ice packs and sitz baths can help to relieve the pain. Some women have found that sitting on a blow-up rubber ring makes hard chairs more bearable, but there are some physicians who feel that these may put extra stress on the stitches and should not be used. Ask your caregiver about this. Women often feel worried about emptying their bowels after they have had an episiotomy because they fear that the stitches will burst open, but in fact the pressure is not in this area and you have nothing to worry about. Drink plenty of liquids, and if you have trouble moving your bowels, ask your physician about stool softeners. (Many physicians prescribe these routinely after delivery.)

If you have had a cesarean section, the incision will probably be quite painful for the first two or three days, but painkillers help considerably and are safe, even if you are breast-feeding. Moving as much as possible and getting up once all the tubes and IVs have been taken away is the best help in making a speedy recovery; staying absolutely still is the worst. Many women worry that their stitches will burst if they move too much, but there is no danger of this, though at first you need to support them by holding a small pillow firmly against the stitches to avoid pain when you sneeze, cough, laugh, or rise up from sitting. The stitches will come out at about the fifth day. Try circling your ankles and gently bending one knee at a time to help circulation and to combat stiffness. Although your baby was delivered surgically, you will still have a vaginal discharge called "lochia," which is normal after birth. At first it is red, then changes to brown. Wear waist-high underpants to avoid rubbing the stitches, and use stick-on sanitary napkins rather than the belted kind.

An unexpected but very distressing complaint after having had a baby can be hemorrhoids, which are varicose veins in the anus. These are likely to occur if a mother has become constipated during pregnancy and may be made much more painful during the second stage of labor, when the pressure of the baby's head may force them to "come down" so they protrude beyond the anus. Suppositories available on prescription can stop the itching, which can be very distressing; so, too, can ice packs and sitz baths. During a bath gently ease the hemorrhoids back inside the rectum, and they should gradually subside. If the problem persists, see your doctor, because they can be treated fairly easily with local medications. The increased levels of hormones during pregnancy predispose women to varicose veins because the walls of the veins become softer and the blood supply is increased. However, in many cases such varicose veins disappear spontaneously without any treatment as the hormone levels subside.

When the milk appears at about the third day after the birth, your breasts may become engorged; this may happen whether or not you are breast-feeding. There are many ways in which you can try to alleviate this. However, it is very important to wear a good supportive bra day and night during this time so the tissues and skin above the breasts are not stretched. This will help your breasts retain their same shape afterward. Because it is so warm in maternity units, many women find their skin becomes very dry after the birth, so it is a good idea to take plenty of moisturizer into the hospital with you. Be comforted by the fact that although in the first few days after the birth you may feel you don't recognize your own body, it really does possess tremendous powers of recovery. Eating a healthy, sensible diet, following postnatal exercises without trying to attempt anything too strenuous too quickly, and giving yourself plenty of time are the secrets of getting your body back to normal. For most women it takes at least six months before they feel their bodies are back to some kind of normality, so don't be depressed if you can't zip back into your jeans by the time you go for your six-week checkup.

Time in the Hospital After Having the Baby
The majority of babies are born in the hospital these days, although the time you stay in afterward can vary from twenty-four hours to eight days or more if there are

complications. Most hospitals discharge mother and baby on the second postdelivery day if all is well. It makes sense to try to get as much rest as possible during this time, and in the early days after the birth your baby is more likely to be sleepy. Many women, though, find hospital wards, hospital beds, and the continual noise of hospital life hardly conducive to any kind of rest! Nevertheless, not having to think about meals or laundry and having an unending supply of fresh clothes for the baby are things to be enjoyed. It is also worth using the time to learn your postnatal exercises if these are recommended.

The Blues—or Postpartum Depression

It is very common to feel emotional, weepy, and even a bit down around the time between the third and the seventh days after the birth. Generally known as "the blues," this state of emotion is largely due to the sudden changes of hormone levels in the woman's bloodstream as the milk comes in. A feeling of being on a high of happiness and excitement one minute, and then bursting into tears with feelings of depression or inadequacy the next is quite normal at this stage. So, too, are feelings of unreality or panic. Usually by the time the baby is about six to eight weeks old your emotions will begin to stabilize, although it is still common to feel more emotional and weepy than you did before you gave birth.

You may be suffering from postpartum depression if these feelings do not go away but actually begin to get worse, with more low times finally developing into a continuously depressed state, when everything seems to be too much effort. Symptoms vary, but continual fatigue, feeling totally inadequate, being overwhelmed with sadness, and being unable to see any hope for the future are common feelings. "Everything in my life seemed to be painted in shades of gray—there was no color in my life at all," was how one new mother described her state of mind.

It is not known whether postpartum depression may be caused by the high levels of hormones circulating in the mother's body, by the actual mental upheaval that adjusting to parenthood entails, or both. However, there is general agreement that exhaustion is likely to make matters worse—new mothers need "mothering" themselves, and having nobody who can help you with practical or emotional support in the early days can make things much harder. Getting to know a few other women who are expecting babies at the same time, avoiding major upheavals at about the time of the birth or immediately afterward, and making arrangements to get as much assistance as you can in the first few weeks after the birth can all help to cut the risks. However, if you do start to feel very miserable or find that the blues develop into something that threatens to be more permanent, make sure you talk to your physician, and explain exactly how you are feeling to your partner. Talking to other mothers can also help—you may be surprised just how many have experienced the same feelings. Support groups may also be available in your area for women suffering from postpartum depression; ask your physician about this.

The most severe form of postpartum depression is termed postpartum psychosis. This has many of the same symptoms as postpartum depression, but in addition a woman may experience delusions, hallucinations, and great agitation. Dramatic changes in mood to mania or severe depression, or swings between the two states, are also symptoms. Fortunately, such severe mental disturbance following birth is uncommon—about one in three thousand mothers may experience postpartum psychosis. The condition obviously requires medical treatment, usually hospitalization. Support and counseling are also important for fathers and for mothers during subsequent pregnancies.

Coming Home

I was so excited to dress the baby in her own clothes at last and to put my ordinary clothes on again. But there was also a slightly panicky feeling when we arrived home and I immediately realized it was time for the baby's feeding. In the hospital you have absolutely nothing else to think about and somehow when you are on your own all the time it all seems so much more overwhelming. I remember asking my husband to find the diapers and get some warm water because I had to change her diaper after feeding her and he said in surprise, "You mean, it's starting already?"

It is a huge change in your life to go from being without children and having no special demands on your time to finding that you have someone who demands attention twenty-four hours a day. Most people feel completely overwhelmed in the beginning and shocked by the way that a baby completely fills their time. Initially, it is hard to come to terms with the fact that you can't run out to the store easily or go to sleep when you like. With a first baby it is also very hard to get any kind of sense of perspective—it just seems that life has changed completely and that this state will go on forever. In fact, it actually lasts for a very short period, and once you get used to being with children all the time, it is just as hard, at the other end of their preschool years, to get used to the fact that there is no one to take to the store with you!

There is no doubt that life is much easier for women who have supportive relatives living nearby or even helpful neighbors who will occasionally watch the baby for them. But friendships with other mothers will be your greatest support—and this is something that is usually available to all new mothers. Such friends can be helpful in both a practical and an emotional sense. In the early days it just helps to recognize that your baby is at his or her most demanding and that things will only get easier. Don't try to force some sort of routine on your baby, but rather set priorities and don't get hung up on trying to live life as it was before you had her. If you tend to get very upset by a messy, disorganized house, it can be hard for you to accept the fact that with a baby, housework has to come pretty low down on your list of priorities. First place has to go to keeping the baby fed, clean, and happy. In second place come your needs and those of your partner. If you are the kind of person whose happiness is at least partially dependent on having an organized home and on being able to serve a home-cooked meal each evening, you will have to reach some sort of compromise. Again, talking to your partner about what both of you expect each other to do and about problems as they arise is very important. Also, if you can afford to pay for help, this is the time to do it. Having someone come in to clean or having meals delivered will definitely boost your spirits. A relative or friend may also be able to help with these tasks. If people offer help, take them up on it! It is important to remember, if this is your first child, that life with a baby is continually changing, because your child develops and changes so very much in the first twelve months of life. This means that just when you have gotten used to the fact that she has two naps, one in the morning and another in the afternoon, she will suddenly go on to needing only one nap during the day, and that probably at a very inconvenient time. And just when you have rescheduled your life around that pattern, then your baby suddenly goes into an awkward phase where she can almost manage to go a whole day without a nap at all, but not quite, and continually falls asleep at about four to five o'clock, which means that she will not sleep at all in the evening! The first year of your baby's life is hard work, but it is also unique, and trying to remember just how short a period it is may help you to feel less frustrated and to enjoy this special time to its fullest.

Organizing Your Life

The other great change that many women having their first baby have to get used to is the difference between working and staying at home, even if you are on maternity leave or plan to return to work eventually. When you work full-time you spend very little time in your own home and consequently rarely know many people in the area, unless it is an area you have grown up in. Work also provides a structure and a framework, not only to each individual day but also to the weeks, to the months, to the years and ultimately to your expectation of life. When you are at home every day of the week there is no structure, and virtually no framework except the one you care to impose on it. Suddenly the times that your partner leaves and comes back to the house have a greater significance because they put some kind of framework around an otherwise formless day and become landmarks that highlight weekdays from weekends and separate day from evening. Everything that happens requires initiative and energy from you to make it happen. All this can be very disconcerting at first, but it does help if you look rationally at exactly how many changes have happened in your life, and don't attribute everything to the baby.

Getting out of the house and seeing other people can be very important to your morale and self-esteem, and this is also true when it comes to maintaining your self-confidence. It sometimes happens that being based at home looking after small children can make some women less confident about their abilities in situations and circumstances they might not have given a second thought to when they were in full-time employment. Probably this is partly the result of doing what is, in effect, quite a solitary job, and partly also reflects the value and worth that society places on the job of parenting. Fortunately this last is changing, although very slowly, and there is more widespread recognition that the job of being a parent is extremely challenging, worthwhile, and important. Certainly it helps not to minimize or underestimate the challenge involved in becoming a parent for the first time and to remind yourself just how many new skills you are learning at this stage in your life—from the practical aspects of child care right through to all the new emotional and psychological demands being made. After a couple of years, dealing with six different things at the same time comes automatically to most women, as does managing their time and energy with maximum efficiency. The organizational skills alone learned during the years when you have preschool children are ones that any management training program would be proud to be able to instill! And, of course, there are tremendous pluses in being able to free yourself from the nine-to-five routine.

While in the early days it may seem that your baby consumes every single minute of your time, there will come a stage when you begin to see a little space that can be used for your own needs—an aerobics class, a weekly adult education class in something which interests you while a friend or relative baby-sits, or even a chance to take up a new hobby or a sport. Of course, you have to plan carefully to make time for these activities—that is where the organizational skills come in—but the opportunity is there and it is well worth thinking about coordinating child care with friends if you do not have relatives nearby who can help by watching the baby occasionally.

Making Love Again

There is absolutely no "right" time to begin having sex again after the birth of your baby. Some women—especially those who have had a very good sex life before, who have had an easy birth without any stitches, and whose babies sleep a great deal at night—may recover their libido very quickly. But for the majority, sheer exhaustion, coupled with discomfort from stitches, can make passion the last thing on their minds. However, it is important not to stop all forms of physical contact and all physical affection between you just because you don't want to have intercourse. It really is very important to talk to each other so neither party feels rejected by the other. Women do need to feel loved, and may often want to be cuddled, even if they don't actually want to have sex at that time. A common misconception is that the six-week postnatal checkup is the time when it is all right to begin having sex with your partner again; in fact, the right time is simply when you feel like it. What happens if weeks and then months go by and you still don't feel interested in sex? The time after having had a baby is a key period for problems to begin between couples, so it is important to take action and not to allow yours to become a sexless marriage by habit. If there have been sex problems before that you have not acknowledged or talked about, then the birth of a baby is often a convenient excuse on which to blame old problems.

Talking to your doctor is one step, and many doctors are willing to try to help. Alternatively, family planning clinics usually have some kind of psychosexual counseling service. Marriage counselors may also be helpful. There are a number of good books available, and if you both read one of these it may make it easier for you to talk to each other.

Spending too much time alone in the house with the baby can often lead to lowered morale and less interest in sex. Too often couples end up seeing each other only against a continual backdrop of diapers and domestic life. Tiredness and the continual demands of a third party, as well as familiarity, prevent them from seeing each other clearly. The solution for this is to get out of the house as much as possible—both on your own during the day and as a couple in the evenings. In the early days, especially if you are breast-feeding, it is often easiest to take the baby along with you, but later it is worth making some effort to make baby-sitting arrangements so you can get a break. Do not be tempted into thinking that it is all just too much trouble to arrange.

To be interested in sex, women need to feel that they are sexually interesting themselves—it is hard to feel this about yourself if you spend too much time alone, have no reason to dress up or be concerned about your appearance, and seldom have the chance to see yourself reflected in other people's eyes. Taking time for yourself and for the two of you as a couple will strengthen your relationship, making you even better parents.

CHAPTER 5

Babies Needing Special Care

How much special care?
Babies needing surgery • The small baby
Having a baby in special care—what it means for your family
The problems of babies in special care
The future for special-care babies
Parents' reactions to premature birth
Babies who may not live
Crib death (Sudden Infant Death Syndrome)

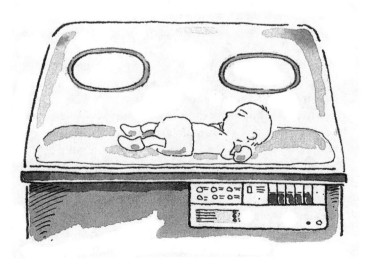

The knowledge, skill, and technology that can save tiny or ill babies are growing all the time. This means that although we can't save every baby, many who would previously have died or been handicapped can now be helped to grow into normal, healthy adults. This is a rapidly changing field, and what seems very timely today may be out of date in the early years of the next century.

How Much Special Care?

Today many babies who used to be taken care of in special-care nurseries can now be kept with their mothers and given any extra observation or care needed in a routine nursery. These may include babies who needed initial resuscitation but are otherwise well, babies born by cesarean section or forceps, those born in the breech position, mildly jaundiced babies requiring phototherapy, babies who need screening for low blood sugar or extra feeding, and babies with conditions that are not life-threatening, such as cleft palate, cleft lip, dislocated hip, or Down syndrome. Even some babies who are too premature to be breast- or bottle-fed, but who are otherwise well and a reasonable weight, can sometimes be tube-fed (fed milk by a tube into the baby's stomach) in a special care unit. Different hospitals will vary slightly in their criteria for admission to a special (or intensive)-care unit.

Another form of intermediate care that may be found in some hospitals is a step-down unit between the postnatal nursery and the intensive-care baby unit. This unit is ideally in close proximity to the intensive-care unit to provide continuity in care between the two units and to allow for open communication between the parents and the unit staff, providing for a smooth transition to home.

The Neonatal Transitional (or Intermediate)-Care Unit

About five babies of every hundred born will need care in a transitional-care unit. A first visit to such a unit can be both shocking and overwhelming for parents because of all the equipment and the fragile appearance of the very small babies. When possible, parents who are expecting a small or a sick baby will find it helpful to visit the unit for a guided tour before the delivery. Modern technology can now help babies to breathe before their lungs can work properly on their own; keep them nourished before they are able to suck, swallow, or digest food in their stomachs; and can also noninvasively measure their temperature, heartbeat, breathing, and the level of oxygen or carbon dioxide in their blood. The most sophisticated procedures are now carried out in most neonatal intensive-care units and in many transitional-care units, as well. Each hospital has its own criteria for admitting babies to special care; very seriously ill babies will need intensive care (see below). The basic principles of special care are, however, still the same as they were when the first nursery for newborns was opened more than a hundred years ago by a French doctor in Paris—that is, to keep tiny or ill babies warm and free from infection.

The Neonatal Intensive Care Unit (NICU)

The whole place was buzzing and clicking and humming with machinery and it was very hot—like a tropical electronic aviary. In the midst of it all were these pathetic scraps of humanity wired up to machines inside incubators. They showed us our son, and my wife began to cry. He looked so helpless and we felt so helpless as well, not wanting him to be fixed to all that machinery and yet knowing he couldn't live without it.

Neonatal intensive-care units in large hospitals, generally regional centers, are where the smallest and sickest babies are cared for with the most sophisticated technology and the highest degree of skill. The broad dividing line between transitional and intensive care is the baby's ability to breathe unaided. While transitional- or intermediate-care units can give extra oxygen, usually through a hood or via a nasal cannula, a baby who requires a ventilator needs to be managed in an intensive-care unit. Babies needing this kind of intensive care may have to be transferred from other hospitals in the area, although in many cases mothers will have been transferred prior to delivery. Amazingly, babies born as early as twenty-three weeks (seventeen weeks early) are now being saved to grow into healthy adults, although for such very premature babies the path to health is seldom straightforward. Having a very small or a sick baby who has to be cared for during many weeks in an intensive- or transitional-care unit places tremendous strains on parents. You'll find more advice on ways to deal with this in the section on "Having a Baby in Special Care—What It Means for Your Family" later in this chapter.

Babies Needing Surgery

Babies born with conditions needing an urgent operation, such as a heart defect or abnormalities of the stomach or bowel, may be transferred to a tertiary-care center. If the diagnosis is made before birth, as nowadays it often is, the mother will be transferred before delivery to a tertiary-care center where pediatric surgery is available. These babies need to be moved to a hospital where there is a pediatric surgeon who is specially trained to surgically correct the anatomic defect. After surgery, babies who are also premature or small may be moved back to their original special- or intensive-care unit for continuing care or stay at the hospital where the surgery was performed until well enough to leave hospital care altogether.

The Small Baby

The nurses told me my son was very small but I was still shocked when I saw just how minute he was. He weighed one pound, fifteen ounces, and he was born at twenty-six weeks. Later, when I could hold him, he fitted easily into my hand, with his legs dangling over my palm. I couldn't believe anything so small could survive.

One of the first things that strikes visitors to intensive- and transitional-care units is that most of the babies are so very tiny. Any baby weighing less than 5½ lb (2,500 gr) at birth is classified as having a low birth weight. Babies can be small because they have been born too soon and have not had enough time to grow and develop—they are called "premature" or "pre-term" babies and account for most of the work of intensive-care units. Babies can also be small because, although they have been born at the right time, they did not get enough nutrition to grow properly inside the uterus. In a sense they have been starved before birth, and these babies are called "small-for-dates." Some babies can be both premature and small-for-dates. Doctors can tell by examining the baby, testing his reflexes and measuring his head, body, and limbs carefully, whether he has been growing at the expected rate, and how mature he is. Premature babies have different problems from small-for-dates babies, and size is not always a guide to maturity. For example, the baby of a diabetic mother can be born prematurely but weigh as much as 8 lb, 12 oz (4 kg) or more.

About 3.9 million babies are born each year in United States, and of these, about 250,000 will arrive prematurely, accounting for approximately 7 percent of all live births. A baby is said to be premature if he is born before thirty-seven weeks of gestation. In general, the earlier he is born, the more care he will need, although each baby's condition and maturity will be different. The reasons for his premature birth, if they are known, and the type of labor and delivery he has had will also make a difference. Because the lungs of premature babies have not yet matured, they often have trouble breathing, and because they have so little body fat they cannot keep themselves warm. They may not have developed the reflexes to suck or swallow food, and the digestive system of very premature babies may still be too immature to work. They have reduced resistance to infection and become ill easily, and they can be prone to seizures and sometimes to episodes of bleeding within the brain, though this may not be as alarming as it sounds. Jaundice is a common problem for both small and premature babies. See "The Problems of Babies in Special Care" later in this chapter.

In most cases, small-for-date babies have been deprived of nutrition only during the later weeks of pregnancy. This means that their normally developed brains will give them a rather large head in relation to the rest of their body and can predispose them to becoming hypoglycemic (low in blood sugar) rather easily. This is because the brain uses up a lot of the body's energy source, glucose, while the liver is too small to store much glucose. Serious problems in small-for-date babies usually arise only if the babies have been deprived of nutrition from early pregnancy, while the brain and other organs are developing. The use of ultrasound during pregnancy means that problems like these may be detected prior to delivery. Continuing research is going on, investigating ways of detecting, very early in pregnancy, which babies will be at risk for poor intrauterine growth. Like premature babies, small-for-date babies also have difficulty keeping warm because they have so little body fat, but they are less likely to have breathing problems unless they are also premature. Although small, their lungs are mature enough to work efficiently, if born close to full term.

Why Are Babies Born Prematurely or Small-for-Dates?

My son was born eleven weeks early for no reason anyone could pin down. I felt I had been too casual about the pregnancy and looking after myself. Somehow if I had rested more or given up work and stayed at home it wouldn't have happened. It didn't help that my mother-in-law believed that as well.

It is usually a terrible shock to parents when their baby is born prematurely—they feel very upset and anxious and often blame themselves. Although there are some known reasons for premature labor, in nearly half the cases doctors will not be able to suggest or discover a reason (see "Problems in Labor and Delivery" in chapter 3). It is very unlikely that a premature birth will have been caused by anything in the mother's lifestyle, whether it is carrying on working, pursuing an active life, having an alcoholic drink occasionally, or enjoying sex. You have only to consider how many babies continue to term and are born healthy despite all sorts of adverse conditions.

The same feelings of guilt are also common in women whose babies are small-for-dates. Again, it is often very hard to pinpoint exactly why a baby fails to grow properly, although certain categories of women are more likely to have small babies, even though the reasons may not be fully understood yet. Known reasons for prematurity and failure to grow often overlap, so it is very common for a baby to be both premature and small-for-dates to some degree. Indeed, small-for-date babies are often delivered early to give them a better chance.

What Do Premature Babies Look Like?

Like a newborn rabbit—I can say that now that he is two, but at the time I felt guilty even thinking it. I just wanted to put him back inside me when I first saw how obviously unready he looked to be out in the world.

In fact many premature babies look like perfect miniatures in every way. Their hands and feet are fully formed. When their eyes are open they can see, and they can hear. If they are born before twenty-six weeks, their eyelids may still be sealed, though these will open naturally in time; their hands are almost translucent, and veins and arteries can be seen through the thin skin. The bones of a premature baby are still quite soft, and the fontanelles are wider. Nurses change the position of babies regularly to reduce prolonged pressure on one part of the body, and it is common to see that their heads have become flattened on the side they have been lying. Eyelashes and eyebrows may not be present but will grow later. Normally ears lie close and flat to the baby's head, but the cartilage that forms the ear is still soft and can easily be temporarily pressed out of shape if the baby lies with the ear bent.

Premature babies have had no time to develop fat under the skin, which is why they have trouble keeping warm. It also makes their bodies look very bony.

Premature babies may have scarcely visible nipples, though these will develop later, and in boys, although the penis is tiny, it is fully formed. The testes have often not descended from the body into the scrotum. They usually descend as the baby matures. The genitals of premature baby girls can sometimes look odd because, although everything inside is perfectly formed, the outer lips around the vagina develop later in pregnancy, and their absence makes the inner lips look bulging or even swollen. Don't worry: Your baby's early birth will not stop the outer lips growing at the same time as they would have done inside the uterus.

Very premature babies will not have had time to develop lanugo, the downy hair that grows to protect their skin while they are in the amniotic fluid, but some later babies can still be covered with this, particularly on their backs and cheeks. It will be shed naturally as the baby develops. Remember that your premature baby is not unformed, just immature. The baby is, in fact, perfectly formed by the end of twelve weeks, from the start of the pregnancy; the rest of the time is spent maturing and growing. The job of transitional or intensive care is to give your baby the time he needs to complete the job of growing.

Weight

Do not forget that normal-term babies lose weight at first and take time to regain their birth weight. Exactly the same thing happens with small and premature babies, although you may be horrified to think they are going to get smaller still. Remember, this is normal and not a sign of your baby's ill health.

Obviously your baby's weight is important information in assessing whether he is able to digest his food and is getting the right amount of fluid and nutrients. Babies are weighed regularly, but it is best to look at his overall weight gain for the week rather than become obsessed with each day's loss or gain; this is not as significant as the general pattern. The more premature the baby, the longer he will take to regain his birth weight. In the tiniest baby, with good care, this can happen in a few days.

Will My Baby Live?

> We were told when my wife went into labor at twenty-seven weeks that our
> baby had only a 40 percent chance of survival and we prepared for the worst.
> But he did live and was taken straight into intensive care. On the third day we
> asked one of the doctors what the real problems would be—up until then we had
> hardly dared hope he would live. We were shocked and frightened when we
> heard of all the possible difficulties and formed an initial dislike for that doctor.
> But after a few days our opinions changed, and in the end we were so glad we
> had been honestly informed. We now hold that doctor in the highest esteem.

Each individual baby's progress and problems will be different, and the road to health will seem intolerably long and slow, with each day bringing one step forward, only to be followed by two steps back. There are some general points that can be made, however. The first is that the majority of babies who go into a neonatal intensive-care unit *do* go home. Most babies born at thirty-two weeks or later will live and grow normally. Only one in seven of babies born at twenty-eight weeks (twelve weeks early) will not survive. Earlier than that, the risks rise sharply, so that babies born more than fourteen weeks early may have a less than 50 percent chance of living, depending on their condition, weight, and the reasons for their premature birth. In each case your pediatrician will tell you about your own baby's chances and answer your questions honestly.

Though this may seem harsh at the time, what often weighs most heavily with parents is not only the life or death of their baby but also his chances of surviving normally without a handicap. Of course, there are risks attached to the life-saving procedures that enable very small babies to survive, but although many more babies are now being saved, the level of handicap is the same as it was twenty years ago. It has stayed at a level of about two in ten, although this figure includes minor handicaps such as slight deafness, nearsightedness or squints, slightly slower development, clumsiness, and shorter height, all of which still allow a normal expectation of life. Only about one in twenty of the very small babies is affected enough to need to go to a special school.

It is difficult to tell early on how a very small baby will progress. In most cases, the only sure test that a baby has not been damaged is time. If, however, the medical staff thinks there is a serious possibility that a baby may have been seriously damaged, they will discuss this in detail with the parents and decide with them whether to continue treatment.

In general, the first twenty-four hours of life are the most dangerous, and most deaths occur in the first ten days. Beyond that there is no definite point when parents can be told their baby is out of danger, though landmarks along the way bring that time closer. Being able to breathe unaided is obviously a crucial step—ventilator treatment can bring problems of its own, but most babies on ventilators do make a full recovery. Usually parents are told to expect their baby to stay in the hospital until the time he was due to be born, although he will not be receiving intensive care all this time but will gradually be promoted through degrees of care until he is sleeping in an ordinary crib in a nursery, being looked after like any normal new baby. Don't be too disappointed if your baby appears to make slow progress—by being tube-fed instead of being fed by mouth, or coming off a ventilator only to have to go back to needing this form of treatment again for a while. This often happens and doesn't mean he has become more ill, just that he is not quite ready for the next step yet. Often two steps forward and one step back is the best way to describe the progress of these babies.

Having a Baby in Special Care— What It Means for Your Family

You will have been shown your baby immediately after the birth, but may not have held him because there is a danger of premature and small babies getting cold easily, and they may need help to breathe. As soon as possible after the birth you will be taken to see him in the transitional- or intensive-care unit. Try not to be overwhelmed if he looks very small or if there seems to be a lot of equipment surrounding him. The nurses will be able to explain everything. If your baby is very premature or ill, he may have to be transferred to a regional neonatal intensive-care center at a larger hospital. Care will be taken to keep the baby warm by in a portable incubator or Isolette. Other family members can travel separately to the referral hospital, and the staff will often take some Polaroid photos of your baby for you to keep.

Physical contact between you and your baby is a very important part of getting to know him and establishing a relationship. No baby is so ill that you cannot put your hand inside the Isolette and hold his hand. In most cases babies are well enough for parents to stroke and fondle them. Even some ventilated babies can be cuddled with the help of a nurse. At first you may be worried about disturbing the equipment, but the nurses will show you what to do. The bright, noisy world inside an Isolette could not be in greater contrast to the dark, protected world inside your womb, and whatever human contact you can offer will help to reassure even the tiniest baby—just as skin contact, warmth and the movement of a mother's body are comforting for any newborn baby. Research is even being done about the benefits of holding a premature baby between a mother's breasts close to her body instead of keeping him in an Isolette—an idea that comes from Bogotá, Colombia, and is called Kangaroo Care—though there is still controversy about this idea. Positive physical benefits have been shown to be linked to close physical contact between parents and babies, so that gently stroking the baby in his Isolette appears to help cut the number of apneic attacks (periods when the baby stops breathing) and even to help the baby gain weight. Premature babies can hear well and, like any new baby, will get to know the rhythm and tone of your voice, so it is important to talk to your baby as well. Very premature babies may still have their eyelids sealed, but once these have separated they can see quite well and, during alert periods, will be able to focus best on your face at a range of about eight to twelve inches.

Unfortunately, some of the procedures which save such babies cause temporary discomfort—for example, having blood samples taken, secretions suctioned from their lungs, or tubes passed into their stomachs. Obviously staff will always be as gentle and as careful as possible and will keep intrusions to a minimum. Once in place, the tubes and fluids they receive are not uncomfortable, but you should always tell a nurse if your baby has moved and if you think he looks distressed or in discomfort, and she will help you to rearrange him in a better position.

Normally, premature babies can cry just as full-term babies can, although the cry will be feebler and not as prolonged because crying is exhausting and premature babies do not have much strength. If your baby is on a ventilator, he will not be able to make any sound because the tube delivering oxygen into his lungs passes between the vocal cords. Nurses will be watchful to notice if such a baby is in discomfort or distress and will investigate the cause.

Premature babies usually sleep a great deal—fifteen to twenty-two hours of every twenty-four. Like normal newborns, they drift easily between waking and sleep, and in their waking hours they vary from being drowsy to being very alert and aware. You can use these aware periods to talk to and especially to stroke your baby and later cuddle and hold him. You should talk normally during feeding, just as you would to a full-term baby. You can encourage your baby to wake up when you are holding him by slightly loosening the blankets and stroking his toes while you talk to him. Because the nervous systems of premature babies are immature, their movements will be rather jerky and uncontrolled, but this lessens as they develop. Small and ill babies are nursed without clothes on because it makes it much easier for nurses to spot any immediate changes in skin color or condition and to address the problem quickly. As he gets stronger, your baby will be able to wear clothes, and you can put a bright, soft toy or a photo or other picture inside the Isolette.

At first all the equipment will seem overwhelming, but never be afraid to ask questions of the nurses or doctors. Early mornings are busy times in the unit because doctors make rounds, during which they discuss each infant and update his condition, and there may be emergencies during the day when the staff has to see to one particular baby urgently. So pick a time when things are fairly calm if you want something explained. Don't forget that the alarms often sound because a monitor that should be stuck to your baby's skin has fallen off, not because your baby's system is suddenly failing.

Babies in transitional or intensive care often need a number of X rays—to check their lungs, or to see that a feeding tube is properly in place. Understandably, parents may feel concerned about the number of times this happens, but it is always kept to a minimum, and with modern techniques the risk to the baby is very small.

Brothers and Sisters
Older children will have been expecting you to bring a new baby back with you whom they could touch and hold. Instead, they may have to cope with your unplanned and early departure to the hospital, longer separation from you, and a new brother or sister who has had to stay in the hospital. Units vary in their policy of children visiting, but if it is possible, arrange for them to come to see the baby, even if they cannot touch or hold him. Generally, children are far less awed by the trappings of intensive care than parents are, but take your cue from them and don't push them to do more than they want. It is as important for them to form a relationship with the new baby as it is for you; to do this they need to see, talk about, and if possible touch or hold the baby. They may like to bring the baby a special toy that can be placed in the Isolette, and it is a good idea if the baby thoughtfully has a small present to give in return. Some children like the idea of putting a photo of themselves or some special piece of their own artwork inside the Isolette. Even if you are uncertain about your baby's chances of survival, it is probably better to bring your other children to see him. If he does not live, your grief will still be part of their lives, and they will probably feel sad and upset, too. Your sadness will have some meaning for them if they have seen the baby themselves, and it will make any reference to the baby less confusing than if they have never seen him. There are some good books available for children about babies in special care.

Fathers
Individual reactions will vary, but fathers who would have wanted to be fully involved with their baby's care in the event of a normal birth will be just as likely to feel the same if their baby needs special care. Sometimes one partner, either

mother or father, tries to protect the other by shouldering most of the responsibility, but this is more likely to lead to stress and resentment later. Whenever possible, couples should see doctors together so they can both ask questions, have a better firsthand understanding, and share decisions.

Fathers need to be both supportive and sympathetic to the many difficult emotions their partners may feel—of course, a premature or a sick baby is a great shock to both parents, but it is still the woman's life that changes more. She has physically undergone the experience of birth and will usually be the one to stay and visit the baby most. Spending long periods in the timeless, isolated world of a hospital can increase her sense of unreality and loneliness, while going out to work or staying home with other children can make it easier for fathers to keep a stronger grip on reality. If possible, it will help couples to take turns staying at the unit so they can understand more of what the other feels. This sharing of their baby's care will help parents to support each other when their baby comes home—a time to look forward to, but also one that can cause anxiety and some mixed emotions as well.

The Problems of Babies in Special Care

Feeding

Sucking reflexes do not usually develop until about thirty-two to thirty-four weeks after conception, and the ability to coordinate sucking and swallowing may be later than this. So babies born prematurely may be unable to suck and swallow and may have problems absorbing food because of an immature digestive system. Fortunately, there are alternative ways to nourish an infant: using a feeding tube, or putting a special solution directly into the bloodstream.

Intravenous Feeding This is also known as total parenteral nutrition, or TPN. Babies who have prolonged breathing problems, who have had operations, or who are too ill or too immature to feed normally through their stomachs, can be nourished with a carefully balanced solution fed directly into their bloodstream through a tube inserted into a vein. If a baby is expected to be fed intravenously for prolonged periods, the solution can be given into one of the larger veins by using "a long line"—this means a long, narrow tube that is introduced into a surface vein and then fed through one vein after another until it reaches a point where the veins are larger. The advantage is that more fluids of different types can be fed in without the worry of bursting tiny surface veins, and the long line can be left in place for some time and not reinserted frequently. Babies can be fed like this for several weeks if necessary, although there is a slightly increased risk of infection in using the technique—the doctor will insert the tube using sterile technique and afterward take an X ray to make sure it is properly in place.

Tube Feeding This is also known as gavage feeding, nasogastric feeding, or orogastric feeding. This is a simple and safe procedure performed by passing a tube down the baby's nose or mouth into his stomach. When the tube is in position, the nurse will draw up some of the contents of the stomach to see if undigested milk is

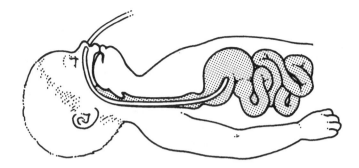

left from the last feeding and to check the contents for acid—a sign that the end of the tube is in fact in the stomach. At the first feeding a baby will have only a tiny amount of acid present, but this will gradually increase. If a very premature baby is having breathing problems, putting food into the stomach may not be suitable because there is a risk of vomiting; instead, food can bypass the stomach and be fed by a tube (called a nasojejunal tube) directly into the duodenum or jejunum parts of the intestine beyond the stomach. A nasogastric tube may also be inserted alongside so the stomach can be kept empty.

Breast-feeding a Baby in Special Care   Mothers often need a lot of support and encouragement to breast-feed a premature or ill baby, especially if he is her first. Some may not have made a definite decision on whether to breast-feed and may choose to express milk for a while until they are sure. The small amounts of colostrum produced before the milk comes in are precious, containing unique nutrients and antibodies that are valuable to a sick infant. If a baby has been born at term, he will have been put to the breast at birth and taken some colostrum. However, premature infants may be unable to feed in this way, so the colostrum can be expressed, frozen, and fed by tube as soon as he is strong enough.

Expressing breast milk enables a mother to produce a good milk supply so the baby can breast-feed as soon as he is able to suck. Expressed breast milk can either be fed to an infant via a tube or frozen until needed. The pumps for obtaining breast milk are either electric or manual (called a hand suction pump). Most hospitals have their own electric breast pumps, which can be used while the infant is still hospitalized.

Ideally, expressing should start as soon as possible after birth, but it is still possible to stimulate milk production after several days or even weeks. Initially, only a few drops of colostrum will be obtained, but frequent use of a pump will gradually increase this. For the first couple of days a mother should apply the lowest suction rate on the pump for a few minutes to each breast every two hours. At about the third day, the milk supply will increase, and the time of expressing can be extended to five to fifteen minutes each side, six to eight times a day.

Few hospitals have pumps for home loan, but it is possible to rent pumps. In addition, breast-feeding counselors, also called lactation consultants, are becoming more available at hospitals to provide valuable breast-feeding advice and support. Also, nurses and social workers can put parents in touch with other families who have premature babies or who have had experience breast-feeding a high-risk infant. Unless there is a medical reason why the baby cannot be picked up, holding the baby to the breast can be comforting and help to stimulate the mother's milk supply. Putting a drop of breast milk onto his tongue together with the skin-to-skin contact can be helpful. Infants develop their sucking reflex at thirty-two to thirty-four weeks, although the exact time can vary.

Breast-feeding can take some time to become established, and many infants may only suck very weakly initially. A nurse or breast-feeding counselor will assist with the correct positioning of the infant so he is pressing around the area surrounding the nipple (the areola). These early attempts will be more successful if he is hungry, has not just been given a tube feeding, and is reasonably awake.

Although breast milk is the best food for a baby, there will be a number of mothers who are unable or choose not to breast-feed. This may be because they find it too stressful or, rarely, because a medication the mother has to take would put the baby at risk. Special infant formulas are available that are designed for low-birth-weight babies and contain extra protein, energy, and some minerals.

Feeding a baby, whether by breast or bottle, can be a very emotional time for the mother. Naturally, if she is bottle-feeding she may wish to be the one who gives her baby his first bottle. The assistance of an experienced nurse can be valuable, and often it will take several sessions before he is able to bottle-feed successfully.

Breathing

If a premature baby has difficulty breathing by himself, this is called respiratory distress syndrome (RDS), sometimes called "hyaline membrane disease." This is very common in babies born before thirty-two weeks.

From about twenty-four weeks of pregnancy, a fatty substance called surfactant begins to be produced that coats the baby's lungs. This substance enables the baby's lungs to expand easily, stretch, and be flexible when he starts to breathe. Surfactant lowers the surface tension in the air sacs so the pressure is evenly distributed and expands them all to the right size, whether the sacs in the lungs are large or small. Because the air pressure is the same throughout the lungs, when the baby breathes out, all the air sacs stay partially inflated to the same degree as well. When the lungs are not well supplied with surfactant to make them stretchy and flexible, a great deal more pressure is needed to blow up each individual air sac. Because the pressure throughout lungs not well coated with surfactant is not equal, at the end of a breath the small air sacs can collapse in on themselves completely.

If premature labor is likely or if the birth has to be induced because of the condition of the mother or the baby, a twenty-four- to forty-eight-hour course of steroids may be given to the mother. It is thought that these steroids stimulate the unborn baby's lungs to produce surfactant. In addition, this mechanism may also be triggered spontaneously to have the same effect when a baby is likely to be born prematurely—for example, because the placenta is ceasing to work properly. Certainly length of gestation alone is no absolute guide to a premature baby's ability to breathe on his own. It is now possible to give babies surfactant after birth directly into their lungs, which reduces the severity of RDS.

Forms of Breathing Difficulties   If a baby is immature or has already been deprived of oxygen, he may have difficulty breathing at birth. Pain medicine given to the mother late in labor can also make babies sleepy and less able to breathe in some cases.

Wet lung (transient tachypnea of the newborn—TTN) is a term used when a baby still has some fluid in his lungs that is making breathing more difficult. The condition may also be due to a mild deficiency of surfactant, but usually disappears within twenty-four hours of birth. In the meantime the baby may need a little extra oxygen.

Hyaline membrane disease occurs when a baby is born without enough surfactant lining the lungs. It often appears in the first few hours after birth. The baby may make grunting noises in an effort to keep the air sacs expanded as he breathes, and his chest becomes deeply sucked in at the beginning of each breath. Often supplemental oxygen and sometimes ventilatory support are needed to help him breathe.

Apnea simply means not breathing. It is very common for premature babies to have apneic attacks. Sometimes, because the nervous system is still immature, the right messages do not always get through, and they simply forget to breathe. Usually, gently shaking or touching the skin is enough to start them breathing again, but if there is a more serious attack, the baby may need to be given extra oxygen or may be started on a medication such as caffeine or theophylline to help stimulate a normal breathing pattern. Repeated or serious apneic attacks need further investigation because they can be a sign of seizure activity, infection, anemia, metabolic imbalance, or other problems.

How Babies Are Helped to Breathe   The air we breathe contains 21 percent oxygen, and babies who are having trouble breathing will not have to work as hard if they breathe air that contains an extra amount of oxygen. The easiest way to give this to babies is to pipe it directly into their Isolette or plastic hood that is placed over their head. Babies who have moderately severe RDS can often be helped with a different method, called "continuous positive airway pressure" (CPAP), when continuous airway pressure is needed to keep the air sacs expanded so the baby can breathe more easily. This is done either by pumping air through a face mask or, more commonly, a small tube is inserted directly into the airway through the mouth or nose.

When neither of the two previous methods is enough, a baby can actually have his breathing done for him by a machine called a ventilator. Ventilators vary, but they usually look like a box that stands to the side of the Isolette with a soft tube that goes into the baby's mouth or nose and between his vocal cords so that the end rests just below the top of the windpipe, allowing oxygen to enter directly into the lungs. It is usually secured in place with tape. A mixture of air and oxygen is delivered in and out of the baby's lungs under carefully controlled pressure, just as in a normal breathing pattern. It is usually moistened before passing into the lungs. With mechanical ventilation some sticky secretions begin to collect in the lungs, so the nurses will frequently take the baby off the ventilator briefly and pass another fine tube into his lungs to suction these secretions out. While he is off the

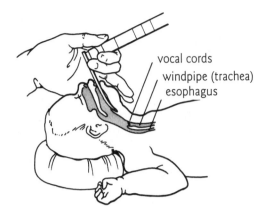

vocal cords
windpipe (trachea)
esophagus

Position of laryngoscope in preparation for
inserting the breathing tube

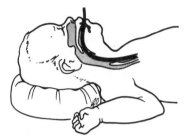

oropharyngeal intubation tube

Extra oxygen supplied through a pipe
inserted directly into the windpipe
through the mouth—naso-tracheal tube
in position

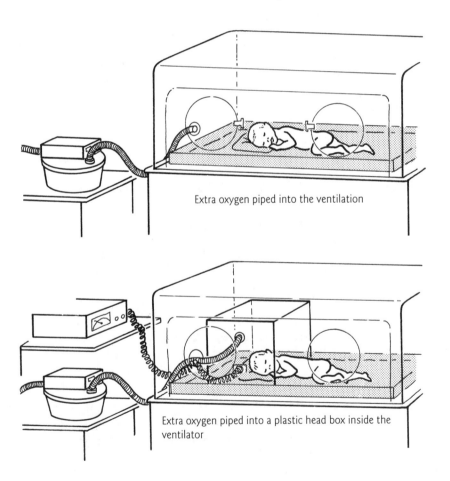

Extra oxygen piped into the ventilation

Extra oxygen piped into a plastic head box inside the
ventilator

Methods of helping babies to breathe

ventilator, they can give him oxygen using a face mask attached to a hand pump. At the same time, the baby may be given physiotherapy to help clear any mucus from the lungs—this involves tapping the chest either by hand or by using an electric vibrator, which helps to loosen the secretions. Changing the baby's position often helps to drain these secretions. Signs that a baby may be ready to come off a ventilator are that he needs less oxygen and begins to make efforts to breathe independently.

While it is very important that a baby has enough oxygen, it is also vital that he does not have too much. Measuring the levels of oxygen and carbon dioxide in the baby's blood ensures that this does not happen. A device called a transcutaneous oxygen electrode can give an estimate of oxygen levels in the baby's blood by measuring the oxygen as it passes just under the surface of the skin. This is achieved with a heated electrode, which looks like a button and is stuck onto the baby's skin. It has to be moved regularly to stop the baby's fragile skin from getting overheated. Other devices, called oximeters, can be attached to a hand or a foot to measure the percentage of blood fully loaded with oxygen; these do not have to be heated. Alternatively, an oxygen-sensitive electrode can be implanted into the tip of a very thin plastic tube, which, inserted into the baby's umbilical artery, gives a continuous readout on a display panel. The more traditional method is to take regular blood samples via a catheter into an umbilical or other artery and analyze them. Measuring oxygen levels very carefully has overcome what used to be one of the biggest risks—that of giving too much oxygen, which may have other damaging effects.

As well as the lowest possible levels of extra oxygen being given, care will be taken that the minimum amount of pressure is exerted when using CPAP or a ventilator. Even so, because premature babies have such tiny, fragile lungs, it is not uncommon for babies having this treatment to get a very small tear in one of their lungs. This is called a pneumothorax, and it has been known to happen even when a normal baby is making strenuous efforts to breathe but is more common if a baby is receiving ventilatory support that provides pressure to inflate the lungs. A small

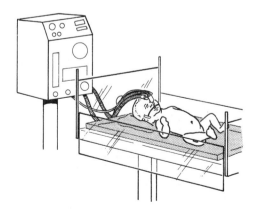

Extra oxygen supplied directly into the windpipe

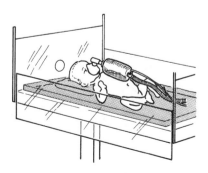

Extra oxygen piped through a face mask.

hole may mend by itself, but a large hole requires treatment (see "More Serious Problems After Delivery" in chapter 4).

Sometimes babies needing to be ventilated or given oxygen therapy for a long time can become oxygen-dependent and will not breathe adequately without it. It is thought that the pressure from the ventilator rather than oxygen levels over a long time may damage areas of tissue in their lungs—the medical name is bronchopulmonary dysplasia (BPD). Such babies may need extra oxygen over months or very occasionally even for one or two years as the tissue recovers, but they can gradually be weaned off to breathe in room air for longer and longer periods. Even babies without BPD who have been ventilated for shorter periods and were very premature may be more prone to coughs, colds, and wheezing from respiratory-related infections for the first year or two of life.

Temperature—Keeping Small Babies Warm

Small babies have difficulty keeping themselves warm because they have very little fat and a large surface area of skin relative to their body mass from which heat can be lost. One of the principal jobs of an isolette is to provide a constant temperature: it has carefully regulated heaters and fans to keep the air temperature inside at the right level. Very ill babies are sometimes nursed in open beds under a large radiant

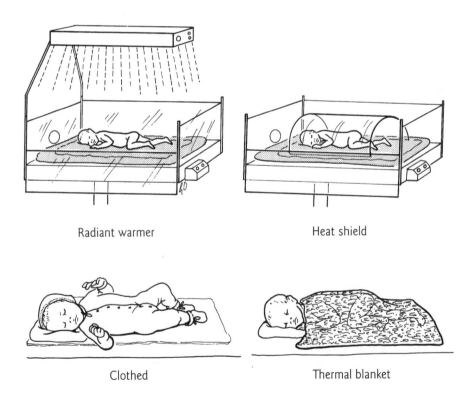

Radiant warmer   Heat shield

Clothed   Thermal blanket

Methods of keeping premature babies warm

heater. Sheets of plastic are also good insulating materials and can be placed over the baby to help to keep him warm.

It may seem odd to parents with all this talk about heat loss that these very small babies are usually cared for without clothes but, as we mentioned, it enables nurses to notice easily any change in the baby's color or breathing. Inside the Isolette the baby may lie on sheepskin or a soft sheet to help maintain warmth. Sometimes small babies may wear a bonnet or some kind of head cover because a great deal of heat can be lost through the scalp, which has a relatively large surface area. Once the baby is better able to maintain his own body temperature, he can be transitioned from an Isolette to a crib with blankets help maintain warmth. At this point he transitioned from an Isolette to a crib, with blankets to help maintain warmth. At this point he will be fully clothed, with a bonnet or cap as well.

Infection

Premature babies have not had enough time in the uterus to acquire antibodies from the mother to protect them against infection. Their skin is thin, and they have many tubes inserted. This makes them especially susceptible to infection. All special- and intensive-care units take the greatest care to prevent infections or a possible spread to other babies. Precautions will certainly include careful hand-washing by all staff and visitors to the unit, and avoiding visitation by anyone with any kind of illness, such as a cold.

Signs that a baby has an infection may be obvious (e.g., an inflamed eye or a fever) or subtle (such as poor weight gain or lethargy). Infections can often make a baby suddenly and seriously ill, resulting in a collapse, and he may need intensive nursing care immediately. To avoid this happening whenever possible, a baby will always be started on a course of antibiotics if an infection is suspected. Samples of blood, spinal fluid, urine, surface skin swabs, and any discharge will be sent to the lab for analysis, and their report will come back in two to three days—this is called a "sepsis workup." If an infection is confirmed, antibiotics will continue, but if not and the baby is better, they will be stopped. If it is not obvious where the source of infection lies, a number of other tests and samples will be taken. An infection of the blood is known as septicemia, one in the lungs is pneumonia, one of the spinal fluid is meningitis, and in the eyes it is conjunctivitis. Most babies who have infections at this early stage respond well to antibiotic treatment and most often recover completely.

Blood and Heart Problems

Bradycardia   This is a slowing down of the heart rate. Usually the baby recovers if he is gently stimulated by rubbing his skin in the same way that an apneic attack is treated. As with apnea, most often this is caused by an immature nervous system but may be indicative of an underlying condition that may warrant further evaluation.

Anemia   Full-term babies acquire stores of iron that will last them four to six months. Premature babies have not always had the chance to acquire sufficient stores of iron, and because of this can more easily become anemic. Breast milk contains very little iron, but the iron that is there may be better absorbed into the intestinal tract than iron-fortified formulas. Solid foods beginning with cereal are usually started at about three to four months and provide extra iron. Fortunately, preterm babies can be helped by giving supplemental iron. If the anemia is causing problems, a "booster" blood transfusion can be given. Blood banks now always screen blood for HIV and hepatitis.

Jaundice   It is estimated that about 60 percent of full-term babies will become at least mildly jaundiced, and the problem is even more common among premature and small babies. It is not dangerous as long as it is controlled, and it can be treated using phototherapy. Rarely, when levels of bilirubin are dangerously high, an exchange transfusion will be performed where a portion of the baby's blood is exchanged with an equal amount of normal adult blood.

Patent ductus arteriosus (PDA)   Because prior to birth he is not breathing air into his lungs and the blood does not need to pass through them to become oxygenated, an unborn baby's circulation is different from that after birth. With the first breaths, the circulation pattern changes and a large artery (the ductus), which has enabled most of the blood to circulate without passing through the lungs, closes. However, it is quite common in premature babies for the ductus to fail to close properly so that it remains open or "patent." When this is present, the doctor may tell you that your baby has a heart murmur, meaning the doctor can hear the unusual flow of blood when listening with a stethoscope. Usually the ductus closes on its own without treatment. If not, drugs may be prescribed to help it close. Occasionally, surgery is required.

The Premature Baby's Brain

All parents of sick and premature babies worry about the risk of their child's brain being damaged. The brain tissue is made up of two halves or hemispheres, in the middle of which are ventricles, which are spaces normally filled with a clear, watery fluid (cerebrospinal fluid or CSF). Because a premature baby's brain is soft and the tissues fragile, it is easy for the small blood vessels lining the ventricles to leak and for a small amount of blood to enter the ventricles, resulting in an intraventricular hemorrhage or IVH. Very often the amount is tiny and the tissues heal naturally, but occasionally it can be more serious, extending into the brain tissue, which carries a higher risk for residual damage. In each case your pediatrician will always discuss your baby's condition and what it may mean for his development.

Many units use ultrasound scans routinely to check the baby's brain growth and to see if there is any excess fluid in the ventricles or signs of bleeding. Sometimes a special type of X ray called a CT (computerized axial tomography) or MRI (magnetic resonance imaging) scan can be used as well.

Seizures may occur in newborn babies, even if they are full-term, and can be due to biochemical imbalances such as hypoglycemia (low blood sugar) or hypocalcemia (calcium deficiency) as well as more serious reasons, such as infection or intraventricular hemorrhage. Although seizures alarm and upset parents, it is important to remember that they do happen more often with ill or premature babies and in many cases do not result in permanent damage. Your pediatrician will examine your baby carefully and carry out tests to try to find a cause.

Twins—and More

Twins are a common sight in neonatal intensive- and transitional-care units because the size the uterus has to stretch to to accommodate two babies makes

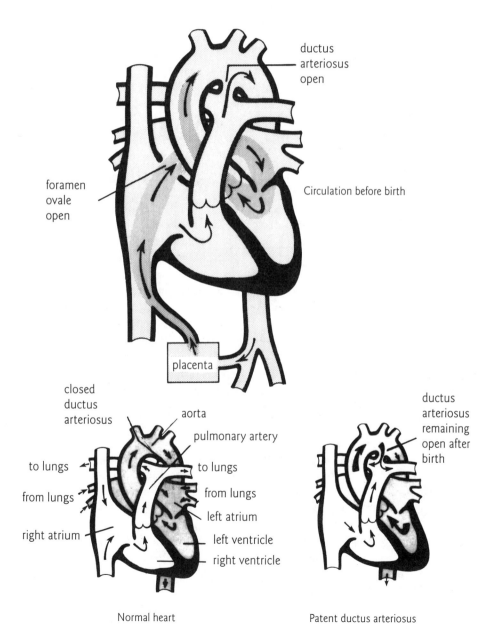

ductus arteriosus open

foramen ovale open

Circulation before birth

placenta

closed ductus arteriosus

aorta

pulmonary artery

to lungs

to lungs

from lungs

from lungs

right atrium

left atrium

left ventricle

right ventricle

Normal heart

ductus arteriosus remaining open after birth

Patent ductus arteriosus

premature birth or low birth weight more likely. As a rule, the greater the number of babies, the more premature the birth is likely to be, so triplets and the far rarer cases of quadruplets or quintuplets are certain to need some degree of special care. The same rule applies to the size of the babies. Twins and triplets are usually smaller than single babies. One twin or triplet may be smaller and weaker, and the difference can sometimes be so great that one baby may need intensive care while the other scarcely needs extra attention at all. Usually the difference in size evens out, though very small-for-date babies can remain smaller into adult life. If possible, both twins may be able to remain in the hospital until they can go home together, but if one baby has to stay for a long time, this will not always be feasible.

All the difficulties already described apply in the same way if the babies are small or premature, but an additional problem is that blood can sometimes have crossed the placenta to pass between twins or triplets so that one may be anemic (too few red blood cells) and very pale, while the other is polycythemic (too many red blood cells) and a dark red color. Fortunately this is treatable, and your pediatrician will explain how if this has happened to your babies.

The Future for Special-Care Babies

Development
Your baby's age will always be taken from the day he was born, but his growth and development for the first year or two will usually match more closely the age he would be had he been born at term. It is important to bear this in mind when it comes to the milestones of development—sitting, crawling, walking, and talking. Parents of premature babies often fear that their child may have been damaged, despite reassurances from doctors, and can feel particularly anxious when their child fails to do things at the "right" age. If they make allowances for the baby's prematurity they will usually find that their child is developing quite normally. The differences between the baby's true developmental and calendar (chronological) age will be most marked in the first two or three years, but obviously all children are different. When it comes to starting school, your child will usually begin at about his fifth birthday; by this time most premature babies are right in line with their peers developmentally.

The hospital may continue to ask you to come back for further checks for some time. This is routine in most cases as part of their follow-up care. Some premature babies can suffer a degree of nearsightedness or a squint, slight clumsiness, smaller stature, slight deafness, and slower development. These are in the minority, and such problems will not impair the child's quality of life. But some handicaps, such as visual difficulties, need treatment to remedy the problem, and hospital specialists who know what to look for are in the best position to do this. In addition, your baby should continue to receive routine developmental and health checkups with his pediatrician, who should be working in concert with the follow-up neonatal program in providing the primary and any specialized care your child may need. Always mention your child's start in life to the doctor or health care visitor making any assessment.

Immunizations

Premature babies should be fully immunized in the usual way, starting with the hepatitis vaccine soon after birth or just prior to initial discharge, whatever their gestation. At two months of age, they should be immunized with diphtheria, tetanus, and acellular pertussis (DTaP), polio, and hemophilus influenza Type B (HiB) vaccines. Almost all can be immunized against whooping cough (pertussis), as there are still frequent cases of whooping cough. This protection should not be withheld, especially now that the risk of side effects is so low using the new acellular pertussis vaccine. If you have any doubts about this, discuss it with your doctor. The remainder of the immunizations should be given in the same way as for full-term infants. In preparation for the fall and winter flu season, anyone caring for a preterm infant as well as older siblings should be encouraged to be vaccinated against influenza by getting a flu shot. If your child is over six months of age and continues to experience breathing problems related to his BPD, he should also receive a flu shot. A baby who has been in special care may be slightly more likely to develop infections than a healthy, full-term baby and so it is wise to keep him away from anyone with an obvious infection. It is important, though, that your other children play with and get to know their new baby brother or sister. They should be encouraged to hold him and participate in his care as appropriate for age as much as possible, but good hygiene, especially hand-washing, should be emphasized.

Infants who have had respiratory problems at birth are susceptible to respiratory infections caused by the respiratory syncitial virus (RSV). A new vaccine is available to protect them and should be given monthly, November through March.

Parents' Reactions to Premature Birth

Giving birth weeks or months before you expected to, producing a baby who may weigh only a quarter of what he should and who needs all the paraphernalia associated with highly technical medical care to survive, is a huge shock. Every parent's story will be different, but it may help to recognize how common some reactions are. Often there is an overwhelming sense of loss—perhaps because they feel one of the most important events in their lives, something they have planned and looked forward to, has "gone wrong." Parents may also feel a sense of loss because the baby looks so very different from the one they imagined. The disappointment continues with the realization of what lies ahead. Instead of the triumphant return home with their baby, mothers very often have to leave the hospital alone. Their isolation is increased because their life as parents with a baby only seems to exist within the hospital. Neighbors and friends cannot share the experience or see them in their new role. Anger is another common reaction—with the baby, with themselves or with the hospital. Again, there is the sense of being cheated out of their expectations.

Leaving the baby in the hospital when you go home is one of the hardest times—anger may turn to depression and a sense of unreality. Try to regard this time as an opportunity to rest and get yourself fit so you will be better able to look after your baby when he does come home. Women often feel it is their fault that their baby was born too early or too small. They may feel they have disappointed their partners, parents, or put an extra burden on their other children by having a baby who needs so much more of their time and attention and takes them away from home for so long. This guilt can surface strongly at later times in their baby's life if he encounters setbacks, even though these may be quite unrelated to his start in life.

Putting these feelings into words does help, so try talking to unit staff and other parents. Many units have specially trained parent counselors and social workers. In all cases it is very important for couples to talk to each other about how they feel. Parents may also worry that their child will survive but be seriously handicapped mentally or physically. For fear of sounding callous and selfish, they feel frightened to say that, in their case, they would rather he or she did not survive. You need to be allowed to talk about these concerns and get help to understand exactly what it would mean if it seems likely that your child will have some disability. Where there is a possibility of serious handicap, doctors will counsel parents as honestly as they can. Medical staff will not take part in euthanasia, but it is important that they know parents' feelings when making decisions about treatment of very sick babies. Always discuss such anxieties with your doctor, nurses, or social worker. When mothers cannot touch and hold their babies freely, they often feel jealous to see nurses so apparently in control. Moreover, parents can get along better with some members of the unit staff than with others. It helps to remember that caring for such tiny babies who require intensive care carries with it a high-pressured responsibility. Having parents so close to the staff increases the tension. Trust is needed on both sides, and this is best arrived at by talking.

It might seem that the time when your baby finally does come home should be one of the happiest, after all the strain of seeing him ill and in the hospital. Yet, surprisingly, mothers can frequently find this a very difficult period. They may feel low, depressed, weepy, lethargic, and have difficulty picking up the threads of life again. Generally, the drama and the crisis of the birth, followed by weeks of uncertainty, have kept them going. Back home there is a chance for all the feelings they have kept at bay to flood in on them. Partners and other relatives can sometimes find this hard to understand, and their impatience and even lack of understanding can make things worse. It may help to know that this is a very common reaction. Don't forget that mothers of first babies often find it hard to adjust to life with a child anyway. Take things slowly and don't expect to transition immediately into a different way of life without any hitches. Understandably, parents who have seen their babies needing expert care to survive will feel even more uncertain of their abilities to look after their baby at home than the parents of normal babies, but remember that all new parents feel nervous and uncertain in the early days. Some hospitals try to arrange for parents to come in and stay a night or two prior to discharge with the baby in a special room on or close to the unit or at the bedside with the nursing staff's and physicians' support close by, if needed. If possible, arrange for your partner to take time off so you can both share your baby's first days at home.

When you leave the hospital you may be given medicines and some vitamins in the form of drops or syrup. Premature babies are sometimes prescribed iron as well if they are anemic. Although each bottle will be carefully labeled, it is a good idea to have these medications and doses of each written down on a separate piece of paper so you can inform other doctors if necessary. The hospital will tell you how to give them, but it helps to make a chart of exactly what has to be given and when and check off each dose through the day. Giving tiny babies a number of exact doses by spoon can be surprisingly hard, but often you can get a plastic medicine measure or syringe from the hospital or pharmacy to improve your accuracy and ease of administration. When you first come home, you may find your baby needs to be fed every three hours or so—or even more frequently—because he cannot take as much milk at each feeding as larger babies can. Usually he will also need night-time feedings for some weeks after coming home. Soon he will be able to take larger feedings and need to be fed less often. He will be ready to begin solid foods about four months from the date when he was due to be born. Some babies are ready for solid foods much earlier than others, and you will soon realize when he is not satisfied with milk alone. Your pediatrician will advise you at this time.

Babies Who May Not Live

Parents can often be frightened to allow themselves to love their premature or sick baby because they are afraid he will not live. By withdrawing from him in anticipation of the death, they feel they will lessen the pain of losing him when it actually happens. Sometimes they have an almost superstitious feeling that if they invest their love in him, it will be tempting Fate. For these reasons they may be reluctant to see, to touch, or to allow themselves to feel close to their baby. Women may also feel very ambivalent about deciding to express milk—dreading to build up a supply of milk that will be such a real reminder of their loss if the baby does not live. Experience has shown that holding back from loving a baby does not help to make his death any easier to accept. It used to be thought that playing down the loss of a baby could help to minimize the distress of parents, but we now know that doing this can deny parents the road to recovery—the opportunity to grieve. The process of mourning and grieving the loss of a child or someone close to us is very necessary, as anyone who has already experienced the death of a loved friend or relative will know. It is easier for parents to grieve for a baby they have known and loved, however short his life, than for a baby they never knew or tried to deny. There can be consolation in knowing you are giving your baby everything and that he died surrounded by love. Suppressing that love can often lead to guilt later. Inevitably, some babies whose chance of life seemed very slim do, in fact, survive. If the parents have already withdrawn in anticipation of the baby's death, this can make it hard for them to reverse those feelings and to form a loving relationship with their child later.

Despite enormous increases in our knowledge and skill, some babies are still destined to live for only a short time. Some are simply born too soon to allow them to survive outside their mother. Occasionally a baby may be born prematurely because his body or brain has not developed normally and, as a result, he may be unable to live the usual length of time. In a few cases, babies born after a very difficult pregnancy, labor, or delivery have suffered so much that they are unable to survive. Sometimes a baby is born with damage to his brain or body, and the severity of this is not immediately obvious. In all these cases the baby may remain alive only with the aid of machines. When it becomes clear to everyone—the parents, doctors, and nurses—that he will not survive without their aid, you may all agree that the help of the machines should be withdrawn. Often, for the first time in his short life, the baby can then be held and cared for by those who love him, without all the tubes and drips and monitors. Try to involve as many family members as you can. Many parents like to have a photograph taken of their baby at this point.

The death of a baby has a profound effect on all those who cared for him. This is a time when parents need help from many different people—from each other, their family and friends, hospital staff, religious leaders, and sometimes from others who have suffered similarly. Baptism or christening can usually be arranged if parents wish. Each of us reacts differently, and some people find that they behave completely unlike their normal selves. It takes a long time to recover, you will never forget your baby, and no matter how many other children you may have afterward, this baby will always be entitled to a very special place in your heart.

The funeral arrangements have to be made. Often there is a special member of the hospital staff who helps parents prepare for the baby's funeral. If the baby's body is to be cremated, this can also be arranged. Help can also be given with any other problems and queries. The family doctor will be informed of the baby's death, and parents are often helped by discussing it with her as well as with hospital doctors who were more intimately involved with his care. In many hospitals it is usual to ask if the baby's body may be examined after death (an autopsy) to determine the exact cause of death and to help other babies with similar problems. The decision to proceed or not is totally voluntary and should be made without any regrets. Often the results of an autopsy can help explain the reason the child experienced such an untimely death. Usually parents are asked to come back some weeks later, when all the results of the examination are available. At this time parents often ask many questions because they have had some time to think about what has happened. These questions are answered as accurately as possible.

The loss of a child, no matter how premature or small, is such a major event that in years to come you must expect to feel the pain more acutely on anniversary dates or at about the same time of year. It is important to realize that this is not abnormal, but part of the very human process of mourning.

Crib Death (Sudden Infant Death Syndrome)

This is the term given to the sudden and unexpected death of a baby that is not linked to any clear-cut cause, such as premature birth. Babies involved are almost always aged between one month and a year, with the highest incidence between three and six months.

Most typically the baby is found dead at home either first thing in the morning or after a period, often very brief, of being left alone in his crib or carriage. "Near-miss" crib deaths, when someone notices a baby has stopped breathing and resuscitates him by picking him up or shaking him, also happen. In such instances parents should take the baby to an emergency department or contact their physician immediately.

Doctors do not understand why babies die like this, but it is thought that the baby stops breathing as a result of a wide range of different infective, circulatory, biochemical, and immunological abnormalities. In about a third of cases there is a story of mild respiratory symptoms—runny nose or slight cough, perhaps—in the previous two to three days.

Most recent research shows that babies should be put to sleep on their back or side, definitely not on their belly. Smoking during pregnancy and after increases the risk of crib death. It is best if no one smokes in the house, and you should try not to take your baby into smoky places. Babies should not be allowed to get too hot or too cold. Indoors, babies do not need more clothes than their parents, although they do need protection from drafts and need adequate clothing to keep them warm without sweating. If your baby is ill he may need fewer clothes (see "Elevated Temperature and Fever" in chapter 17), and if he is sleeping a lot, it is a good idea to wake him regularly for a drink to avoid dehydration and to check how he is feeling. If you are worried, contact your doctor. For more on when to consult your doctor, see "Doctors" in chapter 16.

The shock to parents whose baby dies suddenly and inexplicably is obviously profound. They should be given the opportunity to see and hold their baby after death has been confirmed, and they will need support to deal with the necessary official inquiries and funeral arrangements. Afterward, unequivocal strong support from their pediatrician is very important. The pediatrician should provide a full explanation of the condition and some idea of possible causes. Parents at first tend to experience disbelief followed by deep grief. Some feel guilt that they were not present when their baby died, as though their absence was some kind of neglect. Many feel angry and direct their anger at each other, at professionals who had previously seen the child, or even at other children they may have. Friends and relatives need to allow the parents to talk, and in many cases parents may need further counseling or psychiatric help.

All parents fear a crib death, and parents who have already lost a child in this way will be acutely anxious. There has been considerable debate about the value of home apnea monitors, which sound if the baby stops breathing. See "A Bed for the Baby" in chapter 8 for more on this. The Sudden Infant Death Foundation has a help line and an excellent supply of informational leaflets (see the address section at the back of this book).

CHAPTER 6

Feeding Your Baby

The big decision—breast or bottle?
Facts about breast- and bottle-feeding
If you are not able to breast-feed
If you do not want to breast-feed
Breasts and breast-feeding • Expressing and storing milk
Going back to work • Breast-feeding problems for mothers
Giving up breast-feeding • Breast-feeding problems for babies
Bottles and bottle-feeding • Vitamin supplements
Feeding second and subsequent babies
Problems with early feeding • Weaning from the breast
Eating out • Food intolerance

Many emotions are bound up in preparing and giving food. Eating is not simply about taking in enough fuel for your body to work. In the beginning, sucking milk is a source of great pleasure for a new baby, and feeding the baby is also a source of much satisfaction and enjoyment for a mother. Later, taking trouble to give a child or an adult what we think is something nice to eat is a way of showing love and affection, even if it is only a favorite sandwich. The flip side of the coin is that if that food is rejected, whatever the age of your baby or child, it can feel like a very personal rejection for the giver. It is not surprising that most new parents worry about the way their baby or child is eating, nor is it surprising that later in life mealtimes are so often the setting for family battles!

The best advice is for you to relax and enjoy feeding your baby in a way that gives you both the greatest pleasure—and later, as she grows into a toddler with the whole wide world to explore, don't take offense when the food you offer fails to hold the same fascination for her. By then, both of you will have discovered a whole host of other ways of showing and sharing your love together.

The Big Decision—
Breast or Bottle?

At some stage early in your pregnancy you will be asked how you plan to feed your baby. The best food for babies to start life with is breast milk. It is perfectly designed to meet their every need, and it has unique properties that can never be copied in a formula. The act of breast-feeding itself also helps form a close, emotional bond between baby and mother. But, despite that, it is hard to approach the subject with an open mind and objectively weigh the pros and cons of breast- versus bottle-feeding before making a decision. Your ideas on the subject have probably begun to take shape much earlier in your life, and by the time you get to be a mother, your attitude is likely to be deep-rooted. How you and your brothers and sisters were fed, what your partner thinks about breast-feeding, how your friends feed their babies, and how you feel about your body are factors that may be more likely to draw you toward either breast- or bottle-feeding than the basic facts.

When it comes to weighing the nutritional and emotional advantages of breast- or bottle-feeding, breast-feeding is far preferable. It is right, therefore, to state the case for breast-feeding and to encourage it, except in those few circumstances when it is not medically indicated. However, in the end, each mother must choose what is right for *her*. A woman who dislikes the idea of breast-feeding but is persuaded into it against her real feelings, or who forces herself to breast-feed out of a sense of guilt, will not necessarily be doing the best thing for her baby. Most important of all is that you should feel relaxed and able to enjoy your new baby in a way that suits you best. As long as you take care that feeding is always a time for quiet closeness and for comfort between you both, you will be doing the best whether you are breast- or bottle-feeding.

The Differences Between Breast Milk and Cow's Milk

Breast milk is made of these components:

- *Water* in just the right amount to satisfy your baby's thirst, so breast-fed babies do not need extra fluids.

- *Protein* for body-building, again in just the right amount and in a form most readily absorbed. Colostrum and early milk have higher levels of protein and so does the milk of mothers of premature babies (see chapter 5 for more information on breast-feeding a premature baby). The protein is quickly digested and is vital for a baby's growth.

- *Fat* for energy and growth. Breast milk contains more fat than cow's milk, yet is more easily and completely absorbed by babies. This is one of many reasons why breast-fed babies have different stools from bottle-fed babies (yellow or mustard color, loose, and without smell): they are not excreting any wasted fats. There is a higher concentration of essential fatty acids in breast milk, and it has been suggested that these special kinds of unsaturated fats may be important for the growth of the baby's brain and nervous system.

- *Carbohydrates* in the form of lactose or milk sugar are an extremely important source of energy. Breast milk naturally contains more than cow's milk.

- *Vitamins and minerals*, which are essential in the right amounts for your baby's health and development. As long as you eat an adequate diet that includes sufficient calories, water, and some fruits and vegetables, your milk will contain just about all your baby's vitamin and mineral requirements.

- *Protection from infection*, in the form of antibodies and iron-binding protein, which make the baby's intestines far less vulnerable to bacteria and also give protection against a number of serious illnesses. Gastroenteritis (stomach virus, with diarrhea and/or vomiting) is unusual in breast-fed babies.

Cow's milk is made of these components:

- *Everything for a healthy calf*, but it has to be changed in several ways before it can safely be given to babies under six months old. The same applies to goat's milk and sheep's milk, which are even less suitable for babies.

- *Water* content, which cannot change to suit the baby in the way breast milk can.

- *Protein* levels that are three times higher than in breast milk, are of a different type, and are less digestible. Giving this "foreign" protein to some babies may cause allergic reactions. The protein is diluted to a safe level in formula feeds, but this lowers the calorie content of the feed. Lactose must be added to give extra calories.

- *Fat*, which is far less easily absorbed and again of a different type.

* *Fewer carbohydrates* than in breast milk. Cow's milk has added sugar to make up the same energy value as breast milk. So although natural cow's milk has less lactose, formulas end up containing the same amount as breast milk.

* *Vitamins and minerals,* but not in the right amount for a baby. There are two or three times as much sodium (salt), potassium, calcium, and chloride in cow's milk as in breast milk and six times as much phosphorus—another reason for having to dilute it before it can be used for babies. The iron and zinc in cow's milk is less well absorbed. Some vitamins in cow's milk are destroyed by processing and have to be added again artificially.

* *No protection from infection in the form of antibodies* and other anti-infectious properties. These substances cannot be added artificially.

The Advantages of Breast-Feeding
Breast milk is the perfect food for a baby, with just the right amount of fat, protein, carbohydrates, vitamins, and minerals ready-made, served at just the right temperature and in an ideal container! Here are some of the many advantages: the composition of milk changes as the baby feeds in a way bottle feeds never can; milk at the beginning of a feed, the foremilk, has fewer calories and satisfies thirst; the second part is the hindmilk, which is released with the let-down reflex. It is richer in calories and satisfies her hunger. It is thought that this change may be important in producing a sense of fullness and in controlling appetite. Milk also changes as the baby grows—colostrum and early milk have more protein, and the milk of mothers of premature babies is also known to be different.

* *Protection from infection* is provided by antibodies, macrophages (cells that fight infection), and iron-binding protein, which lines the baby's gut.

* *Protection from allergy.* Families with a history of asthma, eczema, rhinitis, or other allergies are especially advised to breast-feed, as a baby's immature immune system can react to the strong foreign protein in cow's milk by producing allergic symptoms.

* *Less likelihood of obesity,* because breast-fed babies are able to follow the demands of their appetite more easily.

* *Easier digestion.* Breast milk is easier for baby to digest because it is tailor-made for the newborn baby's still immature system. Some breast-fed babies have a dirty diaper after every feed, but it is also common for a totally breast-fed baby to have a bowel movement only once every five or even up to ten days because there is so little waste to excrete.

* *Much greater convenience.* There are no worries about infection, or keeping or carrying milk when traveling. Night feedings are easier because it just means taking the baby into bed and not having to get up to warm bottles. Breast milk is instantly supplied, and there is no tense waiting for milk to warm while the baby screams. It leaves a free hand to cuddle or help another child or even pick

up the phone. The convenience of breast-feeding increases the longer you continue. The most difficult time is during the early weeks, but soon giving a feeding just means sitting down for ten to twenty minutes, and there is no work at the end of the day with bottles to clean and prepare.

- *It provides an instant pacifier,* which can be a boon at awkward moments to calm a young baby who is frightened or upset.

- *Breast-feeding helps you regain your figure* because hormones stimulated in breast-feeding also help contract the uterus to its prepregnancy size and end postnatal discharge more quickly. Full or frequent breast-feeding usually delays the return of periods, a plus if you suffer from premenstrual tension or heavy or painful periods. Weight loss in response to feeding varies—some women lose weight more easily because of feeding, while others do not lose it all until they wean. Nevertheless, stores of fat are laid down in pregnancy for the body to use when making milk, and these can sometimes be harder to shift if you do not breast-feed, especially around the thighs. However, you should not try to diet while breast-feeding.

- *Money saving.* Even though breast-feeding mothers need to eat more—about five hundred to six hundred extra calories a day—the cost of extra food is still less than that of formula, bottles, nipples, and any cleaning supplies.

- *Emotional benefits for mother and baby.* Although this is listed last, it is not because it is the least important factor but because it deserves more detailed consideration. As we have already mentioned, newborn babies need physical love and affection to thrive just as much as clean diapers and warm beds. Being held, cuddled, enjoying the sensation of skin contact and the feel of the human body, comforts and reassures babies so they begin to relax, and to respond to that love. Breast-feeding a baby is the closest physical bond between a mother and her child and combines all the sensations that give babies pleasure. Taking in food is one, but just as important is sucking—a source of great satisfaction and enjoyment to a baby. Breast-fed babies tend to be able to suck for longer and to control how long they continue, and sucking at a warm, responsive nipple is more rewarding than a rubber nipple. Combining feeding, sucking, skin contact, and being held and cuddled adds up to bliss in baby terms! Throughout a feeding there is continual interaction between mother and baby—"emotional feedback" is usually how it is described. The way the baby sucks, moves her hands, arms, and body, and the expression on her face tell the mother what the baby is feeling and needing, and the mother responds. Most women who breast-feed for some time rate this harmony and closeness with their baby as what they enjoyed most. There can also be a physical pleasure for women in breast-feeding, but that is highly individual and varies between just a physical satisfaction at being able to provide milk for the baby and the close contact, through all sorts of reactions to the women who find breast-feeding sexually exciting. Certainly the sexual attitudes of both men and women influence how they regard breast-feeding—some think it is beautiful, some disgusting, and some just a natural bodily function designed for feeding babies. You don't have to be someone who enjoys having her breasts stimulated in love-making to be able to enjoy breast-feeding, and it is quite possible for women who don't like having their nipples caressed at all to be able to enjoy breast-feeding and to do it very successfully.

Facts About Breast- and Bottle-Feeding

- The most difficult part of breast-feeding is usually the beginning. After that it gets easier and easier.

- It may take two weeks to establish breast-feeding and another four weeks for the baby and mother to settle into a pattern—the feeding habits of bottle-fed babies will be just as erratic at first.

- Beginning to sleep through the night depends on the baby, not on whether she is breast- or bottle-fed.

- Mothers who want to breast-feed but run into difficulties should get help from a breast-feeding counselor or lactation consultant who supports breast-feeding and is experienced. Most problems can be overcome or avoided.

- Mothers who switch from breast to bottle because they want to should not have to pretend it was because of problems, but rather congratulate themselves on breast-feeding at the beginning, even if it was only for a few days.

- Caring, sensitive mothers who have to or who want to bottle-feed will have just as close and loving a relationship with their baby as those who breast-feed.

- Similarly, women who have serious problems in becoming a mother and how they feel about their baby will rarely make things right just by forcing themselves to breast-feed. Counseling is advised.

If You Are Not Able to Breast-Feed

There will be some women who cannot breast-feed, either because they are seriously ill, or have to take certain drugs, or have a mentally or physically handicapped baby where breast-feeding is either impossible or very difficult without enormous dedication and support.

There will also be a larger group of women who begin breast-feeding and sadly give up because they run into problems, although many of these problems can be avoided or solved with the right advice and help. Recurrent bouts of infective mastitis or breast abscesses, or babies who, despite all your attempts to build up a supply of milk, fail to gain weight, or even lose weight, may in the end lead to partial or complete bottle-feeding.

Finally, there will be women who feel very strongly that they do not want to try breast-feeding.

If you are in any of these categories, you should not feel you are harming your baby by bottle-feeding. Instead you can be confident in the knowledge that today there are good alternatives that are used to feed babies safely and successfully. In addition, while it is felt that an emotional closeness happens automatically with breast-feeding, it takes only a little thought to foster a rapport between you and your baby during bottle-feeding. Many mothers will do this quite instinctively anyway.

Illness

Serious illness in a mother may make breast-feeding impossible or undesirable. If you are ill and cannot breast-feed, but want to try once you have recovered, you will still be able to produce milk, despite the delay, by putting the baby to the breast as frequently as possible. In general, the longer the interval after the birth, the longer it can take to build up a supply of milk, and if it is several weeks you may never have enough to breast-feed fully. Nevertheless, your baby can still benefit from your milk and you can enjoy the closeness of breast-feeding. If she won't suck at the breast because she has become used to a bottle, seek advice from your pediatrician or a breast-feeding counselor. He may suggest using a feeding supplementer. There are two types available, the Lact-Aid and the Supplemental Nurser System (SNS, Medela, Inc.). The Lact-Aid is a bag, and the SNS is a plastic flask. Both contain formula and hang around your neck, with a tube from the container taped so that the tip ends at the end of your nipple. The baby latches onto both the nipple and the tubing, and receives milk from both the breast and the container. Thus she stimulates the breast, gets used to sucking at the nipple, and has an assured intake at the same time. As your milk comes in, you can gradually reduce the amount of formula. It is best to do this under supervision. Alternatively, you can use a breast pump to express your milk and stimulate your milk supply after the feeding. Use the expressed milk for your baby at another feeding time—it should be stored in a sterilized bottle or container (plastic bag inserts for nurser bottles work well) and can be kept in the refrigerator for twenty-four hours or frozen for two to three months.

Drugs

Drugs (both prescription and over-the-counter) a mother takes are probably always excreted to some extent in breast milk, although in many cases the amounts are so minute they have no effect. As a general rule, breast-feeding mothers should try to avoid taking any drugs at all, but if you need them, always ask your caregiver whether they are safe for breastfeeding.

Premature or Sick Babies

These babies may not be able to suck initially, but you can express milk to be frozen or fed to them through a tube until they are strong enough to feed (see chapter 5). The unique benefits of breast milk are especially important for these vulnerable infants.

Babies with Disabilities

These babies present two kinds of problems regarding breast-feeding. The first is the tremendous shock parents feel when they discover their baby has problems, and the complicated emotions they may experience. Breast-feeding represents a long-term commitment that initially they may feel unable to cope with. The second set of problems are of a practical nature. Mentally handicapped babies have poor sucking reflexes and may be drowsy, and it needs dedication from the mother and good support and advice to breast-feed. Physically handicapped babies who are not brain-damaged can normally suck well enough to breast-feed, but treatment that may entail operations and possibly splints, casting, or traction will mean breaks in breast-feeding when you have to express milk and then feed the baby, who may not be able to be picked up or handled. Mothers have and do manage to breast-feed babies in such circumstances, and it is obviously a source of great comfort to a baby who has to undergo treatment. Your pediatrician should outline exactly what the treatment entails to help you decide. Also, seek out good support, advice, and encouragement whatever you decide.

Abnormalities of the mouth will sometimes make feeding difficult, although a straightforward cleft lip should not produce any problems. When a large area of the roof of the mouth is unformed, the baby may be fed expressed breast milk or formula from a spoon or special nipple. But even though cleft lips and cleft palates can be successfully repaired, the trauma of giving birth to a child with this problem can be quite as great for parents as in cases of more severe problems.

Failure to Thrive
There will be some babies who do not gain weight, or even begin to lose weight despite your best efforts, including extra breast feedings and techniques to increase the supply of breast milk. In this case you'll have to either supplement with formula, or switch over entirely. For more on changing from breast- to bottle-feeding see "Giving Up Breast-Feeding" later in this chapter.

Continual Problems
If a woman has continual problems with breast-feeding such as abscesses, repeated cracked nipples, or mastitis, these may be related to the breast-feeding technique, so ask your pediatrician or a breast-feeding counselor for advice. On rare occasions it may be necessary or preferable to switch to bottles.

If You Do Not Want to Breast-Feed

I dutifully breast-fed my daughter for six months. I hated every minute. I only did it because all my friends did and I was terrified of being branded a bad mother. In fact I had real problems about becoming a mother and couldn't cuddle or show affection to my daughter at all. Thankfully, with professional help, that is now solved, but I was desperately embarrassed about feeding and no one except my parents or my husband ever saw me do it. I couldn't even feed my baby at a mother-infant play group when everyone else was feeding her baby.

Women who do not want to breast-feed will make this decision for a variety of reasons. What your partner, friends, and family think about breast-feeding is certainly going to influence your decision. You may plan to return to work soon after the birth of the baby and leave her in the care of a baby-sitter, mother's helper or nanny, or in a day-care center. You may wish to share the feeding of the baby with your partner. You may not like the idea of being tied so closely to the baby, even in the early weeks. If you have had successive pregnancies very close together, you may feel weary after a period of nothing but pregnancy and breast-feeding and be anxious for your body to get back to normal and belong to you exclusively again. Women with uncertain or unhappy partnerships can feel apprehensive at being tied down and more vulnerable. Some women will feel repelled by the idea of breast-feeding, while others are open-minded about the physical act but very worried about the potential embarrassment of having to feed a baby in public. In fact this is, in practice, much less of a problem than many women imagine. Stores, restaurants, and other public places nearly always have a room you can use, and dressing in loose separates with a large scarf, jacket, or cardigan around your shoulders means you can feed a baby in a quiet corner without anyone noticing. Legislation has now been passed in many states that protects a mother's right to breast-feed her baby in public, as long as it is done discreetly.

If you feel repelled by the idea of breast-feeding, you may find it helpful to talk over these feelings during pregnancy with your partner, a sympathetic breast-feeding counselor, or doctor you can trust who can help you understand why you feel so strongly while at the same time supporting you if your decision is to bottle-feed.

Breasts and Breast-Feeding

The Breast

The breast is made up of fifteen to twenty segments—imagine an orange cut in half. The cells that make the milk are called alveoli, lie at the back of the segments, and have ducts leading down to the nipple. Just before the ducts open onto the nipple they enlarge slightly to form a reservoir. These reservoirs are at the point where the normal skin of the breast darkens into the pigmented ring around the nipple, the areola. Small glands in the areola called "Montgomery's tubercles" produce a fluid that keeps the skin of the nipples and the areola soft and supple. The nipple has not just one opening, but several, which vary in number according to the number of segments and ducts of the breast. The size of the breast does not dictate its ability to produce milk—small ones can be just as efficient as large ones.

During pregnancy breasts become much larger as they prepare to make milk because of an increase in the milk-producing cells and ducts and a greater blood supply, but they do not actually begin to make milk until they are stimulated by a complex hormone response after birth.

Colostrum is the creamy, yellowish substance that is made before the breasts begin to manufacture mature milk. Unlike milk, this is made during pregnancy, and from about the fifth month onward until the end of pregnancy may leak from the nipple a little—it is not significant whether this does or does not happen. Giving your baby colostrum at the start of her life is important. Even if you do nothing more than breast-feed for those first two or three days you will still have given her

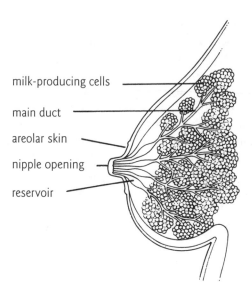

milk-producing cells

main duct

areolar skin

nipple opening

reservoir

something valuable that cannot be artificially reproduced. Colostrum is uniquely designed for the transition your baby makes from placental feeding, when the nourishment she needs is carried in the blood supply through the umbilical cord, to digesting food herself. Colostrum is lower in sugar and fat than mature milk, so it is easier for a baby's immature digestive system to cope with as it gently begins working. It also contains more protein than mature milk and has higher levels of antibodies. These protect the baby from bacterial infection, which is perhaps the most valuable role of colostrum. It will also give protection from illnesses the mother has had or has been immunized against. Colostrum goes on being produced for about ten days after the birth, but after about three days it begins to be mixed with mature milk, which makes the milk seem creamier. Once the colostrum stops, breast milk on its own seems thinner and watery, but do not think your own milk has become "poorer," because this is its natural consistency.

Mature milk is usually present in the breast at about the third day after the birth. Although the breasts have been ready to make milk since about the middle of pregnancy, it is the birth itself that acts as the trigger to milk production. This happens whether you plan to breast-feed or not. A drop in the hormones progesterone and estrogen causes more of the main hormone controlling milk supply to be produced. This hormone is called prolactin. Prolactin starts the milk-producing cells working, although it takes a couple of days for the first milk to appear. This mechanism also operates in the case of miscarriage or stillbirth, because your body has no way of knowing there is no baby to feed, and can be very distressing, especially if a woman is not warned in advance. In the case of a live birth, it is the baby sucking at the breast that stimulates more prolactin and so stimulates more milk for the next feeding.

Breast milk changes during a feeding, from day to day, and as the baby grows. Your health, what you eat and drink, and even your feelings can also change the composition and quantity of milk. As mentioned, early colostrum and milk are higher in protein and antibodies than mature milk, but we still do not know all the ingredients of breast milk nor exactly how the composition changes as the baby grows.

Suckling after delivery has been shown to be a key factor in successful breast-feeding. Women who are able to put their baby to the breast within twelve hours of the birth and, even better, within four hours or as close to delivery as possible, are more likely to be able to breast-feed successfully and to continue longer. But if for some reason you cannot do this, it does not mean you won't be able to breast-feed. The emotional and physical aspects of suckling after the birth are closely inter-woven, since milk production and the release of the milk are governed by hor-mones that are, in turn, affected by our emotions. The baby's suckling stimulates the nerve endings in the nipple. This sends messages to the brain to produce the hormones oxytocin and prolactin. These hormones make the uterus contract to its normal size and get the milk-making cells in the breast working.

Supply and demand is the basic principle of successful breast-feeding. The more the baby sucks at the breast, the more milk the breast makes. In the beginning there may be too much milk and the baby's pattern of feeding will be erratic, but after two or three weeks this will settle down, and as the baby grows, your body will be able to accommodate her needs by making just the right amount of milk, pro-vided you let her nurse whenever she is hungry.

Putting Baby to Breast

> I think men might imagine it's a natural instinct and you know exactly what to do. In fact I felt rather self-conscious and hadn't a clue how to get the baby latched on. I was deeply grateful for a very helpful nurse who sat down and showed me exactly how. I was absolutely thrilled when my baby actually latched on and sucked. At first I still couldn't believe I was a mother and now here was this enormous, perfect baby, doing just what babies are supposed to do!

If you can sit up, make yourself comfortable with pillows and hold the baby so her head is level with your breast; you can put pillows under her as well to support her weight. If you can't sit up you can still nurse lying down and slightly turned to the side with the baby on the bed beside you (if you had a cesarean section, see "Breast-Feeding Problems for Mothers" later in this chapter). To help the baby suck prop-erly without making you sore, put the whole nipple and part of the areola into her mouth with her tongue underneath so that the pressure of her jaws as she sucks is on the areola, not the nipple itself. The baby's father or a nurse can support the baby's head close to your breast and gently guide her into the right position. Touch your nipple against her bottom lip and wait for her to open her mouth wide. At this point bring her head in close so that she takes the nipple fully deep into her mouth. If she is latched on properly, the tops of her ears will likely wiggle slightly as she sucks. If this does not happen, and if you can see her cheeks going in and out as she sucks, or it hurts, put the tip of your little finger gently into the corner of her mouth

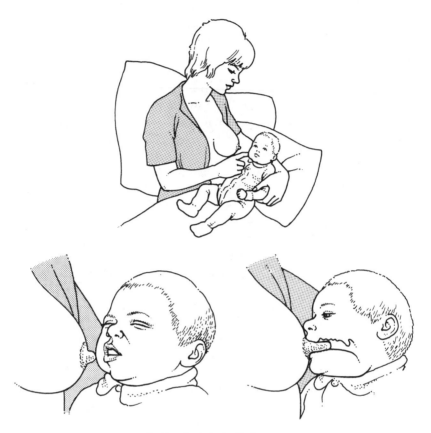

Putting the baby to the breast

to break the suction and try again. Make sure when you are feeding your baby that she is able to breathe clearly through her nose. If you support your breast from underneath with the flat of your free hand against your ribs, this will direct your nipple and breast upward into an easy feeding position for her.

A few doctors may still recommend starting with one to two minutes at each side and building up, but breast-feeding specialists now think this is not long enough to stimulate the let-down reflex. Instead they suggest following your and your baby's preferences from the start. A rough guide is that a feeding takes about twenty minutes, approximately ten minutes each side, although as a baby gets older and sucks more efficiently, she may take less time. You can tell when your baby begins to suck less vigorously and lose interest that it is time to switch her to the other breast. Babies are individuals and feed at different rates, and your body responds differently, too, but if each feeding is taking much longer, it is pretty certain that your baby is just enjoying comfort sucking rather than feeding.

Taking Baby off the Breast

Doing this the right way is just as important as fixing her on properly. Always break the suction first before withdrawing the nipple by sliding a fingertip into the corner of her mouth—do not drag the nipple from her mouth while she is still sucking, as this can cause soreness.

Babies Who Will Not Suck

A baby who will not suck may simply need a little time and patience to get the idea. Loosen any wrappings while still keeping her warm and enjoy stroking her limbs, talking to her and generally discovering the delights of your new baby. Usually babies have a very alert, aware period immediately after the birth, and they have a lot of new sensations to take in. Try her at the breast again when you feel like it, and try to be relaxed. If you have been expressing colostrum, you can try putting a drop on her lips. If she seems very sleepy, let her sleep, and try her again when she next wakes. If you had narcotics close to the time of delivery it can make your baby drowsy, too, and you may have to wait for the effects to wear off. Babies who are jaundiced are also sometimes slow to suck and fall asleep during feedings. Premature babies may not have had time to develop the sucking reflex of babies born at full term. Babies who have swallowed a lot of mucus during the birth may also be reluctant to feed. They may vomit, which will make them feel better; sometimes suctioning with a nasal bulb syringe can help them to bring up the mucus. In any case, do not let your newborn sleep more than 3 hours between feedings, or she may not get enough. This can lead to low blood sugar levels and/or dehydration.

The pediatrician who gives your baby a full examination, usually the day after the birth, will ask about feeding, so seek advice about any problems.

Uterine Cramping

This is caused by the womb contracting back to its prepregnancy size; it often happens during breast-feeding because this stimulates the hormone oxytocin, which, in turn, causes the contractions. If it is very severe in the first days, take a painkiller half an hour before feeding.

Which Side First?

Start on the breast you finished with at the last feed so that each side gets equal stimulation from your baby's stronger sucking at the beginning of a feed. When you change breasts sit your baby upright, supporting her with a hand behind her neck and thumb under her chin, and gently rub her back with your free hand to encourage her to burp. A cloth diaper is a good precaution, as babies often bring up a little milk when they burp because the muscle that closes off the stomach is not yet very strong. If your baby does not burp, do not spend ages thumping her on the back, but continue feeding. Breast-fed babies do not swallow as much air as bottle-fed babies and may not need to burp after every feeding.

Feed Your Baby Whenever She Seems Interested

If she wants to suck, you can be sure you are doing the right thing. She may wake and cry or just start to root around or make sucking movements with her mouth—you will quickly recognize the signs. At times this may be only half an hour after you last fed her, while at other times she may sleep deeply for much longer. Feed your baby whenever she wakes and seems like she could suck. Do not wait for her to cry—this is a late sign of hunger. Most babies gradually settle to a recognizable routine, and forcing a routine on them will only mean several hours with a miserable, crying baby.

When Your Milk Comes In

This is often the most difficult time because it usually causes some degree of engorgement and may coincide with a particularly emotional, weepy feeling at about the third day. Signs are hard, swollen, hot breasts, with taut, shiny skin and even some fever. "I woke up with two rock-hard, aching boulders where my breasts should be—no one told me it would be like this," is how one mother described it.

Don't worry if you get very engorged because it doesn't last more than twenty-four to forty-eight hours. Later breast-feeding is not at all like this. Engorgement at this stage is caused by a greatly increased supply of blood to the breast. It is thought that frequent suckling from birth can help to minimize this. The remedy is to feed the baby often, to empty the breasts. Apply hot, wet compresses immediately before feedings to relieve pain and soften the breasts. Apply cold compresses or ice packs (bags of frozen peas work well!) to make the blood vessels contract and reduce swelling. Alternatively, try sitting in a warm bath and expressing the milk by hand. Try not to pump or express out more than a small amount, as the goal is to get into balance with the baby's needs. On occasion the engorgement causes the nipple to be pulled flat, making it difficult for the baby to grasp. If this occurs, gently compress and pull out the nipple, or use a pump briefly just before latch-on.

At some point, usually after about six weeks, your breasts will become smaller and softer—this is not a sign that you have no milk, but rather that milk production has now settled down and is being made by the milk-producing cells but not filling the breasts until the baby starts to feed and stimulates the let-down reflex.

The Let-Down Reflex

This is stimulated by the hormone oxytocin and causes muscles to contract, squeezing milk out of the milk-producing cells into the ducts leading to the nipple. In fact the process will have been working before the milk came in, but you probably won't have felt it. Once the milk comes in it is very important because although the baby can get what is called "foremilk," which is present in the ducts of the breast, by sucking, two-thirds of the feed is contained in what is called "hindmilk," which is only released by the let-down. The hindmilk has more fat in it and is therefore much richer in calories, which your baby needs for growing. The sensation of the let-down reflex varies, but is usually described as a brief tingling or slight ache and is always accompanied by a rush of milk. Often, milk begins to leak out of the non-feeding breast, and you can see the rhythm of the baby's jaw action change as she begins to take deep swallows and does not have to suck so hard.

Problems with the let-down reflex are a common cause of babies not gaining weight, and mothers of premature babies with a poor suck may be especially prone to difficulties. Anxiety, tension, and stress can all inhibit the reflex, so the cycle gets worse. Try to relax and don't limit the baby's time at the breast, but continue to nurse frequently. Bathing with hot water and expressing milk by hand can some-times stimulate the let-down. You can also ask your physician for a nasal spray of oxytocin (Syntocinon), which can be used effectively to prompt let-down. Once you've experienced the reflex a few times, the let-down will become easier.

Supplementing with Bottles

Supplementing with bottles can spell the beginning of the end of breast-feeding if you start giving them instead of letting the baby suck at the breast, or are too prompt to offer one as a "topping off" without giving the baby enough time at the breast, because your supply will then decrease further. On the other hand, if the baby won't settle and you feel completely wiped out at the end of a day of appar-ently nonstop breast-feeding, then handing her over to your partner for the occa-sional bottle while you take time off to rest and relax can be a real life-saver. It is also useful to have a baby who will take a bottle if necessary to enable you to leave her sometimes. If you plan to bottle-feed at all at some point, it is wise to introduce a bottle by three to four weeks of age and continue to offer one every two to three days. Otherwise you may be faced with a baby who firmly rejects bottles (and is not yet old enough for a cup) when you are returning to work. If you do not want to introduce formula because of the possibility of allergy, you can express and freeze your own milk for bottle-feedings (see "Expressing and Storing Milk" later in this chapter). Many babies are more accepting of the first bottle if it is given by some-one other than the mother. Some babies accept breast or bottle equally well; others will take only the breast, or get used to bottle-feeding in the hospital and will not switch easily to breast-feeding. "Natural" human nipple-shaped bottle nipples, such as Playtex nurser nipples, are available and have been suggested as more suitable for breast-fed babies when they have only an occasional bottle.

Cutting out supplementary bottles can be done, but you need to be determined and prepared to accept a more unsettled feeding pattern for a few days. Aim to build up your milk supply by putting the baby to the breast often and letting her suck as long as she wants. At the same time, try to get extra rest, take in plenty of fluids, and eat well. Give the bottle after breast-feedings. Decrease the bottle-feed-ing by half an ounce per feed per day until you have dropped all the supplementary feedings. Alternatively, leave out the bottle at the feeding when you have the most milk, usually first thing in the morning. Continue to nurse often during the rest of the day, but two days later, drop the next bottle. Allow a week to make the changeover if you have been giving a follow-up bottle at every feeding. Alternatively, if you have been giving only one or two extra bottle-feeds you can try setting two days aside for nothing but nursing whenever your baby seems hungry and abandon bottles outright—your milk supply will quickly catch up with your baby's demands in about forty-eight hours.

Your Food Requirements When You Are Breast-Feeding

Breast-feeding mothers need extra food and should eat regularly, with nutritious snacks between meals. During pregnancy stores of fat are especially laid down to be used to produce milk, and in the early weeks you also need about five hundred extra calories a day to offset the six hundred or eight hundred calories a day your baby may be taking. Your appetite will usually be the best guide, because breast-feeding invariably makes you hungry as well as thirsty—it's a good idea to have a glass of water or fruit juice on hand while breast-feeding, as some women get an overwhelming thirst then.

Examples of five hundred calories are: a meal of meat, potatoes, and vegetables; a scrambled egg on two slices of toast with butter or margarine plus a serving of bacon; one round of ham, or peanut butter or cheese sandwiches plus a yogurt; a sandwich with a glass of milk. Breast-feeding is often a time when you can get away with the occasional indulgence in a rich dessert, but do not rely too heavily on sugary and fatty foods to provide the extra calories, as they have little nutritional value. As feeding is established, your body uses up fewer extra calories, so you can gradually go back to normal eating, but still beware of going for long periods without food; this will affect your milk supply. Aim for small amounts of nourishing food at regular intervals.

Not Having Enough Milk

This is a common worry among breast-feeding mothers. There are three ways to build up your supply: feed your baby more frequently and let her suck as long as she wants; make sure you are eating and drinking enough through the day; and take things easy so the extra calories can be used to make milk. Lots of skin-to-skin contact with your baby may also help. Usually forty-eight hours on this regime will summon up the necessary extra milk. You could try dedicating a weekend or any two consecutive days to try to boost your milk supply.

Babies often go through growth spurts at times. Some typical ages when this may occur are ten days, three weeks, six weeks, three months, and six months, but this is very variable. During a growth spurt the baby will need more milk and will seem hungry and unsatisfied. Many mothers interpret this as a sign that they are not capable of making enough milk for their growing baby. In fact, your milk supply will readily increase to meet this new need within a day or two *as long as you allow the baby to nurse as often and as long as she wishes*. Giving supplemental formula instead will prevent your breast from getting the stimulation needed to respond to the growth spurt. If your baby is suddenly hungry a couple of hours after a feeding, increase your milk supply in the same way.

When to Seek Advice

Talk to your pediatrician about your baby's feedings if the following signs occur in your baby:

- Has less than six to eight wet diapers in twenty-four hours.

- Has less than three to four stools per day during the first several weeks of life.

- Has long periods of sleeping.

- Does not seem satisfied after feedings.

- Has no weight gain over two weeks. If this is not coupled with other signs it may not be significant; however, it should be investigated.

Expressing and Storing Milk

You may want to express milk to relieve and soften engorged breasts, to provide your baby with a feeding in your absence, or because some problem prevents breast-feeding. If cracked or sore nipples or some other problem is making nursing temporarily impossible, gently expressing by hand or pumping may be necessary for a brief time. You can also talk to a lactation consultant about the temporary use of soft plastic nipple shields. Use these only under guidance and only for a brief period.

Expressing by Hand

Choose a time when you feel relaxed and unhurried, wash your hands, and use a clean (sterilized if you are expressing for a preterm infant) bottle or jar with a non-metal lid to collect the milk. After a bath is sometimes a good occasion for a first try, or you can help the let-down reflex by putting hot compresses on the breast before expressing. Start by stroking the breast with a light fingertip touch from the chest wall toward the nipple, moving all around the breast. Thinking about the baby and relaxing help the milk to be released. The point at which you want to apply pressure is where the milk ducts open out into a wider reservoir, which is usually where the dark skin of the areola merges into ordinary skin. Hold the breast between finger and thumb at this point, using left hand to right breast and vice versa. Squeeze rhythmically inward without letting your finger slide on the skin and without touching the nipple. Move around the breast to empty each of the reservoirs in turn and then switch to the opposite breast to give time for more milk to drain down.

You can also collect a certain amount of milk simply by holding a container to catch the drips, which in the early days may leak from the breast the baby is not nursing from. Some people produce quite a lot when the let-down releases the main bulk of the milk. Usually this leaking tails off as nursing is established. But remember that drip milk is foremilk and therefore low in fat and calories. It is less satisfying when fed alone to your baby, and it is important to remember this if the baby is left for a baby-sitter to feed in your absence.

Expressing milk to relieve engorged breasts needs to be done very gently to avoid bruising skin that is already stretched and tender. If you have problems ask your pediatrician, breast-feeding counselor, or another breast-feeding mother to show you how to express milk. Some people get very adept and use this technique

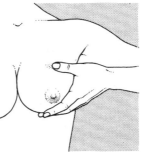

even when having to express full feeds for the baby if they have gone back to work because it saves them from having to carry a pump with them.

Breast Pumps

I didn't like using the pump but it was the only way I could express enough for my baby, who was eight weeks premature. I just used to switch off and imagine it was the baby sucking at the breast. I didn't like it in the beginning, but once I got used to it I could read a magazine and forget what was happening.

Hand Pumps   These can be useful if you *occasionally* express milk for someone else to give your baby. They are not appropriate for working mothers or for mothers of preterm infants. They are inexpensive and readily available in most pharmacies. However, in general, they are tiring to use and far less effective at emptying the breast than battery or electric pumps. Many women find them uncomfortable to use. There are very many different designs on the market. One mother's ideal pump is another one's agony, so look around and take advice from other mothers and breast-feeding counselors. Most pumps tend to be one cylinder inside another, with a funnel shape at the top to fit over the nipple. Drawing out air through the inner cylinder creates a vacuum, which puts pressure on the areola in the way the baby's sucking would. The exact shape and angle of the funnels, the ease with which they are operated, and their ability to come apart to be cleaned vary quite a bit.

Manual pumps that use a bicycle horn-type device are not recommended, as it is impossible to clean the milk out of the rubber horn, and expressed milk can easily become contaminated.

Battery Pumps   These hand-held pumps are available in most large pharmacies and are generally affordable. They use AA batteries, and many also come with an electric adapter (very helpful, as the batteries are drained quickly). They are more comfortable and efficient than manual pumps, but not as good as larger electric pumps. They also do not have the ability to pump both breasts simultaneously ("double pumping"). This makes them most suitable for the at-home mother who wishes to pump occasionally when she is leaving the baby with another caregiver. Most mothers working full-time outside the home will find it difficult to maintain an adequate milk supply using these pumps.

Portable Electric Pumps   These pumps are larger, but still portable. They are available by mail order or in specialty stores. Some lactation consultants may also sell these. They are significantly more expensive than small battery pumps but offer distinct advantages. They generally have the option of double pumping, which helps stimulate greater milk production. The suction oscillates to simulate a baby suckling. They are quite comfortable to use and very efficient at emptying the breasts. These pumps are the best choice for the mother working full-time outside the home, unless she has a hospital-grade pump available at work. The suction strength of these pumps is slightly less than that of hospital-grade pumps. For this reason they are generally not recommended for the mother who is pumping exclusively—that is, not breast-feeding at the breast at all—as they may not be able to stimulate adequate milk production in the absence of breast-feeding.

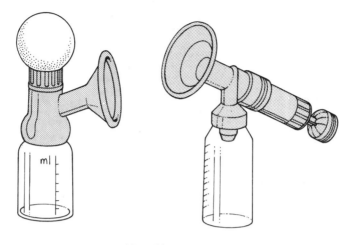

Manual breast pump

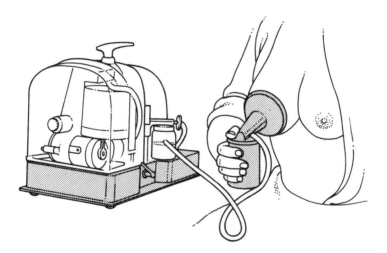

Electric breast pump

Hospital-Grade Electric Pumps   Such pumps are *very* expensive but can be rented from breast-feeding counselors and medical pharmacies and are usually the only effective way of building up and maintaining a supply of milk if your baby is ill or premature and needs to be given expressed milk regularly by tube rather than feeding at the breast (see "The Problems of Babies in Special Care" in chapter 5 for more on this). They are comfortable to use and very effective at emptying the breasts (second only to a baby). A double-pump setup can be used and is recommended. This enables you to empty both breasts simultaneously, cutting pumping time in half. It also stimulates greater milk production. In the beginning, nurses will show you how to use one at the hospital. As with all expressing, it is important to relax. Hot compresses and stroking the breast in the same way as for hand expressing before you start can help the let-down reflex. Like the hand pumps, electric pumps have a funnel or cup that fits over the nipple and areola; the rhythmic suction is provided by the machine. Milk collects in a sterilized bottle.

Containers and all detachable parts of pumps need to be cleaned and sterilized.

Storing Expressed Breast Milk
If it's stored appropriately, breast milk can be kept for:

- Up to twenty-four hours in the refrigerator.
- Up to two weeks in the freezer compartment of an ordinary refrigerator.
- Up to six months in a separate freezer.

Always date milk if you plan to freeze it, and put it in a sterile plastic container every time. Store only 2 to 3 oz in each container to avoid wasting. Label each bag with the amount and date, and use in the order in which they were pumped. Do not thaw frozen milk over direct heat on the stove because it will curdle and be unusable. You can stand the container in a bowl of warm but not boiling water; or hold the container under the tap starting with cold, changing to tepid, and then hot water only as it begins to thaw. Do not allow it to thaw over a longer period at room temperature or leave it standing in the room once it has thawed.

Once thawed, breast milk should be used as soon as possible. Do not keep it for longer than four hours in a refrigerator before using it, and never refreeze milk that has been thawed. Transporting expressed breast milk is best done in a freezer bag, whether you are expressing milk at work to bring home to the baby, or taking a bottle of expressed breast milk to give to a baby while you are out. Keep it as cold as possible by using more than one freezer pack, and observe the storage times as if it were in the refrigerator.

Going Back to Work

Continuing to breast-feed fully or partially once you have gone back to work is perfectly possible if you have the motivation, although it is obviously easier to breast-feed in some jobs than in others. Babies who settle quickly into a feeding pattern can make life easier, but a great deal depends simply on how much you want to do it. Determined mothers will usually plan carefully and make it work for them. Before you go back to work full-time you need to have established a supply of milk, which usually takes about six weeks after the birth. Begin expressing milk and freezing it two to three weeks before you go back, both to build up a store so that you do not begin on day one without any backup, and also to learn the best method of expressing. If you do well expressing by hand, you'll have the advantage of not having to carry, set up, and sterilize a pump. Otherwise, find the pump that works best for you.

It is usually easiest to express at the time when you would normally be feeding the baby. Finding the right place with privacy and enough comfort to express depends on your office. Usually the bathroom is not a good place, though it may sometimes be the only answer. A certain amount depends on having a boss and col-

leagues who do not make you feel bad about disappearing for twenty to thirty minutes occasionally. Take clean screw-top bottles to work (sterilized if you're pumping
for a sick or preterm infant), and if possible store them in a refrigerator afterward. If
not, then use a freezer bag with ice packs. If you work near home it may be possible
to go home at lunchtime or have the baby brought in for one feeding. Make sure
you wear breast pads or easy-access clothes that are loose and dark or patterned so
they will not show if your milk leaks.

To keep up a supply you need to express as often as you would be giving a full
feeding—usually twice during the working day. Let your baby suck as long as she
wants at other times—most babies do tend to take longer over the feedings you give
to make up sucking time they may have missed. This will also keep up your milk
supply.

Some babies may try to reverse day and night, to sleep longer in the day and
demand feedings at night when they can be breast-fed, not bottle-fed. Try not to
encourage this, because it will be too exhausting for you. It is hard to control the
waking and sleeping patterns of very young babies, but as they get older the person
taking care of your baby can try to keep her awake and amused during the day, and
a pacifier can help a baby who seems to miss sucking at the breast. After a weekend
you may find you have more milk because you have been feeding the baby yourself,
and by Friday your milk supply may be down again.

Don't worry too much about trying to accustom your baby to taking a bottle
from you before you go back to work because breast-fed babies often refuse a bottle
from their own mothers but will accept one when they are hungry from someone
else. However, it is a good idea to start offering a bottle containing expressed milk
or water occasionally by three to four weeks of age so that the baby can learn both
bottle- and breast-feeding techniques.

Partial Breast-Feeding

*I did find that being able to come home and breast-feed my baby was tremen-
dously comforting. It seemed an instant way of reestablishing the closeness, and
I think it helped me not to feel guilty or jealous about leaving her.*

A mixture of breast- and bottle-feeding can be a pleasant way to continue enjoying
closeness with your baby after you have gone back to work. Dropping one feeding
needs to be done gradually, and you need to continue to allow the baby to suck
longer at other times—for example, at the morning and evening feedings—to
maintain a sufficient supply. You will probably not be able to maintain part-time
feeding for very long, unless your baby has had time to establish a pattern of full-
time feeding, usually for at least the first ten to twelve weeks.

Breast-Feeding Problems for Mothers

Sore Nipples

These can be caused by the baby sucking on the nipple instead of the surrounding
areola, or being dragged off the breast without the suction being broken first. Other

causes may be wet nipples from soggy breast pads; use of too much soap, which dries the skin; sensitivity to creams or sprays; or the baby feeding at an awkward angle. Thrush, a yeast infection in the baby's mouth, can also infect the nipples and make them very sore.

The way to avoid these problems is to keep your nipples dry and exposed to air as much as possible and to make sure the baby is latched on and taken off the breast properly. Start each feeding with the breast you finished with last time, so that alternate breasts are offered at the beginning of a feed, when her suck is strongest. You can use a hair dryer on the lowest setting, held at arm's length, to dry your nipples, and you can use special plastic "milk cups" with ventilation holes (available from lactation consultants) inside your bra to allow air to circulate and to prevent rubbing. Continue frequent feeding, but cut comfort sucking until soreness has eased. If necessary, a lactation consultant may recommend short-term use of a nipple shield. This is a soft plastic shield placed over the nipple, with holes to allow milk through.

Cracked Nipples

Cracks in the nipples can come from untreated sore nipples or appear without warning. The nipple may bleed through a small crack or split in the skin. If it is not too bad it will not do any harm to continue breast-feeding. You could use a nipple shield, but if it hurts, don't feel you have to put up with the agony. You're better off resting for a day, allowing your nipple to heal, and giving bottles in the meantime. Express milk by hand or pump to prevent engorgement. Rub some of the expressed milk on the nipple and let it dry.

Reintroduce the baby to the breast cautiously for a couple of minutes of nursing at first, and use a nipple shield if necessary until the skin has healed.

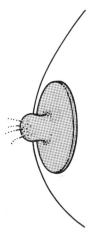

A nipple shield

Blocked Ducts

Blocked ducts cause a tender lump. This can follow engorgement or pressure on the ducts, perhaps from a tight or poor-fitting bra or even an awkward feeding position. Do not stop nursing because this will make it much worse. Instead, try to clear the blockage by massaging the lump gently in the direction of the nipple, applying hot and cold compresses, and offering that breast first at frequent feedings so the baby's strongest sucking at the beginning of a feeding will help to get the milk moving through the ducts again. Positioning the baby such that her chin is pointed at the affected quadrant of the breast can also help clear the blockage.

Mastitis

Mastitis can cause similar symptoms to blocked ducts and may be noninfectious, caused by milk leaking from the blocked duct and surrounding tissue. Fever alone is not a sign that the mastitis is infectious. Other symptoms may include chills, fatigue, and a localized, reddened, painful area of the breast. All the treatments recommended above for engorgement and blocked ducts can help, and the doctor will prescribe antibiotics. Remember to mention to your doctor, even though it sounds obvious, that you need an antibiotic suitable for a breast-feeding mother. It is important to continue breast-feeding, as engorgement will only worsen the situation.

Breast Abscesses
These are rare and sometimes confused with blocked ducts, but they can be nasty. Treatment is with antibiotics, and possibly surgical drainage if antibiotics alone do not correct the abscesses. You may have to stop nursing from the affected breast.

Breast-Feeding After a Cesarean Section
This is easiest following an epidural because you will be fully conscious and alert and able to put the baby to the breast after delivery. Usually a cushion or two under the baby can prevent any pressure on your stitches, but don't be afraid to ask for help to get into a comfortable position and be handed the baby. If you cannot sit in a propped-up position, either because it is too painful because of the restrictions of drainage tubes or drips, or because you feel sick from the effects of general anesthesia, you can nurse lying to one side, with the baby's feet toward your head. Either offer the other side by leaning over the baby more, or get help to move the baby to the other side and shift position. Take special care when nursing in a less than ideal position that the baby gets properly latched onto the breast. Try to vary the angle at which she sucks so the pressure is not always on the same spot. In this way you will decrease the risk of getting sore.

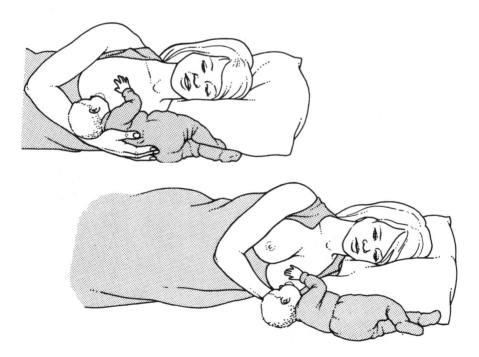

Breast-Feeding Twins

This is perfectly possible. During pregnancy, ask your caregiver how to get in touch with any mothers-of-twins support group in your area. They can give advice, support, and extra literature. Eventually nursing both together saves a great deal of time and avoids the problem of one baby crying while the other is nursing, but in the early days you should feed each separately, both to give you experience of breast-feeding, if these are your first babies, and also to get to know each one individually. Put the baby who wakes first to the breast, and wake the other to follow with a feeding so their hungry times stand more chance of coinciding. Feeding both babies on demand will leave little time for anything else, so you may have to impose some kind of routine on them from the beginning; aim for feedings about every two to three hours.

Once you begin to give all or some feedings together, experiment with a helper to find the position that suits you and the babies best. You can rest them on pillows on either side so their bodies are cradled under each arm and the heads supported on more pillows on your lap, or while they are small you can adapt the conventional nursing position, with both babies lying in the same direction. If one baby has a much stronger suck, always alternate breasts so that each breast receives the same amount of stimulation and thus produces the same amount of milk.

If one baby is much smaller than the other and cannot go so long between feedings, you may have trouble synchronizing feeding times. Begin by nursing both separately and move on to joint feeding times. If the smaller baby wakes less than two and a half hours later, nurse her again, but also wake her for a joint feeding when the bigger baby wakes. If the smaller baby sleeps two and a half hours or longer, then try to buy a little extra time by giving her a small drink and a diaper change and then wake the bigger baby for a joint feeding. It will save more time to nurse both babies every three hours than one baby at three hours and another at four. Gradually the smaller baby should catch up. As long as you let both babies suck as much as they want, your body will produce enough milk for both.

Breast-Feeding Triplets

It is possible to breast-feed three babies, but obviously it needs a lot of dedication and a great deal of extra help and support—as does almost every aspect of caring for three new babies at once. One practical routine is to breast-feed two at each feeding, with the third baby having a bottle on a rotating system so that all the babies have some breast milk.

Whatever problems you may have with breast-feeding, try to take a positive attitude. Even if you manage to nurse for only a very short time, you will still have given each baby a valuable start she would not otherwise have had, both from the anti-infective properties of colostrum and from the physical closeness. If you have to give up because, despite all your efforts, you cannot build up a supply of milk, or your baby does not gain weight or starts to lose weight, remember you can still combine breast- and bottle-feeding and do not have to give up breast-feeding completely. If you do have to switch completely to bottles because of repeated serious problems or illnesses, do not regard bottle-feeding as second best, but concentrate instead on making feeding times ones of enjoyment for both of you.

Giving Up Breast-Feeding

Switching from Breast to Bottle

You should try to do this gradually. Start by dropping the breast-feeding when you have least milk, usually the late afternoon, and substitute a bottle. Drop another breast-feeding session every two to three days and substitute bottles. Drop the first morning feeding and last evening feeding last, as they are the ones that the baby is usually most attached to. You may need to experiment to find the best nipple and hole size to suit your baby. If she is very resistant to the bottle, you could try a natural-shaped nipple, or better still, get your partner or another person to feed the bottle for the first few times. If you are making the switch because your baby is failing to gain weight or you are returning to work, remember that it is perfectly possible to continue with breast-feeding in the morning, in the evening, and during the night or whichever works best for you, in addition to bottles, so that you and your baby can still enjoy the closeness and comfort of breast-feeding.

Some people begin to use bottles for extra drinks. Extra drinks are not necessary for breast-fed or formula-fed babies except in cases of extremely hot weather if there is no air conditioning. If it is extremely hot your baby may get thirsty, so try offering a small amount of plain water in a bottle, cup, or spoon. Don't worry if she refuses, unless you notice signs of dehydration. Breast milk or infant formula are the only drinks that are really necessary for small babies. Older babies may be given diluted natural fruit juices. It is preferable to offer juice from cups rather than from bottles, and use it only at mealtimes to protect the teeth from getting coated with sugar. Avoid giving your child soda and artificial fruit drinks, which have a lot of sugar.

Giving up breast-feeding because of problems may provoke mixed feelings—perhaps of failure if you very much wanted to breast-feed, or guilt if you are relieved to abandon it.

Breast-Feeding Problems for Babies

Babies all nurse differently. Each child's personality, temperament, and maturity will affect the way she takes to breast-feeding. Once you begin to understand and accept your own baby's patterns, the difficulties seem to diminish. Here are some of the types:

The Clock-Watcher

This baby seems to have a quartz mechanism and wakes every three to four hours for a feeding, sleeps regularly and for longer periods at night, and is generally totally predictable. She also tends to be someone else's baby!

The Dreamer

This baby likes to sleep and forgets to wake for meals. As long as she has at least six wet diapers a day, don't worry, but dry diapers between feedings may mean she is not getting enough fluids. Talk to your pediatrician and check that she is gaining weight by having her weighed weekly. Some babies will suck in their sleep, but if not, loosen her clothes, bathe her face, and talk and play with her to wake her up. If she falls asleep after one breast, change her diaper and try again. If she still sleeps, don't worry, and offer the other breast at the next feeding.

The "I Want It Now" Baby

This is the baby who comes to the breast in a panic; roots frantically for the nipple; sucks vigorously; and then chokes and splutters when the milk lets down. She screams with frustration and gets more upset the more you try to feed her. Recognize this baby? The answer may be nursing in a quiet place. She is not the sort to latch on happily when you are chatting to friends around the kitchen table. A little water before the feeding may stem her immediate thirst and help her to start nursing more calmly. If she still panics, let her suck your finger until she establishes a rhythm; then slip the nipple in her mouth. She often appreciates rocking or movement while nursing, so try sitting in a rocking or glider chair or walking around. Best feeding times are when she is half asleep at night in the dark or riding in the back of a car (in a car seat).

The Anarchist

This baby will sometimes wake less than an hour after her last feeding and seem ravenous, while at other times hours pass and she is still uninterested. No two sleeps, feedings, or days are alike, and she is innocently driving you to distraction with her unpredictability. Feed on demand at first, but gradually impose some sort of routine by feeding her when you are ready and distracting her with small drinks, stroller rides, short periods in a bouncing seat, baths, and lengthy diaper changes with lots of exercise and chat when you are not ready. Keeping a written record of her feeding times can help because you can lose track of when she was last fed. Persevere, and gradually a pattern will emerge.

The Piranha

Some babies bite frequently, clamping down on the nipple with their gums toward the end of a feeding. Take it as a sign that she has had enough. She cannot bite and suck at the same time, so sucking can no longer be very important. Older babies may try it experimentally when teething. Withdraw the nipple and say "No" firmly each time. She will sense your disapproval. Between feedings give her teething toys, and if she is old enough, a teething cookie to satisfy the chewing urge.

The Choosy Feeder

This baby will take only from one breast and leave you lopsided. Offer the less favored breast when she is most hungry at the beginning of each feeding so that her sucking will stimulate the milk supply. Try a different feeding position—more upright or lying down. Some babies can be fooled if they are fed tucked under the arm with head toward the front; the change of angle seems to help.

Bottles and Bottle-Feeding

Cow's milk, which is designed for calves rather than babies, is quite different from breast milk, and has to be altered before it can be used as food for babies. In fact, as described earlier, the composition of breast milk changes during a feeding, as the baby grows, and from feeding to feeding in the same woman, so defining what an "average" sample of breast milk contains is difficult. It is not possible to make up an artificial formula that is exactly like breast milk, since we do not know all the properties of breast milk yet, the content varies, and the immunizing and anti-infective qualities cannot be reproduced artificially. But cow's milk can be modified to make a very safe food that your baby can thrive on, though it is necessary to get all the ingredients in the right proportions.

As we have already seen, even though the calorie content of cow's milk and breast milk is the same, cow's milk has two to three times as much protein as breast milk, and this protein is of a different composition. Cow's milk contains less lactose (milk sugar), the fat is less easily absorbed, and the minerals are in higher amounts: sodium, potassium, calcium, and chloride are two to three times higher. In baby formula, the levels of protein and these minerals are reduced by diluting the cow's milk. This will also reduce the calorie and vitamin content to levels much lower than in breast milk. To remedy this, extra lactose and other essential nutrients are added to make it suitable for your baby.

Commercially available formula must be used for bottle-feeding. In the days before formulas were available, mothers simply diluted regular cow's milk and added sugar. Today's formulas are much better tailored to a new baby's digestion, so you should always use one of these when breast milk is not available. Your hospital or pediatrician will advise you which brands to choose from. Once you've made your choice, stick to the same formula unless your pediatrician advises you to switch. You must dilute the powdered and concentrated liquid varieties correctly by mixing the right quantity of clean water. It is not necessary to boil the water in most areas (ask your pediatrician if you are unsure), but it is important to use strictly clean techniques. Wash your hands well with soap before starting. Clean the top of the can before opening it, and pour (liquid) or scoop (powder) into a clean pitcher. Add the correctly measured amount of clean water and mix. It is important to prepare properly diluted formula. Too much or too little water added can make your baby quite sick. Store the prepared formula in the refrigerator for up to twenty-four hours. Fill each bottle with slightly more than the baby usually takes at a feeding. There should always be some left in the bottle at the end of a feeding so you can be sure she took as much as she needed. At some feedings she will take more, at others less, but do not try to force her to finish a bottle once her hunger is satisfied. Discard any formula left in the bottle after a feeding. A ready-to-use formula is also available, which does not need to have water added.

Establishing Bottle-Feeding

I loved taking a warm, fresh bottle of formula and seeing it disappear bit by bit as my baby ate.

After delivery do not let the fact that you plan to bottle-feed deprive you and your baby of the pleasure of physical closeness and contact. Even if you do not want to put your baby to the breast, there is no reason why you should not enjoy skin-to-skin contact in the same way. Loosen her clothing while still keeping her warm and lay her on your tummy or between your breasts, and gently stroke and caress her to help her relax. See "Taking Care of Your New Baby" in chapter 4 for more on handling your newborn.

There is great pleasure in feeding a bottle to a hungry baby, but you need to make an extra effort to see that feeding time stays a time for special enjoyment and closeness, not just another chore to be done by anyone. Always hold your baby very close—at nighttime especially it is easy to cradle her against your skin—and support her in a fairly upright position.

Feed your baby whenever she seems interested in just the same way as if she were breast-fed. Trying to force her into a routine of regular feedings before she is mature enough will only lead to several hours with a crying, upset baby and misery for both of you. Remember that in the womb her body has been nourished continually, and at first her pattern of feeding, just like a baby who is being breast-fed, needs to be in small amounts and often. Offer her a bottle whenever she wakes and roots for food or cries. If she takes only a few sucks and goes back to sleep or loses interest, nothing is lost, and you have given her the comfort of sucking. Do not think that offering her food whenever she wants will encourage her to go on asking for it at irregular intervals. A newborn's digestive system is still immature and needs time to adjust—she is not able to cope with any other way of feeding. Usually, by about two weeks, some sort of pattern is beginning to emerge. Your baby may sleep for three to four hours, perhaps in the morning, and have another time, possibly early evening, when she needs small feedings more often. Do not be tempted to add cereal to a feeding in the belief that it will help her to sleep through the night. Staying asleep for longer periods has to do with the maturity of your baby's brain as well as her digestion, and added cereal will just make her fat and may make her fussy if her digestive system is not ready for it.

Extra fluid may be necessary for bottle-fed babies in very hot weather. If you're in doubt, offer a small amount of clean water once or twice a day between feedings, never in place of a feeding. You can offer an older baby well-diluted, unsweetened fruit juice, preferably from a cup or a teaspoon. If your baby does not want it, you can conclude she does not need it. Avoid sugary drinks, which will cause decay of emerging teeth.

Equipment for Bottle-Feeding
You'll need:

* At least eight wide-necked baby bottles and nipples designed for newborns.

* A large plastic or Pyrex measuring cup or pitcher and a plastic stirrer for mixing formula, or you can measure the water into the baby bottles and add the correct number of scoops of powder directly.

* A bottle brush.

Preparing Bottles of Formula
Everything you use for making up bottles must be clean, including the pitcher and stirrer if you use one, so always start by washing your hands and cleaning all equipment.

It is easiest to make up a day's supply of bottles at one time and store them in the refrigerator for up to twenty-four hours. Make up a little more formula than you think you need—a very rough guide is that babies need about 2½ fluid ounces for every pound of body weight per day, so a 10-pound baby will need approximately 25 ounces of milk in twenty-four hours. However, the real measure is your baby's appetite, and at some feedings she will take more than at others.

As long as you offer her formula whenever you think she might be hungry and do not try to force it on her when she does not want it, you will be giving her what she needs. Discard the rest of the formula and never save bottles to be reheated, because warm milk is an ideal breeding ground for bacteria. You can buy ready-made bottles of formula, which, though expensive, can be useful for when you go out with your baby.

The Pitcher Method   Here are the steps for making formula in a pitcher:

1. Wash your hands.

2. Clean the top of the can of powdered or liquid concentrate formula and open.

3. Empty the concentrated formula or the correct number of scoops of powdered formula into a clean pitcher. Use the scoop provided and use level scoops, not heaping—this is a common cause of overconcentrated feeding. The powder should lie loosely in the scoop; use the flat edge of a sterilized clean plastic knife (not metal) to level it off each time. Never heat powder.

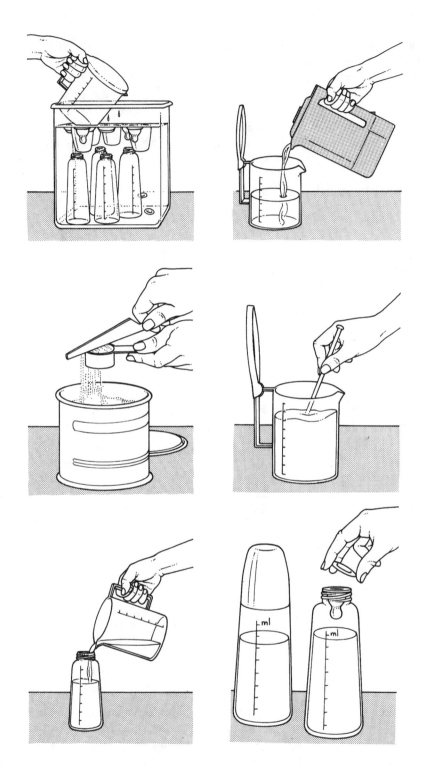

Pitcher method

The most popular brands of baby formula are diluted with one scoop of powder added to 2 ounces of water. Do not be tempted either to increase or decrease the number of scoops recommended unless advised to by your pediatrician.

4. Follow the instructions on the can to pour the right amount of clean water into the pitcher. Make sure the measuring cup is standing on a flat surface, and check the quantity at eye level rather than from above. You can use cool or warm water, although most formulas mix more easily with warm water.

5. Stir the milk until all lumps have dissolved—they could clog the nipples.

6. Fill the bottles to the right level—put slightly more in each bottle than you think your baby will need. Put the clean nipples and nipple covers on, being careful not to keep your fingers around the edges.

7. Put all the bottles in the refrigerator and leave them untouched until needed, but use them within twenty-four hours.

The Bottle Method   Here are the steps for making formula directly in the bottle:

1. Wash your hands.

2. Pour the right amount of clean water into each bottle; make sure the bottle is standing on a flat surface, and check the quantity at eye level rather than from above.

3. As with the pitcher method, make sure the water is cool or warm but not hot.

4. Use the scoop provided and add the right number of scoops of powdered formula to each bottle; make sure there are no distractions, so you can count properly. Level off each scoop with a plastic knife.

5. Take the nipples from the sterilizer, being careful to handle them by the edge, and fit into the bottles upside down. Put the caps, rings, and tops in place. Take out each item separately and put directly onto the bottle.

6. Shake each bottle vigorously to make sure all the formula has dissolved and there are no lumps.

7. Put the bottles in the refrigerator and leave them untouched until needed, but use them within 24 hours.

Giving a Bottle

Here are the steps for giving your baby a bottle:

1. Take the bottle from the refrigerator; warm the bottle by standing it in a bowl of hot water or in a bottle warmer. If a microwave is used, make sure to shake the bottle thoroughly before giving it to the baby since the heat is not evenly distributed and some of the milk may be too hot, which can burn the baby's mouth.

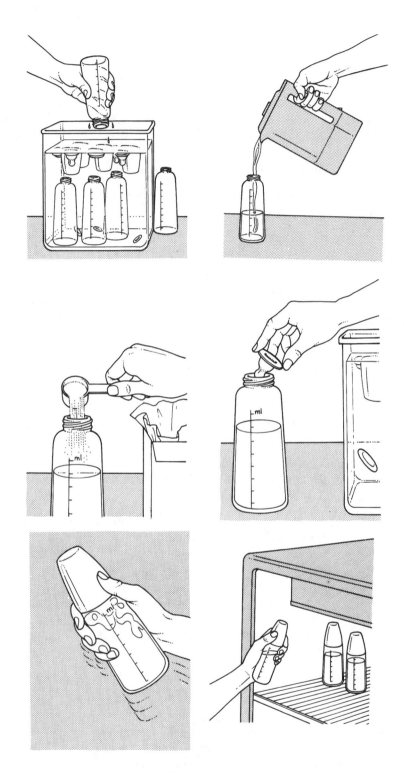

Bottle method

2. Check temperature and flow by testing the liquid on the back of your hand or inside a wrist—it should feel warm or at room temperature, not hot or cold, and flow in rapid drips, not in a continuous stream or too slowly. You can enlarge a hole that is too small with a red-hot needle, but if the hole is too large, you need another nipple.

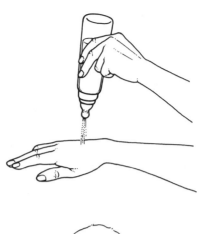

3. Always get yourself comfortable, which means having your back and cradling arm supported; if you are uncomfortable you will be tense and be tempted to hurry the feeding.

4. Touch your finger against your baby's cheek nearest to you, and as she turns her head toward you, "rooting" for food, touch the nipple against her lips. Always introduce the nipple fully into her mouth so that the action of her jaws as she sucks is against the lower half. Tilt the bottle so the opening of the nipple is always covered with milk and to ensure that the baby is not sucking in too much air.

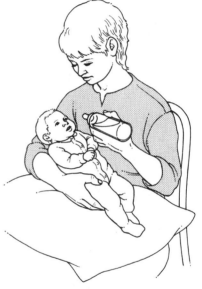

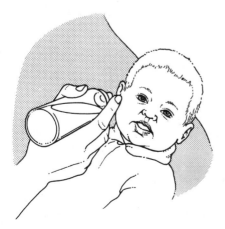

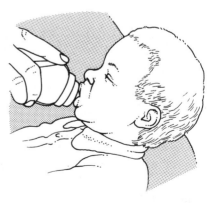

5. You will need to stop feeding at least once to sit your baby up, allowing her to burp up any air (see "Problems with Early Feeding" later in this chapter for more on burping).

6. Do not try to force your baby to take more than she wants; her appetite is always your best guide.

Never keep the remains of a bottle. There is a high risk of germs contaminating warm milk that is left standing around. Throw away unused formula.

Never leave a young baby with a bottle propped for her to drink from because there is a real danger that she could choke. Prop feeding has also been found to increase the risk of ear infections. You are also denying her the closeness babies enjoy during a feeding, which is also the time when they begin to learn the skills of communicating and taking turns that develop when an adult and a baby enjoy a shared task.

Cleaning Bottles and Equipment

Steps for cleaning:

1. As your baby finishes a bottle, rinse it out with water to remove any milk left inside and leave it ready for when you have time to wash several at once.

2. Once a day or so, thoroughly scrub all the bottles, caps, and covers, and rinse with hot, soapy water; a bottle brush is essential, but remember to keep this clean, too, and leave it to dry afterward.

3. Rinse everything well and allow to air-dry.

4. To clean the nipples, turn the nipple inside out and wash thoroughly with hot water and soap. A small nipple brush is also helpful. Thorough cleaning helps to reduce the risk of your baby getting thrush. Pacifiers should be cleaned in a similar way.

Most pediatricians no longer feel that sterilization of bottles, nipples, and water is necessary. If boiling the water is necessary in your area, take special care to allow the water to cool before using it, to avoid burning the baby's mouth.

Other People Feeding Your Baby

My mother was always saying, "Let me feed her so you can do other things." In fact, feeding my baby was the pleasure, and "things" were just chores, but it was very hard to say that I wanted to feed her myself.

Because there is a great deal of satisfaction to be gained from feeding a baby, you may not be short of willing helpers offering to do this particular job—from well-meaning grandmothers to friends and school-age children. Indeed, one of the reasons why you may have chosen bottle-feeding was so you could more easily leave the baby with other people at times, but remember that feeding time is not just an occasion when a baby receives the right amount of calories and protein. It is also an occasion of great pleasure to her and consequently to the person feeding her. It is a very important part of forming a relationship, of getting to know your baby as she and you respond to each other's touch, movement, and facial expressions. This is the main reason why breast-feeding has so many advocates—not only does it provide the best nutrition, but also it provides a regular, continuing form of communication between a mother and her baby.

Naturally, you will be pleased that the baby's father can share in this experience and if it is to be he rather than you who is to stay at home and look after the baby, then it is right for him gradually to take over many of the feedings. But early on reserve feeding times for yourself. Do not be afraid to say that you want to feed your baby yourself, because it is a time when you both get to know each other and feel very close. If any relatives seem offended, you could point out that it is a question that would not even arise if you were breast-feeding. Encourage them to help you with other chores—for example, bathtime, cleaning, shopping, and cooking.

Vitamin Supplements

Before Weaning
If you eat a balanced diet and are healthy, breast milk will give your baby almost all of the vitamins she needs, but if you feel you have not, for whatever reason, been eating well, or have been ill, your baby's doctor can give you the right vitamin supplements in the form of drops for your baby. Vitamin drops may be recommended from six months depending on your baby's diet. Supplemental fluoride may also be prescribed if the water in your area is not fluoridated. If you are bottle-feeding, then the formula does contain vitamins, but in addition some professionals advise the use of the children's vitamin A, D, and C drops if your baby is taking less than 16 to 17 ounces of infant formula daily. These, used in conjunction with formula or breast-feeding, provide a safe dose of vitamins, but never give two different vitamin preparations at any stage, as this could be harmful.

After Weaning
Once you change from formula or breast milk to whole cow's milk (after your child becomes a year of age) and solid foods, it is recommended that you give vitamin A, D, and C drops up to the age of five years, unless your child's diet is sufficiently varied to obtain all the necessary vitamins from food sources.

Sunlight on the skin provides vitamin D, so in good weather give your child lots of opportunity to play outside, taking care to protect a baby's sensitive skin with a sunscreen (after six months of age) and hat in summer.

After you begin solid foods, make sure to sometimes include foods that contain iron, such as red meats and iron-fortified cereals.

Fluoride tablets or drops help to protect teeth if you live in an area where fluoride is not already added to your water.

Feeding Second and Subsequent Babies

You have the benefit of experience, know what to expect, and have gained confidence from bringing up one child, whether on breast- or bottle-feeding. The differences with the second lie in the reaction of your first child to the new baby, your own desire to do the best by both children, and the fact that feeding now has to be fitted into a much more complicated routine. You cannot always feed your baby at the time you expect her to be hungry because you have another child's needs to consider. The best policy is to feed her early, rather than hope she will last and then have to cope with a screaming baby in the background.

When you talk to your older child about the arrival of a new baby, talk also about how she will be fed. If you plan to breast-feed, photographs of you breast-feeding your first child can be a great help. She is quite likely to want to have an experimental suck herself at some stage and try feeding a teddy or doll from her own nipples. The brother or sister of a bottle-fed baby is likely to want her own bottle and to try feeding dolls. Both reactions are quite normal. One mother described how "My daughter was always shoving her doll up her sweater in the supermarket or post office and latching it onto her belly button, saying she was giving it some milk."

There is no evidence that breast-feeding provokes more jealousy in an older child than bottle-feeding, but because it is such an intimate act, mothers are often anxious and feel almost a sense of betrayal to the older child. The answer lies in giving the older child a period of exclusive attention ahead, although not immediately prior to a feeding, and being prepared with distractions while feeding. But it is a fact that however much you involve the first child in the care of the baby, she is unlikely to be captivated by feeding sessions six times a day, and if a child feels jealous, she can pick feeding times to be particularly disruptive.

Make sure you always have a drink and a small snack handy, and keep a treasure chest of interesting knickknacks to be brought out at feeding times only. Boxes of wooden blocks or Lego blocks, different books from the library, or special crayons are useful. Try swapping toys with friends, and change the "treasure" regularly; be innovative—they do not have to be new and expensive, just different. Empty containers make great stacking toys, or you can cut a hole in the lid big enough to push pegs through. Breast-feeding mothers have the advantage of a free hand to cuddle, draw pictures, or turn pages. Older children may like cassettes or short videos, or you can time feedings to coincide with favorite television programs, but avoid sending the older child into a room on her own, or she may feel excluded. Often just making her cozy beside you with a favorite blanket or teddy and talking, singing, or telling her a story about when she was a baby can make feeding times less likely to be occasions for trouble.

Problems with Early Feeding

Burping

Some babies, whether breast- or bottle-fed, swallow more air than others when drinking—you will soon get to know whether your baby needs a chance to burp midway through a bottle or when changing breasts. Hold her in an upright position against your body, or over your shoulder, and gently rub her back. Protect yourself with a clean cloth diaper or towel to prevent a mouthful of regurgitated milk from ruining your clothes. Alternative burping positions are lying face down across your knees, or sitting up with your hand behind her neck and thumb under her chin. If she is perfectly happy and does not burp, carry on feeding. Beware of breaking feedings unnecessarily to burp your baby so that she starts crying and becomes upset and frustrated—it will be the crying rather than the feeding that makes her take in extra air. If your baby seems unduly troubled by swallowed air, try feeding her in an upright position; check that the hole in the nipple allows milk to drip through rapidly and that the bottle is tilted enough for the milk to cover the entrance to the nipple completely. If your baby howls after every feeding time or after specific feedings, she may have colic.

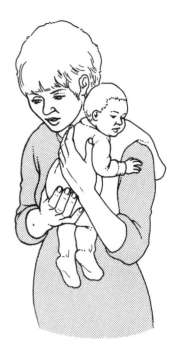

Babies Who Spit Up

These are babies who regularly return part of their milk every time but generally are thriving and perfectly healthy. If you have any reason to suspect that the condition may be a sign of illness, or if your baby is not gaining weight regularly or seems irritable, consult your doctor. Projectile vomiting (which shoots out of the mouth in a forceful stream) is never normal and should be reported to the baby's doctor (see "Pyloric Stenosis" below). Otherwise you just have to be careful to cover clothes, carpets, and furniture, and get used to cleaning up. She will grow out of it as her body matures and as the muscle that closes the opening to the stomach becomes stronger.

Pyloric Stenosis

This is a condition where the muscle surrounding the opening at the end of the stomach (called the pylorus) thickens, narrowing the outlet. Five times as many boys suffer from it as girls, and symptoms usually appear about two to three weeks after the birth when the baby starts vomiting, becomes constipated, and stops gaining weight. The vomiting is often projectile—that means it shoots out and can land feet away. Although the baby does not gain weight, she usually remains bright, and parents may initially think the sickness is due to too much food or a reaction to the milk. Such sickness can lead to dehydration, so parents of babies under three months should seek advice rapidly if this type of vomiting occurs. Diagnosis can be made by feeling a lump in the abdomen over the pylorus, which hardens and softens when the baby is feeding. An abdominal ultrasound is used to confirm the diagnosis. Treatment is usually a simple operation. The baby can be fed only hours afterward and makes a rapid recovery.

Colic

> *My baby never fed without at least an hour of screaming afterward; then she would fall asleep, exhausted. The evenings were the worst—she cried on and off from about four every afternoon until midnight. I had a toddler of twenty-two months and a husband who was rarely home in the evenings. On days when I had no plans to see anyone else I used to feel completely panicked by how I would get through the day.*

All babies cry for a variety of reasons (see chapter 8), but babies with colic cry more—one study diagnosed colic if a baby cried for more than three hours a day and on more than three days a week. Usually such babies act as though they have a stomach ache, drawing their knees up over their stomach during screaming fits and often punching with their fists.

Normally our intestines contract in smooth, rhythmical undulations to move food along the digestive tract, but in some babies this gentle movement may be replaced by spasms, causing the pain and distress termed colic. However, the definitive cause of colic remains open to speculation. Colic rarely begins before about two weeks or after two months, and in the majority of cases stops at about three months, and in all but a very few babies at four months; this is why it is often called "three-month colic." Attacks can last from a quarter hour to several hours. There may be nonstop screaming, or bouts of screaming between which the baby seems miserable or may briefly sleep. Some babies suffer only during the evening, and the usual pattern is that as they get older and begin to grow out of it, they begin to settle slightly earlier each night.

Research has shown that colicky babies are invariably healthy and thriving and basically no different from other babies except that they suffer from colic. The only slight factors to emerge are that weaning too early—before three months—makes colic more probable and that professional couples are more likely to have a colicky baby, though this probably just reflects the fact that such couples are more inclined to seek and get a correct diagnosis. No differences have been picked up between colic sufferers and others in terms of sex, birth weight, birth order, weight gain, feeding method, or the amount of sickness, diarrhea, or constipation they may suffer. Swallowed air used to be blamed as the main problem, but tests indicate that colicky babies have no more air in their intestines than others, although what air there is probably does contribute to pain by getting trapped in loops of intestine during spasms.

Why might some babies suffer from such jittery, jumpy intestines? A favorite theory is that it is simply caused by an immature nervous system that is not yet able to control the intestines properly; this would explain why the problem disappears as the baby grows and matures. Other suggestions include the possibility that it might be related to prostaglandin metabolism and intestinal hormones or to an allergic reaction, most commonly to cow's milk. Certainly among the colic sufferers there will be some babies whose distress is due either to a temporary or long-term intolerance of either cow's milk or other food. In babies whose problems do not disappear by five months, food intolerance should be considered seriously. You will need to discuss this possibility with your family doctor.

An inconsolably screaming baby places an enormous strain on parents; indeed, such babies are more likely to be abused physically than calmer ones. Even though health professionals cannot usually do anything practical to help, just talking about the problem and letting them know the kind of strain you are under can be a relief and enable them to be more supportive.

There are a number of things that are said to help to calm your baby. Some may help; others are not likely to help. Some of these are:

- *Drugs.* The only one now being given is simethicone. Usually the psychological aid of having something to give the baby is more help than any pharmacological effect. Antispasmodic drugs are no longer recommended for babies under six months because although they were used for more than thirty years, in recent years there have been a number of reports of adverse side effects.

- *Fennel tea.* This is an herb said to have a relaxing, calming effect, and it is contained in some drinks for young babies or can be taken as fennel tea. Some parents believe it helps, but there is no good evidence that this is so. Baby teas in general are not recommended.

- *Special nipples and bottles.* These are a waste of money because there is no evidence that taking in extra air causes colic.

- *Sucking.* This is often a tremendous relief for colicky babies, providing comfort and a distraction from pain. Sometimes these babies root as though for food, only to cry again when they begin feeding. As long as you are sure it is the comfort sucking provides, rather than food your baby wants, try offering her your little finger or a pacifier to suck. She may suck furiously, begin to drift into sleep, and then wake with a cry after a short while, wanting to suck again, so that you have to offer the finger or the pacifier once more. Natural-shaped pacifiers are available for breast-fed babies, who are used to sucking with a slightly different technique than bottle-fed babies, but usually a baby who needs the comfort of sucking will not be fussy. See "If Your Baby Won't Stop Crying" in chapter 8 for more on pacifiers.

- *Traditional comforts such as carrying the baby around, rocking, cradling, and stroking.* These are all tried by harassed parents; rhythmic and constant stimuli distract from pain in the same way you use breathing exercises in labor.

- *Swaddling* can sometimes help.

- A *continuous buzz of noise.* Some people turn on the clothes dryer, the television, or even the vacuum to calm the baby. Some stores may carry audiotapes of so-called white noise.

● *A dark, quiet room.* This is also worth trying. Long evenings with a colicky baby can be made easier with a rocking chair so that you can sit and rock the baby on your shoulder or knee to the accompaniment of a favorite television show or video.

Try keeping a diary over seven days in which you record the number of hours your baby cried, plus a systematic approach using one possible remedy each time. This can help you pinpoint which remedy is most likely to be effective and when you most need to ask for extra help. Just writing down what happens may also help to make sense of what may seem one long nightmare and may be therapeutic in itself. Resist throwing every possible remedy at your baby in one evening because you will not know which works (if any) and will have nothing left in reserve to try. Also, too much different attention can add to her distress.

Extra support is invaluable, and so is support between partners. It is not unknown for one partner to stay out later or work longer hours just to escape from a screaming baby. You need to face the problem together, and this means talking and planning how best to cope. Ask a reliable friend or relative if he will come to stay with your howler just for an hour one evening a week so you can get out of the house together and go to a restaurant or just for a walk. Take turns with late-evening and night waking as much as possible so that you both get some decent stretches of unbroken sleep, even if it means sometimes turning in at nine o'clock. Make sure that each day you have one other person visiting or you are going out to see someone yourself. Talk to other mothers about your problem, and let your baby's doctor know so he can be as supportive as possible. If you reach a crisis point and feel you could harm your child, put her in her crib, leave the room, and phone a friend, relative, or health care provider. So common is the problem that support groups have been formed to help parents cope. Ask your baby's doctor if such a group is available in your area.

Introducing Solid Foods

The day will come when it's time to teach your baby to take foods other than milk from a spoon or cup rather than just sucking at the breast or bottle. At the same time, the amount of milk being given gradually decreases as the intake of food increases.

When to Start

Between four and six months is usually the right time to introduce solid foods. Feeding solids before four months is unnecessary because all your baby's needs can be met from milk. Giving solids too early may make your baby fat, which, in turn, may lead to other health problems. It also places a strain on the baby's still immature digestive system, and it increases the likelihood of allergy (see "Food Intolerance" later in this chapter). Some mothers are very tempted to give solids earlier because they think it will make their baby sleep through the night—a thought often encouraged by well-meaning grandmothers. Although babies do wake from hunger, the length of time they sleep is also largely governed by the maturity of their brain (see chapter 8), and stuffing them with food only makes them fat and sometimes more fretful if they are already prone to colic. Cereal or any solid food should never be added to bottle feedings unless recommended by the baby's doctor.

However, just as there are good reasons for not starting too early, so there are also reasons for not starting too late. New babies carry a store of iron in their livers from the last months of pregnancy, which can meet their need for the first four to six months of life. (Premature babies are different; see "The Problems of Babies in Special Care" in chapter 5). As this store runs down they need other sources, and milk alone is not enough. There is also a belief among some pediatricians that babies have "sensitive periods" when they are ready to move on to or learn a new activity—in this case chewing solid food—and that if they do not have the opportunity or are prevented at this time it is very hard to get them to do it later.

What to Feed

At first foods need to be very smooth, strained, or pureed. Avoid egg, wheat, and unmodified cow's milk, since these may cause allergy (see "Food Intolerance" later in this chapter). Some doctors recommend that you do not give these until nine to twelve months and not until a year if there is a history of allergy in the family. If you use a baby cereal to start with, choose one based on rice or other grains such as oats or barley, rather than wheat, and mix it with formula, breast milk, or juice. Pureed vegetables or fruit are starters. If you use vegetables from the family meal, take them out of the cooking water before adding anything, including salt. Extra salt is unnecessary for babies, and it increases the risk of dehydration. Similarly, never add extra sugar to cereals because this may condition your baby to only want sweet things. Use a nonbrittle, smooth, small plastic spoon, or the small metal spoons with white rubber-coated bowls that are designed for infants. Offer just one teaspoon of the chosen food either before or halfway through the lunchtime feeding, and finish off with milk from breast or bottle. Never introduce new foods closer than 3 days apart. In this way you will be able to pinpoint any food that causes an allergic-type reaction.

First Tastes—What to Expect

> I felt it marked a milestone the day I gave my daughter her first teaspoon of solid food. I really enjoyed mixing up a tiny quantity of baby food and putting a bib on her—it seemed to be so much what I imagined having a baby was all about. I suppose it is pretty much what little girls do when they are playing with dolls! But actually feeding the food to her was like trying to put a teaspoon of water into a pitcher that was already overflowing—it all just kept coming out again.

Don't expect your baby to open her mouth and know what to do at first. Taking something from a spoon instead of sucking, having to move the food to the back of her mouth with her tongue, and the taste and the texture of the food itself all add up to a bewildering number of new sensations, and at first most of the food does tend to get pushed out again. Let her get used to the whole experience gradually, with just a teaspoonful once a day for a week. Using a bib is a good idea, even though you are only giving a tiny amount to begin with. Be patient and relaxed. Some babies take very quickly to solids, while others are not interested for some time. But if you persevere in offering a taste once a day, she will eventually get the idea and you can gradually increase the amount to match her appetite. Just as with breast- and bottle-feeding in the early days, her demands are a good guide. Once she is taking some food at one mealtime you can begin to offer something at a second time in the day.

Cutting Down on Milk

At first your baby's needs should still be met mainly by milk. You need to make the change from a diet that is mostly milk to a diet that is mostly solids very gradually. Too much solid food too quickly can make her dehydrated. The first feeding to be dropped will usually be the one following the solids—most babies can learn to drink from a cup or "sippy" cup from about five to eight months. Once a baby starts to have solids, remember he will usually need extra fluids. Offer diluted fruit juice or water after the food. Water or juice may also be offered between mealtimes if you think she may be thirsty. But remember that sucking is still an important source of pleasure and comfort to babies, and make the changeover very gradually—it usually takes two to three months. Many babies continue with a last "comfort" breast- or bottle-feeding for much longer. In addition, breast milk or formula remain an important source of well-balanced nutrition for babies throughout the first year of life. Most babies should continue to receive at least 20 to 24 ounces per day of breast milk or formula in addition to solid foods.

Cow's Milk

Pediatricians now advise continuing breast-feeding or the use of a modified infant formula rather than cow's milk until your baby is a year old. Cow's milk may be a cause of allergy, while formulas are less sensitizing. If you, your partner, or a brother or sister has a history of eczema, asthma, hay fever, or other allergies, this is especially important. So delay introducing fresh cow's milk, or take expert advice from a doctor or dietitian specializing in this field about an alternative. Some babies can also be sensitive to soy and/or goat's milk. Specially manufactured follow-up formulas can be used as an alternative to infant formula after six months (although they offer no proven advantages), provided a variety of solid foods is included in your baby's diet. Skim or fat-free milk is not suitable for children until they reach about five years, and low-fat milk shouldn't be offered until they reach two years.

Weaning from the Breast

As your baby sucks less at the breast, less milk is made. When you first miss a feeding you may find your breasts begin to fill with milk as the let-down reflex works before the next feeding time, but your baby will usually be happy to have the meal that follows early. Alternatively, offer the breast after the baby has had her solids. After a day or two your supply will have adjusted. It is quite possible, and often convenient and a source of pleasure, to continue with just a morning and an evening feeding for some time. This may even be advantageous to babies in continuing to provide protection from infection and allergy.

Some babies discontinue breast-feeding of their own accord and seem to lose interest naturally; others would continue, it seems, forever, and it is you who want to stop. There is no "right" time to end breast-feeding. Some mothers choose to carry on past the first year of life. There is often a touch of sadness about the last breast-feeding. There may be a hormonal component as well as an emotional one (similar to postpartum "blues"), but you can continue to enjoy holding your baby close and cuddling her just as often. Breast-feeding support groups can give you more information about weaning.

Learning About Lumps

From about four to six months your baby has been adjusting to taking some of her food pureed or strained instead of simply having milk. From about six to nine months she is in the next phase, which enables her to make another series of changes so that by about nine months she manages to chew soft, mashed, and chopped foods and finger foods. By the time she is a year old she can eat more or less what the rest of the family eats, with the addition of extra milk drinks and vitamin drops if necessary.

Between six and nine months, whenever you think she is ready, begin to feed her meals with more solid lumps of food. At first you can make food easier for her by mixing grated cheese, chopped, well-cooked vegetables, fish, and finely chopped meat with well-cooked cereal or mashed potato. Soon family meals need be only lightly mashed, although meat often continues to be hard for babies to chew. You have to mince it or cut it very small, and then mix it with gravy so it is not too dry. Boiled chicken is fairly easy to chew. Avoid meats such as steak, which require significant chewing.

If you are feeding mainly prepared baby foods at this point, begin using the junior or stage two or three varieties instead of the strained ones, and start some home-cooked foods as well. Unless you have a special reason to worry about allergy, milk and milk products such as yogurt and cheese and also well-cooked egg yolks should be introduced as an important part of her diet. Avoid egg whites until one year of age. Around three cups of formula a day is a rough guide to what she needs, and may be given mixed in cereal, as yogurt, or in puddings made with formula. Start cow's milk at one year. Three or four well-cooked eggs per week can be included as egg dishes. By this stage at least one or two drinks should be given in a cup or "sippy" cup, and bottles should be discontinued by about twelve months.

Finger Foods

Once my children got to the stage of being able to chew and eat lumps, I used to feed them almost everything by just putting pieces in front of them and letting them pick them up with their fingers—toast, fruit, bits of sausage, and fish sticks, and I have to admit my daughter even used to eat spaghetti like that! It made them slower to learn to use spoons, but it did save an awful lot of hassle.

Once your child can pick up and hold pieces of food in her hand, you can offer your baby finger foods, which give practice in chewing as well as enjoyment. But stay nearby and watch in case she begins to choke on lumps bitten off. Obvious examples of suitable foods are toast fingers, pieces of peeled soft fruit (such as bananas or peaches), and sticks of cheese, but a hungry child will eat almost anything with her fingers if you can stand the mess!

Learning to Feed Herself

Children learn by imitating, and a baby who sits with the family at mealtimes or eats with older children will soon want to try feeding herself with a spoon. Some mothers hate the mess this experimental stage involves so much that they will not let their child try. But stopping a child who is ready to learn a new skill may mean it will be more difficult to teach her later. It can also be frustrating for the child, who may get angry and try to grab the spoon.

It's a good idea to place the high chair on a square of plastic or newspaper, cover your child with a plastic bib with sleeves, make sure she is hungry, and let her eat while you eat your own meal. A small spoon with a deep bowl is easier for scooping things up than a flat, shallow bowl. Special plastic bowls that have suction cups to stick to the table or high-chair tray are helpful. Your baby's natural desire to copy you and any other members of the family, plus hunger, will ensure that she gets some food in. Children who are allowed to try to feed themselves like this when they want to will soon learn to eat with a minimum of mess and save you hours of spoon-feeding. Alternatively, you can give the baby a spoon and let her feed herself while you use a second spoon to pop an occasional spoonful yourself.

Once playing completely takes over from eating, such as when she begins throwing the food on the floor or playing mudpies with it, you know she has had enough and you can offer her some pudding, some fruit, or a milk drink or let her go and play. Do not try to get a young baby to stay in her chair as long as everyone else stays put around the table, unless she is happy.

Eating Out

While babies and small children are unfailingly welcome in some restaurants, other restaurants are far less tolerant. Small babies in infant seats do not usually present too many problems, although if you are nervous you can check with the restaurant in advance. Dressing with a little thought usually makes discreet breast-feeding possible—the table itself provides a screen—or ask beforehand if they have a room you can use.

Most restaurants that specifically welcome children provide high chairs and booster seats; otherwise, ask if you can bring a portable one that fastens to the table or a chair. Taking suitable toys, diversions, drinks in appropriate containers, and making sure your child is hungry, so she spends at least part of the time eating, all help. Timing of sleep to coincide with the meal and rocking her off beforehand in a reclining stroller often works well, or one of you can go out for a few turns around the block to lull her off between courses. Park the stroller inside and within reach.

The most difficult age to eat out with children is between the onset of walking and about three years, although it depends slightly on your child's temperament. All the previous tips still apply, and in addition you can give her lots of exercise beforehand and keep her interest by telling her a bit about what is happening around her. Waiting for food is a sophisticated challenge for toddlers, so bring a private supply of pretzels, Cheerios, or bits of fruit to ward off screams of anguish when the next table gets served first! Generally, though, if the meal out is intended as a treat for you, try to arrange leaving your toddler with someone else for an hour or two.

Food Intolerance

Children may develop physical symptoms and (although this is more controversial) behavior problems because of food they have eaten. The foods that cause the trouble may be natural, such as wheat, eggs, milk, or chocolate, or they may be artificial substances added to food for coloring or as preservatives.

The child's reaction may be caused in a number of different ways. The food may be spoiled or contain chemicals that are poisonous (toxic) to the child: bacteria and viruses may cause food poisoning in this way, but some foods may be chemically toxic to sensitive children even though the foods are not spoiled. The child may be lacking an enzyme to deal with the food in question, so that toxic substances build up and harm her, or she may have an allergy. Normally, the immune system of the body reacts to substances or organisms it thinks are attacking it, such as bacteria, by developing antibodies. The antibodies are formed the first time the substance attacks the body, and the person is then sensitized. When the substance attacks the body again, the antibodies are released again. Usually the result of the antibody release is a healthy one, mobilizing the body's defenses effectively against attack. However, in predisposed children the immune system of the body may also react by producing allergic symptoms such as asthma, eczema, hay fever, diarrhea, and possibly behavior problems, such as hyperactivity.

Doctors use the term "allergy" in an exact sense to describe the body's responses when the immune system is involved, but many people use the term much more loosely; for example, they may say, "I think I am allergic to my boss." It is important to remember that allergy is only one of the ways in which the body can react to substances in the environment.

Food intolerance can run in families, so if you or your partner or a close relative suffers from eczema, asthma, rhinitis (runny nose and eyes), or other symptoms of sensitivity, there is a greater chance that your child may also suffer.

Some preventive action is possible in the case of food allergy or sensitivity. To show symptoms, a baby must first have been exposed to the foreign protein antigen causing the problem; once she has encountered the antigen and begins to react, she is said to be "sensitized." Some specialists suspect this can happen before birth if an allergic mother-to-be eats something that causes her to react. Her antibodies at a raised level enter the baby's circulation, and the baby could theoretically be born with a ready-made sensitivity to that food. Although there is no hard, factual evidence to support this, there is some anecdotal evidence, and it is worthwhile for women with allergies to have their problem identified and controlled as effectively as possible before and during pregnancy and then to follow a safe diet in pregnancy to avoid an allergic attack. Naturally, this applies only to food allergy and not to inhaled substances such as pollen.

Cow's milk is one cause of food allergy. The importance of this lies in the nutritional role of milk in the diet, especially of young children. The immature immune system of new babies is particularly sensitive and may react to the foreign protein in cow's milk. If there is a family history of cow's milk allergy, mothers are particularly advised to breast-feed exclusively for the first four to six months, not to take in too much milk or milk products themselves, and if possible to make sure their baby does not have any baby formula at all—one bottle is quite enough to sensitize a baby. When breast-feeding is not possible, a soy or specially modified formula may be advised, but soy can also affect some children, as can goat's milk, which is not suitable for babies in any case. Your doctor or pediatrician should advise you on this. It may be that you should not give any fresh cow's milk or milk products such as cheese and yogurt until your child is a year old, but continue the formula .

Introduce a small quantity of these foods (a teaspoonful or two) for the first day or two. Stop if there is any reaction. Symptoms vary, but common signs are skin rashes, miserable behavior, failure to thrive or gain weight, vomiting, and occasionally colicky abdominal pain. Remember, however, that babies can get these symptoms from a number of other causes, and if symptoms have started suddenly after months of successful feeding with foods based on cow's milk, it is unlikely that cow's milk protein intolerance is the cause. Remember, too, that if you reduce your baby's milk intake, the nutrients in milk such as calcium, vitamins, protein, and calories must be replaced in the diet to avoid affecting growth.

How Can You Tell If Your Child Has a Food Intolerance?

My daughter was fine while I was breast-feeding, but when I started solids she began getting a rash around her mouth and horrible, dirty diapers. I had a friend who had a child who was allergic to milk and wondered if this could be the same problem. Sure enough, after three milk-free days the rash and the diarrhea disappeared. I tested by giving her a small amount of cheese mixed with potato, and by the end of the meal her skin began to look red around the mouth, and within an hour the rash had reappeared.

The only sure test of any food intolerance is elimination and challenge. This means eliminating, or cutting out, the suspect food from the diet and then, once symptoms have disappeared, challenging by reintroducing a small amount again with the symptoms reappearing. If symptoms do not disappear or reduce significantly within three to five days of completely cutting out the food, you can conclude that this is unlikely to be the problem. If they do disappear and return with reintroduction of the food, it seems likely that this is the cause. When this is done under the supervision of a specialist, it will be strictly controlled to make sure the suspect food really is being eliminated and not taken in other forms, and that the child's diet remains nutritionally balanced. However, more than one food may be the cause, and determining the true source of the problem is definitely a job for an expert.

Parents often try eliminating foods from their child's diet without any medical supervision in the hope it may help a physical or behavioral problem. There are potential hazards with do-it-yourself testing, so children should not be put on elimination diets without expert supervision. There are possible dangers in reintroducing foods to a child who is highly allergic, and it is also sometimes a difficult task to pinpoint exactly what is causing a reaction because it is often a combination of unrelated foods. Seek medical advice to be sure you have a correct diagnosis of your child's symptoms. If you or your physician decide to test your child for food intolerance, be careful to do it safely by keeping in mind these points:

- Symptoms must not be treatable by other means; for example, 75 percent of children with eczema respond to ointment and creams, and only if these fail should a special diet be considered.

- Be objective and do not convince yourself in advance that food intolerance is necessarily your child's problem.

- Cutting out cow's milk to test for a reaction by omitting milk temporarily will not do any harm in the short term in the older child; five days should be enough to see if this is the problem. Some children, however, react to goat's milk and soy-based formula if these are given instead of cow's milk. Others react more severely when milk is reintroduced as a test dose or by accident after it has been omitted from the diet for a time. Ask your pediatrician for advice. In the long term you need advice from your child's physician if your child is to follow a safe, milk-free diet to be sure she is still getting the nutrients she needs. The pediatrician can also advise on the need for supplementary vitamins or minerals and brands of foods that are free from milk.

- If symptoms appear only after you've introduced solid foods, keep a diary of what your child eats and the occurrence of signs such as rashes or diarrhea, but be aware that not all of these are due to allergy. Get the cooperation of your partner or a friend to help you to be objective about the severity of symptoms. Study the diary to try to pinpoint troublesome foods. Wheat and egg are two very common antigens after cow's milk and occur in many foods, but if they are excluded from the diet, nutritional replacements are necessary to ensure that your child grows and develops properly.

- Cut out only one food at a time; otherwise you will not know what caused an improvement.

- Once you've identified a problem food, be careful to cut out all products with that item in. This may mean a lot of label reading. During the time this item is cut out, replace it with something from the same food group so your child still has a balanced diet; for example, if you omit wheat, replace it with rice or rice flour or rice cereals (see "What Is a Balanced Diet?" in chapter 7 for more details).

- Food addiction is often an aspect of food intolerance. Strangely enough, we sometimes crave the things that make us sick. If your child regularly likes and eats a lot of a certain food—say, oranges or milk—try cutting out that item first.

- Be very cautious about reintroducing a supposed problem food. Two reactions are possible after a problem food has been eliminated for a period: either the child may be able to tolerate small amounts of the food again, or she may lose what tolerance she had for the food so that even an extremely tiny amount can make her very sick, and in extreme cases she may go into what is called anaphylactic shock and collapse. For this reason you must test with only a very tiny amount of the suspect food for one to two days in case your child reacts severely, and then increase to a full serving daily for a week. Give the test dose with two adults present and watch your child for the first twenty minutes in case a severe reaction occurs.

Your child may grow out of food intolerance, so do not keep the fixed idea that she can never eat a certain item again. Occasionally test her with a very small amount, and if it seems safe, gradually reintroduce it.

CHAPTER 7

Feeding Your Child Up to Age Five

What is a balanced diet?
Good eating habits—lessons for life
Tips for feeding a young family
Good meals don't have to be a chore
Drinks • Candy • Family eating habits
Eating problems • The overweight child
Behavior problems and food intolerance

A calorie (also called a joule) is a unit of energy. We all need energy, and children need a great deal because they are not only naturally very active, but they are also growing. While a woman of average build, working at home, taking care of children, and running the house, would burn up about two thousand calories a day, her two-year-old son would need about twelve hundred calories. When you consider that he probably weighs only thirty pounds, perhaps a quarter or less of her weight, you can see just how many calories he uses up in the vital process of making extra tissue grow. Children, then, need a great many calories, but energy alone is not enough for the body to stay healthy and grow. We also need protein, vitamins, and minerals. Some foods, such as candy, contain lots of calories but nothing else. Others, such as meat, fish, cheese, and cereals, provide energy along with protein and other nutrients. Bread, cereals (particularly the whole wheat varieties), fruit, and vegetables should make up the major part of the diet. Eating the right mixture is called a "balanced diet."

What Is a Balanced Diet?

A little of everything, but everything in moderation, is probably the best way to describe a balanced diet. Imagine the body as a very complicated machine—different types of foods provide different kinds of nutrients, which the body is able to absorb in just the right amounts to provide the perfect fuel. Missing out on one type of food over a long period means that the body has to try to run on incomplete or poor-quality fuel. Just like any machine, that will inevitably mean a strain on the different parts, which can finally show in malfunction or breakdown—in other words, poor health or illness.

The bodies of children need the best-quality fuel even more than adults because their body machines are also growing and expanding. A poor diet through childhood can mean a child's body never grows properly or has a number of built-in weaknesses. Children who regularly eat nothing but cookies and candy will be short of protein, vitamins, and minerals. At the other end of the spectrum, a child who eats nothing but fruit and vegetables may take in large quantities of vitamins and minerals but miss out on protein and enough calories.

In recent years we as a society have become far more conscious of the ways in which our diet affects our health and of diet-related illnesses. The fact that we Westerners eat far too much sugar and too little fiber, whole grain foods, fruits, and vegetables has been said by some experts to be one of the main causes of illnesses such as heart disease, diabetes, and even some forms of cancer.

Nutritional experts have recommended that the population as a whole cut the amount of fat and sugar it eats and replaces the calorie deficit with whole grain cereals, fruit, and vegetables. But what some parents have overlooked is that it has been specifically stated that these rules should not apply to the children under five. The reason is that their metabolism, the rate at which they burn up calories, is quite different from that of adults. It makes sense to limit the sugary foods and drinks such as sodas and juices because these are empty calories, meaning they provide energy but little else. Too many will only give your child poor eating habits, which may make him overweight, rot his teeth, and deprive him of other nutrients. However, parents who mistakenly apply adult eating rules too zealously to their young children could unwittingly end up depriving them of the large number of calories they need to grow. If growth is affected during this toddler stage, it can have long-term effects on development. This is not a reason, however, to become overanxious about hunger-striking toddlers who go through phases of refusing many foods they previously enjoyed.

Types of foods can be divided into five different groups (see below) for the nutrients they provide. Include some from each group each day to ensure that you are eating a balanced diet. Don't worry if children seem to go from hamburger and fries to sandwiches and cookies one day—just make sure you cut down on fatty and sugary foods the next day, and give them more in the fruit and vegetable line.

Food Groups

Milk and Milk Products   Milk, yogurt, cheese, and cottage cheese provide protein for body building and repair, calcium for teeth and bones, and vitamin A and some B vitamins for good health.

Meat, Fish, Eggs, and Beans   Beef, pork, lamb, liver, kidney, chicken, turkey, herring, mackerel, whitefish, sardines, tuna, shellfish, eggs, peas, beans, lentils, and nuts all provide protein for body building and repair—especially muscle and tissue. Liver, kidney, and egg yolk are especially rich in iron for normal blood. Fatty fish (herring, mackerel, and sardines) are especially rich in vitamin D for strong bones. (Vegetarians can use peas, beans, lentils, and nuts to provide protein, iron, and vitamins, but do not give whole nuts to any child under five years because there is a real danger of choking; peanut butter or ground nuts are allowed.)

Bread and Cereals   Whole grain bread, cereals, rice, and pasta are better than white grain products, which have been stripped of some of their nutritional content and also fiber. These are high-energy foods and contain some vitamins and minerals, too. Fiber makes the intestines work properly and prevents constipation, and eating more fiber in the form of whole grains, fruit, and vegetables may be important in preventing certain types of bowel disease. Most young children happily accept whole wheat bread, pasta, and brown rice if everyone else eats them, but if your child will eat only white bread this is still a good basic food, and he should certainly carry on eating this rather than go without bread at all. Bran is not necessary and should not be fed to young children, except that found naturally in whole grain bread and cereals, as it can interfere with the absorption of important minerals such as calcium and zinc. It may also give a child stomach cramps. Children who do not eat excessive amounts of sweet foods are more likely to have healthier teeth without cavities. Liking and craving sugar is a habit that can be hard to break; you will be doing your child a big favor by not adding sugar to drinks and foods and by teaching him to enjoy dried or fresh fruit as treats, rather than eating too many sweets. Many sugar foods are high in calories but low in other nutrients, which increases the risk of getting fat without providing any of the fuel the body needs to function.

Fruit and Vegetables   All fruits and vegetables contain vitamins that are very important for our health and growth. Vitamin A, for example, is important for our eyesight and also for the health of our skin, hair, and nails; like many vitamins, it can also increase our resistance to infection. Carotene is a substance that is converted to vitamin A in the body and is supplied by carrots, tomatoes, and all green and some yellow vegetables—for example, squash or sweet potatoes. It is also found in dried apricots and prunes. Vitamin C increases our resistance to infection and is important for tissue repair and normal growth. It is found in citrus fruits such as lemons and oranges, in berries, and also in green, leafy vegetables. Unfortunately, the vitamin content of vegetables is easily destroyed by cooking or processing, so whenever possible let your child eat them raw or steam the vegetables. Do not store fresh vegetables for a long time before using them. Remember that frozen vegetables are often as good as fresh ones, and they do not lose their vitamins during the freezing process. Canned vegetables will have lost much of their vitamin content and may also contain chemical additives. While many children go through a phase of refusing cooked vegetables, they will often eat raw vegetables, such as sticks of carrot or celery, and also fresh fruit.

Fats and Oils   Our bodies need some source of fat to protect and insulate vital organs, especially the nervous system. Some fats also contain fat-soluble vitamins A, D, E, and K. Fats can be either saturated, monounsaturated, or polyunsaturated, and recent research suggests that eating too much of the saturated type of fats, which come mainly from animal sources, can be bad for us and in the long term may be linked to heart disease. Red meat, meat fats, and dairy products are high in saturated fats, so replace some of these foods with chicken, turkey, or oily fish such as mackerel or herring, and use cooking oils from plant sources such as sunflower, soy, and corn oils rather than lard. These foods are all higher in polyunsaturated fats. Red meat is a good source of iron and zinc and does not have to be cut completely out of the diet.

For a child under five, try to avoid feeding too much fried food, but there is no need to prevent him from eating butter. Simply use fat for cooking sparingly, and replace some of the foods high in saturated fats with those rich in polyunsaturated fats. Don't give skim milk, because the fat-soluble vitamins contained in milk are found mainly in the cream. Taking away most of the fat from milk not only lowers its calorie count but also reduces the amount of essential fatty acids and vitamins it has to offer. Ask your doctor what kind of milk is best, but usually whole is recommended between ages one and two, and 2 percent milk up to age four.

Good Eating Habits—Lessons for Life

Good eating habits have nothing to do with how you hold a knife and fork but are about the kind of food you eat, your attitudes to food, and the part that food plays in your life. Our ideas start being shaped in the early years by what our parents teach us—both in the example they set and in the foods they offer. This early influence can be far-reaching and carries through into school years and often into adult life. Good eating habits lessen the risk of weight problems and increase the likelihood of good health, so you will be doing your child a big favor if you look objectively at your own eating habits and try not to pass on the bad ones.

* *Do* teach your child to eat mainly at mealtimes. It does not matter that the actual times may be a bit erratic or the meals informal—you are teaching that eating happens at specific times and that life is not a nonstop snack. However, most young children need three small meals and three snacks a day.

* *Do not* feed him frequent high-calorie snacks between meals. He will then not be hungry for the more nutritious food offered at the meal and thus be deficient in some of the essential nutrients. To begin with, babies and toddlers need five to six meals and snacks a day, but that is different from untouched meals and endless chips, cookies, and sugary drinks in between.

* *Do* teach him to enjoy a wide variety of different foods. You need to persist when offering new foods to toddlers and babies, and continue to give small amounts of new items until they get used to the taste.

* *Do not* be tricked into giving only two or three particular foods in the early days to a fussy toddler because that is all he seems to want; keep trying different ideas in between the favorites, and do not get upset when he refuses.

* *Do* set the example you want him to imitate with your own eating habits. Children are highly imitative, and that applies to what you eat, not just how you eat. Share mealtimes and eat the same foods once they are old enough for ordinary family food. If Mom and Dad do not have vegetables, neither will their children.

* *Do not* teach him to crave sweet foods. If you never give sweet drinks and foods, he will never miss them. Mothers often find it hard to feed their children drinks or foods they would not like, but if you already have the sugar habit, resist the temptation to pass it on—too much sugar can rot the teeth and be harmful to health. Try to eliminate it yourself.

* *Do* teach him to enjoy fresh fruit and vegetables by giving him different varieties from an early age and by eating them yourself.

* *Do not* condition him into eating extra salt by sprinkling it over food at the table—it is quite unnecessary. Fast and preprepared foods, and not just the savory ones, contain a lot of added salt, so we are already taking in quite a bit of salt without adding extra. There is good scientific evidence that eating too much salt over a lifetime may predispose certain people to high blood pressure. Giving salt to babies, even in homemade foods, is not advised, since it increases the risk of their becoming ill and at times dehydrated.

* *Do* let him follow his natural appetite in deciding how much to eat. If you do not let him fill up on continuous snacks between meals, his hunger will determine how much he eats at any meal.

* *Do not* insist that he always clear his plate, or try to cajole him into eating more than he wants.

Tips for Feeding a Young Family

Do not be overwhelmed by thinking that feeding your child good food has to mean making everything yourself, expensive trips to the health food shop, or spinach four times a week. There are easier ways.

Fruits and Vegetables

Most children like some kind of fruit. Seedless grapes, bananas, melons, peaches, apples, and pears can all be cut into pieces as soon as children are old enough for finger foods. Once they get to the stage of noticing what they eat, many children stop eating vegetables. Do not force them to try to eat vegetables because you will be enforcing the idea that they are unpleasant. Instead, make sure they have some fruit and a little diluted fruit juice each day for vitamin C, and go on enjoying and experimenting with vegetables yourself. Children are tremendous imitators, and at some stage their curiosity will make them want to try what is on your plate. In between you can occasionally try them with raw pieces of vegetables to eat with their fingers while waiting for the meal to be ready—carrots, celery sticks, cauliflower, uncooked peas and beans in their pod, cucumbers, and tomatoes are all likely favorites. Make sure that the pieces of the vegetables are not too small, to prevent aspiration and choking.

Preprepared and Fast Foods

Manufacturers process foods in many ways to allow them to be kept for extended periods. In general, the more processing a food undergoes, the more additives it will contain. There may be chemical colorings, flavorings, or preservatives. Thus frozen fish is a useful and nutritious buy, but by the time it has been turned into a ready-made frozen fish it will probably need to contain a preservative to keep it fresh. It will also be more expensive. A rough guide is to go for those foods that still resemble their original state—that is, you can recognize them when they come out of a packet or can! Frozen vegetables can be as good as fresh ones because they retain their vitamin and fiber value, but canned vegetables have had to undergo more processing and will usually have had salt added.

Weight Watching

Only a small number of young children are overweight, but the tendency increases by the time they reach their teenage years. Children who are allowed to follow their appetite, who are not encouraged or expected to eat more than they want, and who keep active will rarely get fat, but it makes sense not to offer any child too much sugary or fried fatty foods. Grilled and baked foods are preferable to fried foods—for example, fish sticks and hamburgers can be just as easily grilled. Naturally this makes even more sense with a child who has a tendency to gain excessive weight, but if you have a serious problem you may need expert advice to help him to slim down.

Good Meals Don't Have to Be a Chore

Good food does not have to keep you tied to the kitchen, and if your child is going through a fussy or hunger-striking phase, you will save yourself much aggravation by keeping meals very simple and by spending the time sharing other activities with your child, such as looking at a book, playing a game, or going to the playground. Sandwiches made with whole wheat bread covered with peanut butter and a little jelly, cheese, tuna fish, ham, bacon, tomato, or whatever your child likes in the tasty, not the sugary, line, together with some pieces of fruit and a drink of milk or some yogurt, make a well-balanced meal. If he will not eat sandwiches, just cut up pieces of bread and butter and something like cheese or ham for him to eat with his fingers, or try a hard-boiled egg with fruit to follow. In winter you can toast sandwiches and offer a cup of soup and crackers to dip in it if he is able to do so.

If you cook only in the evening, you can freeze a portion for him to have at a later date, but be sure to defrost quickly by standing the container in cold water, and then heat thoroughly to boiling point before allowing it to cool enough for him to eat. You can also use the microwave to defrost the food, but be sure to test the food for hotness before giving it to your child. If you save a portion for the next day, cool it quickly and keep it covered in the refrigerator, again reheating to the boiling point. Do not save cooked food longer than twenty-four hours in the refrigerator or reheat more than once for a young child—if he does not want it, throw it away and do not be tempted to heat it up.

Most young children have a particular time in the day when they are hungry and eat well—do not necessarily expect him to want a full-size meal every time, but capitalize on his favorite eating time, whether it is breakfast, lunch, or dinner, and feed a variety of types of food. For example, if he always eats a large breakfast, you can give protein in the form of egg, bacon, peanut butter and jelly, or anything else he likes rather than just let him fill up on two bowls of cereal. If he does not eat much fresh fruit, then offer this at his hungriest time, too. If you suspect that he eats well at a certain meal because he is especially fond of what is offered, such as cereal, do not cut this out completely, but feed slightly less, and include other foods or fruit that he may be less likely to take on other occasions.

Avoid very spicy foods for babies under a year, and do not feed whole nuts to children under five because of the danger of choking.

Drinks

Children are usually more thirsty than adults because their bodies do not adjust well to a sudden loss of fluid, such as occurs, for example, with vomiting and diarrhea or during hot weather. A two-year-old needs at least two quarts of fluid a day and a three-year-old at least three quarts, with more in hot weather. The amount and concentration of urine give a guide to the adequacy of the fluid intake.

Most commercial fruit-flavored drinks contain very little fruit and a great deal of sugar and additives, so get your child into the habit of drinking milk, diluted fresh fruit juice, and water instead. The label "natural unsweetened fruit juice" on a drink means it must contain 100 percent fruit juice and no added sugar or preservatives. Concentrated fruit juice is also pure fruit juice, but needs diluting because it has been thickened and reduced in quantity. Fruit nectar contains 25 percent to 50 percent fruit juice, up to 20 percent sugar, and large amounts of water, plus possibly preservatives, but exact quantities must be given on the package label. Fruit drinks have even less fruit juice and more sugar and water. Sodas are acceptable for occasional treats, but are not good thirst quenchers because they are so sweet, they tend to make children even thirstier, are bad for their teeth, and take their appetite away from eating more important foods. The amount of sugar in a typical cola is about 8 percent. Since most older children do learn to love soda, you could let them mix carbonated mineral water with fruit juice to make their own mixtures—cheaper, healthier, and more thirst-quenching.

Candy

My mother-in-law loves giving the children candy, but she won't ask me first, and doesn't just give small items but hands over whole bags of candy or big packets of lollipops. I have tried saying tactfully that it is too much, and after she is gone I secretly take half away, but I don't want to offend her by being so strict.

If you do not give your child candy he will not expect it. Certainly this should be avoided for babies and small children. Once your child knows what candy is, you will have to cope with his demands, even at the checkout counter in the supermarket. The first time you pick up a packet of candy while waiting in the checkout line and hand it to your child, you are showing him that he can sometimes have the candy he sees—and "sometimes" is a very hard idea for a young child to accept. When he wants some the next time, he is more likely to make a fuss if you do not buy any. It is much better to save candy for special occasions, rather than buy it or hand it out routinely so it becomes expected.

In terms of tooth care, allowing your child an occasional piece of candy is better than having him eat it over a longer period—always brush his teeth well immediately after eating the candy, especially the sticky type. Chocolate is also bad for teeth, but unlike other forms of candy does offer some nutritional value in the form of protein and iron. Check the label on the wrapper to make sure it is real chocolate and not just chocolate-flavored or a small amount of chocolate around a sugary toffee.

Spoiling grandchildren is one of the joys of being a grandparent, but spoiling their teeth, making them less likely to eat anything nutritious at mealtime, and teaching them to expect candy is not doing them any favors. Exactly what you say to doting relatives who turn up looking as if they have just raided a candy factory depends on your relationship with them, but you are more likely to get their cooperation if you phrase it as pleasantly as you know how and give them specific guidelines. This may mean saying that only one lollipop or small chocolate bar (preferably give the actual brand name because their idea of "small" may not be yours) can be given, but if they really want to give more they can be saved for a party, special occasion, or to share with friends, though you had better check with the friends' mothers first! Steer relatives in the direction of treats from the fruit and vegetable stand of the supermarket instead, like a bag of seedless grapes, berries, strawberries, or a bag of dried fruit if your child is five or over. A good alternative is a container of good-quality ice cream made from milk.

Family Eating Habits

Table manners differ in every home—your example is by far the best way to get your child to behave as you want because he will inevitably copy your pattern of family eating. Children who are brought up from an early age to sit around a table with other members of the family will soon pick up on adult behavior, learn not to interfere with other people's food, and learn to ask if they want more and to handle the silverware as you do. If meals are sociable times for interesting and fun types of conversation, your children will eventually learn something about taking turns to talk, although this is quite a sophisticated task. Try not to make your baby or young child the focus of too much attention at family gatherings because he can become self-conscious or start to show off. Remember that if eating off your lap in front of the television or grabbing a snack on the move is more your family's style, you cannot expect a young child to know how to behave at the occasional, more formal meal when visiting relatives, friends, or at holiday time, so make allowances for him.

Usually we tend to follow similar patterns of both what and how we eat to those of our parents, but eating rituals vary with different cultures. Children of other nationalities may be brought up with the food and customs of their parents' country and only later learn about the different habits they may see in the homes of friends or when they are out visiting.

Eating Problems

I made her a bowl of rice pudding and she looked at it, and then at me, and then very deliberately picked it up and emptied it onto the floor. I really yelled at her and then felt so guilty.

Most parents have concerns at some stage about how much their child eats, what he eats, or how he eats it. This is quite understandable, especially with a first child when parents do not have any experience with childish idiosyncrasies. Sometimes it is also hard to make the transition from dealing with an utterly dependent baby who has to be fed little, often, and just the right foods to dealing with a young child whose needs are suddenly different and who can let you know when he is and is not hungry and what he wants to eat.

Many emotions are bound up in preparing and giving food. Having food rejected can feel like an insult to the chef, and children quickly find out how much you care, even though they may not understand exactly why.

Toddlers can do all kinds of horrific things with food, some of them innocent, and some, as they get more experienced and smarter, more testing. Obviously you have to let them know what is and what is not acceptable, but beware of making too much of what would otherwise simply be a passing phase about how much or what they eat because that is often how something trivial can develop into a real problem.

The Child Who Won't Eat

My son stopped eating anything much at fourteen months—looking back I realize now it was because the weather was hot and he'd just learned to walk. Eating was boring and he wasn't hungry, but at the time I couldn't see it so clearly and wasted hours following him around with spoons of food, trying to get him to eat. It became a real game to him. If only I had ignored it all, the whole thing would probably never have become such a problem. As it was, he didn't eat normally until he was three and a half and going to nursery school.

All children go through phases of not eating, eating very little, or eating only a few foods—commonly labeled "hunger strikes." They usually begin in the second or third year and reach a peak at about four years, disappearing with the start of school. If you largely ignore the problem and do nothing but offer healthy meals and snacks without making a fuss or letting your child continually nibble in between, his hunger will ensure that he takes what he needs. The more you try to encourage or force him to eat, the more he will discover how important this is to you, and what power he has to demand your attention.

No healthy child will allow himself to starve, so if you have any other reasons, apart from his lack of appetite, to worry about his health, see his doctor. Probably the best test to find out whether he is eating enough is to see if he is growing properly. A check of his height and weight against his expected growth can be plotted on a chart. If this is all right, as it will be for most children, then exercise appropriate indifference to plates of untouched food, but do not allow him to fill up on extra snacks of any kind in between meals or offer other treats instead. Sometimes parents who complain that their child does not eat do not look realistically at what the child is eating between mealtimes in the form of candy, cookies, chips, and other snacks.

Do not forget that drinks are food, too, and often young children who seem to eat nothing are still drinking a great deal of milk and juice. Liquids are also filling, so drinks of any kind before meals will take away his appetite. If this is happening, cut the amount of milk your child drinks to one pint of whole milk per day and do not give sweetened drinks at all, only water. Remember that although after the age of six months milk alone is not enough to meet all his requirements, such as iron, milk is nevertheless an important source of calcium and other nutrients and that most children should drink between a pint and a quart of milk a day.

Often parents worry that even though their child seems healthy now, eating very little will lower his resistance to illness and infection—he will not have the right reserves of vitamins and minerals. Provided your child is healthy, this is not true. You should, of course, if you are worried, continue to supplement his diet with children's vitamins as prescribed by his physician. Very delicate mechanisms operate to ensure that we absorb just the right amounts of vitamins and minerals, and eating a lot or taking massive extra supplements does not mean the body is able to store more; in fact, too much of some vitamins, such as vitamins A and D, is toxic.

Eating and Illness

A loss of appetite is often the first sign of illness, which is usually followed by other symptoms such as a temperature, tiredness, irritability, vomiting, diarrhea, complaints about pain, or a rash. As when he is healthy, the best guide as to what your child needs will probably be his appetite, but remember he will need extra fluids when he's sick. If he does not want anything at all, just concentrate, especially in the case of sickness and diarrhea, on giving him plenty of fluids to prevent his becoming dehydrated. Special solutions are available over the counter that contain a mixture of salt and sugar that you can give your child to prevent dehydration. It is never wise to make up your own mixtures of salt and sugar, since the smallest deviation from a prescribed formula could make your child sicker. If his lips and mouth appear dry and/or he hasn't passed urine for a number of hours (the number depends on the age of the child, but as a guide, four to six hours for a baby under one year and eight to ten for a child from one to five years), go to see or call your physician for advice.

Generally, though, as appetite returns, illness is a time to relax some aspects of eating rules, so try to tempt him with sweetened drinks and interesting but nourishing snacks. Eating problems can often follow an illness when fads have been indulged, and you need to assess carefully when to go back to the "rules" by gradually reintroducing normal eating. This may mean weaning a child who has gone back to having mainly breast- or bottle-feedings onto solids all over again, or reestablishing a pattern of regular mealtimes for a child who has gotten used to eating snacks whenever he wants.

Frequently children are temporarily ravenous after a bout of illness and eat anything and everything. However, although they will need extra drinks and snacks, they sometimes cling to eating habits they were allowed when ill. Parents who have been worried about their child and nursed him through an illness are naturally more anxious and do not want to upset him. However, the same rules apply as at other times—keep him busy and distracted between meals so he forgets about asking for in-between treats; offer such treats at mealtimes sometimes if you think he will like them, as well as two or three extra drinks or snacks for a week or two. Do not make too much fuss or comment if he does not seem hungry.

Children Who Want Food All the Time

Refrigerator raiders are not as common as hunger strikers, but this can be a passing phase that develops into a habit because it gets so much reaction from you. Taking food without asking, especially in other people's houses, is a sure way of getting your attention. It can be a sign of jealousy, for example, about a new baby. Make sure you give your child plenty of attention at other times and keep him busy and occupied in order to take his mind off food. Offer foods and drinks he likes at meal- or snack-times, but explain that extras are not permitted, except water. Play down your reactions to his eating habits generally; often children who seem obsessed with food can also be very fussy and refuse food at mealtimes. This may be another way of gaining your attention or the result of nibbling between meals. If you think the problem has become serious or if your child is getting fat, discuss the problem with your pediatrician (see also the section "The Overweight Child" later in this chapter).

Is Food Too Important?

My mother never cuddled or played with us but spent all her time in the kitchen preparing meals. She would take it as the most personal insult if you weren't hungry or didn't like something she served, and to this day I still can't leave anything on my plate and both of my brothers and I have weight problems. She also had a very martyred attitude to it all—serving up wonderful children's meals at parties but with a stony face that defied us not to enjoy every mouthful after we had caused her so much work.

When long-term battles about food become established, it can often be that the whole relationship between parent and child has come to rest on food and eating alone. If you seem to be at this stage, think about how much of your attention your child gets in other areas of his life. Do you play games or join in activities with him? Do you read stories to him, go for walks together, or sit him on your lap and talk about what he is watching on television? It may be that food is very important to you in some way, or that you find it hard to show affection to your children in other ways and feeding them becomes either the only way to show affection or a substitute for love. Children may make more and more out of what they will and will not eat if it is the only way they can get your individual attention and a genuine response; the fact that you get angry does not make any difference.

Try to take the emphasis off food and concentrate on sharing other aspects of your child's life. If you find this difficult, then talking to your partner, a good friend, or a professional you trust, such as your child's pediatrician, may be helpful.

Using Food as Punishment or Reward

Once children are old enough to understand, it is reasonable to say "no dessert" until they have eaten some of their meal, though there is no need to insist on a clean plate. This is a straightforward reward system and probably what you have been practicing when they were younger. It is also reasonable to deprive a child of a treat if it is set in context—for example, if they behave badly in at the store or supermarket and you are buying them candy or chips, then eliminating the expected treat is an obvious punishment. However, withholding candy or ice cream for bad behavior in a situation that has nothing to do with the food in question, or handing out candy and other treats for good behavior, just puts too much emphasis on food and eating all the time.

The Overweight Child

Exactly what being overweight is, is difficult to measure and even harder to define. There can be many causes and specialists all have different ideas and approaches to the subject. However, there are some general points to keep in mind if you think your child may be becoming overweight, or if you have a weight problem yourself and are anxious about your child.

The first is that prevention is better than cure, and it is probably easier to help an overweight child slim down in the preschool years when you still have greater control over what he eats, when his eating habits are not as fixed, and when the child is distracted from food with less difficulty. Later, when a pattern of eating too much and being overweight is established, it can be very hard to change. So at what point should you begin to watch your child's weight? Start by seeing that your baby does not get too fat because this will make him more prone to respiratory illnesses and he may be slower to do things such as turning over, sitting up, crawling, and walking just because too many rolls of flesh make it more difficult. Most fat babies grow into normal-weight children, and it is only a small proportion of them, about one in ten, who are still fat when they start school. Include a good range of fruit and vegetables, cereals, and small servings of high-protein foods. Distract the older baby with finger foods and smaller quantities of spoon foods at meal- and snacktimes. Usually rolls of fat start to disappear during the second year when the child learns to walk, becomes more active and able to do more, and is usually less interested in food. For these reasons you should always let a child's appetite dictate how much he eats and not try to force or coerce him into eating more.

Probably the best way to prevent a child from becoming overweight is to teach good eating habits in the early preschool years. This means eating a wide range of different foods and not just a very few favorite items—many overweight children are also extremely fussy about what they eat, sticking to just a narrow range of foods, and have a tendency to dislike fruit and vegetables. Offer pieces of fresh fruit or raw vegetables instead of chips, cakes, or candy as edible treats or midmorning or supper snacks.

It is very important for you to teach your child that eating is something that happens at specific mealtimes and to give only a drink between meals to the child who is overweight. Continual snacking will also make children likely to refuse the more nutritious food you offer at mealtimes. Teach your child to drink water right from the start and keep sweet drinks such as sodas or juices for special occasions. If a child stays fat after the first year of life, or after being normal suddenly becomes fat and gets into the habit of eating sweet, high-fat, high-calorie snacks and drinks, his risk of growing into an overweight teenager and adult is greater. If a child is fat at seven he has an almost 50 percent chance of continuing to be heavy into adult life.

Why do some children become or stay fat? We do know what makes them fat: taking in more energy from food than is needed so that extra energy is stored as body fat. But even at that point the matter becomes complicated because all children sometimes eat more than they need—so why do some stay slim and others become fat? Obesity runs in families, so a child with two overweight parents has a much higher chance of becoming so himself. Whether this is because of some inherited tendency to obesity or because families share similar eating habits and attitudes to physical activity is uncertain; probably both factors are involved.

A pattern of eating more than is needed may begin for various reasons—perhaps the child is very difficult and the parent finds giving food is one of the only ways of comforting or appeasing him. This may be true at night as well as during the day, so that a baby or child with sleep problems gets offered far more night feedings or drinks. A parent who cannot show affection except by handing it out on the end of a spoon may put great emphasis on feeding, and in turn a child may try to please a parent by eating everything offered. Parents can also overfeed to compensate for guilt because they feel inadequate about some other aspects of their relationship with the child.

How to Tell if Your Child Is Fat

Look at your child when he is next running around naked or with a bathing suit on with other children of the same age—at bathtime, on the beach, at the swimming pool, or simply in the backyard. If he looks very fat, especially around the thighs and abdomen, in comparison with other children, then almost certainly he is overweight. Think about the clothes you buy for him—do they always have to be two or three age sizes bigger because you can't fasten the waist or because the sleeves are always too tight? The waist in particular is a good guide because tall but slim children may need bigger-age sizes because of their height, but in their case the waist invariably needs to be taken in to fit properly.

Parents with weight problems themselves can often have trouble recognizing or acknowledging a child's problem; if you are not sure, ask a couple of trusted friends for their opinion, but phrase the question so it allows them to answer honestly. "You don't think John is too big for his age?" may get a different response from, "I am not sure if I should be concerned about John's weight. What do you think?"

Weight adjusted to height charts are a good guide, though children who consistently take in more calories than they need tend to be taller than average as well. However, your child's pediatrician may simply be able to decide whether your child is too fat by looking at him.

Helping Your Child to Lose Weight

Many parents do recognize, at various stages, that their child is getting a bit heavy and solve the problem without professional help by just cutting down on high-calorie foods and drinks such as cookies, cakes, ice cream, and other sweets, keeping their child busy to take his mind off food, and encouraging more exercise. The preschool years are a time when you can more easily adjust your child's eating habits before he becomes seriously overweight. These are some simple rules to follow:

- Teach your child to eat only at mealtimes; a young child may need four small meals rather than three, but make them recognizable and definable occasions.

- Sit down and eat the same food as your child; use yourself and other members of the family or visiting children as examples to try to encourage him to eat a wide variety of foods.

- Between mealtimes give only fresh fruit or fresh vegetables as snacks.

- Provide plenty of opportunities for activity—walking, running, and playing with other children are the most easily arranged. Try to take frequent trips to playgrounds and swimming pools.

- Both parents must cooperate to ensure success, and it is important to have the cooperation of relatives and grandparents as well.

If your child is already into the habit of snacking on whatever he wants between meals, then putting these five rules into practice will demand energy and determination. If your child is accustomed to having whatever he wants to eat at almost any time, you will need to encourage him to eat only at mealtime—for example, by making sure he is hungry and by providing appealing but nutritious food. You'll also need to distract him from his usual snacking by keeping him busy and occupied. This may be particularly hard for if you are not, for whatever reason, in the habit of supervising most of your child's day.

Heavy two-year-olds will probably slim down naturally as long as you do not try to encourage or force them to eat more than they want; if you have a demanding new baby, resist the temptation to occupy the older child with food. Instead, plan a few distractions in advance that do not involve eating. By three years, children enjoy having friends over to play and visiting other homes, though you usually have to go, too. Playing with other children is both a distraction and an exercise and, if the other child has good eating habits and is of normal weight, then sharing meal-times can set a useful example. Enlist the help of sympathetic friends or relatives to keep your child busy. If you have a weight problem yourself it may be very hard to ask for help initially, but good friends with the same-age children can be very supportive. Professional help may sometimes be hard to come by. If your child is overweight, do not be tempted to ignore the problem because your doctor says that it is "baby fat" that will disappear of its own accord. If your doctor is unsympathetic try asking for a referral to see a hospital-based nutritionist. Special clinics do exist in some large hospitals but are not widespread for children; if your child's pediatrician is unable to tell you of the nearest one, call the nutritionist at your local hospital or the local county medical society.

Do be careful, though, not to talk about your child's weight in front of him or try to embarrass him into eating less. Instead, try to encourage the whole family to become more active.

Behavior Problems and Food Intolerance

Many young children show patterns of behavior that parents find hard to accept. Among these, disobedience, eating and sleeping problems, temper tantrums, restlessness, and difficulties in concentrating are among the most common. It is often suggested that food intolerance or allergy may be a cause of these difficulties, and there is some evidence that, in a small number of children, this is indeed the case. All the same, before jumping to the conclusion that your child is difficult because of something in his diet, it is sensible to be wary that food allergy or intolerance is the cause.

First, what is problem behavior? One person's uncontrollable home-wrecker can be another's adorable, lively toddler. Children do vary quite a bit in their personalities, and inevitably some are more active, restless, and willful than others. Second, our circumstances affect the way we view children's behavior; single parents with many problems, little support, and bad housing will naturally find the normal phases children go through more of a strain. Your child's behavior certainly is a problem if you find your life is being ruined by it, but the problem may be more in your child's behavior or more in the way you see it. If the problem goes on for some time, and other people, such as neighbors or a nursery school teacher, comment on it, then probably the problem is more in the child than in you. Even if this is the case, the way you are bringing up your child may be important, as well as his personality.

Hyperactivity

> My son never slept for long periods and cried a lot as a baby, but as a toddler he became impossible. He was always restless and miserable and never was calm. He was continually destructive but didn't even seem to get pleasure from that, and the number of accidents he had would fill a book. At nursery school he was aggressive and would never sit down with other children for more than a few minutes at storytime. He just whined or wandered around, darting between activities. Then I read about how sometimes additives can make children ill. I changed his diet, and within a week he began to sleep longer stretches at night, stopped wetting the bed, and sat in my lap and let me read a book to him for the first time.

One type of behavior problem is "hyperactivity." Doctors and psychologists use this term to describe children who are quite excessively active, have very poor concentration, and are reckless and impulsive wherever they may be—at home, with friends, or in a play group. It is often suggested that children with this particular type of problem may be reacting to something in their diets. There are some convincing stories that have been widely publicized, and information about additive-free diets is given below. Before applying a diet, however, remember these points:

* Your child may not be unusual in his behavior at all. The problem may be in the way you are seeing him. Check it out with friends and neighbors.

* There are many causes, other than diet, for children's behavior problems. Try to work out what situation seems to bring out the difficult behavior, and do something about that first. Are you being firm and consistent enough when he wants something he cannot have? Do you have enough time to give him the affection he needs? Does the problem occur only when his young baby sister is on the scene?

* Are there any positive signs that his behavior is likely to be caused by allergy? Does he, or anyone in your immediate family, suffer from other allergic problems, such as eczema? Is his difficult behavior accompanied by physical changes, such as his face becoming flushed or pale? Have you already noticed his behavior is worse after certain foods?

Additive-Free Diets

Additives are chemicals added to packaged food to make it keep safely, last longer, or taste and look as a manufacturer thinks people find most appealing. Preservatives in the form of benzoic acid and the yellow coloring tartrazine are said to be the most common culprits as far as allergies are concerned. There is no harm, however, in trying your child with a diet that omits the common additives listed below for a period to see if physical or behavioral problems improve. In some children simply cutting anything with artificial yellow coloring such as orange squash, lollipops, cakes, candy, and anything coated in bright golden breadcrumbs makes a difference. A number of manufacturers and supermarkets are now producing additive-free foods; the presence of additives is shown in foods on the content label of the package.

If your child's behavior remains a problem after you have tried an additive-free diet, you should consult your doctor. It is quite likely that factors other than diet may be producing the problem. Alternatively, if no other factors do seem likely and there are positive signs that diet may be the answer, then it is just possible that your child is reacting badly to naturally occurring foods such as milk, eggs, wheat, chocolate, or some fruits. To take this further, you must consult a doctor and a nutritionist who will be able to advise you how to cut out certain foods or even, if the problem is a severe one, how to put your child on a diet limited to just a very few foods to see if this makes a difference.

It is potentially dangerous to put your child on a diet cutting out these foods unless alternative sources of calcium and other vitamins and minerals are given, so this diet must be supervised by a nutritionist.

CHAPTER 8

Sleep, Wakefulness, and Crying

"Is she a good baby?"
What is sleep and why do we need it?
A bed for the baby • A book at bedtime
Sleep problems • Crying in young babies
If your baby won't stop crying
Nearing the end of your rope

"Is She a Good Baby?"

There can scarcely be a parent who has not been asked this question about a new baby. What the questioner often means is: "Does the baby sleep for long periods?" and "How much does the baby cry?" One of the biggest shocks of becoming a parent is discovering that the right you took for granted, to sleep when and as you wanted, has been taken away, apparently forever. No wonder that in any gathering of parents with young children there is so much comparing of notes about how much their child sleeps at night. Hearing that someone else's baby settles in for the night at 7:00 P.M. and sleeps without interruption until 6:30 A.M. the following day is certain to bring envy, and possibly a sense of inadequacy, to the many parents whose children seem to spring to life as dusk falls. If, in addition, the child cries a great deal and is very hard to console, the stress for the parents is intense. But be comforted. If your child is wakeful or cries frequently, take some reassurance from these simple truths:

- This is one of the most stressful and difficult times you will have to cope with. Things will get better.

- Babies vary in how well they sleep and how easy or difficult they are to console; you did not cause the problem.

- Although you did not cause the problem, there are things you can do to help.

- Problems with crying and sleeping tend to decrease over time.

What Is Sleep and Why Do We Need It?

Sleep is different from unconsciousness. When we are unconscious our brains hardly respond to any outside stimulation such as light, temperature, or noise, but during sleep our brains are still active, aware of the passage of time, and respond to bodily states such as hunger or anxiety as well as to certain sounds. Exactly why we need sleep is not yet fully understood, but one possibility is that it allows chemicals used by the brain to build up again so they are ready for the next day. Researchers have divided sleep into four stages, stage 1 being the lightest and stage 4 the deepest. During the night we go through several cycles of sleep, moving backward and forward from light to deep sleep. When in stages 3 and 4, the deepest sleep, we are much harder to wake, but when in the lightest stage of sleep we are more likely to wake, and in fact most people, both adults and children, do wake during the night but fall back asleep without remembering this brief period of wakefulness. However, if a child who is often rocked or cuddled to sleep awakes during the night, she may have difficulty falling back asleep without being rocked or cuddled. This child is likely to cause her parents many sleepless nights.

An additional division in types of sleep is between "rapid eye movement" (REM) sleep and non-REM sleep. REM sleep happens in the lighter stages and is when dreams and nightmares are most likely. People who are deprived of sleep fall more quickly into the deeper stages of sleep and also spend more time in REM sleep, as though they need to catch up on dreaming time.

One of the unfair facts of parenthood is that children seem to suffer less from loss of sleep than adults do. This is because children can catnap intermittently during the day—most parents know how impossible it is to keep a drowsy toddler awake in a stroller or car seat. For the adult it is hard to snatch a few minutes' sleep for themselves in a day filled with the demands of small children. Lack of sleep can make adults irritable and depressed, impair their judgment, and slow their reactions. Naturally this makes them less able to keep the problem of their child's wakefulness or crying in perspective and to act rationally. This may be especially true when we are awakened at night, because immediately on waking the mind is less alert—something most people realize only too well! This is also true for your child—the result can be two people who find it difficult to behave very rationally toward each other.

Sleep Patterns in the Newborn Baby

I expected my baby to sleep most of the time and only wake for feedings. It was a terrible shock when all she did was doze for an hour or two at a time.

It is a common mistake to think that new babies are either asleep or feeding. In fact a newborn baby spends six to eight hours of every twenty-four awake, often for an hour or so at a time, and some are more wakeful than others. The length of time that babies sleep between periods of wakefulness depends on the maturity of the brain as much as on their need for food. In the beginning, babies rarely sleep longer than three to five hours, but by four months most can sleep for a six- to ten-hour stretch during the night and can stay awake for several hours between naps during the day.

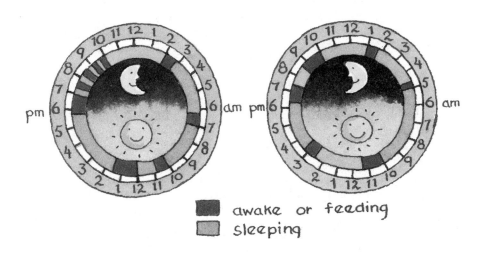

awake or feeding
sleeping

Encouraging a Different Pattern Between Day and Night

Manipulating the waking and sleeping hours of a young baby is not easy, but there are some things you can do to encourage longer stretches of sleep at night:

- Give plenty of stimulation and attention by talking and playing with your baby when she is awake in the day.

- In contrast, make the night feedings as unstimulating as possible—do not encourage your baby to stay awake and play after a feeding.

- Provided the baby does not have a dirty diaper or a diaper rash, it is not necessary to change the baby's diaper during the night. If you are using cloth diapers, it is often helpful to put the baby in double diapers before bed.

- When your baby reaches ten to twelve weeks of age, begin to establish a bedtime routine that the baby can get to know and recognize.

- Allow the baby to fall asleep on her own, so that she develops her own ways of falling asleep and does not rely on you to fall asleep.

Developing a Bedtime Routine

I used to spend hours trying to get my four-month-old daughter to go to bed in the evening when in fact she was having these great long naps late in the afternoon. Then she would stay up until ten o'clock at night. At the time I just couldn't see it because a friend's baby who also had long afternoon naps went to bed each night at seven-thirty. My daughter did not need as much sleep as my friend's baby.

Sometime between three and five months, depending on the baby, a definite bedtime routine will help your baby calm down and prepare to fall asleep. The goals are to encourage the child to be in a calm, relaxed state that is likely to make it easier to go to sleep, to establish a sequence of events the child recognizes as a signal that indicates it is time to go to bed, and lastly to help the child to learn to make the transition from waking to sleeping. You will work out the exact nature of your own child's bedtime routine, but the following points should be considered. The child should be in a clean diaper and should not be hungry or thirsty. In addition, the child must be tired. This last point may sound obvious, but remember that no two babies are alike—some need a lot of sleep, while others seem to manage on very little.

Sleep patterns can change. The baby who never sleeps can grow into a toddler who needs two naps a day, while the baby who sleeps through the night from early on can become a child with frequent night-waking. In the beginning we all settle babies in the way they respond to best—rocking, stroking, patting, and so on. These can help calm the baby during the bedtime routine, but remember that you are instilling habits that may continue into childhood. For this reason it is much better to devise a routine that ends with your baby falling asleep without your help. Hence crib-rocking, patting, or stroking the child until she falls asleep is not a good idea. Many babies fall asleep during a breast-feeding or a bottle-feeding, but again this is not a habit to encourage as a baby gets older. You will want to wean them at some point, and if the only way they have learned to fall asleep is while feeding, they have difficulty learning to fall asleep without the breast or the bottle. For this reason it is much better to finish the last feeding and place the baby in the crib while still awake so she can learn to fall asleep without feeding. You should help the baby to relax, sing a lullaby, pat or stroke her back, but then leave the room and let her actually fall asleep by herself.

Here are some suggestions for a young baby's bedtime routine:

- Bathe or wash her and put on a clean diaper and pajamas.

- Carry the baby upstairs, saying it is time for bed in a soothing voice.

- Give the last breast- or bottle-feeding in the baby's room, but do not let the baby fall asleep during the feeding.

- Sing a lullaby while rocking the baby on your shoulder, but again, not to the point of sleep.

- Settle the baby in the crib, saying good night.

- Leave the room without waiting to see the baby fall asleep or using singing, rocking, or patting to get the baby to fall asleep.

As your child grows, the bedtime routine needs to change to take account of age. From about twelve months, reading a story may be incorporated into the routine.

A Bed for the Baby

It seems that small babies do tend to sleep better in a fairly snug sleeping place. You can buy or borrow a bassinet or a small crib. In a pinch a large cardboard box will do as well, provided it has a firm mattress. A crib bumper is not recommended for babies under a year. Some parents like to take their baby into bed with them, which is safe provided neither parent is taking sleeping pills, drinking alcohol, or using other drugs.

New babies can lift and turn their heads to a certain extent, but they should never be put to sleep on a soft cushion, beanbag, pillow, or anything else that could obstruct their noses, however comfortable you think it seems. If babies cannot lift their heads clear of the material, there is a risk of suffocation. For this reason do not place a pillow or a quilt in a crib with a baby under one year old. A fairly firm mattress covered with one or two layers of flannel or cotton sheets pulled taut is fine. Do not use polyester sheets because they do not allow air through and are likely to make your baby sweaty and may cause mild skin irritation. If your baby tends to spit up, then putting an extra layer of a cloth diaper or folded sheet across the head end saves changing the whole bed every time a little milk comes up.

By about three or four months most babies begin to look rather cramped in a bassinet, unless they were very small to start with, and need to be moved to a crib.

Using the same type of blankets and sheets and transferring familiar toys will help your baby to sleep in the new crib. You can begin to get her used to it by putting her in the crib for a few times during the day, before she sleeps in the crib at night. Most babies make the switch without any problems. When to move your child into a regular bed depends on the child, the space available, and parental preference, but it is usually between twenty and thirty months.

It is important that small babies do not get too hot or too cold. Premature babies have difficulty keeping themselves warm. Several layers of light clothes are best. An undershirt, one-piece suit, and sweater are usually enough indoors during the day. At night dispense with the sweater, provided you use one or two blankets, keeping the room at a steady 65° F (18° C). During the day a baby over a month old need only wear the same amount of clothes as an adult. Choose a warm room for bathing young babies, though. If your baby wears an undershirt, this will avoid undressing her completely when changing sleepsuits or pajamas and help to keep her warmer. Unless your baby has diaper rash, a soiled diaper, or has wet pajamas, there is no need to change her during night feedings. Instead use double cloth diapers or an absorbent disposable with a liberal coating of a protective cream.

As they get older, babies can move out of one-piece suits and into any kind of pajamas you prefer. Remember always to buy those that are flameproof. Remember also that babies under two are especially likely to kick off blankets, and something to keep their feet warm is a good idea in winter. Some people still think it is necessary to put mittens on babies to stop them from scratching their faces. It is in fact much better just to clip their nails short. If you feel nervous about doing this, then baby nail-clippers may be easier to handle than scissors. Putting their hands and fingers to their mouths to suck is an important source of comfort and enjoyment for small babies, and they should not be prevented from discovering their hands.

Position

Recent research indicates that there is an increased risk of crib death if babies are allowed to sleep on their abdomens (tummies). It is better to lay babies on their backs. If they are on their sides, make sure the underneath arm is in front of the body to prevent rolling onto the tummy. Babies develop their own preferences quite quickly, though, and once your baby is able to turn over, she will naturally adopt the position she finds most comfortable. Make sure your baby does not get too warm while sleeping, and make sure that the bedding does not cover her head.

Baby Alarm Systems

There is a lot of anxiety about crib death—quite understandably. If your baby is at risk, then your pediatrician will advise you if an alarm system is necessary; otherwise following the guidelines we have outlined is quite sufficient.

Baby monitor systems are designed to allow parents to hear if their baby is crying rather than act as a warning system to detect apnea. They can be bought from most baby specialty and department stores, and can be useful if you have a house where sound does not carry easily.

Which Room?

While babies are waking quite often and at unpredictable intervals for feedings, most people prefer to have them sleeping in the same room, preferably within arm's reach of the parents' bed. If you find it easier still to have your baby sleeping in bed with you, then go ahead. As long as neither you nor your partner drink alcohol or use drugs, you will still respond to your baby's movements while asleep, and there is no danger she will get squashed. If you are breast-feeding, then having the baby in bed can be a way to catch extra sleep while nursing.

There is no danger that taking a small baby under four months into bed with you will spoil her or get her into the habit of always sleeping with you. Most children go through a phase of wanting to sleep in their parents' bed, whether they were allowed to as a small baby or not. However, parents who do not want their babies in bed with them should not feel guilty or think they are being less loving; we all vary in the amount and type of physical contact we want with our children, and it is simply a matter of choice for the individual.

Some parents worry that if their baby is not in the same room they will not hear her crying in the night. Provided sound normally carries between your room and where the baby is sleeping, that is highly unlikely because we all filter sounds in our sleep, and parents usually respond very quickly to their baby's cry. In fact the opposite is sometimes true, and parents are too sensitive to their baby's nighttime noises so that they wake with every rustle and whimper, without giving the baby a chance to settle again. In the early weeks, when the new baby is not disturbed by light and noise but needs several night feedings, keeping her in your room is usually easier. Once she gets to the stage when you have to avoid making a noise or putting on the light for fear of disturbing her—which hopefully may coincide with longer stretches of sleep—it may help to have her in another room if possible. In many families that means moving the baby in with another child. If the child has to continue sharing the parents' room, it may be harder to set firm limits regarding sleep habits, but all the advice about trying to encourage good sleeping habits still applies.

Comforters and Comfort Habits

> As a small baby my daughter got into the habit of rubbing a blanket against her face and sucking her thumb to go to sleep. When she was two we went on vacation and left the blanket behind on the airplane. It was total murder coping without it—every time she got sleepy she put her thumb in her mouth, reached for the blanket, and then howled and howled when it wasn't there. I tried every kind of substitute, but none would do. Fortunately we had a spare at home, and the minute we got through the front door that was the first thing she went to find.

At about six months of age babies often develop settling habits of their own. Perhaps the most common is sucking—either at a thumb, a pacifier, or a parent's finger. Thumb-sucking in fact often develops much earlier and is the best of the three because the child can find her own thumb in the night without disturbing anyone else. A pacifier can often be useful to soothe a crying baby in the first four months, but it is better to transfer children to sucking their own thumbs after that. At what stage should you begin to discourage thumb-sucking? The longer it persists, the harder it can be to stop, so by age four it is a good idea to discourage daytime thumb-sucking. Continuous thumb-sucking after the age when the permanent teeth begin to appear, usually about five or six years old, may eventually push the top teeth forward, which may entail corrective dentistry later. There is no evidence that children who thumb-suck are emotionally deprived. Most children suck their thumbs only when they are tired, and the attitudes of other children generally encourage even the most persistent thumb-sucker to give it up, at least in public, by the time she gets to eight or nine. Other comfort habits may be stroking something soft such as silky material, rocking, or twirling someone's hair. Children can form an attachment to a special blanket or other piece of material or a particular toy. Some children naturally form their own comfort habits or latch onto a comforter; others can be encouraged to if you think it will help, and other children again are not at all interested. Two points are useful to remember: the comfort habits should not involve anyone else, and the comfort object should have a backup spare or be easily replaced. As time goes on and as the object gets battered and tattered, then it is unlikely an identical new one will be accepted; you might consider rotating identical blankets or whatever in the early days, so that if one gets lost or destroyed it is not such a disaster.

Comfort habits and comfort objects may be used for many years, but eventually children learn to settle without them. In the early years they can be a great help to soothe and comfort in times of stress and separation as well as when a child is tired.

Moving from Crib to Bed

Some children make it quite obvious when they are ready to move—they begin climbing out of their crib, refusing to go in it, or simply starting to want to put themselves to bed in a brother's or a sister's bed. There is no right or wrong time to make the move in terms of age, although it's best to avoid moving them out of a crib just to make way for a new baby. It is more tactful to leave a gap of a few months and present the move to a bed as an achievement so they do not feel they have been pushed out of their crib by the baby.

Many children do not realize at first that they can actually get out of a bed, especially if they never learned to climb out of a crib. Once they do realize, they will inevitably put this newfound freedom to use and keep hopping out every five minutes. The answer is to keep the bedtime routine the same and make sure they are ready for sleep. If they get up, keep calmly but firmly putting them back to bed—do not suddenly weaken and let them stay up or take them into your bed, because you are teaching them that if they try hard enough they can have their own way. It may mean hard work and interrupted sleep again for a short time, but if you persevere for a couple of evenings or nights it will pay off in the long term.

You can use a bed rail or just put large cushions or chairs alongside the bed to stop your child from falling out in the beginning. Check the room again for safety once the child can get up without you knowing in the morning. There should be no unprotected windows left open, for example.

A Book at Bedtime

As your child grows, looking at books together or telling or reading a story is part of a useful bedtime routine because it provides:

- Quality time of quiet closeness for parents and children together.

- Something enjoyable for the child to look forward to in the bedtime routine.

- An opportunity to learn to enjoy books and stories.

By the time they reach their first birthday, many babies enjoy books, although their attention span is short and they often get as much fun from turning the pages as from looking at the pictures. Small children naturally enjoy turning the pages of a cardboard book and often begin to look at the pictures by themselves. Very realistic pictures of things they recognize, such as dogs, shoes, or a crib, tend to mean more than stylized or cartoon drawings at this stage. Naming the objects and talking about them help language to develop. Children like looking at the same book again and again, and a particular picture often holds a special fascination. At what stage you introduce simple stories depends on you and your child. Most children appreciate something more than just naming the pictures at some point between one and a half and two years. Listening to a story and following a sequence of pictures is very much a habit, one that will hopefully give your child a good start in enjoying books.

When it comes to a bedtime story or book, take the child into a quiet room so that you are not competing with television, other children's activities, or adult conversation for their attention. Make the child comfortable on your knee or snuggle up so that a cuddle becomes part of looking at books together. The child may enjoy choosing the books for this session. You do not have to spend a fortune to get nice books for your child. Your local library will have a children's section with picture books suitable for babies and upward, and yard sales are a good place to buy other people's outgrown books inexpensively. If you enjoy making things you can even make an exciting book for your baby by cutting pictures out of catalogs and sticking them on pieces of paper.

Sleep Problems

The most common sleep problems are difficulty going to sleep at bedtime and frequent night waking. It is very easy for a sleep problem to develop without parents being able to see that it is happening. Once the habit is established, they find it very hard to know how to change it. However, research has shown that by changing the way parents respond to their child's behavior they can succeed in changing the way their children go to bed and how they sleep through the night.

Many children stay up very late, sleep in their parents' bed, or will only go to sleep if someone stays near them. If this does not bother you and if your child is sleeping well, then it is not a problem, however unorthodox it might seem to another family. However, if your child is not sleeping well, or if your child's sleeping habits place great restrictions on your life, then these types of sleeping arrangements may be part of the problem.

It is often difficult to see exactly what is happening when you get caught in what seems to be a never-ending battle over sleep. Your own tiredness often prevents you from seeing things rationally or from having the strength to try changing the pattern. Start by keeping a diary of what happens at night, what your responses are, and what the child does. Do this for at least a week or two before deciding on your strategy.

If one parent has been caring for a sleepless child at night, it will be helpful for the other parent to be more involved. This will reduce fatigue for the parent who is managing the child at night, and if the other parent goes to see the child during the night it may help to break the pattern of night waking. This may be especially so if one parent cannot bear to see the child crying without picking her up. The important thing is that both parents agree on the plan to be tried, carry it through consistently, and back up each other. One parent must not suddenly change the plan and begin to criticize and undermine the parent who is going in to see to the child.

Bringing up children alone is very hard work—both emotionally and physically. Single parents may often let children stay up late or sleep in their beds for company. But they also often need the freedom to go out in the evening to enjoy other adult company, and leaving a child who is not used to a bedtime routine with a sitter can be difficult. The methods described here work as well for one parent as for two. Single parents should follow the same rules as couples in being consistent and determined to succeed.

Are You Encouraging Your Child's Bad Sleeping Habits?

> My daughter was still waking twice or even three times a night for a breast-feeding at eleven months. I was so desperate to go to sleep I used to take her into bed and fall asleep with her latched on rather than stand around for hours trying to get her back to sleep.

In this case the eleven-month-old girl was being rewarded for waking in the night by being given a cuddle, a comforting nursing, and being able to spend the rest of the night snuggled up to her mother. This mother was no longer breast-feeding in the day, and once she learned that babies over six months of age do not need to be fed during the night, she decided to stop nursing at night. It was agreed that after the bedtime feeding and during the night the baby's father would offer a drink of water from a trainer cup. If the baby continued to cry, the father would leave the room and return five minutes later. The first night the baby cried, and the father had to go back to her eight times before she fell asleep. Later that night the baby cried again, and the father went to the baby seven times before the baby fell back asleep. The couple admitted they thought it was not going to work and the mother was very upset to hear the baby crying, even though her partner went back to the baby at five-minute intervals. However, the second night the baby woke only once, and after a short bout of crying, during which the father went in three times, the baby fell asleep until morning. The third night the couple had their first unbroken night for nearly a year.

It really does pay, once you have kept a diary for a week or two, to look at what you are doing in response to your child's waking or not falling asleep. Without realizing it, parents are often rewarding, and thus encouraging, the very behavior they want to discourage.

Deciding How to Change Your Response

Each set of parents must work out the approach they think will work and with which they will feel comfortable. They must agree on exactly what is to happen—if one parent is not to be involved, that parent must not criticize the other. Parents exhausted by repeated sleepless nights are often too exhausted to try a new approach. Initially it is true that trying to change your child's behavior could make for more difficult nights—but only for a very short period. If there is no improvement within five to six days, then the plan is not working and you must try something different. Pick a weekend or holiday time to try changing your approach so there is more opportunity to make up for missed sleep in the daytime. The goal of the plan must be to stop rewarding undesirable behavior and to try to get the child to behave in the desired way by being consistent, calm, and firm. In fact, once having made up their minds to try to change their child's behavior, many parents have been surprised by how quickly their child has responded. The key is in their own determination. Being unsure, hesitant, or inconsistent will only show the child that crying for a long time will get her what she wants. With older children of three, four, or five, it is also possible to reinforce desirable behavior with a reward program.

Often, changing the child's sleeping habits will need to be done in stages. For example, the child who will not settle without a parent lying down beside her may need to be "weaned" off this gradually so the parent sits on the bed, then is beside the bed, then at some distance from the bed, and finally in the next room.

Ways of Settling Children at Night

Checking This is a system devised to replace taking the child into your bed, endless rocking, patting, or other nighttime routines and rituals. When the child cries, one parent goes—it sometimes helps if it is not the parent who normally goes to the child—but does not pick up the child. The parent keeps all interaction to a minimum and does not start talking to or playing with the child, but instead briefly reassures her, and tucks her in firmly and deliberately. The parent then leaves the room, even if the child is crying. The procedure is repeated every five minutes. The first night this may be very many times, but as soon as the child realizes she is not going to be taken out of her crib, she will almost certainly settle down.

Night Drinks   Breast- or bottle-feedings are often given to help babies who wake in the night fall back asleep. It is a custom that develops out of night feedings in the early months, to become a habit. If your child is still having a breast- or a bottle-feeding after about six months, it is more of a comfort habit than a real necessity. After this age children are not hungry and are rarely thirsty during the night. There is no such thing as night starvation.

If the child is having drinks or juice from a bottle or a cup, try gradually weakening the strength each night until it is plain water, and also reduce the quantity. If a bottle is used and the child still wakes, try getting her used to a trainer cup in the day and offering it at night. When offering drinks in the night, always keep all interactions to a minimum, and if possible avoid taking the baby or child out of the crib or bed.

Once they are about twenty months old and drinking only water during the night, you can tell them to take their own bottle or trainer cup. Do not give them a bottle or cup with juice or milk in it during the night, as this will cause severe tooth decay. Tuck them in firmly, telling them to go to sleep, and leave the room, even if they cry, using the checking procedure until they settle.

Breast-feeding a baby or a toddler at night poses a different set of questions. Is your child breast-fed only at night, or during the day as well? Do you want to wean off breast-feedings totally or just to cut down the number of feedings? Obviously this does not apply to babies under six months who may still need a feeding in the night.

If your child is not weaned at all, then begin by weaning in the day. Many children get into the habit of falling asleep while sucking at the nipple, so the breast becomes a comforter, like a pacifier, which they need as part of their going-to-sleep routine. You first need to teach the child to settle to sleep without sucking at the breast. Begin by using daytime naps to do this, and progress to settling at night. Once your child learns to fall asleep without the comfort of a nipple in her mouth, there is more chance of her going back to sleep by herself if she wakes in the night. When trying to wean at night it helps if the father, rather than the mother, is the one to go to the child.

Older Children

> My three-year-old daughter was coming into our bed every single night just after we had fallen asleep and then kicking and wriggling all night, making it impossible for us to sleep. I tried bringing a cot into our room for her so she could be with us but not in our bed, and very often one of us ended up sleeping in that while she was in the bed with the other parent.

Older children can be given rewards in the form of star charts made out with days of the week. They are allowed to put a star or a sticker on the chart for every night of desired behavior—for example, staying in their own bed. Five nights of stars can equal a small treat, such as inviting a special friend to play, going on an outing to a favorite playground, or getting a small toy. Make sure the goal is within the child's reach so that she frequently gets the reward—if you set an impossible target, the child is not likely to achieve the goal and soon will lose interest in the reward system. Be firm about not giving stars for undesirable behavior, but do not yell at the child or spend a lot to time talking to her about the undesirable behavior. Give the child lots of praise and encouragement when she does succeed. Never take away or threaten to take away a star or reward the child has won for good sleeping habits.

If you think it would be impossible for her to stay in her own bed for a whole night, start by giving her a star if she stays in her bed once she has been taken back there during the night. At first you may need to take her back several times, using the checking procedure of tucking her in firmly and leaving her even if she makes a fuss. When she finally falls asleep and stays in her bed until the morning, that could be considered a success, and she wins a star. The second night you will probably have to take her back several times again; always be firm and calm, keep interaction to a minimum, and do not give her cuddles and hugs that will encourage her to keep coming back to you.

For a child who repeatedly comes into your bed, check that it is not because she gets cold at night—for example, due to her blanket slipping off.

Children Who Won't Go to Bed

Babies and children who have gotten used to falling asleep with a parent present—for example, falling asleep while being fed, rocked, or with someone lying down beside them—may refuse to settle with another person and take up hours of that person's time. Children who have never had a bedtime routine but who have been allowed to stay up until they fall asleep from exhaustion often stay up until 10:00 P.M. or later, with the result that their parents have no time to themselves. For a child who has never had a bedtime routine, begin by introducing a set pattern of events leading to bedtime. Set a bedtime that you think is reasonable—obviously you cannot go back from 10:30 P.M. to 8.00 P.M. in one or two nights, but gradually move the time backward. As long as you are determined, calm, and firm that this is bedtime, your child will eventually accept this, although for the first two or three nights you may have to take her back to bed many times. Also, be aware that once the child is going to bed earlier, she is likely to awake earlier in the morning.

Babies and children who are in the habit of settling only while nursing, having someone lying next to them, or any other procedure that demands the presence of a parent need to learn to fall asleep by themselves. Begin with a daytime nap when you are likely to have more energy. Settle them in their crib or bed, stroking and speaking reassuringly, and then leave the room. You may have to go back many times using the checking procedure to begin with, but persevere. You may have to make graded moves so they are gradually "weaned" off a routine they have been used to. For example, instead of rocking the child to sleep, rock her for a short time and place her in the crib while still awake, so she can make the transition to sleep without rocking.

No two parents or set of circumstances are the same, and you must devise the plan you feel most able to carry out and one that will best suit your child, but the ground rules still apply—be consistent, be firm and calm, and change your approach in gradual steps.

Twins

It is hard to devise a bedtime routine and to settle two children at once, especially if only one parent has to do this. Twins are also more likely to have had a difficult birth or to have been premature. But it has been found possible to use these methods successfully with twins as long as parents are both consistent and determined.

Medications

Doctors may occasionally prescribe medications for children who will not sleep, or parents buy them on their own initiative. Those most frequently used are antihistamines such as diphenhydramine (Benadryl) or sedatives such as chloral hydrate. Children react to these medications in different ways—some may be knocked out and also sleepy the next day, while they may have no effect on others and still others may become hyperactive and irritable. If your child should have a different than expected reaction to any medication, stop it and immediately notify your physician so that he or she can record it on the child's record. It is common for children to acquire a tolerance so that the drug loses its effect, although if they have a period without it, the tolerance usually disappears. No one knows how much parents' belief in the power of a medication affects the way they handle the child—for example, parents who think their child will sleep because she has had medicine may put her to bed more confidently, which in turn may encourage her to settle.

In general, sleeping problems are much better solved by the management strategies described above. Medications, if they work at all, usually give only short-term relief without tackling the basic difficulty. Nevertheless, in very difficult cases it may be appropriate to use these medications for a short period in combination with appropriate management strategies. In these situations medications may help establish a new sleep pattern, and they may give parents a short break. Children with eczema or other irritating or uncomfortable conditions may sometimes be helped by antihistamines, but using a different approach to night waking or settling will often enable the doses to be cut or reserved only for times when the eczema is especially itchy.

Early Risers

My eighteen-month-old always wakes at six in the morning and begins to scream if I don't get her up. By eight-thirty I feel as though I have already been up for half the day.

It has been found that there are ways for parents to encourage their children to wake later or amuse themselves in their cribs for longer once they do wake. For example:

- *Later bedtimes.* Most children manage to adjust to the hour's difference when clocks are switched from daylight time to daylight savings time, although it takes a few days. Moving bedtime ten minutes later a day over a week can produce later waking, but is more likely to succeed with good sleepers; it rarely helps with poor sleepers.

- *Going to your child before she gets upset.* If you go to your child and get her up before she begins to cry, you will give her confidence to go on playing by herself longer. If you do not go until she gets really upset, you are teaching her that she needs to cry before you will come to her.

- *Drinks and toys.* For children over about a year, a small amount of a drink can be left in a trainer cup at the end of the crib—do not leave them more than they will drink, because it will probably be spilled into the crib. Books and toys can be left for a baby of any age; for many parents the first sign that their child is awake is hearing the sounds of the child playing with toys.

- *Older children.* Once your child is in bed, it is best to set up some interesting toys in your bedroom the night before, plus a drink and a snack. You can then bring her into your room to play, which should mean another half an hour or so in bed.

- *Cues.* Older children often respond well to being given an alarm clock—they can come into your room once the alarm goes off. Do not set it much later than that child awakes, but aim for the child to play in her own room for about fifteen minutes before entering your room. You can gradually make the time later and later. Rewards in the form of a sticker or a star chart help to enforce the idea. If you can arrange for a light to go on at the desired waking time, this enforces the pattern and may be better than an alarm clock because if the child is asleep, she is less likely to be awakened.

Unusual Nighttime Events

Nightmares Nightmares happen to most children at some time—most commonly at about ages three to four. They can be set off by a television program, a story, or a normal but stressful developmental transition, such as going to preschool. They are not themselves a sign of some emotional disturbance. If your child cries out during or after a bad dream, all you need do is cuddle and comfort her and settle her back to sleep.

Night Terrors This is the term given to episodes that happen in the deep stages of sleep. They are different from nightmares that happen during REM sleep and often wake up the child. In a night terror the child usually screams out, often looks terrified, and sweats, but is in fact sound asleep. Thus the child does not respond to anything you say. Although it may worry you to see your child like this, the child will almost certainly remember nothing the next morning—so don't ask about the event then. During the night, wait until the night terror passes and protect your child from falling out of bed. Let your child settle down again—don't try to wake her up. Night terrors are very rarely a sign of emotional disturbance; they happen more often with boys and can occur at any time from ages three to four or older.

Sleepwalking and Sleeptalking   These can also be very worrying for parents, but again they are rarely signs of emotional disturbance. If your child sleepwalks often, the main concern must be safety, so make sure windows and doors out of the house are locked. Like night terrors, they happen during deep sleep—the explanation seems to be that one part of the brain is active while the rest is asleep.

Fear of the Dark   There are many children who do not like sleeping in the dark—most commonly from around three years old and upwards. A nightlight, landing light, or ordinary bedside light with a low-wattage bulb can be left on all night. Do not try to force them to sleep without a light because you will make any anxiety they would have grown out of naturally much stronger. On the other hand, don't keep bright lights on during the night, as they may disturb the child's sleep.

Head-Banging   Head banging or rocking the crib violently can become bedtime settling habits for some children. If the head banging only occurs prior to falling asleep, injury is unlikely. If the child is banging against a hard surface, padding it may prevent bruises or abrasions. Occasionally head banging occurs in children with medical, developmental, or behavioral disorders, but it is not likely to be the only manifestation of these problems; ask your pediatrician or family physician if you are worried. Introducing an alternative settling routine or putting the child in a bed that is not so inclined to rock may be helpful in some instances.

When to Seek Help

If you have tried the recommendations above and the child continues to have persistent nightmares, night terrors, sleepwalking and sleeptalking, fear of the dark, or head banging, you should seek the advice of your child's physician. The physician can assess the child for medical problems that may be associated with these problems and discuss additional emotional or behavioral problems with you. The physician may be able to provide additional recommendations, or may refer you to a child psychologist, psychiatrist, or pediatrician who specializes in developmental, behavioral, or sleep problems.

Crying in Young Babies

In the first few months, crying is an indication to you that there is something the baby wants or needs. Since the baby cannot be more specific about what she needs, determining why she is crying is largely a matter of trial and error. These are some of the things that make a baby cry:

- *Hunger.* Unless you have just fed your baby, this must be the first possibility considered. In the very early weeks breast- as well as bottle-fed babies should be offered feedings on demand.

- *Needs changing.* Some babies are more bothered than others by a wet or dirty diaper. Try changing them anyway if they will not settle. Diaper rash causing soreness is especially likely to upset some babies. Always change a soiled diaper to avoid this, whether your baby is one who is bothered by a soiled diaper or not.

- *Too hot or too cold.* Small babies are not very good at maintaining an even temperature. A baby who is too warm will look red in the face, feel very warm, and may be sweating around the neck. A baby who is too cold will also be fretful—she may be pale, and her hands and feet feel cold. To lower the temperature, loosen clothing and take off a layer of coverings, but check the baby frequently so that she does not cool down too much. To warm up a baby, take her into a warmer room and hold her next to your body with a warm blanket around her. A warm feeding can also help.

- *Uncomfortable position.* Until they can turn themselves over and become more mobile, babies have to rely on you to change their position. Most babies quickly show preferences for sleeping on their back or their sides. A baby who has been in an unusual position in the womb will especially dislike being rearranged into the opposite direction in the early days.

- *Boredom.* Even day-old babies do not spend all their time asleep or feeding. They can spend up to one or two hours awake and can become bored, actually craving human company or something to look at—a human face ranks highest.

- *Need for bodily contact.* All babies find the sensation of being held reassuring, and a baby who will not settle in her crib will often doze off contentedly in her parent's arms or while being carried in a sling. This contact is reassuring to babies and should be provided when possible. However, some babies can be quite demanding. Balancing the baby's needs with the other children's needs, your partner's needs, and your own needs can be quite difficult. If you are in this situation, discuss it with your partner and try to identify friends, family members, or others who can provide assistance.

- *Overtired or overstimulated.*   Small babies may refuse to settle if they get over-stimulated and overtired. They have a limited attention span. If your baby has been awake for quite a while, is not hungry or uncomfortable, but cries and will not settle, this is a possibility. Take your baby somewhere quiet and dimly lit and help her to settle by gentle rocking or providing other rhythmic stimulation such as patting or singing.

- *Pain or illness.*   Consider the possibility of pain from some passing internal discomfort or illness in a young baby who will not stop crying. Usually crying will not be the only sign of an illness. Other signs to look for would be loss of appetite, a fever, vomiting, or diarrhea. A cold that makes your baby congested and unable to breathe well through her nose can increase crying. Children with irritating conditions such as eczema may cry a lot and have difficulty settling.

- *Allergy.*   When they have gone through everything else, many parents wonder if their child's crying could be due to allergy, initially to cow's milk. In a few babies this may be the case. These babies should have other signs of a food allergy, such as rashes, swelling, diarrhea, or blood in the stool. Diagnosing food intolerance requires experience and careful observation of the child. If you have reason to think allergy may be a problem, ask your child's physician for advice. Some children grow out of their initial allergic reactions.

- *Colic.*   Some babies who cry a lot are diagnosed with colic. Often this occurs at about two months of age, which is when babies tend to cry the most. Usually the diagnosis is made when no other cause for the crying can be identified. These babies may cry more because they have difficulty adapting to new situations or changes in schedule. Some babies may be more persistent than others.

If Your Baby Won't Stop Crying

Every day and most of the night seemed to be spent feeding, changing, and pacing the floor with a screaming baby. In fact, looking back I realize she did actually sleep for one good stretch most mornings, but I was so tired from the night I hardly noticed that. Everything just overwhelmed me.

Some babies do cry a great deal more than others and can be very hard to comfort. It is also true that some parents are much better equipped than others to cope with a crying baby. Your own circumstances will make a lot of difference to the way you see your child's behavior and how you cope with it. A parent who already has a few children, who has a supportive partner who is often on hand to help, plenty of friends with children, and perhaps even relatives nearby to enlist as extra helpers is well set up to cope with a rather difficult baby. On the other hand, a first-time parent whose partner is often away or not very supportive, who has no friends nearby and no relatives on hand is more likely to feel insecure and upset when the baby is crying frequently.

Events can spiral so that tiredness, a sense of inadequacy, tension between partners, loneliness, and depression make the parents more and more unable to cope with crying. A loss of perspective can mean parents just focus on the one problem: "My baby won't stop crying." In fact other problems, such as loneliness or inexperience, may be important issues to address, which in turn will increase one's ability to cope with a crying baby.

How to Break the Spiral

- *Recognize the problem.*   You are under great stress; you do need and deserve help.

- *Don't feel inadequate or guilty.*   Your baby is not crying because you are a bad parent or because she hates you. Very many other parents have exactly the same problem.

- *Talk to your partner.*   Be honest about what you feel, and work out how you can each help each other. Single parents should talk to friends or relatives they trust and ask for help.

- *Remember, it will not last forever.*   Perhaps the most important point is regaining a perspective. There are things you can do to help your baby cry less, and crying will decrease over time.

- *Involve other people.*   Tell your child's physician that you are having a very difficult time. Do not expect him to offer a miracle solution, but recognize that talking about the problem and ways of tackling it will help.

- *Get out of the house and talk to other parents.*   Nursing or parenting support groups may provide access to other parents who have dealt with similar situations.

- *Plan a way to get more sleep.*   Both of you waking all the time or leaving it all to one partner is not a good idea. Devise shifts or alternate nights. It may mean getting four hours of sleep between 8:00 p.m. and midnight sometimes. Single parents should ask another parent, friend, or relative to give them a break in the day—remember, most people are flattered to be needed.

- *Accept that you have a temporary problem.*   Stop expecting your baby to sleep three hours between feedings. Stop expecting to get longer stretches of sleep. Behave and plan as though under siege and you may begin to be suddenly surprised by the odd lull.

- *Be systematic in trying different approaches to solve the problem.*   One step at a time, go through each possible reason for the baby to be crying. When you try something, give it enough time to work. If the baby is crying, it may take her a few minutes to realize you have given her what she wants and for her to calm down. Try one approach for at least five minutes before trying another approach to calming your infant.

Ways to Calm Your Baby

Assuming you have already checked whether your baby is hungry, wet, the wrong temperature, in an uncomfortable position, or just wanting to be held and amused and she is still howling, what next? Well, there can never be a sure way of settling any baby, and a method that works well on one occasion may not work the next time. But having a plan of what you will try while the baby is crying can give you confidence and make the baby's crying more manageable.

If you have a young baby who cries a lot, it is better to try going through possible ways of calming her fairly systematically. If you bombard her with everything you can think of in one evening, you are more likely to make her even more upset, and if she does finally fall asleep you will not know which particular trick was most successful. If crying is a regular feature—say, in the evening—then keep a diary over a week. Write down when the crying begins, times of feedings, and what method was tried to soothe her and with what success. At the end of the week you should be able to see which method or combination of methods is most likely to work.

Rhythmic Movement   Parents automatically rock their babies and have done so throughout history. It can be done in a carriage or a cradle, or by holding them. A successful position is often the "parrot" stance (baby on shoulder), but type and speed of rocking are important—vertical rocking has been shown to be more effective, and it should be rapid. This means holding the baby upright and jiggling her up and down swiftly, either on your shoulder clasped facing toward you, or with her back against you looking outward. Slings that hold the baby upright and facing you can be useful, but generally if babies do not get used to them while they are small—say, under two months—they are less likely to accept them later. Some parents find that rocking chairs help for long, noisy evenings when their legs get tired.

Patting or Stroking   Light, rhythmic pats or long, sweeping, stroking movements can sometimes distract a mildly fretful baby enough to drift into the much-hoped-for sleep. You need to have calmed her down enough to lay her in her crib or carriage without full-scale howling.

Sound   Constant, moderate noise has been shown to calm babies under four months; in general, the younger the baby the more effective it is likely to be. Despite lots of records and tapes of womb music (rhythmic heartbeats and pulsing sounds the baby was used to before birth), there is no evidence that this is especially soothing. Any constant background noise will do—a tumble dryer, vacuum cleaner, or television. However, there is no harm in investing in one of the tapes or records if you wish, or you can try your baby with a loudly ticking clock. Parents often try soothing music or their own singing as well—babies do not know if you sing out of tune! Nevertheless, research indicates that noise alone is not as effective as when tried together with one or a number of other methods of settling.

Swaddling

My mother suggested wrapping my baby up very tight in blankets to help her settle. I thought it seemed an awful idea and very old-fashioned.

Swaddling is an acceptable way of calming and helping babies to slip into sleep. Not only has it been tried and tested over centuries, but also modern research has established that new babies often respond well to swaddling. The goal is to give the baby comfort and security by holding her limbs firmly without binding. The rationale behind this is that it resembles the restriction of life in the womb and stops the baby from being upset and disturbed by the freedom of her own involuntary limb movements. Exceptions may be babies who have been in an unusual position in the womb and those who have congenital hip dislocation. Traditionally strips of material were used, but these days a large blanket, or, in hot weather, a cotton sheet will probably do the job just as well. If possible, begin swaddling when the baby is in an awake but calm state; if this is not possible, handle as calmly and as deftly as you can, talking soothingly. It has sometimes been found that the distraction of handling involved in swaddling calms the baby.

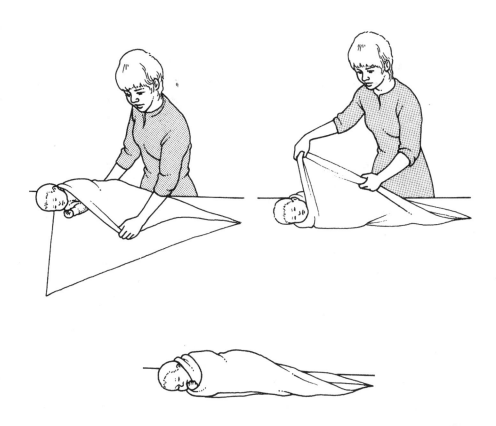

In cold weather, warm the material by ironing it or putting it on the radiator first. Lay the baby on her back on the material. Take a top corner and fold it downward and across. Wrap the rest of the material firmly around the baby's body. Secure it by either laying the baby on one side on the loose end, or use two safety pins. Aim to secure the limbs, but leave hands and lower arms free so that she can suck her hand, fingers, and thumb. Always keep a careful check on the temperature of a swaddled baby, and remove layers and loosen wrapping if she starts to look red and hot.

In cold weather one-piece pajamas and swaddling material plus one or two light blankets tucked firmly over the cocooned baby should keep her warm. In warmer weather use the lightest clothes and swaddling material and a cotton sheet instead of blankets to tuck over her.

Sucking

The only way of calming my month-old baby in the evening was letting her suck at my finger—feeding just made her worse. In the end I bought a pacifier, but I hated seeing her sucking it and only used it at home. I taught my two-year-old it was called a "sucky thing" so she wouldn't talk about the baby's pacifier when we were out.

Sucking is a source of comfort and satisfaction to young babies as well as a way of getting food. Many babies fall asleep at the end of or during feedings and can be calmed if they are upset by being offered the breast or a bottle to suck, even though they may not actually be hungry. Some babies need to suck more than others, and fussy babies in particular can often find comfort in sucking when they cannot be consoled in any other way. There is nothing wrong in using a pacifier for young babies who find comfort in sucking. It is possible to get specially shaped pacifiers for breast-fed babies. Be consistent—if you let your baby suck at a pacifier at home, take it with you when you go out. Always be sure it is not food, comfort, or attention your baby wants before offering the pacifier.

If you dislike the idea of a pacifier but if your baby seems to take comfort in sucking, you can lend her your little finger instead. The disadvantage is that you have to stay anchored. Most babies can be taught to suck their thumbs by about four months and will often do so by themselves. Once your baby has found her thumb you can stop using the pacifier; at this young age it will not have become a fixed habit. If you let your baby continue using a pacifier for much longer it can be harder to break the habit and she may not find her thumb an acceptable substitute. The disadvantage of a pacifier over a thumb is that it requires someone else to find it again when needed, which is especially problematic at night. The disadvantage of thumb-sucking over pacifiers is that sometimes the habit carries on into school age, although dentists now say that thumb-sucking has to continue at a high frequency and intensity beyond five or six years of age to push the front teeth outward.

Letting Your Baby Cry　It is worth remembering that there is a danger of giving a small baby too much stimulation. Sometimes this makes the child very fretful and unable to settle and fall asleep. The baby's crying continues—the parent continues to try to soothe her in every possible way, and the crying gets worse. It is possible that the baby is tired. It is worth putting your baby in her crib, tucking her in firmly, and leaving her to cry for five to ten minutes to see if she begins to settle.

Driving

I tried absolutely everything I could think of and finally in desperation I put her in the car seat in the back of the car and drove around for an hour and a half.

Many parents take to the roads in desperation in the evening hours with wakeful or screaming babies. It is probably the combination of the drone of the car plus the movement that helps them to fall asleep. It is a very bad idea to get an older baby or a child into the habit of being driven around at night to settle them, and much better to try settling them at home in the ways we have suggested. However, as a desperate last resort, it may be worth remembering. If possible, try not to drive alone with a screaming baby. This is very stressful and inclined to make you want to race through yellow lights rather than stop! Always make sure the baby is secured in a car seat, which has to be correctly secured in the car. Keep the infant in the backseat, especially if your car is equipped with front-seat air bags.

Massage   Not a new idea, but one currently being rediscovered. Various articles and books have been written on the subject. Essentially the idea is that a relaxed baby will not cry and also that massage is enjoyable for both parent and baby. In fact, many parents massage their children without thinking about it—stroking their temples, hair, or nape of neck, squeezing and stroking hands, and stroking their whole body to help them to relax. Massage, it is said, is best begun with the baby in an awake but calm state. If your baby rarely combines these two states and is usually crying or asleep, you will have to pick your moment carefully—perhaps after a bath.

The room needs to be warm enough for the baby to be undressed without getting cold. Warm some baby oil on your hands to help them to slide on sensitive skin. Begin by lightly stroking hands, fingers, feet, and toes. Go on to stroke the whole length of the limbs, making your touch a little firmer. Movements can be a mixture of stroking in circular or straight patterns and gentle kneading. Talk soothingly and reassuringly to the baby all the time. She can be lying on something soft in front of you, or cradled in your lap. If she is still enjoying it, move on to the body and reserve the head and neck, which is more sensitive, until last. Stroking the nape of her neck with straight fingers, brushing her temples with the back of your hand, or kneading her earlobes gently between finger and thumb can all be relaxing, and you can do this at any time, without having to undress your baby completely. If, when you begin, or during massage, your baby starts crying, pick her up and comfort her as you would normally, and try again at a later opportunity. Keep each session short to start with and finish before either of you loses interest.

Whether you and your baby come to enjoy regular massage sessions depends entirely on your individual temperaments and personalities. If, after a few tries, you have to conclude that although you may think it a good idea, your baby does not, then don't feel rejected or upset. Nothing has been lost by trying, and if you want, you can try again in a couple of months when she is more mature and settled.

Combining Techniques For generations mothers have instinctively rocked, fed, sung to, and patted their babies to get them to sleep. Now instinct has the backing of modern research, which shows that babies are indeed more likely to be soothed by stimulation of several senses. It is important to remember this and also that too much stimulation can sometimes make a baby fretful. If you have tried every technique singly and waited to see if your baby is likely to settle if left to cry for a short period, it might be worth going on to work your way through a combination of two techniques at a time. Use the same approach for a whole evening or day and write down what happens, especially the time of crying and when it stops. This will enable you to work out the most successful formula. But do not leap to the conclusion that it will necessarily mean rocking, sucking, noise, and swaddling all at once. Remember also that what works on one occasion may lose its charm at another time and you will have to try a different approach.

Nearing the End of Your Rope

At times many parents get so desperate through lack of sleep, personal problems, and a continually crying baby that they feel they just cannot carry on any longer or fear they may actually hurt their baby. If you get to this point or have done something to your child—thrown her into the crib or onto the bed, shaken her, or hit her—you need help. In an emergency these are some immediate measures you can take to stop you from hurting your baby:

- Put the baby in her crib. However furiously she is crying, she is unlikely to get hurt there. Then telephone a friend or a relative. Tell that person just how bad you are feeling at the time; unless you ask for help, no one will know of your need.

- If you have no phone, wrap up the baby and bring her next door to a neighbor or nearby friend.

- If you have no one to call on, put the baby into a stroller, take her out, and walk around the streets. Just being out of the house and walking around usually has a calming effect.

- Consider running a warm bath and getting in it together with your baby. This can be very soothing and often distracts the baby enough to make her stop crying.

- If you are on your own or a single parent, ask a friend or relative if you can come to stay the night with your baby.

- If you are not able to do something that changes the mood of the moment and are not able to get help from a friend or family member, take the baby to a local emergency room that can protect her.

- Once the immediate crisis is past, sit down with a friend or your partner, or a professional, such as a pediatrician, psychologist, or social worker, and try to work out what brought you to this state. Remember that tiredness and loneliness can make any problems seem worse.

How can professionals help? Talking to your pediatrician or family physician can be very helpful—such people are very well aware of the stresses that a crying baby can put on parents. Simply talking things over and knowing that other people are aware of your problem and care how you feel can be a real help. Your child's physician may know of local parent groups or infant play groups that may be a source of help for you. They may also know of other professionals who can help you.

CHAPTER 9

Your Baby and Child's Growth and Development

How your baby grows
Your growing toddler and preschool child
Your child's bones • Your child's muscles and nerves
Food and growth • Physical development
How your child learns to move
Encouraging your child's physical development • Boys and girls

Most of us remember being visited by distant relatives when we were children and having to endure all those exclamations about "Haven't you grown!" One of the most obvious things about children is that they do grow, and at a most tremendous rate—in height, in weight, and in different proportions. For instance, your newborn baby's head accounts for a third of his body weight, but of course the head of an adult is proportionately much smaller than this compared to the rest of the adult's body.

All parents are concerned about their child's growth because it is an important sign of health and progress. However, other signs are just as important, such as intellectual development, behavior, and general health. If you have a very large child you may worry that he is overweight for his age. Of course, obesity, or excess fat, can be a health problem, but if your child is simply big, then this need not affect his health and progress. In general, exceptional smallness, particularly at birth, is more likely to be a cause for concern. However, even if your child looks very small and frail, if he has plenty of energy and can keep up with other children his age, he is probably healthy.

How Your Baby Grows

The way we grow is governed by our genetic and hormonal programming as well as by environmental factors. These outside influences, such as nutrition, love, and education, interact with and affect our genetic programming. The effects of these can never be completely separated. For example, a child who does not get enough to eat will not grow and develop normally no matter how genetically large he is programmed to be. And, not surprisingly, a child who is consistently deprived of love can also fail to grow. Lack of growth can be a symptom of illness, but, given a reasonably healthy, safe, loving home environment, the process of human growth and development will unfold.

How Your Baby Grows Before Birth
When your baby is first conceived, he results from the fusion of two gametes (the sperm from the male and the ovum from the female). Everything the child needs to develop is contained in the genes each parent has contributed. The structures in the cell that contain genes are called chromosomes. The twenty-three chromosomes in each gamete (or forty-six chromosomes in the resulting cell) contain directions for the development of all the bones, organs, nerves, muscles, and other tissues and for the physical and some intellectual characteristics that will make your child who he is.

Your baby will spend about forty weeks growing in the uterus (for more about this, see chapter 2), but anything from thirty-seven to forty-two weeks is considered normal. Your baby's growth within your uterus will be measured in a number of ways—by your own weight gain, by the increasing height of your uterus, and by ultrasound scans. If your baby does not seem to be growing well, special measures can be taken to help to promote his growth, or, if the pregnancy is nearing its end, he may grow better outside the uterus and the birth can be induced early.

Your baby grows very fast in your uterus—reaching a peak rate of growth at about twenty weeks' gestation. At this stage he is growing at a rate of 4 in (10 cm) a month, but after birth the growth rate is approximately 8 in (20 cm) a year for the first year of life; this steadily decreases as the infant ages. Obviously your baby could not continue growing at this fast rate or he would become a giant! In addition to growing in length and weight he is also developing limbs and organs. It is during this very early stage that your baby is most at risk from external damage. There is more about this in chapter 1 on preconceptual care, but basically you have to be very careful not to take any over-the-counter medicines or be exposed to radiation. Be certain to tell your doctor you are pregnant or hoping to become pregnant if she is prescribing any medication for you.

Babies of mothers who smoke are, on average, smaller than babies of mothers who do not. Being small-for-dates can be dangerous for the baby. In addition, heavy alcohol drinking in pregnancy can cause damage, and some doctors suggest that to be on the safe side, pregnant women should not drink alcohol, especially from the time you stop contraception until the end of the pregnancy. It is important for women to eat a sensible, balanced diet during pregnancy; however, in general, babies take what available nutrition there is, even if the mother is undernourished. It is the mother who can end up being nutritionally depleted and potentially sick. There is no evidence that morning sickness, however severe, will affect your baby's well-being.

Intrauterine Growth   One of the most remarkable ways in which nature ensures that your baby will have a safe delivery is that the growth of a baby adjusts itself according to how much or how little room there is in the mother's uterus during the last weeks of pregnancy. The ultimate size a person will be is determined by the genetic characteristics he inherits from both his parents—each parent contributing half of the genetic material. So if the mother is small but the father is large, the baby, who has an equal contribution from both parents, might be too big to be delivered safely through the mother's small pelvis and birth canal. Fortunately, during pregnancy the father's contribution is "suppressed" and the baby grows just enough to fit comfortably into his mother's uterus. After the birth, however, the baby will grow more rapidly, to accommodate the father's genetic contribution, and by the time he is two years old will represent a genetic mix between his mother and his father. In the same way, a larger woman with a generous-size pelvis may give birth to a larger-than-average baby even if the baby's father is small. However, the baby may grow more slowly during his first two years until, again, his parents' contributions are equally represented. His ultimate size will probably be somewhere between the two parents'. Growth after birth also depends on external factors—in particular, nutrition. Even if both parents are large but the baby is undernourished (perhaps because of illness), he will not grow to his full genetic capability.

Birth Weight

While he was in the uterus it was difficult to assess exactly how your baby was growing. After birth it is very important that he should be examined by a physician as a starting point for monitoring his growth and development. The first evaluation of your baby will occur in the delivery room. A nurse or a physician will examine and weigh your baby there. One of many important indicators of your baby's well-being is his weight. The average healthy full-term baby weighs between 6 lb, 6 oz (3.0 kg) and 7 lb, 7oz (3.5 kg). There will always be some healthy babies who come on either side of this range, but this is taken by physicians as a general guideline to what is considered the average birth weight. If your baby is one of the few exceptions outside this range, he will be given special examinations just in case there might be anything that needs extra care.

When your baby is born and you hear the physician saying that he should be checked for smallness or largeness for dates, remember, she is checking, not diagnosing. This evaluation is important, and in many cases all is well. Your physician will discuss any issues with you that may require further evaluation.

Preterm Babies

A baby born before thirty-seven weeks of pregnancy is known as preterm and may need special nursing care because his lungs, digestive system, and nervous system may not be able to work on their own. Such a baby will usually be below 5 lb, 13 oz (2.7 kg), but this in itself is not automatically a cause for concern. As long as he is the correct weight for the pregnancy (gestational) age, physicians will not be primarily concerned about his size. They will be more concerned about his immature bodily functions and will check to see if he needs help with such vital things as breathing, digestion, or temperature control.

Small-for-Dates Babies

A small-for-dates baby is one who weighs less than he should for his pregnancy age. Sometimes failure to grow properly in the uterus can be picked up during pregnancy, and the labor and delivery may have to be induced so the baby can be fed and nourished better outside the uterus. Sometimes the placenta tends to wear out and stops working efficiently before the baby has completed his growth in the uterus. A small-for-dates baby is not just small, he is also undergrown, and this is why women should take seriously warnings about the dangers of smoking, which may cause small-for-dates babies. There is nothing wrong with being small if that is the way you are intended to be, but it is less desirable to be smaller and less well developed than you should be.

Large-for-Dates Babies

Babies weighing more than 9 lb, 6 oz (4.3 kg) should be evaluated in case their mothers may have had undiagnosed diabetes during pregnancy. Many very large babies are not large because of diabetes in the mother but are simply genetically large, perhaps because their mothers are large in build. These babies will not have any problems and, contrary to what many people believe, they will not be unusually difficult to breast-feed. The only other possible danger with a large baby is that he can be difficult to deliver. If prenatal tests show the baby is very large and if the mother is rather small-boned by comparison, the birth may be induced a week or two early, or delivery by cesarean section may be performed. However, it is quite difficult to make such a judgment prenatally, and many physicians are happy to let large, fast-growing babies be delivered normally in their own time. It is quite possible for large babies to be safely delivered without even an episiotomy being needed.

Measuring Growth

Your baby's growth is assessed by measuring his weight, length, and head circumference. Later, when he can stand, his height will be measured instead of his length. In these first few months of a baby's life, his weight can be a major concern of parents, and of health professionals, too, because it is the simplest indicator of growth and whether your baby is getting enough calories. This is particularly true of breast-fed babies, since it is difficult to quantify the amount of breast-milk that a baby is getting. If a baby is gaining weight appropriately, then he is getting enough calories to grow. Another indicator of healthy growth is the measurement of length. Babies have to be measured while they are lying down. This can be quite difficult to do because babies cannot be straightened out very easily! Length is an indicator of whether a baby's frame is growing properly. With proper nutrition your baby will gain weight and grow in length and head circumference. In general, though, you will find that signs of well-being in your baby such as firm skin, alert behavior, and eagerness to feed give you an indication that he is growing well.

How Your Doctor Measures Your Baby's Growth

When you take your baby to the physician's office for a well-baby checkup, your doctor will talk about percentiles. The staff will note your baby's weight, length, and head circumference and check it against what is called a percentile growth curve, which is based on the average of large numbers of babies. This gives an indication of how your particular baby compares to other babies his age. If you're told that your child is on the fifth percentile, this means that of one hundred children of the same age, ninety-five will be larger than your child and five will be smaller. Being below the fifth percentile (or, conversely, above the ninety-fifth) is not necessarily abnormal provided the rate of growth is consistent—that is, if the child follows along his own particular percentile curve. These percentile measures are used to pick out the few babies—about 5 percent at each end of the size range—who might need special attention. Many of the children in the greater-than-ninety-fifth-percentile category and in the less-than-fifth-percentile category will turn out to be normal.

Your baby, when he is weighed and measured, will be placed on one of these percentile curves according to how big he is. If, for example, two babies are both perfectly normal—that is, within the middle 80 percent of all babies—but of different sizes, they will be on different growth curves. The main thing about bigger baby A is that he should grow along the curve appropriate for him; the same thing applies to smaller baby B. If baby A's weight and growth curve started to drop down toward baby B's and stayed there, it would be cause for concern that baby A was not getting enough to eat. Similarly, if baby B's weight gain suddenly shot up on to the level of baby A's and stayed there, while his height remained on its original growth curve, there might be concern that he was getting too much to eat. These curves can be used to measure how well your child is growing through his childhood and will continue to be used to check for the small minority at each end of the size range who may need special dietary help—either more to eat and better care, or less to eat because they are gaining too much weight.

Individual Variations in Growth

It is important for you not to spend too much time worrying about and checking your baby's weight and size. Relaxed, happy parents help children to grow best! In the first few months of your baby's life, fluctuations in growth rates may be quite marked—some weeks he may gain about 8 oz (225 gm), while other weeks he'll gain less or perhaps not at all. This is particularly true of breast-fed babies, who control their own intake of milk in all kinds of subtle ways. The weekly weight gains of normal babies during their first three months are steadily upward but are not always smooth. Other things may cause a fluctuation in weight gain—for example, your baby may have a cold one week and not be feeling well, or he may suddenly have a growth spurt, demand feeding every two to three hours, and put on an impressive amount of weight in a short time.

You will soon develop the practiced eye of an experienced father or mother, and you will know from the way he continually grows out of his clothes, from the changes in his face and body, and from his skin tone, his eyes, and his behavior that he is growing as he should be. There will be no need for constant references to scales and tape measures, although it can be fun, once your child can stand and understand, to measure him against the door from time to time, or against a special wall chart. These are often given away free in magazines, and more elaborate versions are sold in baby specialty shops.

Your Growing Toddler and Preschool Child

Your child's growth rate actually slows down all through the toddler and early childhood years. The amount of weight and height gained by your child gets progressively less over the years until adolescence—although, of course, overall he is still getting bigger all the time. During young childhood, other interesting changes, some noticeable and some less so, will also be taking place. The most obvious will be the changes in proportion. The head looks smaller in relation to the rest of the body; the arms and legs, fingers and toes grow longer; the limbs straighten out; the fat baby tummy becomes flatter; the face acquires its own unique characteristics and loses its baby chubbiness. Less visible changes occur in your child's bones, muscles, brain, and nervous system.

Your Child's Bones

When your baby is born, most of the bones will consist of cartilage: a one-year-old has only three visible bones in each wrist and hand seen by an X ray; an adult has twenty-eight. The bones steadily become harder through childhood: the bones of the hand, wrist, and head harden quite easily, but the long bones of the arms and legs do not become completely hard until the late teens. It is because his bones and ligaments around the joints are so soft that your baby can curl himself up into positions that would be quite impossible for an adult. In addition, the tone of the muscles is poor, which is why he is "floppy" to start with and cannot pull himself up to a standing position until at least nine months of age, or walk without help until roughly twelve to eighteen months—although, as with everything about children's development, there are large individual variations. Some babies can sit up well at six months; others, not until nine months. Some walk before they are a year old, while others do not walk until eighteen months.

The bones of the skull (head) in a young baby are special. He is born with several head bones joined together with soft cartilage or openings called "fontanelles," which enable the head to be "molded" to fit into the birth canal during birth. These soft spots will gradually disappear during the first two years as the bones knit together until your toddler, like you, has confluent bone covering the brain.

As well as increasing in hardness, the bones grow in length, although different parts of the body are growing at different rates. It is bone growth that contributes most to your child's ultimate height. These rates will vary from individual to individual. Contrary to what you might have heard, it is not possible to predict accurately what a child's adult height is going to be from his height at two years old. He may be three feet tall at two, but the old rule of thumb that this is half his adult height will not apply if he is an individual, for example, with medium-size parents. In this case, he is unlikely to grow to six feet and, of course, it is also unlikely that in this case a little girl will grow to this height. Boys and girls differ by 5½ in (12.5 cm) in average height at the end of adolescence, but when they are toddlers there is hardly any difference at all.

Your Child's Muscles and Nerves

Unlike the bones, your baby is born with all the muscles he is going to need, though they will develop in length and thickness as he grows. During childhood there is no difference between the muscles of boys and girls, but in adolescence and adulthood boys will normally develop more muscle than girls. It has been estimated that about 40 percent of the final body mass of a man is muscle, while it is only 24 percent in a female. Muscles are responsible for the strength and flexibility of the different parts of the body. This can be increased by exercise, and both girls and boys should be given many opportunities to exercise and strengthen their muscles.

The brain and nervous system of your baby have a lot of rapid growing to do after birth. Some parts of the brain—those that control attention, absorbing new experience, and the basic baby activities of sleeping, waking, feeding, and getting rid of waste through bowel and bladder—are already working well. However, the parts of the brain that control more complex activities, such as controlled movement, thinking, language, and understanding, go on developing after birth and are nearly, but not altogether, complete by the time he is two. If you think how competent a two-year-old child is compared to a newborn baby, you can see for yourself how many changes have had to take place in his brain and nervous system for him to do the running, holding, planning, talking, demanding, and controlling he can do now.

The brain controls the activities of the body through the nervous system. At first it cannot do this very well because the nerves, particularly those at the extremities of your baby's body, take some time after birth to become fully equipped to carry the brain's messages. Nerves have to be covered with a special sheath called myelin to communicate effectively with the body parts they control. The process of myelinization in the nervous system outside the brain takes up to two years to complete and is not complete in the brain itself until the end of adolescence. Once the nerves are sheathed in myelin they can help your baby to control his movements much more effectively. You will notice that this process does not happen all at once—the baby gains control of his head first, then his limbs and trunk, and finally he gains the very fine control of fingers and limbs that enable him to do delicate and complicated tasks such as building with small bricks or holding a pencil and writing. As his nervous system matures he will also learn to gain control over his bowel and bladder movements. There is more about this in chapter 13, on toilet training, but the important point to remember is that your baby cannot control his behavior as you might like him to until his nervous system has gained the necessary maturity. This takes time.

Food and Growth

Feeding is a vital aspect of caring for and nurturing your children and one that causes so much concern for parents that we have already dedicated two chapters to discuss these issues in depth. Growth and food are fundamentally linked together. All the complex genetic, hormonal, physical, and behavioral developments we have described cannot take place if your baby is not properly nourished. Nourishment is most important during the vulnerable last months in utero and the first months after birth. If a baby is not fed at all, he will die. If he is not fed properly, he will not grow or develop properly. This is obviously a big responsibility for parents, and it is why mothers worry so much about breast- or bottle-feeding and if their children will not eat a variety of foods. You will have read and heard a lot of different advice about eating enough vitamins; getting enough fiber; not eating sweet, sugary foods; and being wary of foods that may cause allergies. It can be very bewildering and make you understandably anxious. In fact, the main point about giving your baby nourishment so he grows properly is actually very simple: he should be given enough to eat. What is enough for him may not be enough for your friend's child, and what is enough for him when he is eighteen months old may not be enough for him when he is three years old, although at this stage he may actually want less to eat because children develop likes, dislikes, increases, and decreases in appetite, just as adults do.

Remember that growing takes a lot of energy, far more than adults use, and, of course, your child will be using energy for all his activities as well. Energy uses up calories, which is why it is important that your child's diet contains enough calories. Different foods are required for different aspects of growth and health. The importance of protein, carbohydrates, vitamins, minerals, and fiber are all explained in chapters 6 and 7. In general, if your child has plenty of energy for his usual activities; if his bowel movements and urine are normal; if he looks well, with clear skin, bright eyes, and shiny hair; and if he very broadly follows his own growth percentile curves, then no matter how little you fear he is eating, you can be sure he is growing and developing normally. Similarly, even if your child eats like a horse and has a passion for what you consider to be unsuitable foods, as long as his growth curves do not rise above what they should be (which may indicate that he is too heavy), and as long as his behavior and looks are normal, you shouldn't worry. More problems are caused by battles and rigid rules about food than are ever caused by food itself. Food provides your child with the energy to grow and to function. It is not a religion or a test of your love.

Physical Development

It is hard to look ahead from those moments when you hold a new baby in your arms and realize that within a matter of months this stage will be long gone, and before two years have passed your child will have developed into a lively little toddler. Watching the way their baby is increasingly able to move different parts of his body intentionally and to control them is a subject of great fascination for all parents. This development depends on the physical growth and maturation of bones, muscles, brain, and nerves. The first eighteen months of a child's life are often described as "the sensori-motor period" of development. This means he is learning about the world around him mainly through his senses and body movements before he can use language and think things through. Like most descriptions of childhood that divide progress into stages, this is a rather oversimplified view. Young babies can solve problems and figure things out for themselves, as you will notice if you leave toys just out of their reach or do something they do not want you to do. Realizing that because you have left the room he will not get his bottle just yet and then yelling in protest actually involves quite a complicated thought process for your nine-month-old. And, of course, the reverse is true as well—movement does not stop being an important way of learning or an aid to learning after the age of eighteen months. Sports, dance, design, even writing or typing all require body movements that embody intelligent processes. Being immobile can handicap mental as well as physical progress, and physical exercise benefits all our functions—not just our physical development.

How Your Child Learns to Move

Watching as your baby is first able to lift his head, then to roll over, to sit by himself, to crawl or to pull himself up, and finally to walk is obviously exciting and rewarding for all parents. There are enormous variations in the way different children develop controlled, confident movements, but in general these developments follow predictable patterns. The medical term for the development of movement is "motor development" and it takes place from the head downward and from the central part of the body outward. At birth your baby already has fairly good control of eye movements and the movements that control sucking and feeding. He will first begin to gain control of head movements and, working downward, he will stand on his feet and finally walk. It means that he will first gain control of his trunk, then of his arms and legs, and finally of his feet, thumbs, and fingers.

There are two other points to bear in mind about your baby's development of movement. First, it is not possible to speed it up. Babies who are given freedom of movement and encouragement to stand and walk do not necessarily walk any earlier than babies who are more restricted, though they do, of course, have a more interesting time! However, babies who are severely restricted—for example, children brought up in inappropriate environments where they are never taken from their beds or stimulated in any way—can be delayed in all areas of development and fail to develop sturdy muscles. Second, early crawling, standing, and walking are not linked to intellectual development. Just because a child walks early does not mean he is more intellectually advanced than other children of his age. Nor does it mean that he is necessarily going to be unusually athletic or energetic later in life. Once a baby is mobile he can explore and discover things for himself. He does not have to wait for them to be brought to him. And once he can walk, he has the priceless advantage of having hands free, which means he can move and hold things and arrange things with his hands all at the same time.

Of course, a baby who is on the move early is more work for you. Toddlers can play havoc with your household at any age, but a baby under a year old who is walking cannot understand when you tell him what he can and cannot do, and can be a real handful. There is advice on arranging your home to make it safe and stimulating for a toddler in chapter 12. Nevertheless, the first steps at whatever age are an exciting moment—physical independence has arrived.

Some of the main stages of the development of movements are shown in the chart on pages 287–290. Your baby might not go through some of them: some babies never crawl, they just get straight up and walk; some babies shuffle on their bottoms instead of crawling; some support themselves on their feet on your lap at two or three months; others just flop down and wait until seven or eight months; some are eager to reach and grasp, while others have to be encouraged to hold things and look at them. Bear in mind with this chart that babies are very individual in the way they progress, and the range of what is normal is very wide. This is just a rough guide.

Gross Motor and Fine Motor Movements

Age	Large-Scale Movements	Delicate Movements
Newborn	Unless picked up he can only lie supine, curled up, and his cheek on one side. His head is floppy. He makes reflex movements such as "walking" and "grasping," but these are not controlled. He will begin to develop synchrony with your movements —setting up feeding rhythms and responding to your touch and handling.	He can turn his head to sound and light, control eye movements, and blink. He can suck and time his own feedings. Although his movements are not well controlled, you will be fascinated by the delicate folding and unfolding of fingers and little movements and breathings while he sleeps. Already different babies have different body language.
About one month	He still cannot support his body, but is beginning to hold up and control his head. He can turn it at will. He will press down with his feet on a surface or your lap. He waves his arms and legs rather jerkily, but already you will see that he does this at certain times—he may enjoy kicking in the bath, for instance. 	He will turn toward sound and your face out of interest. He can follow a moving object with his eyes and head. His facial expression will begin to show interest and excitement. First smiles come at about six weeks and sometimes sooner. He will open his hand to grasp your finger.
About three months	He moves his arms and legs more gracefully now—his movements may be more purposeful, for instance, the beginnings of reaching. He holds his head up and his back straight if you sit him up. If you lay him down flat on his stomach he can raise his head and chest and support himself on his arms. He may roll over, so watch him carefully if he is on a raised surface.	He is doing a lot more watching and noticing with his head and eyes; he will study his hands, perhaps clasping them together. He may get hold of his feet, too. He will begin to enjoy play objects—things he can hold on to for a while, such as rattles and things he can bash and kick. His movements will express his feelings—he may start kicking, arm-waving, and waving his head vigorously as he approaches the breast or bottle, for instance. If he is a thumb- or finger-sucker, he will have become one by now.

Age	Large-Scale Movements	Delicate Movements
About six months	He now has much more control of the upper part of his body. He can lift his head and shoulders when lying on his back, can roll over, will raise his arms to be picked up, can bounce with his feet on your lap, and he may even be sitting alone for a while. He will certainly enjoy sitting propped up. 	He reaches out with his hands to grasp things and holds them confidently. He can pass them from hand to hand. He may deliberately drop them for you to pick up! He watches and monitors everything that is going on. His mouth is an important testing ground now—everything will go into it, including his precious thumb if he is a thumb-sucker. He may suck his thumb when he is tired or thoughtful. He may deliberately bang and rattle things to make a noise. He can hold and suck a spoon, rattles, and large pieces of food.
About nine months	He is almost certainly on the move by now—either wriggling along on his stomach, or crawling or even walking. He will try to pull himself up to a standing position and may take a few steps with support. He can sit up on his own and and lean forward to pick things up. He may be a "bottom shuffler," in which case he may not crawl, but go on shuffling until he can walk. 	He can grasp things well and is beginning to use his finger and thumb to pick things up and to pull them toward him. He can poke with one finger and may be pointing a lot as a way of drawing attention to things, or asking for something. He will take things when offered but may not be able to give them back. When he drops things he will follow them with his eyes and try to get them back. He manages spoons and finger foods quite well, although with some mess (which he will probably enjoy!). He can play games that involve body movements such as hand-clapping, imitating your actions, and peekaboo.

Age	Large-Scale Movements	Delicate Movements
About eighteen months	Much more confident now, he can walk with arms swinging, and is able to stop, start, sit down, stand up, kneel, squat, climb, and carry things around with him.	He will be doing many things with his hands, including some skilled tasks, perhaps with some help, such as threading large beads, building, attempts at drawing, helping you, and using toy tools such as hammers and pegs.
About two years	He can run, walk with confidence, pull wheeled toys around, and safely negotiate obstacles around the house. He can probably walk up and down stairs properly, can push himself along on a pedal tricycle, and can throw, aim a kick if not actually hit his intended mark, but will not be able to catch yet.	Increasing skills in language and thinking should mean he has many more opportunities to exercise physical abilities, too; he can look at a book, turning pages over properly; can arrange things neatly; perform useful tasks such as wrapping and unwrapping parcels; can, perhaps, use scissors; and will be increasingly skillful with hand and eye tasks such as jigsaw puzzles, painting, threading, and construction-toy play. Of course, a lot of practice helps, and so to some extent his skills depend on having opportunities and playthings to practice on. He will probably have some control over bowel and bladder, maybe even complete control, but it will still be variable at times.
About three years	He is quite an athlete now, can jump from a low step, climb on climbing frames, walk backward and sideways, stand on one foot, stand and walk on tiptoes, throw, kick, and maybe even pedal his tricycle. He can carry and maneuver large objects and toys such as strollers or trains.	He will be doing all the things he did as a two-year-old, but better. He may hold a pen or pencil properly now, and draw or paint simple shapes; he will probably be able to model shapes with Play-Doh. He can eat with a fork and make a reasonable attempt at washing and drying himself and also at dressing and undressing, but with some things he will still need help. He may be dry at night.

Age	Large-Scale Movements	Delicate Movements
About four years	He will now be walking, running, and climbing confidently. He can manage stairs and obstacles and find his way around with ease. He can hop, bend, clamber, and swing on climbing frames, and is getting better at throwing and catching—he may even be able to use a bat.	He will have good control of fingers and thumbs now—holding pens and pencils properly, able to draw and build from memory and to copy other people's drawings and building quite efficiently. He should be doing many things to look after himself: using the toilet, washing and drying himself, dressing and undressing (still with help), helping you, and playing with more challenging toys.
About five years	By now you may well have a gymnast on your hands—although children do vary a lot in their physical agility and confidence. A confident child will be climbing balancing, attempting handstands, somersaulting, hanging upside down from the bars of a climbing frame, and probably causing you some considerable nervous strain! Less confident children will still have good control of their limbs, begin to be able to skip, hop, bend, grasp things strongly, throw, kick and dance, or show an awareness of rhythm when moving to music. Physical differences among children will become more apparent, particularly with the more organized activities of school. Some children are never going to be very good at games, or graceful dancers; some may be clumsy or slow or need extra help and patience. Nevertheless, all healthy five-year-olds have in their bodies a very efficient instrument for movement, making, controlling, and mastering the environment you provide for them.	As well as doing the things mentioned above but better, the five-year-old may well be writing, drawing, and painting with confidence and skill. He will be quite good at copying and coloring. He may be able to sew by now—perhaps even to knit or crochet, given help. He can manage tools, hammering nails, using screws and nuts, and screwdrivers—again with your help. He can manage gardening and cooking implements, too. All these skills depend on you giving him opportunities to use his hands and being very patient with him as he learns. However, it is worth spending time teaching your child skills—it will provide a bond between you and him, as well as increasing his ability and confidence. He will also enjoy constructive, creative play with other children—planning large-scale models, digging and tunneling in soil or sand, modeling and painting on a large scale. All these activities will increase and blossom at school, but you can continue to foster them at home.

Encouraging Your Child's Physical Development

The way your baby gradually gains control over his body—his motor development—proceeds fairly automatically, and there is not much you can do to speed it up or hinder it. However, you can do a great deal to encourage and help your child to develop the skills involved in learning different aspects of controlled movement. The most obvious example is giving him plenty of opportunity to practice and exercise each new aspect of movement as he becomes capable of it—for example, providing times for kicking and wriggling on the floor without being hindered by a diaper or clothes, as well as giving him interesting objects to look at and reach and grasp to exercise hand and eye skills; freedom and safety to roll and crawl; furniture to hold as he learns to walk holding on to objects and eventually to walk alone. He will need liberty to explore the world he is discovering, which may mean mud puddles in the park or the ever-fascinating contents of your closets.

Later, as he becomes more controlled, deliberate, and purposeful in his activities, he will want more organized play and events in his life. Having an active child around the house makes a huge impact on your life, and it can be quite a strain to give your child opportunities for free movement and at the same time keep your own life and home in a condition that is comfortable for you. For more on this, see chapter 12.

You may want your child to learn a sport or have dancing lessons. Swimming is an excellent sport, and you can begin to help your baby to be confident in the water as soon as you start to give him his first baths. Once he has had his first immunization, you can take him to the local swimming pool—ask at your local YMCA, YWCA, or other community organization for details of parent-and-baby swimming sessions. Many sports and leisure centers also have special facilities for under-five-year-olds, such as floor mats and climbing bars.

If you enjoy it, it is never too soon to introduce your three- to five-year-old to the delights and disciplines of more organized group games, such as simple versions of football, baseball, soccer, and running. By the time he is five years old your child should have a good grasp of rules, though he will probably still sulk when he is not the winner.

If you are not the athletic type, then walking, climbing, and making trips to the local park together are just as good exercise if you do them regularly.

If your child is agile or is willing to try new sports, he may enjoy dancing or gymnastics. There are many dancing schools in most neighborhoods, and you can get information about them from the library or local education authority. Local sports centers will have information about gymnastics and other sporting facilities for under-five-year-olds. However, if your child is not interested in these activities, do not try to force it. Gymnastics, dance, and other organized activities at this age are only for fun. Too intense coaching could spoil enjoyment and may even do damage to developing muscles and limbs. Again, the value of many sporting activities is that you can do them together as a family. Playing games together, as long as you all enjoy it, is a good way of uniting family members and giving younger members who may have surplus energy a way to let off steam.

Boys and Girls

In the first five years there are virtually no differences in physique and growth rates between boys and girls. They have the same endowment of bones, muscles, and nerves, and on average they are almost the same in height and weight, although, as with everything else, we all know of individual exceptions to this. Yet on some measures of physical skills there do seem to be differences between the sexes. On short runs, girls are faster than boys at the age of five years. Boys are better at throwing and catching and seem to have more strength; girls are better at jobs that involve judgment and precision, such as playing hopscotch. In play groups you visit you may see groups of boys doing heavily physical things such as running around, rough-and-tumble play, or playing with cars, trains, or large-scale layouts; and you may see groups of girls arranging the house play center, reading books, doing jigsaw puzzles, or helping the teacher.

The question of sex differences is a very controversial one, and every family has to decide for themselves how they want to bring up their children. Just because research might show that girls are more likely to become scientists if they are given more opportunity to play with numbers or building toys is no reason for you to deprive your little daughter of a much-loved doll or to deny her the opportunity of helping you in the kitchen. Even scientists will be more complete people if they learn to cook and take care of babies. Similarly, just because research suggests boys can throw and catch balls better than girls is no reason for you to exclude your daughter from games of baseball or basketball. Physically she is just as well equipped as your son, and like him, just needs the chance to practice to become better at a sport. The reverse is also true: if your son is very eager to take dancing lessons, don't discourage him because you think it is not the sort of thing a boy should be interested in.

The question of sex differences has been raised in this particular chapter because the very different ways in which we treat boys and girls are most marked in the amount of physical freedom or restriction we give them. Running, climbing, fighting, riding bikes, and playing ball games are all tolerated or encouraged in boys, but may not be in the families of some girls. Similarly, quiet, orderly, tabletop activities that involve cooperation with an adult are often felt to be more acceptable for girls. There are no physical reasons why this should be so, although you should remember that your child will have considerable pressure from his or her friends to behave in the same way as they do. However, it is important for you to give both your boys and your girls opportunities to do whatever physical activities they are capable of. If you do not encourage your son to talk to adults, take care of other children, help you to cook the meals, and learn the basics of cooking, he will miss out on important chances to learn skills he will need later in life. If your daughter never gets the chance to climb trees, or if you never buy her a bike, she will not get the chance to become physically daring and adventurous. One of the most valuable reasons for becoming physically skilled is the self-confidence it can give a child. If he feels comfortable in his body and feels he can make it do what he wants it to, then your child can be helped to be a more confident person. Both boys and girls need to be raised to accept and be proud of their bodies. There is no genetic or physical reason why little girls should be encouraged to be timid and shy, modest and passive, quiet and still; and there is no genetic or physical reason why little boys should be the opposite. You need to give both sexes the opportunities to do all the activities they might be capable of. It is then up to them to take what opportunities they want to develop into the person they are going to be.

CHAPTER 10

Your Baby's Developing Senses

Your baby's eyesight • Your baby's hearing
Your baby's sense of touch
Your baby's taste and smell

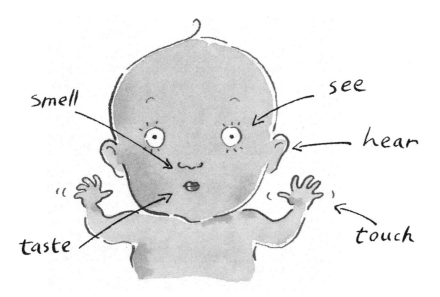

From the day your baby is born she begins to look around her for information about the world. She explores through her other senses, too: she is soothed by touch; she enjoys the taste of milk, but might make a face at something salty; she listens and turns toward sounds; she soon recognizes your smell.

Your Baby's Eyesight

Vision is the richest of all the senses for helping your baby to understand the world. The development of other skills, using her hands, moving around in a controlled way, understanding speech, and learning to relate to people all depend very much on what your baby can see.

The eyes provide a direct pathway to the brain for information about the world. They are the first outpost of the brain to develop in an inch-long embryo. The eyes of a newborn baby receive light rays from objects in the surroundings and build them into an image that is transmitted along the optic nerve to the brain. The brain "sees" the image, but although your very young baby can see roughly what you see—for example, a rattle—she does not yet know what this is. The message her eyes have received has passed to the brain, but it is not until she has more experience of the world that her brain will recognize the image as a rattle. The newborn baby can see, and it takes only a few months for her to recognize, to choose, and to focus on details of all the many objects she sees. This process is known as perception, and it begins to develop from the moment of birth.

Sight at Birth

One of the most common misconceptions is that a new baby cannot see. She is really interested in objects near to her, but cannot yet adjust fully the focus of her eyes for different distances. For example, she sees her mother's face best when she is nursing her in her arms. This first eye-to-eye contact is one of the most important ways in which a relationship is built up between the baby and the person looking after her.

New babies react to very bright light by closing their eyes and turning toward other, more diffuse sources of light. During the first weeks a baby begins to learn to use her eyes to follow moving objects—for example, a dangling mobile. She quickly develops preferences: human faces are more interesting to her than mere abstract shapes. Babies like to be held where they can see faces, and especially your face, clearly.

You may notice that your new baby's eyes seem to be crossing—that is, one eye looks in a slightly different direction from the other. This may just be due to the baby's experimenting with focusing and it may correct itself, but it is sensible to ask your doctor about it if it is always present or if it fails to improve after a week or two.

By about four months some important developments become noticeable. Your baby's sight and her ability to perceive and recognize different objects have been improving all the time. By now her eyes and the visual part of her brain have developed enough to see clearly and three-dimensionally. She can focus on near or distant objects and recognize them, and her interest and ability to see detail far away will continue to improve for some months. While she is immobile, learning will benefit if objects such as toys, spoons, and human faces are brought nearer and if people carry her around to broaden her horizon.

However, one important change happens at about four months that begins to give your baby more control over what happens to her and shows an important link between seeing/perceiving and other skills. At this age your baby has realized that what she can see is a tangible object she can reach out for, touch, and grasp. At first she will notice her hands waving in front of her eyes, and gradually she will deliberately bring them up to where she can see them and will start to play with them. Or she may catch sight of her foot without realizing it belongs to her. If you hold a toy or a spoon or her bottle close to her, she will begin to reach out and try to get hold of it. At first she is not very good at this. Her aim is not always accurate, and she will not always be able to grasp the object because she has not yet gotten sufficient control of her fingers, but it is an important step because it shows the baby is making the link between herself and the outside world. She recognizes there is an outside world and that the things she sees are not just pictures in her head. When she reaches out to touch and grasp she is saying to herself, "That's for me. The world is my oyster, and I am going to explore it."

Make sure your young baby has plenty of safe things to look at and that are within her reach from a few weeks old. A cradle toy suspended over her crib or carriage is great fun; you can make your own and change the objects on it from time to time if you wish. Babies like variety, so give her a mixture of textures—soft and furry, wood, plastic, and rubber. Include a few things that make a noise so she can make things happen. All these experiences will increase her sense of control over the world around her and make her eager to explore more. They will also help to keep her happy and amused. Make sure you carry her around, too, so that she sometimes sees the world from an upright position. Some babies enjoy being carried in a sling close to their mother's body , and most mothers get very good at doing a great many tasks with one hand!

Recognizing and Remembering

When a baby realizes that things and other people have a separate existence from herself, she then has to learn that they go on having a separate existence, even when she cannot see them. You will probably notice that when your young baby of four or five months drops a rattle, or when a person disappears from view, she seems to forget about their existence. At some time between six and nine months you will notice that the baby's memory for objects has improved. When she drops his rattle, she will look over the side of her high chair to see where it has gone. If you hide a toy under a blanket, she will pull the blanket away—and probably urge you to go on playing this game until you are exhausted! At this age peekaboo games in which you hide your face and then show it again are great fun for a baby who has just made the important discovery that people and things are still there—even when they cannot be seen.

From six months onward babies are full of curiosity for the things they can see around them. They love to look at things and reach for them and, if they get hold of them, usually put them in their mouths. The link between sight and touch becomes increasingly closer at this time. The baby's ability to grasp objects improves, although she will not be able to pick up very tiny things until she can coordinate her forefinger and thumb, which happens at about nine months. She likes new things and by about a year will point and babble when something catches her attention.

She is sensitive to faces and their expressions, too. Watch when other adults hold your baby—they usually go to an enormous amount of trouble to get a response from her, by smiling, nodding, wrinkling their foreheads, and talking. Watch how the baby follows, imitates the expressions, and responds. You do this, too, although you are probably not aware of it at the time. From a very early age babies become unhappy and distressed at a sad or angry-looking face and respond happily to smiles and animated faces.

At about nine months, although it may be earlier or later, babies will stop responding happily to all friendly faces and may begin to show wariness of strangers' faces, no matter how friendly they appear. Although this may be inconvenient for you, it does show that your baby has made another important discovery—that the world can be a dangerous place and that caution and suspicion are sometimes needed when she is faced with new experience.

Naming and Playing

As your baby begins to notice and be interested in different objects around her, you will automatically begin to name them for her. Mothers do this even for newborn babies: they will say "Here's Daddy," or "Look at that pretty tree" even though they know the baby cannot possibly understand. However, when your baby begins to point and reach and grasp and show likes and dislikes, you can start using her visual behavior to build up her understanding and awareness of language.

Mothers have many ways of doing this: you may just point and say the single word very clearly, "spoon," or "teddy," or "cracker"; or you may give the baby a running commentary on what she is doing, "Oh, dear, you've dropped your spoon. Let's pick it up and try again"; or you may encourage her ability to learn that out-of-sight objects are still there by saying, "Where's the spoon? Is it on the floor?" and looking down yourself and picking it up with a triumphant cry, "Here's the spoon." Never feel that this kind of behavior is silly or that talking to a baby who cannot yet talk back is pointless. It is not. It is the most valuable learning experience you can give her—and mothers are very, very good at it. There is more about language in chapter 11.

Babies begin to understand the names of things quite a long time before they can say them. If you say, "Where's the cat?" your year-old baby may look around and point or babble if the cat is there. Giving your baby plenty of experience of the "Where's the?" and "What's that?" variety encourages her to learn and build up her store of words and names. Many babies between six months and a year begin to enjoy looking at pictures, too. Simple board picture books can encourage her recognition of objects and their names. Generally young babies like pictures that are very realistic rather than those that are done in a stylized or cartoon design. Good sources for these kinds of pictures are catalogs and magazines, and babies enjoy turning (and tearing) the pages as well. Pictures help her to learn that objects not only exist outside her, they can also be represented. A picture may look very like the real thing, but it is not the real thing, it is just a representation of it.

Television pictures are too complicated for a young baby to understand—she cannot reach out to grasp and handle the objects represented there as she can with real things, and, unlike a book, the image changes very quickly. Although older babies may like to look at television for short periods, they will learn very little from it at this stage, so do not leave your baby in front of the set for long periods. Watching television does not do any harm to children's vision, but it is sensible to encourage older children to sit at least three feet away.

On the Move

Once your baby begins to crawl and then walk, she no longer relies on you to show her things or bring them to her. She can decide for herself what she wants to look at and then take a closer look, and if possible get hold of it. It is just before this stage that you need to look at your house in terms of safety (see also chapter 15). Babies will obviously be attracted to things at their own eye level, so you will have to move all dangerous and fragile things steadily upward from the floor as your baby gets older.

The information she receives through her eyes is the foundation for all sorts of other learning, and the means of learning at this stage is play (see chapter 12). From twelve months onward, and certainly once she can walk and has her hands free, the coordination between your baby's eyes and hands becomes more and more skilled. She will play with things in a more purposeful way, pick up tiny objects and examine them, try to put one object on top of or inside another. She will throw, push, and pull; she will turn things into tools—for instance, she will use a piece of string to pull a toy car toward her. She will observe and imitate. If you give her the chance, the young toddler will also show interest in holding a pencil or crayon and in scribbling on paper. She will be able to use a paintbrush, but expect her to enjoy simply making a mess with the paint rather than actually painting! She can now recognize familiar things and people at a distance of twenty feet or so. The world of the toddler is full of colors, shapes, and sights to be explored and learned about.

Visual Impairment

Very few babies are born completely blind or with severe visual problems. Some of those who are often have other handicaps as well, because something that inter-feres with or damages the formation of the eyes or optic nerve may affect other parts of the baby's or embryo's nervous system—for example, rubella (German measles) in pregnancy, or breathing problems at birth. In some cases severe eye problems can be inherited.

It is very important that such problems are identified and treated early because, as we described above, so much of the baby's early development is linked to her ability to see and perceive. Some visual handicaps are detected immediately after birth, particularly if doctors have been alerted by problems occurring at about the time of delivery, by the mother's illness in pregnancy, or by a family eye problem. Sometimes the baby's visual behavior is the only clue. If your baby's eyes roll a lot, if she is startled when she is touched, or hears a voice but she has no visual clue that someone was approaching, if she does not make eye contact after a month or so or begin to respond to your smiles and movements, then it could possibly be that she cannot see properly. These signs will become more and more noticeable during the first three or four weeks. If you are worried by your baby's lack of visual response, do not hesitate to seek medical advice immediately.

Some eye problems can be cured, and it is important that they are, because after about eighteen months the brain's ability to learn to interpret messages from the eyes decreases sharply. The first six months of life are the most important time in this learning process.

Some conditions, such as cataracts and squints, are treatable. Cataracts affect the lens of the eye and prevent light rays from falling on the retina. They can now be operated on successfully in very tiny babies; the baby is given a contact lens to help her focus. A squint means the eyes do not look in the same direction and therefore cannot operate together. With normal binocular (two-eyed) vision, the two independent images received by each eye are fused by the brain into one. The child with a squint cannot do this and, therefore, relies on the information coming through only one of her eyes and does not use the other one. Eventually the sight in the unused or "lazy" eye, as it is sometimes called, becomes very poor because the brain does not register the information coming from it. Squints can be treated by putting a patch over the good eye, thereby encouraging active use of the lazy one; by glasses; by an operation; or by a combination of these. If you think your baby squints, ask your doctor to advise whether you should take her to see an ophthalmologist for full diagnosis and treatment.

Eye Tests

Most babies and young children in developed countries are routinely tested for sight from six months onward. First tests are designed to find out whether your child has a squint or a minor visual defect such as shortsightedness (myopia). In myopia the eyeballs are longer than average and the image is blurred because it falls in front of the eye's retina instead of on it; the child cannot see things that are far away from her, but can focus on things that are near. Farsightedness (hypermetropia) creates the opposite problem: the image falls behind the retina. Severe farsightedness causes great strain because the eyes have to work to focus on images, even when they are across the room. Normally we only need to make our eyes work to focus on near objects. Both conditions can be corrected by wearing glasses. Another problem is astigmatism, in which the light rays entering the eye are bent because of an irregularity in the eyeball, creating a distorted image. This, too, can be dealt with by glasses. Glasses early on can also prevent the development of squint and lazy eye, as well as helping your child to see clearly.

If any of your family has needed glasses in childhood, or if your baby or young child has not been routinely tested and you suspect there is something wrong with her sight, make sure you ask for a test. The sooner treatment is begun, the better. For more on eye problems, see chapters 17 and 19.

Glasses for Children

Parents, especially if they themselves have never worn glasses, may feel a pang of protective anxiety if their young child needs glasses. The common worry is that their child may feel self-conscious or that other children may comment adversely. In fact these protective anxieties are nearly always entirely adult-based and usually a remnant from our own childhood memories of unattractive frames for children. It is very important that parents, and any grandparents or other older relatives, keep any such feelings very strictly to themselves, as children, and especially preschool children, will usually accept wearing glasses quite happily, provided they are introduced to them in a positive fashion. There is now a wide range of bright, attractive frames for children. Find an optician who stocks a good selection. Those with bendy wire sides that curl behind the ears are usually best for under fives as they stay put during handstands, somersaults, and so on. An alternative is a style with spring sides. Let your child feel she has chosen the style of frame, though obviously a little tactful manipulation may be needed to see that her choice comes within your budget! Make sure they are fitted correctly so they are comfortable, with no red pressure points when they are taken off.

At first glasses will feel a little strange to the child, so it helps to plan some busy days with plenty of activities to help her forget she is wearing them. Glasses may not necessarily need to be worn throughout the day; discuss this with the physician who prescribes them. The mother of a three-year-old who wears glasses because farsightedness made him squint recalled:

> At first I felt sorry about him wearing glasses even though it's a tiny thing compared with real disabilities. It was seeing him crying because he had fallen over, and trying to rub away the tears but finding the glasses got in the way, that slightly got to me. But now they are so much part of his life, to the extent that the other day he came and said, "Mom, I can't find my glasses anywhere," and he was actually wearing them. He's not at all the sort of child I used to think of as "weird" from my childhood days either—he's very athletic and really popular with other kids.

The eyes are the most sensitive information receivers in the body and are able to deal with millions of bits of information every time they look at something. Most of this information is screened out and discarded because it is not needed. The process of becoming ever more selective and discriminating in the perception of all the many objects and people in the world around her is a vital part of your child's intellectual and social development. It is also a source of wonder and delight. Some of the happiest shared experiences between a baby and an adult begin with the word "Look."

Your Baby's Hearing

Although sight is the most important coordinating sense, hearing is a most valuable sense for human beings because it is through hearing that we learn language and are able to communicate with each other. A child or person who cannot hear is cut off from other people, and this will affect her ability to make relationships, as well as the way she learns, unless prompt help is offered and maintained.

The ears work by collecting sounds from the environment and channeling them down into the inner ear by way of the eardrum. The sounds make the eardrum vibrate, and these vibrations are converted by the organs of the inner ear into electrical impulses, which are then passed along the auditory nerve to the brain. The brain converts these impulses into meaningful information just as it does with the light waves coming through the eyes. We take the skills of the brain so much for granted that we do not always appreciate what an impressive performance it is to turn sound vibrations into the lines of a poem, or rays of light into patterns, shapes, and designs, but this is what your baby's brain is equipped to do. And as with vision, her brain will set to work on the task of learning to interpret sounds right from birth.

Your Newborn's Hearing

Once the newborn baby's ears are drained of fluid that is left over from her life in the womb, her hearing is acute, and it will get even better as she grows older. If she hears a sudden noise, she will startle. She may also move her head in response to noise, but she cannot yet tell exactly where a sound is coming from and look toward it. She learns to do this more accurately at about five or six months. New babies soon learn to recognize their own mother's, father's, or caretaker's voice. If your baby is crying and hears you speak to her, she may stop and listen. A strange voice will not be so reassuring. Babies are also sensitive to the sound of other babies. If your baby is in a ward or a nursery with other mothers and babies and one baby starts crying, it is not long before your baby and all the others begin as well.

Many sounds seem to have a special quality for soothing babies—especially rhythmic sounds. Lullabies are an age-old way of sending a baby to sleep, and so is rhythmic rocking. We do not quite know why this should be, but since the ear controls the sense of balance as well as hearing, there is an obvious connection between rhythmic movement and rhythmic sound. You will probably notice that you quite automatically sway backward and forward when holding your baby, you will pat her bottom rhythmically, and you will say simple phrases over and over: "There, there. What's the matter?" and so on.

By about seven months your baby will be well able to recognize and discriminate among different sounds: for instance, the sound of a spoon in a dish will mean food to her; the door opening will mean someone is coming; she can tell angry from cheerful voices, will be upset if you speak angrily, and will perk up if you speak happily. So although she cannot understand words or sentences or speak them yet, she is well on the way to linking meaning with sound—an important part of learning to talk.

Sound Play

Being able to hear is vital to learn to talk, but we do not express ourselves only through speech. Language can also be expressed in signs and gestures (as used by deaf people), and, of course, through print and the written word. There is more about language and its development in chapter 11.

During her first year your baby will learn to distinguish words from other sounds she hears and to associate them with meaningful things, but she will also enjoy being talked to. As you talk to your two- or three-month-old, you will notice that she responds by waving her arms, kicking her legs, smiling, and gurgling. Babies enjoy being sung to as well, no matter how unmusical you think your voice is, so sing and hum to your baby, and let her hear other music, too.

However, babies can be upset by too much noise. Sudden loud sounds can startle them and make them cry. They may get very upset by the vacuum cleaner or the washing machine. We all have a mechanism known as habituation, which enables us to screen out unnecessary sounds once we have heard them a few times; although the noise may be continuing we simply do not hear it. Babies learn to do this in the first few days of their lives, but new sounds may still have to be introduced gently.

Babies and young children in today's cities live in a very noisy environment, with cars roaring past and perhaps the radio or television as continual background noise. You do not want your child to screen out all sounds, so once she is old enough it is sometimes good to be quiet and encourage her to listen for particular noises: leaves rustling; a dog barking; a train passing; a car in the distance getting nearer. Talk about the noises as you hear them and tell her what they mean. As she gets older you can use her hearing skills to introduce important ideas such as loud/soft or high/low. There are plenty of ways to introduce sound play around the home, although most adults find it hard to habituate to sounds such as pots and pans being banged! Five minutes will probably be as much as you can stand.

Most toys are designed to encourage hand-eye activities, but remember that babies play and learn through their ears, too. Once your child is talking, sound remains crucial. This is especially true for blind or partially blind children, who have to learn everything through hearing, touch, smell, and taste.

Hearing Tests

New babies do not have many ways of letting us know whether or not they can hear. If you have any hearing problems in your family, however, or if you had rubella (German measles) or any other illness during early pregnancy, you should tell the hospital pediatrician or your own doctor.

Your newborn baby may be tested using special hearing testing devices to see if she is hearing. Different hospitals vary in their policy toward hearing testing, but this is performed especially if there is anything in your child's medical history that might suggest impaired hearing. During one type of test the baby wears a special device that can measure changes in her breathing in response to a variety of sounds. These can be detected and recorded. A newer test, called brainstem auditory evoked response (BAER), measures cochlear function. The cochlea is the snail-shaped organ in the middle ear that is full of fluid, sound receptors, and membranes and is able to covert the vibrations of the eardrum into nerve impulses that send messages to the brain. In this test a probe bounces sound into the ear and a fraction of a second later is able to pick up an echo bouncing back from the cochlea. If there is no echo, this may indicate that the complicated hearing mechanism is not working properly. If your baby does not pass these tests, other, more sophisticated tests will be arranged to measure the hearing more accurately and to find out if there is really a problem.

Different health providers operate slightly different health screening programs, but most see babies at eight weeks and then again between about eight and nine months. At the first check, which may be done by your pediatrician, hearing can only be tested in a fairly elementary way to see if the baby responds to a loud level of sound. At eight to nine months the hearing test usually consists of sounding a high-frequency rattle and whispering low-frequency words to see if the baby makes a turning response. A baby with a history indicating a greater chance of hearing impairment should be observed more carefully.

The test at eight to nine months involves your sitting with your baby on your lap while your pediatrician or her nurse makes test sounds behind her, to her right and then to her left. If the baby turns toward the sound, it is assumed her hearing is all right. If she does not turn, then it does not necessarily mean she is deaf—she may simply have caught sight of something more fascinating across the room. Bear in mind also that hearing can be temporarily affected by colds and illness. If she does not respond to this first test, you will be asked to bring her back again.

If you are sure she responds to sounds, for instance, you know that you have only to tiptoe across her bedroom floor for her to jump up in his crib—then tell the pediatrician. A parent's own reports on the child are usually taken very seriously, because as one pediatrician with years of experience of testing has put it, "The mother is usually right." Of course, if you are worried about your child's hearing, perhaps because she does not respond to the soothing noises and sounds in the way described above, if she startles when she sees you as if she has had no warning from footsteps or the door opening, and if she is not wakened by sounds, then be persistent in getting her hearing properly checked. Your concerns will usually have some foundation, as you know your child best, and you will be well aware if she does not seem to be developing in the same way as other babies you know.

Your child may also be tested as part of a community screening program at the pediatrician's office or at the time she enters school, when more sophisticated electrical equipment will be used to measure how well she hears the high and the low tones. The age when this is done varies, but most children are tested between three and four. Some children have "high-tone deafness" and cannot hear consonants properly. The speech they hear will seem blurred and will affect their own speech. If your child does seem to have difficulty hearing some sounds, or if she is prone to ear infections and colds that also affect her hearing, ask for the test and tell her day-care supervisors and schoolteachers so they sit her near the front of the group and make allowances for any hearing problems she may have. If she says "What?" all the time or ignores half of what you say, she may not be being difficult. Never rule out the possibility that she cannot hear properly, and make sure she is tested by an audi-ologist—a specialist whose job it is to check hearing.

The Child with Impaired Hearing

Some children are deaf from birth through an inherited disorder of the inner ear or through damage during pregnancy—for example, from rubella, or from a shortage of oxygen at birth. Other children may become deaf later, perhaps because of a severe illness, such as meningitis, or from another childhood disease such as mumps. Many children suffer some temporary deafness during their childhood from middle-ear infection (otitis media) or by a buildup of wax in the ear. Do not try to solve this by using Q-Tips in the ear, as they stimulate wax production and can damage the eardrum. If in doubt, ask your doctor to check her ears—occasionally the ear may be blocked by something your child has inserted, such as a glass bead or other type of foreign object. Since good hearing is very important for the proper development of speech, it follows that poor hearing may affect social relationships. You always need to be aware of the possibility of hearing loss if your child suffers from any of the illnesses mentioned above or from subsequent coughs and colds. Also consider it if her behavior seems absentminded or indifferent, or if her speech is slow to develop. Few children have total hearing loss, and what hearing they have can be the basis for very specialized speech and language training. Once hear-ing loss, whether partial or severe, is diagnosed, it is important for this treatment to begin as quickly as possible.

Hearing Aids

As with glasses, parents usually find the idea of a hearing aid for their child much more difficult to accept than the child does. It is important to keep such feelings from the child and to take a positive and optimistic view of the hearing aid as a real benefit. All hearing aids work on the same principle: they are amplifiers, which make the sounds around louder. With the use of amplification there is always the risk of distortion, but the quality of aids is improving all the time, so this becomes much less of a problem, and the hearing aids are more acceptable to the child.

Small hearing aids worn behind the ear consist of an individually made ear mold in the ear that connects to a small box containing the amplifier and a micro-battery. Under long hair it is invisible. Babies and young children will normally be given bilateral (two) aids, one for each ear. Young babies easily accept a hearing aid, but more tact and encouragement are required between the ages of eighteen months and three years, when many children can be uncooperative about almost anything, ranging from putting on their coat to taking it off again!

Overcoming Deafness

Parents of children who cannot hear properly have to work much harder to stimulate them, drawing their attention to objects and events and associating them with language. You cannot just throw casual remarks over your shoulder—you have to look at the child and speak very carefully so she can also learn to read your lips.

Together with advice from audiologists, medical specialists, specialized teachers of hearing-impaired children, and specialized speech therapists, early language training at home is vital with regular help from the teacher. We all use language in our thought processes, and it is important that hearing-impaired children are able to develop an inner language to use in this way. While the topic of language is controversial, specialists feel that both oral language and sign language should be used to communicate with a profoundly deaf child. There is some evidence that normal-hearing babies of deaf parents who learn sign language early in their childhood do better at reading and writing later than do deaf children who have not learned sign language and who have only limited oral language by the time they learn to read. Young children have a greater facility than adults for learning language—children of bilingual parents are able to absorb both languages easily, while an adult finds tackling a foreign language for the first time far more difficult. In this way the mastering of what are two languages—sign language and oral language—may be easier than an adult imagines for a young child.

Depending on where you live and the degree of the handicap, a child with hearing impairment may attend a special school for the deaf, for which transportation is provided. Alternatively, she may go to a special unit for hearing-impaired children attached to the local primary school. This allows her to live in a hearing community and helps hearing children to be aware of the challenges of the deaf. Many partially hearing children go to ordinary nursery schools, but they need a great deal of specialist-teacher help so they do not miss out on their early education. For more on hearing problems, see chapters 17 and 19.

Your Baby's Sense of Touch

We learn a great deal through our eyes and ears, but we feel through our skin and learn this way as well. This is particularly true of young babies whose vision and hearing are still limited, and even more so for blind children. However, most of us tend to pay less attention to the sense of touch than to other senses.

The skin gives us a great deal of information about what is going on around us—whether our environment is hot or cold, wet or dry. A most important function of the skin is to control temperature. In warm conditions the blood vessels expand, bringing blood to the surface of the body and cooling it. We also excrete sweat though the skin, and as the sweat evaporates, our bodies are kept cool. In cold weather the blood vessels contract to conserve the body's heat. New babies cannot control their temperature through their skin as effectively as older babies, children, and adults can. That is why it is important to keep them in a constant mildly warm temperature, as well as to keep them warmly wrapped up when the weather is cool. There is more about the right temperature for your baby in the section "Taking Care of Your New Baby" in chapter 4.

Our skin also tells us, through its sensitive nerve endings, whether the sensations we are receiving are painful or pleasurable: a caress is pleasant, a spanking is not; warmth is pleasant, sunburn is not. Pain is an important signal of danger to the brain. When we receive a sudden blow, cut, or other painful contact, we instinctively recoil. Pain also indicates illness and damage, and crying can be a sign that your baby is suffering. Always check for uncomfortable bumps in the crib, a sore bottom, or a tightly constricting garment if your baby is miserable.

Babies and young children have more sensitive skin than adults do. What seems pleasantly warm bathwater to you may feel scaldingly hot to a baby. What seems a pleasantly cool breeze to you may be really chilly to a baby. A firm grasp of a toddler's hand may actually hurt her quite a lot, and you cannot really blame her for protesting. A good general rule to remember is that babies and young children often feel things more intensely than adults do. Although babies and young children are resilient and well equipped for survival, they can easily be hurt, so they need to be treated gently and sensitively.

In addition to responding to the environment around you, the skin is affected by the emotional state inside the person. Blushing and sweating when you are embarrassed, excited, or afraid are obvious examples. For some children, skin diseases such as eczema, psoriasis, and acne can be made worse by emotional stress, and emotional upset may even trigger a flare-up of the condition. When you are happy, your skin looks glowing and healthy; when you are miserable, it can look sallow and lifeless. The color, condition, feel, and state of the skin are important signs as to whether a person is well. If your baby's skin changes very markedly and suddenly in any way—whether it is a change of color or temperature, or if there is a rash—take her to the doctor, especially if there are other symptoms, such as fever or loss of appetite.

The Importance of Contact

As soon as a baby is born, one of the first things a mother does, provided she is well herself and has access to her baby, is to reach out and touch her. Research has shown that many mothers have a systematic way of doing this—starting with fingertip touching of hands and feet, and then going on to stroke the baby all over with the palms of their hands. Of course, whether you do this depends on whether you have the baby near you and whether she is naked or wrapped up. Nowadays many doctors and midwives deliver and place the baby straight onto the mother's stomach so they are lying skin-to-skin.

The importance of touch to babies and their parents is beginning to be emphasized more and more. It is certainly true that many mothers, given the choice, love to hold and stroke their babies, to press their cheek against their baby's cheek, to smell and even to lick their babies—after all, humans are animals, too. They want to be as close as they possibly can to their baby's body.

Young babies are also soothed by touch. They like to be held firmly or wrapped up securely. When they are miserable, being carried around in a sling in close contact with their mother's or father's body can sometimes cheer them up and put them to sleep. Holding them against your shoulder, so their stomach and chest are against you, is often especially soothing. Gently stroking their stomach, limbs, or temples can often calm them and, as with other rhythmic behavior such as rocking and singing, can get them off to sleep. This need for comfort through cuddling and touching does not stop with babyhood. A sympathetic touch—just a grasp of the arm or a stroke of the head—can make adults as well as children feel happier and more confident.

Because children frequently have to be carried and have things done for them, they automatically seek and demand a lot of touching, but special forms of touching, such as hugs or a kiss, are ideal forms of reward for children, much better than candy. When your child is being peaceful or cooperative, remember to pat her on the head or give her a hug. If she is having a tantrum, however, hugs may infuriate her even more. It may be better to stay next to her until she has calmed down, and then to touch her gently, perhaps just by holding her hand.

Individual Differences

Many experienced mothers or nurses will tell you that some babies are more cuddly than others. Some babies cuddle cozily into your body, while others go stiff and rigid, nurse in a businesslike manner in ten minutes, and want to get off your lap or be put down. Some adults are like this, too—including mothers. It seems to be a matter of personality, and it is no good quoting research to a baby who does not like people grabbing her all the time! If you have a non-cuddly baby or child, or if you are a nontoucher yourself, don't waste precious energy feeling guilty about it. It should become clear to you from other sections of this book that babies and parents learn and receive mutual pleasure from all the senses in hundreds of different ways. If your baby does not like being on your lap, she may love sitting opposite you in a high chair while you talk to her. If you do not want to carry your baby around in your arms all the time, don't worry. Perhaps the father can do the carrying instead of you, or there might be a grandmother or friend who likes cuddling and carrying. You can give your baby what you feel you do best—it might be conversation or games or trips to the zoo. However, touching and carrying and cuddling are absolutely unavoidable with human babies for many months and even years. If you feel you are not getting any pleasure out of these things and that you see your baby as a burden, talk to somebody about it. Your doctor may be able to help you by recommending one of the organizations that specialize in advising parents on handling these adverse feelings. Touch can also be especially important to newborn babies in incubators. There is more about how you can meet your baby's and your own needs for contact in these circumstances in chapter 5.

One of the most important sensory experiences for a baby is through her tongue and mouth. Sucking is not only necessary to obtain milk, it is also a source of comfort and satisfaction for a baby (see "The Big Decision—Breast or Bottle?" in chapter 6 for more on this). Once a baby can begin to hold things in her hands, she automatically puts almost everything to her mouth for further exploration. By about nine months a baby may still put things in her mouth, but she will show that she is also able to appreciate the sensation of different textures she can touch with her hands—stroking a pet, putting her fingers in her food, playing with sand or water. As she grows, you can help to develop her understanding of different materials in her environment, both natural and synthetic, through everyday experience and play.

If your baby develops an attachment to a toy, blanket, or other object as a "comfort" object you will see clearly how her sense of touch is being exercised. Not only will she clutch the comforter to her or enjoy stroking it, she also will often pull it across her face or hold it against a cheek. Later, if she inadvertently comes across the same texture in a fabric when she is tired—a similar silky or soft piece of material, for example—she may immediately clutch it in the same way and show other going-to-sleep habits, such as thumb-sucking. Your baby naturally explores and tests out the textures of rattles and other toys, and as her awareness grows will increasingly enjoy playing with the water in her bath. Look for textures and sensations to introduce in play—being aware that young babies automatically put most things in their mouths—so your child experiences hard followed by soft, rough/smooth, angular objects such as blocks, and round ones such as balls. When you are out in the garden or park, let her touch the roughness of tree bark, wrinkle green leaves, and crunch crackly autumn ones. You sometimes see parents getting angry with small children for getting messy while playing around in the dirt, but while it is understandable that parents don't want children covered in mud or worse, it is also part of a child's natural curiosity to continually explore and discover.

Your Baby's Taste and Smell

Much less attention has been given to the senses of taste and smell by experts in child development than to the other senses. We do not, therefore, know so much about them, but this does not mean they are not important. Just consider:

- The word "taste" also means a person's own particular preference for things.

- Parents can have battles with their children for years over particular foods because the children do not like the taste or the smell.

- A bad smell is one of the most revolting experiences people can have—literally making them sick.

- Pleasant smells have a powerful effect in attracting people to each other.

New babies can tell the differences among drinks of different degrees of sweetness—they suck most eagerly at the sweetest drink. But since sugar can be harmful to children's teeth, an apparently inborn taste for sweetness does not mean a child should be fed on sweet things. Breast milk is sweet and babies obviously like it, but the sugar (lactose) in it is not harmful to teeth. Babies do not like sharp or acid tastes and almost always spit out things that taste that way.

When you begin introducing solids to your baby, you should aim for a variety of tastes in what you give her so she gets a balanced diet and learns to develop her own tastes. There is more about starting to feed your baby solids and about the problems of food battles and food fads in chapters 6 and 7.

There is evidence that new babies can tell their own mother's smell from that of other mothers. One study showed that babies responded much more often to a breast pad used by their own mothers than to pads worn by other women. A new baby with limited vision, hearing, and understanding of the world may rely on smell as a source of information about where she is and who she is with and also as a source of comfort. A baby may refuse to nurse because her mother smells different, perhaps because she is using scented soap. Mothers sometimes comment enthusiastically on the special smell their own babies have. Some parents can tolerate the smell of their own baby's diapers but find it very difficult to change another baby. It does seem, therefore, as if we use smell as part of the process that helps to attach parents and babies to each other.

The human baby has a potentially wonderful mind—able to use language, to invent, to create, to make jokes, to solve problems—but, especially in the early years, the mind is nourished through the body. What your child sees, hears, touches, tastes, and smells are the raw materials of her intelligence and her personality. Young children try to experience things through all these senses at once. They will see something, reach for it, rattle it, and talk to it; then they will put it in their mouths. This huge appetite for experience can sometimes be inconvenient, but it is essential to your child's development and it can help you, too, to see and experience the world again, as if for the first time.

Language

If someone asked you what you thought was the most impressive human achievement in using the English language, you might think of such classics as Shakespeare's plays, Dickens's novels, or *Webster's Dictionary*. However, the scope of achievement, even in these great works, is not as great as the difference between a newborn baby whose main form of expressing himself is to cry, and the speech of that same child three years later.

A new baby cannot understand what you are saying and cannot talk back to you. A three-year-old can say, "Daddy says I can have some candy tomorrow." In this simple sentence a three-year-old is showing he can report another person's speech, anticipate the future, use a complex combination of verbs ("can have"), hold a conversation, and in this case even use language not quite truthfully as a form of persuasion ("Daddy says"). If you disagree with him he will probably go on to conduct a sustained argument with you!

Children pick up language quickly. This is so basic to our everyday lives that it is easy to take it for granted and to overlook what a vital and complex skill it is. However, there are good reasons for recognizing how important language is to your child and to you. In the first place, it gives contact and closeness between the child and others: it is through talking and listening that you get to know each other and eventually to share each other's experiences. In the second place, it is an important vehicle for learning. For instance, language is the tool that enables a child to tell Mommy what happened at Grandma's house while she was out. Later, language will be used in abstract arguments ("What if . . . ?") and also to solve logical problems. Still later your child will learn the more formal skills of reading and writing as well as talking and listening. Language, or verbal ability, is one important factor in success at school, although it is not the only one.

The roots of your child's verbal ability lie in the early years between birth and four years old. By the end of this period most normal children have mastered the basic rules of their own language and are able to produce original, creative sentences in any number of combinations. And they do it without any systematic training on your part, though this does not mean you have no part to play.

What Is Language?

Language is a system of symbols. They can be sounds, as in speech, or they can be marks on paper. But language is more than a long list of signs that mean something—that would just be a dictionary. Language is also a system of rules used to create new meanings. Through language we can not only produce sentences that are completely original and that nobody has ever heard before, but we can also understand statements we have never heard before, as we do every time somebody talks to us. So when a baby learns language he is not only learning lists of words—mommy, daddy, and cat—he is also learning to use the rules that help him to combine words into completely new and often very delightful statements such as, "Look, I didded it myself." As the word "didded" shows, the way he uses the rules may not be the way grown-ups use them, but it is sensible as far as he is concerned. Babies and young children seem to have a natural ability to learn and use language creatively, but, of course, your child's enjoyment and mastery of language also depend a lot on you and the other people around him continuing to talk and listen to him.

How Language Develops

All babies and small children learn first to understand and then to use language in a fairly standard developmental sequence, but there are big individual variations in the timing of when these developments happen. One child may say his first word (as distinct from babbling "mammam—daddad" sounds) at 9 months. He may say, "bye" and wave, so you know that he realizes the sound "bye" is associated with somebody leaving. Another child will not be able to do this until 15 or 16 months. Yet another might not bother with many single words such as "bye" or "gone" or "teddy" but instead will keep fairly quiet, understanding what you say to him, then suddenly start producing short sentences at 20 months. Some children may be very slow at understanding and producing language, which could be a sign of problems and which should be discussed with your doctor. However, by the time they are three or four years old, most children are using language almost as adults use it, although with smaller vocabularies.

The main stages of language development are summarized in the table at the end of this chapter. This is just a rough guide to what you might expect, so the ages are approximate. Do not be surprised if your baby does something much earlier than the chart shows, although if he is much later—by several months, say—in reaching these stages, you should discuss this with your doctor, who may refer you to a speech and language therapist.

Your First Communications with Baby

If you were alert and well when you had your baby, one of the first things you probably did was to say hello to him. You might then have commented on his nose or his eyes and gently scolded him for being late or giving you a difficult time. Later, when you picked him up for a feeding, you probably asked him if he was hungry, or if he was screaming, you may have told him he needed to calm down or nursing would be harder for both of you. In short, you talked to your new baby as you would talk to another adult. You treated him as if he could understand, although you knew he could not. When adults talk to new babies they use normal adult speech, but they tend to raise their voices and use rather sing-song rhythms. Later, when your baby begins to understand what you say and starts producing his own words, you will not talk to him as you do to another adult. New babies respond to the sound of human voices and seem to prefer higher-pitched tones. They will respond to other sounds by blinking or turning their heads or staring, but human speech seems to have an especially soothing quality for them. One researcher who filmed babies while their mothers were talking to them, and then slowed down the film, found that the babies' arm and leg movements seemed to correspond with the rhythms of the mothers' speech. New babies cannot understand adult speech, but they certainly seem to respond to it, so talking to your baby as you do things for him is important. It is also important for you as a way of expressing your feelings, so don't feel inhibited in case other people think you are odd. Almost everybody talks intelligently to new babies, without even being aware of it. Just watch next time you are at your doctor's office.

Taking Turns

Most people use language in the form of conversations with other people. We talk to tell people something we want them to know, and we listen so they can tell us what they want us to know. We then answer back and develop the conversation, and people respond to what we have said. To have an effective conversation we need to know when it is our turn to speak, and we have to wait until other people seem to have finished. We notice when they pause or accentuate their voice as if to ask a question, or raise their eyebrows as if to invite us to comment. All these signals about whose turn it is to communicate begin to be learned when your baby is very young. They often happen at feeding time because you are close to your baby and noticing his behavior very attentively to see if he is sucking properly, or taking enough from the breast or bottle. While your baby is busy sucking, you may just watch him, but when he pauses for breath and comes off the nipple or bottle, you will take your turn to communicate. You may talk to him, smile, and ask if he has had enough. He may then widen his eyes and gurgle and kick his legs and then, suddenly, he will dive back to the business of nursing and start sucking again.

These exchanges can happen at other times, too, of course, and mothers cannot always gaze down at their babies when they are nursing, particularly if they have older children, or the baby has his eyes closed and is oblivious to the outside world. Nevertheless, feeding time is a good time to develop communication skills with your baby because it is a shared activity that is important to you both, and it gives many opportunities for the baby to let you know how he is feeling and for you to respond. This is why it is a good idea to feed the baby yourself for most of his feedings, even if you are bottle-feeding. It is never safe to prop up a bottle for a young baby and leave him alone with it, because he might choke. Other than the concern for choking, propping him up with his bottle denies him the opportunity to learn the skills of communicating and taking turns that develop when adult and baby are close to each other and enjoying a shared task. These "turn-taking" sessions are the beginning of conversation.

Crying

In his first few weeks, your baby's main means of expressing himself is through crying. Crying is a way for your infant to attract attention and draw people near to him. Language does the same thing: words enable us to communicate with people in another room and even across time and space through the printed word or electronic message. It is much more convenient and efficient as a form of expression than physical gesture or crying.

Most mothers learn to recognize their own baby's cry from that of other babies. They can also detect different kinds of crying—hunger, boredom, fear, or habit. Some babies, for instance, seem to need a good yell just before they drop into a deep sleep. You will quickly learn from experience how to tell this kind of nonurgent cry from a cry of real hunger or distress. Crying is meant by nature to be disturbing—even adults who are not related to a baby find it difficult to ignore, and if you are his mother you will probably find it almost impossible to ignore. There is more about crying and comforting in chapter 8.

Baby's First Sounds

By the time he is a few weeks old, your baby will be producing more pleasant sounds, usually in response to attention from you, but sometimes when he is just lying in his crib, looking at objects in the room or at his own hands and feet. These first sounds will be little cooing noises and gurgles; many babies also seem to enjoy blowing loud raspberries. These are his first exercises in expressing himself vocally, and, of course, they will bring a response from you, which will give you both more practice at conversational turn-taking. However, even if there is nobody around, the baby may enjoy making noises and listening to his own sounds.

Between three and six months these little sounds gradually become more like speech—they turn into babble. Your baby may say one sound over and over, "babababa" or "gagagaga," as if fascinated by the noise. He will begin to raise and drop his voice as if he were talking. This babbling is not really like the adult speech he hears, because even babies with severe hearing loss babble, although they do not develop the speechlike rhythms that hearing babies do. In the early babbling stages, babies produce sounds that do not belong to their native language: babies from all countries seem to make exactly the same kind of noises. It is only later that they make noises that sound like English or Spanish or Chinese. These babbling sounds can give you a lot of pleasure. The fact that the first noises are often "mamama" or "dadada" is also rewarding to parents. Although they are not true speech, they do encourage you to look at your baby and talk to him when he makes them. Other people also talk back to babbling babies. These experiences expand the baby's social world and set the scene for the verbal communication that comes later.

Even after the first true words appear in your baby's vocabulary, he will continue to play with noises that sound like speech but are not. A toddler of 14 or 15 months will wave his spoon and address the rest of the family from his high chair in a long stream of incomprehensible jargon, just as if he were making an after-dinner speech. The rising and falling of his voice will be just like yours, but no words are present. This is very amusing for everybody else, but it is also important for him to practice speech sounds and rhythms and, of course, to take his turn in holding the floor and joining in family conversation.

Listening and Understanding

A baby has to do a lot of listening and figuring out what goes with what before he can produce a word of his own. It has been estimated that he needs to have heard a word five hundred or six hundred times before he says it for the first time. This applies to the first early words he uses: later, when his grasp of the language is better, he will start soaking up new words at a greater rate, including words you would probably rather he did not say!

Before a baby starts talking, you will notice that he seems to understand many of the things you say. If you ask a "where?" question, such as "Where's Daddy?" or "Where's the cat?" he will look around, as if to search. He will understand phrases that are accompanied by gestures, such as you holding out your hand and saying, "Give it to Mommy." He will recognize his own name and the names of familiar people, he will respond to simple instructions such as "Clap your hands," and he will understand "No" and "Don't touch," although he will not always obey them. During this important stage, try to keep background noise such as TV and radio to a minimum when talking to or listening to your child. Research has shown that children's language develops better when they do not have the distractions of continual background noises.

When a baby is at this stage—from 7 or 8 months to the time when he is managing simple sentences—you will notice that the way you talk to him also changes. You now use very simple language and repeat things over and over again. Obviously you do this unconsciously, without thinking about it. You will ask a lot of questions and speak very clearly, saying the names of things distinctly. All this, linked with the gestures you use, helps your baby to learn the names of things and associate words with meaningful actions.

Other processes help him do this, too. As his brain and nervous system are physically developing, which enables him to behave in a more complicated way, he is also learning more and more about the outside world. He knows objects have a separate, permanent existence, and he knows they have uses. When your ten-month-old baby picks up a cup and offers it to his teddy to drink from, he is making a vital connection in learning that the cup has an identity, "cup," and a purpose, "drink." The next step is to realize that the sound "cup" means the object cup.

Baby's First Words

Your baby's first real words are just as exciting as his first steps, but they may be harder to distinguish from his babble and chatter. The first real word is a sound made by your baby that is only associated with one meaning—it may be one object, or a set of objects, but it always means the same thing. Sometimes "mammam" or "dadadad" is the first real word—that is, the baby uses it only when Mommy or Daddy is around. Often the first real word will be something quite different, and indeed it can be a word that the baby has made up himself. Thomas, aged one, coined the word "menem" to mean food. It may have been made up from "mmmm" or "yum yum," but he used it to apply only to food, or to the dish or bowl in which food came, but not to the spoon or the drinks. It was, therefore, a true word, although not English! Most babies' first words refer to objects—"cat," "ball," "dad," and so on, are favorites. Genevieve and Oscar, age one, both hit on something different that for them meant "dog" as a first word. For Genevieve all dogs were "gogs" and for Oscar every dog was a "woof-woof." Babies may also run two or three words together to make one word—for example, combining "what," "is," and "that" to say, "wassat?" Although Eleanor had no idea that this should be a phrase made up of these words, "wassat" was simply a question sound. Another common combination first word is "allgone" which is used simply to mean "gone."

The first word is a very exciting milestone. At last your patient conversations, your pointing things out, your peekaboo games, and your explanations of what you were doing have paid off. Your baby has answered back. He'll add words in the next three to four months. Usually you will be able to keep track of them, and many parents like to keep a record of the words their babies use. They will usually be words that mean something particular to that baby, so they will probably have to do with food, people, special toys, shoes, the car, or a pet. By the time he is about 18 months your baby is likely to know about 20 words and will have added some instructions, "look," "down," "gimme," "again," as well as some adjectives, "big," "pretty," "naughty." He will also have some useful words like "what?" and "where?" He will have some idea of himself—"mine"—as distinct from another person— "he"—although he will probably not say "you" very much.

Don't worry if your baby has a smaller vocabulary than this, as long as he is understanding what you say and is able to grasp the meaning and the purpose of things; he is probably just taking his time about speaking up for himself. However, if he does not appear to understand and does not do what you tell him readily, perhaps you should ask your doctor to have his hearing checked. If your baby's vocabulary is greater than this, and he is already using short sentences by 20 months, that is wonderful. You can communicate with each other much better and share games and stories you could not share before, but don't assume your child is a genius and put pressure on him accordingly. Rapid language development is a good sign that you have a bright child, but it is not the only sign, and you will find that other children usually catch up a little later. The great advantage of having an early talker is that it is so much easier to explain things to him, so you are less likely to have misunderstandings, and there are many ways of entertaining him once he has a good grasp of language. This can make for a smoother and more pleasant relationship.

First Sentences

The very first sentence may be only one word, but it means more than one word. For instance, your fifteen-month-old may call out "cookie." Depending on the way he says it, he may mean: "I want a cookie"; or, if he is leaning out of his high chair and staring sorrowfully at the floor it may mean: "I've dropped my cookie." If he is watching television and sees a cookie it may mean: "That is like my cookie." You will soon be able to interpret what he actually means, and you may put it into words for him. For instance, if he has dropped his cookie you say, "Oh, dear, you've dropped your cookie. Mommy will get you another one." Then, if he angrily throws the cookie down again, you might say, "Oh, so you don't want that cookie, you want this cookie," and you will give him back the one he dropped. If you see the picture on television that he is talking about, you might say, "Oh, yes. That's like the cookie you had, isn't it?" During these chats you are not only encouraging his efforts to tell you things by listening and interpreting carefully, you are also repeating back to him what he probably means in the correct speech and giving him the chance to learn the right way of saying things. Although it may be months, even a year or more, before he actually speaks in short sentences, he is continuing to learn.

If you are worried about your child not speaking when he should and you know his hearing and general development are all right, think about how you respond to your child's attempts to communicate. Sometimes when we are busy it is very easy to say "Wait," or "Here you are," and not use the opportunity for conversation. Young children need adults to give them careful individual attention and listen and talk to them during the day for short periods so they can learn language and communication skills. Remember, too, that they only like talking about what they know—conversations about cookies, toys, buses, shoes, and animals may not be exciting to you, but they are the best things for encouraging him to talk. He will not bother to talk about things he is not interested in or does not understand, so it is wise not to talk too much over his head. There is nothing wrong with baby talk if that is what he enjoys.

Putting Words Together

Putting two words together to make something closer to a real sentence is a very big step. It shows that your child is beginning to grasp the rules. The first simple sentences will still be about familiar objects; for instance, they might indicate belonging: "Mommy shoe," meaning "Mommy's shoe." Then verbs will be added. These sentences show your child understands the importance of word order—a big step. For instance, "go store" means "Let's go to the store" or "I am going to the store." On the other hand, "store gone" with the "go" verb after the word "store" means that perhaps a picture of a store has disappeared, or the bus has gone past the store. The child understands that the subject of the sentence (in the first case "I," and in the second case "stores") has to come before the verb. This is a big advance in understanding and you can help it through conversation and fantasy play—for instance, with dolls going to and from stores, or model stores being on and off the table. On many occasions we automatically do these kinds of things when we are playing with children.

Using the Rules

Once your child starts using these first sentences, usually sometime in his second year, you will find it very difficult to keep a record of the way his language develops. This is because his vocabulary increases in leaps and bounds and will number hundreds of words by the time he is three, but more than this, his use of words will not be just statements you have to interpret. He will start using them grammatically. For example, he will learn to say "going" instead of "go store." He will learn that you have to put an "s" on the end of words to make them express more than one, which shows a development in his knowledge of mathematical concepts as well. He will learn that past tenses usually have "ed" on the end—"played," "jumped," and so on—and, being logical, which young children are, he will put "ed" on all kinds of other words as well. He will say "hitted," or "goed," or even "wented," indicating that he knows "go" becomes "went" when it is in the past, but he sees no reason why the rule should not apply here, so he puts "ed" on the end for good measure.

If you try to correct your child's mistakes, you will probably find he is very resistant to doing it your way. "Wented" fits with the way he sees the language in his particular state of development. He will gradually pick up that "went" is the right way to say it, and as long as you keep saying "went" yourself he will finally get the message. Remember, these errors are not really errors, they are his way of teaching himself the rules and the exceptions to the rules. He will master most of the rules, including turning sentences around to make questions or negatives ("Are we going?," "We are not going") by the time he is five or six. But you could help and encourage his early use of language in many ways; you do not have to leave it all to him.

Talking with Your Child

The main point of being able to talk and listen is to enable the child to communicate with other people, and he will not want to communicate if it is not enjoyable and rewarding for him. The best way you can encourage language skills in your child is to give him plenty of opportunities to practice in ways that arise naturally out of the things you do together. There is no need to sit him down and say, "Now we are going to have a conversation." Conversation comes naturally out of mealtimes, playing with toys, going out, visiting friends, or programs on television.

Here are a few ways you can help your child to learn to talk:

- Talk to him about what you are doing: "I am going to pour a glass of water now because I am thirsty and want something to drink."

- Ask him to tell you what he is doing: "Tell me about the house you've just built with your blocks."

- Ask him what things are for; for example, hold up a fork and ask, "What's this for?" A three- or four-year-old will be able to use the right verb in his construction: "It's for eating." If you say, "What do we do with this?" he will say, "We eat with it." There are several different ways of saying the same thing, and he will enjoy experimenting with them.

- Help him to learn what "in," "on," "under," and "over" mean. There are many games you can play with toys being put in various places.

- Help him to understand what the words "up" and "down" mean—on the swings, for instance.

- Help him to learn the words to use when he wants to compare things: "Which is the biggest block?" or "Is that doll thinner than this doll?"

- Have fun helping him to understand and learn the word that means the opposite of something. For example: "The water is too hot. I need to make it . . . ?"

All the time you are helping him to use language in a more sophisticated way, and these are also aids that will encourage his intellectual development. For instance, knowing the meaning of "big," "bigger," and "biggest" is going to be important when he starts learning math at school. At the end of the day, make a point of talking about what happened during the day. Get him to remember what happened in the morning and then after lunch, which will also help his understanding of time. Ask him what was the best thing that happened that day. What was the worst thing? Children need to be encouraged to put their feelings as well as their thoughts into words. Don't feel slighted if he does not feel like talking, but be ready to listen when he does.

Give him opportunities to talk to other people besides his parents, especially other children. This will encourage him to tailor his speech to be appropriate to different kinds of people, an important social skill. He will need to learn that formal politeness is right with other grown-ups but that he should scale down his conversation for a child who is younger than he is. Children can have a lot of fun playing language games with each other that they would not do with an adult. Listen to your three- or four-year-old playing a fantasy game with a friend and notice how they imitate adults or use nonsense words or spontaneous little rhymes they have made up themselves. When a child is socially ready, then playing with other children is vital for teaching conversational skills such as taking turns in speaking, and asking and answering questions appropriately.

If You Have More Than One Child

Conversation does not only go on between one adult and one child. In everyday life there are not that many occasions when there is only one adult and only one child. Many families have at least two children, and there are very many occasions, even in families where there is only one child, when both parents are present, friends or relatives or other children are visiting, or when the mother and child are talking to people like sales clerks. In other words, it is very common for a child to be in a situation where he either has to compete for the attention of his own special adult, or has to join in with the general conversation.

It is commonly recognized that firstborn children have a head start in many respects because they have your undivided attention for those early months or years, and various studies have shown that firstborn children tend to be more developmentally advanced in the early years. It is harder to find the same amount of time to talk with your younger or youngest children, especially on a one-to-one basis, during the early prespeech and first-word stages. To make sure younger children do have a fair chance of listening, understanding, and replying to you, you have to teach your older children not to interrupt when you are talking to the little one. The older child must take his turn, not only as part of a two-person conversation, but also as part of a three- or four-person conversation. This is quite a hard lesson to learn. Mealtimes are sometimes good occasions to help children to learn to talk like this if you are all sitting around a table, but make sure the baby is not ignored, or that the older child does not keep interrupting when you ask the younger one something. Simple games that involve taking turns, such as naming pictures, or very simple card games, such as matching pictures, can sometimes help once the younger child is able to join in, which is usually from about three onwards. Both parents and other adults, such as grandparents, can help to make sure that each child gets a chance to practice his conversation alone with an adult now and again. In fact, in some circumstances a sympathetic grandma or the lady next door can actually encourage a child's speech skills far more than his mother can. After all, Mom already knows what he got for his birthday, but Grandma has to ask, and the child can really enjoy the opportunity to tell her all about it. That is why it is important for you to give your child a chance to make friends with other adults as well. Apart from their social value for you, these friendships can help your child practice his growing social and communication skills on a wider circle, which will be a great help when he goes on to play group and to school.

Stories, Books, and Television

Stories, books, and television programs help the child learn that information does not come only from his very direct experience—in other words, he not only learns from actually doing things himself, but he will also learn about them from hearing them described in other people's words. In the case of television, he can also learn from watching other people experiencing something.

Babies can start looking at picture books as soon as they can sit up and enjoy spending time on somebody's lap, usually sometime toward the end of the first year. You do not need to invest in a lot of expensive books—big catalogs are very attractive to babies of this age. Recognizing an object in a picture when you ask "Where's the cup?" "Where's the bed?" and pointing to it is a useful skill in learning language. Your baby is learning that some items, like a cup or a bed, can be shown in different ways, in pictures and also in words. Babies love looking at things they recognize, and this means that realistic pictures and familiar objects are more likely to catch their attention and give them more enjoyment than cartoon drawings.

Telling and reading stories to your child is one of the most valuable ways of giving him attention and helping him to learn. Pick a time when he is likely to be interested in sitting down quietly with you—not a time when his favorite television program is coming on, a friend has come over to play, or Grandma is visiting. The time when a child is getting a bit tired but does not actually want to go to sleep yet is an ideal moment for a story. It also gives you a very useful opportunity to sit down and enjoy a cuddle as well. Make sure other distractions are not competing for his attention—that means switching off the television or radio and letting older children know that you are not available for fifteen minutes or so. Sit your child on your lap or beside you with your arm around him.

All libraries have children's sections where there are a number of good, simple stories you can borrow to read to toddlers. When you choose a book for your child, remember that it will make more sense if it has something to do with his own experiences. In the very beginning, with a baby, pictures of familiar objects you can both talk about are probably enough, but by about a year, a very simple story will be enjoyed. Choose one in which the story line is straightforward and about something he understands—for example, going to bed, meeting a cat, or going somewhere in the car. Do not worry if you think your child cannot understand every one of the words you are reading: that is how children pick up interesting new words, by hearing them read in a context they understand. You can also make up simple little stories about things you and your child did together and draw them with your child—he will not mind if you are not a skilled artist! Older children can really enjoy hearing about what they did and what they were like when they were a baby. This is especially true at about the time when a new baby has arrived in the family. Looking at family photographs is also an all-time favorite with children, although in the beginning do not be surprised that your very young child does not recognize himself in pictures, but points to "baby." Do not think stories have to be new all the time, because children love repetition of old favorites. This is especially true of pre-school children. They will soon become familiar with a favorite story and will know immediately if you try to leave out anything or change one word. Nursery rhymes, simple poems, and finger rhymes all help your child's language development and, of course, can give you both great pleasure and amusement.

There are a great variety of children's stories as well as nursery rhymes and songs available on cassette that you can either buy or borrow from the library. Several preschool children can enjoy listening to one of these together at a time when they are a bit tired but do not want to sleep. This is also a great way to keep children amused on long trips if you have a small tape recorder with a headset. You can also buy a blank tape and make up your own cassettes with favorite stories, or something about the child himself. Do not let cassettes become a replacement for reading books with your children, though. Nothing replaces the shared experience of reading.

Television programs are often very popular with young children, but they give a different experience than books do. The biggest difference from a learning point of view is that the child has to follow the program at the pace dictated by the program makers. If he misses something or does not understand something, he cannot stop the program and ask about it, as he can do when someone is reading to him or telling him a story. This is why it is a good idea to sit with your child as often as you can when he is watching television so you can talk to him about what he sees and hears. Television can give children many new topics to talk about and widen their knowledge of the world, but it needs to be backed up by you talking about it and by direct experiences of the child's own.

Can too much television or the wrong kind of television be harmful? The answer is almost certainly yes. Sitting a small child in front of a videotape of his favorite cartoon programs for two or three hours on end is denying him the valuable opportunity to learn by direct experience—that is, by playing, by exploring, by finding out about things for himself.

What about seeing violent or frightening scenes on television? There is no doubt that these can be disturbing and frightening for a young child. It takes a long time to understand the difference between fantasy and reality, and school-age children can still be very confused by realistic scenes staged in television fiction, despite all your reassurance that it is only pretend and actors. A simple example of this is of a two-year-old who saw the video of *Superman III* because it was a rainy day and his older brothers and sisters were watching it. It had the most marked effect on his behavior—he went around making "bam" and "wham" noises and punching everyone who got in his way in a good imitation of Superman fighting the "bad guys." Amusing perhaps when he tried it with an adult, but not at all funny when he directed some well-aimed blows at a few of his playmates at play school the next day.

What is even more worrisome is that a lot of very young children see some of the worst horror movies in their own living rooms. This applies especially to toddlers and young children who are hard to get to bed or who get into the habit of staying up very late in the evening. Parents may think that because very young children do not voice any questions or worries, and do not understand everything that is happening, these images on television have no effect. Older children are all too easily disturbed and frightened by seeing such scenes and can become worried about the dark, begin to have nightmares, be worried about being left alone in a room or about going upstairs to bed on their own. There is no reason to think the effect is any less on a younger child. At the very least, it must give them a curious view of the world to see their parents sitting and watching scenes of people being tortured, terrified, or attacked on television. It encourages them to grow up with the view that such acts are acceptable, and in this way they could be said to be becoming desensitized to violence.

Television is a very powerful influence and is an everyday part of most children's lives. We all need to make sure it is used constructively and not harmfully. Here are some TV do's and don'ts to keep in mind:

- DO NOT use videos or television for hours on end just to keep your preschool children quiet.

- DO make your children be selective about what they watch on television. A reasonable rule as they grow older may be that they can watch for a limited period of time such as one hour, or one or two programs a day, and that they have to choose these programs at the beginning of the day. Obviously, when they are very young you can choose these.

- DO NOT let children see horror movies or violent movies or be playing in the same room when these kinds of movies are being shown on television.

- DO make a point of knowing what they are watching on television. A very simple question to ask yourself, if it is a film or video, is "Would I be allowed to take them to see this at the movie theater?" The use of videos means that we as parents have to be our own censors now. You likely never saw scary movies on television as a child. Is it really fair to subject your child to them?

- DO be positive about the good side of television. There is a lot to enjoy and even learn from on television and in videos—you just need to make sure you are selective.

- DO NOT be pressured by the views of other parents. Make your own decisions in agreement with your partner.

- DO remember that other rules may apply in different households that your child may stay in or visit, including those of relatives. It is worth finding out, tactfully, whether television is used as continual background or if they are likely to be having inappropriate videos on at a time when your child will be around. Perhaps reminding them that you would rather your child did not watch anything you consider unsuitable will make for a more pleasant visit for your child.

Reading and Writing

Talking and listening to your child are two of the best ways you can prepare him for school and formal education, and they cost nothing. A child who has had plenty of experience with conversation, stories, language games, and play generally is much better equipped to start learning formal education than the child who has not been talked with very much and does not know that experiences, knowledge, events, and feelings can all be expressed in words. If your child talks well and can mix with other children easily and also relate to adults, that is the best way to prepare for a good start at school.

Some children are ready to start reading and writing before they go to school, although most do not begin to get the idea until they are five or six. These children will start asking what the words on the side of the breakfast cereal package are, or perhaps when they spot an advertisement in the street they will say: "Look, McDonald's." Many four-year-olds can recognize letters of the alphabet and num-

bers if they are given the chance. Children with older brothers and sisters are more inclined to do this than the firstborn child because they like to copy and will want their own books, pens, pencils, rulers, and erasers so they can be just like the others. Some teachers do not like the idea of parents teaching preschool children to read, because they say it may result in confusion when the child starts school. However, if a child is recognizing letters and words and asking what they are, then it is impossible to stop him from reading. Learning to read is a bit like learning to ride a bike or drive a car—once you learn it, you cannot unlearn it. You can test this yourself by looking at the advertisements on a bus or a train next time you travel and not reading the words. Try to see them as a collection of shapes with no meaning. You will find it impossible.

If your child is showing an interest in making sense of letters and words, encourage it by using books, reading stories, letting him see the text, showing him when it is time to turn over the page, and pointing out letters or words he might know. A common mistake that parents make is to teach children capital letters and to teach them the names of the letters in the way that they may have been taught—for example, a, b, c. Instead, talk about the *sounds* of the letters—for example, the sound "b" as it is at the beginning of the word "book," and the sound "a" as it is at the beginning of the word "apple." If he begins to want to know how to write something—his own name, for example—teach him to form all the letters the right way and to use capital letters where it is appropriate—at the beginning of his name, for example. If children get into the habit of writing and making the shapes of the letters the wrong way, it is very difficult to break this habit later. If you are in any doubt about the correct way to form a letter, ask his nursery or preschool leader. There are many good books available that show the correct letter formation.

It's not a good idea to buy a school reading textbook and go through it with him if he really wants to learn to read because this can confuse the child when he starts school if the teacher's methods are different from yours. He may also get bored if he has seen the books already. Instead, you can make your own books with him about things that have happened to him using very simple words, or pick picture books with a clear, simple text.

Like learning to crawl, to walk, and to talk, parents can find great excitement on the day their child learns to read, but remember, reading is not just an end in itself. The point of it is to convey information and also to entertain. If your child learns to read but does not enjoy reading books, then he is not going to gain very much. On the other hand, if your child sees books as a source of shared pleasure, excitement, and a way of finding out about things, he will not need to be forced to learn to read; he will want to. If your child does not seem to be learning to read very easily when he starts school, don't put pressure on him because, like all the other stages, it is a developmental skill, and when a child is ready, he will often do it very quickly. However, if he does not seem to be making any start at all by the end of his sixth year, discuss it with his teacher and ask about ways in which he can be helped.

Most children want to start drawing, which at first they see as being just the same as writing. You will probably find that your two-year-old can hold a pencil properly. Once he can do this, give him plenty of opportunities to practice. You can encourage him to copy simple shapes such as circles and squares and to try drawing a circle with eyes, nose, and mouth. Drawing shapes with a pencil is more useful for learning to write later on than using a paintbrush, although this can be very helpful in developing artistic skills. Writing involves having very good control over body movements to work the muscles of the hand and the fingers in the correct way. Other skills, such as understanding language, are also involved. Writing is, therefore, usually more difficult to learn than reading. Just as your child understood a great deal of what you could say to him before he could reply clearly, so he may be able to read several things before he can write clearly.

Early Language Problems

Hearing Loss and Language

Hearing is essential in learning to understand and use language. (There is more about helping children with hearing loss in chapters 10, 17, and 19.) If your baby does not seem to respond to sounds or is slow to talk and understand language, then his hearing should be carefully checked. Hearing loss may not be present at birth, but may develop later, perhaps because of ear infections. So if your child's language progress seems to be at a standstill, he should have a hearing test. If he does start to speak, but his speech has certain uncommon abnormalities (not the normal lisping that many young children have, but one in which some consonants are missed), he may have partial hearing loss. If other people find it very difficult to understand your two-and-a-half- or three-year-old, it may be worth getting his hearing checked. Discuss your concerns with his doctor.

Slowness to Understand or Speak Language

If your child is not making vowel sounds such as "oo," or "ah," by five months, babbling by eleven months, and using three or four words apart from "Dada" and "Mama" by 18 months to 20 months, there may be cause for concern, and you should talk to your doctor. Even if your child is more advanced than this, but you are worried about his hearing or language development for any reason, it is worth mentioning it at a visit to your pediatrician.

Slowness in language may be occurring because your child is slow in all aspects of development. You can check whether this is the case by noting his progress in movement and coordination against the chart on pages 287–290. General delays may be due to some problem that may have been discovered already, so you know your child is developmentally delayed. Alternatively, slowness of language may be the first sign that is noted before it is realized that a child is generally delayed. Babies and children with developmental delays need special help to encourage language skills as much as possible. Talk to your doctor about your child getting help and advice from a speech and language therapist or any early itervention program.

Some children are not generally delayed but have a particular problem with language—they have a "specific language delay." If the child is just a little behind, you can probably expect him to catch up, but if his language is only at a level one would expect from a child about two-thirds his age, then you will need to discuss the problem with your doctor and seek advice from a speech and language therapist. Programs of therapy and intensive training have helped many language-impaired children to become more fluent in language than people at first thought possible.

Some children who are especially slow in language also have unusual difficulties in making relationships. They may show little or no interest in other people, turn their eyes away when people look at them, and pull away when cuddled. Such children will require further medical evaluation. You will need to discuss this with your doctor, who is likely to refer you to a developmental specialist. Again, advice from a speech and language therapist will also be needed.

Problems with Articulation

Children may be able to understand well and use sentences but not be able to speak clearly. This may be because they have difficulty saying the various speech sounds or in working out the rules for the speech sounds.

There may be a physical problem or difficulty in coordinating the movements of the lips and tongue that may affect how a child produces a sound. For instance, children with a cleft palate may need therapy to help them pronounce certain sounds. Children with cerebral palsy may also need this type of help; they are able to understand and express themselves, but the physical control of jaw, lip, and tongue movements is hard for them.

In a similar way to learning the rules of language, children also have to learn the differences between sounds and how to use them in words. For example, in English there is a difference in the way we use our vocal cords to form consonants such as p, t, k and the consonants such as b, d, and g. There are rules governing the use of consonants in English that allow us to have three consonants at the beginning of a word—for example "splash" and "string"—but we cannot have six consonants. Some children have difficulty learning to recognize and use the different consonants and rules—their hearing may be normal, but they find it hard to figure out, for example, which sounds go at the end of a word. Because the pronunciation or articulation and the correct use of consonants are complex skills, it is to be expected that many children make mistakes when they are learning to talk. For instance, young children often muddle or miss out a consonant and say "b" for "f," "fing" for "thing," or "poon" for "spoon." If you listen to other children talking, you will realize how common such mistakes are. Some children will mix up consonants and syllables, so that "cat" becomes "tat" and "animal" becomes "aminal." It is not usually helpful for a child to be made to say a word over and over again to change the way he says it. He views words as whole units and probably cannot recognize that there is a difference in only one consonant between the right way and the wrong way.

If your child continues to make many mistakes of this kind and is difficult to understand you should seek advice from a speech and language therapist, who will be able to explain whether the mistakes are part of normal development or whether help is required.

Problems with Voice and Fluency

Some children may have voices that sound hoarse or rough, even though they do not have a sore throat or a cold. Others may sound as though they are "talking down their nose." It is important that you see your doctor about these problems: she may refer your child to an ear, nose, and throat (ENT) specialist for an examination of the throat.

Many children between two and four years trip up over words or repeat the first syllable or consonant of a word before saying the rest of the sentence—for example, "bbbbbbbook." When you think about all the new developments that are happening to a child at that age, particularly in language skills, it is not surprising that they make an occasional mistake—as we all do. However, if the nonfluent speech lasts for more than six weeks or if it is distressing to you or your child, then again seek the advice of a speech and language therapist.

There are many reasons why a child can have a speech or language problem. It is important that he receives appropriate help from the specialists at the right time and that you receive advice about the nature of the problem. Your doctor will refer you to a speech and language therapist, but only if one is needed. The therapist will recommend various activities to help your child overcome his problems, and you will need to work on the therapy activities with him at home to get the maximum benefit and effect.

The ability to understand language and to talk seems to be one of the strongest and toughest forms of human behavior—it is very hard to destroy it. Even children who have been badly neglected and isolated for years can learn to use and understand words once they have been rescued. From the first cry your baby is longing to understand and communicate, and the first time he turns his head toward your voice he is already expecting an answer. Although he'll learn most of the skills of his own language in his first few years of life, the pleasure of talking to other people will go on for the rest of his life.

Stages of Development

0–1 month

- Responds to sounds, especially familiar voices, and quiets when picked up.

- Begins to establish feeding patterns.

- Communicates through crying, grunting, and sighing.

- He will enjoy the time you spend talking with him, as he begins to coo.

1–4 months

- First smile is usually at about 5 to 6 weeks.

- He will begin to recognize you and familiar faces.

- Anticipation of being picked up with arm-waving and kicking.

- First laugh.
- Cries become more expressive—of hunger, tiredness, impatience, etc.
- He may imitate sounds as you talk to him.

4–6 months

- Recognizes and responds to familiar sounds, voices, and objects.
- Reacts to tones of voices—is upset by anger, cheered by smiles and brightness.
- Babble begins—"ga" and "goo" sounds are joined together.
- Begins to make noises to show his feelings of pleasure or distress.
- He will begin to have a variety of experiences—with solid foods and learning to hold toys.

6–9 months

- Begins to show understanding for certain phrases/signs—"up," "down," or "Daddy's coming."
- Responds to his own name and other familiar objects.
- Makes appropriate gestures, such as raising his arms to be picked up.
- Continues to babble and tries out a few single syllables.
- Imitates clapping and playing peekaboo.
- You can now tailor your speech to his new level of understanding.

9–12 months

- Understands games such as dropping and picking up a toy.
- Understands "please give it to me" and "no."
- Follows instructions such as " kiss the baby doll."
- Enjoys songs and rhymes.
- Understands own daily routine.
- May produce first words—"Dada," or "Mama," or "bye."
- Expressive babbling.
- Plays with toys and objects and shows that he knows how they work.
- Your own speech will be designed to respond to his, such as naming things repeatedly, giving him instructions, and asking him questions.
- Other people, such as relatives and friends, will be talking with him, and he will learn to respond to them.

12–15 months

- Follows simple commands.

- Can point to pictures of things he knows as well as some body parts.

- Laughs at humorous events, such as funny faces.

- May say two or three words, but tends to "jargon" (speech-like chatter with no understandable meaning).

- Shows he knows the use of things by more complex play, especially as he is more mobile.

- Still echoing his words and pointing out new ones.

- You will continue to have more detailed conversations that are based on real events as his world becomes more complex.

15–20 months

- He will now recognize more objects and pictures of objects.

- Flipping through books and "telling" the story will be a favorite pastime.

- Begins to understand "in," "on," "me," and "her."

- Single-word vocabulary will continue to increase and will include words such as "more," "all gone," and "no" as well as some verbs and object names as he attempts to imitate all he hears.

- Your child may use his vocabulary for requesting and commanding.

- Vocabulary increases to about ten to fifty words.

- This is a fascinating time as your child is now physically independent, very inquisitive, and beginning to respond more verbally.

20–24 months

- Understands longer sentences and recognizes objects and pictures in greater numbers.

- Can match familiar objects.

- Understands "more," "here," and "now."

- Enjoys stories.

- Vocabulary increasing to sixty to seventy words with some joined to make two-word sentences.

- Makes up his own stories and will tell you about things that have happened.

- You will need to interpret much of what he will say to others, as you will understand him best.

24–30 months

- He will have more understanding of concepts such as, "big," "small," "one," and "a lot."

- He will be able to pass on messages.

- He will enjoy stories and remember many details.

- He will begin to understand cause and effect, such as, "If you bounce on the bed, you will fall off."

- His vocabulary will be impossible to keep track of, with his words increasing to two hundred to four hundred words.

- He will begin to use plurals and verbs and will form many questions.

30–40 months

- He will describe actions, understand size differences, remember events, and tell you about them.

- He can recognize and correct inaccuracies in stories or messages.

- Categories will be recognized by him, such as "A cat is an animal."

- He will be able to tell you what he is going to do.

- Remembering nursery rhymes and playing pretend games are his favorite activities.

- He is now able to hold a conversation and will enjoy talking to family and friends.

CHAPTER 12

Play and Early Education

Different types of play
How you can help your child have richer play experiences
Play stages • Arranging play
The importance of messy play • More than one child
Getting into a routine • Making friends
Play for sick children • Preschools and child care
Beginning elementary school

Play is serious business. It is important in every single aspect of your child's development and education and is the way she will acquire the skills and knowledge she needs to prepare her for adult life.

Different Types of Play

You'll notice that your child plays in different ways. The variety is important because each type helps her develop in unique ways.

Physical, Energetic Play

Physical play—running, jumping, climbing, and so on—allows children to develop their muscles and learn to control and coordinate their bodies. Infants' and toddlers' play is almost exclusively physical. They will practice new skills such as crawling and walking endlessly until they have them mastered, then move on to the next challenge. Older children also need large doses of physical play to help them accomplish more difficult feats such as climbing up and down playground equipment, up trees, and over rocks; throwing, catching, and kicking balls; and balancing on a stone wall or tricycle. Some young children are fearless on the playground, while others approach each new move cautiously. Most are in between. When you know your child's tendency you can decide how best to help her stay safe and develop her abilities.

Experimental Play

In one sense all play is experimental for young children—they are testing their powers and finding out what they can and cannot do. But some kinds of play lend themselves to discoveries about the physical world. For example, a baby banging a rattle is learning about how the rattle responds to her movements and the noises it makes when it meets the floor. Putting objects into containers, stacking blocks, and fitting shapes into a sorting box teach toddlers and preschoolers in direct ways about things adults take for granted, such as volume and gravity.

Creative Play

There is great joy and triumph to be had from making something all by yourself when you are young. Art also gives children a way to express their ideas and feelings better than they yet can in words. And it develops fine-motor control and coordination. Children never tire of using markers, crayons, and paints to create. Gluing, cutting, and sticking are other favorites. Using their bodies to show how butterflies fly or kangaroos hop is another area of creativity for children. Younger children generally do "art for art's sake," learning about the different materials they are using and exploring color, shape, and form. By three and a half or four, most children begin to use art materials to represent things they see around them. To make the most of creative play, give your child a few basic supplies and keep out of it. Children create instinctively, but if you "show her how it's done," she will lose faith in her own abilities.

Fantasy Play

Acting out with toys, or with friends, things that happen in their lives helps children make sense of the world around them. Children everywhere play house, school, mommies and daddies, hospitals, and babies. The subject matter of these games has not changed since you were young because this is the stuff of life. Two-year-olds' fantasy play is usually a direct reenactment of their own experiences or things they see you do, such as talking on the telephone or driving a car. As children get older their fantasy play takes off, including pretend people, plots, "costumes," and, ideally, playmates to act with. Fantasy and pretend games at this age can also be flights of pure imagination—witches and wizards, flying astronauts, or underwater fish. Another favorite is to play imaginative and fantasy games in miniature, setting out farmyards, dollhouses, cities made of Legos, and so on.

Messy Play

Also called tactile play, playing with sand, water, dough, or some other malleable substance helps a young child explore, discover, and experiment with the properties of these different materials. As children get older they also use these objects to create. This kind of play is very satisfying because children can mold the materials as they choose, and they will change and respond immediately in the child's hands. This play also has a very soothing and calming effect on a child when she is overexcited or just out of sorts. Parents may overlook this kind of play at home because of the mess involved or because they associate it only with a beach, sandbox, or pool. Yet, tactile play can keep children entertained for hours. And it doesn't have to be that messy. Later in this chapter the section on the importance of messy play will give you ideas for making the most of it while keeping the mess under control.

Playing with Friends

Having an opportunity to play with other children is important because it will teach your child how to share, to develop social skills, and also to have a sense of fairness. She will learn how to express her feelings during a disagreement and then learn how to make friends again after. By age four or five your child will begin to keep rules and work together with others toward a shared goal.

How You Can Help Your Child Have Richer Play Experiences

As all parents quickly learn, small children do not have to be encouraged to play. Perhaps the simplest way to enrich your child's play experience is by talking to her about her discoveries through play, and often, though not always, by playing with her. Playing with your child helps her to learn the skills she needs to play with other children and is an important part of learning about relationships and building on her understanding and ability to express herself. Games and playing are also an important part of the way children learn to talk and understand what is being said to them. Early baby games, such as peekaboo, ring around the rosy, pat-a-cake, and this little piggy, are all great fun for you to play with your child while your child also learns about listening, anticipating, and responding. There is more about how children learn to understand and use language in chapter 11. Almost from birth, babies and small children are observing, listening to, and absorbing information about the world. The fuel for their behavior is curiosity—they want to find out what is going on, and they will explore and discover in the best way they are able at each stage of development. What a baby does with the objects she is interested in is often described as play; for example, when we see her holding a rattle and chewing on it we may say, "She's playing with her rattle." But the baby does not know she is playing. She is exploring naturally and instinctively. To her the rattle is not a toy because it is no different from the spoon or the bunch of keys. It is simply a hard thing that makes intriguing noises.

As a new parent, you'll soon discover that part of the huge effect your child has on your life is the impact she makes on your home. Once the baby begins to move, you will have to rearrange rooms so they are safe and interesting for a child to play in, while still being comfortable places for you to work or live. Arranging your home so your child can play safely but still leaving clean, comfortable spaces for adults is an important contribution you can make to your child's play.

From a safety point of view it is important that you make changes to your home before your child progresses to the next stage of mobility. With a first child it is not always easy to anticipate when this may be, but chapter 15, on protecting your child, gives some helpful suggestions. Being one step ahead of your baby's growing abilities means being careful about putting her down on sofas even before she has learned to roll over, and not leaving her on the floor near potentially dangerous objects, even if she has not yet begun to make those first wriggling movements forward. Later it is important to keep chairs tucked underneath the table, anticipating the time when she will learn how to climb onto them and reach cupboards or work surfaces that were previously out of reach. Consider gating off rooms that cannot be childproofed.

Obviously the way your child plays and what she needs changes considerably as she grows. The chart in this chapter gives some ideas of what your baby might require at different stages, and some suggestions for playthings. It also lists some ways in which you might meet her developing needs. As you can see, giving children things to play with does not have to be expensive (that is especially true at the baby stage), but it does take a certain amount of thought and planning.

Play Stages

Age	What Your Child Can Do	Playthings	What You Can Do
Birth to three months	Listen, observe, begin to recognize people, objects, and places. Smile and coo. Kick, wriggle, turn head, try to roll.	Colorful, tinkling mobiles to look at and listen to; cradle gym in crib; pictures or post-cards inside crib or stroller to look at; music boxes, music from records or radios; mirrors. Warm rug to lie and kick on. Jingle toys that she can bat with hands and feet. Soft toys attached to stroller or crib.	Carry her around on you, facing out or facing you. Talk, play, and sing. Lie her where she can see things—trees, people, moving objects, other children. Give her changes of scenery. Give her exercise times—take clothes and diaper off after bath or when she seems restless and bored to allow her to kick and move more freely.
Age three to six months	Reach, begin to grasp, chew, put things in mouth, roll, squirm. Follow objects with eyes.	Rattles and smooth objects she can hold and gnaw on. Different textures—rubber, plastic spoons, wooden spoons, sponges; different cloths, such as furry teddy bears, leather gloves, woolen blankets, cotton scarves. These must be safe for baby to be able to put in her mouth. Different shapes—balls, square board books, cubes, "squishy" toys that can change shape. Floor play.	Sit her in a reclining chair with a tray with different objects on it. Vary toys—give different things at different times. Put things just out of reach so she has to reach for them. Look through your kitchen drawers for safe wooden and plastic utensils.

Age	What Your Child Can Do	Playthings	What You Can Do
Age six to twelve months	Make sounds to communicate with others. Recognize people. Learn that things and people go and come back. Crawl or wriggle across floor. Pull herself up. Decide what she wants and go to get it. Reach, grasp, pick up small objects, pass them from hand to hand or to mouth. Give and take objects. Increasing hand control and coordination between eye and hand. Understands the use of things.	Other people, teddies, dolls, soft animals, etc. Simple games with others such as peekaboo. Safe, stable furniture to hold on to. Warm rugs and carpets to move around on. Things she can put other things into and take out of—stacking blocks, plastic cartons, boxes, saucepans with lids, blocks, cupboards and drawers with safe objects such as pans, plastic dishes, and utensils in them. Balls to roll, activity centers that require different actions—a ball and ring, a bell to ring. Simple books or pictures from catalogs of objects she will recognize.	Talk and listen to her. Take her where she can see other people, for example, to the store, play groups, place of worship. Play games with her. Once baby is on the move, arrange all rooms she is likely to be in so they are safe. If you cannot supervise all the time, a playpen may be necessary plus safety gates on the stairs or in doorways. Give her freedom to explore; increase your tolerance of the level of mess considerably! Learn from her exploring behavior what she's most interested in and talk about it—language is developing now. Play giving and taking objects, showing her how to put things inside other things, stacking towers for her to knock down.

Age	What Your Child Can Do	Playthings	What You Can Do
Age twelve to twenty-four months	Walking, climbing, greater control over all movements, including hands. Activities now purposeful; she wants to get somewhere when she moves and to do things with the objects she handles, not just explore them. Holds crayons and brushes. Language developing from single words to short, conversational sentences.	Push-along toys, wheeled trucks, trains, pull-along animals, low, stable furniture to climb on and off. Greater control means she can now enjoy some messy materials: sand; Play-Doh; water; soil in the garden; painting with large brushes, thickly mixed powder paint, and old newspapers or rough paper. "Painting" with plain water outside is a favorite. Big crayons and chalk for drawing. Simple puzzles. Shape-sorter boxes. Balls to kick or throw. Pretend household objects such as tea sets, model cars, trucks, also dolls and their equipment begin to be used in make-believe play. Picture books of familiar objects and those with very simple stories. Other people, other children—for conversation, singing, finger rhymes, and simple stories.	Give her toys to encourage all these new abilities. Make sure gifts from others are suitable, safe, and sturdy. Keep some back, let her get the most out of each new plaything. Arrange a corner of the kitchen or yard for messy play. Put her in comfortable clothes, and invest in large plastic bibs and smocks. Read to her and go through books with her (see chapter 11). Buy her toys that encourage these skills— not just girls' or boys' toys. Join the local children's library for her. Talk and listen to her; give opportunities to talk to others, for example, keep her up later in the evenings to talk to Dad or to both parents together. Join a play group or some group where you meet other parents and children. Read and sing to her, and encourage others to do so, too. Sympathy, firmness, a supply of novel playthings and safe objects as distractions. Enjoyment of songs and rhymes and beginnings of fantasy play.

Age	What Your Child Can Do	Playthings	What You Can Do
Age twelve to twenty-four months (continued)			Toys that encourage fantasy such as models (e.g., Duplo), toy cars, houses, dolls, dress-up things. Book to look at. Blocks and toy telephones. Comforters, toys she had as a baby. Unbreakable things. Musical toys—drums, shakers; banging toys—hammer toys.
Age twenty-four to thirty-six months	Walk and climb confidently. Good control over hands. Can pay attention to activities that interest her for a long span now, but may still get bored and moody.	Toys to ride and climb on such as bicycles, safe climbing towers, and frames. She needs space to run in—a yard or trips to the park. Water, sand, dough, and paint will give more creative opportunities now.	Use everyday life to talk about colors. "You chose your red socks today." Count the stairs, the knives and forks as you use them. Simple musical instruments, records, and songs. Story and picture books and good children's television will give her new ideas and experiences. The garage and cars and other "miniature worlds" will become deeply interesting. Give opportunities for more outdoor play and exercise. Scout garage sales for secondhand bicycles and large outdoor toys if you cannot afford new ones. Your yard can now be adapted—a sandbox, safe climbing frame and/or swing, plus space to dig and make a mess. If you have no yard, try to take her out regularly.

Age	What Your Child Can Do	Playthings	What You Can Do
Age twenty-four to thirty-six months *(continued)*	Throw, kick a ball. Beginning to learn colors, numbers. Language will be more conversational and adult. May be able to sing now. Re-create domestic situations, make-believe, and role-play.	Also enjoyable are threading beads, building models with construction toys, simple puzzles, wagons, books, glove puppets.	She will need her own space to play in the house or apartment. You can start teaching her how to arrange toys and put them away. Your conversations will be more natural now, but still be aware of ways in which she is learning. Be ready to answer any questions; listen and watch her when she is playing to help you to understand what she is trying to ask. Continue reading to her and talk about what you see together in books or on television. Let her play with other children whenever possible. Join in make-believe games with her.

Age	What Your Child Can Do	Playthings	What You Can Do
Age three to four years	She will have many skills, both physical and mental, that she will need in adult life. They still need developing and refining. For example, she can perform more delicate tasks with fingers, although she may still have trouble with hand-eye coordination—she will not see why a puzzle piece is placed the wrong way. She can run, balance, climb, and may be able to hop. She will enjoy some activities such as swimming and running, although walking long distances depends on the individual child—but most three-year-olds still just want to play. Talking, being read to, watching children's television programs, preferably with you as much as possible. Doing things for herself; having own clothes, hangers, and storage spaces, own soap, towel, toothbrush in their own places.	Toys that need more skill such as basic Lego, more complicated picture puzzles, modeling games, memory games, and board games that require turn-taking. Other children will be important partners, but in more sophisticated activities such as board games, she is best playing with you to begin with. Playing board games with another child and no adult supervision comes later. She will enjoy "helping" you cook and using safe implements and tool sets. Doll and model play is very important—pretend houses will be made in all sorts of corners. She will enjoy going to places of interest, and animals become fascinating now. Make sure she has the opportunity to be with and play with other children, perhaps in a play group or nursery school. This is usually the stage when, if she has not already done so, she can benefit from spending a regular part of some days of the week away from home in a supervised setting.	You are finally resigned to the fact that a large part of your house will be permanently occupied by toys and children's equipment, plus children themselves! Give your child a wide variety of playthings, not forgetting the inexpensive, reliable standbys of empty boxes, dough, water, sand, and safe household utensils.

Age	What Your Child Can Do	Playthings	What You Can Do
Age three to four years *(continued)*	A peak age for dress-up clothes, which continues through six or seven. Will talk more fluently, understand more than she can say, be sensitive to other people's feelings, be able to show sympathy and helpfulness as well as anger or hurt. A three-year-old still often indulges in parallel play—playing alongside rather than with other children—but she is much better able to cooperate with other children in pairs or groups now.	Normally at about this age she begins to have friends over to play and to go out to visit other people's homes—perhaps without you if she feels confident enough.	

Age	What Your Child Can Do	Playthings	What You Can Do
Age four to five years	Now she will be able to cooperate far better with other children, either in pairs or in groups. She has a better understanding of games with specific rules—at this age children understand well and love party games. Drawings with properly held pencil will give clues about how to see the world. Some children may begin to recognize written words by now, especially their own names, but just like all the other milestones, learning to recognize words and write them develops at very different ages with different children.	She can manage a bigger range of board games, is safe with toys with smaller parts, and messy play becomes much less messy as she learns better control, so that arranging painting, sand and water, and Play-Doh activities at home is easier, although you still need to cover up and be prepared for some mess. Four- to five-year-olds are also better able to manage some gluing and sticking on their own, although you need to be nearby—most children can manage to cut with blunt-ended scissors at about this age.	Children this age have the stamina and understanding to enjoy more sophisticated days out. Point out and talk about places such as the police station, fire station, and car wash. You can now explain the reasons for the safety rules you have already instilled. For example, talk about why she shouldn't cross the road, swallow dangerous substances such as bleach, or run around with sharp, pointed objects, although you still need to be vigilant in safety precautions. Now it can be an adventure to stay away from home for a night with a friend. Looking at wildlife brings great pleasure—the birds

Age	What Your Child Can Do	Playthings	What You Can Do
Age four to five years (continued)		Can usually manage to pedal a first bike with training wheels or a tricycle. A good age to fix up rope swings from garden trees or invest in some kind of outdoor play gym—an expensive purchase but one that should last and that can be used by siblings.	in the backyard, collecting tadpoles, or following an ant trail. By now your child will be aware of the stage ahead, big school. Making sure she has mastered some self-help skills such as putting on her own socks, shoes, and jacket, going to the bathroom by herself, and recognizing her name are essential skills to give her confidence.

Arranging Play

The way you organize your life and home when you have a young child makes a great deal of difference to her freedom and ability to play. The following points all have to be considered.

Freedom

Babies, toddlers, and small children all need increasing amounts of freedom to move around and explore for themselves. This is why making your home safe is so important. If you are constantly saying "Don't touch" or "Keep out" to your child, you are not only making harder work for yourself but are also inhibiting her natural curiosity, which enables her to learn about the world and test it. Every small child needs the freedom to:

- *Move.* That means space, both indoors and out, where she can kick, crawl, roll, toddle, climb, bounce, and run. If you live in an apartment without a yard, it's important to try to get out to a park or other open area every day.

- *Explore.* That means having things she can open, empty, dig into, spread around, tear up, pile up, spill, drop, pick up, and, eventually, put away.

- *Learn from her own mistakes.* This means you allow her to figure out how to do things on her own instead of always doing everything for her. She needs to be free from too much interference, criticism, and control so she can learn the limits of her own initiative and attention and be allowed plenty of time to do what she is doing without interruption. She needs to be praised for her own efforts. Later it's good to have a special space for displaying her artwork. That old standby the refrigerator is still a great place, or you can use a bulletin board hung in her room or elsewhere in the house.

Order

Anyone familiar with lively toddlers will know that the list of freedoms above would sound like a recipe for chaos if it were not for the reverse side of the coin of freedom, which is control. A child cannot really be free if she cannot learn how to make order in her life, how to find things that are lost, how to handle things so they do not get broken, how to correct mistakes, how to ask for an adult's help, how to win adult approval by cooperating with her parents' requirements, and how to make and keep friends because she knows when to compromise and sympathize with other people's needs.

Regarding order, important points to remember about storage are:

You will soon discover as the collection of toys grows that being able to find things and put them away easily is crucial for both you and your child. It is valuable for your child to know that each set of objects, whether it is crayons, blocks, toy cars, books, or stuffed animals, has its own place. This helps her to learn that things belong in groups. She can also learn that small things can fit together into bigger things—for example, crayons, markers, and coloring books all go on the shelf for writing and drawing materials; cars go in the white box, trucks go in the blue box, and both boxes are stored on top of the model garage—these are all transportation toys.

Help your child not only to be neat and to find things easily, but also to learn about sets and groups, by giving each set of toys its own storage container. You do not need to spend a lot of money: plastic wipes boxes or cardboard shoe boxes are excellent. Make a picture label to stick on the outside, and a printed label with its name to help with prereading skills. Just cut the pictures off the container the toys came in for the labels. Your child will enjoy looking for the right labels with you. Obviously there is no need to be too rigid about this and get annoyed if she puts the crayons in the car box. She will eventually get the hang of putting everything in a place where it can be found again.

Small containers like these are better for general neatness than putting all the toys in one big box, basket, or drawer. To find anything, your child has to dump all the contents out on the floor every time. It also becomes impossible to keep small pieces of toys or games assembled together. Try making only some toys available at any one time, and to keep others put away so you can rotate them every now and then. Bringing out a toy she has not seen for four or five weeks is as good as giving her a new present and can be especially useful when either you or she is not feeling well, it's the third rainy day in a row, or there is just some special occasion.

Safety

There is more detail about this in chapter 15, but remember the following points about play safety:

1. Choose playthings and activities that are right for your child's age and stage of development—see the chart on pages 337–345. A general rule is that the smaller the child the larger the toy needs to be, apart from large exercise-type toys.

2. Check toys you buy or those given as presents for loose parts, sharp edges or pins, and loose fluff that could be swallowed or inhaled.

3. Make sure all soft toys are washable.

4. Never let your child play with plastic bags; paper ones are fine, but you need to supervise any children under eighteen months.

5. Do not allow children to "mouth" balloons.

6. Once your child starts to move around, make sure that all dangerous, small, breakable, or poisonous things are kept well out of reach. Keep one step ahead of your child's increasing mobility and anticipate when she may begin to be able to pull herself up, climb onto chairs, and so on. Once a child can climb, dangerous things must be locked away. Small children do not know the difference between cleaning fluids and cosmetics that can be poisonous and bottles of things to drink, so keep all such items well out of reach. Putting them under the sink or on the bureau leaves them accessible to a young child.

7. Put a barrier around any heat source—gas or electric.

8. Use a safety gate on the stairs until you are sure your child can manage them.

9. Block off electric outlets so she cannot put her fingers or other objects into them—use dummy plugs. Be sure electrical cords are out of reach.

10. Consider using a playpen if you have another child or have to leave a child unsupervised for a few minutes—for example, if the telephone rings or if your cooking area is too small for you to work safely with her under your feet. Children usually accept being in a playpen more easily if you get them used to it when they are very young.

The Importance of Messy Play

Playing with sand, earth, water, dough and clay, paint and glue is relaxing and soothing for children. Messy play, as it is sometimes known, does not actually have to make a big mess. It also gives children a marvelous chance to experiment by pouring, sifting, measuring, shaping, moistening, hardening, coloring, sticking, and unsticking. Working with those malleable materials, as opposed to structured and specific toys and playthings, a child is able to impose her own ideas. This is not only satisfying and rewarding but also stimulates the imagination. For you, the plus side is that these activities cost virtually nothing and mean that with a little planning, your child can be happily occupied for hours. Messy play brings so much pleasure and contentment that you will find building this activity into your child's day will have a beneficial effect on her temperament, making her calmer and much easier to cope with.

Messy play can take place outdoors where there is more space and you do not have to worry so much about protecting furniture or floors and about cleaning up afterward. But indoor messy play is also possible no matter how small your house or apartment, if you plan in advance. Decide where in the house it matters least if water, paint, glue, or Play Doh gets dropped on the floor. The bathroom and the kitchen are naturals because they usually have linoleum or tiles, which can be easily cleaned. Always cover up your child's clothes so you do not have to worry about them—cutting the sleeves off an old T-shirt of yours and tying a belt around the middle makes an effective smock, which can be put over whatever your child is wearing. Provide a reasonable work area and cover it all with old newspaper, or better still, invest in a couple of plastic tablecloths to cover the floor or table. You need to stay on hand to supervise under-fives with messy play, although the older they get, the more they can do unaided, and their actions also become far more controlled, thus minimizing accidental mess.

Here are some simple ideas for outdoor and indoor messy play.

Outdoors

1. **A sandbox.**   Make one yourself with an old box sunk into the ground, or buy one, but be sure it has a lid to stop neighborhood cats from using it as their litter box at night. Sand from garden shops or hardware stores is best. Do not use builder's sand, which is yellow and stains clothes and skin. Adding water to the sand adds a whole new dimension to the game and provides children with magical experiences as they watch the sand change and the water soak away. Remember, though, that small children do not know when to say "when," so you need to supervise to make sure the whole sandbox does not get flooded. You can make cardboard combs to use for patterns in dry or wet sand, and almost any plastic household containers and implements, including teaspoons, measuring cups, and plastic knives, will add to the fun. You can even turn an old cardboard box on its side next to the sandbox and tell your child it is her oven and she can put all her sandpies and cakes into it. Of course, if she decides it is a refrigerator or a tool bench and not an oven, that is fine, too.

2. **Water.**   Water is popular for all ages, but you must always supervise. *Never* leave a young child alone in a kiddie pool or near any water, even for a minute. Once she can sit up, a small baby will enjoy sitting in a couple of inches of water, and older children adore bigger pools and sprinklers. You can even purchase water tables for toddlers on up. Again, provide lots of plastic household containers and implements, including watering cans, and bottles and jugs for pouring. Make holes in the sides of margarine tubs or plastic containers so the water pours out of the sides in little jets. Your

child may also enjoy washing dolly's or teddy's clothes or bathing dolly with real soap or a drop of mild baby shampoo.

3. **Painting.**   Most young children will not spend as much time painting as they will playing with sand, water, or modeling materials, but it is still a fun and valuable activity. The easiest way to set this up is to invest in a few paint pots with lids and holes for brushes so that they cannot be tipped over and spilled and insert the brush through the hole. A smock is essential, and even outside you may want to cover the ground with old newspaper. Your child doesn't have to paint a specific picture. Young children have lots of fun painting empty cardboard boxes or other leftover material. You can cut a door and windows in the box. You don't have to invest in an expensive upright easel to pin the paper on. In fact, painting on an upright surface is quite difficult. Laying the paper flat on the ground and taping it down is probably easiest to begin with.

4. **Sidewalk chalk.**   This is another easy outdoor coloring activity. You need to supervise little ones, but if you can give them a little square of sidewalk or a patio to chalk on, the result will be cleaned away later by the rain. You do need to explain carefully that this is the only area your child can chalk in, because it is confusing for a child to be told she can chalk in one place, and then find you are very angry when she does the same thing indoors, on the kitchen floor. Keep chalk, paints, and crayons safely put away when your child isn't using them.

Indoors

1. **Homemade dough for play.**   The homemade variety is softer for little fingers and much cheaper than harder commercial modeling clays such as Play-Doh. In a saucepan, mix two cups of flour, one cup of salt, two cups of water, two heaping teaspoons of cream of tartar, and two tablespoons of vegetable oil. Combine until it is smooth—your child will likely love helping you mix and stir. Color it with a few drops of food coloring, and then cook slowly over low heat, stirring all the time until it binds together and forms a soft dough. Store it in a plastic container with a lid or in a plastic bag to stop it from drying out between play sessions. You can give your child a small rolling pin, plastic cookie cutters, and plastic knives, plus cut-up straws for "candles" so she can make a birthday cake out of this dough. Again, adding a cardboard box as an "oven" is usually fun. Playing with this dough is a very easy activity to set up, and it does not actually make much mess. It helps to cover the floor with a plastic mat if you have one. Avoid the problem of your child tracking dropped bits of this dough over the rest of the house by sweeping all around the mat and floor under the table before she gets down when she's finished.

2. **Washing dishes.**   Cover your child in something waterproof and provide a secure chair for her to stand on at the sink. If you fill an old dishwashing

liquid container with water, tell her it's soap, and give her a few plastic cups and saucers, it can keep her happy for some time. You can also give her jars and ladles for pouring water. You need to stay close by when a young child is standing on a chair, but this is a perfect activity for when you need to prepare dinner.

3. **Bathtime.** This can happen at any time of day—you don't need to wait until nighttime. Putting two young children in the bath together is a good way to let them enjoy water play even in the middle of winter. Of course, you need to stay in the bathroom with them, but it can be an opportunity to have a cup of coffee or to clean the rest of the bathroom. You don't need to make it deep. Just a few inches of water along with toys and plastic containers will provide lots of fun.

4. **Gluing and sticking.** Your child can do this outdoors or indoors. Again, you do not need any special equipment. You can make paste from flour and water or buy a simple bottle of school glue. Add a few popsicle sticks for spreading paste and some leftover egg cartons, cereal boxes, and milk containers, and your child can glue together fantastic sculptures. Cover your child in an old smock and protect the table and floor with newspaper from the inevitable dropped globs of glue. Scraps of fabric and wool as well as dried pasta, rice, and other dried foods are fun to glue as well. If you enjoy crafts, you might even find yourself getting carried away, but let your child do as much as possible herself. If crafts aren't your thing, you may still need to give your child one or two ideas to get her imagination working. Can she make something that looks as though it might fly? Or, very simply, can she make something as tall as her teddy? Can she make an extra-special boat? Older children love making very simple toys—for example, binoculars, by taping two cardboard toilet paper tubes together, or a telescope that folds up from several different-size tubes fitting inside each other, or taping together several tubes to make a tunnel for marbles or little cars.

5. **Rice.** You can make an indoor version of a sandbox by putting dry rice in a large container. Your child can spoon, shovel, and pour the grains to her heart's content. Hiding small objects in the rice is another favorite.

These are just some suggestions; you will probably have many more ideas of your own.

More Than One Child

If you have more than one child, particularly when they are at different and equally demanding stages, you need special patience and ingenuity to provide regular opportunities for messy play. The oldest child may well be able to manage something without too much difficulty—for example, a three- to four-year-old can enjoy painting, gluing, sticking, and all sorts of other activities without your constant

are cared for in homes at first and enter a school or center later on. Every family must weigh a variety of factors, including finances, personal preferences, and the availability of different types of care, to decide when a group situation is right for them and their child.

The move to being part of a group can be an adjustment. Yet it offers advantages, increasingly so as children get older. At a preschool or child care center, your child will have a much broader range of play equipment than you can offer at home. She will also have the fun of playing with this equipment with others, learning to share and to take turns, pretending to be on a spaceship, in a hospital, a school, or whatever anybody feels like doing. In addition to having the companionship of other children her own age and learning to play with them, she will have the chance to form relationships with other adults and to learn that she can trust and like people other than her parents. Her language skills will improve as she learns to communicate with a wider variety of people. When your child can settle in happily at preschool or day care, she will gain the valuable experience of comfortable separations, learning that she will be all right without you for a while, and that you can go and come back reliably. These experiences increase her independence and confidence. Schools and centers may also involve you in activities with other parents and children that are rewarding.

Types of Programs

There are a few broad categories of group situations for young children. In the past these categories were quite distinct, but their differences have blurred over time as programs evolved to meet parents' changing needs. The result is many options for families, though the different names can be somewhat confusing.

- **Nursery schools.**   Nursery schools were begun to provide enrichment and social stimulation to three-, four-, and five-year olds. This remains the focus of most programs, but many have dramatically extended their hours. In this type of program, you can now opt for a traditional part-day, part-week program, or choose to send your child for more hours or more days. Some schools are open for forty or fifty hours per week, the same hours as day-care centers. Nursery schools are regulated by the state's department of education, though this may vary from state to state.

- **Child care or day care centers.**   These programs generally operate from about 7:00 A.M. to 6:00 P.M., twelve months a year, and are used almost exclusively by working parents. Some centers will accept children as young as six weeks old; others begin somewhat older. Depending on your state, centers may be regulated by a department of health, human services, or social services. All centers are required to be licensed and meet basic operating standards, addressing such things as building safety, the maximum number of children who may attend, and sometimes the training requirements for teachers. The quality of child-care centers varies a great deal. Some provide "custodial care," tending to children's basic needs but not much more, while others offer carefully planned education and enrichment programs. The National Association for the

Education of Young Children (NAEYC) publishes recommendations for high-quality care that include health and safety, curriculum, and teacher-child relationships. Child-care centers and also nursery schools can choose to undergo an evaluation process and receive NAEYC accreditation if they pass. Parents can look for accreditation as the mark of a quality center or nursery school; however, participation in NAEYC and this process is voluntary, so an unaccredited program might also be a fine place for your child.

- **Religious programs.** Churches, synagogues, and other places of worship house a large number of nursery-school and day-care programs. Some of these programs are religious in nature; others rent space but are not otherwise affiliated, and so are comparable to other schools or centers. If you are considering a church-based program, ask questions to be sure the relationship between the church and school is what you are looking for. Is the curriculum based on religious teachings? Are the teachers members of the church or synagogue? What holidays (if any) are celebrated in the classroom? Many church-based programs are in basements, so you'll also want to be sure the atmosphere is cheerful and there is sunlight, or at least frequent opportunities to play outside.

- **Montessori.** This is a popular type of preschool and tends to be expensive. The programs use specific Montessori materials, including things such as letter blocks made of sandpaper or beads for counting. The emphasis is on independence, mastering concepts and skills, and progress at each child's own pace. Strict Montessori programs may have limited social interaction for children, but most programs combine cooperative play with the more traditional Montessori activities. All teachers are required to be trained in Montessori methods and to do an internship in a Montessori program to receive certification.

- **Head Start.** Begun in 1965 as part of the war on poverty, Head Start is a federally-funded child care program available only to children of low-income families. Initially it served as a traditional part-day nursery school for four-year-olds, but like other programs, it has expanded its hours and age range. Head Start's goal is to meet the educational, health, social, psychological, and nutritional needs of its children. Parent involvement and special services for children with disabilities are also key components. The quality of care in Head Start programs is quite good. Each site adheres to national Head Start program standards and is evaluated every three years.

- **Family child care.** Family child care or home day care is different from other types because it takes place in a home. Providers receive licenses from their state regulatory board to care for a limited number of children. The quality in family child care homes can be poor to excellent, but state requirements are usually minimal, so it is up to you to decide if a particular home is a safe, nurturing place for your child. Like centers, child care homes can be accredited by their professional organization, the National Association of Family Child Care (NAFCC), providing a "seal of approval" of good-quality care.

Choosing a Nursery School or Child Care Center

The easiest way to find out about local schools and centers is by asking other parents. You can also get information at your local social services or health department, a reference library, or even the yellow pages. Child care resource and referral agencies are another source and sometimes list prices and hours of operation. Call Child Care Aware at 1-800-424-2246 to find one in your area. If you work, your company might help you locate a school or center.

It is worth taking time in choosing a nursery school or center, especially if your child is going to spend many hours of her day there. But if you have a choice in your area it is often a good idea to put your child's name on several waiting lists while you make up your mind because the most popular ones often fill up early. This is especially true if you are looking for a center for an infant or a toddler; such centers are often in short supply. In addition to talking to other parents about the programs that interest you, be sure to spend a morning at each one. Schedule time to speak with the director and visit a classroom, and bring along your child, too. Things to consider are:

- Are you made welcome and introduced to the staff? If the supervisor does not like the idea of your staying to watch, be suspicious. Talk to the staff to find out their views on discipline, shy or anxious children, and free play, and ascertain whether they match yours. By watching how children and teachers interact, you can quickly gauge if this might be a good place for your child.

- Is your child also made welcome, perhaps introduced to other children? She may be invited to play, but no attempt should be made to force her to join in or do anything until she is ready.

- Look at the space the children have to play in. Church halls can be drab, but interesting activities and a happy atmosphere can transform them. Does the place seem crowded? Numbers of children per square foot are governed by state and local regulations, but some schools let their numbers creep up. A space for outdoor play on nice days is important.

- Look at the toys, equipment, and play materials available. Do you get the impression that the same old puzzles are put out in the same area every day? Are a number of activities such as painting, sand, water play, Play-Doh, and dressing up available all the time? You may have to drop in one or two times to find out if they vary the week's activities, and introduce special topics such as woodwork or cooking. Look for an area to play house; dress-up clothes that are imaginative and in good repair; plenty of construction toys and puzzles; large-layout toys, such as railways and big building blocks; toys that encourage fantasy play such as models, dolls, vehicles, road layouts, or toy villages. Look also for large equipment such as climbers, slides, and play tunnels; and a quiet corner where children can go to look at books. There may also be theme tables that involve the children bringing their own contributions, such as a nature table or a color table. Most important, do the children look excited and seem interested in what is there?

- There should be a good ratio of adults to children Required ratios vary from state to state, but the National Association for the Education of Young Children (NAEYC) recommends a minimum of one teacher for every ten preschoolers, six two-year-olds, five toddlers, or four infants. Are the adults listening and talking with the children? How do they deal with squabbles and destructive or disruptive behavior? Do they seem to be calmly in control? Are they affectionate with the children? Do they make a point of helping the shy, lonely, or aggressive child to join in more constructively? Is there provision for children with special needs? Do the adults spend most of the time with the children rather than chatting with each other? Do the children spend most of their time playing in small groups, and some time with the whole group together? If they do most of these things most of the time (nobody is perfect!), then this is probably a good program. The atmosphere of the group should be busy and buzzing, but you should not feel the place is out of control.

- Are boys and girls treated without discrimination? Do boys get encouraged to do the quiet, creative activities that promote language skills and prepare for schoolwork as much as the girls? Or are they allowed to run about in groups and spend a lot of time with sit-on toys and cars without much adult attention? Similarly, are girls encouraged to join in with the physical play and large-toy activities? Do boys and girls play together? Both boys and girls need physical, energetic play, construction play, and quiet, creative periods with adult attention. If you are concerned that your daughter is not getting a balance, talk to the teacher about it. Often, busy teachers and supervisors are not really aware of what is going on, and if you say, "I'd like my daughter to have the chance to paint, thread beads, and dress up, as well as run around," the teacher may suddenly realize that she has not done these things yet, and will arrange for them to happen.

- Are ethnic and cultural differences recognized and valued? If your child or other children in the school are from a different ethnic group from the majority, is there positive recognition of this in the attitudes of the staff, in play material, and in illustrations on the walls and in books? Are children helped to respect and value racial and cultural differences?

- Singing and storytime can tell you a great deal about a program. Songs should be varied and fun, with lots of action rhymes and percussion. The children should be obviously enjoying the singing. If you get the impression that this is a session that most children would like to skip, then something is not going well. Storytime should also be something children look forward to. The story should be chosen so it holds the children's attention, and be well read so it keeps their interest quite naturally without continual interruption, telling the children to pay attention or sit up. Unfortunately, a few schools use storytime as a way to keep everyone still while the assistants tidy up, or take it in turns to shepherd the children in and out to go to the bathroom and wash their hands.

If the school seems happy and potentially welcoming to your child, but there are a few things that do not measure up to what you would like, why not approach the teacher or director and offer to help? Many schools welcome the ideas and skills of parents, so you may be in a position to change things.

Preparing Your Child to Start a Nursery School or Center

Before your child goes to school, it helps to get her as familiar with the program as you can. If possible, bring her to see the classroom and meet the teacher ahead of time, and even arrange a few play dates with her future classmates. Reading some books about schools and perhaps having a pretend school day at home will be helpful. If your child is old enough, let her talk openly about her feelings of excitement and nervousness. Many children feel more secure bringing a favorite toy or blanket at first, and schools should allow this. Another trick is to slip a family photo into her pocket or tape one to her teddy, so she can take a quick peek if she starts to feel lonely. You can send familiar bedding and crib toys if your child is an infant or toddler to ease the transition from home to center. Also, tell the caregivers as much as you can about your child's home routines so they can be imitated at care.

On her first day you may perhaps feel apprehensive or even sad, but try not to let your child know that this is how you feel. She might think if you are worried, there must really be something to worry about. Stay positive and assure her that you will be back to pick her up.

Some children sail into this experience without a backward glance, but often your child will want you to stay for the first few times. Be suspicious of any program that does not encourage parents to stay as long as they like. If your child cries a great deal or refuses to stay, talk about it with the teacher, who may be able to help.

Good-bye rituals are comforting to many children, such as three kisses, then a wave from the door. Many children cry when their mothers leave and calm down quickly the moment they are out of sight. If your child is one of these, leave her with a trusted teacher or assistant who can distract her after you go. But don't sneak away. It's tempting, but it will only cause clinginess because your child will always be afraid you are about to disappear. If your child has real trouble separating over a long period of time, you may have to rethink your decision. It may be a good idea to wait for a month or two and try again. If that isn't possible, a smaller group or a different teacher could be the answer.

When your child starts school she will probably come home very tired. Much as you want to know what she has been doing, don't badger her with questions. Sometimes there has been so much going on that she will be too confused to reply, and as likely as not she will remember the best parts later on and tell you on her own. Many schools post the day's activities, so you can use these to start conversations when she is ready. If your child is an infant or toddler, insist on written reports or at least a good conversation with the caregiver at the end of each day to let you know about eating, napping, diaper changes, and your child's general well-being.

Beginning Elementary School

In the first years of your child's life, it is hard to imagine that she will go off one day to "big" school, but that day will come sooner than you expect! Most parents send their children to the local public school, as it is free to parents, usually convenient, and children will know one another from the neighborhood. Sometimes groups of children are bused from a school in one neighborhood to another. Some parents choose parochial schools because of their religious values, or because these can provide an alternative to a below-average public school district. A smaller number of parents send their children to private schools, which usually are expensive and require interviews and tests to gain admittance. In a small number of cities some public schools, called magnet or charter schools, function more like private schools in that children must apply and not everyone who lives in the area will get in. Admittance may be by test or via a lottery system. A handful of districts, usually in cities, are even experimenting with schools run by for-profit companies. The best ways to find out about schools in your area are to ask other parents with older children, call your local school board, or for private schools, to consult a reference library or the yellow pages.

Five is the standard age at which children begin kindergarten in the United States. But it is common for children born near the cutoff date, especially boys, to wait an extra year. This can give youngsters extra time to mature and may help their performance and adjustment in the early grades. But educators are beginning to notice a cost down the road when children reach puberty much earlier than their peers. If your child will be one of the youngest in her class, it's best to talk with her current preschool teacher and the school's kindergarten teacher, guidance counselor, or other professionals to decide if she is ready.

Making a Good Start

Even if your child was happy and confident at preschool, she may still feel nervous when it comes to leaving you on the first day at the "big school." Don't be surprised or annoyed if there are a few unexpected tears. The sheer number and size of the other children around, the noise, and the long, crowded hallways can all seem foreign and scary. Good kindergarten teachers will help your child adjust and feel welcome and comfortable at school. Moving up with a group of friends from a preschool or the neighborhood makes the changeover easier, but not all kindergartners are so lucky. You can help by inviting a few likely friends over to play in advance of the big day. The school secretary may be able to supply names of other families interested in getting together, or you may meet some parents at a before-school meeting or orientation. There are also a number of good books about starting school that you can read with your child.

It helps most to talk about things that will be new—riding a bus, eating in a cafeteria, moving in lines in the hallway, playing outside at recess —as these are areas that are likely to cause the most problems. Find out what you can about how these transitions work so you can prepare your child. Some children are also apprehensive about learning to read or other "big kid" academic challenges. Reassure your child that she can handle whatever comes up, and that her teacher and you are there to help if she needs it. Remember, though, that some children go to school happily and adjust with no problems, so don't look for trouble if it isn't there. Also, don't bombard your child with information all at one sitting. It is best to answer questions as they arise or talk about subjects when it is appropriate. For example, when you go to buy her lunch box or are having lunch together at home, you can talk about what all the children will be doing at school.

Take practical steps also to ease your child's way into kindergarten. Be sure she is well used to using the bathroom without help. It helps to have clothes that are easy to get in and out of: elastic-waist pants or skirts instead of buttons, or overalls; pull-on T-shirts instead of buttoned shirts. Only a few children can tie shoelaces at this age, so Velcro fasteners are helpful. Make sure all clothes and belongings are clearly labeled and that your child can recognize her own name, whether it is on a backpack or a picture. It helps if she can write her name as well, but don't worry if she can't—that's part of what she will learn this year. If your child will be eating lunch at school, be sure that she can open her lunch box and the containers inside. And if you don't read to her regularly already, take the time to start. This will help her know what to expect during storytimes at school and give her a jump on learning letters and sounds.

Like the first days of preschool, the first days of kindergarten can be quite exhausting. Try to restrain your curiosity to know every detail of her day. She will probably tell you more in her own time if you don't quiz her too hard, and instead have an informal conversation later, perhaps at bathtime or bedtime. Even then, general questions like "What did you do today?" may not get you very far. Instead, ask specifics: "What story did your teacher read today?" "Did you do any painting?" "Whom did you sit with at lunch?" Also, don't make the mistake of thinking your child is not learning anything if she says all they did was play. Many good kindergartens follow what are called developmentally appropriate practices, which are all about helping children learn through play activities. "Real" learning in reading, writing, and math is still going on. Your child's teacher should be able to explain more about this kind of curriculum and how it works. If you are concerned about your child's academic progress over time, though, you should, of course, feel free to speak to the teacher about it.

Once school gets under way, teachers often welcome parent volunteers. Parents can give teachers time to give extra attention where it is needed, or facilitate special art, cooking, or other projects that require close supervision. Children at this age generally love Mommy or Daddy to come visit, and it can be very pleasant for you to spend time in the classroom if you can. You'll get a clear picture of your child's life at school and build your relationship with your child's teacher. In addition, the Parent–Teacher Association will always welcome enthusiastic newcomers to help out with projects.

CHAPTER 13

Toilet Training

Body waste
How do you know when your child is ready to start toilet training?
Early setbacks in toilet training • Potty or toilet?
Common problems with toilet training
Illness and infection

Understandably, most parents look forward to the day when their child is toilet trained—partly because nobody enjoys dealing with dirty diapers, and partly because it really does seem to signal the end of babyhood. So the day when your child first steps out in "big kid" underpants (and is still wearing the same pair at the end of the day!) is just as big a milestone as when he learns to walk or to talk. Just like those other developmental milestones, there is a wide variation in the age range at which children achieve bowel and bladder control.

Mothers used to spend hours holding their tiny babies over potties. If the baby was regular in passing a bowel movement, the mother hoped to strike it lucky by providing the potty at the right time and saving a dirty diaper, though, of course, this did not mean that the child was able to control bladder and bowel movements. There are still some parents who want to start training their babies in the first year by trying to catch regular bowel movements—for example, by placing them on the potty after meals. If a baby is regular, this may condition him to move his bowels when he sits on the potty, although he still does not have conscious control. The danger of this approach is that when he does learn to understand and control what is happening, in his second and third years, he may decide not to cooperate and you have to start training him all over again. Nowadays, with disposable diapers designed for toddlers making life much easier, most parents prefer to wait until their children show some signs of becoming ready to use the potty. But before we embark on the whole subject of how your child learns control, it is useful to know a few of the basic biological facts.

Body Waste

The food that healthy people eat is automatically processed by the digestive system. We eat fats, proteins, carbohydrates, vitamins, and minerals, and we drink liquids. These are distributed through the bloodstream to fuel growth and to give us energy to function. But there is some waste matter that the body does not need, and this has to be passed out at regular intervals. Liquid waste, urine, is produced by the kidneys and stored in the bladder until a feeling of fullness signals a need to pass urine. It is then passed out through the urinary tract. Solid food is passed from the stomach through the small and the large intestines, which are responsible for extracting what the body needs and which then push out the waste through the rectum and its external opening, called the anus. Normal people vary in the number of times they need to pass this waste—most urinate several times a day and have a bowel movement from once or twice a day up to every few days. Obviously these functions vary according to what and how much you eat and drink. This may vary depending on the weather (when it is hot you may drink more and excrete more fluid, or if you do not drink, you will sweat more and pass less urine), or on your state of mind (when you are nervous your digestive system becomes more active), or, of course, when you are ill.

Newborn babies produce and pass this waste automatically and have actually started doing so in the womb. Although they often seem to know what they are doing—they usually become very quiet or red in the face when passing a bowel movement—they actually have no conscious control over the process. Conscious control means being able to recognize the signs of wanting to empty bowels or bladder, and then waiting until you are in the right place to do so—bathroom or potty. This only comes with age and maturity. It happens because both the parts of the brain and the nervous system supplying the bowel and bladder become more mature. The rate at which this happens is under control of the genes, so it is not surprising that delay in gaining bladder control tends to run in families. Most children are able to achieve this conscious control at some time between eighteen months and three years, with a few exceptions on either side. Bed-wetting at night goes on longer in most children, although a few whose bladders can hold urine for long periods are dry earlier. Wetting at night (eneuresis) isn't abnormal in children under five years, although if a child has been dry and then starts wetting again you need to check to see that there is nothing wrong physically or emotionally.

How Do You Know When Your Child Is Ready to Start Toilet Training?

Sometime during his second year your child may give you some of these clues that he is ready to start learning how to use the potty:

- He may show that he is aware when he passes urine or a bowel movement. For example, he will tell you when he has done something, or he will stop what he is doing and look uncomfortable.

- There may be longer intervals between wet diapers so that when you go to change him the diaper is either completely dry or suddenly absolutely soaked through. You may notice that he starts being regular with bowel movements—for example, always after breakfast—when he wasn't before.

- He shows an increased interest in passing urine or a bowel movement—for example, looking at it and talking about it.

- He may want to copy other children or parents and may play with the potty, if you keep one around, or play at sitting his toys on the potty or lavatory.

If he does not show any of these signs by the time he is about 20 to 22 months, you can start introducing the idea of the potty or toilet yourself. There are all sorts of stylish potties available now, often designed as cars, turtles, and so on. Some even come with lids, which is very handy for traveling. Show him the potty and explain what it is for. It is sometimes a good idea to buy a pair of grown-up underpants at the same time, for the idea that he is moving on from the baby stage can be especially attractive if your child has older brothers or sisters. However, it is probably a bad idea to start potty training a child just at the time when you are expecting a new baby, or immediately after the birth, because this is a time when he may want to be babied himself. Remember that it is also quite common for toddlers who have been dry for some time to start wetting or soiling again when a new baby arrives. Be prepared for this and try to remain patient. If necessary, put the child back into diapers for a while. The phase will usually pass if you make sure you give the older child plenty of love and attention at other times. Alternatively, some children become very independent soon after the birth of a baby and start managing to use the potty or go to the toilet by themselves. It is not a good idea to start potty training a toddler at about the time when there may be other pressures—for example, if you are moving, or if either you or he is likely to have to go to the hospital shortly, or if you are planning a vacation somewhere where accidents would be a particular problem, such as going to stay in the newly carpeted home of friends or relatives!

Probably the best incentive for a toddler to start using the potty or the toilet is to see other children slightly older than himself using it. If he has no older brothers or sisters, or you do not know older children who come over to your house and are willing to demonstrate, then it helps to get some books that show pictures of children using a potty. Let your child sit on the potty with his diaper or pants on—many toddlers feel very insecure about sitting down on what appears to be a seat with a hole in it without diaper or pants, so do not force him. If he wants to play by sitting a teddy or a doll on it, that is fine as well. When you think he understands what the potty is for, you can start sitting him on it at regular intervals—shortly after meals is a good time. At first you will probably only catch a "peepee" or a "poo," or whatever his name is for it, by accident. This is a big milestone, and when it happens you should take the opportunity to praise him, and tell him how clever and grown up he is, and give him lots of attention. It is much easier to potty train a child in warm summer weather because you can let him run around outside with no diaper or pants on and the potty ready at hand. In winter you will have to accept that some accidents are inevitable, and try the same technique in rooms where you do not value the floor covering too much! It helps if you can have more than one potty around so there is one in every room where he is likely to need it—perhaps you can borrow one or two from friends. Some people like to give a child a positive reward when he actually manages to produce something in the potty—such as pretzels, a piece of apple, or a chocolate bar. Usually your praise and a big hug are a child's greatest reward—plus the pride in becoming grown up—and he does not need any more than this. If he does not do anything, or does it in his pants soon after he gets off the potty, do not blame, scold, or get angry. This will only give him the idea that potty training is a big issue and a possible battleground. Instead, just say, "Never mind, we'll try again next time," and keep persevering with good humor and plenty of encouragement. Once you have started potty training, as long as you are sure that your child has shown signs of readiness, it is best to keep going and remain consistent despite accidents and setbacks. The very first time you leave the house with your child in a pair of pants it can feel like a trapeze act without a safety net, but be brave—training pants with plastic coverings can serve to stem the flood, and it helps to have regular potty stops at every outing. Nevertheless, taking several pairs of underpants, pants, and socks with you is pretty essential in the early stages. Naturally, as soon as he begins to get the hang of using the potty, you're better off avoiding dressing him in overalls, pants with buttons, or any other complicated clothes. Stretchy pants or dresses that are easy for your child to manage without help are best. Children of this age do want to learn and to cooperate with parents, despite bouts of awkwardness, so capitalize on this and keep going.

Early Setbacks in Toilet Training

If the process is very slow or does not happen at all, then ask yourself if perhaps your child is not yet ready—check again for the signs of readiness covered in the previous section. If your child seems to have discomfort or pain upon his passing urine, if his urine dribbles out rather than passes in a strong stream, or if there is blood in the urine, this may be a sign of an infection or other problem, so consult your doctor right away. See the section "Illness and Infection" later in this chapter. Usually children gain control of bowel movements first and take a bit longer to make it to the potty or bathroom every time they have to urinate. However, some children become dry first and are more reluctant to "let go" of their bowel motion—they may prefer the safer feeling of performing in their night diapers.

When children begin toilet training and are really ready and able to cooperate, the whole process can be very quick—only a few days for some children. This is much more satisfactory from the parents' point of view than starting much earlier, but taking months or years over the whole process with many accidents on the way. Becoming dry at night takes longer, but most children are able to achieve this before they are five and, at the latest, before they leave preschool. About one in ten children is not dry, even by this time, so if your child is one of these, remember, there are many others like him. Bed-wetting tends to run in families and is more common in boys than in girls. It occasionally occurs because the child is upset and cannot get into a routine, or alternatively because the child has general developmental delays and is showing this in other ways besides being slow to obtain bladder control. At about the age of five years, or at the time of entry to school, it is a good idea to ask for advice from your doctor to see if the process can be speeded up. She may wish to rule out an infection by testing the urine, and will also want to know whether the child is wetting because he is upset—perhaps because there is too much pressure on him to be dry, or for some other reason.

Probably trying to remain relaxed about the problem and just being confident that eventually, if you don't get too anxious about it, the child will become dry, is the best approach. However, there is no harm in cutting out fluids shortly before your child goes to sleep, or, for a few days or weeks, waking up your child before you go to sleep yourself and getting him to pass urine. It is important to try not to be angry in the morning after a wet night if you possibly can, as bed-wetting really is not the child's fault. Of course, it is even more important to show pleasure if the child does have a dry night.

Potty or Toilet?

Most people find it easier to start their child on a child's potty, as it is more comfortable and feels safer. The toilet can feel insecure and alarming to a small child, and he may be worried by the flushing noise. He can also be encouraged to use a potty himself; as already mentioned, it is a good idea to have more than one around the house. When he becomes confident and reliable he can be introduced to the toilet, either sitting on a special child seat or, in the case of boys, standing on a step. Boys can be encouraged to urinate in the potty standing up from the start, but don't worry if he'd rather sit down. If his father or an older brother will do a bit of demonstrating, he will soon get the idea of standing up to pee! Remember that all children are different—while some toddlers accept the whole idea very readily and are quickly dry with hardly an accident, for others it takes a lot longer.

Using strange bathrooms can sometimes be a problem, so if your child is worried about urinating at day care or nursery school, explain or write to the teachers so they can help to reassure him.

Common Problems with Toilet Training

Constipation

Constipation is actually a common problem in young children, but it is not always recognized. Constipation indicates that an abnormal amount of waste matter has built up in the lower bowel, which then becomes so hard and uncomfortable that the child is afraid or unable to pass it. Once a child has had pain or difficulty passing a bowel movement, he is more likely to withhold subsequent bowel movements, and this vicious circle makes constipation yet more likely.

What causes constipation in the first place? It can be a poor diet with too many bland, sweet, and fatty foods and not enough roughage. It can also occur after an illness; it may follow a bout of diarrhea in which the child has been deliberately holding on to the movements. Sometimes a hard movement can cause a crack or fissure in the anus; if you see little specks of blood in the stool, it may come from such a crack. The pain of this can make the child want to withhold his bowel movements.

Constipation can also result from overenthusiastic toilet training by parents. If you put too much pressure on a child to perform on the potty, he can deliberately choose not to do so.

Inconsistent toilet training, when it is not clear to the child what he is expected to do, can have the same result. Sometimes a child just isn't ready, and you need to ease up in your demands a little and not worry about accidents.

Mild or occasional constipation can be corrected by increasing the amount of roughage or fiber in his diet and giving more fluids, particularly drinks such as prune juice. Some doctors may prescribe laxatives; others may not be happy about giving them regularly, as the bowel needs to be encouraged to make its own muscular efforts to expel waste, and laxatives can make the passage of the waste too easy. If your child is prone to occasional bouts of constipation, make sure his regular diet has a lot of whole-grain bread, cereals, fresh fruit, and vegetables in it. You should

also encourage him to go to the bathroom regularly. Be careful not to be too insistent about this, though, as it can increase his anxiety. Reward him when he does go. With a child who is having problems, an external reward is sometimes necessary. A child old enough to understand such a system can have a chart with stars for success on it. Children who are too small to understand a chart can just be given praise or a little treat every time they sit on the potty or toilet and try to have a movement, until the habit is established.

Untreated constipation can go on for weeks and become a serious physical and emotional problem. When this happens the child becomes completely incapable of moving his bowels because the muscles have become overstretched and will not work to push out waste. The sensation of wanting to pass a stool mass may be lost as a result. Liquid waste matter may dribble out from around the hard mass in his bowel; this may look like diarrhea but is in fact due to constipation. It is very distressing for the child because he cannot help it, and yet may be scolded by parents and teased by other children. If your child is soiling his pants in this way, think back to what his bowel habits have been in the past. Busy parents may not notice that a child has not had a bowel movement for a while.

When constipation gets to this chronic stage, medical treatment is needed. Laxatives may work, or the child may need to be admitted to the hospital so the stool can be removed manually or with an enema. Fortunately, the stretched muscles do recover their elasticity and can be retrained to work normally over a period of time.

Bowel Movements—in the Wrong Place

Sometimes children who have no physical problems with their bowel movements deliberately pass them in their pants or on the floor, although they are quite capable of getting to the potty or the bathroom. This condition (the medical name is encopresis) happens in children who are old enough to be toilet trained and know the difference between the right and the wrong place to have a bowel movement.

It does *not* apply to young toddlers in their early stages of toilet training—who often go and hide behind the sofa when they are having a bowel movement. Do not get angry when this happens, because what the young toddler needs is understanding, sympathy, and patience from you. Some children feel very vulnerable when sitting on the potty to have a bowel movement, and ensuring that they have secure privacy is often a great help. You could put the potty behind the sofa or let the child sit on it alone in the bathroom—making sure, of course, that he cannot lock himself in! Soiling is a very common problem in young children, and there is nothing shameful about it—so don't make the child feel ashamed because this will make the problem worse.

In an older child, passing a bowel movement deliberately in the wrong place is sometimes a sign that the child is emotionally disturbed or unhappy about some-

thing, or he may want to get back at you if you have been scolding or punishing him. Alternatively, he may simply be teasing you to see if you react to his actions. Annoying and worrying though this may be, it is important not to react, but to stay as cool and unconcerned as possible, pointing out that the floor is not the right place to have bowel movements and encouraging and rewarding him when he does go in the right place.

If your child starts doing this regularly after having already been toilet trained, think about whether anything could have upset him recently. A big change in his life, such as the arrival of a new baby, separation from one of his parents, being in the hospital, or some other emotionally upsetting experience, can produce this reaction. If you cannot think of any such problem or you feel you cannot handle this behavior, seek help from your doctor. Referral to a child guidance clinic or psychiatric department may be necessary on rare occasions.

Toddler Diarrhea

Some one- to four-year-olds, particularly boys, can have episodes of very loose stools for a few days. The loose stools may contain bits of undigested food. The condition passes, stools are normal for a while, and then there is another bout of looseness. It is probably caused by the intestinal muscles being overactive, perhaps because the nerves that supply them are not working properly, and the food passes through the intestines quickly, without being fully absorbed. The condition is not dangerous, though it sometimes occurs when the child is under stress. It passes with age, so if your doctor can find no other symptom of illness, don't worry about it. Just be sure to remind the child to go to the bathroom regularly so he does not have an accident. If he does have an accident, be reassuring and sympathetic because it can be very upsetting for him—particularly if it happens somewhere like nursery school or day care.

Accidental Wetting

When a child has been dry for a while and starts wetting again, this is usually because the habit of being dry has not been very well established in the first place, and something has happened to upset the child's routine. He may have had flu or one of the infectious illnesses of childhood, such as chicken pox. Alternatively, some upsetting event—being in the hospital, a parent being away from home, or the birth of a younger brother or sister—may have occurred. Occasionally a recurrence of wetting may be due to an infection—this is a possibility if the child has pain passing urine, if the urine is cloudy, smelly, has blood in it, is passed more frequently, or if your child dribbles urine after passing it in a proper stream. There is also the possibility of diabetes. If you notice any of these symptoms, consult your doctor. Accidental wetting after a period of dryness can be annoying both to you and the child, but it will usually stop after a few days or weeks. Try using the techniques you used to help the child become dry in the first place. If it persists beyond a few weeks, but if the child has been dry previously, you should talk to your doctor.

Illness and Infection

Intestinal Infections

As most parents quickly learn, stomach "bugs" are common—few children reach school age without having had at least one bout of vomiting and/or diarrhea. The cause is usually viral but rarely a bacterial infection of the intestine, and mild cases usually resolve spontaneously. Children do not usually want to eat when they have an intestinal bug, but they should be given plenty of fluids, since the biggest danger of these infections is dehydration—the smaller the child, the greater the risk.

Mothers of breast-fed babies sometimes worry that their babies have diarrhea because the normal stool is so liquid, can be very frequent, and often seems to come out with great force! But as long as the movement is the usual yellow color and there are no other signs of illness, there is no need to worry. A continuing change in the color and the consistency of the bowel movement could be a sign of illness, so if you see this, check with your doctor.

Once children are eating solid food, there is usually no doubt about when they have diarrhea. The first signs of an intestinal infection are vomiting or stomach pains and/or diarrhea—loose, watery stools that will look and smell differently from normal stools.

A child who is vomiting and has diarrhea can easily lose too much fluid and become dehydrated. These are the warning signs:

- He doesn't urinate.

- His eyes become sunken.

- His skin loses its elasticity.

- The child becomes weak and has little energy.

- He begins to breathe rapidly and have a dry tongue.

- His pulse rate is rapid.

- In a young baby the fontanelle or "soft spot" on his head will be sunken.

Because dehydration can develop so rapidly, a child with these signs will almost certainly need to be taken to the hospital. There they will be able to replace the fluids, sometimes through giving oral fluids, but in some cases an intravenous infusion may have to be given.

Breast-feeding helps to protect babies against intestinal illnesses, and if your breast-fed baby does contract such an infection, breast milk may help his recovery. (For advice on treatment see the section on "The Intestinal Tract and Its Problems" in chapter 17.)

The best prevention is for you to be scrupulous about washing hands after handling diapers or using the toilet, and before handling any food. As your child grows, get him into the hand-washing habit, too.

Urinary Infections

One cause of wetting accidents, particularly in girls, is an infection in the upper urinary tract or bladder. If your daughter starts wetting her pants when she has already been toilet trained, check with your doctor for the presence of an infection. A sample of her urine will need to be tested. Other signs of a urinary infection are foul-smelling urine, complaints of pain when passing urine, dribbling urine rather than passing it in a stream, and general symptoms of ill health, such as loss of appetite and vomiting. Abdominal pain and vomiting may also be caused by an infection in the urine. If you have any reason to suspect that your child is particularly prone to urinary infections, see your physician, who may want you to check your child into the hospital for an evaluation to be sure there is not a structural abnormality of the urinary tract that predisposes to infection, such as vesicoureteric reflux. This means that some urine is not passed out of the bladder but goes back from the bladder into the kidneys. If this is not diagnosed and treated, it can cause damage to the kidneys. Fortunately, once it is detected this condition can usually be treated with antibiotics or occasionally by surgery. Your child will be taught how to empty her bladder completely and to drink plenty of fluids.

You can help your child to avoid the chance of infection by encouraging her to pass urine regularly and to make sure her bladder is really empty. Try not to let your child get constipated, since this may interfere with bladder emptying and can increase the chance of bladder infection. All-cotton underwear is the best choice, since synthetics can cause soreness and predispose your child to infection. Let your child have plenty to drink, and be sure to teach your daughter to wipe from front to back so she doesn't bring bacteria from her stool to her vagina or urinary tract.

Serious Kidney Disease

The kidneys are vital in getting rid of waste from the body, so if they stop working or are seriously damaged, a person cannot survive. Today many people with kidneys that do not work can be helped by transplants or by having regular dialysis—either by a machine that does the work of the kidneys in cleaning the bloodstream, or by allowing the poisons in the blood to pass into fluid that is instilled into the belly and changed regularly.

Signs of kidney disease in a child include slow growth or failure to grow well, being very thirsty (especially at night), and passing much more or much less urine than normal. Blood in the urine, frothy urine, or swelling of the child's eyelids, abdomen, or feet (due to a buildup of fluid in the body) are all signs that the kidneys may not be working properly. If you notice any of these symptoms, see your doctor immediately. The condition requires specialist investigation and hospital treatment. Complete kidney failure is very rare.

Congenital Disorders

The earlier in life that symptoms of gastric or urinary illness show themselves, the more likely it is that there may be some underlying disorder that the baby has been born with.

The first bowel movement normally passed by a new baby is called "meconium" and looks black and sticky. After a day or so the baby's bowel movements change according to how he is being fed. Breast-fed babies have soft, sometimes almost liquid stools that are bright mustard-yellow. They can be as frequent as every feeding—or, particularly as the baby gets older, as rare as every few days. In a breast-fed baby this does not mean constipation. A formula-fed baby's bowel movements are paler, firmer, and smell unpleasant. A formula-fed baby may become constipated, or the stools may become harder, and the baby may show signs of straining and discomfort. In this case, check that you are making up the formula exactly in accordance with the directions, and try to give the baby more water or a little fruit juice between feedings.

If the new baby's bowel movements do not show normal patterns, this could be a sign that something is wrong with the bowel or digestive system. A baby who does not pass meconium in the first twenty-four hours may have a condition that prevents his bowel muscles from working properly and may require surgery. Some babies are born with blockages in their intestines, and these, too, can be operated on. Some babies have the opposite problem and have a condition that gives them continual diarrhea. Because they are losing too much fluid and too many essential chemicals from their bodies, they need to have these substances replaced by an intravenous drip into their veins as well as normal feeding. However, once they are past the first few vulnerable weeks, these babies can grow up normally and live with their condition, provided they drink enough fluids and follow the instructions of the doctor and dietitian about diet.

Babies can be born with urinary problems, too. Boys in particular can sometimes have an abnormal valve in their urethra (the tube leading from the bladder to the opening at the tip of the penis) that prevents them from passing urine properly. If your newborn baby boy's urine only dribbles out instead of shooting out in a stream, it may be a sign of this condition, which can be corrected with an operation. Signs of a urinary infection in a baby include strong-smelling urine or apparent discomfort when wetting, but also lethargy, vomiting, and being disinterested in feeding. An infection could mean that there is an underlying structural abnormality. (This may require antibiotics to prevent infection, or surgery.) Urinary infections are much more common in girls, so if you are at all worried about your daughter or if she seems ill for no other apparent reason, it is important to have her checked for underlying problems.

The most common of the serious inherited illnesses (a disease passed on through the genes) is one that also affects the digestive system: cystic fibrosis. This affects the pancreas and prevents the body from absorbing most foods. It also affects the lungs by making the mucus that is normally present in them very thick and difficult to cough up. Fibrocystic babies are very sweaty, have large amounts of salt in their sweat, and have very offensive-smelling bowel motions. The disease can be controlled in childhood by special diets, enzyme replacement, physical therapy, and courses of antibiotics. For more on this, see the section "Cystic Fibrosis" in chapter 18.

CHAPTER 14

Relationships

Your baby • How your baby learns
You and your baby • Separation
Leaving your baby • Your baby and other people
Social problems • Aggression • Sharing
Good behavior • Children's fears
Going back to work—who takes care of the baby?
Communicating with your child

*W*hen I have my baby I will feed her whenever she cries. You have to rearrange your life around the baby, don't you? You have to meet her needs.

I am very worried about spoiling the baby. I don't want to give in to every demand. That would be bad for him, wouldn't it? I want to still continue with my life—the baby will learn to fit in.

These are two mothers-to-be talking in a prenatal class before the birth of their first babies. Both are already thinking about how their babies are going to become part of their lives and using words such as "rearrange" and "fit in." They already see their babies as people who have needs, who can be upset, who can be spoiled. All expectant parents have these kinds of ideas about their babies, while parents who have already had children may base their expectations on the children or the child they already have. In fact, the baby always seems to turn out at least a little different from the one who was imagined, and parents also often behave in ways they would not have predicted. How will you and your baby adjust to each other?

Your Baby

A baby arrives in this world with certain features that parents often interpret as a personality. The baby may be large, suck strongly, and yell loudly for feedings. "She's quite a pig," you'll say affectionately. "She doesn't like to be kept waiting, she's got a mind of her own." Another baby may be very calm and placid, with slow movements and a deliberate way of doing things. You will adjust your own movements to hers, speaking slowly and softly. "She's so calm," you'll say. "She's a good baby."

You can probably think of hundreds of other examples of the ways in which parents attribute personality characteristics to babies. If you do not yet have a baby, you may think the parents imagine these characteristics—all new babies seem to look the same. But they are not. Babies are unique in looks and behavior. These influence how people respond to them. Thus your personality and your baby's personality will both contribute to your interactions with each other.

In addition to the way your baby behaves and reacts, physical factors make a difference—the sex and size of the baby, for example. A small baby or one who has been sick may arouse more protective feelings than a big, healthy one. The position in the family and the sex and age of siblings can also influence the baby's development and behavior. As you can see, many factors interact to shape and form a baby's personality. Furthermore, just as there are various recognizable stages in her cognitive development, so there are also certain stages of social and emotional development that all babies go through, although at different rates and with their own individual ways of doing things.

The chart "How Your Baby Learns" shows your baby's social development in the first five years.

How Your Baby Learns

Age	What She Can Do	What You Do
Birth to four weeks	Hear and respond to voices, turn toward them. Show signs of recognizing you. Respond to touching and being picked up. Move in rhythm with you and your voice. Cry.	Respond to crying, pick her up, talk and sing, exchange long looks with her, feed, clean, clothe, and become confident in handling her.
Four to six weeks	First smile—a genuine, pleasurable reaction to your face or voice.	Talk and smile back to her, which encourages more smiling.
Six to twelve weeks	The first laughs. Noises and gurgles other than crying. Beginning to enjoy play, such as in the bath; activities such as splashing, tickling, and hearing songs. Can grasp something put in her hand; turn her head to interesting noises and objects, but not yet with accurate focus. Can wait for feedings. Is awake for longer without crying.	Respond in the same way. Talk back to the baby as if her noises meant something. Give opportunities for play—splashing her, rocking her, and so on. Give her things of different textures to hold, different shapes, colors, noises to look at and listen to. Life becomes more predictable, and you may feel more relaxed.
Four to six months	She can use her eyes and control movements to reach for things and focus attention. She will be showing pleasure in you with special smiles, reaching out to you. Solids often introduced—this means she can join in mealtimes, a real social occasion.	You may be pointing things out, watching to see when she learns to follow where you are pointing—a big step. You will learn to recognize your baby's preferences—if she likes company, try to provide it; if she is wary, do not force her to go to other people. Other people can now feed your baby solids. Take care not to start fighting over food. Early solids often introduced but are not vital solid nutrition yet.
Six to nine months	Begins to show wariness of strangers. On the move—perhaps crawling; probably rolling toward things and people. Enjoys games like peekaboo, which shows she realizes people are still there even when out of sight. Laughs in response to play. Will give you things as well as take them. May become more clingy, protesting when you leave the room.	You have to be much more vigilant and make the home safe. More playthings needed, and more mess will be made. More impact on your life now. You can make up games to play that will test skills such as crawling after an out-of-reach ball. You may have to take a clingy child everywhere with you at this stage, and your life may seem very baby-dominated.

Age	What She Can Do	What You Do
Nine to twelve months	Babbling begins to turn to wordlike sounds such as "mama" or "baba." Understanding what you say: "Where's Daddy?" will make her look around. Will imitate your actions, become more adventurous, and need more supervision.	Respond to early word sounds and encourage by repeating and saying the things that have caught your baby's attention. She will begin to get into things, and the word "no' will enter both your vocabularies—yours first and then hers!
Twelve to eighteen months	First words will come soon. She can feed herself if allowed to, holding her own cup and spoon. Will probably be weaned from breast and bottle. She will understand much of what you say and may do things for you; for example, she will "go and get the cup" for you. Can wave bye-bye and perhaps hug and kiss you.	When language comes, you will begin to hold conversations. Your baby will also delight other people at this stage, as they can enjoy talking to her and getting answers. Weaning may have made you sad, but independence gives new pleasures. She can also amuse herself more and do more things for herself so you feel freer.
Eighteen to twenty-four months	Tantrums and refusals may start now. She develops a will of her own. May be destructive or aggressive, but there are compensations. Language is developing fast, and toilet training may begin.	A lot of patience needed now, and recognition that this is a phase that will pass. Other people can be of great help, so cultivate them. Positive achievements in language or first use of potty may emerge.
Two to three years	Tantrums and arguments may continue, but she becomes more competent at everything now, and you can distract her by giving her new things to play with. Talking is becoming more like yours, short sentences and connected conversations. She can answer questions, follow instructions, and give her own. Fantasy play with dolls, models, and household objects. She imitates you and helps with chores. Begins to understand others' point of view, such as in stories and through sympathy for other people. Can play with another child for a short period.	You can help her to learn to start taking care of herself by feeding herself, perhaps helping to dress herself and make more of her own decisions. Try to find ways of sharing pleasant activities together—conversations, books, activities, visits to friends. Treat her as a person living in your house and not just a baby under your control. You will certainly need a break from her from time to time.

Age	What She Can Do	What You Do
Three to four years	Still needs help with some things, but has at least the beginnings of the social skills that you have, such as conversation, doing things with others, helping, hindering, deciding, and organizing. May be able to be away from you at a play group or nursery.	The range of toys, books, and play activities you can give are as great now as they will ever be. She still enjoys baby toys, but also skillful ones and playing with other children. You may have another baby by now, but do not try to force independence too early.
Four to five years	She can probably be independent for part of each day and will do most things for herself, although she will still need help with coat buttoning and shoe tying. She will be able to go to the toilet by herself and may be able to put her own things away, partly depending on your help and attitude in this respect. Her language is almost as articulate as yours, although she knows fewer words. She will choose her own friends, and may become more attached to another grown-up, such as a teacher, than she sometimes seems to you. In a safe setting she can even take simple responsibilities such as running an errand—her memory and sense of responsibility will be good enough. She will be getting ready for kindergarten.	You will be handing her over to other people on a much more regular basis. Teachers are not substitutes for you; they are part of her life and they will be her grown-up friends, not yours. The same is true of friends she chooses at nursery school. She needs less constant monitoring now and becomes more of a companion, but she will still need babying sometimes, especially if she is sick or sad, and she may still have moods and tantrums.

Note: There are wide variations in the rates at which children achieve these abilities, but consult your child's doctor if your child is definitely behind these milestones.

You and Your Baby

Adjusting to Motherhood

However much you have wanted a baby, there may be times after the birth when you feel completely overwhelmed by the responsibility of caring for another human being who is so dependent on you. However equal a mother's relationship with her partner, the change in her life is still greater because she is the one who carries the baby in pregnancy, gives birth, and often nurses the baby. This all gives mothers special responsibilities and a unique relationship with the newborn baby. Physically mother and baby often spend a great deal of time together. With the birth of the baby, a mother's life, body, and hormones have undergone a dramatic change. Thus, initially mothers may have more difficulties than fathers in adjusting to having a baby. But don't worry too much—there are qualities in both babies and mothers that help with this adjustment.

Anyone watching parents in different delivery rooms with their newborn babies would be struck by the similarity with which they often behave. They keep saying "hello" to the baby and then talk about the way she looks and whether she has her father's nose or eyes. From the beginning parents treat their baby as part of the family and as a person. Similarly, although the baby cannot talk, she has already begun responding to you. Parents need to spend time with their new babies, so whenever possible most hospitals arrange it so that babies are not taken away immediately and put in a nursery. When you are able to lie next to your new baby, to pick her up, to watch her and talk to her, you will soon notice that she responds to you in all sorts of special ways. She will gaze steadily into your eyes, react to the sound of your voice, and stop crying when you pick her up. When you feed her, you will gradually develop a pattern of feeding that allows you time to rest and talk to her. You will learn to know from her face, body position, the sound of her cry, and the time of day whether she is hungry, upset, or just about to drop off to sleep. Most mothers-to-be worry about whether they will know what to do with their babies: "How will I know if she's hungry?" "How will I know if she's just tired?" In fact, most mothers do learn how to read their own baby's signals and tune in to them. A new baby means lots more hard work, sleepless nights, and a big change in lifestyle, but being sensitive to your baby's needs and meeting them when possible decreases the stress in this early period. There will be time enough later for your baby to learn to wait and to fit in with others, as inevitably she will.

A happy, mutual understanding between parents and their babies often takes time to develop, though. Even when things have been going well, there will always be times when the baby starts behaving differently—for instance, suddenly wanting to be fed every two hours again just when you thought you had established a schedule. There will also be times when it is difficult to be responsive to your baby's signals—if you are sick, tired, depressed, preoccupied with other children or responsibilities, or are sore from stitches just after the birth. Babies are very sensitive and will pick up that their needs are not being met as quickly. Thus the baby may become more demanding just when you are least able to cope.

What do you do when the baby is screaming for no apparent reason and you are not feeling well yourself? The first thing to remember is that you are *not* failing as a mother by asking other people to take over now and then. Even if you are breast-feeding, the baby's father, grandmother, or a friend can bring the baby to you for a feeding and then take her away afterward to rock her, play with her, or take her out for a walk. Don't refuse offers to help just because you are worried someone else will take over your special role with your baby. It won't happen, and the time you spend with your baby will be much more special and fun if you allow yourself a break when you need it.

Separation

Sometimes it is not possible for mother and baby to be together immediately after the birth. This may be because you or your baby is sick. If the baby is sick, she may need to go to special care or intensive care (see chapter 5). Even if you are well enough to be able to visit the unit, you may not be able to pick up your baby or cuddle her right away because of life-support machinery and equipment. Obviously this will make it more difficult for you and your baby to get to know each other in the first hours or days, but it is important to know that such difficulties are usually overcome and good relationships are established.

There will be other separations in your child's life later—for example, you or she might have to go to the hospital for a few days. You may have to go away for a short time, or she may be going to stay with relatives or friends. Perhaps you are going back to a part-time or full-time job soon after the birth. Most mothers, whether they work or not, eventually need to have some time away from the baby. It may be simply a shopping trip, a chance to read a book, or an opportunity to take an older child to the movies or a swimming pool. Successful separations are part of a healthy parent-child relationship.

What is a successful separation? It is one where both parties—child and parent—feel secure and are not upset. If you are comfortable leaving your child, try to ensure that she has secure, happy experiences when she is away from you, such as brief trips with grandparents or occasional afternoons with a friend. If separation is linked with pain, illness, or fear, such as may occur if a child is taken to the hospital, then, of course, it will be distressing and upsetting to the child. In this situation it is best to try to stay with your child as much as you can; for more on this, see chapter 20.

How can you tell if arrangements for leaving your child are successful? After all, a baby cannot tell you what happens when you are not there. You'll need to rely on your instincts and common sense. Is the person with whom you have left your baby someone you trust, who understands how to take care of the baby and is physically able to do so? Did she pay attention and ask questions when you were telling her about your baby's routine? Be wary of the person who brushes aside details of your baby's likes and dislikes with a cheery, "Don't worry. We'll be fine." Are you happy that your baby will be safe where you have left her? First-time mothers who are not used to the curious and boisterous ways of toddlers can be horrified at the thought of an eighteen-month-old let loose anywhere near their tiny newborn baby. The friend who takes the trouble to reassure you that she will make sure her own children do not interfere with your baby is a good friend.

Do not forget that grandmothers and friends with older children may not have homes that are safe for crawling babies or lively toddlers. Do not be afraid to remind them tactfully about the dangers of small objects the baby can choke on, low-level glass and china ornaments, and electrical sockets. Bring your own stairgate for them to use. Again, it is reassuring if they have already thought of all these things in advance. Some people may be fine for watching your child for an hour or two while you go shopping, but are not suitable to care for the baby all day. For example, another mother who already has a baby herself as well as a toddler just simply will not have the time and energy for another baby on a regular basis, however willing she may be. Grandparents who may have adored sitting cooing with a new baby may find a lively toddler just too taxing but may not want to admit it.

Later in this chapter there is more about leaving your baby with someone else while you go back to work. In general, any separation from your baby will be much more successful if the person who watches her is loving and familiar and makes sure that your child has a good time.

It is potentially damaging if a child is switched from one person to another and never has the chance to build up a permanent, long-term relationship with any parent or parent figure. This may happen not only with children in institutional or foster care but also in disturbed or disorganized families or even in loving families who often switch caregivers. In this situation a child may be handed from one person to another and never really get the chance to attach herself to anyone in particular.

Leaving Your Baby

Sometimes you might feel unsure about leaving your baby, even when you want time to yourself and you know that the person caring for the baby is trustworthy and loving. Anxieties about leaving your baby may be related to memories of your own unhappy separations in childhood. These feelings may also be caused by guilt instilled by other members of the family or friends—perhaps your mother-in-law thinks you should not have a part-time job, or a close friend has told you she does not think the local day-care center is a very good place to leave a small baby. First-time mothers who do not have a wealth of experience to fall back on can be easily upset by casual remarks!

Whatever the reason, it helps to remember that babies are like blotting paper, tremendously good at soaking up your feelings. Hovering around anxiously, lingering over the good-bye, and generally behaving strangely when you leave will immediately give your child all the clues she needs to become clinging and anxious in return. A parent who is confident when leaving the baby is more likely to have a baby confident of leaving her.

In the beginning allow yourself time to separate so you do not just dump your baby and rush off, but make sure the baby is properly settled and that the person looking after her has everything needed and knows the baby's schedule and routine for sleeping and feeding. Always make a point of actually saying good-bye and telling your baby where you are going and that you will be back soon. This may seem silly with a very tiny baby who will not understand your words, but children very quickly get to understand your feelings, both from the tone of your voice and your actions as well as by your actual words. Do not linger too long over saying good-bye—a quick cuddle, a kiss, and "Bye-bye, Mommy's going out now but she will be back soon" is fine. Do not try to force children into waving bye-bye or make the whole ritual unnecessarily drawn out and long. Doing this is much more likely to bring tears.

Between six and eighteen months your child may enter a phase when she is more sensitive about your absences and may become clingy and cry when you leave. During this period you may be tempted to sneak out secretly without saying good-bye because you dread a scene, but do not do this. It will only increase your child's anxiety. Remember to be calm and matter-of-fact about leaving, since your anxiety can fuel the child's anxiety. As you leave, a skilled caregiver will have a distraction ready, such as a game, a drink, or something really fascinating and new to look at, such as their cat or a pretty flower in the yard. If saying good-bye does get hard, then talk about the routine with the person who is caring for your child and suggest ways by which the child can be cheered up and distracted once you are gone. No matter how hard it gets, do not just suddenly vanish without telling your child you are going. This would be likely to result in your child becoming more fearful and less trusting in other situations, such as when you are visiting friends or going to a play group. Your child will think that you may suddenly vanish again. She may also spend a great deal of time looking for you while you are away.

It can be just as upsetting if there are tears again when you return. This does not mean your child had a bad time. You can see this yourself when you come upon a peaceful, happy scene, with your child sitting in her stroller or being amused on the floor, but then suddenly she looks up to see you and her face crumples into tears. Try not to allow reunions to become too emotional—snatching up a baby, hugging and kissing her, and clinging to her are going to make your child think her experience was much worse than it really was. By all means pick her up and cuddle her, but then make a point of letting her get on with some activity while you talk with the person who has been watching her. This changeover time when the child has both of you sitting there is quite important, as it takes the emphasis off the fact that you go and come when the other person is present and makes for a more normal, everyday atmosphere for the child. You will also want to know how your child has been behaving and how she and the caregiver have gotten along together in your absence. A good caregiver will tell you exactly what happened and how long your child was upset if at all after you left. She should not try to pretend that everything has been easy when this has not been the case.

Always give the person who takes care of your baby a good idea about how long you will be away, and come back at the time you said. Leave a phone number whenever possible or the phone number of a relative, your partner, or someone else to contact in an emergency. Make sure there is a good supply of bottles, and if your baby is breast-fed, express the milk and leave it in a bottle. If the baby is more than four months old, also leave some food that is appropriate for her.

Your Baby and Other People

Mothers have intense feelings for the little baby to whom they have just given birth. This is just as true for mothers whose babies are sick or for other reasons must be separated from the baby after birth. Although the feelings after birth are the unique experience of the biological mother, other people besides the biological mother will become very attached to the baby, too. Adoptive parents are an obvious example, and other people in the family and among your circle of friends and acquaintances will form relationships with the baby as well. From the baby's point of view, the person she feels closest to is the person who cares for her, talks to her, loves her, and remains constant through her life. This person may not be her biological mother. Although babies and children often have happy relationships with multiple adults, it does seem to be crucial for children's well-being and security as they grow up that they have at least one constant, loving person in their lives who does not go away or abandon them. This "mothering" relationship is a foundation for good relationships with other people. In practice it is usually provided by the child's own mother, but other adults can also have this important role in the life of a child.

Fathers

Most fathers are present at the birth of their babies today. Even as recently as twenty years ago this was not common, but professionals now realize that *both* parents should be involved in the preparation for and the birth of their baby. Fathers are encouraged to attend prenatal classes; they often shop for baby clothes, read baby books, and feel more free to talk among themselves about the pros and cons of natural childbirth or epidural anesthesia.

If you are a father reading this, how important do you think you are to the well-being of your child? And what can you do in practical terms to bring her up? There is plenty of evidence to suggest that children from homes where there is no father can be at a disadvantage, although single mothers should note that these disadvantages are often not because of the absence of the father. Families with only one parent often face financial difficulties, and the parent may lack the emotional support of other adults. Parents who feel supported, both financially and emotionally, will more easily be able to meet their children's needs.

A father also provides a male example for his children: for a son, a man to model himself on; for a daughter, a way to begin to learn about the opposite sex. At certain times most children prefer the company of their fathers to that of their mothers. As a child gets older, he may be the person the child seeks out to dry tears or put a bandage on a cut knee. This may be especially true when a second baby comes along. A father can do a great deal to help an older child come to terms with not being the baby of the family anymore, especially if he has built up a good relationship with the first child beforehand. Mothers cannot do everything and be everywhere, particularly when there is more than one child in the family. Children suffer if their mothers are depressed, overworked, or feel isolated, so this is another important reason for fathers to share child care from the beginning.

There is evidence that children do better at school when their fathers take a close interest in what they do. However, if a father has not been involved in the early years, it will be difficult to suddenly become involved in the children's lives when they start school or when they become teenagers. Fathers do need to start getting to know their children and to read their signals right from birth, just as mothers do. Of course, this helps the child and the family. But there are many rewards for the father, too. Those first beaming smiles, first brief sentence— "Daddy kiss"—the triumph as your toddler struggles to her feet and stands on them for a few seconds are just as exciting for fathers as they are for mothers. It may be harder for men to express these feelings, but far more men now talk among themselves about their babies' growth and development.

Feeling Left Out   Fathers can sometimes feel left out after the birth of a baby, both in their relationship with their partners and in their relationship with their baby. Mother and baby may seem locked into a perfect mutual relationship, and the father does not quite know where he is supposed to fit in. One important issue that highlights this is breast-feeding. When a mother breast-feeds her baby she is actually physically joined to the baby in the most intimate way. If her partner feels strongly about this it may have something to do with the way he regards her sexually, perhaps feeling possessive about her body or breasts. But many men do not feel excluded in quite such a personal or physical sense, just a little superfluous. Although feeding is a very important part of caring for a baby in the early stages, there are many other things fathers can do for their babies, such as changing diapers, burping, and dressing. It is also worth remembering that many mothers lack confidence when they are breast-feeding their first (and sometimes later) babies and need the father's support and encouragement.

Sharing the Workload   Because babies increase the workload of the household, fathers need to help even more than usual with the chores. This is even more necessary if the mother works or when a second or subsequent baby arrives. This should not be a matter of the father "helping," but of sharing the workload fairly. If the two of you decide to make arrangements for child care, household help, or babysitting, it is best if the father takes some responsibility for these, too. Following is a list of some of the regular things (as distinct from occasional things such as decorating) that fathers need to think about when having a baby, a young child, or more than one child. Look through it with your partner and see how many each of you does or shares responsibility for.

Care of Home
- ❑ Shopping
- ❑ Preparing food
- ❑ Cooking
- ❑ Doing dishes
- ❑ Cleaning kitchen floor
- ❑ Vacuuming
- ❑ Dusting
- ❑ Putting garbage out
- ❑ Laundry
- ❑ Ironing
- ❑ Putting children's clothes away

Care of Baby
- ❑ Feeding
- ❑ Changing
- ❑ Bathing
- ❑ Dressing
- ❑ Taking to the doctor
- ❑ Making up bottles (if applicable)
- ❑ Putting to bed
- ❑ Playing with

Care of Older Children
- ❑ Taking to/picking up from day care/ nursery school
- ❑ Reading stories
- ❑ Listening to children read
- ❑ Attending day care/school special events
- ❑ Choosing schools
- ❑ Talking to day care/schoolteacher
- ❑ Putting to bed

Financial and Practical Responsibilities
- ❑ Wage earning
- ❑ Paying household bills
- ❑ Paying other bills
- ❑ Arranging baby-sitters
- ❑ Baby-sitting yourself
- ❑ Inviting friends' children to play
- ❑ Cooking dinner for friends' children and own
- ❑ Other family responsibilities (e.g., elderly relatives)

- ❑ Choosing child-care arrangement
- ❑ Paying for child care
- ❑ Managing household help/paying household help
- ❑ Cleaning the inside of the car
- ❑ Cleaning the outside of the car
- ❑ Insuring the car

Mark each box with your initials, and at the end you will see how many jobs you share, how many fall to one person, and who does each job.

If one of you is doing nearly everything on this list, perhaps you should both ask why. Of course, you may have consciously decided to do things this way, perhaps because one of you works shifts or does very heavy work or because one of you is not going out to work. Nevertheless, it's better for your child to see you both as people who care for her and take responsibility for her if your relationship is to be close and trusting. This may mean that you'll have to drop some extra commitments at work or in your sports or social life for a while. This can be a difficult decision, particularly if work is very important to one or both of you. With some couples, one parent exchanges some opportunities for fulfilling work ambitions for the rewards of a close relationship with their children. Each couple has to work out these solutions in their own way, but it's a good idea to talk about the issue, preferably both before you have children and as they grow up. As you do, remember that it's best for your children to see you generally agreeing with each other or at least settling any disagreements you may have in a friendly and fair way.

If fathers are to share the work and the rewards of parenting on an equal basis, they need a partner who is prepared to relinquish some of the special mothering responsibility. This can be harder than some women realize or are prepared to admit. Some men deliberately make such a big deal out of doing any job involving the baby that in the end their partner stops asking them, but some mothers complain when their partner does not do things the way Mommy does. If you feel that your partner never helps out with the children, you may want to ask yourself if you are really able to accept your partner's different way of doing things with your child. Sometimes, for the father to take on more responsibility for his child, the mother has to learn to give up some of that responsibility.

Some decisions need to be reached by mutual agreement, since it would be confusing for a child if both parents had completely different ideas about what behavior was acceptable. But women who expect their partner to stick rigidly to their patterns in all the more mundane aspects of child care—for example, how children are fed, how they are dressed, or even how they are bathed—are setting their partner up for constant criticism and taking away some of the rewards involved in child care. On the other hand, fathers who rarely look after their children should not adapt the routine simply for their own convenience. For instance, a father who usually goes out to work but is watching after the children for one Saturday may not worry about feeding them potato chips and cookies and letting them watch television most of the day. He knows perfectly well that the rest of the time his children are being fed balanced, nourishing meals and are engaged in stimulating activities, so that one day of a different regimen will not harm them. Similarly, it does not matter to him if the baby skips her afternoon nap, because he knows his partner will be home in the evening to help out with the cranky baby who is overtired. If the same father took care of his children for most of the week he would probably behave quite differently!

Brothers and Sisters

When you're expecting a second baby, often your biggest concern is the effect on your first and older child. However much you want another baby, you might feel a little bit sad at the prospect of losing that special one-to-one relationship you had with your first child. "I feel I'm almost betraying her by having a second one," said one mother. This feeling is perfectly normal. You may worry that the older child will be jealous of the baby and wonder how you will manage the work of two children while still giving enough individual time to each. With so much attention given to the problem of jealousy and rivalry, we sometimes forgot that children can have a positive relationship between or among themselves despite occasional skirmishes.

The extra work you may fear as a second-time parent is often much more of a reality than the jealousy problem. Often, second-time parents get little sleep, have far more work to do, and have much less time to spend with the new baby than they had with their first. Although most of your concern may be for the older child, often it is actually the second one who misses out on the attention—she may be left to cry longer for a feeding, or be parked in a high chair while you do a double load of laundry instead of playing with the child. Mothers often report an instinctive need to be with and get to know their new baby. You must find time to meet this need. This may mean allowing your older child to spend time with others even if you have previously been uneasy about separation. But in the first few weeks of a second or third child's life it is likely that she will not receive as much of her mother's attention as previous children.

This is not necessarily all negative. The older sibling provides some compensation for the decreased adult attention second and third children receive. The opportunities and interests they share with the younger child will depend, to a large extent, on the age gap. Even quite young toddlers can be protective and helpful toward a new baby. As the baby grows up and begins to move around and be capable of doing things, the children can share many activities. The baby also gets to watch a bright, noisy toddler bouncing around.

One very valuable aspect of being a brother or a sister is mutual teaching and learning. The older child shows the younger one how to do something and in the process learns herself. She has to put into words exactly how you make a tower by putting one brick on top of another. She has to break down a process into its different parts to show the unskilled baby how it is done. She learns to understand the point of view of someone who is less able than herself, for she can see that the baby is not as advanced as she is. She has to figure out how to explain things simply, in terms the baby can understand. Of course, some of this teaching/learning process may go on in directions you will not find very helpful—like the time the toddler shows the baby exactly how to haul everything out of the closet for the umpteenth time! But in general it is a valuable process that parents often overlook.

You may worry that with more than one child you are not doing as much with either of them as you did when you had just one baby. Relaxed times when you could let the baby kick without her diaper or lie down beside her on the floor talking, hours of letting her sit on your lap while you talked to friends or looked at stories with her, or simply the amount of time you carried her and talked to her—all these may seem like things of the past. The loss of this one-to-one closeness can be quite sad for both you and your first child. Be prepared for tears and tantrums sometimes (and some strong emotions on your part as well), but be sure that you talk to your child about what is happening and about what you feel, and listen to what she has to say to you. Remember, small children understand far more than they can put into words.

You may be tempted, in your efforts not to upset your older child, to pretend that tasks and chores involving the baby are nothing more than a bore—"Oh, that baby's crying again," or "Silly baby needs her diaper changed; what a nuisance." The thinking behind this approach is quite understandable, but it can lead the older child to think that the baby himself is nothing more than a nuisance and a bore, and this will not help the two children to form a relationship. Research findings suggest that a better relationship develops between older and second children when the mother talks to the first child about the needs of the baby and about the baby as an individual. She should also seek the older child's opinion about what is happening and what she should do, inviting her to think about and to share the experience of looking after the baby: "She's crying now. What do you think she wants? What can we do?" The older child may think the baby wants a toy, or a feeding, or rocking in the stroller—try out her ideas so she can, with you, find out which idea works. Help her to understand how the baby thinks and sees her— "She's looking toward you because she heard your voice," or "She likes looking at you jumping around because you've got that nice, bright shirt on," or "She doesn't know my name or your name yet, but she is going to get to know her name the more often we talk to her and say it." Talking about what the baby sees, understands, and feels about the world around her and especially about her very important older sibling seems to help the older child understand and be interested in her younger sibling. This is the start to a good relationship between the two. Of course, talking like this about the baby and inviting the older one to share the decisions and help are not always appropriate, so try to be sensitive to when it's the right time. If your toddler is tired, engrossed in play, in a hurry to go out somewhere, or has a friend visiting, she is unlikely to be interested.

Once you have more than one child, sharing such things as bathtimes, mealtimes, trips to the park, and dentist appointments all become a way of life. Of course, it makes sense to share as much as possible so you do not have to do everything twice. But sharing can be fun for your children, too—even a very new baby can enjoy splashing in a bath with an older sister or brother. However, try to reserve some private times between you and your older one and you and your younger child. It is very important to create opportunities when each child has some time alone with you. The founder of the Methodist movement, John Wesley, was from a family of seventeen children. One of his mother's principles was to give five minutes each day to each child individually! With fewer than seventeen children you could probably spare more than five minutes—perhaps ten or fifteen, or even an hour occasionally. For instance, you might take the older child out for a special treat while Grandmother looks after the younger one. As the younger one grows up, she, too, needs times alone with you. This may happen naturally when the older one goes to school or out for a play date. Of course, the children will often be happy playing together, but it is worth trying to give each one some special time. It may be a special game you play together, a story or two at bedtime, or a private conversation in the bedroom away from everybody else.

Dividing up the work of two children often means that the father takes the older child and leaves the mother to look after the baby. Why not make conscious efforts to do it the other way around sometimes? This will give the father a chance to spend time getting to know his new baby by being responsible for routines such as changing her diaper and dressing her while the mother spends some time alone with the older child. Giving your older child individual attention even for a short time will make her feel less likely to feel the need to demand attention in ways that are irritating and upsetting, such as tantrums, whining, or being aggressive toward the younger child.

Grandparents

A few days after I came out of the hospital with my first baby, I was feeling really down and miserable, and when my mom came to see me, she could see I wasn't myself. She took care of the baby for an hour or two a day, and in a few weeks I was fine again. Now she is really fond of my two-year-old and it's heartwarming to watch them together. I don't know what I would have done without her.

My mother-in-law had never breast-fed any of her children, and although she said it was a good idea, I don't think I truly believed this. It was her first grandchild and she was desperate to show him off to all her friends and even talked about his coming to stay with her when he was only a few weeks old. She didn't really like the fact that he was still tied to me because of the breast-feeding and used to talk to him, saying things to him that she really meant to say to me, like, "When you have finished with all that nursing you are going to come and stay with me, aren't you?" I don't think she was aware of what she was doing consciously, though.

Grandparents are often very important people in children's lives. The part grandparents play in your child's life depends on how near they live, on the type of people they are, and how physically able they are, as well as on the relationship you had with them before the first baby arrived on the scene. If that relationship was already a bit strained and tense, there may be clashes as they take on the grandparent role. But whatever your own personal feelings, try to stand back a little and let them develop a separate relationship with your child, because there are big rewards to be had on both sides.

It is important to remember that raising a child today is much different from when your parents raised you. Grandparents may expect you to use the same methods they used and cannot understand that times have changed. Try to be patient and not hurt their feelings, but rather say something like, "I'll think about trying your way" or "Let me run it by my partner." But don't try to please your parents at your partner's expense. It is much more important that you and your partner agree on child-rearing methods so that you are consistent rather than each of you trying your own method. Working together promotes confidence not only in yourselves but also in your child.

Many grandparents (especially grandmothers) have trouble realizing that their children are capable of raising their children on their own, especially if it is the firstborn. You need to encourage grandparents to step back and give you the opportunity to succeed in your new role. Ask for suggestions when you want them, but let them know that you find negative criticism demoralizing. If you are concerned about how your own parents or your partner's parents are treating you or the child, talk it over with your partner and figure out a way to gently discuss the matter with them. This can be a matter of walking on a tightrope. Some grandparents feel entitled to make plans for the baby and suggestions to the new parents just because they are grandparents. On the other hand, in most cases you should allow the grandparents to develop their own relationship with the child. Many children grow up with wonderful memories of their grandparents.

How soon, how often, and in exactly what way you want your parents to be involved with your child is highly individual. Some mothers welcome their own mother or mother-in-law coming to stay right away on the return from hospital and helping take care of things at home. Others very much want to keep their relatives at bay until they are settled in and have become confident in their new role as a parent. It is very common in the early days for new parents to feel just a bit tense if a slightly domineering grandmother gives too much forceful advice or wants to start taking over responsibilities.

Some issues, such as potty training, table manners, the giving of presents, and discipline, are especially likely to be sensitive and provoke strong feelings between grandparents and parents. On the positive side, grandparents can often be a tremendous source of support and comfort. If they live nearby they may be able to give you a break from baby care, baby-sit in the evenings, and help out in all kinds of practical ways. Be careful not to abuse their goodwill and start "dumping" your children on their doorstep more often than you think they want. Part of the joy of being a grandparent is being able to indulge your grandchildren and then to hand them back to their parents after a relatively short time! If grandparents are forced into taking on a more regular child-care or a substitute-parent role, that special relationship may change and can become soured if the grandparents resent this role. If your own relationship with your parents-in-law or parents works well, these problems are less likely to arise, but if things do get difficult, it is worth remembering just how much your own children will get out of what their grandparents can give.

It is especially worth maintaining contact with the grandparents if you and your partner separate or divorce, for it is in these sad circumstances that grandparents most often fear losing touch with their grandchildren. And it can be an additional loss to children who no longer live with both parents if they also lose regular contact with grandparents and other relatives who love and care about them. Obviously, to maintain that contact it is important that grandparents show tact and sensitivity by not taking sides, criticizing, or putting undue pressure on couples to get back together again.

On a purely practical note, do not forget, when you are visiting older relatives or leaving them in charge of young children, that however many children of their own they may have had, they might have forgotten about some of the safety aspects of child care. So do not be afraid to point out, gently and tactfully, of course, about the need, for example, to keep stair gates in place, and to cook with saucepan handles turned toward the center of the stove so they cannot be pulled down by a toddler.

Friends

Other parents with children of a similar age can be a great support. Lifelong friendships often spring out of meetings at childbirth classes, hospitals, or parent groups, and your child's first encounters with other babies or toddlers will probably be a result of your need to see your friends. Even babies can enjoy themselves by gurgling at each other, touching each other, and imitating each other's sounds and movements. As your child gets older you may also take her out to more organized play activities such as "Mommy and Me" classes, play groups, and nursery school. At first she will want to play with others only within your sight and sometimes even insist on being in physical contact with you. You will need to be there to help with squabbles over toys and to prevent accidents, but there will come a time when your child definitely does not need you to be there every minute. She'll prefer going off with her friends to play house, make a tent, or play school. She may have a special friend to whom she will become very attached. Even in very young children such special friendships can be long-lasting. If the friend moves away, your child may remember that friend for years to come.

Same-age friendships are very valuable for your child's emotional and social well-being. Children also learn from them. To communicate, a child has to learn to tailor her conversation and reactions to the other child. Listen, for example, to a three- or four-year-old talking to a friend and note how the subject matter is sustained, then changed, and how friends react emotionally to each other. For example, here is a four-year-old sympathetically listening to her slightly older friend David telling her about his first day at school:

KATIE: *"What did you do at school?"*

DAVID: *"We played a game called Superfriends. Paul Bryant made up the game. There were twelve boys and twelve girls. The boys chased the girls."*

KATIE: *"Did you chase the girls?"*

DAVID: *"No, I didn't want to play."*

KATIE: *"What did you do?"*

DAVID: *"I played with a girl and we hid in a corner of the playground. The teacher came and told Paul to stop. He had to go inside."*

KATIE: *"What did you have for lunch?"*

DAVID: *"I had peanut butter and jelly and chocolate chip cookies. What did you have?"*

KATIE: *"I had hot dogs and baked beans."*

It is unlikely that David would have given his mother so many of the details about the game or expressed his anxiety about Paul's getting into trouble. Moreover, few adults would have had the tact to ask for the supremely important details about lunch at just this point in the conversation.

How do you help your children learn the skill of making friends? In the beginning you need to stay nearby when they have another child of the same age visiting. At this stage it is very difficult for them to take turns with toys and share. Without constant nagging, gently tell your child to give things to the other child or say, "Now it's Mary's turn." Also use distraction if there is going to be a dispute over a toy. Distracting a toddler by offering a different toy is much better than letting things escalate to a tantrum, with both children yelling and both tugging at the same toy. At the toddler stage, children tend to play alongside each other rather than together, but you can help them by showing them little simple games they can play with you—such as building a tower of bricks and then both of them knocking it down, or getting a big cardboard box they can both fit inside and pretending it is a car or a boat, or even pulling them together in a wagon. Show them how to play traditional games such as peekaboo or Ring Around the Rosey with each other. If you do something simple like this with one child, the other child will probably stop and watch and then may want to come and join in herself. The first child will then stop and watch the other one. They are learning that the same things make other people laugh, as well as observing and noticing what other people do. As they grow older they will begin to do some of these things together without your help.

Do not expect to just put two children of any age in each other's company and see them immediately hit it off and start playing together. Left alone, two very young children are more likely to end up having a fight over a toy. They'll almost always need your help with introductions and easing them into a game together. If your child has a visitor, encourage your child to show the newcomer where the toys are. Then get something out and help your child demonstrate how it works, and then give the visiting child a turn. Talk to them about what the other child wants to do—"Have you got one of these at home?" or "Do you know how this works?"—and then you can invite your child to show her friend or help her, a role your child will probably enjoy. Once your child can see that the visiting child is friendly and is not going to take all her things away, she may relax and begin to learn that it can be fun to show off her own things to a newcomer, rather than just grabbing them back all the time and saying, "No, mine!"

You also need to show young children how to share very simple games. If it is summer, for example, you can bring them outside with a small bowl of water and demonstrate how they can get plastic cups and pour the water in and out of different containers. If children never experience any of these simple turn-taking skills, enjoying activities together and showing other children how to use toys or playthings, then their behavior may appear very antisocial when they are first playing with a group of same-aged children—at nursery school, for instance. Children quickly learn to watch each other to see what kind of reaction they are likely to get. If one child immediately grabs a toy in a possessive way or takes it from another child, the other child is likely to have the same kind of reaction, and before you know it there is a full-scale battle going on.

What do you do if your socially skilled toddler, who is normally very friendly and sharing, finds herself on the receiving end of grabbing, snatching, or aggressive behavior? Most parents feel terribly upset when this happens—there is more about it in the section on aggression later in this chapter—but in general it is best to explain to your child that this little boy or girl does not yet know about sharing or is not yet used to playing with a lot of other children and does not understand about taking turns. If you find it easy to encourage children into sharing kinds of play, then perhaps you can help this other child learn the rules.

When a child is worried or in trouble, having another child to talk to will be an important outlet, especially if the trouble is with adults in her life. When parents are angry with a child, or with each other, the child may need a friend she can turn to for support. This process can begin to work at a very young age if your child has the chance to meet other children regularly. Brothers and sisters can also be confidants for each other, although they are sometimes the source of trouble! Other grown-ups, such as a neighbor or the teenager who comes to baby-sit, can be friends as well.

Social Problems

Difficulties in Making Friends

Some children find it difficult to make friends. They cling to their parents when they are at a party or at a friend's house. They sit by themselves in a corner at nursery school or play group and seem to prefer solitary activities such as reading or playing with their toys to joining in games with the crowd.

Children have to learn to take turns

Others have problems for very different reasons. They seem to have no idea at all about taking turns. They barge to the head of the line for the slide, snatch the Superman outfit from the child whose turn it was to wear it, and push over anyone who gets in their way. If another child protests, these children tend to hit or even bite. Aggressive children like this can be just as lonely and friendless as shy children, although the problem may be more difficult to detect.

Children need to learn the *skills* of making friends. These do not necessarily come automatically for every child. They need to learn to ask the right questions at the right moment, as Katie did of David in the passage quoted above. They need to show tact and sympathy. They also need to be able to show trust and be willing to confide in the other child, as David did with Katie. If your child has difficulty getting along with other children it may be because she just does not know how. You can help by giving her opportunities to talk about what she has been doing, and planning supervised outings with other children. It can be helpful to invite other children of the same age home to play, but avoid forcing them into each other's arms. The ideal companion is a more confident, generous child like Katie or David who will be sympathetic to a shy or awkward child and will set an example of friendliness, or a younger child to whom the child will appear grown up and important. Children who have difficulties making friends for whatever reason are usually better with just one friend around than when they are one in a crowd of children.

You might also ask yourself about your own social life. Do you have a circle of other mothers you see? Do you have people coming to visit your house bringing their children along so your child has the chance to meet new people at her own home? Sometimes, if a child's parents are shy and find it difficult to make friends, their child may have fewer chances to learn all the social skills of friendship, because she meets fewer people. The time when you have young children is often a key one for making friends, and even if you are not naturally very chatty or sociable, you can often enjoy an hour or so in the company of other parents with whom you may not have much in common except the children. Ask at the local library or recreation center about a parent group in your area. Contact the groups, and tell them you do not know many people in the neighborhood. If you find a friendly, well-run group, the leader is sure to invite you to come along and make a point of looking out for you on your first visit so she can introduce you to one or two other parents. This may be easier than simply showing up and hoping that someone will talk to you, for even in the friendliest such group newcomers can sometimes be overlooked at the first visit in the midst of all the chaos.

Aggression

Aggression shows itself in various ways and at different stages. A child who has learned to walk is often tempted to give a younger, tottering toddler a little experimental shove. She can then be amazed at the amount of attention this attracts, and may want to create that kind of commotion again. Instead of rewarding the behavior with attention, say "no" very firmly but without shouting. Then immediately take your child away into another room by yourselves and tell her again quietly but firmly that she must not do this. Aggressive action from you will not help, so stay calm and resist any temptation respond to the child's aggression by hitting or shaking her.

Children learn hitting from each other as well as from adults. Be prepared, for example, for your child to become more aggressive if she sees this aggression in older children at a play group or school. In a well-run environment this will not go unchecked, but in calm moments it helps to tell your child why this kind of behavior is not allowed and to give her some guidelines for coping with problems that lead to hitting.

What is sometimes harder to deal with is if your child is the subject of aggression from another child or children. We generally teach children not to hit back, on the principle that two wrongs don't make a right. Hitting should be detected by the adults supervising the situation, and the child who is hitting should be punished. If hitting occurs repeatedly there may be too little adult supervision, and it is worth investigating alternative play groups or schools where adults are quicker to step in to help toddlers resolve quarrels without fighting.

Biting.   As an aggressive act, biting is not any different from hitting or pushing, but it deserves separate attention because parents are often more shocked if their child starts biting or is on the receiving end of such action. Some parents believe that biting the child back to show her how much it hurts is the best way to stop such behavior, but this only teaches the child that it is appropriate to bite in some situations. Tell the child firmly but without shouting that biting is not allowed because it hurts other people, and immediately remove her to a place by herself— the other end of the hall or another room. Allow her back when she has begun to calm down, usually after a few minutes.

If biting develops out of an excited game, then calm things down and show the children how to play the game without actually biting, again making it clear that real biting is not allowed. If they cannot play the game without things getting out of hand, switch their attention to another activity. If your child starts to bite after being bitten by another child, you will need the cooperation of the other parent or teacher—it is possible for epidemics of biting to spread through groups. All of the parents need to supervise carefully to stop the habit.

Some children begin biting while teething, initially without aggressive intent. You still need to give a clear signal that biting is not acceptable by saying "no" firmly and moving a slight distance away from the child. But again, try to avoid overreacting, since that might cause your child to do it again to "push your buttons."

Aggression between Brothers and Sisters

Seeing your own children being unkind or aggressive to each other can be upsetting. Invariably parents get most upset when they see an older child being aggressive to a younger one. Jealousy and rivalry are triggers. It is important for you to be fair and not to always demand that the older child give in or allow the younger one to get away with provocative behavior. A good way of dealing with this type of problem is to help the aggressor think through the consequences of her actions and the alternative responses that would be more appropriate. Helping the aggressor to see the other child's point of view may be helpful. Try to avoid intervening in all disputes between your children, because this will prevent them from developing their own coping skills. Codes of behavior between brothers and sisters are set very early on, and sharing objects, activities, and also time and attention is the basis of family cooperation.

Sharing

Babies and young children are self-centered. Learning to understand that other people have needs and that some things may belong to another is a long process of social learning that begins toward the end of a baby's first year and is especially important in the second and third years. As with all behavior, example is the first lesson: point out when you or another child is sharing with your child. Remember that a one-year-old thinks everything belongs to her. "Me" and "mine" are often among the first words. First children are especially likely to believe that they own everything, since their parents often give them a lot. They may not have much experience competing with another young child for toys or other possessions. For many children this phase will pass quickly as they begin to have more contact with other children who want their toys. Sometimes parents can get too involved in disputes about sharing, especially between brothers and sisters, and where possible it is best to let the children resolve their own sharing disputes unless they involve aggression or you see one child taking advantage of another. Don't always make older children give in to younger children. It is reasonable to keep possessions belonging to older children, which may be broken or which are unsuitable for the younger one, out of the way. It may help younger children to accept this if they in turn have some prized possessions that are special to them and not freely available in the collection of household toys.

Practical solutions to sharing problems:

- If you are not sure who had the toy first and if neither is willing to give it up, take it away from both and distract them with another activity.

- If one child has grabbed a toy from another, calmly take it back and give it for a short time to the child who had it first. Explain to the grabber that she has to wait her turn. Reward the child who asks and waits by encouraging the other child to give the asker a turn.

- If the owner of the toy simply cannot be persuaded to give it up, try distracting the other child with a similar or more interesting toy. You may need to develop clear rules about when sharing will be expected. It is sometimes helpful to allow your child certain toys that she does not have to share. Set these aside when friends come over.

Good Behavior

Handling Young Children

Getting your child to cooperate and to behave the way you would like often becomes more difficult once she has learned to walk and is fully mobile. When this happens, so many more activities are within her range that you have to teach her basic rules of safety. For example, you need to tell her not to climb up on the table and have her accept that this is not allowed. At this stage it becomes even more important that you take safety precautions, such as keeping all the chairs pushed in around the table. However, do not rely on these precautions to keep her safe. She will surprise you with the ways she can get around these precautions. It is essential to check what she is doing very frequently.

Other issues, such as accepting that she cannot have a lollipop or cookie every time you go into a store, cooperating with putting appropriate outdoor clothes on, waiting until you finish setting the table before eating, or helping another child before getting her a drink, are the types of family rules that often lead to toddler tantrums. These tantrums may be upsetting to you, and you may sometimes be tempted to bend the rules to stop a tantrum. Some parents worry that enforcing rules that result in tantrums will harm their relationship with the child. However, in the long run having a child who has learned to follow your family's rules will be very important to a good relationship between you and your child, so it is worth enforcing the rules even if you have to deal with a few tantrums.

How can you make it most likely that your child will do what she is told? First-time parents learn by trial and error, and few of us escape those embarrassing public scenes when a child stages a major tantrum because she wants to be allowed to push the stroller when you are in a hurry or does not want to hold your hand when it would be unsafe for you to let go. However, there are some general principles that are the basis of all child management, whatever the situation:

1. Your love and the expression of your love in the form of cuddles, praise, and attention are more important in helping your child to be "good" than threats or punishments. Always make a point of expressing your pleasure and telling your child she is good when she stops touching things when you ask, or climbs into her car seat obediently. We all have a natural inclination to correct children when they do not do as required more often than we praise them for good behavior. It is important to notice when children are being quiet and playing well. Giving attention at these times indicates that this is what you want the child to do rather than only giving attention for what they shouldn't do.

2. Cut back on the number of demands you make. Children become less receptive to a continual stream of "Don't do that" and "Stop touching those." If you look carefully at the rules and commands that really matter, you will find there are relatively few. If a command is not really important to you, you may not be willing to enforce it. For situations that are not important enough to use commands, there are other means of encouraging your child to behave. For example, playing with or distracting the child will often redirect the child to more appropriate behavior. Reserve commands for those instances when it is most important that your child follows your instructions.

3. Carry through what you say. This means when you tell her to stop doing something, you must be prepared to actually intervene if necessary and brave the ensuing screams. If you say "no" to something and then give in after the child makes a scene, you are teaching that you will give in if she screams loudly enough.

4. Be consistent. Firmly stopping a child from doing something one day, then allowing it the next, is confusing to the child. Talk to your partner about what is and what is not allowed; if parents cannot agree, then a child can easily play one off against the other.

5. Remember that it is possible to be firm and loving at the same time. You don't have to sound angry when you say "no" to something. You can follow a "no" by affection when your child complies.

6. Playfulness and humor are important tools in managing the behavior of young children. Play and joking around are very effective ways of distracting a young child who is upset over something trivial. Humor also helps the child learn to make the best of things and not get upset over small matters. However, especially with older children, be careful not to mock them, or appear to minimize something that is really upsetting to them.

Discipline

The main goal of discipline should be to teach children principles that will enable them to make judgments and to decide for themselves on socially and morally acceptable ways to behave. Spanking children only teaches them that you are angry with them at that moment, and it may encourage them to hit other children. It does not teach them what you want them to do, so that oftentimes, the minute you turn your back, they indulge in the behavior you have just disapproved of. If your child is generally fairly well behaved, then she would respond to another form of discipline, and if she is usually naughty, then spanking her probably has no beneficial effect. It certainly does not help children to develop any form of social understanding and code of conduct. Think about it. Children are strong imitators. Does spanking mirror any behavior that you find acceptable in other relationships? We do not approve of children hitting each other or adults settling matters by violence.

If you do lose control and slap your child, it is best to tell her afterward that you are sorry and that you were wrong to hit her. Remember that all children go through difficult phases and that all parents suffer times of stress and lack of confidence or patience. Talking to other parents of similar-age children is a great help because many problems are extremely common, and hearing how other people cope can help.

We've stressed the importance of your praise and approval, but do not underestimate the impact of your disapproval and withdrawal of affection. This does not mean you should give your child the "cold shoulder" for a long period or make disturbing threats that you will cease to love her. Instead firmly state, "I don't like your doing that because it's making a big mess." If necessary, stop her from engaging in the behavior. Try to keep your disapproval focused on the behavior, not the child. Don't say, "You're bad." Instead say, "We don't allow hitting." In general it's not very effective to defer punishments, such as later in the day not allowing her to do something she enjoys. This is particularly true of two- or three-year-olds, who live very much in the present and will have forgotten the incident an hour or two later. Even with older children, if you are withdrawing a privilege or treat, it is better to pick something due to happen in the next few hours or at least by the end of the day, not something occurring a day or two later. It is reasonable to withdraw food treats if the bad behavior occurs in relation to the treat—for example, if a child stages a scene in a store, not to give him candy or whatever item has been promised. It is better, however, not to use food too much in punishment (e.g., no dessert) or reward (e.g., extra candy), as it lays too great an emphasis on the enjoyment and the importance of eating. In a few children this can make problem eating phases extend into something more permanent.

Probably the most effective and immediate punishment for young children is that described in the section on aggression, simply to isolate them for a few minutes from the scene of the crime. When you do physically distance a young child by putting her out of the room you are in, keep the time to only a minute or two. Such separations quickly register your disapproval, and keeping her apart from you for longer than a few minutes may be unnecessarily frightening for a young child. Afterward try to change the mood with a distracting activity. Later, when she is calm, you can briefly explain why you put him in the room or chair, but don't dwell on the incident. Obviously, different situations call for different tactics—distancing yourself from the child who is refusing to let you put a coat on her is unlikely to work because you have to return to the same battleground. Making a game out of it is much more likely to be successful.

Humor is a very powerful tool in managing young children, who have a strong sense of fun and playfulness, but summoning up the ability to be humorous is not always possible. You have to be very resourceful and able to use a wide variety of skills to manage your young children. It is not surprising that we find our children most difficult to handle when we are under pressure or feeling tired. So even if you aren't feeling playful, it is worth stressing again that it is important to praise your child and show your affection and pleasure when she does comply with your wishes or is helpful. This gives much greater emphasis to the times when you show displeasure, while an undiluted stream of negative commands and criticism leads children to ignore the comments or to build a very poor self-image.

Learning to Wait

One of the things that is particularly exhausting about caring for small children is the nonstop stream of demands for help and attention. The process of growing up is largely one of children learning to develop some awareness of other people's needs and feelings and to control their own demands and behavior accordingly. You need to help your child to learn to wait. Pick the right moments. When a toy is trapped, it is not a good time because your child's frustration will make her oblivious to anything else. Other requests, to come and see something, to help with a puzzle, to give her a cookie, may not be so pressing. Try not to say, "Just a minute" all the time, because this does not have any meaning in terms of time for your child. Instead, be specific. Say, "When I've finished setting the table, I'll do that for you." The child can then see for herself when you will be ready. Do not ask her to wait for everything or make the waiting time too long, and remember to praise her when she does wait.

Young children tend to amuse themselves best if you put a little thought into the planning of their day so that activities and pace are varied and periods when you are busy are interspersed by times when you give them some of your undivided attention. For more on this, see chapter 12.

Children's Fears

Fear of the dark, of insects, dogs, thunder, water, and the noise of the vacuum cleaner or even the washing machine are very common in toddlers and can often lead to what parents see as difficult behavior. It is true that sometimes children can pick up a parent's fears, and many adults struggle to control their natural reactions to spiders or going to the dentist in an effort to show calm unconcern to their child. Most childhood fears will fade or pass if you reassure your child and stay calm. It is only when the fear is so strong that it seriously disturbs your child's normal behavior that it is termed a phobia—for example, a child who becomes hysterical at any prospect of getting in any kind of water. Here are some guidelines for helping children overcome fears or phobias:

1. Take your child's fears seriously and do not laugh, disregard them, or tease her about them. Your sympathy is important.

2. Do not force contact with the feared object, but rather try gentle tactics, allowing the child to have some control over her approach so she can retreat or draw closer as she feels able.

3. If your child's fear is so intense that even a gradual approach sparks panic, avoid the object of anxiety and only try to approach it again when she is happy and relaxed. Stop before she becomes anxious again.

Fear of the Dark

This is more common in school-age than in preschool children and can be sparked off by a story in a book or by television, by a change from summertime to wintertime, or by some other event. Point out that your child can still call for you in the dark. Talk to her about where everything is in her room while her eyes become adjusted, or make the room less dark with a nightlight or a hall-light. As with all other fears, never force a child to confront the fear by leaving her in the dark. For more on sleep problems, see chapter 8.

Fear of Doctors and Dentists

It's a good idea to make your child familiar with the doctor or dentist at times when treatment is not required. When possible, take your child on your own checkup visits. If some treatment is required, explain in advance what will be happening. There are a number of well-illustrated books you can read together. If your doctor or dentist has children or grandchildren of his own, try mentioning this and talking about them in a family context. This can be reassuring for three- and four-year-olds. For more on children in the hospital, see chapter 20.

Going Back to Work—Who Takes Care of the Baby?

Of all mothers married and unmarried, more than 50% with children under age six are in the workforce. Most employed mothers work full-time even when their youngest child is under three years. When the mother either wants or has to return to work, it is sometimes possible for the father to take over, especially if the mother only works part-time. But more often, other plans have to be made. Making arrangements for someone else to take care of your baby is very personal and one about which you will probably have some strong, instinctive feelings. There are many questions to consider in trying to choose the best arrangement:

1. Are you still breast-feeding? Do you plan to continue? It is perfectly possible to return to work and continue to breast-feed—for more suggestions, see the section "Going Back to Work" in chapter 6. Even if you are not breast-feeding, the age of your baby is a key factor in choosing the best day care for your needs.

2. How long will you be away, including traveling time? How often? There is obviously an enormous difference in the kind of arrangements you need to make for a part-time job as opposed to a full-time job with long hours.

3. What choices do you have? Is there a relative or a friend who can help? Is there a day-care center at or near the place where you work? How much money can you afford to pay?

Your Child's Changing Needs

It is best if the arrangement you make can adapt to and grow with your child so she does not have to cope with too many changes, but that is not always possible. It may help to consider the different needs that arise at different stages.

In the first year of life a baby needs to relate to one person. She needs that person to get to know her and her wants. This does not mean that it always has to be a one-to-one relationship exclusively, but if your child is to be cared for in a day-care center, then look for one where the same person will always take care of your child. Be sure that person has time to give your baby enough individual attention. A constantly changing flow of different people looking after many babies does not allow for them to get to know each other.

Obviously you will want the person who looks after your baby to know all about babies' needs, to have some experience with them, and also to be interested in knowing about your particular baby and her needs and wants. This can be very labor-intensive—as you know yourself!—so make sure the person you choose has enough time to spare. A caregiver who already has two other small babies to care for is unlikely to be able to spend much time talking to and playing with each one on her own. Find someone who can provide the kind of day you would like your baby to enjoy, which may mean some time outdoors, some time playing, some time reading. The environment should be as loving and as stimulating as the one you would provide yourself.

How can you be sure what will happen when you are not there to see what goes on? There is more public scrutiny and accountability in a licensed day-care center, but a home day care with three children from different parents and where the parents arrive and leave at different hours will have a busy and open house that should give you some reassurance.

If you can afford it, employing a person to come to your own home may be a good arrangement, but it requires you to carefully select the person, since there will be no one watching her while you're gone. If this is what you plan, it is a good idea to start the new arrangement at least two weeks before you plan to return to work, so the two of you can get to know each other and establish trust before you go back. It also helps to introduce the person you employ to as many of your friends and neighbors as you can, as well as places where she can take the baby. Ask them all to give you feedback on how the caregiver is with your child.

In the second year of life, continuity and closeness of attention are still very important, but other factors now come into consideration. This is the year that your child goes from being a baby to being a toddler. She will begin to run around, to explore, to get into everything. A baby needs a lot of nurturing, but with a toddler continual but less intensive attention and a different kind of caregiving come into operation. Is the person who is going to look after your child fit and active, and alert to danger without being repressive? The care of a doting grandparent may have been ideal in the first year of life, but they can find that a lively toddler is just too much to cope with for a full day. Obviously their love and attention are still invaluable, but you may want to rearrange the day so part of it is spent with somebody else. Most toddlers enjoy the activity, excitement, and lively atmosphere that surround other children, although they play alongside rather than with each other at this stage. It is also important for their own social development that they begin to mix with and see other children.

Nursery schools and day-care centers differ in the ratio of caretakers and the type of care offered for the children. Most nursery schools require that a child be about three years old, although some have programs for twos or those two and a half. Once your child reaches this stage, you may need to review your care arrangements. Can your child's caregiver take her to the nursery school of your choice? And while your child will be taken care of for part of the day, there are still the rest of the day and holidays to consider. By now, however, your child will really love having other children around. A rather solitary arrangement where she is cared for at home by one person who comes to the house is only satisfactory if that person can invite the child's friends over and provide the sort of social life you would offer if you were home.

Sometimes working parents prefer to juggle hours with a young baby or toddler so they can keep her up late in the evening and spend time with her, but once a child begins to go to nursery school regularly, she needs to have a more stable routine and to go to bed at a reasonable hour. As the child's week begins to become more structured, weekends, other times off, and holidays begin to be more important as opportunities to spend time as a family.

The Choices

There are many different child care options available. The best choice for you depends on where you live, what your family circumstances are, how much you can afford to pay, and more other factors than we can name. Here's an overview to help you sort your options.

1. *Licensed day-care centers have their pros and cons.*   Good centers tend to be expensive. If you cannot afford the full fee for this type of care, you may find that there is an eighteen- to twenty-four-month wait for a place in a subsidized program. So begin investigating early.

   If you can afford this option, you need to be very careful in selecting the right place because quality does vary. Following is a checklist of questions you can use when evaluating a day-care center. These guidelines have been reviewed by the Committee of Early Childhood, Adoption, and Dependent Care of the American Academy of Pediatrics:

1. Is the child care facility licensed? (Ask to see the current license.)
2. Is the location convenient to your home?
3. Is your initial reaction to the facility positive? (Trust your feelings.)
4. Are all the costs written out and easily available for you to read?
5. Is there extra after-hours care available in case of emergency or inability to reach the facility at your prearranged pick-up time?
6. Can you visit the facility during regular operating hours before registering your children in the program?
7. Is the number of adult caregivers sufficient for the children present?
8. Do the caregivers TEACH in addition to seeing after the usual basic needs?
9. Does the staff appear to enjoy caring for the children?
10. Is the staff at eye level with the children when engaged in activities with them or do they stand above them when playing or instructing them?
11. Does the facility appear to be clean?
12. Will the staff allow you to examine the entire premises?
13. Can parents visit whenever they wish? (Restricted visiting times are improper.)
14. Do the children already in the facility appear happy/sad? (Circle one.)
15. Do the adults and children interact?
16. Does there appear to be enough space for the number of children present?
17. Is there a sleeping (quiet) area large enough to accommodate all the children?
18. Are beds, hammocks, or mattresses available to sleep on?
19. Does each child have a specific place for his/her own belongings?
20. Are all the medicines and poisonous substances LOCKED UP? (Ask to check.)
21. Is a list of the meals/snacks readily available? (Ask to see it.)
22. Are the meals/snacks nutritious and balanced?
23. Are infants fed lying down? (Bottle propping is unhealthy.)
24. Can your child get a special diet if necessary?
25. Are all the toys to play with at the facility chosen with safety in mind?
26. Are there many toys present for your child's particular age?
27. Is there an outside area available for play activities?
28. Does the outside area appear to be planned for safe playing? (Hard surfaces and rocks, high climbers, slides, and swings are dangerous.)
29. Is there a written plan for play activities? (Ask to see it.)
30. Are inside *and* outside play supervised all the time?
31. Are the older and younger children playing together or in their own age groups? (Mixed play leads to a higher percentage of accidents.)
32. Is a large part of planned activities television viewing? (This is not recommended and may be harmful if programming is not carefully supervised.)
33. Are the parents encouraged to become involved in any activities? Are learning experiences available through the facility for the parents? (Some child care centers have parenting and other classes scheduled.)
35. Does the staff regularly meet with individual parents? (Ask how often.)
36. Do the caregivers have a written policy concerning discipline? (Ask to read it.)
37. Are there policies for the care of ill children? (Ask to see them.)
38. Is there a holding area for ill children?
39. Will the caregivers administer prescribed medications to your children?
40. Is there a physician consultant for the child care facility?
41. Have personnel had training in first aid and infectious diseases?

2. *Home day-care providers.* This is someone, often a mother or a grand-mother, who cares for other people's children in her own home. Most home day cares are not licensed. You can find them by asking friends and neighbors, looking for ads in the local paper, asking at local places of worship, and at your pediatrician's office. Common sense plus the recommendation of other parents are the best guides in choosing this person. Ask for the names of people such as other parents who can give a character reference. Ask if you can stop by, unannounced. Be suspicious if that is discouraged. Children in this person's care will follow her routine, so you need to know and to feel happy with the daily life your child would lead.

3. *Nannies, mother's helpers, and au pairs.* These are all people who take care of your child in your home. Experience and training vary greatly, so be sure to investigate at the time of the interview and when you check references. Generally a nanny only deals with extra jobs relating to the children, such as cooking for them and doing their laundry. Any extra responsibilities, such as light housework, should be negotiated at the interview stage. A live-out nanny will ask a higher salary than one who lives in and has her room and board included.

Reputable nanny agencies charge high fees but in return should screen applicants. However, because supplying child care has become a booming industry, some agencies simply act as an introductory agency, passing on names of clients and applicants without any checking. Alternative ways of finding a nanny are to advertise in your local paper, or to ask other nannies for referrals.

Always ask for character as well as work references, and always check the references. Ask lots of questions, and follow up if the references seem hesitant or curt. If the references are good, you must ultimately trust your own gut feelings about who the right person is for the job. Decide in advance exactly what time you want your nanny to start and finish work, and exactly what jobs you want her to do. Also decide whether she has to take her vacations at the same time as you, and what your policy is to be on sick pay, should you be unlucky enough to hire a nanny who then breaks her leg on a skiing trip. Find out what the going rate of pay is in your area, then calculate what her take-home pay will be and what you will have to pay in taxes and insurance. Outline what extra perks the job offers—for example, occasional flexible hours, an especially nice room or private bath if she is living in, or perhaps vacations away with you sometimes.

If you only need part-time help or if you work from home, a mother's helper might be a good solution. These are usually adolescents who have no training in child care but will also do some housework or entertain the child while you attend to other activities. You need to be sure that the person you find is intelligent, reliable, and interested in learning about your child. You can find a mother's helper by asking neighbors or calling local schools. Again, you should decide exactly what the job will require before interviewing.

Au pairs tend to be the least expensive option, but may not be suitable if you are working full-time and need someone to take sole care of a baby all day. Usually families take them on through an agency on the basis of a letter, references, and a telephone call, so what kind of person you get and how much experience she has with child care are highly variable. Au pairs can come from other countries or other parts of this country. They can be a good solution for parents with older children, or to help out by baby-sitting for a few hours for parents who work part-time or just need a little extra help. Many au pair employers make the mistake of expecting the au pair to do too much and are then disappointed. The expectations vary by agency, but generally au pairs are supposed to do up to five hours a day of light housework or child care with at least one day a week free, but preferably two. If you imagine a niece coming to stay to help out and fill in time between high school and college and treat the au pair accordingly, you have a better chance of making the relationship work.

4. *Relatives.* Having a relative, often a grandmother, care for the child is very common and can be ideal. Many parents feel much more secure with this arrangement, and it is often the most affordable. As with other types of care, however, the situation is most likely to be successful if you establish up front what the guidelines are and how you would like the relative to interact with your child. The relative needs to respect that you are the parent, and should be willing to follow your lead. You'll need to be able to communicate your position on such things as feeding, discipline, and television viewing. Also, in the case of an older relative, you need to be sure that she has the stamina necessary to care for a young child and will be able to lift a growing baby or toddler and take the child outside to play.

Checking References

Whenever employing somebody to look after your child, whether in your home, in that person's home, or in a day-care center, ask for references, or ask if you can talk to at least two previous employers or clients. Make sure at least one of these is recent (within the past 12 to 18 months), and always follow up all references. Anyone who has left a lot of child-care jobs suddenly and without apparent reason, or who cannot give you the names of at least two employers who have found them satisfactory in a similar job, will not give you the kind of confidence you need. If this is the person's first child-care job, ask for character references as well as references from other jobs. If you will be around a lot when the person starts working for you or if you have older children, providing a first job may be more acceptable than if you are going to be leaving a young child with the caregiver for long periods of time.

Managing Your Child's Care

It is important from the start to be very specific about the kind of care you would like for your child—this may be more difficult to talk about with relatives who are giving their services free than with people who are being paid. It helps to write down a plan of how you would like your child to spend the day. This should include not only details of feedings, sleep schedule, and so on, but also the kind of fun and play times you would ideally expect her to have. Good communication is the key to a successful relationship between you and your child's caregiver. You need to be honest, detailed, and accurate from the outset in explaining and writing down just what you expect from that person.

Continuity of care is important, but if you are worried about some aspect of your child's care, it is better to trust your instincts. If the problem cannot be resolved by talking to your child's caregiver, you may have to make changes. Often the burden of having to choose a caregiver and form a relationship with her falls primarily to the mother, but it is much better if the job can be shared between both parents. Then you can discuss any worries between the two of you rather than let any problems become one person's sole responsibility.

Single Parenthood

Financial restrictions limit the choices of child-care arrangements, since full-time nannies are expensive and hard for a single wage earner to afford.

The facilities offered in a particular area or by an employer will be especially important if you are a single parent. It may be worth considering moving to another area or changing jobs to take advantage of good-quality, economical child care. Many employees offer workplace day care, flexible hours, or allowances to help with the cost of child care. If you work part-time, you may be able to consider teaming up with another parent so you watch the children while the other works and vice versa.

In practical terms you can try to lessen your workload and the strain of bringing up a child alone by building up as effective a support system as possible. It will be beneficial for your child if she can continue to know and have a relationship with the parent she does not live with if that's possible. But other relatives and friends who want to take an interest in her or help you can make a great difference to your quality of life as well. It is very common for single working parents to feel that finding a baby-sitter and arranging to go out are just too much trouble. This simply increases their isolation, however. It is important to have some kind of adult social life and ultimately to make an effort to create a balance in your life.

All parents, whether single or in a permanent relationship, find the friendship of other parents with similar-age children a valuable source of support. These friendships allow you to share and compare experiences and perhaps offer practical help by looking after each other's children. Prenatal classes, parent groups, play groups, and nursery schools are common places to form these friendships.

Communicating with Your Child

When my mother, who lived nearby and was very close to us all, died, my three-year-old son asked if he could go and see her. I tried to explain that her death meant he wouldn't ever see her again, that she was gone. He then asked if he could have her car when he was older. I found it very upsetting.

I never married the father of my two-year-old daughter and we separated when she was six months old, but he has tried to get custody and comes to see her once a week. On most of these occasions he and I end up arguing in front of her. She sometimes says things like "Daddy bad," but I worry that what happens may affect her in the long term.

All parents find some subjects much harder to talk about with their children than others, although exactly what those subjects are varies from household to household. Common topics that cause us to stumble are death, religion, divorce and separation, and sex.

Young children often cannot use language to accurately describe their feelings or the relationships between events. This is especially true of very young children of two or three whose ability to put into words questions and worries may be limited, but whose awareness and anxiety about events they cannot fully understand are nevertheless real. The result is that quite often when parents come up against a subject that is difficult or painful for them to talk about and that may make them feel guilty or anxious, they either avoid young children's questions or put them off with something that has a weak link with the truth. Studies of children whose parents separated when they were under ten, for example, show that in a great number of cases the children were never offered any explanation. Often the parent remaining with the children felt that what had happened was obvious and no words were needed, but the children's version of events showed that this was far from being the case. Obviously, exactly what you choose to say to your children about difficult subjects will always depend on individual circumstances, but there are some broad guidelines that hold true in most instances:

- *Children can understand more than most parents realize.*   This means not only are they likely to be aware of changes in their lives or to pick up information from television, overheard conversations, and things they see, but that they can understand simple explanations better than we often realize.

- *Children are very sensitive to parents' reactions.*   A child might ask questions or begin a discussion, but if an adult's manner and behavior tell the child this is a "no go" area of conversation, if her parents ignore her questions or get angry if the subject arises, the child will quickly pick up on this and generally avoid the topic. Remember, though, that if a child avoids a topic, this does not mean she has forgotten it. Avoiding a topic may lead the child to develop inaccurate and confusing explanations of her own, perhaps more anxiety-provoking than the truth. Remember that not talking about a sensitive subject usually has more to do with sparing our own feelings rather than those of the child.

- *A child's view of the world is generally self-centered.*   Learning to be sensitive to other people and think about how they feel is a slow learning process. This means you do not need to burden a child with long, involved explanations relating to your own feelings. Rather, a child usually wants her questions answered directly and related always to how something will affect her. This child's-eye view can often lead to questions or statements that may upset parents—for example, "Can I have Grandma's car?" on learning of her death, or "Will my daddy still come to see me on my birthday?" Don't think it is just your child being selfish or unfeeling. All young children share this view.

- *Keep explanations simple.*   Do not think that because a child asks questions about complex topics, the child wants to know all the complexities and adult issues involved. Many parents find that after they take a deep breath and launch into a carefully thought-out explanation, the child loses interest after half a sentence. Keep it simple and answer the question she has asked.

- *Information needs updating.*   Parents often breathe a sigh of relief once they have tackled a difficult subject, feeling that now that their child has been told, there is no need to go over it again. The fact is, though, that children forget, sometimes events change, and, as their understanding develops, they need more sophisticated and fuller explanations. Telling a three-year-old everything about how babies are made and are born does not mean you will not have to cover the same ground in different terms for your child as her understanding develops through childhood and adolescence.

Marriage Difficulties

Even in the best marriages, there may be times when you and your partner are not getting along well. You may often be quarreling and arguing, or alternatively not speaking much to each other. These emotional difficulties will affect the way you care for your children. If you are unhappy and under pressure, it is much harder to cope with the demands of young children and to be a strong source of stability in their lives. There are, however, various ways in which you can reduce the effect that your relationship traumas will have on them and minimize the chance of long-term emotional damage.

- Do not criticize the other parent when you talk to your child, or even to friends if your child is nearby. However you may feel personally, it is important for children to be able to appreciate the good sides of their father and mother. Speaking negatively about the other person will be confusing and in the long term potentially damaging for your child.

- Do not threaten to leave home. This is very frightening to a child and undermines the very core of her security.

If events have actually arrived at a point where one of you is going to leave, then it is vital that you talk to your child, prepare her as much as possible, and reassure her that you will both still love her and will still be her father and mother. Give your child details about who is going to take care of her and when and where the leaving parent is going to see her.

Try to continue talking to your partner about the welfare, care, and future of your child.

Separation and Divorce

It is often hard to put aside your own feelings about your ex-partner. But whatever has happened, it's best for your child to be able to go on loving and being loved by both parents. If the other person is not able to fulfill that parental role, then you will have to try to explain this in simple terms. Expect your child to be sad and to grieve this loss, even if she has been abused. Make it very plain that the events are not the result of the child's action or behavior. A young child sees everything in terms of herself and thinks it is her fault if Daddy or Mommy goes away. Emphasize your love and reassure her that she will not lose you. If you feel bitter toward your partner, it can be hard to find that your child still loves and wants that other person, but do not feel angry that your love alone does not seem to be enough. Your child's reaction is a plea for more reassurance.

In the long term it is better for a child if she can maintain a relationship with both parents. It is one of the hard facts of life that long after love has changed to loathing or indifference, you both still have to go on being parents, and the more you are able to communicate, to set aside differences, and to make arrangements based on your child's needs, the better it will be for her.

It is at times like these that other relatives and friends can be very helpful, so turn to them if you can. Grandparents, aunts, and uncles, as well as close friends can all give your child extra love and security and can often talk more dispassionately than you can about events. Their detachment may enable a child to ask questions she senses are taboo with you.

If your young child does not ask you direct questions, don't assume she has not noticed anything. Trying to make sense of events and feelings through play is common. Uncertainty may show in changed behavior—for example, regressing to wanting a bottle when she has left that stage behind, wetting the bed at night, disturbed sleeping, or simply difficult behavior. It is also common to find that children in this situation often start to be more clingy and do not want to let the remaining parent out of their sight, whereas before they were happy to go to school or to play alone for a while. Try to be patient and reassure your child that you will return to pick her up or, in the case of playing in another room, that you are not going to leave suddenly. There is a fine line to be drawn, however, because parents can often assume that every little problem with their child is due to their own marital difficulties and end up doubling their guilt load. Remember, children go through difficult stages anyway, no matter what happens in your family life.

Death, Illness, and Disability

Young children can seem very insensitive when talking about death, especially the death of a loved grandparent. They often ask very practical questions like, "Where is Grandpa?" and "Can I see him?" after hearing of his death because their concept of people is rooted in the physical reality of the body. The idea of a personality and a spiritual presence that can cease to exist is beyond their grasp. Talking about the way in which plants or flowers grow and die, or the way animals die, can help them to understand, although the finality of death is beyond their understanding so that they do not usually show the grief an adult feels. Still, young children may miss and feel the loss of a loved friend or relative who dies. They may ask about the person some time after his death, even though you thought they understood that they would not see him again. Be prepared to be patient and explain simply—exactly what you say will be tempered by your own religious or other beliefs. If the child enjoyed happy times with the person who has died, recall those occasions.

When someone in your child's life is ill, you need to explain the facts simply to her so that she understands the changes in that person's behavior toward her. The way you answer your child's questions about people she may encounter personally or see in the street who have some noticeable disability or handicap is also important in influencing long-term attitudes. If he embarrasses you by pointing and asking loudly in front of the person concerned, give a simple explanation—for example, that person is in a wheelchair because his legs do not work well enough to walk. Later you can tell her that not everyone is as lucky as she is to have a perfect body and mind that work so well. Go on to explain that people whose bodies do not work as well as hers may look or behave differently, but they probably get tired of people asking what is wrong, so it is better to ask later instead of in front of them. Young children are simply curious—prejudices such as fear or pity will be picked up from the way you and other people respond to that curiosity.

Religion

How you answer questions about God as well as about death will naturally depend on your own religious beliefs. If you are ambivalent, expect your child to be influenced by the much more definite views she may hear from peers or at nursery school. It is probably best to be honest about your own feelings while giving your child an idea of the prevalent religious beliefs she will encounter. If you belong to a religion that is a minority in your area, it's a good idea to explain to your child that many people believe certain things but that your family has other beliefs.

Sex and Sexual Abuse

With widespread public advertising about the threat of AIDS, more young children may ask specific questions. "What is a condom?" is just as likely from a four-year-old as "Where do babies come from?" The arrival of a second or a third baby in the family or the birth of a friend's baby may prompt questions. There are many good books if you need help in explaining how babies begin and grow in the womb, but remember that children will forget, and they will need a fuller explanation as they grow older.

Young children are very interested in babies—though it is important to teach your child to touch and hold them (under supervision) with care and gentleness and not allow her to view a baby as a doll she can play with. Strangely, though, young children are often quite unperceptive about the changing shape of their mother or a friend during pregnancy. Most parents find the growth of the unborn baby inside the womb quite easy to explain to young children, using one of the many picture books that are aimed at under-fives. It is often less easy to answer questions about exactly where and how the baby gets out and just how "Daddy's seed" got into the womb in the first place. Even if you find it easy to cover the facts, including the correct anatomical terminology, instilling a sense of discretion as to the time and place for discussion can still prove difficult. One mother, in the seventh month of pregnancy, remembers her four-year-old daughter's clear and merciless questioning in the line at the grocery store: "When exactly did Daddy give you his seed?" In fact, young children usually accept factual information about intercourse and birth without the embarrassment of much older children. Again, be led by your child's questioning, and do not burden her with more information than she wants and is ready for. Use the language and the words you feel comfortable with and also follow your instincts about how and what to tell your child.

Quite separate from the question of how a baby is made is the question of warning your child about sexual abuse. From a very early age—certainly by about two or three—most children have a good understanding of what their "private parts" are. You should choose the language and words you are comfortable with, but the simplest message to give your preschool child is: "Your body is special and it is your own—if anyone touches you in a way you don't like, tell them not to, and tell me right away." Growing public awareness that child sexual abuse appears to be relatively widespread and the resulting media attention have left many parents both fearful for their child's safety and uncertain about what is normal sexual development in a child. A degree of healthy suspicion and awareness is not a bad thing, and some pedophiles do seek out positions of authority and trust that will put them in close contact with children. But at the other end of the spectrum, a few parents may begin to feel anxious about enjoying what is simply a child's natural sensuality. This may take the form of hugging, caressing, and stroking, all of which are perfectly normal. There is nothing wrong in finding pleasure in the sensation of a baby's soft cheek against your own face, in stroking her limbs, or in admiring the perfection of a diminutive body. What is not normal is to find the natural sensuality of children sexually exciting.

What should you do if your child says something that may indicate she has been a victim of sexual abuse? The most important thing is not to panic and overreact: this may decrease the chance of ever discovering what happened. Take what your child says seriously, but also remember that while most children do not make up stories, they do say funny things that, on investigation, turn out not to mean what an adult may think. For example, a three-year-old who said, "I don't like snakes because they go up your bottom," revealed, after a bit more conversation, that this was based on a story from an older child about how a snake could live in the toilet. Also be careful, in your desire to coax your child into telling the truth, not to prompt her with leading questions or to put words into the child's mouth. This is less likely to happen if you let your child tell you what happened in her own time and in her own words, but it is all too easy for an anxious parent with a not very forthcoming child to ask specific questions about what someone did. There is good evidence that young children are likely to say "yes" to this sort of question, and then the question may be repeated by the child as a statement and become part of "the history" of what happened—irrespective of the facts. Cultivating a natural patience when talking with your young child and allowing her to volunteer information at her own pace and in her own words is a valuable skill for any parent to learn. This is true whether you're talking about what she did at nursery school or potential abuse. A child under five is, however, unlikely to be able to make up a sequence of events, including a person and a place.

Physical signs of sexual abuse may be a sore bottom, vaginal discharge in girls, disturbed behavior such as wetting or soiling by a child who has been potty trained for a long while, a disturbed sleep pattern, refusal to eat, anxiety, clinginess, or awareness of sexual acts in speech or behavior. Problems other than sexual abuse can cause these signs and symptoms, so it is important to have these signs and symptoms evaluated by your child's physician immediately.

Sexual abuse may have occurred inside or outside the home. The latter is easier to deal with, because the child is still able to continue to trust those people she loves and still has their support. Abuse inside the home by a member of the family entails an abuse of power and of trust. Insensitive investigation can be traumatic for children, and it has come to be recognized that steps taken to ascertain the truth and then to protect the child from further abuse can in themselves cause as much distress to the child as to constitute secondary abuse. As the parents, you must decide what steps are necessary to protect your own and other children. Teams of physicians, psychologists, and social workers who specialize in the evaluation of suspected child sexual abuse are available at many regional pediatric hospitals to help families with these decisions.

Sexual play and exploration involving looking and touching without the use of force with children of the same age is a normal part of growing up; sexual abuse is not. Sometimes sexual play can get out of hand, and, for example, a brother can seriously abuse a younger sister. If you suspect anything, try to find out what has actually happened by talking to the children separately. If you are worried about this or any other sort of sexual abuse but have difficulty talking to your children, or if you suspect that there has been a case of sexual abuse, contact a social worker or talk to your child's physician as soon as possible.

Research has shown that the attitudes of the parents are relevant to the long-term effects of both the abuse and the investigation, and that children fare best when the parents are very supportive but calm. To do this, parents may need a good deal of support themselves, particularly if such an incident revives memories of sexual abuse a parent may have suffered as a child. Research shows that parents who were sexually abused in childhood are more likely to talk to their own children about sex in general, probably because they are especially aware of the need to educate and protect early.

Children are naturally very curious about bodies—talking about what they can and cannot do is a way of learning about what different parts of the body are called and how they work. Learning about how a child's body differs from an adult's helps to foster a sense of pride and confidence in their own bodies that will lead toward having a good self-image. You can channel this curiosity to encourage your child to learn the basic skills of taking care of her body—brushing teeth and hair, washing hands, taking baths, going to the toilet, choosing the right kind of clothes according to the weather and season, and eating healthy food. You can explain that smoking and eating things that may be harmful—toxic substances that occur naturally like berries and leaves, for example, as well as household poisons—can damage a healthy body.

CHAPTER 15

Protecting Your Child

Safety
Parents' checklist—how to protect your child from injuries
Emergency first aid • Hygiene

Safety

M y eighteen-month-old climbed up onto a stool to try and reach something on the kitchen counter and knocked a cup of hot coffee all over his chest and stomach. He had never climbed up onto a stool before, and I didn't even know he could do it so I thought the coffee was perfectly safe.

We were at a family wedding when my three-year-old started choking on some peanuts he had helped himself to. Fortunately there was a nurse among the guests, and she told us to go straight to the nearest emergency room. It turned out he had inhaled a peanut right into his lung and had to have an operation to get it out before it caused an infection. I had no idea peanuts could be so dangerous for little children.

I left the front door unlocked while I was taking out the trash. I was only out in the backyard for a second, but when I came back inside I found that the front door was wide open and that my two-year-old had gone right out and was standing on the sidewalk. I managed to get to him before he stepped off the curb into the traffic, but I was shaking for a long time. We live on a busy street, but I had no idea he could pull the door open.

M any of the injuries that happen to children could be prevented. With children under age five the problem is that dangers and risks change daily as the child grows and becomes more mobile and curious. It is harder for first-time parents to anticipate and to spot potential dangers when they have no experience of the ways in which children develop. Generally, parents tend to react to the threat of danger rather than anticipate it. But once their child has managed to climb over the safety gate and fallen down the stairs, or moved enough to roll off the changing table, they will recognize these hazards and will not rely on the safety gate or leave their baby alone on the changing table again.

What we all need to do is protect our children by being one step ahead of them and spotting the dangers before an injury happens. When you have a small baby in a crib it might seem a long way off before you need to think of safety gates, the dangers of electrical outlets, long appliance cords, and all the other hazards that might harm a crawling or walking baby. But in fact it is not; many babies are mobile by seven to eight months and can pull themselves to their feet with whatever is handy well before they are a year old. In addition, once you have a baby, you are more likely to be visited by people who have slightly older children. It is better to child-proof your home from the start.

What Are the Most Common Injuries?

According to the National SAFE KIDS Campaign, in the United States, injuries are the single most common cause of death in children ages one to four. In addition, each year, one in four children is injured seriously enough to require medical attention. Babies under age one are most likely to die from suffocation, injuries in motor vehicle crashes, choking, fire and burns, and drowning. For preschoolers ages one to four, drowning is the leading cause of death from injury, followed by fires and burns, pedestrian injury, injuries in motor vehicle crashes, and choking.

PROTECT your child by taking safety measures around the home and when you are out. Always be one step ahead of your child's ability and anticipate what he will soon be able to do.

TEACH about avoiding dangers by what you tell him and by showing him what you do yourself in various potentially dangerous situations.

Buying Products

Many of the products that you buy are regulated by the U.S. Consumer Product Safety Commission (CPSC). The CPSC is an independent federal regulatory agency that was created in 1972 by Congress in the Consumer Product Safety Act. In that law Congress directed the commission to "protect the public against unreasonable risks of injuries and deaths associated with consumer products."

The CPSC has jurisdiction over about 15,000 types of consumer products, from automatic-drip coffeemakers to toys to lawn mowers. The CPSC works to reduce the risk of injuries and deaths from consumer products by:

- Developing voluntary standards with industry.

- Issuing and enforcing mandatory standards; banning consumer products if no feasible standard would adequately protect the public.

- Obtaining the recall of products or arranging for their repair.

- Conducting research on potential product hazards.

- Informing and educating consumers through the media, state and local governments, private organizations, and by responding to consumer inquiries.

To report an unsafe consumer product or a product-related injury, call the CPSC's toll-free hotline at (800) 638-2772, or at (800) 638-8270 for the hearing- or speech-impaired.

Here are some things to pay attention to when purchasing consumer products. Electrical appliances such as hair dryers and lamps should bear a sticker or a mark stating that the product is "UL Listed." This means that the product meets safety standards established by the Underwriters Laboratories.

When purchasing children's products such as cribs and nursery equipment, look for a sticker indicating that the product is certified by the Juvenile Product Manufacturers' Association (JPMA). Experts have developed performance standards (tests) for high chairs, playpens, walkers, portable hook-on chairs, carriages and strollers, gates and enclosures, and full-size cribs because these products are basics that are used often and strenuously. The standards are published by the American Society for Testing and Materials (ASTM), a highly regarded nonprofit organization. Industry members, consumer groups, and staff from the U.S. Consumer Products Safety Commission are involved in developing the standards.

To become JPMA-certified, a product must be tested by an independent testing facility for compliance with the specific ASTM standard. If a product passes the tests, JPMA allows the manufacturer to label it with the JPMA-certified seal. If you are interested in a product but are unsure if it has been JPMA-certified, ask your retailer for assistance or call the manufacturer.

Toys

When purchasing toys, keep an eye out for labels that indicate the age of the child for whom the toy is designed. Choose toys with care. Keep in mind the child's age, interests, and skill level. Look for quality design and construction in all toys for all ages. Be a label reader—look for and heed age recommendations such as "Not recommended for children under three." Look for other safety labels, including: "Flame retardant/Flame resistant" on fabric products and "Washable/hygienic materials" on stuffed toys and dolls.

Under the Federal Hazardous Substances Act and the Consumer Product Safety Act, the CPSC has set safety regulations for certain toys and other children's articles. Manufacturers must design and manufacture their products to meet these regulations so hazardous products are not sold.

Protecting children from unsafe toys is everyone's responsibility. Careful toy selection and proper supervision of children at play are still—and always will be—the best ways to protect children from toy-related injuries.

Parents' Checklist—How to Protect Your Child from Injuries

Choking and Suffocation

Babies are most at risk for choking and suffocation, but older children can be at risk when playing on their own.

One of the first places to check for hazards is the nursery. An unsafe used crib could be very dangerous for your baby. Each year in the United States, about fifty babies suffocate or strangle when they become trapped between broken crib parts or in cribs with older, unsafe designs. A safe crib is the best place to put your baby to sleep. Look for a crib with a certification seal showing that it meets national safety standards. If your crib does not meet these guidelines, destroy it and replace it with a safe crib.

A safe crib has:

- No missing, loose, broken, or improperly installed screws, brackets, or other hardware on the crib or the mattress support.

- No more than 2⅜ inches between crib slats so a baby's head or body cannot fit through the slats.

- A firm, snug-fitting mattress so a baby cannot get trapped between the mattress and the side of the crib.

- No corner posts over 1⁄16 of an inch above the end panels (unless they are over 16 inches high for a canopy) so a baby cannot catch his clothing and be strangled.

- No cutout areas on the headboard or footboard so a baby's head cannot get trapped.

- A mattress support that does not easily pull apart from the corner posts so a baby cannot get trapped between the mattress and the crib.

- No cracked or peeling paint, to prevent lead poisoning.

- No splinters or rough edges.

- DO NOT ever leave a baby alone with a propped-up bottle because he can easily choke on it.

- DO make sure babies cannot get anything pulled tightly around their necks—don't use strings or ribbons to attach pacifiers. Watch for open-weave cardigans and jackets, especially with ribbons or threads around the neck that can catch on a hook or knob and be pulled tight. Open-weave or lacy shawls, blankets, or clothes can also allow fingers to be caught and trapped—babies have actually lost fingers that were trapped and cut off like this. Beware of potentially lethal drawstrings on parkas for older children.

- DO check that there are no hanging cords—for example, from a window blind or curtain—that can catch around a child's neck and strangle him if he falls; again, such tragedies have happened. Make sure no cords or threads are within reach of the crib, and keep string and rope away from children. Teach toddlers never to put things around each other's necks in play, and make sure older children grow up with this message.

- DO keep all plastic bags away from babies and children, and teach children never to put these bags on their heads. If they do, they can suffocate. Very flimsy plastic—for example, on dry cleaning bags—often attracts babies and toddlers because of the rustling sound it makes, but it could easily obstruct breathing if held over their faces.

- DO NOT let your baby or young child get hold of small items such as coins, marbles, Legos, hearing-aid batteries, and buttons, because once he can pick up things it is an automatic reflex to put them into his mouth, and he can easily choke on them.

- DO check that all toys you give to babies and young children are safe, with no small parts that can come loose, or sharp points that may be dangerous.

- DO NOT leave babies alone with finger foods such as carrots, cheese, popcorn, and so on, because pieces can break off and cause choking. Always be on hand when your child is eating. Make older children sit down to eat—do not let them run around, since there is more chance of choking. Always chop up babies' food to a size small enough to swallow. This is especially important with round foods such as hot dogs, carrots, and grapes.

- DO NOT give large, hard candy to babies or young children, and always supervise eating and drinking.

- DO NOT give peanuts to children under four years old because they can easily choke on them or inhale them into their lungs, often without anyone realizing it at the time. A child who has inhaled a peanut or other object will usually begin to wheeze or cough. Take him to your doctor immediately, or to the nearest emergency room if you know he has inhaled something. Peanuts can splinter and cause infection, and the risk of local lung damage rises the longer the nut stays in place. In cases where the peanut is left longer than seven days, more than half the children suffer some damage. Be especially careful on occasions such as weddings or parties or when visiting other homes.

Scalds and Burns

As children learn to crawl, climb, and walk, the risk of burns or scalds increases; be one step ahead of your child's growing curiosity and make safety measures a habit from birth.

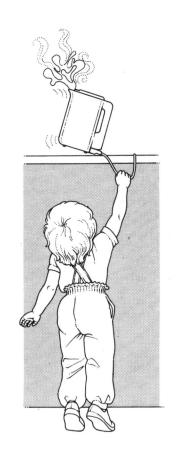

Hot drinks and hot water can scald badly enough to scar permanently, and children have died from severe scald burns. Never drink a hot beverage with a child on your lap, and do not pass hot drinks over the heads of children. Keep all hot drinks in drinking containers or teapots away from the edge of tables, where they can be reached. Do not place containers with hot fluids on tablecloths, which young children can pull down on top of themselves.

Appliances should always be well out of reach and with short electrical cords that do not hang down. Remember, steam can be dangerous and scald badly, so do not leave a kettle simmering unattended.

Stoves can be made safer with a guard around the edge. Make it a habit to always turn pot handles inward and use the burners at the back if you are cooking with only one or two pots. If possible, keep a young child in a playpen or high chair while working in the kitchen. Do not take pots off the stove—for example, to drain spaghetti—with a child under your feet. Never leave a child alone in the kitchen with the stove on. Turn things off and take the child with you to answer the phone or the door. Teach him not to touch the oven door or try to open it.

Do not let your child get into the habit of climbing on chairs to reach kitchen cabinets, cupboards, or anything else near the stoves.

Irons are a common cause of burns. Do not iron where children are likely to be playing, and always unplug and put the iron away completely out of reach to cool down. Do not leave an iron unattended with a child around—remember, an unplugged iron that is still hot can burn badly. Young children love to copy things they have seen grown-ups do. A toy iron and their own ironing board is fine, but emphasize the message that they should never, ever try to iron with your iron.

Always test bath water before putting a child in the tub—children have died from burns they received in baths of very hot water. Always put cold water in first and then add the hot. A plastic strip thermometer is now available to stick to the inside of the tub to check the water temperature. If you do not have a thermometer, test the water with your elbow. Never leave a baby or a toddler alone in a bath, even for a minute when answering the phone or door. Instead, wrap him in a towel and take him with you or let it go if you can. Do not set the thermostat so high that water is very hot when it comes out of the tap because it can burn older children when they go to wash up. You can have your boiler thermostats reset by plumbers or electricians.

Matches and lighters must be kept well out of reach. Do not let children play with matches—again, they will try to imitate you and strike them. Do not indulge in any "blowing out" games with matches or lighters.

The CPSC estimates that half the deaths and one-third of the injuries resulting from electric heater fires occur at night when family members are asleep and the heater unattended. The CPSC is also concerned about the use of power or extension cords that can be too small to supply the amount of current required by the typical portable electric heater. Here are some things you can do:

- Make sure that any heaters are at least three feet away from upholstered furniture, drapes, bedding, and other combustible materials.

- Make sure that the extension cord (if used) is marked #14 or #12 American Wire Gauge (AWG).

- Make sure all heaters are placed on the floor.

- Make sure the heater is turned off when family members leave the house or are sleeping.

Operate heaters away from combustible materials. Do not place heaters where towels or other items could fall on the appliance and trigger a fire. Avoid using extension cords unless absolutely necessary. If you must use an extension cord with your electric heater, make sure it is marked with a power rating at least as high as that of the heater itself. Keep the cord stretched out, and do not let the cord become buried under carpeting or rugs. Do not place anything on top of the cord. Never place heaters on cabinets, tables, furniture, or the like, and never use heaters to dry wearing apparel or shoes.

Preventing Fires

Here are some way to prevent common causes of fires:

* Use a thermostatically controlled deep fat fryer.

* Do not leaving burning cigarettes in ashtrays.

* Never smoke in bed.

* Install automatic smoke detectors—alarms that go off in reaction to smoke. Check their batteries regularly. Make sure you and your family practice a plan for escaping safely from your home in the event of a fire.

* Frequently check that plugs are wired correctly and sockets are not overloaded. Consider installing a circuit breaker to make it impossible to electrocute yourself.

Traffic Injuries

Children as Pedestrians   Outside the home, traffic is the single greatest danger to your child's life. Children under five years old need continual close supervision, and it is worth remembering, as your child grows, that children are not totally reliable in traffic as pedestrians until they are about twelve years old. Judging the speed and distance of traffic from several directions and reacting quickly is too complicated for young children. Many children think that cars can see them and stop. Many children are killed each year just a few hundred yards from their own homes—remember, injuries do not only happen on busy streets. Be just as careful in quieter neighborhoods. Hold your child's hand near a street and in parking lots. Make sure you always cross streets in a safe place. Setting a good example is an important way to teach pedestrian safety.

When your child is old enough to ride a three-wheeler or a bike on the sidewalk with you beside him, teach him to be careful of other people walking on the sidewalk. Do not let him ride across the street—always make him get off and either carry the tricycle over yourself, holding the child with your free hand, or get him to wheel it across beside you to a safe place. Children should ALWAYS wear helmets.

Streets in rural areas or the suburbs without sidewalks can present a special hazard. Keep children between you and the side of the road, and walk so you face oncoming traffic. At dusk or after dark make sure you can be seen clearly by wearing light clothes and a reflective armband, coat, or vest.

Children as Passengers in Cars   We all dread the possibility of a serious car crash, but you can give your children a much better chance of surviving or escaping a crash without serious injury if you ensure that they are safely secured every time they travel in the car.

Protect your kids in the car. According to the National Highway Traffic Safety Administration, the safest place for any child twelve years old or under is in the backseat. Every child should be buckled in a child safety seat, a booster seat, or with a lap/shoulder belt if it fits.

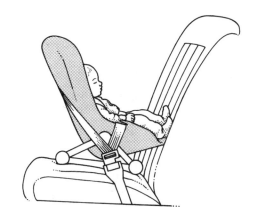

Riding with babies. Infants up to about twenty pounds and up to one year old must ride in a rear-facing child seat. The child seat must be in the BACKSEAT and face the rear of the car, van, or truck. Babies riding in a car must never face the front. In a crash or sudden stop, the baby's neck can be hurt badly. Infants in car seats must never ride in the front seat of a car with air bags. In a crash, the air bag can hit the car seat and hurt or even kill the baby. Never hold your baby in your lap when you are riding in the car. In a crash or sudden stop, your child can be hurt badly or killed.

Riding with young kids. Kids over twenty pounds and at least one year old should ride in the backseat in a car seat that faces the front of the car, van, or truck. It is best to keep kids in the forward-facing car seat for as long as they fit comfortably in it.

Older kids over forty pounds should ride in a booster seat until the car's lap and shoulder belts fit correctly. The lap belt must fit low and snug on their hips. The shoulder belt must not cross their face or neck. Never put the shoulder belt behind their back or under their arm.

Remember:

- All kids are safest in the backseat, in a safety seat or seat belt.

- Always read the child seat instructions and the car owner's manual.

- Test the child seat to ensure a snug fit by pulling the base to either side or toward the front of the car.

Drowning

A baby or a toddler can drown in just two inches of water, so do not let a young child play with water unattended, and never leave a baby or a toddler alone or with a sibling in the bathtub, even for a second. If the doorbell or phone rings or another child needs your attention, take the baby with you.

When children are paddling in a pool or playing at the seashore, at a swimming pool, or beside a river, stay nearby and watch them closely. It's best to have one supervisor for each child.

Teach children to swim as soon as possible, and make sure they learn about water safety, but when your child has learned to swim do not assume that he is drownproof. Being confident about water does not mean he is necessarily safe.

Do not use five-gallon buckets around the house. One child drowns every week in these buckets. They are very attractive to toddlers, who often fall head-first into the buckets while trying to look inside and then cannot get out.

If you have a swimming pool it should be surrounded by a four-sided fence that is at least five feet high and has a self-latching and self-locking gate. Most of the children who drown in swimming pools were seen by their parents just a few minutes before they were found floating in the pool.

Cuts and Other Injuries through Play

Glass around your home is one of the biggest dangers to a young child. It may be in a front or a back door, and is in most patio and French doors. Toddlers can easily trip and go right through a glass door, and older children can crash into a sheet of glass in a door when they get excited and run around. All this may seem a long way in the future when you have a small, helpless, newborn baby who cannot even turn over for himself, but as we said at the beginning, anticipation is the key to preventing injuries.

Check your house and replace glass in doors with either wooden panels or special safety glass. While ordinary glass easily breaks into lethal jagged pieces and splinters, safety glass does not. There are two types—laminated glass is two sheets of ordinary glass stuck to a layer of plastic in between. Although laminated glass rarely breaks, if it does, the pieces stay in place. The second type of safety glass is made by a special process of heating and cooling that makes it less likely to break; it is called "toughened" or "tempered" glass and must be ordered to size. If it does break, it will shatter into small pieces that are relatively harmless. As well as panels of glass in doors or glass doors, look at your low-level windows, especially interior ones, and at glass panels or doors in showers or bathrooms. Glass that is frosted or patterned is unlikely to be safety glass.

Measures can be taken to make glass safer by fixing a plastic film over panels in doors or other areas. Mark dangerous glass with colored strips to make children notice it is there, or board up the area. Do not let toddlers or young children walk around with a glass or anything made of glass in their hands, as they could easily fall and cut themselves.

Keep all knives, scissors, tools, and other dangerous objects out of the way of babies and young children. As they get older, teach them to use dangerous tools safely and only with you beside them. Remember again that children are highly imitative, and keep scissors and razors in the bathroom well out of reach.

Teach children:

- Always to carry scissors, screwdrivers, sharp pencils, or anything else pointing downward, and to walk, never run with them.

- Never to run with a pencil or with a lollipop stick in their mouth.

- Never to touch electrical outlets or plugs. Socket covers are a cheap and useful way to make outlets safer.

- Not to slam doors or play with doors. Fingers can easily get pinched in hinges as well as by the door itself. A device can be fitted at the top of the door to prevent doors from slamming—check at your local hardware store.

Toys

Check all toys periodically for breakage and potential hazards. A damaged or dangerous toy should be thrown away or repaired immediately. Edges on wooden toys that might have become sharp or surfaces covered with splinters should be sanded smooth. When repainting toys and toy boxes, avoid using leftover paint, unless purchased recently, since older paints may contain more lead than new paint does. Examine all outdoor toys regularly for rust or weak parts that could become hazardous.

New toys intended for children under eight years of age should, by regulation, be free of sharp glass and metal edges. Older toys can break to reveal parts small enough to be swallowed or to become lodged in a child's windpipe, ears, or nose. The law bans small parts in new toys intended for children under three. This includes removable small eyes and noses on stuffed toys and dolls, and small, removable squeakers on squeeze toys.

Toys with long strings or cords may be dangerous for infants and very young children. The cords may become wrapped around an infant's neck, causing strangulation. Never hang toys with long strings, cords, loops, or ribbons in cribs or playpens where children can become entangled. Remove crib gyms for the crib when the child can pull up on hands and knees; some children have strangled when they fell across crib gyms stretched across the crib.

Keep toys designed for older children out of the hands of little ones. Follow labels that give age recommendations—some toys are recommended for older children because they may be hazardous in the hands of a younger child. Teach older children to help keep their toys away from younger brothers and sisters.

Even balloons, when uninflated or broken, can choke or suffocate if young children try to swallow them. More children have suffocated on uninflated balloons or pieces of broken balloons than on any other type of toy.

Electric toys that are improperly constructed, wired, or misused can shock or burn. Electric toys must meet mandatory requirements for maximum surface temperatures, electrical construction, and prominent warning labels. Electric toys with heating elements are recommended only for children over eight years old. Children should be taught to use electric toys properly, cautiously, and only under adult supervision.

Poisoning
The Bathroom

- Remember, medicines can poison if used improperly. Many children are poisoned each year by overdoses of aspirin. If aspirin can poison, just think of how many other poisons might be in your medicine cabinet.

- Your aspirin and other potentially harmful products must have child-resistant caps. Aspirin and most prescription drugs come with child-resistant caps. Check to see that yours have them and that they are properly secured. Check your prescriptions before leaving the pharmacy to make sure the medicines are in child-resistant packaging. These caps have been shown to save the lives of children.

- Throw out all out-of-date prescriptions As medicines get older, the chemicals inside them can change, so what was once a good medicine may now be a dangerous poison. Flush all old drugs down the toilet. Rinse the container well, then discard it.

- All medicines must be in their original containers with the original labels. Prescription medicines may or may not list ingredients. The prescription number on the label will, however, allow rapid identification by the pharmacist of the ingredients should they not be listed. Without the original label and container you can't be sure of what you're taking.

- Your vitamins or vitamin/mineral supplements that contain iron must be in child-resistant packaging. Most people think of vitamins and minerals as foods and, therefore, nontoxic, but a few iron pills can kill a child.

The Garage or Storage Area   Many things in your garage or storage area that can be swallowed are terrible poisons. Death may occur when people swallow such everyday substances as charcoal lighter fluid, paint thinner and remover, antifreeze, and turpentine.

- All these poisons should have child-resistant caps and should be stored in the original containers.

- The original labels should be on the containers.

- Make sure that no poisons are stored in drinking glasses or soda bottles.

- Make sure that all these harmful products are locked up and out of sight and reach.

Make sure that whenever you buy potentially harmful products, they have child-resistant closures and are kept out of sight and reach. Post the number of the poison control center near your phone.

Falls

All children fall, but there are things you can do to try to make sure they do not fall too far or too hard. Babies most often fall because they roll off tabletops or other raised areas, so never leave your child alone on a changing table, work surface, bed, or sofa, even if he has not learned to roll over. The next time you turn your back to go to answer the phone may be the first time your child learns to roll over. Rolling over on a bed against a hot radiator is a cause of burns to babies. Do not leave your child in a baby walker near steps or stairs.

When your child begins to crawl—or even before—you need to use a safety gate to guard stairs and doors out of the house that might be left open. A playpen can be useful to put your child in when you need to leave a door open for a short period—for example, while taking the garbage out, or when you want to answer the phone or check on another child.

As your child becomes more mobile, check that there are no lamps or furniture he can pull down on top of himself. Keep chairs pushed into the table or well away so he cannot climb up. Falls from windows, balconies, or roofs are likely to be much more serious, so check that windows are fitted with safety guards. Do not rely on screens for protection—they are meant to keep insects out, not children in.

Use a harness when you put your child in a high chair, stroller, swing, or other baby seat. Remember to anticipate your child's growing ability to climb, move, and show curiosity. Things that could once be easily put out of reach on a table or low shelf may suddenly come within reach when he learns to climb. The safety gate that kept him safe may suddenly become an obstacle to try to climb over, especially if he has seen older children do this. Once your child starts to crawl, teach him to come down stairs backward on all fours.

Beware of dangers such as balconies, stairs, and windows when visiting other houses, or in homes decorated for the holidays that may not be geared to a young child.

Emergency First Aid

In the United States there are approximately 24 million emergency department visits annually. Many more emergency visits are made to doctors' offices. The goal of this section is to help you deal with everyday emergencies.

The best you can do is to take steps to prevent many childhood injuries and other emergencies. But you also need to learn how to recognize and respond appropriately to emergency situations, including how to access local emergency medical services. It is a good idea to learn basic life support procedures, including cardiopulmonary resuscitation (CPR) and the Heimlich maneuver.

In a life-threatening situation, you should call 911 or your local emergency number. However, when your child is sick or injured and it is not life-threatening, your pediatrician or family doctor should usually be the first person contacted. Make sure that the doctor's office is prepared for childhood emergencies: the staff is trained in pediatric emergency care, and the office is stocked with infant- and child-size emergency equipment. Talk to your doctor about how to respond to emergencies: How long should you wait after your child's illness begins before calling the office? How do you reach the office after hours or on weekends?

Basic Life Support/Cardiopulmonary Resuscitation

First, assess the child's condition carefully: the extent of his injuries, his respiratory status, and his state of consciousness. A child who has traumatic injuries, particularly to the head, neck, or spine, should not be moved unless absolutely necessary. An unconscious child or one who has difficulty breathing needs immediate attention. If possible, send someone for help while you take care of the child. If you are alone with the child, administer cardiopulmonary resuscitation (CPR) for one minute and then get help.

To assess consciousness, shake the child gently and shout out his name while watching for movements or changes in his level of alertness. Signs of unconsciousness include a deep state of unresponsiveness, drooling, eyes rolling back, and the tongue falling to the back of the throat. Unconsciousness may be a sign that the child's brain is receiving an insufficient supply of oxygen and that basic life support measures are necessary to ensure that oxygen will be delivered to the brain and other essential organs.

CPR should always be performed in a specific sequence, which can be remembered by the letters ABC—**A**irway, **B**reathing and **C**irculation.

Airway. First clear the child's mouth by sweeping your finger sideways inside the child's mouth. Place the child on his back on a firm, flat surface and then tilt his head and neck so that the airway will be open. To do this, place your hand on the child's forehead and use one or two fingers of your other hand to lift his chin up slightly and tilt his head back until his nose is directly above his ears. This position should be maintained throughout CPR. If you can see something in the airway, try to remove it, but be careful not to push anything farther down into the airway. If you think your child may have suffered a neck or back injury, do not move the child's head or neck. Instead, leave the child in a neutral position. Specialized training is needed to provide CPR to a child with a back or neck injury. You can learn this technique in a CPR class.

Breathing. Once the child's airway is open, you should evaluate his breathing. Look at the child's chest and abdomen for the rising and falling motions that accompany breathing. Listen for breath sounds by positioning your ear close to the child's nose and mouth. Move your cheek over the child's mouth to *feel* the child's breaths. If the child is not breathing, you must breathe for him. This part of CPR is called artificial respiration or artificial resuscitation.

With the head still in the head-tilt/chin-lift position, provide two slow, gentle breaths. The technique for doing this varies depending on the child's size. On a baby, make a seal between your mouth and the baby's nose and mouth; on a larger child, pinch his nose closed and make a seal between your mouth and the child's mouth.

Inhale first, make the seal, and give two slow (1 to 1.5 seconds), gentle breaths. Pause after the first breath you deliver to take in a replenishing breath; this will ensure that your rescue breaths are oxygen-rich. Deliver only enough air to make the child's chest rise; for a baby or a small child, your breaths can be delivered in small puffs, as if you were blowing out a candle. Watch from the corner of your eye to see the child's chest rise. If the chest does not rise or if you have difficulty delivering the breaths, the child's airway may be obstructed. Try to reposition the head and neck to open the airway, then try artificial respiration again.

If this still does not clear the obstruction, you should perform the techniques described below in the section on choking. Between breaths, look and listen for the chest to fall and air to be exhaled. If the child begins to breathe on his own, continue to maintain the open airway, and watch him until help arrives. If the child does not resume breathing on his own, you should assess circulation by checking the pulse before continuing.

Circulation. After providing two breaths, make sure the baby or child's heart is still beating and blood is still circulating. To do this, take the child's pulse. Continue to maintain an open airway while you take the pulse. On an infant, feel for the *brachial pulse* on the inside of the upper arm between the elbow and the shoulder. On a larger child, feel for the *carotid pulse* on the child's neck by placing two fingers in the groove between the neck muscle and the Adam's apple. Feel for the pulse for five to ten seconds. If you do not feel a pulse, have someone else call for emergency help immediately, and continue CPR by doing chest compressions. If there is no one else present to call for help, perform chest compressions for one minute, then leave the baby briefly to summon help yourself. If a pulse is present but the child is not breathing on his own, continue artificial respiration at the rate of twenty breaths per minute for an infant, fifteen breaths per minute for a child.

To perform cardiac support, or chest compressions, place the infant or child flat on a firm surface. (However, do not move a back- or neck-injured person.) Continue to maintain the child's open airway by tilting the head slightly back, with one hand on the child's forehead. Use the other hand to compress the chest.

First locate the proper position for chest compressions. On an infant, imagine a line running between the nipples and over the sternum or breastbone (the bony structure in the middle of the chest). Place three fingers (index, middle, and ring) on the sternum, with the index finger just below the imaginary line. Lift the index finger; this leaves the middle and ring fingers in the proper position on the lower half of the breastbone. Compress the chest at a rate of a hundred compressions per minute (five in three seconds or less). After five sets of compressions, breathe for the baby once; then continue with the compressions. Your compressions should be hard enough to push down on the chest to a depth of about .5 inch to 1 inch.

CPR Summary

Airway

1. Clear mouth and airway with fingers, sweeping sideways.

2. Position head with head-tilt/chin-lift maneuver.

Breathing

1. Look, listen, and feel for breaths.

2. Inhale.

3. Make a seal over baby's nose and mouth or child's mouth, with nose pinched.

4. Deliver two slow, gentle breaths.

5. If chest doesn't rise, reposition head and neck and repeat procedure, or clear obstruction with Heimlich maneuver.

Circulation

On an infant:

1. Feel for brachial pulse on inside of upper arm.

2. If pulse present but not breathing, continue delivering breaths at rate of twenty breaths per minute.

3. If no pulse present, position fingers as outlined on page 429 and deliver chest compressions at a depth of .5 inch to 1 inch (1.3 to 2.5 centimeters) and rate of a hundred compressions per minute.

4. After five sets of compressions, deliver one breath.

5. Reassess condition after ten cycles of five compressions, one breath.

On a child:

1. Feel for carotid pulse on side of neck.

2. If pulse present but not breathing, continue delivering breaths at rate of fifteen breaths per minute.

3. If no pulse present, position hands over sternum and deliver chest compressions at depth of 1 to 1.5 inches (2.5 to 3.8 centimeters) and rate of eighty to a hundred compressions per minute.

4. After five sets of compressions, deliver one breath.

5. Reassess condition after ten cycles of five sets of compressions, one breath.

Choking and Suffocation

Choking and suffocation are significant causes of fatal injury in infants and children up to four years old. In many of these cases, babies and young children choke on food, especially hot dogs, candy, nuts, and grapes. Other items that frequently cause choking include balloons, small toys or parts of small toys, coins, and screws or other small pieces of hardware.

Relieving Choking in Infants and Children   Take a Red Cross or hospital-sponsored class in how to do the Heimlich maneuver. An infant or child who is choking on something will try to clear it himself by coughing, and you should not take action as long as the child is able to cough, cry, or talk. When the baby or child is unable to make any sounds other than a high-pitched, weak cry or a weak and ineffective cough, you should begin the Heimlich maneuver.

Infants.   For infants, the American Academy of Pediatrics and the American Heart Association recommend back blows as the safest and most effective way to clear an obstruction in an infant younger than one year old. Have someone call for help while you begin the back blows. If you are alone with an infant who is choking, perform the back blows first before you call for help. Place the baby face down on your forearm, using your hand to support the baby's head and neck. Rest your forearm on your thigh with the baby's head lower than his chest. With the heel of your other hand, deliver up to five forceful blows high on the baby's back between the shoulder blades.

If this does not clear the blockage, turn the infant over and place him on your forearm, which is resting on your thigh, with the baby's head lower than the body. Place your fingers over the lower half of the baby's breastbone and deliver up to five rapid downward (toward the head) chest thrusts. To position your fingers properly, imagine a line running between the nipples. Place three fingers on the breastbone, with your index finger just below this imaginary line. Lift the index finger; this leaves the middle and ring fingers correctly placed.

Repeat both procedures if the object has still not been dislodged. If the object has been ejected from the throat but has not come out of the baby's mouth, continue to hold him in a downward direction and open his jaw with your thumb over his tongue and your fingers around the lower jaw. If you can see the object, remove it by making a sideways sweep with your fingers. Be careful not to push the object farther down into the baby's airway.

If the baby continues to choke and is unable to breathe, he may quickly turn blue and lose consciousness. If this happens, you will need to perform CPR. First, call for help or send someone to get help. Remember the ABCs of CPR: First, make sure the Airway is open. Second, assess Breathing and deliver artificial respiration if necessary. If you are unable to deliver breaths because of an obstruction, turn the baby over and deliver back blows and/or chest thrusts. Repeat these procedures until you are able to deliver two breaths, then assess Circulation by taking the baby's pulse and apply chest compressions if necessary. If you are not able to clear the obstruction, do not apply chest compressions.

Children More Than One Year Old.   Remember not to intervene if the child is coughing or able to speak or cry. The Heimlich maneuver can be done on a child who is sitting, standing, or lying down. If the child is sitting or standing, kneel, sit, or stand behind him and wrap your arms around him as follows: Make a fist with one hand and place your fist on the child's abdomen below the ribs and above the belly button. Place the second hand around the fist and deliver quick inward and upward thrusts up to five times or until the obstruction is removed and the child is able to speak or cry.

If the child is lying down, kneel at his feet and place the heel of one hand on the abdomen between the ribs and belly button. Place the second hand on top of the first and deliver inward and upward thrusts to dislodge the object. If the child continues to choke and is unable to breathe, he may quickly turn blue and lose consciousness. If this happens, you will need to perform CPR. First, call for help or send someone to get help. Remember the ABCs of CPR: First, make sure the **A**irway is open. Second, assess **B**reathing and deliver artificial respiration if necessary. If you are unable to deliver breaths because of an obstruction, position the child on his back, kneel at his feet, and deliver abdominal thrusts as previously described. Open the child's jaw by placing your thumb over the tongue and your fingers around the lower jaw. If you can see the object, remove it by making a sideways sweep with your fingers. Be careful not to push it farther down into the airway. Repeat these procedures until you are able to deliver two breaths, then assess **C**irculation by taking the child's pulse and apply chest compressions if necessary. If you are not able to clear the obstruction, do not apply chest compressions.

Choking Summary

Is the child choking?

- Child is unable to breathe or speak.
- Child may be turning bluish.
- Child may have high-pitched, weak cry or weak cough.

DO NOT initiate Heimlich maneuver or back blows if child can cough or speak; call your doctor.

Choking relief for an infant or child:

Tell someone to call 911 or your emergency number. If you are alone, attempt choking relief before calling 911.

Infant less than one year:

1. Place baby face down on your forearm resting on thigh.

2. Deliver up to five back blows with heel of hand.

3. If blockage not cleared, turn baby over and deliver up to five rapid downward (toward the head) chest thrusts.

4. Use sideways sweep with fingers to remove foreign body only if you can see it.

5. Apply CPR if child stops breathing.

Child, sitting or standing:

1. Place fist on abdomen below ribs and above belly button. Wrap second hand around fist.

2. Deliver up to five inward and upward thrusts.

3. Apply CPR if child stops breathing.

Child, lying down:

1. Place heel of hand on abdomen between ribs and belly button. Place second hand on top of first.

2. Deliver up to five inward and upward thrusts.

3. Use sideways sweep with fingers to remove foreign body if you can see it.

4. Apply CPR if child stops breathing.

Scalds and Burns

The most frequent cause of burns in infants and toddlers is exposure to hot liquids, either from spilled food or drink or from immersion in too-hot bathwater. The injuries can be quite serious in infants and toddlers because their skin is so thin. Children age three or older are more likely to be burned when their clothing catches fire. These flame burns are often extensive and deep.

Burns are usually categorized by their seriousness.

* First-degree burns involve only the surface of the skin, causing redness but no blistering. Sunburn is usually a first-degree burn.

* Second-degree burns extend into the second layer of skin, causing oozing blisters, redness, and severe pain. Sometimes the surface skin may pull off and parents may not see the blister phase.

* Third-degree burns involve the top two layers of skin as well as part of the tissue underneath, causing blanched, charred, or blackened skin. These burns may destroy the nerves as well, producing a severe injury without severe pain.

When a child is burned, not only his skin is affected. Burns also cause the smallest blood vessels to become leaky, leading to excessive fluids in the tissues and loss of fluid from the blood vessels. Thus dehydration and shock are major concerns after a burn. Other damage also may occur to various physiologic systems in the body.

In a Burn Emergency   For third-degree burns (waxy, pale-looking, charred, or blackened), do the following: First, smother flames (by wrapping child in a blanket or other cover and rolling the child) and remove smoldering or wet clothes, but not clothes that stick to the burn.

CALL 911 OR YOUR LOCAL EMERGENCY NUMBER. WHILE WAIT-
ING FOR THE AMBULANCE, do the following steps:

- Assess **A**irway, **B**reathing, and **C**irculation, and give CPR if child stops breath-
  ing. (Deliver two breaths by artificial respiration before calling 911 if child is
  not breathing.)
- Cover burned area with a clean cloth.
- Elevate burned extremity.
- Treat for shock if necessary by elevating legs to be higher than the level of the
  head.
- Keep child warm and reassured.
- DO NOT put ice on burn.
- DO NOT put grease or butter on burn.
- DO NOT cover burn with fluffy material that could stick to wound.

For second-degree burns (reddened, blistered, painful), do the following:

PROVIDE FIRST AID AND TAKE CHILD TO THE EMERGENCY
DEPARTMENT.

FIRST AID:

- Remove smoldering or wet clothes.
- Immerse burned area in cool water for five minutes or cover with a clean, wet
  cloth.
- Wash burn with soap and water and pat dry.
- Cover burned area with a clean cloth.
- Elevate burned extremity.
- Take child to the emergency department as soon as possible.
- DO NOT put ice on burn.
- DO NOT put grease or butter on burn.
- DO NOT break blisters.

For first degree burns (reddened areas, no blistering), do the following:

PROVIDE FIRST AID AND CALL YOUR DOCTOR if burn is larger than
the child's hand.

FIRST AID:

- Remove clothing covering burned area.
- Immerse burned area in cool water for five minutes or cover with clean, wet
  cloth.

- Wash burn with soap and water and pat dry.

- Leave burned area uncovered, or cover with loose, sterile, gauze bandage.

- Give acetaminophen for pain.

- DO NOT apply grease or butter, as these can lead to infection.

Chemical Burns

If your child does get a caustic chemical on him, flush immediately and thoroughly with cool water. Hold the affected area under cool running water for at least five minutes, making sure not to let the water and chemical splash into your child's eyes. If the chemical gets into his eyes, see "Foreign Body in the Eye."

In a Chemical Burn Emergency

PROVIDE FIRST AID AND CALL YOUR DOCTOR OR POISON CONTROL CENTER, OR TAKE YOUR CHILD TO THE EMERGENCY DEPARTMENT.

FIRST AID:

- Flush area immediately with water for at least five minutes or until all traces of chemical are gone.

- Shower your child and remove any of his clothes that may have chemical on them.

- Cover burned area with cool, wet cloths.

- Follow instructions given by doctor or poison control center.

Electrical Injuries

PROVIDE FIRST AID AND CALL YOUR DOCTOR, OR TAKE YOUR CHILD TO THE EMERGENCY ROOM.

In an Electrical Injury Emergency

FIRST AID:

- FIRST, SEPARATE VICTIM FROM SOURCE OF CURRENT.

- Do not touch victim if he is still in contact with the current. Stand on a dry area (newspaper, blanket, rubber mat, etc.), and use a nonconducting object such as a wooden board or broom handle to knock cord away from victim; or pull child away from cord with a rope or strong cord looped around his arm or foot, or turn off power at main switch or fuse box.

- CALL 911 OR YOUR LOCAL EMERGENCY NUMBER if there has been any loss of consciousness or cardiopulmonary arrest. Administer two breaths first before calling.

WHILE WAITING FOR THE AMBULANCE:

- If child has been thrown and back or neck injury is possible, immobilize his back and neck with firm pillows or rolled-up blankets or towels placed around his head, neck, shoulders, and torso.

- Assess **A**irway, **B**reathing, and **C**irculation, and give CPR if child has stopped breathing.

- Treat burns (see above).

- Keep child warm and treat for shock if necessary.

- DO NOT move child if back or neck injury is suspected.

- CALL YOUR DOCTOR if there has been no loss of consciousness and if injuries appear less severe.

Falls

Children who are drowsy, limp, or pale after a fall, or those who vomit or who appear dazed, should always be taken to the emergency department. The key things to check are whether your child is conscious, whether he is breathing, and whether there is any bleeding. If the child has stopped breathing, give mouth-to-mouth resuscitation and then get him to the hospital. If the child is breathing but is unconscious or very drowsy, it can be dangerous for him to remain lying on his back because the tongue or any vomit may block the throat and stop his breathing. For this reason it is important to place him in what is called the recovery position (see illustration below) and then get him to the hospital.

If your child is conscious but you think he may have broken a bone or have some kind of internal injury, don't move him unless you absolutely have to. If you don't know what is wrong or you think the child may be seriously injured, always call an ambulance.

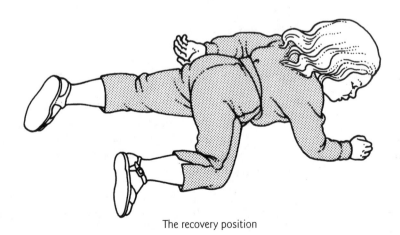

The recovery position

Bleeding

External Bleeding   Most minor cuts or scrapes can be taken care of at home by cleaning the wound gently with soap and water and then covering it with a sterile bandage. Observe the wound for several days for signs of infection such as redness, tenderness, warmth, and/or swelling. If these signs appear or if the wound is deep, call your doctor.

Wounds that are deep or that gape open or bleed heavily may require emergency medical care. Blood spurting from a wound indicates that a nearby artery may have been cut and that emergency action is needed. The first priority in treating any serious bleeding injury is to prevent excessive blood loss. Direct pressure to a wound usually will stop even severe bleeding. But sometimes applying direct pressure may cause further tissue damage. In such cases you can apply pressure to the main artery that supplies the injured area. The main arteries can be accessed in the armpit (if an arm or a hand is bleeding) and the groin (if a leg or a foot is bleeding). After bleeding has been controlled, attention must be given to preventing infection and promoting healing. Some wounds, especially those on the face and neck, require stitches. If you aren't sure whether stitches are needed, take the child to your doctor or to the emergency department to have the wound evaluated. Tourniquets are no longer considered necessary for stopping bleeding in children, and can cause serious damage.

If a body part is partially amputated, stop the bleeding by direct pressure and by compression on the main arterial supply. Then wrap the wound carefully to immobilize the injured area. If a body part is totally amputated, wrap the severed part in a clean cloth and then in a plastic bag. Keep the part cool and take it with you to the emergency department.

In an Emergency

CALL 911 OR YOUR LOCAL EMERGENCY NUMBER if the child is bleeding severely or if bleeding won't stop or if the child shows signs of respiratory distress or shock.

WHILE WAITING FOR THE AMBULANCE:

- Apply direct pressure to wound.

- Assess **A**irway, **B**reathing, and **C**irculation, and give CPR if child stops breathing.

- Keep child warm, rested, and reassured.

PROVIDE FIRST AID AND TAKE CHILD TO EMERGENCY DEPARTMENT IF:

- You are unable to stop the bleeding.

- An object is impaled in the wound; immobilize object before moving the child.

- Wound has a gaping appearance.

- Wound is on face or neck.

FIRST AID:

- Apply direct pressure to wound.
- Press sterile gauze or clean cloth against wound.
- Hold with firm pressure for fifteen minutes or until bleeding stops.
- If blood soaks through cloth, add more gauze or cloth, but DO NOT remove the first cloth from the wound.
- If severe bleeding continues, apply pressure to main arterial supply at the groin or armpit.
- Elevate the wound above the level of the heart.
- Bandage the wound, leaving gauze or cloth compresses in place.
- Wrap and tie bandage firmly, but not so tightly that you cut off circulation; make sure you can still feel a pulse in the extremity.
- Watch child for signs of breathing difficulty or shock.
- DO NOT remove an impaled object.
- DO NOT apply a tourniquet.

FOLLOW-UP:

- Check if child has had a tetanus shot in past five years; if not, get a booster shot.
- Watch wound for signs of infection (redness, swelling, heat, tenderness, or discharge); if present, call your doctor.

Internal Bleeding   A child who has sustained a sharp or crushing blow to the body may bleed internally even when there are no apparent signs of injury on the outside. Thus, if your child has been injured, or if he has fallen, you should observe him carefully for signs of internal bleeding.

In an Emergency

CALL 911 OR YOUR LOCAL EMERGENCY NUMBER if child shows these signs of shock or respiratory distress:

- cold, clammy skin
- rapid or weak pulse
- pallor
- restlessness
- breathing difficulty

WHILE WAITING FOR THE AMBULANCE

* Assess **A**irway, **B**reathing, and **C**irculation, and give CPR if child stops breathing.

* Keep child warm, rested, and reassured.

* Elevate child's legs to maximize blood flow to the brain.

CALL YOUR DOCTOR IMMEDIATELY if your child has these symptoms of internal bleeding:

* Blood coughed up from the lungs: bright red and/or frothy.

* Vomited blood-vomit may be red or brown in color, with consistency of coffee grounds.

* Blood in the stools or urine.

* Hard and tender abdomen (feels full when child is resting, and it hurts when touched).

* Bleeding from nose or ears.

Poisoning

Make sure you have the phone number of a nearby poison control center posted near your phone. Certified poison control centers that are staffed twenty-four hours a day are located in about half of the states and are able to provide callers with immediate information about thousands of poisons. The number for your local poison control center should be listed at the front of your telephone directory, along with other emergency numbers. If you have trouble locating a local poison control center, call the nearest hospital and ask them whom you should call in case of poisoning. Post that number near your phone.

Whenever you suspect an accidental ingestion, call the poison control center immediately, read to them the label of the substance your child has ingested, and follow their directions carefully. They may recommend that you give your child syrup of ipecac, a substance that will cause your child to vomit. Syrup of ipecac is available without a prescription at most pharmacies; however, it is sometimes kept behind the counter, so you may have to ask your pharmacist for it. Keep some on hand as long as there are toddlers or infants in the house, but do not give it to your child until told to do so by a doctor or poison expert. Some poisons will do more damage to your child if they are vomited. Activated charcoal is another agent that may be used in a hospital setting in cases of poisoning. This is a gritty material that will absorb poisons in your child's digestive tract so he can eliminate them safely. Most children will not swallow activated charcoal willingly, as it has an unpleasant taste and texture. Try adding it to chocolate syrup. In the emergency department, if necessary, activated charcoal may be given to your child through a tube connected to his stomach.

Has Your Child Been Poisoned? You may find evidence of an accidental ingestion before any symptoms of poisoning have appeared. For example, your child may tell you he ate something, or show you an empty container. Or you may not realize your child has ingested a poison until you notice symptoms. The symptoms your child exhibits may help identify the poison he has ingested. However, many poisons produce symptoms that are nonspecific, meaning that you may not even recognize them as symptoms of poisoning.

Nonspecific Symptoms

- Sudden change in child's level of alertness or consciousness

- Changes in his heart or breathing rate

- Muscle weakness, lack of coordination, stumbling, or falling down

- Dilation or contraction of the pupils or blurry vision

- Flushed, pale, or sweaty skin

- Vomiting

- Excessive drooling

- Unusual breath odors

Consider the possibility of mushroom poisoning if your child has gastrointestinal symptoms in late summer or early fall. Symptoms may occur ten to fourteen hours after ingestion and may include violent abdominal pain, vomiting, fever, diarrhea, blood in the urine, and rapid heartbeat. These symptoms may be followed by apparent remission, but they can ultimately lead to kidney failure, coma, and death.

What to Do if Your Child Has Been Poisoned

Call the poison control center immediately if your child has ingested, inhaled, or been splashed with a known poison or a substance that may be poisonous. If possible, have one person call the center while another person stays with the child to provide first aid. Pharmacists and doctors who staff the center have access to a computer database that contains detoxification information on hundreds of thousands of substances. They will be able to tell you what to do. In general, you want to minimize your child's toxic exposure, either by diluting it or eliminating it from his body. Elimination is usually accomplished by inducing vomiting. Poisons that are caustic, such as drain cleaner and paint remover, should not be vomited, however, as they can cause further tissue damage on their way up the esophagus. Many household products give exposure information on their labels, but this information is not always up-to-date. You will be better off if you rely on the poison control center.

In a Poisoning Emergency

If you know what your child has ingested:

CALL THE POISON CONTROL CENTER OR EMERGENCY DEPART-MENT.

Tell them what your child ate or drank, when he ate or drank it, how much of it he ate or drank, and your child's condition now. Wait for the poison control center to give you instructions.

If you are told to induce vomiting:

In addition to a glass of water, give child syrup of ipecac as follows:

- One teaspoon for infants less than one year of age
- One tablespoon for older babies and children
- Two tablespoons for adolescents

If you don't have syrup of ipecac, give your child milk or lukewarm water, then tickle the back of his throat with your finger. If vomiting does not occur, repeat the procedure once. When your child vomits, have him hold his head down between his knees so he will not swallow vomit. Hold a baby face down across your knees. Save material vomited.

If you are told NOT to induce vomiting but to dilute poison:

Give child one or two glasses of milk or water.

If you don't know what your child has ingested:

CALL THE POISON CONTROL CENTER OR EMERGENCY DEPART-MENT and tell them what you do know. Wait for their instructions.

CALL 911 OR TAKE YOUR CHILD TO THE EMERGENCY DEPART-MENT if told to do so by the poison control center. Take to the hospital:

- empty containers that contained ingested substances
- any vomited material

WHILE WAITING FOR THE AMBULANCE:

- DO NOT induce vomiting or give liquids to a child who is unconscious or convulsing.
- Assess **A**irway, **B**reathing, and **C**irculation, and give CPR if child stops breathing.
- Treat for shock if necessary.

Drowning

Rescue the child without putting yourself at risk. A large child or teenager, panicked by fear of drowning, may flail and fight if you jump into deep water to save him, and unless you are a very strong swimmer and knowledgeable about life-saving techniques, you may find yourself pulled down by the "victim." A safer approach that you can use is to lie down on your belly at the edge of the pool or lake and reach out to the child with your hand or foot, or with a board, stick, or rope, with which you can pull him to safety. If you must wade out away from shore to reach the child, take with you a rope or buoy he can grab onto. In this way he will not have to grab onto you, and you will be able to maintain your balance as you pull him back to safety. If you cannot reach the child without swimming to him, again, take something for him to grab onto. When you throw a rope or a buoy to a drowning victim, try to throw it past him, then pull it back to within his reach.

Give breathing assistance to a child who is not breathing. If a child in the water is not breathing and if the water is shallow enough for you to stand up, you can begin delivering breaths while the child is still in the water, floating on his back. After delivering a few breaths, make sure someone has gone for help and then move the child onto flat land.

Assess Airway, Breathing, and Circulation and deliver CPR if the child has stopped breathing. Continue to provide CPR until the child begins to breathe on his own or until emergency personnel arrive. Treat for shock if necessary. Keep the child warm and rested until help arrives. Any child who has lost consciousness, stopped breathing, or possibly aspirated (inhaled) water into his lungs should be evaluated in an emergency department, even if he appears to have been revived successfully. Water aspirated into the lungs can lead to later complications, including lung infections and cardiopulmonary dysfunction.

In an Emergency

1. RESCUE THE CHILD without putting yourself at risk.

2. PROVIDE TWO BREATHS BY ARTIFICIAL RESPIRATION to a child who is not breathing.

3. CALL 911 OR YOUR LOCAL EMERGENCY NUMBER, THEN CONTINUE CPR if child is not breathing.

WHILE WAITING FOR THE AMBULANCE:

- Monitor Airway, Breathing, and Circulation, and give CPR if child stops breathing.
- Keep child warm, rested, and reassured.
- Treat for shock if necessary.
- Treat for hypothermia if necessary.

4. TAKE CHILD TO EMERGENCY DEPARTMENT if at any time he lost consciousness, stopped breathing, or possibly aspirated water into his lungs.

5. CALL YOUR DOCTOR if child was submerged for longer than a moment, even if he seems to have suffered no ill effects.

Head Injuries

Of all the injuries your child may sustain, head injury is potentially the most serious. Head injuries are responsible for most injury-related deaths in children and are also the most frequent cause of disability. Yet most head injuries are minor and represent little more than bumps and scrapes. Since the scalp is so richly supplied with blood vessels, however, even small cuts may bleed profusely, and minor bruises may swell to the size of an egg. While these injuries may look serious, they usually can be handled at home with proper attention to signs of complication.

More severe head injuries produce immediate unconsciousness and demand immediate emergency management. In between these two extremes are those head injuries that may appear minor at first but may develop into something very serious. This can happen, for example, when the injury causes bleeding inside the skull; only when the bleeding begins to put pressure on the brain do symptoms appear. Unless treated, this type of injury can be fatal. Head injuries also may be associated with other serious injuries, especially to the neck and back.

In an Emergency

CALL 911 OR YOUR LOCAL EMERGENCY NUMBER IF:

- Child loses consciousness for longer than five minutes.

- Child may have injured his neck or back.

- Child shows symptoms of severe head injury within one hour of injury:
    — repeated vomiting
    — drowsiness or lethargy
    — irritability
    — seizures
    — vision, speech, or mobility problems
    — persistent severe headache
    — dizziness
    — unequal pupils
    — liquid oozing from ears or nose
    — pallor
    — unconsciousness (inability to be wakened)

WHILE WAITING FOR THE AMBULANCE:

- If child may have injured neck or back, immobilize by placing firm pillows or rolled-up blankets or towels around his head, neck, shoulders, and torso.

- Monitor **A**irway, **B**reathing, and **C**irculation, and give CPR if child stops breathing.

- Use direct pressure to control bleeding.

- Apply ice to reduce swelling.

- Keep child warm, rested, and reassured.

TAKE CHILD TO EMERGENCY DEPARTMENT IF:

- Child loses consciousness, even briefly.

- Open wound has gaping appearance or bleeding cannot be stopped.

- Child appears stunned, confused, or disoriented.

- Child has no memory of the event.

- Child shows symptoms of complications within seventy-two hours of injury:
  — headache
  — vomiting more than two or three times
  — inability to be wakened
  — unusual drowsiness or sleepiness
  — unusual behavior, agitation
  — seizures or shaking spells
  — confusion
  — one-sided weakness
  — unsteady gait or balance problems

FIRST AID:

- Stop bleeding with direct pressure.

- Apply ice for swelling.

Foreign Bodies

Foreign-body aspiration—breathing in a small object—is one of most common causes of fatal injury in children under five years old. It should be suspected whenever a child has a sudden onset of coughing, choking, or gagging. When a child over one year of age is choking and is unable to speak, you should immediately begin the Heimlich maneuver. If the child can still speak, the airway is not completely obstructed, and the Heimlich maneuver should not be used, as it can turn a partial obstruction into a total obstruction. Instead, a child with a partial obstruction should be taken immediately to the emergency department for removal of the foreign body. Foreign bodies that lodge deeper in the respiratory tract—for example, in the trachea or bronchi—can be more difficult to recognize. A child with this problem may have a mild cough and wheezing, or he may suddenly appear exhausted, limp, and bluish, with a slow breathing and heart rate, with tongue protruding, and with blood-tinged drool. This is a medical emergency and demands immediate attention in an emergency department.

Foreign Body in the Ear   Children like to put small objects, such as peas, beans, and beads, into their ears. These can cause pain and decreased hearing and should be removed by your doctor. Don't try to remove an object yourself with either a swab or tweezers, as you may push it in farther and damage the eardrum. Insects also may crawl inside a child's ear and become trapped. This can be extremely painful as well as upsetting if the bug continues to wiggle and buzz. If this happens to your child, put several drops of warm mineral oil or alcohol into the ear canal to kill the insect; then take your child to a doctor to have the insect removed.

In an Emergency

CALL YOUR DOCTOR if you saw the child put something into his ear or if he has symptoms of a foreign body in his ear such as:

- ear pain
- decreased hearing

FIRST AID:

- If an insect has crawled into the ear: put several drops of warm mineral oil or alcohol into the ear canal; then take child to the doctor.
- DO NOT try to remove the object yourself unless you can grasp it with your fingers; don't use swabs or tweezers.

Puncture Wound/Embedded Foreign Object   Puncture wounds range in severity from splinters to bullets and include wounds caused by any sharp objects that puncture the skin and deeper tissues. Puncture wounds often cause little visible bleeding. However, deep penetration by the offending object may lead to serious infections, tetanus, internal bleeding, or organ damage.

In an Emergency

CALL 911 OR YOUR LOCAL EMERGENCY NUMBER for deep puncture wounds or embedded object. Try not to move your child.

WHILE WAITING FOR THE AMBULANCE:

- Monitor **A**irway, **B**reathing, and **C**irculation, and give CPR if child stops breathing.
- Keep child warm, calm, and reassured.
- Keep injured area elevated if possible.
- Treat for shock if necessary.
- Immobilize the object by carefully wrapping wounded area with bandages or clean cloths.

DO NOT attempt to remove the object.

FIRST AID for shallow puncture wounds:

- Wash your hands with soap and water.
- Cleanse the wounded area with soap and water.
- Use gentle pressure to encourage bleeding of wound.
- Inspect the wound to see if part of object still remains. Apply pressure again until object is gone.
- Bandage the area with sterile dressing.

FIRST AID FOR MINOR PUNCTURE WOUNDS OR SPLINTERS:

- Wash your hands with soap and water.

- Carefully remove object with tweezers sterilized in rubbing alcohol or over an open flame. (Allow tweezers to cool.) Pull the splinter out at the same angle at which it entered the skin. Tiny splinters need not be removed, as they will work themselves out. If a small splinter is embedded, you may need to loosen it with a sterilized needle and then pull it out with tweezers.

- Use gentle pressure to encourage bleeding of the wound. If an object is deeply embedded, see your doctor for removal.

- Wash area with soap and water.

- Bandage the area with sterile dressing.

FOLLOW-UP:

- Call your doctor to review your child's tetanus immunization status.

- Watch for signs of infection: redness, warmth, swelling, pus, tenderness.

- Seek medical attention if necessary.

Foreign Body in the Eye   Any foreign body that gets into an eye must be removed or it can become embedded in the eye or scratch the cornea. Small particles may not be obvious at first, but they can cause red, teary eyes, pain, and possibly visual problems. Some particles can be removed easily at home; however, after removal, you should continue to watch for pain and swelling, which may be signs of corneal abrasion.

In an Emergency

TAKE YOUR CHILD TO THE EMERGENCY DEPARTMENT if:

- An object is embedded in his eye.

- The object cannot be removed by procedures described below.

DO NOT try to remove an embedded object; loosely cover the involved eye before going to the emergency department.

REMOVAL OF A FOREIGN BODY IN THE EYE:

- Wash your hands before examining your child's eyes.

- Tell your child to blink repeatedly; tears and blinking may flush out small particles such as dust.

- If you can see a small particle floating on the surface of the eyeball, try to dab it out with the moistened corner of a clean cloth or tissue, or flush with water from an eye dropper.

- If the particle is still present, gently pull the upper lid down over the lower lid and hold for a moment.

- Check lower eyelid by having your child look up while you gently pull out the lower lid.

- Dab the particle out with the moistened corner of a clean cloth or tissue.

- Check the upper lid by having your child look down while you place a cotton-tipped swab across the eyelid. Gently pull the eyelid up and over the swab to expose the inner lid.

- Dab out the particle with the moistened corner of a clean cloth or tissue.

- DO NOT let your child rub his eye.

- DO NOT touch your child's eyeballs with your fingers.

Foreign Substance in the Eye   Chemicals that are splashed into a child's eye should be flushed out immediately by holding the eye open and pouring large amounts (3 to 4 quarts) of water directly into the eye. Hold the child so the injured eye is lower than the other eye, so the water will not run into the healthy eye. Although your child may scream or cry, it is important to wash out the chemical quickly, immediately, and thoroughly (continuously for ten minutes or more) to avoid damage to the eye. Cover the eye loosely with gauze and take the child to the emergency department. DO NOT let your child rub his eye. Take the container with you that held the substance.

In an Emergency

PROVIDE FIRST AID AND TAKE CHILD TO THE EMERGENCY DEPARTMENT if a chemical is splashed in his eye.

FIRST AID:

- Flush the eye immediately by holding the eye open, and pour 3 to 4 quarts of water onto the eye.

- Make sure the chemical doesn't splash into the other eye

- Continue to flush the eye for ten minutes or more

- Cover the eye loosely with gauze.

- Take the container that held the chemical with you to the emergency department.

- DO NOT let the child rub his eye.

Foreign Body in the Nose   A foreign body in the nose is also quite common in children. You may or may not be aware that your child has put something in his nose; however, suspect a foreign body when your child has difficulty breathing on one side or a foul-smelling discharge from one side.

Using an instrument called a rhinoscope, the doctor will be able to look up the nose and may be able to remove the object in her office, or this can be done in the emergency department. Occasionally surgery is required for objects that are pushed back too far.

In an Emergency

CALL YOUR DOCTOR OR TAKE CHILD TO THE EMERGENCY DEPARTMENT IF:

- You are unable to remove an object in your child's nose.

- Your child has symptoms of a foreign body in the nose:

  — difficulty breathing from one side

  — foul-smelling discharge from one side

FIRST AID:

- Tell your child to breathe in through his mouth and then blow out through his nose.

- Hold the noninvolved nostril closed, forcing all the air behind the foreign body.

- Repeat this several times.

- If you can see an object and can reach it with your fingers, try to remove it carefully.

- DO NOT insert anything into your child's nose that could push the object in farther.

Swallowed Foreign Body   Children under five years of age frequently swallow small objects such as stones, toys, and coins. Rounded, smooth objects smaller than 20 mm in diameter (less than 1 inch, or about the size of a quarter) usually will pass through the gastrointestinal tract with no complications. However, sharp, pointy, or long objects may become lodged in the esophagus or the intestines and may need to be removed in the emergency room. In addition, an alkaline battery as well as objects that contain mercury or lead may cause poisoning and must be removed immediately.

You may know or suspect that your child has swallowed something because he may tell you. Or your child may come to you complaining of pain in the upper part of the chest and difficulty swallowing, and he may salivate heavily. These symptoms indicate an esophageal obstruction. If you suspect that your child has swallowed a foreign object, call your doctor immediately. You may be directed to take your child to the emergency department. If the object is known to be small, smooth, and not lead or mercury, the doctor may suggest waiting for a few days to see if the object is passed spontaneously. Abdominal symptoms such as fever, pain, vomiting, or blood in the bowel movements suggest a possible abdominal perforation and may require emergency surgery.

In an Emergency

TAKE YOUR CHILD TO THE EMERGENCY DEPARTMENT if he has swallowed a foreign object and has any of these abdominal symptoms:

- fever
- abdominal pain
- vomiting
- bloody bowel movements

CALL YOUR DOCTOR IMMEDIATELY if you think your child has swallowed a foreign object. Symptoms include:

- complaint of pain in the upper part of chest
- difficulty swallowing
- heavy salivation

Eye Injury   Eye injuries may result from a foreign object or substance getting into the eye or from a blow to the eye. All eye injuries should be taken seriously, as the consequences of damage to the eye may be severe and long-lasting. Even if at first an injury appears minor, your child should be watched carefully to ensure that he has not received a serious but less obvious injury. For example, a scratched cornea cannot be seen by the naked eye but is extremely painful and requires medical treatment to promote healing and prevent infection. Inconsolable crying in an infant may be a reaction to a scratched cornea.

Blow to the Eye

A blow to the eye may produce swelling around the eye socket, a black eye, a laceration to the eyeball or eyelid, or other damage to the eyeball that may not be obvious at first, such as a scratched cornea, fracture of the bone around the eye, or bleeding into the eye.

In an Emergency

CALL YOUR DOCTOR OR GO TO THE EMERGENCY DEPARTMENT if your child has suffered a blow to the eye and:

- Eye is bleeding.
- Child experiences double vision, loss of vision, or severe pain in eye.

  FIRST AID:

- Apply an ice pack, covered with a towel, if there is swelling and/or discoloration but no bleeding.
- If there is bleeding, loosely cover the eye but do not apply pressure.

- DO NOT bandage both eyes if only one is injured; covering both eyes can frighten a child unnecessarily.

Shock

Recognizing and Treating Shock "Shock" is the word used to describe the shutdown of the body's systems when the tissues are deprived of oxygen. It is different from electric shock, which refers to an electrical impulse that causes a "short-circuiting" of the nervous system. Shock can result from trauma-induced bleeding; from fluid and electrolyte loss caused by diarrhea, vomiting, or other illnesses; from fluid loss associated with severe burns; from heart disease; from a severe allergic reaction called anaphylaxis; or from a massive bacterial infection (septic shock). Shock can be difficult to recognize and can appear to come on quite suddenly. This is because the physiological events that lead to shock often occur without any apparent symptoms. Thus your child should be treated for shock whenever he has suffered a traumatic injury, or if he has lost significant fluids due to persistent diarrhea, or if he has a high fever, is lethargic, has difficulty breathing, or in any other way appears seriously ill.

When a child goes into shock, his lips, gums, and fingernails may appear bluish, and his skin may appear mottled and clammy. These signs indicate impending circulatory failure. SHOCK IS A MEDICAL EMERGENCY. If possible, have one person stay with the child while someone else calls 911 or the local emergency number. If you are alone with a child in shock, check his breathing first and apply CPR if he is not breathing; then call 911. The next steps are designed to maximize blood flow to the vital organs such as the heart and brain, to minimize blood loss, and to make sure the child is able to breathe. If the child has suffered a traumatic injury and may have hurt his neck or back, DO NOT MOVE HIM. If no neck or back injury is suspected, move the child to a safe place and lay him down. Cover the child to keep him warm and try to keep him quiet and calm until help arrives. If the child is conscious and not bleeding heavily, elevate his legs to maximize blood flow to the brain. If he is unconscious or bleeding heavily, turn him on his right side and watch carefully to make sure his airway is open. Apply moderate direct pressure to wounds to stop bleeding. Stay with the child until help arrives, keep him calm and reassured, monitor his condition, and provide CPR if necessary.

Sprains/Broken Bones/Dislocations

Children of all ages frequently suffer bumps and bruises, strains and sprains, and sometimes even broken bones or dislocations. For babies and toddlers, falls are the most frequent cause of these injuries. Older children often injure themselves on the playing field or on bicycles, skates, or skateboards.

Only a few situations call for emergency medical care requiring ambulance transportation. The most critical of these is a neck or back injury. Children with these injuries must not be moved, as any movement may cause further damage to the spinal cord. If you suspect a back or neck injury, immobilize the child's head, neck, shoulders, and back with firm pillows or rolled-up blankets or towels. Do not lift the child's head, even a little, to place something underneath.

In an Emergency

CALL 911 OR YOUR LOCAL EMERGENCY NUMBER IF:

- The child is unconscious.

- Back or neck injury is possible.

- An arm or a leg is in an unusual position.

WHILE WAITING FOR THE AMBULANCE:

- DON'T move child if back or neck injury is suspected.

- DON'T move child if an arm or a leg appears broken.

- Assess **A**irway, **B**reathing, and **C**irculation, and give CPR if the child has stopped breathing.

- Keep the child warm, and treat for shock if necessary.

- DON'T give the child anything to eat or drink.

More frequently, your child's injury will be less severe and you will need to deal with pain and swelling in an extremity. If your child cannot put weight on the limb or move without significant pain, he may have a broken bone (fracture) or a sprain. Your child may know that the limb has been broken; for instance, he may have heard a snapping sound at the time of the accident. If this happens, or if the limb looks broken—for example, bent in a way that it shouldn't be or out of alignment—immobilize the limb in the position you found it and then take your child immediately to the emergency room. There the injury will be examined and X-rayed. If the limb is out of alignment, the doctor may give your child a local anesthetic before straightening it and applying a cast. If the injured part is very swollen, casting may be delayed until the swelling comes down. The table on page 452 shows what to do for a variety of common injuries.

Often you will not be able to tell if your child has suffered a sprain or a broken bone. There may be pain, swelling, and discoloration, and he may or may not be able to move the limb without significant pain. This type of injury can be treated at home initially. Rest the limb, apply ice, and elevate the injured area above the level of the heart. Call your doctor for instructions on what to do next. Your doctor may want to have the injury X-rayed immediately, or she may decide to wait for a while to see if the pain and swelling persist. You also may give the child acetaminophen for the pain.

Dislocations occur in a joint when the ends of the joint are pulled out of their socket. These injuries are frequently sports-related, but they may also occur in young children who are picked up and swung by the arms or who are jerked by the arm as a means of gaining compliance. The most common type of dislocation is a dislocated radial head, commonly called nursemaid's elbow. It acquired its name because it may occur when an adult, walking with a toddler in hand, holds the child's hand tightly when he stumbles or falls, thus pulling the radial head of the lower arm bone out of its socket in the elbow. A child with this type of injury may exhibit few signs except to stop using the arm. This type of dislocation does not need immobilization on the way to the emergency department, where it can easily be treated. All types of dislocations need prompt medical attention to ensure that the bone is realigned in its normal position.

Injury	Symptoms	Treatment
Strained muscle	Pain Stiffness No swelling	Rest Apply warm compresses
Sprain	Pain Swelling Inability to move or bear weight	Rest Apply ice Elevate
Fracture (broken bone)	Pain, numbness, or tingling Inability to move or bear weight Swelling or discoloration	Immobilize limb Bandage open injury Apply ice Take to emergency department
Dislocation	Pain Inability to move or bear weight Swollen or deformed appearance	Immobilize limb Apply ice Take to emergency department

To immobilize an injury, use a splint made of something you find around the house, such as rolled-up newspapers or magazines or a broomstick. Make sure the splint is long enough to immobilize the limb itself and the joints on either side of it. Pad the splint if necessary, and tie it to the injured limb. Make sure the ties are not so tight that they cut off circulation. Likewise, if you use an elastic bandage to wrap the injured area, make sure you don't wrap it too tightly. Check the extremity below the bandage for signs of impaired circulation (discoloration). Arm injuries should be both splinted and placed in a sling, to relieve weight on the injury.

Bites and Stings
Insect Stings   Insect stings are frequent complaints of children, yet in most cases the pain lasts only a few hours and no further complications are seen. When insect stings cause more serious problems, they are usually allergic reactions of varying degrees. These range from localized pain and swelling at the site of the sting to life-threatening, systemic reactions. Stinging insects include honeybees, bumblebees, wasps, hornets, yellow jackets, and ants. All of these except ants are closely related; thus if a person is allergic to a honeybee, for example, he is likely to react to a yellow jacket sting as well. Honeybees differ from the other stinging insects in that their stingers are barbed and stick into the victim's skin. The bee dies after leaving its stinger behind; thus it can sting only once. The other stinging insects, however, can sting many times. Among the ants, only fire ants cause significant problems.

In an Emergency

CALL 911 OR YOUR LOCAL EMERGENCY NUMBER when your child shows any of these symptoms of an impending severe allergic reaction:

- difficulty swallowing
- change in voice
- wheezing or difficulty breathing
- severe itching or hives
- severe swelling of lips, eyelids, or site of the sting
- stomach cramps, nausea, or vomiting
- dizziness
- unconsciousness

WHILE WAITING FOR THE AMBULANCE:

- If you have gotten a prescription for epinephrine from your doctor, give your child an injection of the dose prescribed at the first sign of a severe allergic reaction.
- Assess Airway, Breathing, and Circulation and give CPR if child is not breathing.
- Keep child lying down and comfortable.

CALL YOUR DOCTOR IMMEDIATELY if your child has a known sensitivity to insect stings. If you have gotten a prescription for epinephrine from your doctor, give your child an injection of the prescribed dose first, then call the doctor. Take the child to the emergency department.

FIRST AID for a honeybee sting:

- Remove stinger by flicking it or scraping it out with a knife blade edge or fingernail; this reduces the amount of venom entering the body. Don't squeeze or use tweezers on the stinger.
- For local pain, swelling, and redness, place cold compresses on the site of the sting.
- For generalized itching, redness, and swelling, or hives:
  — Apply ice or cold compresses.
  — Immobilize stung area if possible.
  — Keep child lying down and comfortable.
  — For child older than two, give antihistamines as prescribed by your doctor.

Tick and Other Insect Bites   Most insect bites, including those of mosquitoes, fleas, chiggers, and bedbugs, cause only local redness and itching and can be treated

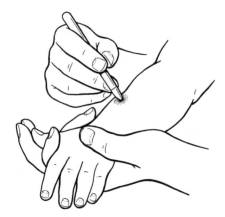

by washing well with soap and water. Cool compresses and calamine lotion also will help relieve this irritation. Occasionally a person develops an allergy to the saliva of one of these insects; however, the allergic reactions are usually not as severe as those brought about by the stinging insects already discussed.

Tick bites are treated differently from bites of other insects. Usually tick bites cause only local reactions similar to those of other insects. However, ticks may cause serious illnesses, including Rocky Mountain spotted fever, Lyme disease, babeosis, Erlichiosis, and tick paralysis. Ticks are widespread in many areas of the United States. The deer tick, which can pass both tick paralysis and Lyme disease, is endemic in many parts of the United States, such as along the East and West Coasts and in Wisconsin and Texas; while the dog tick and Rocky Mountain tick, both of which can pass Rocky Mountain spotted fever, are most frequently found in the southeastern United States. Deer ticks are smaller in size than dog ticks and often are not noticed at the time of the bite.

Whenever you find a tick on your child, take care to remove it as quickly as possible. Studies have shown that the incidence of disease increases with the length of time the tick is attached. Usually ticks take about one to two hours to become firmly attached to the skin. The method of removal is important, as tick fragments left behind can cause illness.

Removing a tick:

- Covering the tick with petroleum jelly or mineral oil for about thirty minutes may make removal easier.

- Using tweezers, grasp the tick as close to the skin as possible.

- Pull with steady pressure.

- DON'T crush or squeeze the body of the tick.

- DON'T use a lighted match, fingernail polish, or rubbing alcohol to try to get the tick to loosen its grip, as these may cause the tick to release more infective agent into the wound.

- Cleanse the area with soap and water, and disinfect with rubbing alcohol.

Lyme Disease Symptoms

- a rash that spreads outward in a circle

- malaise

- fatigue

- fever

- headache

- swollen and painful joints

Rocky Mountain Spotted Fever Symptoms

- headache

- malaise

- fever

- rash (beginning three or four days after tick bite; appearing first on wrists and ankles, then spreading to hands, feet, forearms, and elsewhere on the body)

- swelling around eyes and eyelids

ROCKY MOUNTAIN SPOTTED FEVER CAN BE FATAL; SEEK HELP IMMEDIATELY.

Spider Bites Although more than a hundred thousand species of spiders are known, only two are associated with severe reactions in humans: black widow spiders and brown recluse spiders. It is often difficult to determine whether a child has been bitten by one of these spiders, as reactions to the bites are somewhat delayed. In addition, young children may be unable to describe the spider adequately. Spider bites usually occur singly. If there are multiple bites, consider something other than a spider.

Black widow spiders are shiny black with bright red hourglass-shape markings on their undersides. Only the female is dangerous. She is larger than the male and will attack to protect her eggs or if she is otherwise provoked. Black widow spider webs are found in out-of-the-way places such as woodpiles and dark corners. The venom of black widow spiders is more toxic than many snake venoms and can lead to death from cardiovascular collapse if not treated. An antidote to the venom is available and will be given to any child who is suspected of having been bitten by a black widow spider.

Brown recluse spiders are small (about 0.5 inch, or 1 to 1.5 cm long), brownish spiders with dark, violin-shaped marks on their backs. They are usually found outdoors but may also be found indoors, inside closets. They are shy and will attack only if provoked. A bite is usually not noticed until two to eight hours after it occurs, when the child develops a local reaction, characterized by redness, blisters, and pustules at the site of the bite. The local reaction spreads over the next three to four days and can range from mild to severe. Some people, especially small children, may develop a systemic reaction one to two days after the bite, with fever, chills, weakness, nausea, vomiting, and joint pain. In the worst cases this can proceed to renal failure.

In an Emergency

CALL 911 OR YOUR LOCAL EMERGENCY NUMBER if child shows signs of respiratory difficulty following a spider bite.

WHILE WAITING FOR THE AMBULANCE:

- Assess **A**irway, **B**reathing, and **C**irculation, and give CPR if the child stops breathing.
- Keep child lying down and comfortable.

PROVIDE FIRST AID AND THEN CALL YOUR DOCTOR OR TAKE THE CHILD TO AN EMERGENCY ROOM if he has symptoms of a black widow spider bite or a brown recluse spider bite.

Black Widow Spider Bite Symptoms

- severe pain and cramping in thighs, abdomen, flanks, and chest
- possible nausea and vomiting
- chills
- headache
- abnormal sensations (tingling, numbness)
- respiratory distress

Brown Recluse Spider Bite Symptoms

Early symptoms (at the site of the bite; develop within two to eight hours after bite, spreading over next three to four days):

- redness
- blisters
- pustules
- systemic reactions (twenty-four to forty-eight hours after bite):
  —fever
  —chills
  —malaise, weakness
  —nausea, vomiting
  —joint pain

FIRST AID:

- Keep the child quiet and avoid unnecessary movement.

- Keep bitten area below the level of the heart.

- Place a constricting band between the bitten area and the heart. The band should be loose enough to fit two fingers between it and the body and should be placed 2 to 4 inches above the bite.

- Apply ice to the bitten area.

Snakebites   Most snakes found in the United States are harmless. However, certain species of snakes, found mostly in the Southeast and the Southwest, can cause severe reactions, especially in children. Ninety-nine percent of venomous snakebites are caused by a family of snakes commonly known as pit vipers. This family includes rattlesnakes, water moccasins, and copperheads. Other poisonous snakebites are caused by coral snakes or other exotic, imported snakes.

To differentiate a pit viper from a nonpoisonous snake, look for the following: triangular head (rather than oval), elliptical pupil (rather than round), and two curved fangs that advance forward when the snake bites. Rattlesnakes also have rattles, but copperheads and cottonmouths do not. Unlike the pit vipers, coral snakes have round pupils and a blunt head; however, they can be identified by their distinctive coloration: the snout is always black, followed by a yellow ring, a black band, and then alternating red and black bands, with narrow yellow rings bordering the red bands. The nonpoisonous king snake looks very similar to the coral snake, except the yellow rings are within the black bands, and the red and black bands are directly adjacent to one another. This rhyme can help you remember which is the poisonous type: Red on yellow, kill a fellow; red on black, venom lack. Also, coral snakes have fangs, whereas king snakes do not. The fangs of poisonous snakes leave distinct marks when they strike, which can help you identify a poisonous snakebite even if you did not get a good look at the snake. The reaction to a snakebite varies depending on the size of the snake, the type of snake, and the size of the child.

In an Emergency

CALL 911 OR YOUR LOCAL EMERGENCY NUMBER if child shows signs of respiratory distress, shock, or has convulsions.

WHILE WAITING FOR THE AMBULANCE:

- Assess **A**irway, **B**reathing, and **C**irculation, and give CPR if the child stops breathing.

- Keep the child warm, rested, and reassured.

PROVIDE FIRST AID AND TAKE THE CHILD TO THE EMERGENCY ROOM if the child has any of these symptoms of a snake bite:

- fang marks

- local burning pain, redness, and swelling within minutes

- numbness

- metallic taste in mouth

- nausea, vomiting

- weakness, lethargy

- chills, sweating

- fainting

- difficulty swallowing

  FIRST AID:

- Keep the child rested and reassured.

- Immobilize bitten area.

- Keep bitten area below the level of the heart.

- Keep the child warm.

- DO NOT apply cold compresses or ice.

- DO NOT give the child anything to eat or drink.

Marine Life Stings   At the seashore, a number of marine animals can present dangers to children playing in the water or on the beach. These animals include stingrays, jellyfish, Portuguese men-of-war, corals, sea anemones, and hydras. Most of these animals are not harmful to humans, but those that are can cause serious, even life-threatening reactions. Stings are the most common type of marine injury. Stings can be quite painful but are not usually dangerous. However, some stinging animals produce extremely toxic venoms. Children are especially in danger when exposed to these venoms because of their small body size. Some stinging animals may wash up onto the shore and appear dead, yet they are still capable of stinging and delivering their toxin. Thus children (and adults) should learn to watch out for marine animals lying on the beach and not go near any animal even if it appears to be dead.

Stingrays
These account for most marine life stings. These fish may bury themselves in the sand until stepped on by an unsuspecting swimmer. Then they strike with a barbed tail that contains a potent venom and may cause serious lacerations. Children stung by stingrays must, therefore, be treated for two types of injuries: bleeding from the cut, and toxic reactions to the venom.

In an Emergency

CALL 911 OR YOUR LOCAL EMERGENCY NUMBER if the child shows signs of respiratory distress or shock.

WHILE WAITING FOR THE AMBULANCE:

- Assess **A**irway, **B**reathing, and **C**irculation, and give CPR if the child stops breathing.

- Control bleeding with direct pressure.

- Keep the child warm, rested, and reassured.

PROVIDE FIRST AID AND TAKE THE CHILD TO THE EMERGENCY ROOM if the child has any of these symptoms of a stingray injury:

- immediate pain

- bleeding

- localized pain and swelling, peaking within ninety minutes

- fainting

- weakness

- nausea, vomiting, and diarrhea

- anxiety

- cramps

FIRST AID:

- Irrigate the wound with cold salt water to remove venom.

- Control bleeding with direct pressure.

- Keep the child warm, rested, and reassured.

- Watch for signs of respiratory distress or shock.

Portuguese Man-of-War
This looks like a jellyfish but is really a floating colony of hydrozoa. The tentacles that hang from the colony release one of the most powerful neurotoxins known. These tentacles can be long and transparent and virtually invisible to swimmers. Even when the animal appears to be dead on the beach, the tentacles can release toxins. A sting from this creature can cause local pain and irritation as well as headache, muscle ache, fever, abdominal rigidity, pain in the joints, nausea, vomiting, pallor, and breathing difficulties. If the area stung is large in comparison to the victim's size, the sting can lead to coma and even death. Most true *jellyfish* cause only mild, local skin irritation. One exception is the lion's mane, a highly toxic creature found along both the Atlantic and Pacific Coasts. A lion's mane can grow as large as 8 feet wide, with shaggy clusters of golden-yellow tentacles that resemble a lion's mane. The sting may cause severe burning, possibly muscle cramps, and respiratory failure.

Other marine creatures may also injure children. These include sea anemones, coral, starfish, sea urchins, and sea cucumbers. Most of these are only mildly toxic or dangerous, causing little more than burning, redness, and some swelling. Sea urchins have spines that can pierce the skin and lodge in the tissues, causing intense pain, redness, swelling, and aching. These spines must be removed and the wound treated to prevent infection. Coral cuts can be dangerous, as they can cause bleeding as well as a toxic reaction to the venom. For either of these types of injuries, call your doctor or go to the nearest emergency room after applying first aid. A doctor will clean the wound thoroughly and treat the child with antibiotics.

In an Emergency

CALL 911 OR YOUR LOCAL EMERGENCY NUMBER if your child shows signs of respiratory distress or shock.

WHILE WAITING FOR THE AMBULANCE:

- Assess **A**irway, **B**reathing, and **C**irculation and give CPR if the child has stopped breathing.

- Keep the child warm, rested, and reassured.

PROVIDE FIRST AID AND TAKE THE CHILD TO THE EMERGENCY ROOM if he has any of these symptoms of a Portuguese man-of-war sting:

- local pain and irritation or severe burning

- muscle aches or muscle cramps

- fever

- abdominal rigidity

- painful joints

- nausea, vomiting

- pallor

- breathing difficulties

FIRST AID:

- Rinse the area with cold salt water.

- Cover the area with vinegar or rubbing alcohol to neutralize the venom.

- Wrap your hand in a cloth or wear gloves, and try to remove tentacles.

- Keep the child warm, rested, and reassured.

- Watch for symptoms of respiratory distress or shock

Convulsions/Seizures

Seizures are not uncommon; about 4 to 6 percent of children will experience seizures or convulsions at some time during their lives. Fortunately, only a small fraction of these children will develop recurrent seizures (epilepsy). Seizures may be experienced in a variety of ways: one child may seem to "space out" while another child may collapse, with rhythmic twitching and jerking motions. By definition, a seizure may appear as a brief loss of consciousness or an altered state of consciousness; or as a change in behavior, motor activity, sensation, and/or autonomic function (bladder incontinence).

Seizures occur when nerve cells in the brain misfire, causing a brief interruption of normal brain activity. This misfiring can be initiated by a number of factors, including high fevers, infections, head injury, brain tumors, metabolic disturbances, or toxic reactions. Seizures that are caused by high fevers, also known as febrile convulsions, are the most common type seen in infants and young children. Most seizures last ten to fifteen minutes or less. Thus, when you take your child to the emergency department when he seizes, the seizure may have stopped before you get there.

Seizures themselves are more frightening than dangerous. If your child seizes, he is not in danger of biting off his tongue. The only real danger is that he could suffer from a lack of oxygen during the seizures. Another danger is that a child may injure himself on furniture or other objects when he falls or during the convulsions. A child will have no recollection of the seizure afterward. Thus, if you can stay calm, your child may not experience any significant anxiety after the seizure. Any child who has had a seizure should be seen by a doctor. The first time a child has a seizure, parents frequently call an ambulance or paramedic unit to transport the child to the emergency room. If the child is still seizing upon arrival, the attending doctors will often administer an anticonvulsant medication to stop the seizure. Then the doctor will try to determine the precipitating cause of the seizure and make sure that condition is being managed effectively. She will also want to rule out serious illnesses or injuries; and she will consider other possible conditions that may resemble seizures—for example, breath-holding spells, hyperventilation, migraine headaches, night terrors, or narcolepsy.

Your child is likely to be very tired after a seizure and will want to sleep. Continue to monitor his breathing and fever while he sleeps, and make arrangements to have him seen by a physician immediately.

In an Emergency

CALL 911 OR YOUR LOCAL EMERGENCY NUMBER if your child fails to regain consciousness after a seizure or if he shows signs of respiratory distress.

WHILE WAITING FOR THE AMBULANCE:

- Assess **A**irway, **B**reathing, and **C**irculation, and give CPR if your child stops breathing.
- Keep your child warm, rested, and reassured.

CALL YOUR DOCTOR OR TAKE CHILD TO THE EMERGENCY ROOM as soon as possible after the seizure has stopped.

IS MY CHILD HAVING A SEIZURE? Here are some signs:

During first 10 to 30 seconds:

- Child may fall to ground.
- Face becomes pale.
- Pupils dilate (become larger).
- Eyes roll backward or to sides.
- Muscles stiffen.
- Child may grunt or cry.
- Child may have frothing at mouth.

The second phase may last up to ten or fifteen minutes:

- Rhythmic jerking of arms and legs.
- Child may lose control of bladder or bowels.

WHAT TO DO:

- Stay calm.
- Move nearby objects that could injure your child if he hit or fell on them.
- Loosen tight clothing around neck and waist.
- Place the child on his side so he does not aspirate mucus or vomit.
- Assess **A**irway, **B**reathing, and **C**irculation, and provide CPR if your child stops
- breathing.
- DO NOT force anything between the child's teeth.
- DO NOT try to restrain the child's movements.
- DO NOT give the child anything to eat or drink during seizure.
- DO NOT put the child in the bath to stop seizure.

Hygiene

While he grows and matures in the womb, the unborn baby is protected from out-side infection by the sterile amniotic fluid in which he swims. This fluid is con-tained within a membrane or sac known as the amniotic sac. However, once the baby leaves the sterile and watery world of the womb and is born, he quickly becomes host to millions of invisible, teeming microorganisms—or germs. This happens in the cleanest of hospitals or homes. Fortunately, most of these germs, which cover not only our skin, but also the lining of noses and throats, respiratory tracts, and intestines, are quite harmless. In a few cases, some of them are actually helpful; for example, certain bacteria present in digestive juices help in the process-ing of food. But, of course, there are also germs that cause disease.

In understanding why and how it is best to protect babies and children from germs that can cause infection and disease, it helps to know a little about germs and about the body's way of protecting itself.

Germ Know-how

Germs come in three basic types: bacteria, viruses, and fungi.

1. Bacteria: These are very tiny, single-celled organisms, and although some can actually be useful and essential as described above, there are very many more that can cause an enormous range of illnesses. Fortunately, our bodies can cope very well with the vast majority of bacteria that are around—our skin and the mucous membrane lining prevent most bacteria from invading. In addition, body fluids such as saliva, breast milk, and tears contain natural antiseptics. Inside the body the bacteria or the poisons they produce can be conquered by antibodies produced by our immune system. If the body's own natural defenses fail to cope and illness or disease results, then antibiotics can be used. Certain types of bacteria are more easily defeated by certain types of antibiotics; however, in a few cases the frequent use of antibiotics has resulted in some strains of bacteria becoming resistant, so we need to be careful not to overuse antibiotics.

2. Viruses: These infective agents are very much tinier than bacteria. They work by getting inside the cells of the body and altering the way the cells function. Our bodies can produce antibodies to defeat them, and both this and immunization help our resistance to viruses. They cannot in general be treated by antibiotics.

3. Fungi: Certain types of fungi occasionally cause infection, the most common of which is thrush, caused by the fungus *Candida albicans*. However, fungus infections are more easily treated, though not with antibiotics.

It also helps to know that it takes more than the mere presence of germs to cause illness. If a doctor takes a swab from your child's throat, the doctor is likely to be able to grow all kinds of germs that are capable of causing a variety of illnesses, from pneumonia to sore throats. Yet your child stays healthy. This is both because changes need to occur in germs to make them more likely to cause infection, which is called "virulence," and also because the body has a natural defense mechanism that keeps germs under control—our immune system. At birth a newborn baby's immune system is still very immature, and it takes several months before it begins to work reasonably effectively, and even longer before it works as well as that of an older child or adult. Fortunately, new babies are not born completely unprotected. During the last three months in the womb, antibodies from the mother cross the placenta and enter the baby's bloodstream so the baby is born with a ready-made set of antibodies to protect him against certain infections the mother has already suffered. This is called "passive immunity." In addition, colostrum and breast milk are very rich in both antibodies and anti-infective agents that lessen the likelihood of gastroenteritis and other infectious illnesses. This passive immunity does not last forever, but as it fades, the baby's own immune system begins to work more efficiently and is able to produce its own antibodies. Further protection can be given with a vaccination program that gives your baby a lifelong immunity from certain diseases. This is called "active immunity."

Your New Baby—Hygiene in the First Six Months

New parents usually feel rather anxious but also quite confused about what sort of safety measures they should take to protect their new baby in terms of cleanliness and hygiene.

In fact, the basic rules are very simple:

Wash your hands with soap and water before handling a baby under three months old, and ask other people who hold your baby to do the same. This very simple measure really does help to stop the spread of germs. It is especially important to wash your hands after changing a baby's diaper, wiping another child's bottom, or going to the bathroom yourself, because the bowel/hand/mouth pathway is one of the most common ways by which germs are spread, usually causing diarrhea and vomiting. It is also essential to wash your hands before making up bottles or preparing any food.

Do not let people who have colds or other illnesses breathe on, cuddle, or kiss your new baby, and tactfully discourage visiting toddlers and older children from doing the same. However, your baby is at far less risk from germs within the family, so there is no need to be quite so restrictive with older brothers and sisters who have a runny nose.

It will also reduce the chance of infection if in the first three months you try, tactfully, to cut down on the number of people who handle your baby. Obviously, this does not bar all the family who want to have a look at the new arrival, but it is probably better not to have him passed around at large gatherings, such as a christening.

Breast-feeding is generally much safer than bottle-feeding. However, if you are unable to breast-feed, be meticulous about sterilizing bottles and making up feedings. Milk is an ideal breeding ground for bacteria, which is why you have to be especially careful. Bacteria grow most quickly in warm milk—boiling kills bacteria, and storing at refrigerator temperature slows down the rate at which bacteria can multiply. This is why you should always cool milk quickly and not leave warm bottles of milk standing around or reheat or warm up a bottle that has already been used. For the first five months, nipples also need to be sterilized, but when mixed feeding is introduced at about four months, plates and implements just need to be washed well in hot water and soap in the usual way.

Toys and other playthings are not usually carriers of germs because germs that cause illness do not live in the dust found on a kitchen floor but are more likely to thrive in cooked food or milk. There is no need to sterilize playthings once your baby begins to hold and grasp things and put them in his mouth (usually around four to five months); just keeping them socially clean is enough. However, try not to let playthings that have been sucked or played with by babies or toddlers who have illnesses be passed on to your baby without thoroughly washing them first.

Do make sure your baby is given the vaccinations to protect him against potentially harmful illnesses, unless there is a medical reason to the contrary. Your pediatrician can give you advice about this.

How long do you sterilize bottles? By about five months your baby has become a human vacuum cleaner, taking hold of almost anything that comes within reach and putting it automatically into his mouth. Fortunately, by this time the immune system is better developed and beginning to work more efficiently. By five months most babies can begin to take drinks from a feeder cup and bottles can gradually begin to be phased out. There is no need to carry on sterilizing bottles after six months as long as they are kept reasonably clean. Whole milk should be started at one year of age. However, you still need to be just as careful about cooling milk quickly and storing it in the fridge, and not leaving warm bottles of milk standing around or reheating a bottle that has already been heated previously.

Keeping Your Baby Clean

Change your baby's diaper regularly so the skin does not get sore, and then give him a bath once or twice a week. Most babies quickly begin to enjoy bathtime, and then it is up to you whether you bathe him every day or every other day. Once babies begin to move around, sit on the floor, reach for things, and eat solid food, they quickly become dirty. Many parents find that a bath at the end of the day is a good prelude to the bedtime routine.

Older Children

After about the age of five months there is no need to go on trying to keep your child away from colds and coughs, although serious illnesses are different. If you keep your child away from other children for too long, he may acquire a worse bout of the illness once he comes into contact with his first infectious bug, as he has had no chance to build up any immunity.

Safety rather than hygiene dictates that you gradually begin to teach a toddler not to put absolutely everything into his mouth. Tiny pieces of Legos, the cat's food, or something unmentionable he found in the garden are obvious examples. However, one habit is important to instill in him for life—to wash his hands before handling food, before having a meal, and after going to the toilet. The same applies to other adult members of your household who have not already picked up this habit!

Pets

Children can pick up worms from dogs and cats—these are roundworms (toxocara). The eggs are transferred when a child puts his hands in his mouth, and they then hatch out into larvae in the child's intestines. This is why it is important to worm your dog or cat regularly. The rear end of pets is potentially more harmful than the front end, and children are more likely to become infected after touching an animal's excrement and then putting their hands to their mouth than by having a dog or cat lick their face. However, it is better to discourage animals from getting near babies' faces and to tell children not to let animals lick their faces for safety reasons. Toxoplasmosis is an infection that can be spread by cats and is also in uncooked or improperly cooked meat. It can cause serious damage to an unborn baby in the first three months of pregnancy. That is why pregnant women are advised not to change cat litter and to wear gloves when gardening. Fleas can also be passed on to children from animals, so make sure your pet is kept free from fleas. When buying a pet of any kind, have it checked over first by a vet.

Your Home—How Clean Is Clean Enough?

Most people worry from time to time about whether their home is kept clean enough, especially when a new baby comes along. It is also an anxiety well recognized by companies who make cleaning products for use in the bathroom and kitchen, whose commercials go a long way to suggest that without their product your home will be a hotbed of highly infective germs. In fact, as with most aspects of hygiene, common sense is your best guide. If the toilet looks dirty, then it probably does contain more germs, but keeping the toilet bowl looking clean and the toilet flushed is all you need to worry about. In fact, water in toilets—provided the toilet is kept flushed—has been found to contain surprisingly few germs. Do not waste time worrying about "invisible" germs, and remember that germs do not breed in household dust, but rather in food and drink. Keep your home clean to your own standards, but don't go into overdrive when a new baby arrives. In fact, it can be harmful for your baby to be constantly exposed to fumes from detergents.

Preparing Food

Scrupulously clean and careful preparation of food is the best way to avoid stomach upsets. If you prepare food in advance, cook it thoroughly, put it in the refridgerator immediately, and warm it up when it is needed. Food less carefully cooked and then reheated is likely to carry germs that can cause stomach upsets, so always reheat food very thoroughly to as high a temperature as possible rather than just warming it up. Then allow it to cool so your child or the rest of the family can eat it. Always wash your hands with soap and water before preparing food, and never prepare food if you have any kind of infection on your hands. Even touching your nose when you have a cold and then going on to prepare food is a way of giving your germs to the rest of the family. If you are storing leftovers, always cover them and keep them in the refrigerator. Alternatively, food that has been cooked can be frozen and then thawed and reheated thoroughly, but do not freeze food a second time.

*Adapted from *The Children's Hospital of Philadelphia Parent's Guide to Childhood Emergencies* by Lisa J. Bain, published July 1993 by Delta book, a division of Bantam Doubleday Dell Publishing Group, Inc., New York, NY.

CHAPTER 16

Doctors and Medications

Doctors • Changing primary care physicians
How to get the best from your primary care physician
Referrals • When to call the doctor • Medicines
Giving medicines • Taking the medicine . . . without tears
Antibiotics—why they are not always the answer
Allergic reactions • The pharmacist
Over-the-counter medicines • Immunizations
Visiting nurses and health clinics • Your child's teeth
Teething • Taking care of your child's teeth
Food for healthy teeth • Going to the dentist

Doctors

Choosing a Primary Care Physician

I was expecting my third baby and saw my primary care doctor for the early part of my prenatal care. My morale sank below zero the day he poked my tummy and said: "Hmm, of course, your stomach muscles are shot to pieces—that's why you're so big."

We all remember the bad moments from medical encounters for many more years than we remember the good ones, and it is especially important that your primary care doctor is someone you like and trust. Women having babies and then caring for small children are among the most frequent visitors to primary care physicians, and their doctor can be a valuable source of support during these important and sometimes stressful years.

How do you make the right choice of doctor? The success of the relationship will depend on what you expect from the doctor you choose, whether that matches up with what that particular doctor intends to provide, and on how you both get along together. The neighborhood hospital can give you a list of doctors in the area, and you can see from that whether they all work together in a large health center, in a small partnership of two or three, or by themselves. Big, though, as far as a practice is concerned, is not necessarily better. There is also a *Directory of Doctors*, including medical specialists, which is available from your local medical society. It contains not only a list of the doctors in the area but details of the service provided. You may already have some feelings about whether you would like a man or a woman doctor, someone recently qualified or more experienced. You can find out when they qualified and whether they have any specialist qualifications by inquiring at the local medical society or your nearest hospital. At times doctors who specialize in family practice will provide prenatal care, deliver your baby, and then care for you, the new baby, and other members of your family.

Go to the practice and ask the receptionist or practice manager about the services offered; just looking around the waiting room and picking up the general atmosphere will help you to decide. Is the receptionist easily available across a counter or locked away behind a glass partition or closed door with a "Please Knock and Wait" sign? Are there toys for waiting children and interesting and useful notices and information on the walls? Many GPs put up photos of themselves in the waiting room with their names so patients will know who they are, and practices often produce their own information leaflet explaining how to make an appointment, how to contact a doctor out of office hours, and any special services that are available. But the real lowdown on what a doctor is like inevitably comes via the local grapevine—in other words, by asking young children's parents whose attitudes and judgment are in sympathy with yours. Your local pharmacist, local medical society, your obstetrician, physician friends, or local hospital referral service may all be useful sources of information, too.

While you may hope to pick the ideal doctor, he is not obliged to accept you, however perfect a patient you think you might prove. It is quite common for a primary care physician to ask to see you before taking you as a patient. In addition to giving you a chance to see if you like his approach, the doctor will also want to know about special conditions that you or your family may have that need long-term care—for example, epilepsy, a heart condition, or diabetes—so mention anything of this nature when you have your first visit with the doctor or when completing a patient information form.

Changing Primary Care Physicians

If you are unhappy with your doctor, find he no longer provides the kind of service you need, or just lose confidence in his ability, you can ask to have your records transferred to another doctor. If you decide to change doctors, you should be polite enough to tell either the doctor or a member of his staff the reason or reasons for your decision. You may have a perfectly legitimate reason for wishing to change—perhaps you are moving to another area that makes it inconvenient for you to go to that particular doctor, or perhaps you would prefer to have a woman doctor. You should be prepared for the fact that the thought may occur to your prospective doctor's mind that perhaps you are an unreasonably demanding or difficult patient who has simply exhausted the patience of your previous doctor and should explain to the new doctor or his staff the reason or reasons for your decision. Naturally, there are always several sides to such cases, and the new doctor will usually take you on and see how the relationship works out, although he will probably want to see you first and ask you more questions about why you want to change. If problems should arise and dissatisfaction occurs on both sides, then a doctor can tell an individual or a family he will no longer care for them as patients. He will give several options of other physicians who could provide medical services.

How to Get the Best from Your Primary Care Physician

Find out how the practice operates by asking a receptionist who can tell you about the appointment system, contacting doctors after office hours, the handling of emergency situations, routine questions, whether there is a telephone hour, etc. Making friends with the receptionist can be the key to good relations with the doctor—she can often give useful advice when you are unsure about bringing a child to the office. Many office nurses can also give useful advice when your child seems to be sick.

Keep appointments, and be on time. Always phone if you are likely to be delayed or want to cancel the appointment.

Take your child to the doctor's office whenever possible, rather than taking the child to a local emergency room. Babies and small children are easily transported, and if you protect them from the elements you can take them to the doctor's office even if it is raining or snowing. If you do not have a car, see if a friend can help, or call a taxi. If your child is so ill that physically moving her is difficult, call the doctor's office and explain the situation—your doctor will give you advice as to how to handle the situation. Convulsions, severe injuries, ingestion of toxic materials, etc., constitute such situations. However, apart from such cases, a doctor can usually do far more for your child in his office where there are more facilities and equipment than at home, and a doctor can see many more people at his office in the time that one home visit would take.

Warn the receptionist if you intend to bring in a child with a rash or a suspected infectious illness. She may arrange for you to wait in a separate room or come at the beginning of the office hours to avoid spreading it to other people. Many practices arrange for young children who are acutely ill to be seen quickly by the doctor.

Calling the doctor at night is something people usually feel worried about. Although most doctors can come up with stories about the rare call for something totally unnecessary–calling about a mild diaper rash is such an example—in general parents know when their child is ill and needs attention. Obviously parents tend to learn with experience, and first-time parents are likely to be more anxious and make more calls than seasoned veterans of childhood illnesses, but it is best to trust your instinct. If you are truly concerned about your child's condition, then call for advice.

Most doctors often share night and weekend duty with other doctors working in the same area. It is, therefore, quite possible that you will not be able to speak to your own doctor at night.

It is worth remembering that a child's temperature may rise in the evening, and coughs are likely to get worse when the child lies down. Parents who have wondered all day about whether to take a child to the doctor see the symptoms getting worse, and panic about getting through the night. Tell the doctor on the phone what you are most worried about and answer questions as accurately as possible. Do not necessarily expect your child to be seen right away by the doctor, since this may be a case for telephone counseling. For example, the doctor might tell you how to try to lower your child's temperature, but he will always ask you to call again if the suggested treatment does not work or you are still anxious.

What should you do if you are very seriously worried and the doctor you have called refuses to see your child? Well, it may be that he is justified and your fears are needless.

However, young babies in particular can deteriorate very rapidly. If you are still concerned, call the doctor again or bring your child to the nearest hospital emergency room. After your child has been evaluated, ask the examining doctor to contact your child's doctor and fill him in with the details of the illness. If your visit to the emergency department turns out to have been unnecessary, then be prepared to learn from experience and listen to advice, but do not feel ashamed or guilty. If, on the other hand, your child does need treatment, then be relieved that you had the courage to trust your instinct and that your child has been helped.

Do not expect your doctor always to have an answer, because for many problems there is no one single answer but a variety of possible solutions or causes you need to discuss together, or even no obvious answer. A relationship between the doctor and his patients or the patient's parents is a two-way contract, not simply a matter of pronouncement and a few pearls of wisdom plus a prescription. A doctor has expert knowledge about how bodies in general work and about some aspects of how people behave; you have expert knowledge about your own or your child's body and behavior. A combination of this knowledge will help you to arrive at some possible answers. If you always expect a definite solution, you put pressure on a doctor to come up with one instead of being able to say he is not sure or does not know, which can lead to a more comprehensive attempt at finding one.

Do not expect a prescription for a medication (especially antibiotics) every time you see a doctor, because it will often not be necessary. Explanation, advice, and/or reassurance can be far more valuable in many instances than medicines. Do not feel your visit was unnecessary or unsuccessful because you leave without a prescription—the doctor will certainly not have felt that. Sometimes a patient's expectation and unjustified faith in medicines can put pressure on a doctor to give a prescription he knows is medically useless, simply to reassure a parent or a patient. Remember that there is not a medication for every problem; teach your child the same philosophy. Most children with mild fevers and minor complaints get better in a few days without medicine.

Always ask questions if you do not understand what your doctor has told you. Parents today are better informed, and they generally welcome a doctor's taking the time and trouble to explain something about their child's condition and treatment. Doctors in turn now view a large part of their work as education, and the old-style physician who feels threatened or affronted by parents or patients who ask informed questions is rare. Remember, though, that while a doctor will be happy to discuss a problem, he will have good reason for advocating a particular course of action, even though you might disagree with his advice.

The real reason for your visit may not actually be your child's cough/cold/behavior but some vaguer or less tangible emotional problem that is much harder to ask for help with. In general, the doctor will try to exercise a sixth sense to pick up your less obvious anxieties, but if you do have some insight into a deeper reason for your visit, try to help eliminate the doctor's detective work and say what it is.

Make separate appointments for each person needing treatment. Do not show up to an appointment booked for only one child, then suddenly say, "While I'm here . . ." and launch into details about your own or other children's ailments. If you have other children requiring attention, tell the receptionist when making the original appointment—she will not only allow the proper time, but also make sure all the relevant charts are in front of your doctor. It may be helpful to jog your memory by writing down in advance a few particularly important questions you want answered.

Listen to advice and carry it out. Doctors are trained to listen to what patients say—we need to take in what is said in return. This is not always as easy as it sounds when at least half your attention is on your child, and often we only pick up part of a sentence or latch onto a few words without taking in the rest. Some practices have well-written brochures available for conditions such as asthma. These can be a useful addition to verbal advice. Taking advice is also a relatively new skill patients have had to cultivate in place of simply picking up a prescription. Before you go back with a problem that has not been resolved, think whether you have actually tried what was suggested.

Referrals

If your child needs specialist help—for example, for a vision or a hearing problem, or if your doctor is not sure what is causing the trouble—he can refer you to a specialist. However, many conditions that used to be reasons for referral are now dealt with by the pediatricians themselves, as the offices can arrange most tests and now have many more facilities and resources at their fingertips. Your doctor will sometimes ask if you have any special preference for a hospital, if needed. Most doctors get to know a great deal about specialists in the hospitals by feedback from patients, by the kinds of letters they send, and by the general treatment and management patients receive. A children's hospital is usually a good choice because its entire focus is on children.

Occasionally you may be reluctant to ask your physician for a referral—for example, if you feel he may disapprove of your wish to see someone practicing alternative medicine, a homeopathic doctor, or someone specializing in allergy. If you really feel your doctor is totally opposed to such ideas and would oppose your concerns, then that may be a reason to consider seeing another doctor in the practice or even to change doctors. But give your own physician the benefit of the doubt first, and explain why you are worried and what you hope for. His referral is very important because he is your protection against medically unqualified or unscrupulous practitioners who may take your money and do nothing or else do genuine harm. He is also your protection against going to perfectly good specialists who may not be suitable for you for various reasons.

When to Call the Doctor

In general, parents should trust their instincts—no one else knows your child as well as you do. If your child's condition is worrying you, then it is right to call the doctor.

Babies under six months   Because young babies cannot yet move around, talk, or understand questions, determining that they are ill and finding out what is wrong require some detective work and picking up clues. Most parents quickly notice changes in their baby's behavior and condition. Because a young baby's condition can deteriorate very quickly in certain circumstances, it is best to play it safe and see a doctor if you are worried, especially if your baby is only a few weeks old. The following symptoms are certainly reasons to seek advice:

"Not himself"

Not responding to you, not smiling or "talking" as much as usual, not as interested in her surroundings, or sleeping more than usual.

Fever

This may be accompanied by other signs. Try reducing temperature in the ways described on page 494. If the baby cools down, is still feeding, and is not otherwise distressed, just keep a watch. If she stays feverish or has other symptoms listed here, call the doctor.

Not eating

If she takes less than usual for several feedings or does not wake up for feedings at usual times.

Vomiting

If there is more than normal regurgitation on several occasions, particularly if it shoots out to a distance of 3 to 4 feet in babies less than three months old (called projectile vomiting), or is green (bile-stained vomiting), or contains blood.

Diarrhea

If this is profuse and watery, with or without blood, on several occasions. If you are breast-feeding and have taken any laxatives or eaten more fruit than usual, etc., this might cause temporary diarrhea.

Dry diapers

If her diapers are much drier than usual because she has not passed urine, which may indicate that she is dehydrated—usually as a result of poor feeding, vomiting, diarrhea, or a combination of all three. Dehydrated babies may appear to have sunken eyes, loose skin, may be lethargic, or are more irritable than usual or hard to console.

Rapid or difficult breathing

Her ribs may appear sucked in with each breath, or she may make an unusual noise with her breathing. She may find it difficult to feed as well.

Persistent coughing

If she coughs in spasms lasting more than a few seconds. Long spasms often end with vomiting.

Blue discoloration of the lips or tongue

A lot of babies have blue hands and feet if they are cold. However, if the baby's lips and tongue look blue or mauve (compare with yours) after a bout of coughing, or with breathing difficulties or feeding, she needs to see the doctor immediately. There may be a congenital defect of the heart or lungs.

Seizures or convulsions

During a seizure a baby either goes stiff or else rhythmically jerks her arms or legs for a period lasting up to several minutes. Her eyes may roll up, she may drool or go blue, and she is unresponsive to you. All babies jerk their limbs once or twice, for instance, if they are startled by a sudden movement or a loud noise, but this is quite normal. It is only if the jerking continues that you need worry. After a seizure the baby may be floppy and sleepy. If your child has had a seizure, call your physician or 911 immediately.

Screaming

If this is continuous and unusual, even after you have checked that she is not hungry or thirsty, wet or dirty, too hot or too cold, etc., call the doctor. He may not find anything wrong upon examining the baby, but it is reasonable for the baby to be checked.

Head injuries

If your baby bumps her head and loses consciousness, no matter how briefly, or vomits or remains floppy and lethargic, take her to the doctor or the local emergency room.

Any other injuries should be seen by the doctor unless very minor.

Burns

These happen particularly when the baby reaches out for a cup of tea or coffee you have just poured, so remember to keep hot things well out of the reach of children. Remove the hot, soaked clothing immediately, because they retain the heat and make the burn worse, keep the affected part under cold running tap water for five minutes, pat dry very gently, and cover with a clean, dry cloth. Then take her to the doctor or to the nearest emergency room. Some people recommend covering the burn with butter, but this should not be done.

Rash

Most rashes are due to mild infections. An urgent examination by a physician is necessary if the child is also unusually irritable or not responding to you as usual.

If your young baby is obviously ill and your doctor cannot see your child quickly, then play it safe and take the child to the nearest hospital accident and emergency room.

Babies six months to a year Much the same rules apply to this age group, although changes in behavior and clues as to the cause of an illness may be easier to pick up. As babies get bigger and stronger they are better able to withstand bouts of illness, but breathing difficulties and persistent coughing, vomiting, and diarrhea need to be treated seriously and acted upon promptly. If your baby has vomiting and diarrhea, always take this seriously—stop feeding her solids and milk (unless you are breast-feeding) and just give her plenty of a commercial salt and glucose preparation available at pharmacies until the diarrhea stops and her symptoms seem to have settled. Most babies can then return to full-strength milk and a normal diet gradually after a day or so. She may lose weight very slightly but will rapidly regain it once she starts feeding normally again. If her symptoms do not subside after twenty-four hours or if she vomits everything, including water, she needs to see a doctor. In the case of slight fever in a baby who is still taking fluids and is otherwise alert, try giving fever-reducing medications for babies as directed by your doctor, and sponge her down with lukewarm water to reduce the fever. Seek medical advice if the baby continues to refuse food and fluids, seems in pain, is reluctant to move an arm or a leg, or is listless and unresponsive.

Children aged one to five   Loss of appetite is a good indicator as to how ill your child is—if she begins to eat something, it is usually a sign she is getting better. Always be sure to give plenty of fluids—a child who is so ill that she will not drink anything during a day needs to see a doctor. Fever that does not respond to fever-reducing medications for babies, that is accompanied by other worrying signs of illness such as pain or crying, that is bad enough to make a child delirious, or that continues for more than after twenty-four hours needs assessment. There are, however, no hard-and-fast rules—again, trust your own judgment. Breathlessness due to croup or asthma can be serious and needs treatment.

Between the ages of one and five years children become increasingly able to tell you what is wrong—although not always accurately! They may describe pain felt anywhere as "tummy ache" and, conversely, a wide variety of illnesses—such as infections, pneumonia, urinary infections or gastroenteritis—may give them abdominal pain, so the site of the pain does not necessarily indicate the cause. Call the doctor in the following cases:

Severe or prolonged pain

Judging the seriousness of your child's pain is not always easy. However, if she complains of a belly ache but continues to play actively, there is unlikely to be anything seriously wrong, whereas if she just wants to be cuddled or lies on the sofa all morning, she is probably fairly ill.

Children's ability to tolerate pain varies quite a lot, just as in adults, and you will know best whether your child is the stoical sort who does not complain until the pain is very severe.

Diminished level of activity or generally "not herself"

This is a good, though nonspecific indication of illness.

Loss of appetite

This is another nonspecific indicator of illness. Conversely, once she starts to eat again, you know she is feeling better. Parents sometimes worry that their child may lose weight and try to make her eat while she is ill. However, this is not necessary and she will not come to any harm provided she drinks plenty of fluids. Once she is better, she will rapidly regain any lost weight. She should, however, drink enough fluids to be able to urinate four or five times in a twenty-four-hour period to prevent dehydration.

Fever

Particularly if she is generally ill without any obvious reason to account for it. Fever is almost always associated with a loss of appetite. However, she may be developing one of the childhood illnesses, such as influenza or chicken pox, so it is worth asking friends or the nursery school if any of these illnesses are in your area.

Not drinking, prolonged vomiting, or diarrhea

Children may become dehydrated, although not as quickly as small babies. Indicators include a dry tongue and passing very small amounts of concentrated (dark) urine.

Urinary symptoms

Pain on passing urine, passing small amounts of urine very often; "fishy"-smelling urine; funny color—pink or Coca-Cola-colored; not passing as much urine as usual while drinking normally.

Puffy eyes, face, or ankles, particularly in the morning

This is usually associated with other urinary symptoms.

Severe earache

This may be due to an ear infection but can also be due to a sore throat or early mumps. Ear infections often need treating with a full course of antibiotics to ensure a quick recovery. Not all children with ear infections suffer from earache—fever and vomiting can also be signs. Bright red ears may occur if your child is hot or has been crying or running around and do not indicate an ear infection. Ear-pulling can be a sign of pain, but well babies often pull at their ears, so this alone may not mean she has an ear infection.

Severe sore throat

This may make swallowing painful. Give fluids, ice pops, or cold, soft foods.

Sore mouth

Particularly if your child has also become sick, with a fever.

Difficulty in breathing

Or making loud noises when breathing in (stridor) or breathing out (wheezing). She will usually have a cough as well.

Seizures (convulsions)

With or without a temperature.

Not walking, putting weight on one leg, or using one arm or walking with a limp

When previously normal and no obvious accident to account for it.

Bleeding or bruising

If you are unable to account for any bleeding or bruising from an injury. A sick-appearing child, with or without a fever and a rash that looks like little early bruises, may have a serious infection.

Accident

Unless it was very minor, you should notify your doctor, particularly after a head injury, if your child has been knocked out, or vomits, or if she has eaten or drunk any medicines or household items.

If your child has any of the symptoms described above, she should see a doctor within twenty-four hours and in some cases earlier. However, she may have other symptoms that worry you and that need discussion with a doctor, though not so urgently. Some of these worries—for instance, about your child's hearing or vision—may be serious. Others, such as "fussy" eating or constipation, may be less serious medically but still important to you, and it may be helpful to discuss them initially with the doctor's office staff.

Medicines

Your Attitude toward Drugs

Drugs include not only aspirin or antibiotics, marijuana or heroin. We all use a variety of drugs in our everyday lives. Coffee, tea, some carbonated drinks, and chocolate all contain varying amounts of caffeine—a stimulant. Tobacco contains nicotine—a very powerfully addictive drug, as smokers who have tried to give it up will know. Alcohol is a drug that for many of us is an aid to relaxation, enjoyment, or getting through tough times.

The problems of cigarette smoking, heavy drinking, glue sniffing, or heroin addiction may seem a million miles away when you have tiny children, but one factor that may make children more likely to abuse drugs of any type when they are older is the example they are set in childhood. Obviously this is by no means the only factor, but because small children subconsciously absorb attitudes and ideas from the way the adults around them behave, it is worth considering. There is a much greater likelihood of children smoking if both their parents smoke. The children of heavy drinkers are themselves more vulnerable to following suit.

It is no good saying "Don't you ever do this" while lighting up a cigarette. Children quickly pick up hidden or double messages and are more likely to follow example than empty exhortation. So what does this mean in practice when it comes to the under-fives? Parents who are very dependent on some form of drugs, whether alcohol, tobacco, tranquilizers, or one of the illegal varieties, need to think seriously about the effect this will have in the long term on their children's attitudes. Talk it over with your partner and, if possible, with a doctor you trust or one of the organizations aiming to help with advice. But all of us can be more aware of the messages we are giving in word and deed by looking at this list of do's and don'ts.

- DO NOT teach that for every problem there is a drug to cure or to soothe. For example, by coming back from a hard day at work and immediately reaching for a large drink or cigarette and saying, "I needed that." Instead, make an effort, and some considerable effort may be required, not to present a drug as the answer to stress or problems.

- DO NOT give your child an infallible belief in the power of medicines. If you always expect a prescription every time you go to the doctor, you may give your child the same idea. Do not teach that medicine is the only answer, that it always works, and that nothing will get better any other way.

- DO be honest about your own use of drugs. If you smoke and cannot give it up, tell your child you wish you had never started because smoking can give you a bad cough and may make you ill. Most children are very antismoking and want their parents to stop. Even a young child can understand something about addiction. Once you start taking something, your body gets used to it and you just cannot do without it, even though it is bad for you. It is better not to start. It may be much harder to be honest about dependence on alcohol. Try not to set the example that adults can never be happy or have fun without a glass in their hands.

- DO NOT develop medicine rituals. Small children can think taking medicine is "grown-up" and, therefore, attractive, so do not develop elaborate procedures around medicine-taking or make too much fuss about it. Don't encourage children to believe a medicine always makes everything better so they ask for cough medicine, for example, when they are just tired, or for vague "off" days.

- DO teach that the right amount of medicine can sometimes help—but twice as much is not twice as good. Young children can understand that a little may make them feel better, but too much can be bad for them. When they get older you can explain that drugs always have more than one action and should therefore be treated with respect.

- DO make sure always that all medicines, especially brightly colored pills that look like candy, are kept safely out of reach.

Giving Medicines

Here is a list of essential points when medicines are prescribed for your child.

- Store all medicines well out of reach of children and in childproof containers.

- Store medicines at the right temperature—that is, in the refrigerator or away from direct heat if that is the direction on the bottle. When the course is finished, destroy any remaining medication by flushing it down the toilet.

- Know what you are giving. The name of the medicine should be written on the label on the container. If your doctor forgets to explain what he has prescribed, do not be afraid to ask. The days of talking blindly about the "red pills" and the "yellow liquid medicine," without having any idea what they are supposed to do, are over. If you leave the doctor's office without knowing whether it is antibiotic or cough medicine you are giving your child, ask the pharmacist, who often includes written information sheets when filling the prescription.

- If your child is taking any medicines and you have to see another doctor—for instance, a specialist—make sure you know the name and the dose, or take the medicine with you.

- Make sure you understand the instructions for giving the medicine before leaving the pharmacy, how much, how often, and when. Lots of people misunderstand instructions without realizing it. For example, four times a day does not mean four randomly spaced doses, but one dose every six hours. Giving it wrongly can make medicine less effective. Check whether the medicine should be given before, with, or after meals.

- Measure doses of medicine accurately, using a marked measuring spoon for liquid.

- Make sure the medicine is swallowed—sometimes that is easier said than done with babies or protesting toddlers. Vomiting or diarrhea may mean medicine never has a chance to get into the system; if this is a continuing problem, ask your doctor's advice.

Taking the Medicine . . . Without Tears

Do not try to give medicine to a baby or child who is upset—calm her first if at all possible. Try to give the medication to your child before a feeding, unless otherwise directed. When hungry, your child is more likely to take the medicine down quickly, thinking it is part of her usual meal.

Measure medicine into a spoon before picking up the child yourself, or getting someone else to hold her for you. You can balance it on a clean plate with something under the handle to level it or use a test-tube-style medicine spoon, which stands up by itself. Bottle-fed babies may take thin, though not syrupy, medicines from a nipple or small bottle.

Do not give medicine to a child lying flat, as she may choke, nor to one sitting upright, as she is more likely to dribble or spit it out. Lay her back slightly with your arm supporting her head, trapping her arms so she does not grab at the spoon. Put a small baby in an infant seat.

Babies who have been weaned will usually open their mouths for a spoon; give the entire spoonful at one time so they do not taste and decide they do not want it, although many children's medicines are sweet. Smaller babies will open their mouths if you touch the spoon against their top and then their bottom lip.

Once the medicine is in the mouth, use your free hand to gently lift their chin upward—this will keep their mouths closed, stop the medicine from coming out, and encourage them to swallow. Very lightly stroking a finger across the outside of a baby or small child's throat will usually produce a swallow motion.

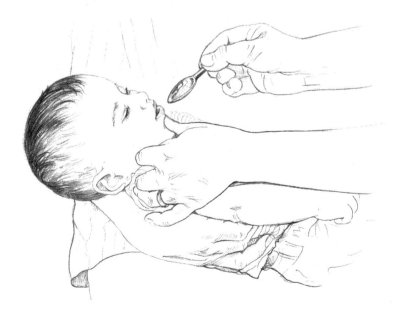

If the child begins to choke, do not keep trying to force her to swallow and holding her mouth shut; let her sit up and gently stroke her back while she recovers; and do not worry about the medicine. Try again when she has calmed down; giving it in two smaller doses may help, or pouring it into her mouth more slowly.

If your child needs to take medicine contained in syrup regularly, remember to brush her teeth afterward to prevent dental problems from developing. An increasing number of medicines are now sugar-free.

Antibiotics—Why They Are Not Always the Answer

Antibiotics have revolutionized medicine, but do not make the mistake of thinking they will cure anything and everything. Their use is strictly limited—they work by killing off bacteria. So if an ear infection or sore throat is caused by bacteria, antibiotics can be the answer. But if a virus is causing illness, then antibiotics will not be of any use. Viruses are smaller organisms than bacteria and, although research continues, so far there are few successful antiviral drugs.

How does a doctor know whether illness is due to bacteria or a virus? Only by taking a history, looking at the symptoms, and using medical knowledge. In general, pus indicates bacterial infection, but redness and soreness could be due to either. If an antibiotic is given by mouth in the form of liquid medicine or pills, this is said to be a "systemic" form of treatment—that is, it treats the whole system. If an antibiotic in a cream or ointment is just applied directly to the skin, then the treatment is said to be "topical"—it does not affect the whole system but just the area on which it is used.

Antibiotic medicine is always prescribed for a specific period of treatment—five, seven, ten, or fourteen days. Although symptoms may disappear very soon after taking antibiotics, it is important always to complete the course. Otherwise not all the bacteria may have been killed, and the symptoms will start to return as soon as you stop the medicine.

Different antibiotics work better against different bacteria. Repeated use of the same antibiotic encourages bacteria to become resistant, so they are not killed. Bacteria that survive an only partially completed course of antibiotic may be especially likely to develop resistance to the antibiotic given. Giving medicine at irregular intervals instead of the prescribed interval also allows germs to fight back and multiply when the level of antibiotic in the system falls; this can also lead to resistance.

Allergic Reactions

If your child starts to show signs of allergy while taking medicine, stop giving it and call the doctor's office for advice. Skin rashes and swelling are the most common signs—rashes may be raised or consist of red blotches and cause itching. Swelling may show as puffiness of the face or extremities. If possible, take the child to the doctor's office so your doctor can see the reaction—it could be due to something else altogether. Most nonirritating rashes will be caused by the infection that led to the child becoming sick. If it is thought to be an allergic reaction, a note will be placed on your child's medical record, because once a sensitivity develops, she will probably react to that drug again and could become more seriously ill next time. For this reason you should be sure you know what it is your child is thought to be allergic to so you can tell any other medical staff who may need to treat your child in the future.

The Pharmacist

The pharmacist at your local pharmacy can be a valuable help —he can advise about over-the-counter medicines and will always tell you if he thinks you should take your child to see a doctor. It is part of the pharmacist's training to make sure you understand how a prescription is to be used, and he will tell you exactly what it is if you are unsure. Just ask the counter assistant at the pharmacy if you can speak to the pharmacist if you need this kind of advice.

Over-the-Counter Medicines

Do not give any over-the-counter medicines to a baby under six months old except on the advice of a doctor.

Immunizations

The body's immune system is its defense mechanism against potentially harmful bacteria and viruses. When the body is invaded by bacteria or viruses there may be a localized response in the form of inflammation and a general reaction, including fever. There is also a specific immune response when the body recognizes the bacteria as foreign and, along with other defensive measures, produces antibodies that combat the particular bacteria. Once antibodies to particular bacteria have been produced, the body retains a "memory" of the invading foreign cells so if the body encounters the same bacteria again, the antibody system is immediately ready to combat the disease.

We do not have to wait for our children to catch potentially life-threatening diseases, though, to acquire an immunity. Instead, we can protect them by having them immunized. There are two forms of immunization—active and passive. Active immunization means that a weak form of the infection is deliberately given to a child; this stimulates her body to produce antibodies so she will be able to resist future infections. With passive immunization the antibodies are produced by another person or animal and injected into the child to give temporary immunity. Very few, if any, immunizations last a lifetime, while others, such as for influenza, only last a short time. The program of immunization for infants and preschool children is designed to give them protection from many diseases that are potentially life-threatening or that can do permanent damage. Babies are born with some natural immunity because during pregnancy some of the mother's antibodies pass over into the baby's bloodstream, but the immunity usually lasts only for a few months. Breast milk also contains antibodies, so that babies who are breast-fed are also more immune to infections than are bottle-fed babies.

Very many parents today do not even know what diphtheria is because it has been so successfully combated by the use of vaccines, but this may create a sense of false security, which could make parents less conscientious about having their child immunized.

Before vaccines were available, many thousands of babies and young children became ill each year with serious infections such as polio, diphtheria, smallpox, and whooping cough. Some of these affected children died; others were left permanently damaged. Since the introduction of vaccines, and improvements in hygiene and sanitation, these terrible illnesses have become rare in most parts of the world. Polio, diphtheria, and tetanus still occur commonly in underdeveloped countries where vaccination is not widely available. As these diseases are now rare in the developed world, it is very easy to forget how devastating they were in earlier times. However, diphtheria, tetanus, whooping cough, and polio are still present and could again cause serious illness and death to many children if widespread immunization did not occur. Even in recent years, there have been cases of diphtheria and polio in many parts of the world, including Europe, in children who did not receive vaccines. The Hib vaccine prevents some cases of bacterial meningitis, pneumonias, and serious throat infections. Although there has been some publicity given to the side effects of immunization, the dangers of the diseases that are prevented by immunization are many times greater than the dangers of immunization, which is now extremely safe.

Why bother immunizing against rare diseases? You may ask why you should have your baby immunized against a disease like diphtheria, which is very rare nowadays in the developed world. The problem is that when a disease becomes rare, but is not completely wiped out, an unexpected outbreak could damage large numbers of individuals if they are unprotected. Of course, when a disease has been completely wiped out worldwide, as has smallpox, then vaccination is no longer necessary.

How is it done? Most vaccines are given by injection into the thigh. The polio vaccine can given by mouth or by injection. Either route is effective.

Most parents dislike taking their children for any procedure that may cause pain or discomfort to the child. One mother said: "I felt that I was betraying my baby by taking her to the doctor for something that was going to hurt her. It seems awful to let someone stick a needle in them when they are so trusting and unsuspecting."

If you personally dread injections or going to the dentist, you may be especially reluctant. However, it is worth remembering that the vaccines are being given to prevent serious illness, and the small discomfort of the injection is very minor compared to the severity of illnesses such as whooping cough, measles, or polio. Remember that some babies are scarcely upset at all, and most cry for less than a minute. They certainly will not be permanently upset by the experience or have painful memories, and it really is not worth putting your child at unnecessary risk to avoid minor discomfort. If one parent feels reluctant to take the baby, perhaps the other can take over.

When is it done? Doctors sometimes differ slightly in the ages at which they recommend immunizations, but the following is the timetable recommended by the American Academy of Pediatrics (except as noted, the times indicate the age of the child, not intervals between immunizations; the times indicated are ideal, but if not strictly adhered to, the series can be continued):

Hepatitis B vaccine
> First dose: two days
> Second dose: two months later
> Third dose: six to twelve months later

Triple vaccine (diphtheria, acellular pertussis, tetanus) and Hib (Hemophilus influenza b)
> First dose: two months
> Second dose: four months
> Third dose: six months
> Fourth dose: twelve to fifteen months (Hib should be given after fifteen months)

Polio vaccine (suggested routes)
> First dose: two months (injection of killed vaccine)
> Second dose: four months (injection of killed vaccine)
> Third dose: twelve to fifteen months (oral route)

MMR vaccine (measles, mumps, rubella)
> First dose: twelve to fifteen months
> Second dose: four to five years

Booster DPaT (Diphtheria, acellular pertussis, tetanus) and polio
> Four to five years

Varicella vaccine (chicken pox)
> (optional but advisable) twelve months

Booster, tetanus and polio
> Thirteen to eighteen years

Tuberculin test
> Nine months
> Five years
> Adolescence
> As indicated for possible exposure

Reactions

Triple vaccine (DPaT).   A few hours after the injection there may be a small lump where the injection was given, and some reddening and tenderness around it. About half of all children vaccinated have a mild fever, and many seem cranky. Very occasionally the fever may be quite elevated and the child may seem quite ill. Most of these symptoms subside within a few hours or settle after giving antifever medications for babies prescribed in the proper dose by your doctor, but very occasionally (less than one in every hundred thousand children vaccinated) more severe illness may occur, with convulsions or even coma. If you are worried, consult your doctor. If the baby has had a reaction to the triple vaccine, this is most likely due to the whooping cough part of the vaccine (see below). With the new acellular vaccine, reactions are almost nonexistent.

MMR vaccine (Measles, Mumps, Rubella).   Some babies may have a slight fever and a faint rash for a few days two to fourteen days after the injection. A few get swollen faces, like mumps, about three weeks after. This will gradually go away. If your child is hot and irritable during the first days after the injection, you can give the proper dose of antifever medication to lower the temperature. The chance of a reaction is less after the second dose of the MMR vaccine. None of these reactions is infectious. If you are worried about a vaccine, consult your doctor.

Reasons for Not Giving the Vaccines

Babies should not be immunized while they have an acute illness with fever (not just a cold) or if they have had a severe local or general reaction to a previous DTaP vaccination. In such a situation you should discuss this with your doctor. In the case of an acute illness, your doctor will want to wait until the baby is better before giving the vaccine. Where a severe reaction has occurred, the doctor may decide to leave out the whooping cough part of the vaccine so the baby can still have the diphtheria, tetanus, polio, and Hib vaccines. If you have concerns about any of the vaccines, consult your doctor or an infectious disease specialist.

Contraindications for Live Vaccines   Live vaccines should not be given to children who are in direct contact with individuals who are immuno-compromised—that is, those whose natural immunity is at a low level or those who have no immunity at all. These are individuals who may have been born with a lack of natural immunity, individuals being treated with anticancer drugs or high doses of steroids, or those individuals who may be suffering from an acquired immune deficiency, such as AIDS. The vaccines in question are the oral polio vaccine and the MMR vaccine.

Babies can be safely immunized if they have an allergy or if there is an allergy in the family.

Babies can be immunized even if another member of your family had a bad reaction following immunization.

If your baby was born prematurely, or had a low birth weight, it is still important to give the first vaccination two months after birth.

Breast-feeding does not interfere with immunization.

Even if you think your child has had measles or rubella, the vaccine should still be given. There is no extra risk from being immunized, and the diagnosis of measles and rubella is often difficult to make clinically. There are blood tests that can determine if you have antibodies against these diseases.

Immunization can go ahead even if your baby has been in contact with another child with an infectious illness.

Visiting Nurses and Health Clinics

If you think your child is ill, you should contact your doctor, but there is also another level of health care designed to help parents and to monitor children's development. Community health care is the general term for this, although the way in which it works will vary slightly according to the practice of different physicians. Essentially the aim of the service is to provide a surveillance system that can offer both support and advice to parents about their child's health and be watchful to pick up any developmental or health problems that may need further investigation or treatment. Much of the work of the community health service is aimed at preventing ill health—ensuring that all children are covered by a program of immunization to protect against certain dangerous diseases is most important. These facilities are usually located throughout larger cities and provide routine well-baby care, including the administration of immunizations.

Visiting nurses provided by many of the insurance health plans can be a valuable source of support in the early days. In addition to wanting to know if you and your baby are well and making good progress, they will also have time to talk about the more intangible aspects of parenting. If you feel a bit low, disoriented, or overwhelmed by the changes in your life, they can be a sympathetic and often constructive support. Unfortunately, there are rarely any magic solutions to age-old problems of babies who cry a great deal and do not sleep, but it is surprising how someone looking objectively at what is happening can often make helpful and positive suggestions. The nurse will also be able to suggest ways in which you can meet other new parents, although very often such friendships spring from meetings at the health clinic or the doctor's office where you will go to visit once you get out and about. At the first home visit your the nurse will probably weigh your baby, examine her, and answer many of your questions. You will then bring your baby to the doctor's office or to the health clinic at two weeks of age for further follow-up.

Developmental Checkups

New babies will receive their first checkup within twenty-four hours of birth, and this will be done either by a neonatologist, a pediatrician in the hospital, or by your family doctor before you are discharged from the hospital. The next checkup is at two weeks, again either by a doctor at his office or at the local health center. You should call for this appointment shortly after coming home from the hospital.

On this occasion the doctor will ask about your baby's feeding and sleeping routine and will be looking to see how alert and responsive she is. He will see how well your baby is beginning to support her head, listen to her heart, and check to make sure the hip joint fits properly into the socket. The doctor will see if your baby follows objects with her eyes, and ask if you think she reacts to noises, but screening for hearing defects is not usually done until the baby is about seven or eight months old, unless there is cause for suspicion.

Exact timing of further checkups varies according to the practice of different doctors, but in most instances the next checkup will be at about eight weeks, four months, six months, nine months, and then at a year of age. Again the doctor will be looking to see how generally alert your baby is and ask about patterns of eating, sleeping, and behavior as well as about any illnesses your baby may have had. By six months most babies can sit unaided, push themselves up on their forearms when lying on their bellies, and will reach out to grab an object such as a block placed in front of them. The doctor will test her hearing by making a series of sounds behind her and seeing if the baby turns her head in response. If the child fails to respond to the noises it is more commonly because she is tired, distracted by something else, not interested, not familiar with the test sounds, or has wax blocking her ears rather than that her hearing is actually impaired, but the test will be repeated a few weeks later, and if she fails to respond again, she will be referred to an audiologist. All the same, if you are worried about your baby's hearing at any age, tell the doctor so that, if necessary, more accurate tests can be carried out.

After this visit at one year of age, visits to the doctor usually occur at fifteen months, eighteen months, twenty-four months, thirty months, and at three years of age. Yearly checkups are then the rule. Depending on your child's age, the doctor will be looking to see if she has reached various developmental milestones, using a variety of tests to measure these, as well as making sure she is in good health and has no problems with hearing or sight. The ages at which children learn to walk, talk, are toilet trained, and so on vary tremendously, but the chart in chapter 9 gives an idea of what to expect at various stages. Most doctors will be happy to explain the point of various tests. If you have any specific worries about your child, always ask. If you still think there is some abnormality in your child's hearing, sight, or development, your doctor will likely refer you to a specialist who can give a detailed assessment.

Your Child's Teeth

Your baby's first set of teeth, or milk teeth, are forming in her gums before birth. Rarely, a baby is born with the first tooth and if this is wobbly, it may have to be taken out. But if it is firmly embedded, it may be left because removing it means the child may have a gap until her second teeth begin to come through. An early tooth may also interfere with breast-feeding. Usually babies cut their first tooth, which will be one of the middle upper or lower teeth (called a central incisor), at about six months. Do not worry, though, if your baby does not cut teeth until a little later; some babies are still giving toothless, gummy smiles at the end of their first year! Total absence of teeth is very rare.

Teething

Babies may become a little disturbed when teeth start to erupt. They usually like to bite on something hard, such as a teething ring. You can also rub the gums to give relief. Do not give teething preparations or pain relievers, but discuss all forms of medication for teething with your doctor. It is important to remember that teething does not cause fever of more than a hundred degrees or excessive irritability. If these symptoms develop, call your doctor.

This is the order in which your baby's teeth will usually appear:

Age	Teeth	Position
6 months	Incisors	Two central bottom and two central top teeth
8 months	Two more incisors	Top and bottom, making four top and four bottom front teeth in all
10–14 months	First molars	Double teeth for chewing
15–18 months	Canines	The eyeteeth or "fangs"
2–2½ years	Second molars	The second set of double teeth at the back

In total there are twenty primary or "milk" teeth—twelve less than the full set of thirty-two permanent teeth we have as adults. Most children have a full set of primary teeth by the time they are about two and a half years old, and these last until about the age of six, when the teeth that were the first to appear, the middle front or central incisors, become loose and fall out as the second teeth begin to push through the gums. These primary teeth continue to fall out until the age of about twelve.

Taking Care of Your Child's Teeth

Teeth are made up of a soft, sensitive center called pulp, which is well supplied with nerve endings and blood vessels and is protected by a hard outer casing of dentine and then enamel. Dentine is softer than enamel. Enamel does not have nerve endings and is therefore not sensitive. Teeth become decayed when acid eats through the protective coating of enamel and begins to attack the sensitive inside of the tooth—this causes a toothache. So a toothache is not the first warning of decay, but actually means the enamel has been eaten away at some point, leaving the less hard dentine vulnerable to decay.

How does the acid that eats through the protective enamel coating come to be on our teeth? The answer lies in a substance called plaque, which cannot easily be seen by the naked eye but which forms a sticky film covering the teeth. The attacking acids are produced when bacteria present in the plaque react with little bits of leftover food. Cleaning plaque off the teeth, therefore, is the most important protective measure you can take to safeguard your child's teeth. This can be done by daily brushing.

When to start cleaning teeth? Teeth need cleaning as soon as they appear, and that is true of the primary teeth just as much as of permanent teeth. The idea that the first teeth do not matter because they are going to fall out is wrong. The first teeth need taking care of just as much as second teeth, first, to avoid pain and distress, and unnecessary extractions; and second, if the primary teeth are allowed to decay so they have to be taken out long before the second teeth are ready to come through, this may lead to loss of space for the permanent successors and thus can lead to orthodontic problems.

If children have not been encouraged to take care of their teeth by cleaning them carefully and not having too much candy and too many sweet drinks, they are unlikely to change their ways when they reach the age of six, when their second teeth start to come through. Sound teeth look good. Your child should have a nice smile, so why risk a mouth of discolored stumps instead? Toothache is quite painful, and children do not have to suffer from it if their teeth are properly cared for.

Your baby's first teeth are best cleaned by wrapping a clean, nonfluffy piece of material like gauze around your finger and simply rubbing the teeth and gums gently to wipe away the plaque.

In the second year, you can introduce a toothbrush—choose one with soft bristles, and brush the teeth starting at the base of the tooth and moving away from the gum—that is, upward if you are brushing the lower jaw and downward if you are brushing teeth in the top jaw. As your child grows, she will want to take over some of the brushing herself. Teach her to brush in the same way that you do and always insist that you have a turn at the end to make sure her teeth are properly clean.

When is your child old enough to brush her teeth completely by herself? This depends slightly on the individual child but usually not before five years old, although obviously she will have been taking over more and more of the brushing, with you supervising and having a turn at the end to reach those difficult back molars.

How often should you brush a child's teeth? The ideal would be every time she eats something, but obviously this is not practical. Compromise with a routine where you brush morning and evening, and always make a point of brushing teeth after she eats candy. You must make sure that the last tooth-brushing session at night is never followed by anything else to eat or drink, which will leave a coating of plaque and bits of food in her mouth during the night. Be very firm about this from the start and it will become a routine with your child.

Toothpaste.   Toothpastes are mixtures that have a slightly abrasive action to aid cleaning. The one active ingredient that is added to nearly all toothpaste today is fluoride, a mineral that occurs naturally in the water in some areas. It has been found that fluoride can cut down dental decay, although too much can cause teeth to become mottled—mottling varies from small white flecks to brown staining, with large amounts needed to cause the latter. In this country it is left to individual counties to decide whether to add fluoride to their water. You can find out by asking the local water department or by calling your pediatrician whether yours is an area in which the correct amount of fluoride has been added to the water. If not, taking fluoride during pregnancy will not help make your unborn baby's teeth extra strong, but you should give fluoride drops or tablets to your child from the age of six months until she is twelve years old, the period during which teeth are developing in the gums. Fluoride has been shown to strengthen the developing enamel against tooth decay. Where the water contains an adequate amount of fluoride or you are giving the child drops or tablets, restrict the amount of toothpaste you put on the child's toothbrush to a pea-size drop, as most of this is swallowed.

Food for Healthy Teeth

Sugar is a natural enemy of teeth and the biggest single cause of tooth decay. Children who do not eat candy or drink sweet drinks do not get decayed teeth that need fillings as often as children who are continually bathing their teeth in sweet fluids. But eliminating candy and sugary foods from your child's life completely can be very difficult and unnecessary. You will be doing well to protect your child's teeth if you follow these simple rules:

1. DO NOT make candy a habit, but instead save it for special occasions and treats.

2. DO encourage children to think of other foods as edible treats—for example, fruit or cheese.

3. DO NOT give children candy to be eaten slowly over a long period—for example, chewy taffy candy or a lollipop to be sucked. It is far better to have a sweet-eating binge and then to clean teeth thoroughly afterward.

4. DO save candy or sweet drinks for after meals, when a tooth-brushing session can take care of all the plaque.

5. DO NOT give anything to eat or drink after teeth have been brushed before your child goes to bed.

6. DO NOT allow your child to go to sleep with a bottle containing milk, juice, or any other fluid containing sugar, since this will lead to a condition known as "baby bottle caries." This results in serious cavities in the teeth and requires extensive dental rehabilitation.

7. DO feed your child a healthy, balanced diet.

This last rule means plenty of the kind of food that needs chewing. Whole-grain foods such as whole wheat bread tend to need more chewing, as do uncooked vegetables such as carrots or celery and fresh fruit such as apples. Chewing these all exercises jaws and makes for healthier teeth and gums.

Do not forget that carbonated drinks and most of the fruit drinks that have to be diluted with water contain a tremendous amount of sugar, which is just as damaging for your child's teeth as actually eating candy. Even when the label says there are no added sweeteners, some drinks are naturally very high in their own sugar content—for example, apple juice, which is best rationed to drinking at mealtimes only and then made up in very weak solution (one part juice and three parts water). A steady supply of these very sweet drinks in between meals has the same effect as regularly giving your child candy to eat. Because they are so high in sugar they are also very poor thirst quenchers. The acid in the juice dissolves the surface enamel. If this continues for long periods the teeth are eroded and cavities result. Sodas taken in excess can also damage your child's teeth.

Never dip a pacifier into sweetened drinks such as sugar water or some super-sweet fruit juice. This is the quickest way to rot teeth, and your child will end up with a row of blackened stumps instead of pearly white, gleaming teeth.

Going to the Dentist

Try to pick a dentist who is sympathetic and friendly toward children and who is prepared to take the time and patience needed to care for the teeth of children. The best way to find out about good pediatric dentists is to ask other parents about a dentist where children are made welcome or to call the local American Dental Association. If you make an appointment as a family and take your baby with you, she will grow up being used to visiting the dentist and seeing her parents sitting in the dentist's chair. Try hard not to convey any apprehensive feelings or fears you may have yourself—parents can find themselves putting on their most convincing acting performance when they find themselves in the dentist's chair under their child's watchful gaze! In fact, it is important that you remember that modern dentistry has come a long way since you were a child. Your child does not have to end up with a mouth full of fillings, as you may have done, if adequate preventive methods have been taken. Modern treatment using local anesthetics is rarely painful. If your child does need fillings in her first set of teeth, remember that the primary teeth are less sensitive than the second teeth.

In the beginning, the dentist will just want to look at your child's teeth as she sits on your knee; as she gets older she will learn to open her mouth so the dentist can see better using a small dental mirror, and she can progress to actually sitting in the dentist's chair, but do not force this until she is ready. Some health centers have visiting dentists who are used to dealing with small children and have more time to deal with a nervous one. Although the primary teeth may show minor irregularities such as crowding, there is very rarely an indication for treatment until the permanent teeth start to erupt.

CHAPTER 17

Common Health Problems

Elevated temperature and fever
Infectious diseases causing fever
Colds, coughs, and sore-throat colds
Tonsils, tonsillitis, and adenoids • Croup • Skin problems
Sunburn and heatstroke • Stings and bites • Parasites
Mouth problems • Nail problems • Ear problems
Eye problems • Bladder and kidney infections
The intestinal tract and its problems
Minor orthopedic problems • The clumsy child

Reading descriptions of symptoms and wondering if they fit your child's complain—often in the small hours of the morning—is an experience few parents escape. Usually they will not find it difficult to decide whether to ask for help from a doctor, and there are some suggested guidelines in chapter 16 about when to consult a doctor. In reading this chapter and the next, however, it is important to remember that all children are special individuals, which means the body of each one will react slightly differently when there is something wrong. Your child may be sick yet have quite different symptoms or reactions from the ones described. In general you should trust your instincts; if you are in doubt or really worried, get professional help anyway. Doctors understand that children's ill health is a major source of anxiety to a parent. If the problem turns out not to be serious or does not require treatment, they will still feel your visit is justified, as they will have been able to offer information and reassurance.

When using these chapters to seek information about a complaint, remember that the same condition can, in its mildest form, be a common health problem, while in its more severe form it merits classification as a serious illness—eczema and asthma are just two of the conditions that fall into this category.

If your child is unlucky enough to suffer from a long-term or chronic condition with severe symptoms, the whole family will inevitably end up becoming experts on the subject, but do not make the mistake, if your child does start to show mild symptoms of being ill, of jumping to conclusions and anticipating that a host of problems inevitably lie before you.

Elevated Temperature and Fever

An elevated temperature or feverishness are symptoms of so many childhood illnesses that it seems helpful to set out the general principles for treating the problem, even though the cause will naturally vary.

Normally the temperature control mechanism in the brain keeps the body's temperature constant—this is the body's thermostat. When bacteria or viruses attack, the toxins they produce affect this thermostat and interfere with it working properly. The result is often shivering, shaking, and feeling alternately hot and cold while the body temperature is actually elevated; this is fever.

A child's temperature can often rise without his being particularly sick. Running around, getting upset and screaming, hot weather, or being wrapped up too warmly may all make his temperature rise temporarily. It is very important to look at his overall condition, not just his temperature alone, to assess how sick he is. Children can run quite high temperatures that would make an adult feel very ill and still have nothing very much wrong with them. Conversely, small babies may have only a slight temperature but still be quite seriously ill. Most parents can tell just by feeling how hot their child is and looking at his appearance and behavior whether he has a temperature. Probably if you cannot be sure in this way, the temperature is either normal or only slightly raised.

If your child is under six months old, fever alone is usually a good enough reason to see a doctor. However, as long as he is still feeding, has no other symptoms, and is not excessively irritable, you can see if you can cool him down by loosening clothing and using tepid sponging. Do not think a baby or child with a temperature needs to be wrapped up warmly, whatever other people may say, because excessive covering with clothes and blankets will elevate the temperature even higher. A child under six months old should not be given any over-the-counter medication without talking to a doctor.

Babies and children over six months can be given antifever medications for babies in the dose recommended for their age. If the fever continues and is accompanied by any other symptoms, you need to take the child to the doctor. How promptly you act depends on the child's age and the severity of symptoms. Babies may safely be taken to the doctor's office.

Aspirin, in any form, should never be used for any child under the age of twelve years without a doctor's advice because it has been associated, although only in a few cases, with a very rare and serious condition—Reye's syndrome—which causes inflammation of the brain. Do not worry if your child has had aspirin in the past; there is no danger now.

Taking Your Child's Temperature

Thermometers measure temperature in Centigrade and/or in Fahrenheit. Degrees of temperature are marked off along the thermometer, sometimes with an arrow or an "N" to mark the normal point. Normal body temperature is 37 degrees Centigrade or 98.6 degrees Fahrenheit. Make sure the mercury column (the thin line) starts well below normal. To do this hold the top end of the thermometer and shake it with a wrist-snapping action, like cracking a whip. For children under three put the bulb end of the thermometer under their armpit (with no shirt on) and keep it there by holding their arm across their chest or abdomen for one full minute before reading the temperature. Older children may be able to manage to

Fahrenheit and Centigrade Comparison Chart	
F	C
95	35.0
96	35.6
97	36.1
98	36.7
98.6	37 (normal)
99	37.2
100	37.8
101	38.3
102	38.9
103	39.4
104	40
105	40.6
106	41.1

keep it under their tongues—again, it needs a full minute—but if you have problems, put it under the armpit. If you are telling a doctor the temperature, mention if it is an armpit (axillary) temperature, because this is slightly lower than a mouth (oral) reading.

After using the thermometer shake it down again, wash it with cold water, and store it well out of the child's reach. It is important that the child understands he is not to bite the thermometer when you put it under the tongue.

Tepid Sponging to Lower Temperature

- The air in the room should be comfortably warm—not hot or cold and drafty.

- Lay the child on a towel across your knees or the bed and gently remove his clothes, talking soothingly.

- Sponge his body, limbs, and face with tepid (lukewarm) water. As the water evaporates from the skin it absorbs heat from the blood and in so doing it cools the body.

- DO NOT be tempted to think that the colder the water, the more effective the treatment. Cold water makes the blood vessels in the skin constrict, so less blood flows through and less heat can be lost. Consequently the temperature will stay high or even rise.

- As the child cools down, pat his skin dry with a towel and dress him only in a diaper or underpants. Cover him with a cotton sheet. DO NOT bundle him up with blankets.

- Keep checking his body temperature to make sure he does not get too cold and shivery. If he does, cover him with more light clothes and wrappings but keep the coverings loose.

- His temperature may begin to climb again. If he starts to get hot and irritable, keep repeating the spongings every ten minutes until the temperature lowers.

Taking Care of Children with Fevers

Your best guide as to how to treat a child with a fever is the child's behavior. As has been said, it is possible for a young child to have an elevated temperature and not be acting particularly sick, in which case there is no need to do more than keep a careful eye on him to make sure he does not suddenly deteriorate. Cover him up fairly warmly when going out in cold weather. He may be incubating an infectious illness, so it makes sense to keep him out of places such as day care, nursery school, etc., until he is well and to warn other mothers whom you would normally see in case they have a special reason for avoiding infection.

Children who feel sick will naturally limit their own activities. Young children like to be near their parents, so make a bed up on a sofa downstairs if he wants to sleep so you can be close to check on him and still do what you have to do. Try to get a child who has an elevated temperature to drink plenty of fluids, but do not worry if he does not want to eat. If you have to take him out in cold weather—for example, to the doctor's office—no harm will come to him if you wrap him up warmly. It makes sense to keep him indoors until he is feeling better.

Fever (Febrile) Convulsions (Seizures)

My eighteen-month-old daughter ran a high temperature very suddenly because of a sore throat. I was alone in the house, except for another toddler of two and a half, when she had a convulsion. I completely panicked. She went stiff and rigid and began to turn blue in the face. I ran next door with her to the neighbors, who called the doctor and began giving her mouth-to-mouth resuscitation, though I don't know if that helped. After that I learned a great deal about convulsions, and two years later, when my son began to make jerky movements while running a high temperature, I recognized the signs. In this case he just went pale and limp, not stiff, and quickly came around. I undressed him and tried to cool him off.

The words "convulsion," "fit," and "seizure" mean the same thing. We all have electrical activity going on in our brains all the time, but a convulsion occurs when there is a sudden unusual release of electricity in the brain. Although it is very frightening for parents if their child has a convulsion, be reassured that they are rarely dangerous. About one in thirty to forty children will have a convulsion as a result of running a high temperature—medically these convulsions are known as febrile (meaning feverish) convulsions. A young child's immature brain cannot cope with the sudden rise in temperature—it is the suddenness of a sharp rise in temperature that seems more likely to provoke the convulsion than the actual level that the temperature reaches. Such convulsions are most common between the ages of six months and three years. About a third to a half of all children who have one febrile convulsion will have another, and there is sometimes a family tendency to have such convulsions. These are not harmful in the long run.

What are the signs? While running a high temperature a child may begin to make jerky limb movements, seem distressed or frightened, or cry out beforehand. In other cases there may be no such warning signs. The essential feature of a convulsion is that the child loses consciousness. Usually his body and limbs go rigid, his eyes may roll upward, the teeth become clenched, and there may be trembling or jerking of the limbs. During this phase his breathing may be interrupted and, more unusually in children, he may become incontinent of urine. Some children may become stiff for only a brief period of time and then become limp and very pale. After regaining consciousness your child may seem confused but then go to sleep.

What should you do if your child has a convulsion?

- Stay calm.

- Turn his head gently to one side so that if he should vomit, there is less likelihood that he could aspirate the vomit into his lungs, which could cause a serious pneumonia.

- Do not try to put anything into his mouth or to restrain his movements.

- Stay with him while the convulsion is occurring.

- When he regains consciousness, reassure and comfort him.

- Take immediate steps to lower his temperature by taking his clothes off, giving fever-reducing medications if he is able to drink, or administering the medication rectally. Sponge him with tepid water.

- When his temperature is lowered and he is comfortable, telephone the doctor.

When Emergency Action Is Needed

- If the convulsion continues for more than ten minutes or if the child has a second convulsion after the first, immediately contact your doctor.

- If you are unable to reach the doctor, call 911 or take the child straight to the nearest emergency room where, in the majority of cases, it will be possible to stop the convulsion within a few minutes by the use of medications.

Long-Term Treatment   Nearly all febrile convulsions that are not associated with other problems are quite short and uncomplicated and will not harm the child or affect his development. Even children who have several such convulsions will usually "grow" out of them without any problems, although if they are very frequent your doctor may discuss giving anticonvulsant medicine to prevent the attacks from occurring until the tendency to have convulsions is outgrown.

A useful alternative to giving regular anticonvulsant medication to a child with a tendency to have febrile convulsions is to give diazepam (Valium) rectally . Until recently it was thought that diazepam had to be injected directly into the bloodstream to stop convulsions. However, it is now known that it often works almost as quickly when given rectally. The best preparation is one that allows the liquid to be pushed in by squeezing a plastic container rather like a "squeeze" bottle—your doctor will explain how to use it. Suppositories do not seem as effective, since the outer coat has to be melted before the drug can be absorbed. Many parents whose children suffer from convulsions now make use of this method in an emergency, and it will usually control the convulsion and make admission to the hospital unnecessary. In the case of children who give warning signs of a possible febrile convulsion, as some children do by appearing ill, the same method will often prevent the convulsion from occurring. However, this is not helpful in all cases, and you should discuss it with your doctor. In most children with febrile convulsions, the risk of later epilepsy is probably about one in a hundred.

Infectious Diseases Causing Fever

Chicken Pox

This illness is caused by a virus that has an incubation period of ten to twenty-one days. First symptoms are of general ill feeling, and possibly headache, slight fever, and a blotchy rash, which disappears when the typical chicken pox spots appear. These look like little red pimples, and the first ones may be mistaken for flea bites, but they change into oval blisters filled with clear fluid that break and then crust over. The spots usually take up to a week to appear fully. The child is infectious for twenty-four hours before the first spots appear and until all the spots are covered with crusts.

Treatment consists of making the child feel as comfortable as possible, choosing nonitchy clothes; give him plenty to drink, a light diet, and fever-reducing medications if a low-grade fever should develop. NEVER give aspirin to a child with chicken pox! It is better if he does not scratch, but do not get upset if he does, because it is very itchy. Calamine lotion dabbed on the spots helps, plus a tepid bath with two cupfuls of sodium bicarbonate dissolved in it. Keep his nails short and try to distract him by keeping him occupied with toys, games, etc.

Scratching can sometimes lead to the complication of infection of the lesions, which might produce large scars. More serious complications are rare, but occasionally chest infections can develop or, very rarely, inflammation of the brain and nervous system. If your child begins to have convulsions or is unexplainably drowsy and confused, contact your doctor at once. Children can catch chicken pox if exposed to an adult with shingles. An inactivated live virus vaccine is now available to protect a child from acquiring chicken pox and should be given at 12 months or older.

Rubella (German Measles)

This is a very mild disease for children caused by a virus, but it is potentially very dangerous for the unborn child of a pregnant woman. The incubation period is fourteen to twenty-one days, and during this time the child may have a runny nose and possibly tender, swollen glands in the back of the head. The child may be a little irritable for a day before a slight pink rash begins behind the ears and on the forehead and then spreads to cover the whole body. The spots usually do not run together, but in some children the rash is very faint or hardly perceptible. It is not itchy, and no special treatment is needed for children with this mild disease beyond giving them plenty of fluids. The danger, however, involves pregnant women who have not been immunized in the past and hence are unprotected. If they develop rubella during the first three months of pregnancy it may seriously damage the unborn baby. Deafness, cataracts causing blindness, and malformations of the heart can result, while some women will miscarry. Unfortunately, a child with rubella is infectious for seven days before the rash appears, as well as when the rash is present and for up to a week afterward. If you think your child may have been in contact with the disease or has it, warn friends and relatives, and your child should avoid contact with pregnant women as far as possible. Warn the doctor if you are taking your child to her office, so she can arrange an appointment at the end of office hours when the waiting room is empty or can isolate your child away from others in the office who are at risk of contacting the illness.

Because rubella can be so dangerous to the unborn baby, vaccination should have been completed for all children between the ages of ten and fourteen. This is included in the MMR vaccine against measles, mumps, and rubella, which is given to all babies at twelve to fifteen months, with a second dose given at four years of age.

Measles

Also caused by a virus, this is a very infectious illness that is easily passed on by tiny droplets from the nose and throat from infected individuals that are inhaled from the air. The incubation period is ten to fourteen days, and the rash often appears on the fourteenth day after exposure. Children are initially vaccinated against measles between twelve and fifteen months of age as part of the MMR vaccine and then again at four years to boost their immunity against the disease because this can be a very serious and deadly disease. The first symptoms are fever, a cough, a runny nose, and red, sore eyes. There are often small white spots on the lining of the cheeks inside the mouth, and they may also extend down the throat. These are not painful. The rash appears two to three days later as small red, flat spots that join together to form irregular patches. Usually the rash begins behind the ears and on the nape of the neck, spreading down to cover the whole body. As the rash erupts, the child's temperature usually rises sharply, and he will feel very ill. The rash itself is not itchy, but it is not uncommon for children to develop an earache and swollen glands in the neck. Call your doctor, especially if your child has not been immunized.

Keep his temperature down by giving fever-reducing medicines, sponge him with tepid water, and give him plenty to drink. His eyes may be sore, and this will be relieved by keeping the lights dim in his room. However, no harm will result from bright lights.

Measles can cause eye, ear, or chest infections as complications that need treatment with antibiotics, and more rarely complications of the brain and nervous system are possible, including convulsions. If your child seems unusually drowsy or confused or begins to have convulsions, call the doctor at once.

Mumps

Mumps is not as infectious as measles but can be passed by droplet infection in the same way. The incubation period is fourteen to twenty-one days, and children are infectious immediately before the symptoms appear and for about seven days after. Mumps is caused by a virus that usually attacks the parotid glands, which produce saliva and which are just below the ears. Usually the first sign is swelling and pain on both sides or one side of the face close to the angle of the jaw. Sometimes the swelling may be preceded by muscular pains (especially in the neck), fever, and a headache. The salivary glands seem to produce less saliva so that the mouth is dry, and eating and drinking are painful, particularly first thing in the morning. Giving pain-reducing medications usually eases the pain, but warm compresses applied to the painful areas can also help. The exact location of the swelling may vary slightly depending on the glands involved and can affect both sides sequentially, only one side, or both sides simultaneously. The illness can be mild or can make a child very uncomfortable for a day or two. The MMR vaccine, against measles, mumps, and rubella, is given between twelve and fifteen months and again at four years to prevent this illness.

The most common complication of mumps is mumps meningitis (one in four hundred), which can cause headache, stiff neck, and sometimes nausea and vomiting about ten days after the onset of the original illness. There is no special treatment for this, and fortunately most children recover completely, but consult your doctor if you suspect your child has such symptoms. In adult men especially, the infection may spread to the testicles, which can be painful but is fortunately unusual, and even if this happens it rarely affects both testicles to cause complete infertility. In women it may spread to the ovaries, but again this is rare. Sometimes the pancreatic gland in the abdomen can be affected in both adults and children, causing abdominal pain. Mumps can occasionally also affect the hearing nerve, leading to deafness, usually only in one ear, but this is also very rare.

Scarlet Fever

This disease has an incubation period of two to four days and is caused by bacteria called hemolytic streptococci. These bacteria can cause throat and ear infections without a rash or be carried without producing any symptoms at all. Scarlet fever itself is usually a fairly mild illness that is spread by droplet infection and results in a sudden fever, sore throat, and loss of appetite. A day or two later a pinpoint rash spreads over the face and body, except for the area around the mouth. The skin becomes quite dry and flaky.

If you suspect your child has scarlet fever, see your doctor. She will do a throat culture and may start a course of antibiotics. If the culture is positive for the streptococcus, the antibiotics must be taken for ten days. If the culture is negative, the antibiotics can be discontinued. This can still be a very serious illness, and your doctor will keep an eye on your child to make sure he makes a full recovery and does not suffer one of the rare complications. These include ear infections or, more unusually, a subsequent kidney inflammation. This is most likely about three weeks after the rash first shows—signs are vague and include general malaise, abdominal pain, passing red-brown urine, and puffiness of the face and limbs. A very rare complication is rheumatic fever, which makes joints ache and can cause serious damage to the heart valves that can be permanent. This complication can occur up to three months after the acute illness.

Whooping Cough (Pertussis)

Whooping cough has three distinct stages, beginning with the "catarrhal" phase, with a runny nose, slight cough, and mild fever. After seven to fourteen days the child develops the characteristic whooping cough—this is a series of short coughs followed by a "whoop," which is caused by the noise of air being breathed in through a partially restricted windpipe. The child suffers uncontrollable spasms of coughing and may turn blue or gray during an attack because of lack of oxygen. The spasm is often followed by vomiting. This phase (the paroxysmal stage) may last two weeks or more. During the final, "convalescent," phase, the child ceases to be seriously ill but continues to cough and whoop more mildly; this can last for up to three months. In subsequent colds and coughs the child may continue to whoop simply out of habit. Giving an antibiotic (erythromycin) in the early phase may help to shorten the illness, but there is no medicine that will cure the cough.

Family members are usually treated with erythromycin for five days to prevent spread of the disease to others.

Small babies may not develop a whoop, but may stop breathing for short periods of time—up to thirty seconds. They are most at risk of serious complications, including developing a hernia, convulsions, pneumonia, brain damage, and even, in rare instances, death. Severe cases of whooping cough may have to be admitted to the hospital for special nursing care. Patients may need to have their air passages cleared, given oxygen, and be tube-fed.

It is important that all children are protected against the disease, with the triple vaccine first given at two months. By doing this the incidence of the disease will decline, and tiny babies of less than two months will be at very little risk of contracting it. There are a very few specific reasons for not vaccinating, which are outlined on page 484.

Colds, Coughs, and Sore-Throat Colds

Most babies catch a cold sometime in their first year—they are more likely to do this if they have older brothers or sisters at play group or school, because there is more chance of a cold being brought home, or if they attend a day-care center. It is reasonable to avoid known infection in the first three months as far as possible, but as long as your child is normally healthy, it is not worth turning your life upside down to keep him away from minor coughs and colds.

Why do we catch colds? Not from actually getting cold or not wrapping up warmly enough, although it is important to keep your child warm. Colds are infections of the nose and throat caused by viruses called rhinoviruses. Because there are so many different strains of these viruses and because the immunity we develop against one strain only lasts a short time, it is not possible to protect by vaccination. Nor, as has been suggested, has any research shown that taking vitamin C makes us less likely to catch colds or to shake them off more quickly. Obviously a good diet and general good health make us better able to resist or to fight viruses of all kinds, including cold viruses, but sadly the cure for the common cold seems as far off as ever. If your child catches a cold, all you can do is to relieve the symptoms and make him as comfortable as possible.

Babies under six months. Babies breathe mostly through their noses. When a small baby catches a cold, the most serious problem is usually that the nose gets blocked up and the child cannot breathe through it—this in turn makes it very hard to suck at the breast or bottle. Your baby may begin to feed and then stop, crying with frustration as he tries to breathe in through his nose and cannot. Mucus is best removed from the baby's nostril before feedings by using a 3-oz suction bulb, obtainable from the pharmacy. If mucus in the nose is thick, it can be thinned with a few drops of saltwater solution, also obtainable over the counter at the pharmacy. Put several drops into each nostril before using the suction bulb. Gently cover one nostril while you aspirate the other side. Repeat this process on the opposite side.

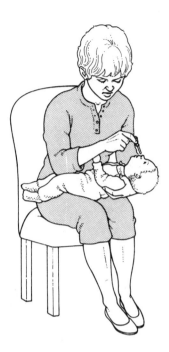

Your doctor can prescribe fever-reducing medications if the cold is making your baby feverish—do not give small babies medicine without your doctor's advice. Be prepared for your baby to be more fretful and demanding and for feeding and sleeping routines to become disrupted.

He may have a sore throat as well, so offer frequent breast-feedings, or extra drinks of water if he is bottle-fed. Coughs that go with colds in small babies are usually a reflex action to clear mucus that trickles down the back of the throat.

Obviously babies cannot blow their noses, so keep gently clearing away mucus from around the nose with soft tissues. If he wakes clogged up with dried crusts of mucus after a sleep, wash them off using a cotton ball and warm water. Applying a little petroleum jelly around the nostrils waterproofs the skin and helps it from getting sore. It looks a bit messy, but it gives the skin a chance to recover. Make sure not to block the nose itself.

Some babies seem more prone to diaper rashes when they have a cold; be particularly careful to change his diapers frequently and use protective cream if the skin starts to redden.

Babies over six months and older children. Saltwater nose drops can be useful for older infants, as they will probably still be taking some breast- or bottle-feedings. They are completely safe and can be used as long and as often as needed. Sucking is also an important source of comfort, and some children are very reliant on thumb-sucking as a bedtime habit. They can get very distressed by a blocked nose, so if the cold is making it difficult for them to breathe, insert the saltwater solution to the nose and aspirate the nose as often as necessary.

A baby more than six months old can be given fever-reducing medicine in the correct dose for his weight if he is warm, but in many cases dressing him in loose, comfortable clothes that are not too hot and giving plenty of fluids will be sufficient. Babies with elevated temperatures should not be wrapped up tightly or given extra covering. If you are at all worried by his condition or if the fever lasts more than a day it is best to ask your doctor's advice.

Over the age of a year fever-reducing medicines are still the best way to reduce fever if the cold is bad. Not many children under three years old can blow their nose, so keep using soft tissues to catch the drainage, and use a cream locally if the nose starts to look sore.

Do not try to force your child to eat if he does not want to, but make sure he has plenty of fluids—if he will not drink either and seems unusually sick, seek the advice of your doctor for babies under a year. In older children seek advice if they are still not drinking well, continue to appear ill, or specifically complain about a sore throat, ear pain, etc.

Be prepared to be patient when children are under the weather with colds. They may be more clingy and want to sit on your lap instead of going off to play by themselves. Your undivided attention and a bit of comforting will be as useful as any medicine in making them feel better. If a child has a cold or a cough but does not seem too sick and is eating normally, there is no need to keep him indoors in cold weather provided he is dressed warmly. A child who is acting sick or feverish will not want to play outside, but it will do him no harm to leave the house to take him to the doctor's office or on any other necessary trip—again, make sure he is protected against the cold, and if possible take him in a car. If possible avoid taking a child who feels ill on a bus or a train, as it involves so much more disruption, although babies and small children can be more easily wrapped up and taken in infant seats or their parents' arms.

Coughs

There are many different types of cough, and there are various reasons for coughing. Many people believe that the answer to any cough is cough medicine, but this is not the case. No cough medicine can cure a cough, although some can suppress coughing. However, in many cases coughing is a reflex action to some form of irritation in the throat or lower air passages and is often a way of clearing or coughing up mucus. This will help recovery, so suppressing a cough is not always useful.

While colds are infections of the nose and upper air passages, coughs may result from infections of the throat and lower air passages. These are the areas that may be affected. There are various types and causes of coughing:

- *Coughs that happen with colds.* These are usually a reaction to mucus running down into the throat and are a way of clearing it. They may be worse at night, when the child lies down. Suppressing such a cough with cough medicine is not a good idea.

- *Coughs that follow colds.* This usually means that the virus causing the cold has moved down to infect lower air passages as well. If mucus has dried up but if the cough is irritating and disturbs sleep at night, then a cough suppressant may help.

- *Throat infection.* Colds often begin with a sore throat, but viruses or bacteria can also limit their attack to the throat alone. It is up to your doctor to decide whether the infection is caused by bacteria, in which case it will respond to antibiotics, or to a virus, in which case antibiotics are of no use. Sore throats in children are often due to mild tonsillitis.

- *Short, hacking coughs.* These may be the first sign of one of the infectious childhood fevers, such as measles or whooping cough. They can also indicate a viral bronchitis—virus infection of the windpipe.

- *Chest infections.* Chest infections can often follow colds or sore throats and mean that the bacteria have traveled downward. The cough sounds "mucusy," and the child may be short of breath and wheezy. It is up to your doctor to decide, by listening to your child's breathing and looking at his condition, whether antibiotics will help.

- *Bronchitis and wheezing.* Bronchitis is a specific form of chest infection, meaning that the air tubes in the lungs (bronchial tubes) are inflamed and full of mucus. It can develop from an infection higher up in the air passages, such as a cold. It begins with a dry, hacking cough, which changes into a loose, rustling one in a day or two, and the child begins to cough up mucus, which is often swallowed. This, together with the coughing, can make the child feel nauseated and may cause vomiting.

  A child with bronchitis may begin to wheeze—a form of asthma. It is more common in children who are overweight but tends to be far less common after about the age of seven. Usually bronchitis is due to a virus and so will not respond to antibiotics. Coughing up the mucus to clear the tubes is important; in bad cases physiotherapy can be used to help.

It is important to remember that persistent coughing can occur because a child has aspirated something into the lungs without the parent knowing—such as a peanut, a bead, or a piece of a toy. This is potentially dangerous, so if you know or suspect this has happened, take your child to the nearest accident and emergency room, where an X ray can check if this is the case.

Tonsils, Tonsillitis, and Adenoids

Tonsils and adenoids are made of special lymph tissue—an important part of our natural defenses against diseases. It is their job to "capture" germs that threaten to enter the system by being breathed in through the throat or nose. The tonsils guard the throat entry to the body. Adenoids guard the nasal route.

Taking the tonsils out (tonsillectomy) used to be the most common operation for children before the 1960s, so many parents today have had their tonsils taken out as children. Now we know that if a child's tonsils are enlarged, it is usually just

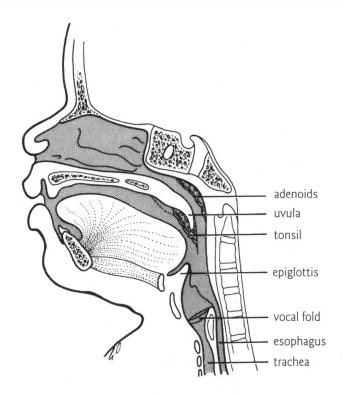

A young child's nose, mouth, and throat in cross-section

a sign that they are working well. Between the ages of about one and four years they are likely to be larger because they are especially active as the child begins to come into contact with more potentially harmful bacteria and viruses.

Sometimes, however, the tonsils are overcome by the germs and become infected. Tonsillitis can be very mild and simply part of a passing sore throat, but it can also be severe and make the child feel quite ill. Children under the ages of five or six years hardly ever complain of a sore throat even when it is very inflamed. This may be because a bad throat does not hurt as much in young children, but probably also because small children cannot locate exactly where the pain is coming from. They may say they also have a bellyache because glands in the abdomen can be enlarged and tender as the system tries to fight off infection. This can occur in children two years of age and older.

Treatment of tonsillitis is only effective if it is caused by bacteria. Antibiotics can then very quickly make the child feel better. If the tonsillitis is due to a virus, antibiotics will not work, and a doctor can only treat the symptoms—fever-reducing medicines lower the fever, and cold drinks will ease soreness. Only a throat culture sent to a laboratory for analysis can tell for sure if a sore throat and tonsillitis are due to bacteria or a virus infection, but if a child is very ill, doctors will usually start treatment with antibiotics anyway while waiting for the result. An operation to remove tonsils is rarely done now before the age of four years because the tonsils are an important defense against germs. After that age an ear, nose, and throat surgeon may suggest taking them out if they have become scarred and pitted and are no longer doing their job but instead seem to be the source of infection. Adenoids are usually removed at the same time. Tonsils and adenoids are sometimes removed because of severe snoring and obstructed breathing during sleep.

There may also be ear problems, and a specialist may suggest that adenoids be taken out at the same time as the middle ear is cleared of fluid and tubes are inserted into the eardrum. This is because it is thought that without adenoids the eustachian tubes may drain better. If your child has a history of frequent sore throats as well as frequent ear infection, tonsillectomy will probably be suggested at the same time, with the idea that the tonsils may not be working very well and may even have become a source of infection that is spreading to the middle ear. Having both tonsils and adenoids taken out means the child staying in the hospital until he is drinking a lot of fluids. He may be admitted to a children's ward or a day surgery unit until he has been able to maintain adequate fluid intake. You will probably be able to stay with your child and encourage him to drink enough. Tonsillectomy makes a child feel miserable because the throat is obviously painful afterward. This should not be a problem with good pain relievers, and the quicker a child can begin to swallow food, the quicker the throat will heal.

Croup

If your child begins to lose his voice and if his breathing sounds hoarse or has a high-pitched or barking noise when he breathes in, then an infection has affected his larynx (voice box). This can lead to attacks of croup—spasms of coughing that sound like crowing or seals barking, and difficulty in breathing in, so the child may struggle for his breath. A croupy cough can sound very similar to whooping cough—the main differences are that whooping cough has three distinct phases, while the croup cough often starts soon after or at the same time as the child becomes sick. An attack can be very alarming, but keep calm because if you make your child upset this will make things much worse.

If you imagine that a child's windpipe is only the width of a drinking straw, you can see how easily it can be narrowed further by swelling and inflammation. Panic makes this worse. Attacks of croup happen most often at night. This is what to do:

- Pick the child up, speaking soothingly and reassuringly.

- Holding him upright, take the child into the bathroom and start to fill the bathtub with hot water, or turn on a hot shower.

- Keep the door shut and sit with the child on the toilet or a chair, fanning the steam toward his face, still talking calmly to him. Usually, as soon as a little moisture in the form of steam is breathed in, the breathing will become easier.

- Continue to sit with the child in the steamy atmosphere for at least ten minutes or so until his breathing is easy again, although it may still sound noisy.

- If steam doesn't work, try bringing your child outside to breathe in cold air. Bundle him well if the weather is very cold.

- After the immediate attack has been relieved, phone your doctor if you are still worried or if you think breathing is still very labored.

You need to watch your child's condition to take action if another attack occurs. Make him upright by raising the head of the bed or by propping him up with pillows. Croup often follows a cold because the virus has spread downward. Antibiotics are of no use against viruses, although if the croup continues for several days, or if the child has become suddenly worse or is under six months old, you should see your doctor, who can decide whether it may be due to bacteria and, therefore, treatable.

If the breathing is getting worse, take the child to the hospital for emergency treatment, which involves administering humidified oxygen if necessary. In severe cases, nebulized adrenaline is given. Some pediatricians may give a short course of steroids. In rare instances, if the child continues to deteriorate, a small tube may have to be passed temporarily into the windpipe to improve breathing and deliver oxygen directly to the lungs.

Prevention is not always completely possible, but once you know your child is susceptible to croup, there are certain measures you can take. Watch for signs that a cold has begun and may move down to affect the larynx; use a vaporizer or a humidifier when your child is resting. Make sure that the vaporizer/humidifier is out of reach of the child to prevent further injury from scalding. There is no need to put any medication in the water that will be humidified, since many of these solutions, when inhaled, may irritate the lungs even more. If an attack seems likely, steam the bedroom using the vaporizer/humidifier before his bedtime and again before you go to bed yourself. Keep the heat low in the room and leave the window open a crack to make the air less dry; cover your child with extra blankets if it is a cold night.

Skin Problems

The skin is a waterproof barrier that helps to keep germs out of and body fluids inside the body. It also assists with temperature control to help us cool down or warm up. The layer of fat just under the skin provides insulation and fuel storage for emergencies.

Skin Problems in the Newborn and the Young Baby
Newborns and young babies often have tiny yellowish-white spots on their faces, especially around the nose. These are quite normal and are due to blockage of the little glands. These spots nearly always disappear in a few days, although the glands may become blocked and larger ("milia"), in which case they last a little longer. There is no need to do anything about them. Nearly half of all babies develop a blotchy red rash, sometimes with tiny white blisters as well, about one or two days after birth. It occurs over the chest, back, and face. It is called *erythema toxicum*

(toxic erythema), and goes away in a few days without treatment. It does not itch or cause any discomfort to the infant.

The skin problems of newborn babies are discussed in more detail in chapter 4.

Heat Rash   Young babies may also show a heat rash because their sweat glands are not yet properly formed and functioning. This red rash, in which there may be some raised bumps, is called milaria, and is more likely to appear in hot weather. It occurs especially in the groin, armpit, and behind the head on the neck. To treat it, all you need to do is keep the baby as cool as possible and the skin dry with corn-starch powder, especially in the creases.

Diaper Rash   Almost all babies get occasional bouts of redness and soreness in the area of their diapers. Treatment for skin that is irritated by being wet and in contact with urine and stools is to change the diapers frequently. This is more common with the disposable diapers, which tend to trap moisture in the diaper area. Whenever possible, allow your baby to go without a diaper so the air can get to his skin as much as possible, and apply a protective covering such as zinc ointment at every diaper change. If the rash does not begin to clear in a week, it may have been complicated by a yeast infection—candidiasis or "thrush." This turns the skin a more fiery red color with a scaly edge and has single areas of rash (satellite lesions) that eventually become part of the generalized rash. If the rash does not respond to the usual treatments, it probably needs a cream prescribed by your doctor (an anti-fungus ointment). The rash usually responds to this within a week or so.

Reactions to detergents, especially the biological ones, can cause rashes, so if your child keeps getting sore and you are using cloth diapers it is worth trying an enzyme-free powder for washing.

Skin Problems in Infants and Older Children

Dry Skin   If your child has dry skin it may become extrasensitive in the coldest part of the winter. Try using a soap that contains cream for washing; it will leave a protective, waterproof film. A thin layer of a moisturizing cream will help to heal lips, cheeks, or noses that have become sore. Avoid pure wool or nylon next to the skin if these irritate, and use cotton or cotton blend clothing.

Eczema   Doctors use the word "eczema" to describe a group of skin problems, but there are actually different types of eczema with different causes. The common type dealt with here is called atopic (allergic) eczema. About one in eight of all children will show symptoms at some time, and these can vary from transient dry patches to very severe symptoms that persist over years.

Itchy Skin   This is very common, and there are a large number of different causes. Some of them are infections, usually produced by organisms such as bacteria and fungi, themselves invisible to the eye. Some are infections caused by worms or tiny insects—pinworms and scabies are examples. But there are also other skin conditions not caused by infections, of which eczema is the most common.

Impetigo   This is a bacterial skin infection. It is itchy and very infectious and can easily spread through a play group, school, or family. It begins with small blisters, and these turn into areas of pus covered with very thin skin. Raw, weeping patches then occur, and finally drying produces yellowish-golden crusts. Healing usually starts from the center and leaves temporary rings of red skin. Treatment with antibiotic cream and at times antibiotics by mouth will usually be necessary. The infected areas should be carefully cleansed and the crust removed. The antibiotic ointment should be applied to the raw areas. Be careful to wash your hands very thoroughly after touching an infected area, and keep the child's towels and clothing separate, because impetigo can spread so easily. It is best to keep play-group-age children away from other children until the rash is under control.

Molluscum Contagiosum   These are little whitish-yellow, pearl-like spots that can measure up to about one-quarter of an inch in diameter but are usually much smaller. They may occur singly or in clusters. They are caused by a virus. They usually disappear spontaneously within a few weeks or months and often do not need to be treated. If treatment is required, it involves freezing, the application of a drop of a special acid, scraping, or a combination of these procedures. Even after treatment, it may come back and need treating again.

Moles   These can be flat, raised, hairy, or smooth. Moles present at birth should be seen by a doctor for evaluation and regular follow-up. Moles appearing after birth in children are almost always harmless and should be watched carefully, especially if someone in the family has had a malignant melanoma. In this case the opinion of a dermatologist should be sought. If there is a rapid change in the color, shape, or size, you should consult a dermatologist for an opinion as to whether further treatment is required.

Pimples and Boils   Redness, warmth, and pus-filled areas are signs of a skin infection. Sometimes these infected areas develop because bacteria have entered into the skin after its surface has been interrupted by an injury, so keep cuts and scrapes clean. These infections might itch, so try not to let your child scratch, because this may spread the infection to other areas. Keeping pimples and boils covered with loose cotton clothes, so they can dry out, is better than putting adhesive tape or Band-Aids on. If the infection does not clear, visit your doctor, as an antibiotic cream or a course of antibiotics by mouth may be needed.

"Ringworm"   This is not due to a worm at all, but to a fungus, and in childhood it is often caught from other infected individuals. It most often affects the scalp, and little patches of hair may come out, leaving a bald and painful patch. Your doctor will need to see it, but it can be successfully treated with an antifungal cream you can purchase from the pharmacist with a doctor's prescription. More severe cases will have to be treated with oral medication for six to eight weeks.

Warts (Verrucae)   Warts are raised growths caused by a virus and are quite harmless. Children usually get them between the ages of six and twelve, although they can occur in younger children. Over half of them disappear by themselves within two years. If they do persist or grow larger they can be treated by your doctor or a dermatologist, usually by freezing or applying certain acids to them. A wart on the sole of the foot may hurt because of pressure. They are easily picked up in swimming pools, but swimming pool attendants warn against wearing rubber protective socks because there is such a danger of slipping on wet tiled surfaces. Over-the-counter applications are less effective and take much longer to work. These warts can be treated either by special acids or removed by freezing, but the treatment often fails, and unless a wart is painful it is probably best left untreated, as it will eventually disappear naturally.

Birthmarks

Babies may be born with a whole variety of marks on their skin, sometimes called nevi.

Stork Bites   These are pink areas that may appear on the back of the neck, the upper eyelid, or the forehead. They are not caused by bruising from the bird that carried the child to the delivery room, but that is how they got their name! Those on the eyelid and forehead go away after a few weeks; those on the back of the neck are usually permanent but are almost always covered by hair so as not to be noticeable.

Strawberry Marks   These are raised red patches with white marks that may occur anywhere on the body. They are usually not present at birth, but begin to appear in the first month or six weeks. They may become quite large but then usually resolve completely over the first few years of life. See chapter 4 for more details. If there should be bleeding from trauma to the red area, it can be controlled by pressing a clean dressing firmly over the bleeding area for about ten minutes. If bleeding persists you should contact your doctor for advice. If these marks are large or involve an upper eyelid, laser treatment may be warranted. If you have any question about the treatment of these marks, discuss it with your doctor.

Port-wine Stain   These are present at birth, usually on the side of the face, and they are much less common. They tend to be permanent and, especially if they are large, your child may need laser surgery to prevent further growth of these marks.

Sunburn and Heatstroke

Babies and children can easily get sunburned because their skin is more sensitive—fair or red-haired children are likely to be more susceptible. Skin only begins to burn and redden *after* the damage is done, so do not wait for signs but take preventive action in advance.

- DO NOT leave a baby unprotected in direct sunlight.

- DO expose children to sunlight gradually at the start of the summer or when on vacation.

- DO NOT leave the baby in areas where sun can reflect from surfaces such as water, pavements, etc.

- DO NOT let them go out in the midday sun or for more than half an hour at a time on the first day of direct exposure.

- DO protect them with light-colored, cotton clothes and hats and shade protection in the strong sun. This is the most important protection. If your child is older than six months, use a good protective sunscreen with a high (factor 15) sun protection factor on any exposed areas. The sunscreen is ideally applied one hour prior to the exposure. If your child has been swimming, reapply the sunscreen if there is going to be prolonged exposure. If your baby is younger than six months, keep him covered and in the shade rather than using sunscreen.

- DO NOT ever leave a child alone in a closed car in warm weather—the temperature inside can rise very quickly and could be dangerous, causing heat prostration or heatstroke, and could even prove to be fatal.

- DO give children plenty of fluids to drink in hot weather.

If your child should get sunburned, apply a cold, wet, and soft cloth to the painful areas to reduce pain and administer a mild pain-relieving medication. Find a cool place out of the sun, such as an air-conditioned room. You might apply an anesthetic spray to the painful areas. These are available over the counter at the pharmacy. If blisters occur in the area of the sunburn and/or if your child should develop a high fever, you should consult your doctor. Heat rash can appear as a reaction to the sun or because a baby has been wrapped up too warmly and has become overheated. Cool the baby down as you would do for a fever by loosening the clothes, fanning, and tepid water sponging. Heat rash may be itchy, so you can use calamine lotion or cornstarch powder to ease the discomfort.

Heatstroke can be serious to babies and children. Children may not have sunburn but could still suffer from heatstroke. They will appear flushed and feel very hot, with a temperature higher than 106°F (41°C). Their skin is dry and there is no sweating. Their movements are often uncoordinated, and they may seem confused. In serious cases where nothing is done they may even become delirious, fall into a coma, and die. Early stages of heatstroke can be treated by tepid water sponging and fanning, but very rapid cooling can cause other problems, so if your child has heatstroke, seek medical advice rapidly. Take the child immediately to the nearest emergency room for care.

Stings and Bites

Stings

If your child is stung by any type of insect, stay calm and reassure him—fright rather than pain is usually what will make him most upset. The only occasions when you need medical advice are if your child has been stung several times by bees or wasps, if he has been stung in the mouth or throat, or in the rare event of his being allergic to the sting. In a very few individuals this can cause sudden swelling of the lips, mouth, and throat and needs emergency medical treatment, so if this should ever happen, take him to the nearest emergency room. If you know that your child is allergic to bee or wasp stings, your doctor can prescribe an "anaphylaxis" kit (Epi-kit), which should only be used in an emergency following a sting.

Bee Stings   Bees leave their stinger, complete with poison sac, in the skin. Pick off the stinger carefully with tweezers, aiming for the point nearest the skin so you do not squeeze more poison into the puncture. Apply ice to the area of the sting. If you then apply a paste made of meat tenderizer you can relieve the discomfort almost immediately. An anesthetic ointment applied to the affected area will also decrease the discomfort.

Wasp Stings   Wasps do not leave the barb in the skin, so there is no need to do anything about it. Again, ice and the same treatment as for bee stings are best for killing pain.

Jellyfish   These do sting, but only a sting from a Portuguese man-of-war needs medical treatment. This species is easily recognized by the transparent bluish-white bladder that floats on top, above the water level. Otherwise ice and an anesthetic spray to take the pain away are the only treatments.

Bites

Mosquitoes   Insects like mosquitoes that bite rather than sting are more interested in quietly feeding off the person they bite than hurting them. This means that neither you nor the child may know when the biting is going on. The first sign may be a series of itchy bumps, or a rash. You can protect children aged six months or older with an insect repellent if you know there are likely to be mosquitoes around. Anesthetic sprays are more effective than calamine for stopping the itching. Over-the-counter cortisone ointment will help in relieving the discomfort.

Snakes   There are three poisonous kinds of snakes in the United States: the rattlesnake, the water moccasin, and the cottonmouth snake. If your child is unlucky enough to be bitten by one of these snakes give him the highest recommended dose of over-the-counter pain relieving medicine and take him to the nearest doctor or hospital. Do not suck the poison out.

Ticks   Diseases contracted by tick exposures are becoming more and more prominent in the United States. The most common tick-borne disease is Lyme disease. The deer tick is the common carrier of the organism, and although this disease may occur in just about any state, it is most commonly found in the Northeast from Massachusetts to Maryland, in the Midwest in Wisconsin and Minnesota, and in California.

Other diseases, such as relapsing fever, Rocky Mountain spotted fever, babesiosis, and Ehrlichiosis, are carried by ticks but are far less common in occurrence.

Some precautions to take in avoiding tick bites are:

* Avoid tick-infested areas.

* Clothing should cover as much of the arms and legs as possible.

- Tuck pant legs into the tops of boots or in stockings.

- Spray tick repellents on clothing and exposed parts of the body.

- Daily inspection of oneself and family members is important, with prompt removal of any ticks.

- Daily inspection of pets and removal of ticks are indicated.

Spiders   In the United States there are two spiders that have powerful enough fangs or potent enough venom to endanger human beings.

The most common, the black widow spider, has a red spot on the bottom part of its body. The bite produces immediate pain at the site of the bite, and a burning, swollen, and inflamed area develops around the bite site. Systemic symptoms can occur within thirty minutes, and prompt treatment with specific antivenom is necessary. A diagnostic clue as to the bite of this spider is double fang markings at the point of the bite.

The brown recluse spider, found mainly in the central and southern states, is recognized by a dark, violin-shaped mark on the top surface of its body. They inhabit dry cellars, closets, and outbuildings. Their bite causes severe local pain, with rapid swelling that progresses to a deep ulcer at the site of the bite. Systemic symptoms develop less rapidly than for the black widow spider bites. No specific antivenom is yet available, but cortisone preparations hasten the healing process.

As with tick prevention, careful observation, using long clothing, and insect repellents are advisable in preventing bites from these spiders.

Parasites

Fleas

Flea bites can produce itchy red bumps on the skin, usually in clusters on the shoulders, arms, or other exposed parts of the body. Nearly always the fleas will have jumped onto the child from a cat or a dog. The child may be the only person affected in the house, because though other people may be bitten, some children are hypersensitive and their skin reacts more to the bites.

If fleas are suspected, then regularly use a spray on your cat or dog, or take it to the vet for checking. You may need to suggest this course of action delicately to neighbors if you suspect their animal is involved! The child's skin is best left alone to get better by itself. Antihistamine medicine or cortisone ointment from the pharmacy may reduce the itching. If in doubt about the cause of the skin problem, take your child to the doctor. If you suspect that your pet is the source of the fleas, be sure to fumigate the house (with everyone being out of the house at the time), and treat the rugs and furniture that may be contaminated.

Head Lice

When my friend's child had head lice I was horrified. Then it turned out my daughter had them as well—we all began to feel itchy all over immediately.

Although parents are always horrified when they first encounter head lice in their children, it is in fact a very common complaint in all social groups. It is usually discovered when a child complains of severe itching on his scalp.

Lice cannot jump or fly but move by climbing along the hairs. They can only spread from one head to another if the hairs are actually touching, so they are passed on when children put their heads together or use each other's comb or hairbrush. Although they live on the hairs, they actually feed off blood by making pinpricks in the scalp and sucking blood through the little hole. Soon after moving on to a head the louse, a six-legged insect the size of a match head, lays eggs, which are cemented to the hair with a special gluelike substance. The eggs are called nits and after the lice hatch they show up as white pinhead-size specks. To check if your child has nits look behind the ears, on the nape of the neck, and the crown for any dots stuck to hairs close to the scalp. Try to remove them by running finger and thumb up the hair—if they come off, this is probably dandruff and not nits.

Do not panic if you find them—treatment is easy and effective. Your local pharmacy has over-the-counter lotions that are usually effective. If the symptoms persist and the nits continue to increase, consult your doctor for more effective prescription medication. Do not use a shampoo; lotions will work best. Sit your child on a stool with a towel around his shoulders and, if possible, an old headband around his forehead to catch drips. If you do not have a headband, another towel will do. Soak the dry hair thoroughly with the lotion. It is very important to let the hair dry naturally, not blow it with a hair dryer, and although the smell may be offensive, you must follow the directions prescribed carefully. Do not allow the child go swimming or wash the hair until the prescribed time period is up; then use an ordinary shampoo. It is important that all affected children and adults in the family are treated, or the problem will recur.

There is no need to go through the head with a fine-tooth comb—an unnecessary and unpleasant experience for the child. School nurses and the doctor's office staff will always be happy to check for nits, but parents should also do this themselves as an ordinary part of child care.

Pinworms

I first knew my daughter had worms when I went to empty her potty and saw these two tiny white threads waving at me. I felt revolted at first—that live "things" could be wriggling around inside her. Then I felt terribly guilty thinking that only a child who wasn't properly taken care of could have worms.

Most parents are horrified at the idea of worms—as with head lice, they are socially unacceptable, linked in our minds with unhygienic homes. But, as with lice, this is misleading. Pinworms are so common that nearly half of all children under ten have them at some time and so do many adults, often without realizing it.

To get worms a child has to swallow the microscopic eggs—these are usually picked up on the hands or under the fingernails and passed into the mouth on food or when the child sucks his thumb or puts a finger in his mouth. Once inside, the fluids in the intestine stimulate the eggs to hatch, and the tiny worms travel through the body, feeding on the contents of the intestine. After mating occurs in the intestine, the males disintegrate, having fulfilled their purpose in life, and the females then travel to the rectum. They emerge to lay their eggs on the skin of the perineum and around the anus—this is what causes the itching that is the main symptom of worms. The egg-laying usually happens at night, when the child is still and warm. Worms are equally common in boys and girls, but in girls the worms can crawl forward into the vagina, causing even more itching and at times urinary frequency, burning, and vaginal discharge. The cycle is continued when children with worms scratch their bottoms because of the itching—often without even waking up—and the eggs are caught under their fingernails again, ready to be transferred back into the mouth.

Treatment is simple and effective. A strawberry-colored drug called piperazine or an orange-colored drug called mebendazole is taken; these paralyze the worms so they cannot lay eggs and are passed out of the system—the drugs may stain the stools red or orange. A second dose is taken two weeks later to catch any worms that may have hatched in the meantime. Because the eggs are so easily transmitted by hand, the whole family should be treated at the same time. To make sure the cycle is broken, scrub carefully under the fingernails of the affected child in the morning and put him to bed in cotton underpants to prevent scratching in the night. All members of the family should be careful to wash their hands after going to the toilet and before meals, and anyone preparing food should wash her hands before starting to cook.

Roundworms

These are much more unusual than pinworms. The only way you would know if a child has roundworms is to see one passed in a stool or vomited out—they are like earthworms but are whitish in color. Although rare, they are not particularly harmful and can be easily treated with medications. They are more common in hot, humid climates where there is poor hygiene. If someone who has roundworms handles food without carefully washing her hands, she may contaminate the food with the worms' eggs.

Roundworms from Dogs and Cats (Toxocariasis)

These are different from human roundworms.

Puppies that have not yet been wormed should not be allowed in too close contact with small children nor taken out for walks in places where children play because their excreta contain large numbers of eggs from these worms. Although most infected children do not have symptoms, some may develop a rash, cough, fever, or wheezing. Infection can occasionally be serious, with a risk of it affecting the eyes, the liver, or causing epilepsy.

Scabies

This is caused by a tiny insect, an eight-legged mite that burrows into and under the skin. There may be just a few small, itchy bumps, sometimes filled with pus, on the skin. This occurs particularly on the hands and feet of young babies but often spreads over other parts of the body, too. It may look like eczema, and it may become infected. It is very infectious, and other family members and friends often catch it.

Scabies needs treatment with a lotion, permethrin, and you will need to see the doctor so the rash can be diagnosed and you can get a prescription. Everyone in the family should be treated at the same time. The itching may continue for a week or so, even after the rash has been successfully treated. In babies the treatment needs to be applied to the face and scalp as well as the rest of the body.

Mouth Problems

Thrush

This is common in babies under a year old and shows as white, furry patches or spots on the tongue and inside the cheeks that cannot be wiped off.

Thrush is caused by an organism called *Candida albicans*, which is normally present in our bodies but which can sometimes get out of control to produce these symptoms. Babies most usually get it because many mothers have *Candida albicans* in the vagina at the time of delivery, so that the baby's mouth becomes infected during birth. It can easily be cleared up with a variety of treatments. Most commonly prescribed are nystatin drops, but there are many alternatives.

Mouth Ulcers and Cold Sores

A virus called herpes simplex often causes mouth ulcers between the ages of one and five years. They show as little, flat, yellowish-white spots and can appear anywhere inside the mouth. They may make it so sore that the child will not eat and is reluctant even to drink. The lesions can take up to two weeks to disappear completely. After that first attack the virus may persist in the skin around the mouth and may later cause recurrent sores. These are not actually caused by the cold virus, but are due to reactivation of the herpes virus, likely to occur when the child is ill—often the case when they have a cold. Cold sores can also be triggered by cold weather or overexposure to sunshine.

Severe attacks of mouth ulceration caused by herpes simplex can be treated by a drug called Acyclovir, and if your child has such an attack take him to the doctor as soon as possible. Local anesthetic lozenges and sprays can help him drink and eat more comfortably. Try giving drinks through a straw and avoid fruit juices because the acidity will be painful. If a child is having trouble eating anything at all because of the pain, try Jell-O, ice cream, rice pudding, and Popsicles to suck if the child is old enough. You can maintain your child's nutrition by giving milk shakes and other protein drinks. Make sure that your child is drinking enough fluids to allow him to urinate five to six times within a twenty-four-hour period.

Single mouth ulcers   These are not usually due to the herpes simplex virus but can also be painful and last a week to ten days. Their cause is not known, and treatment is rarely helpful. Try to give soft and cold foods that are not salty or acidic and will not be so painful to eat. Ice cubes and Popsicles can help to deaden the pain in older children and ensure adequate hydration.

Nail Problems

These are not common in under-fives, but sometimes young children do get infections of the nails. There may be an acute, painful swelling, and this will probably need antibiotic medicine from your doctor. If your child sucks his thumb or bites his nails, there may be chronic infection with swelling and redness around the nail area. Keep nails short by filing them. Do not cut them too short since this could cause infection, also.

Ear Problems

My six-month-old baby became feverish and miserable and wouldn't feed. I thought he must have a sort of flu bug, but the doctor looked in his ears and said it was an ear infection.

Ears have three sections. The job of the outer ear—the part you can see—is mainly protective, and it funnels sound to the middle ear. It is separated from the middle ear by the eardrum, a sheet of membrane that vibrates in response to sound. The job of the middle ear is to amplify sound by producing vibration of the eardrum. The middle ear is filled with air and has three tiny bones stretching in a chain through from the eardrum to the inner ear. When the eardrum vibrates it sets off a reaction in these bones, which transmit the noise vibration to the inner ear. This part of the ear is filled with fluid, and here the sound vibration finally stimulates a nerve so the message is sent to the brain. A tube called the eustachian tube leads from the air-filled middle ear to the top of the throat and equalizes the pressure in the middle ear. We are most aware of this happening when we go up in an airplane and our ears start to "pop" as the pressure drops. The same thing happens in reverse when coming down and the pressure rises again. Because the eustachian tube opens into the throat, swallowing can help to counteract the change in pressure that gives that popping sensation.

Middle Ear Infections

Earache is most usually caused by an infection in the middle ear (otitis media). Because it is so common in babies and young children, a doctor will always look inside their ears with an instrument called an otoscope during an examination.

An ear infection is caused by a buildup of pus in the middle ear, putting pressure on and stretching the eardrum, thus causing the pain of earache. Looking inside the ear, a doctor can see if the eardrum is inflamed and red or if it is bulging.

The reason why young children get earaches so often is because their eustachian tube is narrow and lies horizontally, which makes it very easy to become

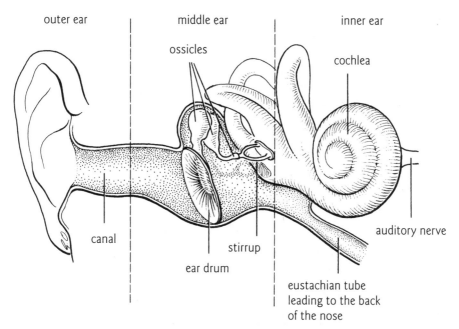

outer ear   middle ear   inner ear

ossicles

cochlea

canal

stirrup

ear drum

auditory nerve

eustachian tube
leading to the back
of the nose

The ear in cross-section

blocked, especially after a cold. The end of the tube is also surrounded by lymphoid tissue located next to the adenoids. Germs from sore throats can very easily travel up to the ear. Babies spend a lot of time lying down, which makes the problem of drainage worse. But even the most trouble-prone ear sufferers experience fewer infections because, as children get bigger, the eustachian tubes become wider and move into a more sloping position, thus facilitating better drainage during a cold. Most children with ear infections may run a fever, be miserable, stop eating, vomit, or have diarrhea. Others may not seem particularly sick but may still be found to have an ear infection. Even if they are old enough to talk, young children rarely say they have earache, although it can be very painful indeed. This is because they are not good at locating exactly where a pain is coming from, though sometimes they may put a hand to their ear. The only way to be sure if there is an infection is for a doctor to look inside, for a middle ear infection will not make the visible outer ear look any different.

A ruptured eardrum (perforation) may usually result if a child with a middle ear infection is not treated. After a period of acute pain, which may come on very quickly, the child may suddenly seem better, but blood and mucus will be seen coming from the affected ear. A ruptured eardrum is nature's way of relieving the pressure and hence the pain. However, perforation should be avoided if at all possible because each time it happens it leaves a small amount of scar tissue when the eardrum heals. Scar tissue is thicker than normal tissue and makes the eardrum slightly less flexible to noise vibration; repeatedly ruptured eardrums can, therefore, make a child's hearing poorer.

If you cannot get treatment in time to prevent a ruptured eardrum, clean the discharge from the outer ear with alcohol and a cotton swab, but do not put a Q-Tip into the ear canal. Take the child to a doctor as soon as possible, because antibiotics may still be needed to clear the infection. The eardrum usually heals in about two weeks or less—your doctor will want to see him again to check that it has healed properly. In the meantime, do not let water get in the ear, for this may stop the infection from clearing; be careful at bathtime, and avoid swimming.

The treatment for middle ear infections is with a course of antibiotics. If you suspect ear trouble, take the child to a doctor without delay. Children over six months old can be given the maximum recommended dose of acetaminophen (the best-known brand is Tylenol) for babies because the pain is severe. Do not cancel the doctor's appointment if the painkiller works and your child suddenly seems all right again—the ear infection is probably still there, and he will become cranky again when the effect of the acetaminophen wears off. Holding a warm, soft cloth next to the ear can be comforting—put the cloth on a radiator or iron it to make it warm. Older children may use a hot water bottle wrapped in soft cloth.

Other causes of earache include infections of the outer ear canal, which will be painful, especially when the outer ear is moved. There may be a discharge. The treatment in this case is antibiotic drops placed right into the ear canal.

Foreign Body in the Ear

A bead or other tiny object in the ear is always a possibility with small children. This may cause infection and pain. They may even have poked something into the ear canal that has damaged the eardrum. One of the reasons parents should never put Q-Tips in their children's ears is that it encourages the child to do something similar; it is also unnecessary and dangerous in that the eardrum could be damaged if the Q-Tip is placed too far into the canal. If you know your child has put something in his ear, take him to the local hospital emergency room or to an ear, nose, and throat specialist. In some cases a light general anesthetic may be needed to remove the foreign body.

Serous Otitis Media and Glue Ear

This condition is being diagnosed in many more children today, partly because of better hearing tests and greater skill by doctors in detecting fluid in the middle ear (serous otitis media). In order to amplify noise properly, the middle ear should be filled with air. But very often the eustachian tubes get blocked and the ear fills with fluid. Recurrent middle ear infections can contribute to this, and it is thought that in some children allergy may also be partly responsible. Unlike the pus caused by an infection, this fluid is sterile, although it can cause short episodes of mild earache. But because the bones and eardrum cannot vibrate so well, it can cause some hearing loss. It is presumed that seventeen of twenty children will have had this condition at some point by the time they are six years old. Usually the fluid is thin and eventually drains naturally, but sometimes it becomes thick and gluelike—hence the condition is commonly known as "glue ear." The danger is that poor hearing may affect a child's speech development and his ability to learn and to form relationships at a most crucial period. At school a child who cannot hear may well be considered slow or lazy unless the real problem is picked up. Getting through to a child who does not hear well can place a great strain on the whole family.

Doctors can tell if there is fluid in the middle ear by looking at the condition of the eardrum, testing the hearing, and measuring the middle ear pressure with a machine called a tympanometer. The ear, nose, and throat specialist will usually want to wait several weeks to see if the fluid will drain by itself, and may sometimes prescribe a decongestant to be taken during this period.

If the fluid does not drain by itself, then the only way to remove it is by making a tiny opening in the eardrum (called a myringotomy) under an anesthetic, and aspirating it out. Specialists vary in their exact approach to the problem, but most suggest fitting grommets or tubes in the eardrum at the same time the fluid is drained. These are tiny, plastic, hollow tubes that are fitted into the eardrum, allowing air to circulate freely in the middle ear and any further fluid to drain out of the middle ear cavity. Some surgeons recommend taking out the adenoids at the same time to help drainage. Depending on the routine of the surgeon, having tubes put in usually is usually done as same-day surgery in the day surgical unit of the hospital, though it can be longer if the adenoids are to be taken out at the same time. Tubes normally stay in place from six to eighteen months and are then rejected by the ear and fall out naturally. The hole in the eardrum heals in about two weeks and, usually, the middle ear stays free of fluid. The child's hearing is restored to normal within about a week of the operation, but if he has been very deaf he may notice a difference immediately and think everything sounds very loud.

Sometimes the ear fills up with fluid again after the tubes come out and another set has to be put in. If this seems likely to keep happening or if the tubes fall out very quickly the surgeon may put "long-stay tubes" in; these work the same way but

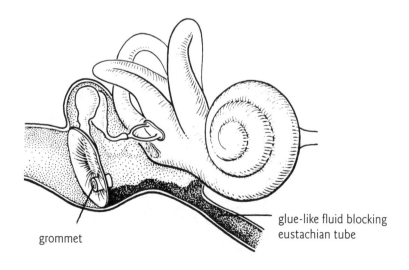

grommet

glue-like fluid blocking eustachian tube

Grommet inserted into ear drum to allow air to circulate freely in the middle ear

have a different design, opening out into a wider shape behind the eardrum so they cannot fall out naturally, and will have to be taken out by another operation.

Most children have fewer problems as they get older, because the eustachian tube widens and becomes more upright. Glue ear is very unusual after about eight years old. For more serious ear problems, see chapter 19.

Eye Problems

Always see a doctor if your child's eye seems infected, the cornea is hazy, vision is affected, or there is swelling and redness of the eyelids, especially if this spreads to the surrounding skin and he complains of sore eyes.

Sticky or pussy eye is very common in the first forty-eight hours after birth and is due to the chemicals that are used to prevent certain serious illnesses.

Continually Watering Eye
If this occurs in the first four months of life it may be because of a blocked tear duct; the baby needs to be taken to the doctor to check on this. It usually clears itself over a period of time and usually responds to repeated massaging of the tear ducts. Often there is an associated drainage from the eye. If the white of the eye is red this usually indicates an infection and requires specific treatment, usually but not always with antibiotics.

Bloodshot Eyes
These are sometimes due to a smoky environment, which can make an eye bloodshot, or they may be caused by something irritating the conjunctiva, the moist lining over the eye. Such problems are more often uncomfortable than serious. The first step is to check if there is anything in the eye, such as a speck or an eyelash. Usually the eye waters so the tears wash it away or at least move a foreign object to

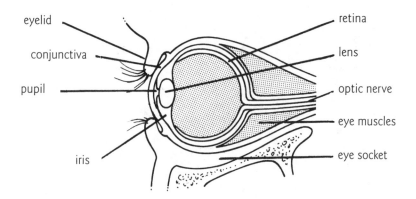

The eye in cross-section

the outside of the eye, where you can pick it off the lid with a clean tissue without touching the eye itself.

To look at your child's eyes, wash your hands and gently pull the skin below the eye slightly downward to reveal the inside of the lower lid. To look under the upper lid, hold the eyelashes between finger and thumb and very gently pull the lid forward and upward. Ask older children to look up while you check the lower lid, and down while you check the upper lid. Do not try to remove any foreign material from the middle of the eye, but wait for it to move to the outer edge; blinking helps this, but rubbing is likely to make it worse.

If you cannot see anything, the soreness and inflamed blood vessels that make an eye look red may be due to infection from bacteria or a virus. See your doctor, who will probably prescribe antibiotic drops or ointment.

To give eyedrops, lay your child down, speaking soothingly, and try to put the drops into the inner corner of the eye so that blinking sweeps them across the eye. You can ask older children to tell you what color the ceiling is or how many spiders they can see on the lampshade to get them to look up; asking them to blink ten times afterward often distracts them and stops them from getting upset.

To ease the discomfort, try pressing warm compresses or a clean, warm cloth softly to the eye. Clean away discharge using a cotton ball and warm water. Wipe away from the eye and use separate swabs for each eye to avoid continually reinfecting each side. Children with eye infections should not share clothing or towels, and try to get them to avoid rubbing their eyes.

Sometimes conjunctivitis caused by a virus can spread through a group of children at nursery school or play group, and there is not much that can be done to prevent this. Viral conjunctivitis can be accompanied by fever, mild rash, and a sore throat, and always occurs with measles. There is a viral conjunctivitis that is associated with otitis media and that you can simply treat symptomatically with pain relievers and warm compresses to the eye once your doctor has made the diagnosis.

Crusty Eyelids (Granulated Eyelids)

The eyelids may be sticky and irritated or have crusts of dried discharge, especially after sleep. This can be caused by specks of dandruff, by a tendency toward eczema or allergy, or by an infection. If your child has dandruff, treat this with dandruff shampoo and cleanse the eyes in the way described above. If this does not seem to be the problem, seek your doctor's advice; an antibiotic cream may be needed for infection, or the short-term use of steroid cream if the trouble seems to be eczema.

Red Eye

This is due to a burst blood vessel and looks far more alarming than it is—it shows as a bright red spot that then spreads out, making half the eye look red. Red eye can happen as a result of pressure from fierce nose blowing or from a bad spasm of coughing (especially in whooping cough) or violent vomiting. It can also happen for no apparent reason. It is not painful, and there is no need to do anything—it will gradually fade.

Styes

Styes are the result of an infected eyelash hair follicle. They show as red, swollen lumps on the upper or lower eyelid and can be painful. Warm compresses help discomfort, but if they are very sore see your doctor, who can give some antibiotic ointment.

Allergy

Allergy to some kind of pollen, fungus spores, mites in house dust, or animal fur can show as watering, swollen, sore, or itchy eyes. There may or may not be other symptoms. Allergy tends to run in families, so if close relatives have hay fever, asthma, or eczema, your child is more likely to suffer. Allergic conjunctivitis is the medical term for inflammation of the eyes due to allergy. You may find the complaint is seasonal, coming on when a particular pollen or fungus spore is in the air, or it may occur only when the child is in contact with a particular animal.

There is no cure for allergy. Some children may have less trouble as they grow older, though sometimes it returns in adult life. In bad cases antihistamines can be taken by mouth. Steroid eyedrops or cream may also be used, but only for a very limited period under strict supervision. Sometimes the eyelids can become so puffy that they start to sag, and a slight muscle weakness may make this more severe on one side. Your doctor may suggest you consult a specialist both to rule out other causes and to discuss possible treatments.

Squint (Strabismus—Crossed Eyes)

A squint is present when the two eyes do not point in the same direction when the child is looking at something. It may occur for a variety of reasons—the child may be farsighted (hypermetropic) or there may be a defect in the eye itself or in the nerves supplying the muscles moving the eye. There is a hereditary factor, so you may know of other members of the family having been affected in a similar way.

Squints may be diagnosed when routine testing for them is carried out, but, much more commonly, parents are the first to notice them. It is important to take a child for an examination as soon as you can. We need the use of two eyes (binocular vision) to see things properly in depth. If a child has a squint, only one eye is used. The "lazy eye" gradually loses its function, and unless the squint is corrected, the child will have defective sight in that eye (ambylopia). Of course, it is also important to correct squints for cosmetic reasons.

If your child has a squint, he will probably be referred to an ophthalmologist, a specialist eye doctor. Treatment may involve patching the good eye with special glasses, to ensure that the lazy eye has to work. Children may need glasses anyway to correct a refraction error if they are myopic (nearsighted), astigmatic, or hypermetropic. Older children may benefit from eye exercises, which an orthoptist (a specialist in this area) can recommend. Finally, it may be necessary for the child to have an operation to correct the squint. This will correct the appearance, and, if carried out early enough, may also help the lazy eye to work better. Day surgery for surgical treatment of a squint is usually all that is necessary.

Farsightedness and Nearsightedness

Children will not be able to see clearly unless the light coming into their eyes is focused exactly on the retina, the light-sensitive screen at the back of the eye from which messages are sent to the brain. The eyeball may be slightly the wrong shape, so the distance between the front of the eye and the back is too long or too short. If the eye is relatively short, the light coming into the eye will be focused behind the retina, causing farsightedness (hypermetropia), or, if the eye is relatively long, the light is focused in front of the retina, causing nearsightedness (myopia). In either case the child is said to suffer from a refractive error. A refractive error in one or both eyes is sometimes first detected because it leads to a squint. In other instances parents may notice that the child cannot see clearly unless he puts objects close to his eyes. He may seem clumsy because he is not able to see things clearly. Alternatively, vision testing at the doctor's office at the eight-month or three-year screening examination may show that the child's sight is not as good as it should be.

If any of these problems exist, the child should have a proper eye test to check out how severe the refractive error is. For the young child this is done by retinoscopy—examining the eyes with a special light after paralyzing drops have been put into them so the pupil stays wide open and the eye cannot focus. Trial lenses are then held between the light and the front of the eyes until the error is corrected. Glasses can be prescribed that will bring objects into focus when the child looks at them.

Small children vary quite a bit in how well they tolerate glasses, but most manage surprisingly well, particularly if their eyesight is greatly improved (see chapter 10 for more on introducing glasses to under-fives). Explaining to an older child why glasses are necessary, and giving praise when the child wears them, are more effective than applying heavy pressure or forcing them. It is important that young children who need glasses have their eyes checked every year, and occasionally more frequently, as the refractive error can change quite rapidly when they are growing fast, and new lenses may be required. Older children usually need less frequent testing.

Children with squints are often farsighted and, in this case, the glasses do not usually greatly improve the vision, but are used to control the squint. For more serious eye problems, see chapter 19.

Bladder and Kidney Infections

Bladder Infections

Girls get bladder infections far more often than boys because the tube leading from the bladder to the outside (the urethra) is much shorter and germs from outside do not have as far to travel as they do in boys. In girls the opening of this tube is also very close to the anus, and it is, therefore, easy for germs from the bowel to get into the bladder. This is the reason why it is very important always to wipe a little girl's bottom from front to back and to teach her to do this, too, so that germs are not wiped from the anus forward into the vagina and urethra, causing infection.

Symptoms of a bladder infection in children are not the same as in adults, and infection is much harder to diagnose. It is impossible to tell whether a baby in diapers is urinating more often than usual. Smaller children will usually have fever, seem irritable, or have symptoms that suggest an upset stomach such as vomiting or diarrhea. If checking for other sources of infection such as the ears or throat reveals nothing, then a urinary infection may be suspected. Occasionally the urine has a bad odor, but this may be just because the child is drinking less and the urine is more concentrated and stronger. It sometimes also smells of ammonia, which does not mean that it is infected.

Ideally a midstream sample of uncontaminated urine should be collected and sent for analysis, and after this the child may be started on a course of antibiotics. In practice some doctors prescribe antibiotics without sending a urine specimen first, since this can be awkward to collect properly until the child is old enough to use a potty or a toilet.

Unfortunately, if the doctor does this no one knows whether there is a urinary infection present; if possible, a sample should be checked before treatment is started. Bladder infections are easier to diagnose in children past the diaper stage, who may complain of pain when urinating and may need to do so more frequently. The suspicion of a bladder infection always needs prompt treatment with antibiotics, but a urine specimen must be sent for analysis first, even though a laboratory may not confirm it for several days. If left untreated there is a danger of the infection spreading upward to the kidneys, with the risk of permanent damage.

Foreskin Infections

There is no medical reason for circumcision at birth. Before the age of about four years the foreskin is joined to the penis, and trying to force it back can cause infection. Infection of the foreskin can occur in older boys after it has separated. There is then a risk that it can become "fused" back onto the penis. Symptoms of infection are soreness, especially when urinating; redness; and a yellow discharge. The infection can be treated with warm soaks and an antibiotic cream, and if the foreskin has become fused it is worth trying to ease it gently back as far as it will go each night when the child takes a bath and then covering it with an antibiotic ointment or cream. It may take several months for it to separate again fully. If this does not work, then a small operation is necessary to remove the foreskin (circumcision).

Circumcised babies can get ulcers on the tip of the penis from contact with wet diapers. This can spread into the opening of the urethra and be very painful when the child urinates. Treatment consists of frequent diaper changes, and the use of disposable diapers is helpful. Protect the tip of the penis with petroleum jelly to allow it to heal.

Vaginal Discharge

If this occurs with soreness, redness, and itching, it is usually due to thrush. Babies can get this if their mother has thrush at the time of the birth, and the candida organism can spread from mouth to bowel, where it easily infects the vagina, especially in a baby in diapers. In older girls the candida organism can also be spread from bowel to vagina easily because the openings of the anus and the vagina are very close. Always teach little girls to wipe their bottoms from front to back after a bowel movement to avoid this. Treatment involves using one of a number of creams—usually nystatin—and is very effective.

Pinworms can also cause vaginal itching and soreness.

Persistent vaginal discharge may be due to the child putting something inside her vagina. She may have forgotten or been too shy or ashamed to let you know she has done this, so her doctor will need to do a careful examination. At times this must be done under anesthesia to adequately examine the vagina.

Some little girls may develop itching and discharge as a reaction to detergents, so make sure all panties are well rinsed, and use cotton in preference to synthetics. Bubble baths and shampoo are also frequent sources of irritation and should never be used in the bathwater.

Kidney Infections

The kidneys perform a number of vital functions: they excrete waste, which is passed out of the body as urine, but they keep some useful substances in the body that would otherwise be left in the urine; they produce a substance that stimulates bone marrow to make red blood cells; they maintain the body's balance between acidity and alkalinity, and they also play a part in controlling blood pressure. So you can see that any infection that might damage the kidneys has to be taken seriously.

Kidney inflammation can follow throat, or more rarely, skin infections from bacteria. The inflammation is not caused by the bacteria themselves but is a result of the body's reaction to fight the infection, so antibiotics are not usually necessary. Children with this problem pass small amounts of blood in the urine, which make it look darker and brownish rather than red, and may also have slight swelling of the face and hands and feet, and possibly fever, headache, and abdominal pain. Treatment may just involve rest and observation, but even in mild cases this might mean admission to the hospital initially for observation.

Inflammation of kidneys caused directly by infection is usually the result of infection moving up the urinary tract from the bladder. Much more rarely it can reach the kidneys via the bloodstream. Treatment in either case is with antibiotics. Children who get urinary infections will need to have an ultrasound scan and X rays to make sure there is no blockage or delay in the passage of urine from kidneys to bladder or, in boys, no blockage in the urethra. Their kidneys will also need to be checked to make sure they have not been damaged by the infection.

A common cause of repeated kidney infection is faulty valves in the tubes (ureters) leading from kidneys to bladder so urine flows back upward, spreading any infection from bladder to kidneys. This can be detected by doing a special X ray in which a radio-opaque dye is placed into the bladder through a fine hollow tube or catheter via the urethra, and X-ray pictures are taken while the dye is passed back out again. Another test, using radioactive material, can also give useful information, not only about the anatomy of the kidney but also about its function. Sometimes this problem needs to be corrected by surgery, but since it has a tendency to resolve as the child gets older, treatment often consists in giving an antibiotic regularly to stop the child from getting infections until the problem has resolved itself.

The Intestinal Tract and Its Problems

The first bowel movement passed by a new baby is called a meconium stool and looks black and sticky. After a day or so the baby's bowel movements change to the normal color and texture of a newborn according to how he is being fed. Breast-fed babies have soft, sometimes almost liquid stools that are bright mustard-yellow. They can be very frequent—at every diaper change—or, as the baby gets older, occur only every few days. In a breast-fed baby this does not mean constipation. The bottle-fed baby's bowel movements are usually firmer, smell slightly more, and may be a variety of colors. A bottle-fed baby can become constipated. This is likely if the stools become harder and the baby shows signs of straining and discomfort. In this case check that you are making up the formula correctly, and try to give the baby more water between feedings.

If the new baby's bowel movements do not show these normal patterns, this could be a sign that something is wrong with the digestive system. Some babies are born with blockages in their intestines or at the anus, a condition that needs an operation. This needs to be investigated by the pediatrician. Usually the baby is still in the hospital and will not be discharged unless he passes the meconium stool. If your baby doesn't pass meconium in the first twenty-four hours after birth, alert your doctor.

Infections in the Intestinal Tract

As most parents quickly learn, stomach infections are common—few children reach school age without having at least one bout of vomiting and/or diarrhea. The cause is either a virus or bacteria in the intestine, and for mild cases, the child usually gets better without any treatment. Gastroenteritis is an infection of the bowel—the cause of most cases of abdominal upsets. Dysentery is acute gastroenteritis caused by a number of specific bacteria that invade the bowel wall. It is not as common as viral gastroenteritis but is just as infectious and can spread through a play group or nursery quickly. If laboratory analysis confirms certain types of dysentery, treatment with antibiotics is occasionally suggested.

Germs are spread from the bowel of someone with the infection to someone else, usually via unwashed hands touching food. It is all too easy not to wash your hands very thoroughly after a bowel movement or after changing a dirty diaper. A contaminated hand may then touch some food or another person's hand before that person puts his hand on food or in his mouth. There is a special need to wash hands thoroughly before preparing food, making up babies' food, or eating meals, and after having a bowel movement, urinating, changing a dirty diaper, or wiping a child's bottom. Be especially vigilant about washing hands when someone in the family already has an intestinal infection.

Germs causing diarrhea and vomiting can also lurk in the nose and infected spots or cuts, so try to remember not to touch your nose or the source of any infection while handling food.

The first signs of an infection are vomiting or stomach pains and/or diarrhea—loose, watery stools that will look and smell different from normal ones. Mothers of breast-fed babies sometimes worry that their babies have diarrhea because the normal stool is so liquid and the movements can be very frequent, and often seem to emerge with a great explosion; but as long as the movement is the usual yellow color and there are no other signs of illness, there is no need to worry. On the other hand, a continuing change in the color and the consistency of the bowel movement could be a sign of illness and should always be checked with your doctor. Once children are old enough to have solid food, there is usually no doubt about when they have diarrhea.

However, diarrhea or vomiting or both can signal the beginning of an illness other than a stomach upset—for example, whooping cough, meningitis, or a urinary or ear infection. If your child is drowsy and weak, in pain, or feverish as well as having diarrhea and vomiting, see your doctor.

Treatment for Babies

There is a serious risk that a baby or small child with diarrhea and/or vomiting can quickly lose too much fluid and become dangerously ill with dehydration. The smaller the baby, the greater the risk, so very young babies who are seriously ill with diarrhea and vomiting may need to be admitted to the hospital. How soon you consult your doctor depends on the age of the baby, whether he is taking any fluids at all, how severe his symptoms are, and whether he has other symptoms. As a rough guide, do not let a baby under four months go longer than twelve hours if he is not taking in any fluids and has both diarrhea and vomiting. With an older baby you can afford to wait twenty-four hours to see if his condition improves with treatment. But if you feel very worried for whatever reason, then call your doctor for advice. Call immediately if your baby stops urinating, his eyes become sunken, his skin loses its elasticity, or he becomes weak and breathes rapidly. Babies with these signs will most likely need to be admitted to the hospital.

The actual treatment of diarrhea and vomiting is the same whatever the age. Stop all milk and solid forms of food for twenty-four hours, and give fluids to prevent dehydration. For babies a number of carefully designed glucose and salt mixtures can be purchased at the pharmacy. These will prevent dehydration and are much safer than homemade mixtures, which should not be used. Try to encourage your child to take frequent small sips rather than one large drink to avoid further vomiting. Aim to give at least as much as your child usually has from his total daily feedings, and enough to satisfy his thirst. A very small number of babies may not like the salty taste, and the flavored varieties that are available may also be rejected. If you have problems getting it down, try mixing the plain version with very small amounts of table sugar.

Once the diarrhea and vomiting stop, reintroduce milk and solids slowly—half strength for bottle-fed babies for the first twenty-four hours, then use normal strength. Breast-milk feedings can be continued while the baby has diarrhea, but he should be offered extra glucose water as well. You can cautiously reintroduce solids as soon as milk feedings are tolerated, and you can introduce a normal diet over three to four days. If diarrhea and vomiting begin again, go back to clear fluids for another twenty-four hours, and see your doctor if the diarrhea continues after this. Once your child is better he may be extra hungry, so feed him as often as he wants to help recover the weight he has lost.

Hospital Care

Hospital care may be necessary for very small babies in cases where there is severe dehydration and where intensive nursing cannot be given at home. Fluid and basic nutritional requirements can be given directly into the bloodstream using an intravenous infusion to replace the fluid and salt that may have been lost.

Older Children

Treatment is the same—stop all food and milk for twenty-four hours and use specially designed salt and glucose preparations, liquid Jell-O, or non-caffeine carbonated drinks only. Frequent sips are best. Once the symptoms stop, gradually reintroduce food, beginning with something quite plain, such as a piece of toast, a plain cracker, or a pretzel. Or you can try what's called the BRAT diet, offering your child bananas, rice, apples, and toast. If diarrhea or vomiting begins again, go back to plain fluids only. See your doctor if the child does not respond after forty-eight hours of fluids only, or if you cannot get him to take any fluids. If there are other symptoms, such as fever, drowsiness, or lack of response to pain, see your doctor at once. Again, once recovered, the child may be extra hungry and will quickly regain weight if he has adequate food.

Drugs

Most cases of diarrhea and vomiting are due to viruses, so antibiotics are of no use. The most common cause is the rotavirus. Laboratory analysis on samples (your doctor will tell you the best way to collect them) will show if a bacterium rather than a virus is the cause. For some bacterial infections your doctor may prescribe an antibiotic. Antidiarrheal drugs such as Kaopectate, Lomotil, or Imodium should not be used for acute diarrhea in children.

Caring for a Child with an Upset Stomach

My two-year-old was seriously ill with diarrhea and vomiting for a week and I had a four-month-old baby as well. At the time I kept going because he needed me so much but as soon as he began to recover I felt totally drained. Being stuck in a house that smelled of disinfectant and vomit for so long and doing nothing but soak and wash piles of horrible clothes and sheets got me down almost as much as the worry about his health.

Caring for any sick child is a strain, but continually cleaning up after children who are vomiting can be especially demoralizing. Even though you may not like leaving your child with someone else, try to get out of the house once a day because you will be of more use to him if you stay reasonably sane. Ask a friend or a relative to sit with your child for just an hour in the day, or try to get out when your partner can be home.

Minor Orthopedic Problems

In-Toeing
This means that one or both feet point inward—hence the name in-toeing. It can affect just the foot, the foot and lower half of the leg, or the whole leg. In a new baby who is otherwise normal this can be due to an awkward position in the uterus during pregnancy. Naturally, parents worry about any problem in their child that might affect development, so you might want to consult a doctor when the child begins to walk. In 90 percent of cases the foot will straighten out by itself by about three or four years old. In the few cases that do not right themselves, treatment can still straighten the foot out. Waiting will not have jeopardized this.

Clubfoot
As opposed to in-toeing, where the foot is otherwise normal, clubfoot involves a structural abnormality of the bones in the foot so it is twisted out of shape. The foot may be turned in so the sole of the foot faces to one side and the child walks on the

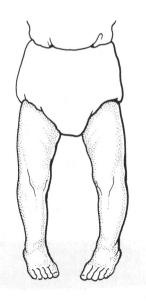

In-toeing

edge of the foot and heel instead of in the normal way. This is a congenital abnormality. If you suspect your child has a clubfoot, see your doctor early for advice and treatment. It requires application of a series of casts, and ultimately corrective surgery is necessary.

Bowlegs
All babies' legs bend outward at the knees to some degree, but nearly all of them straighten up by the time they are five years old. It is only in cases that are so severe that they interfere with a child's walking that treatment may be needed. Rickets, caused by a deficiency of vitamin D, can very occasionally be the cause. There is no evidence that walkers or early walking will cause bowlegs.

Knock-Knees
Three-quarters of all children between two and four and a half years have knock-knees to some extent, but as long as it is not part of a more widespread problem there is no need to do anything. The majority of cases will correct themselves, and the child will walk and develop quite normally. There is no evidence that special shoes, splints, or exercise make any difference. If it is still a problem after the start of school your doctor will refer you to an orthopedic surgeon, but even then treatment is unlikely to be considered before the child is about ten or eleven years of age.

Flat Feet
All children begin life with flat feet and only develop an arch when they are about three to four years old. For those whose feet continue to be flat, the majority are otherwise quite normal and will not have any special problems from being flat-footed.

However, a few children may have other symptoms, such as pain, stiffness, weakness, or muscle spasm. In this case a flat foot can be due either to a bone irregularity or to an inflammation of the foot itself. It may also occur in conditions such as cerebral palsy or Down syndrome.

Loose Joints (Hyperflexibility)
When someone can bend a joint in both directions—for example, bending fingers backward as well as forward—people often say they are "double-jointed." In fact all it means is that the joint is very lax or loose so it can bend in both directions. This can often be no more than a familial characteristic causing no problems, but do discuss it with your doctor because in rare cases widespread joint looseness can be part of a more general disorder.

The Clumsy Child

Kevin had been a good baby and his talking had started very early. But at four years old he seemed delayed in some ways. In particular he was always bumping into things, he was not able to ride a tricycle, and he showed no interest at all in playing with blocks or kicking a ball.

No child is born perfectly coordinated; even one who grows up to be a champion ice skater will stumble over early steps. This leads some people to believe that all young clumsy children will "grow out of it," a prediction that is true for most but by no means for all. Clumsiness can be seen in large movements, such as walking or throwing (gross motor skills), or finer skills, such as using scissors or buttoning buttons (fine motor skills). "Motor" here means what makes movement. Clumsiness involves more than just body movement; children also have to learn to judge their world visually. If they are trying to catch a ball they must first learn to watch it, anticipating its speed and direction. This kind of judgment is usually referred to as a perceptual skill, and some authorities would rather talk about children with perceptual motor problems, arguing that the word "clumsy" carries with it immediate ideas that the child is inferior. In everyday experience there is, indeed, a danger that clumsy children will be seen as generally delayed, and they may even come to think of themselves in this way.

Recognizing clumsiness is not always easy, for the general pattern is that the child can move around well, but the quality of his movement is poor, rather like the child who can swim but has not progressed beyond the dog paddle. Clumsy children seem to have great difficulty organizing and planning movements, so that, although they may know what they want to do, they are not able to organize their bodies to produce a smoothly planned set of movements.

Rhythm and force are two further difficulties: the accomplished child will learn to skip at an even pace, while the clumsy child will turn the rope around far too fast. Dealing with tasks in a sequence may be an obstacle as well, as anyone who has watched a child put on his shoes before his pants will appreciate. Slowness is another characteristic, and if they are hurried, such children usually become flustered—they are no different from many adults in this—which leads them to greater problems.

Another distressing consequence is a lack of friends. Other children may be intolerant of the clumsy child constantly bumping into them; they will shun the child at games, and this can easily produce loneliness leading, possibly, to behavior disturbances.

There are many causes of clumsiness. It is always worth having a child's vision tested, but the central area of difficulty is more likely to be that the brain is not working as efficiently as it is in other children. It is important to note that it is not appropriate to refer to clumsy children as brain-damaged or spastic. Children with cerebral palsy are often clumsy, but not all clumsy children have cerebral palsy.

If you are concerned about your child, discuss your anxieties first with your child's doctor, who may feel that an opinion from an occupational therapist or physiotherapist would be helpful. When helping a so-called "clumsy" child it is useful to follow certain ground rules:

- Spend some time on what the child can do, to maintain his confidence.

- Keep practice to short periods, with tasks in short, manageable steps. Allow your child to go at his own pace.

- Never ask the child to do something he clearly cannot. This sounds obvious, but some adults think they can teach children by humiliation. This is a mistake, and can cause further damage.

Children with severe problems in this area are unlikely to become ballet dancers or carpenters. But if you help such a child appropriately, he can learn to reach acceptable levels of skill. And if you can help him escape hurtful labels, you will have achieved a lot.

CHAPTER 18

Serious Illness and Treatable Congenital Defects

Asthma • Eczema • Epilepsy (seizure disorders)
Serious infectious illnesses • Kidney (renal) problems
Jaundice • Hemophilia • Childhood cancer, including leukemia
Sickle-cell disease • Thalassemia • Short stature • Diabetes
Cystic fibrosis (CF) • Celiac disease • Heart problems
AIDS • Cleft lip and palate • Genital problems

In this chapter we look at a variety of illnesses and conditions that are potentially more serious than those described in chapter 17, which dealt with common childhood illnesses. Some of these pose only short-term problems; others are more long-term and some lifelong, but none of them need necessarily impair the quality of life, and many can be treated successfully. We have also included some minor congenital defects that are easily treatable.

Obviously, in their most severe forms, each of these conditions poses far more difficulties than cases where children are only mildly affected; each child must be assessed and treated on an individual basis.

Asthma

I had asthma badly as a child and still get occasional attacks. My daughter also gets it now. I think it's important to remember that generally an asthma attack doesn't feel nearly as bad for the sufferer as for the person watching.

About one in six children will have an asthma attack at some time. When this happens breathing becomes more difficult because the branching tubes (bronchi) leading from the windpipe through the lungs become inflamed and narrowed. It is difficult to have enough air pass through these narrowed tubes, and the effort of forcing air out causes the labored breathing and wheezing sound of an asthma attack. It is easier to breathe in than to breathe out, so some of the air gets trapped in the lungs and makes the chest expand more than normal.

No one knows the cause for sure, but it seems that the airways of asthmatic children are oversensitive or possibly hyperreactive. They react to various triggers by producing excess mucous from inflammation and coughing and by narrowing through a muscle spasm in the airway walls.

Causes of Asthma Attacks

There are several factors that can work together or singly to bring on wheezing or an attack. Here are some of the most common culprits. Try to determine which make your child especially susceptible.

Allergy   Many children with asthma are allergic and, in most, allergies to pollen, house dust, and furry animals may produce coughing and sneezing. Grass pollen, which is around from mid-May to late June, is the worst offender among pollens. Cats are the most common animal causes of allergy, but dogs, birds, horses, guinea pigs, and hamsters can also cause reactions. Sometimes horsehair alone in the form of upholstery padding can be enough. In dust, it is the dust mites that cause the trouble. They are little creatures that live in bedding and furniture and feed off human or animal scales of skin that are shed. Food allergy may also act as a trigger for asthma.

Infection   This can act as a trigger to asthmatic wheezing or a full attack. Respiratory infections such as upper respiratory infections—especially the RSV (respiratory syncitial virus) infections—are particularly common triggers for asthma in the infant and toddler age group and may cause prolonged flare-ups lasting several days.

Emotion   Great excitement or upset can bring on an attack of wheezing in an asthmatic child, and general tension or anxiety often results in worsening of the episodes of wheezing.

Smoke   Smoke, especially from cigarettes, can trigger wheezing, so it is even more important not to smoke if your child is asthmatic. Obviously smoking is a harmful habit for asthmatics of any age. Smoking in another room or outside is helpful, but remember that the smoke will cling to your clothing, and this secondary smoke is almost as harmful. Some industrial fumes, paint smells, and perfumes can also be irritating.

Weather   Sudden changes in climate can provoke asthma. Sudden sharp cold or wind are particularly likely to irritate.

Exercise   Exercise, especially running, can make asthmatic children start to wheeze, but this is not a reason to avoid sports and games, as the wheeze usually settles rapidly on resting. Using an inhaler beforehand can enable most asthmatics to take part in any sports and improve their endurance and performance.

Treatment

Prevention   Where possible, avoid likely triggers to asthma—for instance, smoky atmospheres or specific animals that cause an allergic reaction.

Drugs   *Bronchodilators* are medicines that make the muscles around the airways relax and so widen or dilate the bronchi or airways; and the most common bronchodilator is albuterol. It is up to you and your doctor to work out the most effective treatment for your child, for these drugs can be used in various forms, including syrups, tablets, aerosol sprays, inhaled powders, and mists. Theophyllines are also bronchodilators, but cannot be taken by inhalation. Sometimes a bad asthmatic attack fails to respond to bronchodilator treatment. This should be regarded as a warning sign that you should contact your doctor.

Sodium cromoglycate is a drug that can prevent asthma attacks by its action on the lining of the airways. It has to be taken regularly and is inhaled deeply into the lungs as a dry powder, spray, or mist. A device called a spinhaler or aerochamber is used to deliver the medications, and children can be taught how to use it from about three to five years old. Alternatively, before this, treatment can be given as a mist using a nebulizer. Older children can manage the inhalers.

Steroids are hormones that affect the body's reactions to inflammation. They can be very effective in the prevention of asthma, and are also useful in the treatment of acute attacks when bronchodilators fail to work well. If taken by inhalation, the steroid is delivered directly to the lung, and only a small dose is required.

Inhaled steroids may be used on a long-term basis to prevent asthma as an alternative to sodium cromoglycate. If steroids are given in the form of syrup, tablet, or injection, a larger dose is required, and given in this way they need to be used with caution. If taken regularly for a long time they can have many side effects. There is no need to worry about this if your child needs just a short course of steroid treatment, but if he needs longer-term treatment, discuss all aspects with your doctor, who will keep a careful check and use the lowest possible level of these drugs.

Antibiotics do not make any difference to an asthma attack but may be prescribed if an infection due to bacteria has triggered the attack.

What to Do if Your Child Has an Asthma Attack

At the first signs of an attack (labored breathing, coughing, and wheezing) sit her down, speaking calmly and reassuringly, because if a child gets frightened or panics, this can make matters worse. Immediately give her a dose of the bronchodilator prescribed. Stay with her and tell her to breathe deeply and regularly. It may help to sit a young child on your lap and do the breathing with her.

If an asthma attack does not begin to respond to increased use of the bronchodilator, call your doctor at once. Parents with asthmatic children soon get to recognize when an attack is not responding to treatment.

Hospital treatment may involve the use of oxygen, nebulized bronchodilators, and often steroids. Extra fluid may be needed, and is given, if necessary, in the form of an intravenous drip. Steroids can be given through a drip or by the oral route.

Living with an Asthmatic Child

Provided you learn how to handle the condition properly, there is no need to handle an asthmatic child any differently or to stop her from taking part in games or activities suitable for normal children. Together with your doctor, work out the best way of preventing attacks and of treating them if they occur.

Preventive drugs such as sodium cromoglycate must be given regularly if they are to work. Do not try to make your child manage without them in the belief that it will toughen her up. It will not, but it will make an asthma attack more likely.

Give preventive treatment with drugs such as albuterol before events that may trigger wheezing—for example parties, games, or sports.

Treat symptoms of wheezing calmly and in a matter-of-fact way, and help your child to have a sensible attitude to her condition. Do not undermine her confidence by panicking and being obviously overanxious.

Learn as much as you can about asthma so you are best placed to help. Your The American Lung Association can provide you with very valuable information as well as contact with parent support groups. The American Lung Asslociation can be reached at (800) 586-4872.

Will My Child Grow Out of Asthma?

Only one in five asthmatic children will still have persistent symptoms in early adult life, but it is difficult to predict in which children they will persist. Perhaps it is more important to remember that today's treatment of asthma is so effective that the great majority of asthma sufferers can lead just as full and active lives as anyone else.

Following are a few indications about the likelihood of asthma continuing, but they are not hard-and-fast guidelines.

Factors for Having Fewer Problems Later in Life

* When the main cause of wheezing is infection, resistance to most infections often develops at about seven to eight years of age.

* When the cause of asthma is allergy to environmental substances, there is a good chance of having less trouble in the teen years.

Factors against Having Fewer Problems Later in Life

* If a child with other allergies—for example, eczema or hay fever—develops wheezing attacks or a persistent cough in the first two years of life, then the chances of it disappearing are not quite so good.

* If the asthma is very severe and the child needs be hospitalized often, or if a close relative or relatives have asthma, this seems to lessen the chances of it disappearing in early adult life.

* It is important to remember that asthma is a chronic illness that lasts for life. As a rule, most people with this illness have fewer and fewer problems as they get older but will experience occasional recurrences, often triggered by the same conditions that triggered the recurrences during childhood.

Eczema

My daughter was covered from the age of about eight weeks until approaching five with an agonizingly itchy red rash that was often raw and weeping. The irritation bothered her so much that she used to tear at her skin even when it was raw and bleeding. She couldn't sleep at night, and one of us had to stay with her every single night. It was terrible to see her suffering so much.

The word "eczema" is a label doctors use for a group of skin problems. There are many different types of eczema, which have different causes. The most common type is called atopic eczema. About one in eight of all children will get it at some time. Usually it covers only a small part of the body and only lasts a few months, but occasionally it is more severe, and it is the severe type that is mainly described here.

What Causes Atopic Eczema?

No one knows for sure, but there are many different schools of thought. One explanation, which many leading skin specialists (dermatologists) subscribe to, is that the immune system of atopic people is oversensitive. Our immune system is our defense against disease, but if it is oversensitive, reactions occur to normally harmless substances. These can be foods, or airborne substances such as pollen, house dust, minute scales from animal hair, skin or feathers, or fungus spores. For more on allergy see "Food Intolerance" in chapter 6.

An atopic person's body makes extra amounts of a certain type of antibody. The tendency to do this is inherited, and is passed on from parents to children in their genes. Some atopic people may be perfectly healthy all their lives and never know they are atopic. But it seems that making extra amounts of this antibody does make such people more likely to suffer from asthma, eczema, and hay fever. Tests can be done to find out if someone is atopic. Even if she is, it is only a problem if the person suffers from one of the atopic diseases.

Eczema can affect children very badly over a long period, or it can be mild and disappear quite quickly. Usually the rash begins to appear on the cheeks at the age of about three to four months and can get raw and weeping. It may start to fade, or appear later on other areas of the body. Typically it occurs in the creases at the elbows, wrists, buttocks, knees, and ankles.

The hallmarks of an eczema rash are:

- **Itching** This is the worst aspect because it can be so upsetting for the child. It also makes her scratch, which itself can lead to more rawness, soreness, and infection.

- **Redness** This is caused by extra blood flowing through the blood vessels in the skin in the affected area.

- **A bubbly, grainy appearance to the skin** These are tiny, fluid-filled blisters just under the skin called *vesicles*.

- **Weeping** This happens when the blisters burst, either by themselves or because of scratching, and the fluid oozes out onto the surface of the skin.

- **Crusts** These are scabs that form when the fluid dries.

- **Scaliness** Children with eczema often have dry, scaly skin. This may be a result of the disease but may also be the natural skin type of that family, which, in some people, can predispose them toward developing eczema.

- **Depigmentation** Pale patches of skin can appear because eczema can disturb the production of pigment that controls our skin color. The effect does fade and disappear.

- **Lichenification** This means a leathery, thicker skin area in response to scratching. It fades if treatment is helpful.

Other effects of eczema can be:

- **Infection** Skin that is broken and damaged is more likely to be infected by bacteria or yeasts. One very common type of bacterium (*Staphylococcus aureus*) produces yellow crusts or pus-filled spots.

- **Thirst** If eczema is widespread, too much fluid can be lost through the skin, making the child thirsty.

- **Poor temperature control**   Too much heat is lost through inflamed skin, so the body attempts to compensate by trying to adjust its thermostat. The result is that the child can feel cold and then when moving into a warmer atmosphere very quickly gets too hot. Eczema also stops the sweat glands from working properly; sweating is one way of losing heat when we get too hot.

Treatment

If a child's eczema is not so bad as to disrupt her own and her family's life, it can probably be managed by avoiding likely sources of irritation and using bath preparations, moisturizers, and suitable steroid creams (see below). It is up to you and your doctor to work out what is best for your child and to remember that this may change. In severe cases where the eczema is so bad as to interfere with the child's life and put a strain on the family, your doctor may need to refer you to a specialist (usually a dermatologist) who can help.

In treating eczema there are various lines of approach:

- **Avoiding irritants**   Various things can irritate sensitive, eczema-prone skin; avoiding them can make a great difference. The key here is to be vigilant about noticing what seems to cause a reaction.

- **Selecting fibers**   Use pure cotton or cotton mixtures for clothing instead of wool or synthetics.

- **Choosing soap**   Try not to use any soap at all, but if you must, use one that contains moisturizers. Add bath oils to bathwater, and use emulsifying ointment or a water-dispersible cream. Examples are aqueous creams. Don't bathe too frequently and keep baths to a short duration, since water can dissolve the natural body oils. In mild cases this will probably be enough by itself. Avoid enzyme detergents in washing clothes.

- **Avoiding acids and chemicals**   Some acid fruits and vegetables such as tomatoes and citrus fruits and also very salty foods cause a reaction on hands and around the mouth; avoid all direct use of antiseptics and solvents.

- **Protecting from heat, sunlight, and cold**   These can irritate some children, so protect from these elements, or avoid them as far as possible if they are found to irritate your child.

- **Moisturizing the skin**   Washing with water alone rapidly results in drying off, but adding bath oil to water will help to moisturize dry, eczema-prone skin very effectively. Your doctor can tell you what is available, and you may need to experiment to find the best product for your child.

- **Treating infection**   As mentioned, eczematous skin is prone to infection. This can be treated by a course of antibiotics taken by mouth. Some doctors initially use antibiotic cream, but serious infections always need to be treated with an internal antibiotic.

- **Using steroids**   These hormones can be very useful for their ability to calm down the inflammation the body produces in an allergic reaction. Unfortunately, they can also have undesirable side effects if not used properly, so parents need to pay close attention to advice about using them. We now know that taking them internally (by mouth or injection) regularly for long periods can stop the body from producing its own supplies of steroid hormones and can ultimately slow down growth and have other undesirable side effects. However, steroids can be useful in controlling eczema and safe if they are used as creams or ointments directly on the skin. It is important to use the minimum amount of the least potent preparations that will keep the condition under reasonable control. Steroid creams should not be put on like face cream, but instead applied to the rash only in the very smallest amount that can hardly be seen. The best time to do this is after a bath containing some form of oil because the skin is better able to absorb it then. There are about sixty brand names of different steroid creams and ointments available by prescription, and they come in different strengths. The mildest is hydrocortisone, which has various brand names, in strengths that are marked on the tube as a percentage beginning with ½ percent and going up to 2½ percent, with ½ percent and 1 percent hydrocortisone available over the counter; 1 percent hydrocortisone is most suitable for long-term use for babies and for use on sensitive parts of the body such as the face. Slightly stronger forms of hydrocortisone are suitable for longer-term use in older children if the affected area is not too large. Medium-strength preparations can be used short-term for sensitive areas (but not on the face). Strong steroids should be used carefully and only under the direction of a dermatologist. Most skin specialists now think these should not be used undiluted on children for more than a few days, and only very occasionally. Because they are easily absorbed, some of the hormones from these creams and ointments can enter the bloodstream, so if very strong preparations are used over a large area the risks are the same as for steroids taken internally. Too much of a strong steroid can also thin and stretch the skin itself, which then appears like stretch marks after pregnancy, with loss of skin elasticity. Thinning of the skin means blood vessels show through. This can show as a reddish complexion on the face. Ask your doctor if you think your child's skin shows signs of damage. Using a nonsteroid cream or a weaker steroid can usually reverse damage if it is caught in time. But stopping a strong steroid suddenly can make the rash much worse, so weaker preparations need to be given over a week or two.

- **Tar**   This sounds strange, but tar is soothing for inflamed skin and comes diluted as ointment or paste, sometimes mixed with steroids. Tar paste bandages can be very helpful.

- **Elimination diets**   These are now very popular in treating eczema. Probably only a few children with eczema can be helped by special diets, but in these cases they may make a great deal of difference. Avoid artificial colorings and benzoate preservatives. For more complicated diets, especially those in which natural foods such as milk are eliminated, you should consult your doctor and a dietitian.

- **Antihistamines**   Most of these do not relieve itching but may take the edge off it, and the drowsiness they cause can be useful at night to eliminate sleeplessness caused by irritation. In some children they stop working after a while, so it is best to reserve them for bad periods and have times in between without them. In a few children antihistamines do not work at all. They may even have the reverse effect and make a child overactive.

- **Bandages**   You can use these to stop your child's scratching at night. Bandages made into cotton mittens can be very helpful. Children often begin scratching in their sleep and then wake because of extra irritation and soreness. Medicated bandages saoked with medicated ointment can also be very soothing in especially troubled areas.

- **Wet wraps**   The basic principle is that a wet dressing is applied directly on the skin, and left in place for several hours following application of a cream or an ointment. There are many modifications of this general approach, which has proved very effective in treating more severe and widespread atopic eczema.

  Although wet wraps can be used to some effect with just a moisturizing cream, they work much better if a mild steroid is applied under the dressings. Generally this approach is most suitable for use overnight.

  Exactly why wet wraps work so well remains unclear, but important factors may include prolonged cooling of the skin as a result of gradual evaporation, which appears to provide relief of itching; wetness, which appears to aid healing; physical protection against the harmful effects of scratching; and a better penetration of the steroids.

- **Light treatments (phototherapy)**   The observation that atopic eczema often improves during holidays in sunnier climates, such as around the Mediterranean, has led to treatment with artificial light. The therapeutic effect of light is not due to visible light at all, but to the invisible shorter wavelengths known as ultraviolet radiation (UVR). UVR can itself be subdivided into two types, longer-wave UVR, known as UVA, and shorter-wave UVR, known as UVB.

  UVB alone appears to be of rather little benefit as a treatment for atopic eczema. On the other hand, there have been reports of good results from treatment with combined UVA and UVB, resembling natural sunlight, and, more recently, from treatment with narrow-band UVA. To date, though, the most effective form of phototherapy has been a treatment known as *oral psoralea photo chemotherapy* (PUVA), which comprises a combination of UVA and a drug given to the patient before exposure, called a psoralen. This has proved to be a highly effective way of treating atopic eczema in older children, particularly adolescents who have had eczema for many years and for whom other treatments have not proven effective. Although it can be a very effective treatment, it is difficult to administer because very expensive equipment and highly trained staff are required, and because the patient will have to travel, sometimes for long distances, for regular treatment sessions. Administering PUVA is also difficult, and requires great skill, because it can lead initially to an increase in irritation of the skin.

Helping Your Child Cope with Eczema

One of the worst things about having a child with bad eczema is other people's reactions. They will stare and look repulsed and horrified. The older and more aware your child is of her condition, the more protective you feel.

Once you have learned about eczema, explain to relatives and friends what it is. People still tend to think that any kind of skin rash must be catching. As your child gets older there is a good chance she will "grow out" of it. If the eczema appears in the first year of life there is a 50 percent chance it will not be a problem by age five. Even if it continues into school age, only one in twenty will still have trouble in adult life. In general, the later it first appears the greater chance there is that it will persist. But even children who first develop eczema at five years old have about a 50 percent chance of it clearing within the next five years. There are no hard-and-fast rules, and each case is different.

Eczema can leave physical scars if it continues for long periods of time. As a parent, it will be vital to you to protect your child from psychological scars. This involves allowing your child to lead a normal life, even if some activities do make the rash worse in the short term. Help your child forget her skin problems by keeping her busy and encouraging her interest in other people and activities. As she gets older explain, in simple terms, that the rash is caused by an allergy. She will certainly be asked by other children and possibly adults and needs to know how to answer. Do not be overprotective or hide your child away. Talking to other parents whose children have the same problems can be a great help. Your dermatologist can supply you with useful information and get you in contact with parent support groups and local and national organizations.

Epilepsy (Seizure Disorder)

We had so many fears and anxieties about the epileptic fits our daughter had. We worried about brain damage, about her being less intelligent, about her future aspirations. In fact, there is no reason why someone with epilepsy should be less healthy or less intelligent than anyone else, but it took counseling to help us understand this and to sort out our fears.

There is a great deal of ignorance and misunderstanding about epilepsy, and this in turn often leads to fear. In fact, there are quite a few school-age children in the United States with epilepsy, and the vast majority go to ordinary schools. If there is no other associated condition, there is no reason why they should not be as intelligent and as healthy and not lead as full a life as anyone else. Epilepsy is not an illness in itself but a symptom of several different conditions with different causes, and in a great many cases the reason for its appearance is not known, even after extensive tests. So there is no such thing as an epileptic child; rather, a child who has a seizure disorder.

Electrical activity takes place in everyone's brain, but an epileptic fit or seizure (the two words mean the same) happens when there is a brief disruption of this normal activity and a sudden, unusual release of energy—a sort of electrical storm that sends the system out of control for a few seconds or minutes. Anyone could have seizures in theory. Those who do simply have a lowered resistance to certain stimuli, not all of which can be identified. Unlike febrile convulsions, which may affect one in thirty to forty children at some time, an epileptic seizure is not usually triggered by high temperature and typically occurs out of the blue. (For more on febrile convulsions, see "Elevated Temperature and Fever" in chapter 17.)

A seizure disorder is not diagnosed as such unless the seizures are recurrent. There are several different types of seizure disorders, all of which can affect children, but the most common are *petit mal* (minor) and *grand mal* (major). These names are the French for "little illness" and "big illness," respectively, and are used because French doctors were prominent in writing about epilepsy years ago, when the different types were being recognized and described. Many doctors today prefer a more modern, scientific classification, but these old names still have some value and seem to be familiar to many nonmedical people.

Petit mal attacks are "absence" or blank attacks involving a brief lapse of consciousness. The child may seem to be daydreaming or going blank for a few seconds, often with rapid blinking of her eyelids, but she does not usually fall down, and may even continue to perform simple actions such as walking, though she is not really aware of what she is doing.

Afterward she will have no recollection of what happened, but may be aware that there has been a gap in her experience. Usually she can pick up the threads of her conversation or activities at once, but sometimes she needs to be reminded. If the attacks are infrequent they are unimportant, but if they are frequent the child may be literally bombarded with unconsciousness, and her schoolwork and social life may suffer as a result. Schoolteachers often suspect petit mal as the reason for a child doing less well than they think she should. Sometimes they are right in their suspicion. Much more often the child is just not paying attention because she is uninterested or anxious, or perhaps has attention deficit disorder (ADD).

Petit mal is rare. Less than one in twenty children with epilepsy suffers from it. These attacks seldom occur under age three and rarely persist beyond adolescence, so the outlook is usually very good. They also tend to respond well, even dramatically well, to appropriate medication.

Grand mal corresponds to the kind of seizure most people think of as epilepsy, and it often generates fear because of lack of information. The attacks usually occur suddenly, without warning. The child may become rigid and stiff, lose consciousness, and have trouble breathing. Her limbs jerk convulsively and she may have excess saliva, which is blood-tinged if she has bitten her cheeks or tongue, and she may be incontinent of urine. The movements gradually stop and the child may fall asleep for a few minutes or even longer before waking, often confused and irritable. There is no set pattern to how often seizures occur—it varies with every individual.

Some children with a different kind of epilepsy have warning signs, which they learn to recognize before a seizure occurs. Older children may be able to describe these events. Such children may go on to stare as part of the attack, have repetitive movements, and may only be seen to have a change of behavior over a few seconds. These children may have a *grand mal* attack as a later part of the seizure in some cases. One mother said her three-year-old used to sense when an attack was about to happen and would lie curled on the floor in readiness.

What to Do During Major Seizures

- Loosen any tight clothing around the neck that might be constricting, and remove surrounding objects that might also endanger the child.

- Turn her on to one side, preferably her right side.

- Stay with the child while the attack is taking place, but do not try to put anything in her mouth, especially your finger, or restrain her limbs.

- After the seizure, making sure the child is still on her side so she can breathe more easily, put her somewhere comfortable to rest or sleep. When you are sure your child is safe, call your doctor for advice.

- In the rare event of a seizure lasting more than five minutes or those occurring one after the other without the child regaining consciousness, it is best to call your doctor, or the rescue squad if your doctor is not available, and have your child taken to the nearest emergency room. It is most unlikely that any harm will result, but appropriate medical attention is indicated.

Treatment

There is no cure for epilepsy in the sense that antibiotics can cure tonsillitis or pneumonia, but treatment of the tendency to have seizures with anticonvulsant drugs is often highly successful in preventing them from happening. It is a bit like giving a cough medicine to suppress a cough, rather than giving treatment to cure the cause of the cough such as bronchitis, pneumonia, or whatever.

Many effective drugs are now available, and the more modern ones have the advantage of being less likely to cause troublesome side effects than the older ones. Although the doctor will know the most likely drug to be effective depending on the type of seizure, it is not always possible to stop the seizures immediately. More than one drug may need to be tried before the best result is achieved. The dose is always carefully calculated for each child, based on her weight, and the aim is to produce and maintain a level of the drug in the blood that is neither too low to be effective, nor so high that it produces drowsiness or other side effects. The doses will be very low to start with and gradually increase, so this is another reason why the drugs may not be effective immediately. To be effective the drug must be taken regularly, so you'll need to gain your child's cooperation. Sensible older children can often be entrusted with their own medication but still need careful supervision. The doses are usually taken two or three times a day (occasionally only once at bedtime), and do not need to be given at precise intervals, though a routine is obviously desirable and more reliable. The drug should never be stopped suddenly, as this can sometimes provoke more seizures. If you are unhappy about the medicine, perhaps because of side effects, you should discuss your concerns with your child's doctor. Sometimes a change to another drug proves very helpful. Unfortunately, it is not possible to predict just how long a child will need to continue treatment. Each case is different. It is like asking, "How long is a piece of string?" In some cases, and with certain types of seizures, the attacks come under control very quickly, whereas in others they respond less well. There is a tendency in children for spontaneous improvement with age, and many children "grow out" of their epilepsy. This has something to do with maturation of the nervous system. The seizures can cease at any age—the popular idea that they stop at seven, fourteen, or twenty-one has no basis in fact. They could just as well stop at six, twelve, or eighteen There are many children, but few adults, who have epilepsy, so somewhere along the line most children stop having seizures.

Lifestyle for a Child with Epilepsy

Being overprotective—that is, preventing the child from taking part in normal activities, or giving in to her every wish for fear of causing upset—will do more harm psychologically in the long term than the epilepsy itself. You need an opportunity to discuss your concerns and to find out as much about the condition as possible. Your neurologist can supply you with useful information and direct you to parent support groups and local and national societies. In general, children with a seizure disorder should be treated quite normally, although simple safety measures must become a way of life. A good rule of thumb is to be cautious where activities would endanger safety if a child were to have a seizure during them—do not, for example, leave the child alone for a long time or let her lock herself in the bathroom. These precautions apply to all five-year-olds and under anyway, though obviously as the child gets older and more independent the questions get harder. But parents of children who don't have seizures have to keep making decisions about what is and what is not safe, based on their child's age and ability and the circumstances of the activity. If your child has seizures, you have to make the same decisions but also have to take into account the nature and frequency of the seizures.

Swimming and bicycling may be especially difficult to decide about, and again the child's condition, age, ability, the level of supervision, and the place of the activity must be considered. One specialist with several decades of experience suggests that children with frequent seizures should only swim for brief periods in a pool with a competent assistant alongside them all the time. Children with occasional seizures or with controlled epilepsy could swim for longer periods in a pool if a trained lifeguard or a competent swimming companion is present and aware of the possiblility of a seizure. Such children should also not be encouraged to bicycle on busy roads, though bicycling on a bike path or, with young children, on the sidewalk is safe enough. Make sure the child always wears protective gear, especially a helmet. Children with frequent fits should not be allowed to climb trees, use jungle gyms in the school yard, or climb ropes in gym classes.

Education and Seizures

There is no reason why the vast majority of children with seizures should not go to mainstream schools. As long as your child has no associated problems that may need special attention, go ahead and pick a day care or nursery school as you would with any child. Naturally, you should tell the teacher of your child's condition. Some parents want to conceal the fact of the child's seizure disorder from teachers, and though the impulse is understandable, this is unfair to both teachers and child and is most unwise. If she then has a seizure at school, the panic and alarm that will result will be far greater than if you had been honest and informative.

It is important to make sure the teachers understand what to do in the event of a seizure. Obviously that also applies to other helpers who will be in charge at different times. Young children need careful supervision anyway using wading pools, climbing on playground equipment, on swings, and so on. As long as a helper is always on hand and supervises carefully, there is no reason why your child should be restricted. Usually your instinct will tell you if this is the kind of day care or nursery school that will suit her needs. If she takes medications that may make her drowsy, make sure the staff also knows about this. When it comes to primary-school activities, much the same applies. As long as there is good supervision, most activities are suitable, though you may need to use your judgment about swimming. If you are concerned that drowsiness due to drugs may cause a problem, talk to the teacher, though be aware that most children, whether or not they are on anticonvulsant drugs, can feel tired when faced with something they do not want to do!

The Future

Each case is unique, so there can be no certainties but many possibilities. Most people with epilepsy do marry and have children, do drive cars, do get insurance and mortgages, and do take up the careers they hope for. The possibilities depend on the nature of the individual's condition as well as all the other factors that influence all of us, such as personality, temperament, and talent.

Serious Infectious Illnesses

Tetanus

Another name for this is lockjaw, so called because the bacteria cause the muscles of the jaws and neck to go into spasm. Fortunately, immunization has now made this disease very uncommon, but even so, some people still get it each year in the United States, and almost all of them die. A common misconception is that tetanus can only be caused by a wound from a rusty object. In fact, bacteria grow in the soil, so any cut can potentially allow the bacteria to enter. Symptoms usually show between two days or two weeks, but occasionally they occur after months, making diagnosis difficult. Spasms in the jaw and neck are first signs. A child thought to be suffering from tetanus would immediately be admitted to the hospital, but immunization as part of the triple vaccine is routinely given to all babies to protect them. Three doses of the vaccine are given during the first year, with a booster at 12 to 15 months and then another before starting school.

Poliomyelitis (Polio)

Thanks to routine vaccination, this potentially fatal or crippling disease is now very rare in the United States. It is caused by a virus that affects the brain and central nervous system, causing paralysis of the limbs but sometimes of the whole body so breathing is affected and the child may need a respirator. The first symptoms, seven to ten days after infection, are mild fever with sore throat, headache, and vomiting. Before a vaccine existed many children died of this horrible disease and others were left disabled due to paralysis. Because immunization has largely conquered polio it is easy to forget just how frightening the threat of it can be and consequently to become more casual about immunization. Once children begin to be unprotected against polio it is possible it might occur again because it is still common in other countries and could be reintroduced. The vaccine is given in the form of drops or injection at the same time as the triple vaccine two times in the first year of life, with a booster at twelve to fifteen months and again before starting school. There is significantly less danger of developing active poliomyelitis from the injection than from the oral vaccine. However, if only the oral is available, it is still safer to take the vaccine than to risk the child's getting the disease.

Diphtheria

There are many parents who have no idea what diphtheria is because, like polio, it has virtually disappeared from this country since routine immunization was introduced. It is caused by bacteria that multiply in the throat, sometimes blocking the airway and forming a grayish membrane over the tonsils. Sometimes the nose is the main site, causing a blood-stained discharge. The bacteria produce a potentially lethal poison (toxin) that affects the heart and nervous system and can cause heart failure or paralysis of the muscles used for breathing. The first symptom, two to seven days after infection, is usually a severe sore throat. Immunization is provided by the triple vaccine, which includes diphtheria, and is given three times in the first year, at twelve-to-fifteen months of age, and once before starting school. Like polio and tetanus, it is essential that parents do not become complacent about immunization just because the disease is now very rare.

Meningitis and Encephalitis

A child at my daughter's day care center had meningitis, and although he made a complete recovery I don't think there was a mother there who didn't begin to have concerns if their child complained of a headache or a stiff neck. It may not be contagious among children, but fear of meningitis is certainly infectious among parents.

The meninges are the covering of the brain and spinal cord, and in meningitis they become inflamed because of infection by bacteria or a virus. Bacterial meningitis can be treated with antibiotics, and if it is diagnosed and treated early the outlook is usually good, although there is a very low risk of brain damage, deafness, and blindness. There is no special treatment for viral meningitis, which can follow a virus infection occurring elsewhere in the body, such as mumps, but usually children make a complete recovery. What are the symptoms? Unfortunately, in children under two years old and in babies in particular the symptoms can be very vague. Poor feeding, drowsiness, vomiting, and extreme irritability are general signs that may be due to meningitis, or to other causes. A high-pitched cry, convulsions, and tension or bulging of the fontanelle (the soft spot on top of the head) are much more definite signs. A nondescript rash that becomes hemorrhagic (looking like small bruises) and does not fade on pressure should be looked for. The only sure way to diagnose meningitis is to test the fluid surrounding the spinal cord, and this is done with a lumbar puncture (see below). In older children symptoms such as a headache, stiff neck, and vomiting may occur, but do not leap to the conclusion that your child has meningitis every time she complains of any of these symptoms, especially if she seems well in all other ways. Sudden mood changes and irritable or uncharacteristic behavior coupled with vomiting and possibly fever, stiff neck, and headache are reasons to call a doctor. If you are concerned that your child may have meningitis, take her without delay to her pediatrician or to the local emergency room.

Inflammation of the brain (encephalitis) is usually caused by a virus. This is a rare complication of infections such as measles, mumps, chicken pox, or whooping cough. Symptoms are similar to those of meningitis.

Lumbar puncture. The process is somewhat similar to having an epidural anesthetic, except that fluid is being removed for study instead of being injected. The baby or child needs to lie curled on one side so the spines of the vertebrae stick out. In young children this is not a difficult procedure. The doctors and nurses will use sterile precautions to avoid any risk of infection, and the cooperative child need only be held gently so she does not move. Local anesthetic is used to numb the area before a needle is inserted into the area surrounding the spinal column to draw off some of the fluid that surrounds the spinal cord. It does not hurt, although it may feel uncomfortable, so that reassuring and comforting the child to ensure that she is not frightened by what is happening is important. If the spinal fluid shows signs of infection, intravenous antibiotics are started immediately. Further laboratory studies, such as cultures, will exactly determine the specific bacteria causing the infection; antibiotics known to eliminate the infection are then used.

Kidney (Renal) Problems

Many kidney problems are now being detected prenatally. Problems that can be detected include some genetically inherited diseases, but more commonly, obstruction or malformation of the urinary tract. Sometimes abnormalities detected prenatally disappear after birth and cause no further problems. It is important that any abnormality that is detected beforehand is followed up by a pediatrician after birth. Sometimes these abnormalities require antibiotics to prevent infection, sometimes they need observation but improve spontaneously, and sometimes they may need surgery. If one kidney fails to work, the other kidney, if normal, can take over its function very satisfactorily. However, if both kidneys fail, the child will either need dialysis or a new kidney, transplanted from a donor. Complete kidney failure is rare; it only occurs in one or two children in a million and often occurs after a prolonged period of decreasing function. Many kidney diseases can be completely cured by treatment, but a few are long-term and chronic and may require nursing and medical treatment throughout life.

Dialysis can either involve the passage of special fluids into and out of the abdomen by a specially inserted tube, or the child's blood being passed through a machine that purifies the blood. Both systems carry out the functions of a normal kidney. When the abdomen is used the process is called peritoneal dialysis. When the blood is passed through a machine the process is called hemodialysis.

Peritoneal dialysis can be carried out at home, whereas hemodialysis for children takes place in the hospital or dialysis centers. Renal transplantation provides the best quality of life, although some kidneys may be lost due to rejection either acutely or slowly over the years, in which case the child has to return to dialysis or can be given a second or even a third kidney transplant, should this be necessary. A well-functioning transplant restores energy levels and improves growth, which can be affected by chronic renal failure.

Long-term problems with the kidneys (chronic renal failure) involve much stress, both for the child and the parents. The lighter burdens fall in those cases that can be treated without resort to prolonged dialysis. This means either a successful transplant or, if the disease is not so severe, drugs or diet, alone or in combination. Stress for the child arises either from the direct effects of the disease or from its treatment. One effect of kidney disease is that the child tires easily and so cannot keep up, in games or at work, with children of the same age. Growth can be stunted in some cases. Stress from treatment comes especially when dialysis is needed.

In the longer term, children who have experienced kidney failure may be more prone to anxiety. It has been suggested that this may be because at a time when they should be taking pride in increasing control over their body, they find instead that it is not functioning to such an extent that they have to undergo dialysis. Sympathy and support help, but parents also experience considerable stress in view of the endless and time-consuming nature of the treatment. If home dialysis is not possible, treatment in the hospital or dialysis center can be extra-stressful for the parents because of the burden of organizing a program to allow for the constant trips to the hospital.

Your kidney doctor (nephrologist) can give you information about parent support groups and local and national societies. These can offer much-needed advice and support.

Jaundice

The word "jaundice" describes the yellow color of the skin and eyes that develops when a yellow pigment (bilirubin) normally excreted in the bile builds up in the blood. This happens when the liver, which produces bile, is not working properly. The pigment that gives bile its color is not properly excreted and backs up into the blood. It then is deposited in the whites of the eyes and the skin, producing a yellow color to the whites of the eyes and a suntanned color to the skin. Jaundice can be caused by a variety of factors. Newborn and premature babies are especially prone to it. Jaundice in the first ten days of life is usually not due to a problem in the liver or bile ducts. If, however, jaundice persists after two weeks of age or if it is associated with dark urine and pale stools, it is important that doctors check for liver disease. In older children jaundice can be caused by infectious hepatitis, which can be passed on in the form of a virus, just like a cold or flu. There are various kinds of hepatitis virus. Most cases in the United States are due to hepatitis A virus. A vaccine to protect against hepatitis A is now available and its use is optional. The hepatitis B virus is also widespread, and this is why vaccination to give protection is advised routinely for children and adolescents. Other types of hepatitis have been identified and include C, D, and E types. Symptoms of infectious hepatitis are loss of appetite, headache, nausea, abdominal pain due to an inflamed liver, and sometimes fever. The yellowing of the skin does not usually begin for a week, and once it does, the child may begin to feel a bit better. The urine becomes dark because it is also stained with bile, and bowel movements are pale because the bile is not finding its way into the intestines. Because it is caused by a virus there is no specific treatment, but viral hepatitis is a mild childhood infection, and children usually recover well. Rest and a high-protein diet are the treatments. The virus is very infectious, so take care to wash hands after diaper changing or taking a child to the bathroom in order to avoid catching hepatitis yourself.

Hemophilia

At first we just thought Peter bruised very easily. I had one very unpleasant session with our doctor when it was obvious she thought that all these bruises might be the result of us actually spanking him. I got very upset, but after that she suggested we get some blood tests. These indicated that he had a bleeding disorder. We were referred to a hematologist, who made the diagnosis of hemophilia.

Of course, nearly all bruising in children is caused by minor injuries, usually accidents, but occasionally it is inflicted by parents or other caregivers, so the doctor's concerns were understandable. A very small number of children, about eight in every one hundred thousand, have an abnormality in the mechanism that causes blood to clot and the flow to be stopped when a blood vessel is damaged. By far the most common variety is hemophilia A. This is caused by the lack of one of the substances (Factor VIII) involved in clotting. In this and other related conditions, spontaneous bruising occurs in the absence of injury.

Children with hemophilia vary a good deal in how many times they bleed spontaneously. In some it occurs several times a week; in others, only two or three times a year. The bleeding often occurs into joints, which may become painful and stiff and then become red, swollen, and tender. Bleeding episodes usually come out of the blue, but sometimes they seem to be brought on by a change in the weather or emotional stress, and there is sometimes an increase in the frequency of bleeding around adolescence.

Hemophilia is inherited as a sex-linked recessive condition. The defective gene is carried on one of the mother's two X chromosomes, and almost always males are affected. Rarely, this illness can be seen in females. If a couple have a boy with the condition, there is a 50 percent chance of any subsequent boys being affected. If a woman in this situation becomes pregnant, there is the option of a termination if she is carrying an affected boy. It is now possible, in some specialty centers, to carry out a test in or about the tenth week of pregnancy to check on the presence of the abnormality in the unborn baby.

Parents are understandably shocked when they first learn of hemophilia, especially if it has never been detected in the family before, and many women feel guilty because they have carried the defective gene but are healthy themselves. It is a very natural reaction to want to protect a child with this condition, but being overprotective—for example, not letting children play with sharp toys—can lead to additional emotional and social problems. Parents with young children obviously have to be more careful, and letting toddlers lead an ordinary life while trying to avoid bumps and bruises is very stressful. Extra backup to help with housework is important because parents of hemophiliac children need to be more observant. But there is no reason why a child with the condition should not go to day care or nursery school.

Living close to a hemophilia center helps, as does learning to give treatment at home, because after a while parents feel more confident, and this in turn gives the child confidence. In the preschool years parents can find it hard to leave their child with baby-sitters or relatives, but it is important to continue to have a life together. Sensible precautions, such as making sure the sitter is fully briefed, are sufficient. Later in life the choice of job for a man with hemophilia may be limited if the hemophilia is severe, but most affected men find and keep satisfactory jobs.

Treatment

Although there is no cure for the condition, it is possible to stop the bleeding when it occurs, and indeed it is most important to do so. Repeated bleeding into joints can result in crippling arthritis, so when an episode of bleeding occurs, children should receive an infusion of the missing clotting factor into their bloodstream as soon as possible. Until recently this could only be carried out in a specialty center, but, increasingly, home treatment is becoming possible. Tragically, a number of children with hemophilia who received such infusions were infected with HIV (human immunodeficiency virus) because they were given contaminated blood products. Many of these went on to develop AIDS (acquired immmune deficiency syndrome). Infusions are now carefully checked to ensure that blood for transfusion will not be contaminated with HIV.

Children with problems in their blood-clotting mechanism also need special care when they have dental treatment or more serious surgical operations for other reasons, so their families need to keep in touch with specialty centers. The National Hemophilia Foundation can provide further information. They can be reached at (800) 424-2634. The address is: 116 West 32nd Street, 11th Floor, New York, NY 10001.

Childhood Cancer, Including Leukemia

Many adults do not realize that children can have cancer, and just hearing the word can be a great shock. It is still a life-threatening condition, but modern treatment means that the chances of cure, or at least of long-term remission of the illness, are very much more likely now than they were even ten years ago.

Normally the cells of the body increase in number to replace those that die. In children more cells are produced as the body is growing, but the process of cell multiplication is very much under control. Cancer is a condition in which the cells in the body do not obey the rules; they multiply in an uncontrolled way, sometimes spreading to other parts of the body.

Although the causes of some cancers in adulthood are now known—for instance, the link between cigarette smoking and lung cancer—the causes of nearly all cancers in children are still unknown. There is no evidence that anything children or parents themselves have done could be a cause.

In theory, the cells of any part of the body can get out of control and a cancer can develop, but in reality, in children there are only certain organs that are usually affected. Leukemia, a cancer of the white blood cells, is the most common variety, but occasionally cancers of the brain, the eye, kidney, glands, liver, bones, testes, ovaries, and connective tissue can occur.

The signs that a cancer is developing will obviously depend on where it is situated. Most children with leukemia first show tiredness or a predisposition to infection because of anemia, that is, the blood is not able to carry enough energy-giving oxygen to the tissues, or easy bruising. But, of course, leukemia is a very rare cause of tiredness.

Pressure from swelling produced by a tumor is usually the first sign of other sorts of cancer. One of the most common forms of brain cancer affects the cerebellum, a part of the brain that is important in helping the child to keep a sense of balance. So cerebellar tumors often show themselves with the child starting to stagger rather than walk properly.

To make an accurate diagnosis of a cancer it is often necessary to take a biopsy—that is, to remove a sample of tissue, under anesthetic, and examine it under a microscope. If leukemia is suspected, a biopsy of the bone marrow, where blood is manufactured, is taken, usually from the hip.

The treatment varies, not only according to the type of cancer but also according to the age of the child. There are three main approaches that can be used:

- Surgery to remove a malignant growth. This is not possible in leukemia.

- Chemotherapy (drugs) to shrink a growth or to control leukemia cells in the blood tissues.

- Radiotherapy. Radiotherapy consists of concentrated x-ray treatment to the specific part of the body that is invaded by the cancer. This therapy kills all the tumor cells that are irradiated. The outlook for children varies according to the type of cancer and what stage it has reached. The overall cure rate in the late 1990s is 70 percent, but some have more than a 90 percent chance of cure. For others the prospects are much poorer.

For most children the side effects of treatment are the worst part. They may lose their hair (something that does not upset young children very much at all but that can be distressing for teenagers), and they may feel very sick because of the drugs rather than the illness itself. This can lead to them asking why they have to go to the hospital since they go in feeling well and are then made, as they see it, worse.

The psychological care of the child has to take into account the stress caused to the whole family. Uncertainty about the outcome is characteristic of many cases, if not all, and is one of the most powerful causes of distress. It is better if parents are truthful and prepare children as much as possible for investigations and treatment.

Children are resilient and can cope, providing they trust those who are caring for them. Older children should be reassured that the doctors and nurses will be able to take away most of the pain or other sorts of distressing symptoms they may experience by giving medicines or injections. Brothers and sisters need support as well, and, if they are older than the affected child, may need to be given more detailed information so they understand what is going on. The hospital doctors, nurses, and social workers will be pleased to discuss how to talk to children about the illness. They have often had a good deal of experience in these situations.

Further information can be obtained from the Leukemia Society of America, which has local and national chapters. Call (800) 955-4752.

Sickle-Cell Disease

Sickle-cell disease is a group of inherited blood disorders in which there is an abnormality of the red blood cells, causing them to become rigid and sickle-shaped, hence the name. Sickle-cell anemia (Hb SS) is usually the most severe and common form, but there are other types, such as sickle trait disease (Hb SA), Hb SC disease, and sickle beta-thalassemia. Sickle-cell disease mainly affects people of African and Caribbean origin (about one in two hundred) and is also found in people from the Mediterranean, Asia, and the Middle East. Although there is no complete cure for sickle-cell anemia yet, research has improved the treatment now available.

A child is born with sickle-cell anemia because he has inherited a gene from both parents, each of whom is a carrier with sickle-cell trait. People who have sickle-cell trait are not affected and have no symptoms themselves. This is because people with sickle-cell trait have an identical but healthy backup gene to do the job (see "Genetic Factors" in chapter 1 for more on dominant and recessive genes). But if both parents have sickle-cell trait then there is a one in four chance that every child they have will be born with sickle-cell anemia. There is a one in two chance that each child will inherit sickle-cell trait—that is, be a carrier of the gene but not be affected themselves. If only one parent has sickle-cell trait, each child has a fifty-fifty chance of inheriting either the trait or normal hemoglobin. If one parent has sickle-cell anemia and the other has sickle-cell trait there is a fifty-fifty chance again that the child could be born with sickle-cell anemia or sickle-cell trait. A special blood test can tell if a person has sickle-cell trait, and it is now possible to test the unborn child for sickle-cell anemia, although at present this is only being done at certain specialty centers.

Symptoms

The rigid sickle-shaped blood cells cannot flow smoothly through small blood vessels. This can cause blockage of the blood supply with subsequent pain and, more rarely, damage to bones, muscles, and lungs. A further problem is that these sickle-shaped blood cells do not live as long as the normal 120 days of healthy red blood cells, and this causes chronic anemia. Episodes of pain are known as crises and can be prompted by dehydration, strenuous exercise, infection, pregnancy, and anesthetics. Both the symptoms and their effects can vary greatly from one individual to another. Symptoms very rarely start until the child is more than six months old and may include painful swelling of hands and feet. As a child gets older, sickling, causing mild or more severe pain, may occur in any part of the body, with the joints, abdomen, and chest being common sites. Anemia is always present but can become dramatically worse, so that a child may become jaundiced at times because of increased destruction of red blood cells. Young children with sickle-cell anemia are more prone to bacterial infections and are treated with prophylactic antibiotics. During adolescence other features may occur, such as leg ulcers and delay in growth.

Treatment

Drinking extra fluid regularly helps to keep the blood flowing smoothly, and taking folic acid tablets compensates for folate deficiency. Taking penicillin regularly protects against serious infections. If your child has the condition, you need to learn how to let your child lead as normal a life as possible while avoiding triggers that may cause sickling, such as dehydration, sudden change in temperature, infection, or strenuous exercise. You also need long-term support from skilled and sensitive professionals to help you cope with your own emotions and be as supportive as possible to your child. Genetic counseling can help you understand the long-term implications of the disease and equip you with information regarding future pregnancies. During a crisis, the child needs painkillers to give pain relief, fluids, bed rest, and possibly antibiotics. With help and advice you can learn how to recognize the early warning signs calling for urgent medical attention, such as fever, pallor, lethargy, and swelling of the abdomen, as well as how to manage mild symptoms at home. The most vulnerable period for those with sickle-cell disease is early childhood, but improved treatment means the prognosis is much better, and most sufferers live into adulthood.

Thalassemia

This is an inherited abnormality of the blood that is found among people from Mediterranean countries. As with sickle-cell disease, people can carry the thalassemia gene without being affected, but when two adult carriers of the gene have children, there is a one in four chance with every pregnancy that their child could have thalassemia. The blood of thalassemia sufferers cannot produce hemoglobin efficiently, which makes them anemic unless they have good treatment. They can also suffer skull deformities, fail to reach their full potential height and thus be of shorter than normal stature, and fail to enter puberty.

The symptoms, which usually show in the first six months of life, are anemia and failure to thrive. There is currently no complete cure, but with babies bone-marrow transplantation may be successful. This is a new field. The prognosis has improved with better treatment to combat symptoms so that most thalassemia sufferers now live to adulthood. Treatment consists of blood transfusions, which children need to have every two to four weeks to prevent them from developing anemia. It is now often possible for this to be done in an outpatient setting, decreasing the number of hospital stays necessary. However, because of the iron in the transfused blood, there is a buildup of iron deposits in the tissues. A drug (desferoximine) has to be injected to induce a process called chelation, the freeing of iron deposits. This substance has to be injected into the vein or under the skin.

Obviously the treatment is not pleasant for children, and they need a great deal of support and help from parents and other members of the family, both to minimize the stress of medical procedures and to help them have as full and as enjoyable a life as healthy children as possible. Parents and relatives in their turn will need counseling about the disease and opportunities to talk about their feelings. In common with most inherited diseases, parents may feel great guilt, and parent support groups have proved of value. Fortunately, genetic counseling, fetal imaging with ultrasound, and amniocentesis to detect thalassemia in the unborn child can help to decrease the incidence of the disease.

Short Stature

Obviously children vary in height, and the great majority of small children are perfectly normal. Such children have a normal rate of growth. They usually have parents who are not very tall either, and thus have probably inherited a tendency to be small.

Some children, however, are very small, so that, for example, a five-year-old might only be the height of an average two-year-old. There are various reasons for this. The child may have a definite, inherited syndrome in which failure to grow is one feature. Such children are often small at birth even if they are born at the expected time. Very occasionally there is a lack of the growth hormone normally produced in a gland at the base of the brain (the pituitary gland) and necessary for ordinary growth to occur.

Treatment

Tests can be carried out to see if the child is suffering from growth hormone deficiency and, if this is the case, the child can be given injections of artificial hormone to stimulate growth. Children brought up in socially stressed conditions also tend to be small, and, in circumstances of severe deprivation, the amount of growth hormone put out by the pituitary gland is sometimes reduced. This situation is reversible if the child is placed in a more suitable social environment.

Education. Unless failure to grow is part of an inherited syndrome that has other problems, small children are of normal intelligence and go to ordinary schools.

Lifestyle. Children who are tiny for their age face many kinds of problems. People often think they are much younger than they really are and talk down to them. They may develop ways of coping with this that are not very helpful, such as acting much younger than their age. Parents will usually have no problem dealing with this themselves, but they need to be able to help others treat their children more appropriately if secondary difficulties are to be minimized.

Helpful information can be obtained from an endocrinologist, who can give you literature on the subject and get you in touch with parent support groups and local or national societies.

Diabetes

Our daughter became very listless and then sleepy. It was a terrible shock when she actually went into a coma. All sorts of awful thoughts went through my mind, so when they came and told us at the hospital that it seemed likely she had diabetes but would be all right, our first reaction was tremendous relief. In fact neither of us knew anything at all about it; otherwise we would have recognized the classic warning signs, such as thirst, increased appetite, weight loss, and urinating too frequently. We had a great deal to learn about how it was to affect her life.

Every year many children in the United States develop diabetes mellitus, sometimes called sugar diabetes. There is no cure, but medical advances mean it is no longer the killer it once was, and with good management a person with diabetes can lead a perfectly normal, full life. Most people know that diabetes has to do with blood sugar, but unless they have a relative or a friend who is diabetic they are often understandably unclear about the exact nature of the problem.

First of all, diabetes is not caused by eating too much sugar, nor is one of the symptoms a liking for sweet things. The problem lies with a gland called the pancreas, which is positioned near the stomach. The pancreas produces a hormone called insulin. It is insulin that breaks down the body's fuel, glucose, and enables it to be used as energy, to repair body tissues, or to be stored in the liver. You may think that you do not actually eat much glucose in the form of sugar, but a great deal of ordinary food and especially carbohydrates are broken down into glucose by the digestive juices. When someone has diabetes, the pancreas fails to work properly and either produces very little insulin or none at all. Because no insulin is made to convert the glucose, it stays in the bloodstream until it reaches the kidneys, when it is passed out of the body in urine. Because glucose carries water with it, this means passing a great deal of urine, and this in turn leads to another symptom, excessive thirst. Finally, since the body is being deprived of the fuel it normally has in the form of glucose and begins to use up fat stores, it sends out signals for more food by making the sufferer extra-hungry. So the symptoms of diabetes are excessive thirst, passing urine very frequently, eating a lot but losing or failing to gain weight, and glucose in the urine. Of course, the last of these can only be detected if the urine is tested, but if your child has the other symptoms, seek your doctor's advice. It is important that diabetes be diagnosed early, because if it is not treated, a child can become very drowsy and tired, go into a coma, and even die.

Treatment

Because the body cannot make its own insulin, it has to be given by injection. Adult diabetics can sometimes manage the condition with diet and tablets alone, but children always need insulin injections, usually three to four times a day. They continue to need them even when they are ill and not eating.

Normally the balance between the amount of insulin produced and the amount of glucose to be converted is regulated by the checks and balances of the body's own systems. But when insulin has to be given artificially it is much harder to keep the balance right, and that is where diet comes in. Diabetics must try to keep the levels of glucose in their body fairly constant, which means eating little and often. Three main meals with snacks in between so there are six regularly spaced intakes of food are needed, and a child with diabetes must not be kept waiting for meals.

Because diabetics' bodies cope so poorly with glucose, they must avoid loading the system with sudden surges of it. For this reason, children with diabetes should not eat candy, and the intake of foods high in carbohydrates, such as potatoes and bread, must be controlled. But diabetics do not have to eat special food. They eat the same things as anybody else but always as part of a balanced diet. In fact, a diabetic diet is very healthy for the whole family, high in fiber, low in fat, and with little sugar.

Young children quickly adapt to both the diet and (something that often surprises parents) to having injections of insulin. Many can give the injections themselves by the time they are about seven or eight. To check that the level of glucose is staying under control, parents have to check the glucose levels in the blood as well, with a glucometer. These are simple procedures that children can soon learn to do for themselves.

Insulin pumps are available for difficult to control diabetes. These are battery operated and release insulin slowly and constantly. For the most part, their use is experimental.

What Happens When the Balance Between Insulin and Glucose Is Wrong?

Various things can upset the balance—too little food, too much sweet food, extra exercise that burns up a lot of glucose in the form of energy, the changing needs of a growing body, or infections.

Hypoglycemia occurs when the body has too little glucose. It may be the result of too much insulin having been given for the amount of food to be processed, because too little food has been eaten, or because exercise has used up a lot of glucose. It comes on suddenly, and the signs to look for are lack of concentration, sweating, dizziness, vagueness, inability to respond to questions, bad temper or crankiness, and sometimes difficulty in speaking.

If untreated, hypoglycemia can lead to a shock. This is why everyone with diabetes needs to carry or have on hand something sweet to eat at the first warning signs that the blood sugar is falling. A piece of hard candy will do, and orange juice to drink is a good idea as well. Once the person has begun to recover, she should eat some other foods. If a child does become unconscious, call a doctor and get her to the nearest emergency department immediately. Food or fluids should not be given to anyone unconscious because of the real risk of choking or aspirating the material into the lungs.

Hyperglycemia means there is too much glucose in the body. This is the situation when a child first begins to develop diabetes before she gets treatment. It is usually slow to develop and, after treatment has begun, may be because too little insulin has been given, an insulin injection is overdue, too many carbohydrates have been eaten, or because the child has an infection. The signs include tiredness; excessive thirst; hunger or frequent urination; a dry tongue; a sweet, fruity smell on the breath; and deep breathing.

Extra injections of insulin may be needed, but if the child is dehydrated, treatment in the hospital may be necessary.

Lifestyle for a Child with Diabetes

Children with diabetes need to eat regularly, need to eat a balanced diet, and need to have insulin injections. But these are not restrictions that will prevent them from having as full and as active a life as any normal child. Try not to be overprotective or overindulgent. Being matter-of-fact about diet and treatment will help your child to accept it as part of life. Obviously you need to be sure that child care providers and nursery and primary-school teachers know and understand about diabetes and how to treat suspected hypoglycemia. Food should not be a problem because so many children take packed lunches these days, and the child can take an additional snack for playtime. Both you and your child will become experts in keeping the balance between insulin and glucose.

In the beginning you may well need to talk over both the condition and your own emotions with informed counselors or a doctor you trust. You may have many different feelings about the subject, but support and help are available both through other parents and through the Juvenile Diabetic Foundation, which has local chapters in most large cities. When the child gets older she, too, can find valuable support from meeting other diabetic children at specially arranged summer camps.

Cystic Fibrosis (CF)

In this condition all the glands that discharge their secretions directly into the body are affected. The secretions are thick and sticky instead of runny (another name for the condition is mucoviscidosis), so they block up a number of the connecting tubes in the body's system.

The condition occurs in about one in two thousand births, and is an inherited disease caused by the presence of a recessive gene. About one in twenty people is a carrier of the CF gene, but it is only when two carriers have a child that there is a one in four chance of that child inheriting both genes and having cystic fibrosis. The chance is the same for each pregnancy, though some couples never have a CF child so they never know they are both carriers of the gene. In other families all the children may be affected. The CF gene mainly, but not exclusively, occurs in Caucasian (white Indo-European) people. Some children are affected less severely than others. CF mainly affects the way the lungs and the digestive system function, but CF also has an effect on other parts of the body that may at first seem unrelated. What links them is the presence of secretory glands. The problem may be diagnosed at birth when a baby fails to pass meconium, a tarlike substance present in the gut before birth, or if the feces are unusually bulky and very foul-smelling. Sometimes the gut is obstructed, which must be dealt with by surgery. More commonly the problem is discovered in the first months or few years of life because the child suffers repeated chest infections, does not digest food properly, and passes frequent, pale, foul-smelling bowel movements. The diagnosis is confirmed by carrying out a test on the child's sweat, which is abnormal in the amount of salt it contains (sodium and chloride) because the sweat glands are affected, or by detecting the genes in a saliva or blood sample. The principal symptom of CF is that the mucus in the lungs is very thick and difficult to cough up and can easily become infected. Sometimes this mucus blocks the bronchial tubes, tiny air passages into the lungs. This can cause lung damage and air cannot pass through the mucus on breathing in or out. Bacteria invading the mucus will then also cause lung damage.

To clear the mucus, parents of CF children, and later the child himself, must learn physiotherapy, which is practiced several times a day, to loosen the mucus. CF children need to learn how to cough up the mucus their lungs produce, and they also need regular antibiotic treatment to prevent bacteria from infecting the mucus. The antibiotics are sometimes taken through a nebulizer, a device that makes mist out of a liquid by blowing air or oxygen through it so the medicine can be delivered directly into the lungs. The final part of the daily treatment routine is taking digestive enzymes to replace the enzymes that would normally be produced

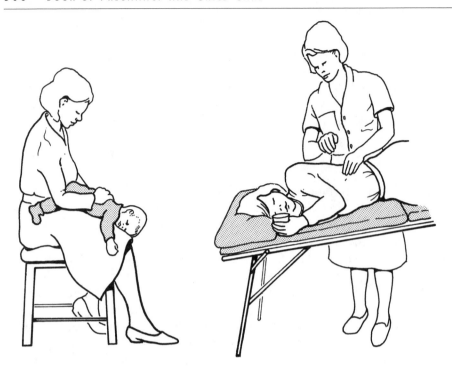

Physiotherapy is needed for babies and older children to loosen lung mucous

by the pancreas to break down and help the body absorb food. Fats are especially difficult for CF sufferers to digest, and without drugs they require a very-low-fat diet. Enzyme capsules now have a special coating that prevents them being destroyed in the stomach before they reach the small intestine and that enable CF children to eat an entirely normal diet.

CF children need plenty of high-energy food and vitamin supplements to ensure that they get the nutrients they need to grow and develop properly. In addition to physiotherapy, exercise is very important. Playgrounds, swimming, and gym play geared to the under-five age group are all a good idea. Later, learning a sport such as tennis or archery, dance, and drama is part of an active lifestyle that helps keep the lungs clear and that strengthens muscles.

In 1989 geneticists identified the CF gene, making a test available to detect whether a person is a carrier of the faulty gene. This will be performed by blood analysis or by using a special mouthwash. Research has provided a means of screening for cystic fibrosis in the unborn baby, although at present this is only offered to families known to be at risk.

Sadly, as yet there is no cure for CF itself, although advances in treatment mean that both the quality of life and the life expectancy for CF children are now vastly improved. When CF was first recognized as a disease in the late 1930s, children died very young from lung infections or digestive problems, but now 75 percent live to enjoy adult life. Apart from the development of gene therapy in the future, work is also being done with heart-lung transplants when a point is reached when these organs begin to fail. As with all organ transplants, though, an insufficient number of donors limits more widespread use of this technique. The Cystic Fibrosis Foundation can provide further help and information. There are local chapters in most large cities. Phone 1-800-FIGHT CF or 1-800-344-4823.

Celiac Disease

Most children who fail to gain weight properly are not suffering from physical disease; for one reason or another they are just not getting enough to eat, perhaps because they are living in families under stress because of difficult social circumstances. However, there are a small number of conditions in which children fail to thrive even though they are getting a very adequate diet; celiac disease is one of these. In this condition the child is unable to tolerate the gluten (a protein) in wheat or rye. Consequently, foods such as ordinary bread, cakes, and biscuits will make her ill. The bowel movements are pale and bulky and smell offensive. The child not only fails to grow as well as she should but also is often irritable and miserable.

The condition is diagnosed by passing a tube through the nose into the small intestine just beyond the stomach and snipping off a tiny segment (taking a biopsy) of the lining of the gut, so this can be examined under a microscope. The lining has an abnormal appearance in children with celiac disease. The usual velvety appearance is replaced by a flat layer of cells lining the intestine.

Usually children do very well on a diet free of gluten, but they need to stay on the diet for the rest of their lives. As the diet is quite restrictive, it is important that the diagnosis is made properly. The biopsy may be repeated when the child is on a gluten-free diet, to make sure the appearance of the lining of the gut has returned to normal.

Heart Problems

Congenital heart disease is a term used when a baby is born with something wrong with the structure of her heart that affects the way it works. The heart is formed very early in pregnancy, between the sixth and the tenth weeks, after which it grows with the baby. We know that if the mother has rubella (German measles) in the first three months of pregnancy it can affect the formation of the baby's heart, and it may be that other viruses also have this effect. If the mother has diabetes there is also a slightly increased risk of her child having heart disease, but in the majority of cases we do not know the cause. About eight in every thousand babies born alive have some form of congenital heart disease, but in a third of these children the abnormality is very mild and does not need treatment.

The job of the heart is to receive blood that has already been circulated through the body and given up some of its oxygen (blue blood); pump it to the lungs, where it becomes oxygenated again and turns red; and then to pump this red blood back around the body again. It helps to imagine the heart as two pumps, each with its own reservoir, the right side filling with blue blood from the body and sending it to the lungs, the left side filling with red blood from the lungs and pumping it back around the body. The left side of the heart has to be stronger and has more muscle, as it has more work to do than the right. These two sides of the heart are separated by partitions or septa so the blue blood and the red blood do not mix. There are four valves, which open completely to allow the blood to pass through and then close to prevent the blood from flowing backward. The pumping action followed by a resting period, which allows the heart to fill with blood, is controlled by an electrical circuit directed by nerves.

Heart Murmurs

A murmur is simply the noise made by the blood flowing through the heart and big vessels. It is very common for doctors to discover that a child has a murmur by listening to her heart with a stethoscope during a routine examination. This is not the same as finding that the child has heart disease. In most cases such murmurs are what doctors call innocent, which means they are not due to heart disease or any other illness. An innocent murmur does not influence the way in which the heart works and will disappear as the child grows. In many cases, at times when a heart murmur is found to be due to a heart defect, it may correct itself by the time the child reaches school age. In other children the murmur comes from an abnormality that will need treating.

Common Heart Disease Abnormalities

There may be a hole in the muscular part that separates the two pumping sides of the lower chambers of the heart. This means that extra blood from the left side of the heart, where the pressure is higher, enters the right side; consequently more blood is being sent to the lungs, and the heart has to work harder. This is commonly known as ventricular septal defect. Children with small defects do not show any symptoms, and the hole usually becomes smaller and closes on its own, although it may take some years, and they may have more chest infections than normal children. If the hole is large and causing symptoms, an operation may be necessary to correct it. Children can have another abnormality when a narrowing occurs at some point in the arteries or valves so the heart has to work extra hard to pump the blood through. In some babies the tube between the two arteries, known as the ductus arteriosus, remains open. This normally closes after birth as the lungs begin to work (see "First Reactions" in chapter 4). The effect is that the blood from the main artery going to the body (the aorta) is allowed to flow to the lungs. Again, the lungs receive extra blood, and the heart has to work harder. This can be corrected by an operation that has a very low risk and that will enable the heart to work normally.

Sometimes the veins or arteries are wrongly connected to the heart so blood with a lower amount of oxygen than normal, and which is therefore blue in color, is circulated to the body. This will make the skin have a bluish tinge, hence the description, cyanosis. Procedures are possible to make the condition less severe and to allow more oxygenated blood to reach the body, but major surgery will be needed to correct the abnormality. This may be done shortly after birth or deferred till

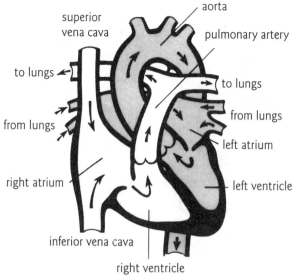

Normal heart circulation

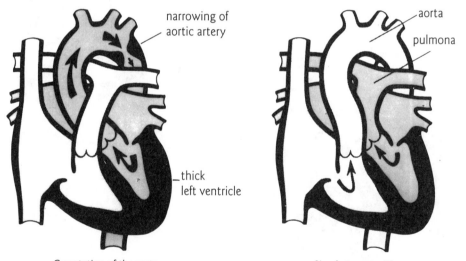

Coarctation of the aorta

Simple transposition

later, depending on the particular problem and baby's progress. More rarely one side of the heart may be weaker than the other. This is known as the hypoplastic left heart syndrome and should be considered a life-threatening condition that requires immediate surgery.

Symptoms

Many babies and children with minor heart problems do not show any symptoms and are not affected. Others get out of breath when walking or running or, in the

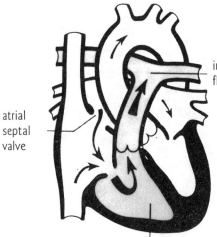

atrial
septal
valve

increased blood
flow to lungs

enlarged
right ventricle

Atrial septal defect

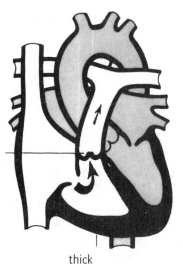

thickened
pulmonary
valve

thick
right valve

Pulmonary valve stenosis

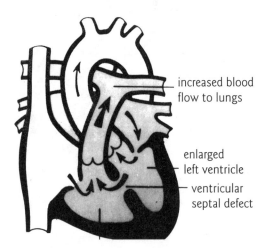

increased blood
flow to lungs

enlarged
left ventricle

ventricular
septal defect

enlarged
right ventricle

Ventricular septal defect

case of an infant, when feeding. This may mean that the baby cannot finish the feeding and consequently grows more slowly. Some children may have less energy, may tire more easily, and may have more chest infections. In the first instance doctors will carefully examine your child, listen to the heart with a stethoscope, and may plan some tests, although many children do not need any.

Investigations and Tests

A chest X ray may be needed, and by attaching wires painlessly to chest, arms, and legs, doctors can test the electrical activity of the heart (electrocardiogram or ECG) and take a tracing. An ultrasound scan of the child (echocardiogram), similar to the one done in pregnancy, will show a picture of the heart on a television screen. Sometimes doctors need to measure the pressures inside the heart. This test involves an overnight stay in the hospital. The child is given a sedative and a tube is inserted into a vein and/or artery, usually at a point in the groin, and steered with the blood flow into the heart chambers. Special dye can be injected through the tube, which shows up on X ray so that a clear outline of the heart and any defects can be seen. The procedure is not painful, and the child is usually sedated while it is being done. Sometimes this test can be used to treat heart problems—for example, to stretch narrow valves.

Lifestyle

Most children with heart disease can lead ordinary lives and go to ordinary schools. More than half the babies born with heart disease need some kind of investigation in the first year of their lives, and some need an operation at this time. Often doctors prefer to wait until the child is much bigger before undertaking any corrective surgery and treat them in the meantime with medicines. Understandably, parents feel anxious about their child and, unless the condition is fully explained, may fear that the condition may suddenly worsen and the child collapse. In fact this is extremely unlikely. If the child's condition does worsen, the only signs will be a gradual slowing down of activity and eating. The most beneficial thing you can do is to allow your child to enjoy a normal childhood. If there is a real reason for a child not to do too much in the way of games and exercise, the heart specialist will explain why. Otherwise it has been shown that children with heart disease are usually very sensible and naturally limit their own activity when necessary. Parents sometimes wonder if crying can harm a baby with heart disease, but this is not the case. Such babies should be comforted in the ordinary way. Children with heart disease should be immunized at the normal time. Occasionally such children can get a special sort of infection in their hearts from having decayed teeth, significant dental work, or other operations. To prevent this they will be given antibiotics by the doctor or dentist just before a dental or surgical procedure.

The majority of children are able to go to normal school. In a few, fatigue, tiredness, and blueness may cause lack of concentration, so extra help may be necessary. The great majority of girls who have heart defects should be able to have children when they grow up. However, each case needs to be considered individually. A full range of careers is possible for most heart disease patients, but in a few cases heavy, strenuous outdoor work is best avoided. The armed forces are not willing to take people who have had heart operations, even though they may be healthy.

AIDS

HIV (human immunodeficiency virus) is a virus that can attack the immune system to produce symptoms of the illness called AIDS (acquired immune deficiency syndrome). It can lie dormant in the body without causing any symptoms for five or more years, although in some people this period may be shorter. The HIV virus is transmitted from one person to another by an intermingling of blood, by sexual contact, or from an infected mother to her child through the placenta or by breastfeeding. It cannot be passed on by touching or in urine, sweat, or feces. The number of children in the United States with AIDS is growing rapidly, especially in the newborn and adolescent age groups.

A large proportion of infected babies are born to mothers who have been intravenous drug abusers or who have acquired the AIDS virus through sexual contact. A large group of children with AIDS are hemophiliacs who, tragically, were given a blood product that carried the virus. Hemophiliacs need to be treated with infusions of the clotting factor their bodies lack when they are injured. All blood and blood products are now screened to be sure they are free of HIV, but in the early 1980s supplies of the clotting factor were contaminated with HIV.

Most of the other infected children acquired the virus from their mothers before or during birth in the same way that other viruses, such as rubella, may be transmitted. Only about one in five of the babies of women carrying the virus is infected. An HIV antibody test will not suffice to make a diagnosis in an infected infant because antibodies are transmitted across the placenta from mother to baby. Only if the antibody persists in the baby's circulation beyond eighteen months of age is the baby truly infected. Fortunately, we have now developed more rapid techniques to diagnose HIV-infected infants. The most commonly used is the PCR (polymerase chain reaction) test, which indicates if there is virus in the blood. We can be fairly sure if an HIV infection is or is not in the blood by about three to six months.

Unfortunately, some babies who acquire the virus from their mothers do show signs of disease, sometimes serious and occasionally fatal, by the age of eighteen months. The rest appear to remain well for some years, some surviving at least into their teenage years.

Treatment
Although there is no cure for HIV, many drugs have now been developed that suppress the virus. It is hoped that, in the future, the disease will respond better to multiple antiviral drugs so that patients can remain healthy for long periods of time.

Lifestyle
There is no reason why children infected by HIV should not lead normal lives. The biggest social problems they face are the fear and prejudice of other parents who

mistakenly think they pose a threat to their own children. There is no reason why these children should not go to nursery schools and make friends in the ordinary way. The only occasion when care needs to be taken is in the event of an injury where the child with HIV bleeds. Even in these circumstances the risk of infection is extremely low. Provided that the contaminated blood does not come into contact with another child's open wound, or possibly a mucous membrane, there is no risk of infection. If an infected child does bleed, the area should be thoroughly washed and then cleaned with a disinfectant. Anyone who gets contaminated blood on his hands should wash them immediately and thoroughly.

Cleft Lip and Palate

Seeing a baby who has been born with a cleft lip is one of the most distressing experiences of parenthood. So much attention is focused on a newborn's face; when people say "What a lovely baby," they invariably mean "What an attractive face." The child born with a cleft lip is really not beautiful.

A cleft is a split, and a cleft lip is one with a split so that the upper lip is separated just under the nose. Clefts can also occur in the palate, and in either place they can be single (unilateral) or double (bilateral). It is the most common birth defect in the head and neck region, about one in seven hundred babies being born with the condition. The exact cause is unknown. There is a small hereditary element, in that if there are clefts in the family there is an increased chance of the condition recurring, but this is only part of the story. What is more certain is that it happens during the first three months of pregnancy (at approximately seven weeks of gestation).

Fortunately, the outlook for children born with clefts is generally good. One of the most reassuring experiences the parents can have is to see a set of photographs of other children before and after surgery, when they can begin to answer for themselves what is usually their first question, "Can anything be done?" Once information has been given and parents have had a chance to express their entirely natural feelings of anxiety and disappointment, the initial shock passes quickly—within a matter of days, in many cases—and plans can be made for the future.

The first task is to manage feeding. Usually there is no real problem, but when the palate is cleft it has a gap in it and milk taken into the mouth regurgitates out through the nose (nasal regurgitation). A feeding can take up to two hours. There are now several specially designed nipples and feeding bottles. Physicians and specially trained nurses and speech therapists should be able to give advice.

Next, generally, come plans for surgery. The timing of each stage will depend partly on the nature of the cleft and partly on the surgeon's practice. Many think it best to operate for the first time at about three months, but others now begin surgery within the first week. This first-stage operation brings together the edges of the gap in the lip, leaving only a slight scar in most cases. The gap in the palate is usually left until after six to eight months of age. By now parents will have met most members of the cleft lip and palate team: plastic surgeon, orthodontist, speech therapist and audiologist, pediatrician, and social worker.

Children with cleft lip and cleft lip and palate normally need a further operation at about ten years of age. This consists of bone grafting to complete the repair of the tooth-bearing part of the upper jaw. Audiology is of the utmost importance, since hearing loss is frequently associated with clefts, and it is essential that full hearing tests are given to all children with them. A full test is one given in a specially equipped clinic; no one should be satisfied with a crude assessment in an ordinary consulting room.

Speech therapists play a key part in the treatment of children with cleft palates. Make contact early, well before your children starts to talk, since you will be the main teachers. If helped, your child can get off to a flying start.

Nursery school and meeting other children is the next challenge. At this point parents and children meet a big hurdle, the difficulty of explaining to others the nature of the cleft. The simplest explanation is the best: "I was born like that. Some people are born short or tall, with blue eyes or brown; I was born with something wrong with my mouth." Parents often worry about the emotional adjustment of children with clefts; there is some need for concern, but they have no more behavior problems than are expected in any group. Nor is there any particular personality pattern in cleft-lipped children, although there is a slight tendency toward shyness in school.

There is no reason either to anticipate any greater than normal difficulties in schoolwork later on, providing there is no hearing loss, although there is one point that should be guarded against: Teachers may underestimate the intelligence of children with a cleft.

Later surgery may be necessary, sometimes not until the teens are reached and the child has stopped growing, sometimes before. The childhood of children with clefts is not all roses, but providing there are no other complications present the outlook is firmly optimistic.

The Craniofacial Association has branches within the United States in most large cities, and their phone number is available in local phone directories or through major children's hospitals.

Genital Problems

Hypospadias

When a baby boy is born, it may be obvious that the opening that is normally at the tip of the penis is situated toward the underside. This is one of the most common types of failure of normal development, and surgery by a pediatric urologist can usually correct the problem. Most specialist surgeons carry out the operation in one stage when the infant is between twelve and eighteen months, but surgery may be performed later in life.

As children with this problem get older, it is particularly important that they are given a good explanation of how they are different from other boys, and what the operation will do. Until the operation is performed, unlike other boys, they will have to urinate sitting down, and they need to know why this is. The outlook is usually good, and there is no reason why sexual function should be affected later on.

Undescended Testicles

The testes begin to develop in the abdomen during pregnancy, and, before the baby is born, normally descend into the scrotum or bag under the penis. Sometimes the descent does not occur properly and the testicles stay in the abdomen or fail to complete the entire journey or take a wrong turn and finish up in the groin.

The problem should be detected at birth when the doctor carrying out the newborn examination notices that he cannot feel two testicles in the scrotum. If the condition is not noticed immediately after birth, you may notice it later, or a checkup with your pediatrician may reveal the problem. Children with this condition need a corrective operation because testes left undescended may develop complications at puberty or in adult life. A surgical operation can usually remedy the problem quite easily, and this is usually carried out when the boy is between one and four years of age.

Again, it is very important to explain to boys who are affected in this way what the problem is, why they need an operation, and what is going to happen during the operation and afterward. You may be embarrassed yourself about giving explanations, but this will make your son even more anxious. So if you are worried about what to say to your three- or four-year-old, ask your family doctor or the surgeon who is going to carry out the operation to explain the problem to your child simply.

Disabilities

Some children have disorders or impairments that can be helped but that will affect them all through their childhood and into adulthood. It is not possible to draw a clear line between chronic illness and disabilities. For example, many children have just one or two attacks of asthma, or eczema, but occasionally these conditions can become chronic problems, lasting through childhood and having disabling effects.

It may be surprising to realize that some very mild conditions can be more profoundly problematic than conditions some people regard as really severe. For example, a boy with hearing loss who doesn't want to wear a hearing aid might be teased at school and called "stupid." He might refuse to go there, missing weeks of schooling. A child who uses a wheelchair could go regularly to school and not suffer the same harm. Yet most people would think that mild hearing loss was much less important than being unable to sit without support or walk. If your child has a problem that cannot be completely cured, you need to do your best to help him reach his maximum potential and feel good about himself, including his disability.

Why Do Disabilities Occur?

Genetic (inherited) causes: Either the sperm or the egg involved in fertilization may contain genetic material that is incomplete. Sometimes both sperm and egg are affected. If there is some serious imperfection, then usually the mother has a miscarriage—this is nature's way of making sure that, as far as possible, children are not born with impairment. Genetic conditions may not always be obvious at birth. Some conditions, such as cystic fibrosis (see chapter 18), may be obvious at birth, or they may only show up when the child is a few months or a few years old.

Congenital disorders: Congenital means the child has been born with the condition. It may have been inherited, but not all congenital disorders are inherited. If the child has been damaged in the womb or at the time of birth, then the problem may be congenital but not inherited.

Other causes: Some chronic problems or disorders are caused by events after birth. Injuries due to accidents and infections (especially those affecting the brain, such as head trauma and meningitis) are the most common. Sometimes the causes of chronic conditions are just not known. For example, the Fragile X syndrome, one reason for learning difficulties, was identified only relatively recently.

Types of Disabilities

A child may have a physical disorder affecting the body, a learning disorder, or an emotional or behavioral disorder. Unfortunately, some children are multiply disabled and show not only physical disorders but also learning and emotional difficulties as well. Although many of us tend to think of physical problems as the most problematic, in many multiple-handicapped children it is the learning difficulties that limit the child's potential the most.

How Are Disabilities Discovered?

If there is a particular reason to think your child has a disability, then sometimes it can be discovered while the child is still in the womb, by methods of prenatal detection (see "Genetic Counseling" in chapter 1 for more on this). Down syndrome is an example of a condition that can be detected prenatally.

Immediately after birth, your child will be examined by a pediatrician to make sure he has no condition that is detectable by examination. Some problems, such as heart defects, undescended testicles, or Down syndrome, may be discovered in this way. A few days later, your child will have a heel prick to take a drop or two of blood. This will be examined to see if your child has a lack of a thyroid hormone or a disorder of body chemicals (phenylketonuria). If either of these is detected, your child can be treated and impairments can be prevented.

The way a disability is detected after birth will depend almost entirely on what the problem is. Some conditions, such as some forms of learning difficulties, may be suspected in the first year, but there may be a period of uncertainty lasting months or years before it is clear that there really is a problem or, more happily, that the development in this respect is going to be normal.

Living with a Disability

How you are likely to feel when you know your child is going to have a disability depends a good deal on how mild or how serious the problem is, on how quickly you learn about it, on how well or how badly you are told about it, and on your own personality and the way you react to other stresses of life. If the problem is a severe one and you hear about it suddenly, you may experience a wide range of feelings; these are those feelings associated with loss, in this case the loss of a "normal" child, and include:

- **Numbness.**   A kind of blanking out, as if the shock is so great you cannot understand exactly what is being said. This is why you will likely need explanations of your child's condition more than once, so you are able to absorb the information fully, to think, and then to ask questions.

- **Disbelief.**   A feeling that the bad news simply cannot be true. Many parents search desperately for another explanation. Perhaps the doctors are mistaken. Perhaps the test results have been switched with those of another child. This stage can pass very quickly or can last for months.

- **Anger.**   Many parents direct anger at themselves, at each other, or at health care providers, including doctors. "If only," parents may say to themselves, "they had noticed something earlier, if only [their doctor] had sent him to a hospital sooner, if only the hospital doctors had acted differently."

- **Despair.**   A feeling of bleakness without hope. It seems as though the future can hold only despair and misery.

● **Acceptance.** You eventually begin to feel more in control. You learn to accept the reasons and the fact that it may not be possible to receive a full explanation. You can begin to plan for the future.

These feelings typically occur in this order but may overlap and recur. Sometimes, especially if the problem is less obvious, or if you can only understand that there is a problem slowly over a period of months or years, reactions may be very different, and be mingled with relief at the prospect of finally getting help. One mother says:

> I began to suspect he couldn't hear properly when he was only about five months old. As he got older, I kept noticing other signs, but my pediatrician said there was nothing to worry about. They clearly thought I was just overanxious because I had problems at home and my marriage had broken up. It wasn't until John was nearly two years old that my doctor agreed he wasn't learning to talk and sent us to a specialist who found he was practically deaf.

With problems that are not immediately obvious, parents are often the first to notice or suspect a child's disability. If you have tried for some time to get the doctor to confirm your suspicions, it may come as a tremendous relief to have your fears finally acknowledged and know that you can now get appropriate help.

Most parents, when they realize their child has a disability, experience a mixture of feelings toward the child himself. Part of you may feel that he needs extra love, care, and protection, so you'll want to stay closer to the child than you normally would. This is understandable, but can hinder the child's developing independence. Part of you may feel a sense of dislike for the child. This is common and does not mean you are a bad parent. Fortunately, this kind of feeling does not usually last very long. Part of you will likely feel a continuing sadness, but also a determination to make sure your child has the chance to grow up as normally as possible. Which of these feelings is predominant will often change over time, but traces of each of them may persist over years.

Parents of disabled children may also have a harder time, not just emotionally, but also financially and in their social lives. Medical insurance may not cover all expenses associated with care for a disabled child. If you had planned to go back to work, you may find this is impossible because of the extra demands your child requires. One or both of you may have to pass up promotions so the family can live near a particular hospital or school. There may be extra problems finding a competent baby-sitter, so you may feel cooped up and irritable. Sometimes, too, differences between parents about how a child with a disability should be treated may lead to arguments that might not have occurred otherwise, or perhaps might have happened, but around some other, less painful topic. Brothers and sisters of the child with a disability may feel left out and neglected, or perhaps upset because they do not understand what is wrong with the affected child.

With all these possible problems, it should be good news to know that most families with a disabled child cope remarkably well. Parents usually come to accept the nature of their child's disability and make realistic plans for the future. It is sometimes not easy to explain to relatives—grandparents, for example—and friends about a child's problems, but if you can, you will probably find that you get more help. Neighbors, friends, and relatives may, of course, sometimes not believe that the child has a condition doctors cannot cure. This can be exasperating, but in time other people usually come to accept the situation, too, and can be helpful.

Try to be open and frank with any other children you have about the disabled child's problems. Almost all brothers and sisters adjust well when they know the facts. They will perhaps experience at least occasional feelings of resentment against the child who needs extra attention, but they may also grow up to be more caring people than they otherwise might have been.

Coping well with a disabled child is not just luck. The people who seem to do best are those who follow certain rules. They deal with problems one at a time rather than allowing themselves to be overwhelmed by a whole mass of difficulties. They use a number of different people to give them information and provide help and support, rather than relying entirely on one person. They are encouraged by small improvements, even when they know that if the child was without impairment, progress might be much faster. They prepare themselves for disappointment as well as success with each new treatment approach.

Most parents of children with disabilities are usually able to talk freely to each other about their feelings and resolve differences of opinion about the best thing to do for their child in a friendly fashion. Divorce rates are *not* higher in parents of disabled children. Having a disabled child certainly changes your marriage, but it does not need to make it worse, and it may even make it better.

If you are a single parent bringing up a disabled child on your own, it is particularly important that you seek outside help from relatives, friends, and professionals.

For all disabling conditions, except the very rare ones, parent organizations exist, and many of these have local branches. Your doctor can give you information on this. Get in contact with the appropriate one if it is at all possible. You may find it extremely helpful and, if you are dealing well with the situation yourself, you will have a lot to contribute to the organization and others in it who are less fortunate than you are.

Deafness and Other Severe Hearing Problems

Deafness is better described as "hearing loss" or "hearing impairment." Only about three in a thousand children need a hearing aid because of moderate or severe hearing loss, but between five and ten in every hundred cannot hear properly at times. This larger group of children should not be described as deaf, but their mild hearing loss is very important because it may affect speech and language development.

Mild hearing difficulties can occur because sticky fluid, due to chronic infection, prevents vibration of the tiny bones that transmit sound in the ear; this is called "conductive hearing loss." More severe hearing difficulties are usually, but not always, caused by "sensorineural dysfunction"—the organ of hearing or the nerves for hearing are damaged or fail to develop properly. Some children have a hearing loss only for high-pitched tones, which makes the speech of others difficult to understand.

Your child should have regular screening tests for hearing, but if you suspect a hearing loss has been present for more than a few days you should seek advice promptly, even if he has recently passed the test. Hearing losses can come and go, and the child may have developed a hearing loss since the testing was done. Remember that by six months your child should be turning to a voice across the room or to a quiet noise made on either side and by a year should be responding to hearing his name and to other familiar words. An older child may be inattentive or not respond to requests (selective hearing). Of course, this is much more likely due to hearing loss if he fails to respond to all requests, rather than just to those you think he might not want to hear!

Some hospitals can now test newborn babies' hearing with special techniques—for example, the "acoustic cradle"—but most routine testing is first carried out at seven to eight months old. If your child is suspected to be deaf after routine testing, further tests may need to be carried out. Tympanometry, for example, involves putting a tube into the ear canal and measuring the air pressure on the eardrum to give an idea of whether there is a fluid buildup. This gives a good indication of how well the ear is conducting sounds, and it is quite painless. Older children are tested by formal "audiometry" with headphones on each ear; this test is usually too difficult and thus inaccurate for children less than four years of age.

Treatment

Most mild deafness is conductive and due to a problem in the middle ear. It usually improves on its own but, if needed, can be successfully treated with medicine or minor surgery (for more, see "Ear Problems" in chapter 17).

A child with more severe hearing loss needs a good deal of extra help with his communication from the time the problem is first detected. Most will be helped by hearing aids, but remember that the ear molds need to be regularly changed as the ear gets bigger. If your child has severe hearing loss, it is important that he be able to see your lips and face when you are talking, so he can use his eyes as well as what limited hearing he has to understand you. It is important to remember that in a deaf child as in a hearing child, he'll be able to understand speech before he can express himself.

In a more seriously affected child you'll have to consider the use of sign language. There are a number of these available, but the most common is Signed English. At one time it was thought that use of sign language might prevent spoken language from developing, but most experts now agree that deaf children should be encouraged to communicate in every way possible, including signing. Of course, it is important that as many children as possible, not just parents, know what the signs mean.

Frustration at not being able to understand people and express needs can be major problems in a child with a hearing loss, but you can do a great deal to reduce this by being aware of the situations in which your child becomes upset and by paying special attention to his needs at those times.

Education

A child with permanent hearing loss will be able to go to an ordinary school, a special unit attached to an ordinary school, or a special school. The right choice for your child will depend on the seriousness of the child's problem and on what is available locally. Obviously, if your child is in an ordinary school, teachers will need to make special arrangements, such as sitting the child in the front of the class. Unless the cause of the hearing loss is due to a brain defect, a deaf child's intelligence is likely to be normal, but difficulties in communication will sometimes result in slow educational progress.

Visual Impairment

Total blindness is very rare. Of all those registered as blind, about 90 percent have some sort of vision, and we should be careful to distinguish among degrees of impairment. A very rough rule of thumb is the distinction between blindness and partial sight: the partially sighted person has a significant visual loss, sufficient to get in the way of some activities, but has enough vision to read normal print, sometimes with the help of magnifying devices. A blind person must use Braille to read.

The causes of visual loss are varied. Sometimes the eye fails to develop normally. This may be the result of an illness while the mother is pregnant (rubella was the most likely illness to cause this in the United States until the vaccine was developed, but in many countries toxoplasmosis is more common), or it may be inherited. Sometimes the optic nerve or visual part of the brain is damaged at birth, or during an illness, or by an accident. About half the children registered as blind have additional impairments, such as learning or movement problems. The proportion with additional impairments is smaller among partially sighted children.

The outlook for a baby born with a visual loss depends partly on the extent of the loss and partly on the presence or absence of other problems. With good educational opportunities and a supportive family, a blind child who has no other disabilities can reach the highest levels, both personally and professionally. Seeing babies learn a great deal through eyesight, so babies born blind or with severe visual impairment will benefit from expert developmental guidance and support. Consider, for example, the behavior of a very young child when a familiar adult enters the room. A sighted baby may wave arms and legs excitedly, gaze at the adult, and be generally rewardingly responsive. A blind baby will tend to lie still, presumably so that he can use his hearing to its full effect. This lying still can appear to be "aloofness" and may puzzle you, unless you understand that it is an indication that the baby is trying to find out what is going on.

Other areas of difficulty for severely visually impaired children include feeding problems (solid, chewy food is often resisted) and sleeping difficulties (a bedtime routine is hard to establish when day and night are not considered different). All children with loss of sight tend to have a reduced vocabulary—how do you explain the word "ceiling" to someone who has never seen one? These problems can often be considerably overcome with expert help. The sensation of feel can be most helpful.

Education

Educational opportunities have changed in the United States, especially since the recent movement away from segregated special education. There are schools for the blind and for the partially sighted, but the general trend is to provide extra support for the visually impaired child in a mainstream school.

Despite inevitable strains and stresses, and many downs as well as ups, many blind people can hold their own in open employment, go on from school to higher education, and can and frequently lead full, happy lives, with rewarding jobs and happy marriages. The world of the severely visually handicapped may be tough, but it is not necessarily one of devastation.

Cerebral Palsy

Cerebral palsy is the name given to conditions in which children have a disorder of movement or posture because the brain has failed to develop properly during the pregnancy or has been damaged during pregnancy or at birth. It is "nonprogressive," which means it does not get worse as the child gets older, though obviously as he grows older and bigger the problems will change. It occurs about twice in every thousand babies.

A child with cerebral palsy may suffer anything from a very mild disability with slight weakness of one hand to a much more severe disability with paralysis and uncoordination of arms and legs. Occasionally just the muscles involved in feeding and swallowing are affected. Although the affected muscles are often floppy in the first year or two of life, they often become "spastic" or "stiff." If just one limb is affected, this is called "monoplegia." Children with an arm and a leg affected on the same side are "hemiplegic"; if both legs are affected, this is "diplegia"; and a child with all four limbs equally affected has "quadraplegia."

The condition may be suspected early because of the presence of abnormalities the pediatrician may discover in examining the newborn baby. More often, however, the baby is slow to hold his head up, or sit and stand, and may be more floppy than usual. As the child gets older it becomes more obvious that there is something wrong, and, except in mildly affected children, other problems may be revealed.

The fact that the brain is damaged may lead to difficulties in addition to movement disorders. The child may have mild or severe learning problems, impairment of vision or hearing, or may develop seizures. Despite these problems, there are many positive points about children with cerebral palsy. Although they often have learning difficulties, they may well be brighter than they appear. The difficulties in movement may make it hard for them to communicate their feelings and ideas, but there are now many mechanical and electronic aids to improve not only movement but also communication, so many frustrations can be reduced. This is particularly likely in athetoid cerebral palsy, in which the movement problem is one of mobile movements.

Behavior problems are common in some types of cerebral palsy and may be the most disabling features of the condition.

Treatment

If your child is diagnosed as having cerebral palsy, it is important that you get a full assessment of his physical state and abilities. This may be done in the pediatric department of a hospital or at a child development center, often attached to a hospital, or by the United Cerebral Palsy Foundation. A number of different specialists, as well as pediatricians, may be involved. Audiologists, physiotherapists, speech therapists, occupational therapists, psychologists, and orthopedic surgeons may need to contribute to a full assessment and to advise you about the best ways to help your child to develop as well as possible. It may be difficult for you to think of ways to help a child who cannot crawl or walk easily to learn about the world, but these professionals will have much useful advice about how to tackle the problem.

A child with cerebral palsy will probably need regular physical therapy. The physical therapist will work with you on how to build this therapy into your child's day. This will help to make the child more mobile, but, of course, it cannot cure the problem.

Many different methods of treating cerebral palsy have been developed, and some are highly intensive. There is no conclusive evidence that the outcome is better in the intensive rather than the traditional regimes that are used in most U.S. programs for children.

Education

Children with cerebral palsy often have associated learning difficulties. These may be severe, but some do have normal or near-to-normal ability. Parents, of course, are the people who know the child and his abilities best, but a skilled assessment will still help you uncover and develop intelligence present in even a severely physically disabled child. Whatever their ability, all children are entitled to receive education up to age nineteen. For a child with cerebral palsy this may begin in a nursery school for normal or disabled children, in a special unit that may be attached to a child development center, or in a school for the physically disabled. In a good unit you will have access to professionals such as physiotherapists and speech therapists, who may work in the school or visit it regularly.

Spina Bifida

When I first knew Bobby had spina bifida, I prayed for him to die. But he hung on and now he's three, and I just can't imagine our family without him.

When a baby has spina bifida, it is obvious at birth. There is a swelling in the center of the back: this may be quite large, and the covering over it may be broken. The baby's brain and spinal cord grow rapidly during pregnancy. The spinal cord is encased in the spinal column or backbone. If the vertebrae making up the backbone do not close completely in the back when they are developing, the child is said to have spina bifida. If the defect in the back is large, the covering of the spinal cord or even the spinal cord itself may protrude through the defect. If it is just the sac or the bag that protrudes through, and it contains spinal cord lining, this is called a meningocele. If the spinal cord itself is contained in the sac, this is a myelomeningocele. The defect may occur at any level of the spinal column. Wherever it occurs, the spinal cord and nerves below it will be affected, so, broadly speaking, the lower the defect the less the child will be disabled. In the most common form the defect occurs at a level that affects the nerve supply to the legs, bladder, and bowel, producing weakness of the legs and inability to gain control of bowel or bladder.

Another defect that may occur, either alone or with spina bifida, arises from obstruction to the circulation of the fluid (cerebrospinal fluid) that fills the brain cavities and drains down into and around the spinal cord. As a result of this blockage, the brain cavities may become enlarged with fluid (hydrocephalus), and the brain tissue may be damaged by increased fluid pressure. It may be necessary to put a tube with a valve into the head to allow the fluid to drain away.

All causes of spina bifida are not known. There is a tendency for it to run in families, and this may be because there is a genetic or inherited factor, or it may be because family members tend to share the same environment.

It is likely, though not absolutely certain, that a vitamin deficiency, including folic acid, may be one factor. If you have had a baby with spina bifida, and wish to consider becoming pregnant again, consult a doctor about the risk of a recurrence. If you decide to become pregnant, ask your doctor and a dietician about diet and specially prescribed vitamins as soon as you begin trying to conceive.

About five in every two thousand children are born with spina bifida, but figures are falling, partly because of the increased use of screening. Spina bifida can be diagnosed early in pregnancy by an ultrasound scan, blood test, or by amniocentesis (see chapter 2 for more on this.)

Children with spina bifida will nearly always need special help—for example, from physical therapists, pediatricians, orthopedic surgeons, and urologists—to help them to be as functional as possible. Depending on where the defect is, some will need wheelchairs, while others will be able to get around with crutches or even without any special aids. Development of control of the bowel and bladder may well present problems, but there are a number of techniques that can be used to help with these problems.

Treatment
There is no cure for spina bifida, but surgery is often performed to cover the spine and prevent infection, and this means that children can live longer. Hydrocephalus can also be treated by inserting a tube into the brain to drain the fluid to another part of the body—the name for the whole apparatus is a "shunt," while a valve is part of the apparatus.

Education
One survey done in the United States showed 40 percent of children with spina bifida were at mainstream schools, only needing help with toileting, provided the layout of the school was adapted for the handicapped. Spina bifida children tend to

have uneven educational ability, so they often learn to read without trouble but find math very difficult. Like other children with neurological damage, they tend to be easily distracted and have poor handwriting. Much depends on the severity of the condition, but before your child enters school, take him to a psychologist for assessment and advice about stimulation and further education. Children with hydrocephalus often have a lower IQ, while in those with spina bifida but not hydrocephalus the range of intelligence is closer to normal.

Lifestyle
This depends on the extent of the impairment. Some children have normal intelligence, can walk, although with difficulty, and have less of a problem with incontinence, which can usually be greatly helped by modern management. Others are more profoundly and multiply affected.

Muscular Dystrophy

This rare condition usually becomes noticeable between the ages of two and five years. The child will usually not learn to run well and will develop difficulty climbing. The muscles become steadily weaker, and the child's walking is affected, so he may begin to stumble, fall, and eventually have difficulty climbing stairs. The most common type, Duchenne muscular dystrophy, which affects only boys, is rapidly progressive, so that by the age of ten years most affected boys are confined to wheelchairs and have a limited life span.

The Duchenne type is inherited, and is a sex-linked recessive condition caused by a defective gene. This means the affected gene may be carried by the mother on one of her two X chromosomes. If a couple has a boy with the condition, the mother may carry the gene, in which case there is a 50 percent chance of any subsequent boys being affected, but no girls will be affected. In some cases, the abnormal gene may arise in the boy alone as a mutation, in which case the risk is different. Genetic counseling in this situation involves discovering if the mother is a carrier, and if so, offering intrauterine detection and the option to terminate an affected pregnancy. See "Genetic Counseling" in chapter 1 for more on this.

Another sex-linked form of muscular dystrophy that is milder and rarer than Duchenne is known as Becker dystrophy. Limble-girdle and facio-scapulo-humeral muscular dystrophies are also milder, and are inherited in a different manner. If increasing difficulty in walking is occurring, the family doctor will probably refer the child to a pediatrician or neurologist who will examine him. A blood test will be carried out to check whether there is an excess of a chemical substance that circulates when muscle tissue is being destroyed.

Treatment
Sadly, there is no known cure for muscular dystrophy, but the course the disease takes is well known. From the time of diagnosis you will have to plan for the future, which will eventually include a wheelchair and special educational needs. Management, as with all disabilities, splits into physical and psychological

problems, both of which require advice and sympathetic help from specialists. A reasonably controlled diet is important so obesity does not become an added burden, so consult your doctor about this as well.

Education

There is an overall reduction of intelligence by about 20 IQ points with muscular dystrophy, but most young children with the condition will be able to attend a mainstream nursery school.

Lifestyle

> When we were told our son had muscular dystrophy, we at first really had no idea what it meant. The consultant was very sympathetic but very frank. At the time it seemed cruel because what he had to tell us was so horrifying to hear, but as time went on I was glad he had been honest from the start.

Parents of a child with progressive muscular dystrophy have a hard time, as do their children. All the same, much can be done. One couple with two sons with the condition were plunged initially into a state of severe shock and grief. After a couple of years they began to accept the situation, and from that point some positive action was possible. Neither had ever traveled abroad, but when the mother took a cleaning job at the boys' school, this enabled them to save for vacations, which the entire family enjoyed to the fullest extent. Their father said: "Since we know their lives will be limited, we want to pack in as much as we can now, so that when we look back we will never say 'If only' but rather 'Didn't we have good times.'" You may find it easier to cope with your own distressed feelings if you share them with each other, as well as with relatives, friends, and sometimes professionals. As with parents of children with other physical disabilities, it will often be helpful to learn more about the condition and perhaps, at some stage, meet other parents of affected children.

Severe Learning Difficulties

Inevitably, some babies and toddlers will develop faster than others. This will be true not just of the speed with which their bodies grow, but also of the rate at which they develop in their language and in the coordination of their movements. Some will be quick to speak and understand; others will be slow. Some will be quick to walk and able to undress and dress themselves; for others this will take longer. The speed of development of a baby or toddler does not allow us to predict how intelligent he will be when he grows into a schoolchild, and gives no indication at all of how bright he will be as an adult. But if a child is very slow to develop in the early years, there may be something wrong with the way his brain is working and, of course, this will mean that he is likely, or perhaps in some cases certain, to have learning difficulties later. This is particularly true for language development. Children who are slow, even sometimes very slow, to walk often do well later unless they have some reason (such as cerebral palsy) to explain their slowness. A high proportion of children who are slow to understand and talk, however, who are not, for example, speaking in little two- or three-word sentences by the age of three years, will have definite learning disabilities in school, and some of them will have severe learning problems.

Causes of Severe Learning Difficulties

About three in every thousand children have severe learning difficulties. There are numerous causes, but there is usually something wrong with the way the brain has developed, and some degree of brain malfunction (dysfunction) or even brain damage is present. Usually this has occurred because of an inherited condition, a problem that has been present from the time the egg was fertilized. The most common of these is Down syndrome, which alone accounts for about one in three of all children with moderate to severe learning difficulties. Other, less common, genetic causes account for a further one in seven chance, so altogether more than half of all case of severe learning difficulties are caused by genetic factors. About one in ten affected children has had damage to the brain at birth, and another one in ten has had an illness or injury to the brain after birth. Then, in quite a high proportion, about one in four, the cause is unknown.

How Are Severe Learning Difficulties Detected?

Sometimes it is obvious at birth that a child is probably going to have some degree of learning difficulties. This is true of Down syndrome and children born with very small heads (microcephaly). Sometimes, however, the baby will appear normal at birth, and only gradually, perhaps not until the age of two or three years, will it become obvious that the child is developing very slowly. Often it is the child being very slow to speak that suggests there is a real problem, but the child with severe learning difficulties is also likely to be slow to respond socially with smiles, gurgles, and babbling in the first year of life and may be slow to sit and stand. If the birth has been very difficult, it may have resulted in brain damage, but it is important to remember that most children who have difficult births grow up to be perfectly normal later.

What Can Be Done about Severe Learning Difficulties?

If your child is one of those thought to be normal after birth, but suspected possibly of having learning difficulties because of very slow development later, your family doctor or pediatrician will be able to help you determine whether your child is just a bit slow to develop, which presents no great problem, or whether there is real cause for worry. Your doctor will ask about what your baby can do and check on the child's progress. If your child is definitely slow to develop, blood and urine tests and often special X rays will be done to see if it is possible to establish a cause. Unfortunately it is most unusual to find a definite cause that is treatable, but it is important to find a cause if possible, because of the possible genetic implications— a risk that you may have further affected children, for example.

The process of diagnosis is often somewhat obscure. There may well be a period of one or two years when severe learning difficulties are suspected but no one can be sure. Some children are very slow to develop in the first two or three years, but then pick up, while in others the presence of learning difficulties becomes more obvious as time goes by.

Inevitably this realization will be a time of great anxiety, sadness, and disappointment, and you will need to share your feelings with your partner, with other members of your family, with friends, and with the professionals who are trying to help you. You may well have angry feelings as well as being sad and worried. These feelings may stay with you for weeks or months, and may keep coming back over the years, but you should try to make sure they do not prevent you from helping your child to develop to the best of his abilities.

Children with severe learning difficulties can and do learn, but they take longer and need a good deal more help. Almost certainly, a child with learning difficulties will be doing more on his fourth birthday than on his third, more on his fifth than on his fourth, and so on. Progress may be slow, but it does occur. It is always better to check on progress by comparing your child with how he was a year or so ago than by comparing him with other children of the same age who do not have learning difficulties.

If your child has severe learning difficulties, your pediatrician will refer you to other professionals, such as a psychologist and a speech therapist, who will work in partnership with you to promote the development of your child. If your child has particular communication difficulties, he may be helped by using a system of communication by signs. Ask your pediatrician if there is a special child development center you can attend locally, such as an Early Intervention program, where you can meet other parents with children with similar problems and get more intensive help. It is especially important that your child gets regular checkups on vision and hearing because children with severe learning difficulties are particularly prone to have sensory difficulties. As time goes on, and certainly before the age of five years, if it is clear that your child has severe learning difficulties, there will need to be a plan to meet his special educational needs. In the United States, this involves a number of professionals coordinated by the educational psychologist pooling their opinions and, with your help, making a "statement" (Individual Educational Plan—IEP) to describe the schooling your child requires

Down Syndrome

Down syndrome is the largest single cause of learning difficulties and is because of a chromosomal disorder. Normally people have twenty-three pairs of chromosomes (for more details see chapter 1), but Down children have an extra chromosome—usually this is a third chromosome, at position twenty-one. The medical name for this condition is trisomy twenty-one, meaning there are three number twenty-one chromosomes at the twenty-one position. In the remaining Down children there is an abnormal rearrangement of chromosomes. Trisomy may be present but only in some cells, a condition called mosaicism. This mistake in cell division is more likely in older women, though we do not understand why this is. One child in seven hundred is a Down baby, but the risk begins to rise with a mother who is over the age of thirty-five years, so that in mothers over thirty-eight years the figure is more than likely to be one in two hundred.

Down syndrome is named after the Victorian doctor John Langdon Down, who first identified the condition. For a long time it was known as mongolism, though this term has fallen into disrepute now and is no longer used. Down babies are nearly always identified at birth because although they may be very attractive, there are distinct physical characteristics: slanting eyes with folds of skin along the lids to the inner corner (epicanthic folds); a wide bridge to the nose; short, stubby toes and fingers; distinctive creases on palms and soles; and a large tongue. Down babies tend to be floppy and to grow slowly, so they tend to be short in height. Some Down babies have heart or intestinal abnormalities that need to be corrected with surgery. They tend to suffer from infections, especially bronchitis, more than other children.

If your child is diagnosed as having Down syndrome at birth or shortly afterward, the pediatrician will usually see both parents together to break the news as soon as possible. She will also tell you if your baby has been found to have any other problems. Inevitably the news will be extremely upsetting and, as with parents of other children with disabling conditions, you will probably find it helpful to share your feelings with others.

In fact, the range of ability shown by Down syndrome babies is quite wide. All will have learning difficulties, but while with some this will mean that they are only able to express themselves poorly with a few words in simple sentences, with others it will be possible for education to occur in a mainstream school, where the child will fit in with other children of lesser ability. Progress in the first year or two of life is often very encouraging, and after this it gradually becomes clearer to what degree the baby with Down syndrome will be limited in ability. For further information on promoting ability in the disabled see the section above, "What Can Be Done about Severe Learning Difficulties?"

Many children with Down syndrome are placid and lovable; a very few are noisy and boisterous. As he gets older it will gradually become clear to you what sort of personality your Down syndrome child has—as with any other children, you will probably find characteristics you love and others of which you are less fond!

Fragile X Syndrome

This is the second most common form of mental retardation known today. About one in ten boys with mild or severe mental retardation suffers from it. It is caused by a defect on the single X chromosome in boys and on one of the two X chromosomes in girls. Although girls do sometimes suffer from its effects, most girls with an affected X chromosome are of normal intelligence—their unaffected X chromosome is making up for the one with the defect.

Many children with Fragile X look normal, but some have a characteristic appearance of a high forehead, protruding ears, and prominent jaw. It is much less easy to diagnose a child with Fragile X from appearance than is the case with Down syndrome. Special DNA testing is the only way to make the diagnosis with confidence. A sample of blood is taken when the condition is suspected, and the DNA is analyzed. The chromosomes are also examined using a special technique.

The mental retardation that occurs in Fragile X may be quite mild or severe. Girls are often more mildly affected or not affected at all. At one point it seemed that Fragile X syndrome might be a common cause of autism (see below). It now seems more likely that all children with severe mental retardation commonly show autistic features. Those with Fragile X also often show some such features, but they do not usually have the full picture of autism.

The genetics of Fragile X syndrome are complicated. Like Duchenne muscular dystrophy, discussed earlier in this chapter, it is a sex-linked condition, but unlike most such conditions, girls can be affected. So if your child is found to have this syndrome, you should seek expert advice from a clinical geneticist. You and other members of the family should be tested.

Autism

As quite a high proportion of children with autism do show learning difficulties in addition, the problem is described here.

Autism was first described by an American child psychiatrist, Leo Kanner, in 1943. Children who develop the condition may have it from birth, or it may occur after a period of normal or near-normal development for up to the first two or three years. Boys are affected about four times as commonly as girls.

If your baby has the problem from birth, he will usually be born after a normal pregnancy and delivery. He may be rather unresponsive in the first few months of life, not showing much interest in you or his surroundings, but being quite happy to be fed and cared for. Toward the end of his first year it will become more obvious that things are not going well. He may babble a little or not at all. He may dislike being cuddled and seem to prefer to lie in his crib. When you try to look at him he may, as if deliberately, turn his face away (gaze avoidance). He may spend a lot of time looking at his hands. In the second and third year of life his language delay may become more obvious. He will probably be very slow to understand and to speak, so it is quite likely he will not be speaking even in single words by the age of three years. In contrast, he is likely to have walked at an early age, and he may be quite good at doing puzzles, such as table jigsaws, or pasting shapes. By this point he will often have developed fixed patterns of behavior he hates to have disturbed, getting very upset if his routines are disrupted.

His way of relating to other people, including his parents, may be odd and unusual. If he wants something, rather than asking or pointing, he may, for example, take the adult by the hand and lead to where he wants to go. If language does develop, it may be slow and mechanical. The child may also echo things said to him. Normal children do this, too, but usually only for brief periods while they are learning to speak. The child with autism is likely to have mannerisms—particular habits such as jumping up and down and flapping his hands when excited, putting his hands in front of his eyes and waving them repeatedly, or gazing at his hands while he moves them in front of his face.

If autism is suspected, your pediatrician will check to see if there is a known physical cause and then will probably refer him to a psychologist or psychiatrist. In most cases a cause is not detectable, but there is strong evidence that the problem is not caused by anything the parents have done but by a dysfunction in the brain. In many cases this is likely to be caused by one of a number of faulty genes, but at this time it is unusual to be able to pinpoint exactly the nature of the error in the genes.

Not surprisingly, because of the problems, it is very difficult to make a relationship with a child with autism. You may find it helpful to get counseling from a psychologist or a psychiatrist to help you deal best with your child. A child with autism may have associated learning difficulties, but is likely to benefit from attending a child development center where there are a number of children with severe learning difficulties. The kind of help provided for children with learning difficulties or language disorder (see above) will likely help a child with autism, but the child and parents may need additional help with the behavioral problems associated with autism.

Education
As with other children with learning difficulties, as the child nears school age, you, local professionals, and the school staff will need to work out an IEP for his educational needs. This must involve several people, including teachers experienced in educating children with communication difficulties and severe behavioral problems. The outlook for a child with autism depends on the severity of the condition and on whether the child has learning difficulties as well. Unfortunately, quite a high proportion of children with autism will persist in having serious difficulties of communication and problems in their social relationships. Autistic children change but do not "grow out of" their condition. Many will need extra care, and will find it difficult to manage independently after they leave school.

CHAPTER 20

If Your Child Has to Go to the Hospital

Preparing your child for a hospital stay • Operations
Who's who in the hospital • Common hospital procedures
Staying or visiting? • Breast-fed babies
How parents can help • Taking care of yourself • Coming home

Every year in the United States many children under five years of age are admitted to the hospital, and more than two million children go to accident and emergency rooms. So the chances that you will have to take a child to the hospital are, unfortunately, quite high—especially if you have more than one child. Obviously we would all prefer that our children not be frightened by a hospital visit. It is encouraging to know that many children cope with a hospital encounter with the sort of casual attitude we only wish we could manage ourselves, and some of them actually enjoy the novelty of the experience.

How your child reacts to a hospital visit will depend especially on her age, personality, the reason she is in the hospital, the way she is admitted, her previous experience of hospitals, the investigations and treatment she needs, the attitude and manner of medical and nursing staffs, the atmosphere in the hospital and in the ward or room, and, of course, on your own anxieties and how well you are able to cope with what is often a very worrying situation.

It is easy to see how these features can combine to make a hospital visit less likely or more likely to be upsetting. The first six features you cannot change, but you can learn to allow for them. The last three you can sometimes influence for the better. Every child will react differently, but usually children between one and four years old are most vulnerable when it comes to hospital visits. This is because they are aware of what is happening but are not able to understand it all. They are also less likely to have stayed away from home before or to have been separated from their parents.

It is more difficult to know how babies under a year old react to hospitals, but this is an important time when the bond between mother and baby is still being formed. We do know that babies often behave differently when their routine is changed; staying with your baby and keeping as much as possible of her life the same will help. Taking care of very young babies in special-care units presents different problems, which we have talked about in chapter 5.

If your child has already visited or stayed in a hospital, what she felt about it will influence the way she handles another visit or stay. If it was distressing or frightening, then think why that was, and do what you can to change things; if your child is old enough, tell her how and why it can be better.

Do not forget that young children pick up all sorts of ideas about what happens in hospitals without ever having been a patient. Visiting her mother after the birth of a new baby is a very common experience for children under five. If all they know about the hospital is the inside of a maternity unit full of little babies in plastic boxes on wheels, and if they have been told that is where they were born too, then hearing they have to go to the hospital can fill them with confusing ideas. Visiting sick adults in the hospital can also leave misleading or worrying impressions, or simply hearing that someone they knew died in the hospital can have the same effect. As one mother recalled:

My mother died in the hospital when Lucy was just two. She did come with me once to see her grandma and I suppose she realized that I was very upset when we got the news of her death soon afterward. Then a year later she had to go into the hospital herself to have her tonsils out. I don't know if it was the hospital smell or the sight of the nurses, but when we got there she got very quiet and clingy and eventually said, "I won't have to go to heaven, will I?"

Your own attitude toward hospitals and medical treatment will certainly affect your child's attitude. Parents have a vital role in helping children through what is bound to be an unusual experience for them. You can only carry out that job by staying with your child as much as possible and by giving her the right kind of preparation.

Preparing Your Child for a Hospital Stay

Ask most two- to four-year-olds in a hospital why they are there and they may well say they feel fine and that there is nothing wrong with them. From their point of view there is no need to be there at all. Small children may find it very difficult to make the connection between a series of sore throats in the past and an operation to have their tonsils out now. Many conditions do not make children feel bad at all, such as squints, or middle ear problems that may cause loss of hearing. So do not assume, from past trips to the doctor, that your child understands why she is going to the hospital. Explain it in simple terms.

When to Tell Your Child

It is probably best to mention the subject first after visiting the doctor or hospital where the decision was made. It is less likely at that point to seem like something you have decided out of the blue. Small children have little idea of the passage of time, so tell them at the same time that going to the hospital will not happen for a while and that you will tell them all about it when the hospital notifies you for preadmission testing and subsequent admission. If surgery must be done very soon or even immediately, you of course must tell them this.

While You Wait

While you are waiting for the hospitalization, read a few books about hospital visits that will mean something to your child at her age and read them with her once or twice—without necessarily talking directly about her visit, but just about hospitals as places where children go to be made better. If your child asks specifically about her visit, then answer questions honestly, but do not burden her with too much information. Most common questions tend to be "Will you stay with me?" and "Will it hurt?" If you cannot stay with her or do not know yet whether you will be able to, do not lie. Say something along the lines that you do not know yet, but if they don't have a bed you will stay with her until she is asleep—only you can decide exactly what is best to say to your own child. On the question of pain, again, do not lie and say something will not hurt if you know it will. It is better to tell her that it may hurt for a little while but then it will be over. Try to say in very simple terms why it needs to be done to stress the positive side so she does not feel it is just being done to hurt her.

Be Well Informed

Find out for yourself as much as you can about what will happen to your child so you know in advance about anything that might upset her. If this is a planned admission, ask if there is an opportunity to visit the ward or room with your child beforehand. This can have disadvantages if the child sees something upsetting, but you can talk this through. Nearer the time of the visit you can tell her in a bit more detail what will happen—but again, in very simple terms. Like adults, children vary in how much they want to know. If they are old enough to understand, tell them a day or so before they go into the hospital some of the simple things that will happen, especially details of the admission procedures. Often children can be upset by little things such as having to pass urine into a special sort of bottle or pot to give a urine sample or sitting on scales with a chair to be weighed. This is usually because they are generally confused, bewildered, and anxious, and think almost everything is potentially painful. Procedures such as blood tests that might worry a child are best not described in detail until shortly before you have to deal with them.

Before you go into the hospital, describe to your child, with the help of picture books, what the hospital will be like. Most children find the idea of having their own night table beside their bed attractive—talk about what you can put on there. Talk about the doctors, nurses, and other people. Even very small children can understand that some of them are also mothers and fathers with children at home and the hospital is where they come to work rather like their own daddy or mom or other relatives they know who go off to work. This is often a very reassuring idea. Explain that hospitals have to stay open all the time, so nurses and doctors have to take turns working all night as well as all day. Tell them that lights stay on all night in the wards or rooms and that there is always someone there to look after them.

How much very young children—say from one to two and a half years old—can understand in advance is very variable. But do not forget that their understanding of language is often far in advance of what they can actually say. Good, realistic pictures of hospital wards or rooms and nurses are invaluable in helping very young children understand something of where they are going. Most libraries have a selection of books, or you can look in your local bookstore if you want to invest in one or two.

Packing

Most children enjoy packing a little suitcase to take to the hospital. Children usually regress when they are feeling ill or in unusual surroundings, so choose toys and books that are on the young side and not too taxing. Steer them away from very precious toys that might easily be broken, because one of the enjoyments of life in a ward or room is showing other children what they have brought with them. Make sure favorite comforters, such as blankets, bits of special clothing, toys, pacifiers, or whatever, are taken along, plus a spare if possible. This is definitely not the time to start thinking that your child is far too old to have a pacifier, bottle, cup with a lid, or to be in diapers. Do not be embarrassed and think it will reflect badly on you because they are too old and should be beyond this stage. All children have habits that parents think perhaps they should have grown out of, but this is a time to put your child's security before your own feelings, so make sure you take everything she could want if she was home.

Playing at being in the hospital can help older children, especially three- to five-year-olds. Use play to bring in some of the facts about the operation, such as the face mask and hats that operating room staff have to wear. Old pajama tops, striped shirts, and plain white shirts can be used for "uniforms." Children very often hate putting on the hospital gown. If you can get the idea across in play that the patient puts on a back-to-front white gown to keep clean, too—maybe by dressing his teddy bear up—this might help.

Do not spend a fortune on an expensive doctor's set. You will be annoyed if your child is not interested. For young children a cardboard box with a big red cross and a string handle packed with things such as bandages, a syringe (a meat baster), medicine (an empty plastic bottle with a label stuck on), plastic scissors, and perhaps your eyebrow tweezers will provide as much fun. Even a "stethoscope" can be made out of a length of plastic clothesline with a cotton spool. Friends and relatives can also be sources of doctor's equipment. Your child might like to take her medical kit in to show off to the nurses as well.

Operations

If your child is going into the hospital for an operation, give her some realistic idea what to expect, regardless of her age. For most children the essential facts are that they put on a special gown like the doctors' white coats to keep them clean, have something to make them sleepy, and are taken on a gurney to the operating room, where nurses and doctors wear specially clean clothes (often green or white), caps, and masks. Then they will be given something to make them go right to sleep until it is all over. When they wake they will usually be back in the ward or room with you. Sometimes, though, children wake up in the recovery room without you, and you should ask beforehand if this is a possibility so you can prepare your child. She may feel a bit sore, but she will begin to get better soon. The younger the child, the simpler this version becomes. Obviously you have to be the best judge of exactly what to say, but do not deliberately mislead your child, and make sure you prepare her, however young she may be. It may seem silly to talk to babies about this, but many mothers find it reassuring themselves when they tell a baby what is going to happen. The precise details of what happens on the day of the operation depend on the surgeon, the anesthesiologist, the type of operation, the age of the child, and hospital routine.

Most hospitals have a "holding area" where the parents may wait with their children until they are partially sedated or taken into the operating room.

Before the operation, an anesthesiologist—if possible, the one who will be giving the anesthesia—will come to see your child. Tell your child that this is the person who is going to put her to sleep so she won't be awake during the operation, but warn her that when they meet again in the operating room the anesthesiologist will look different because he will be dressed in special clothing, with a hat and a mask. Most children who are old enough to understand find it reassuring to have met the anesthesiologist in more normal circumstances and discover that he is just an ordinary-looking person outside the operating room. Ask the anesthesiologist how the premedication and the anesthesia will be given so you can prepare your child for what to expect and can answer her questions. Sometimes premedication may be omitted.

The premedication is an important part of the operating procedure since your child is fully awake and aware, and it is often what children remember most about the whole event. One six-year-old, confident of her facts, gave this description of her operation to her fellow patients: "Do you know what having an operation means? It means having a needle in your bottom, that's what." The premedication can be given by an injection, or as medicine to be swallowed. What is prescribed for your child depends on the child's weight, age, and the type of operation she is to undergo, as well as the practice of the particular anesthesiologist. Generally children are put to sleep with gas initially. Many anesthesiologists do not put a mask over the child's face but hold the end of the tubing delivering the anesthetic gas in their hand, cupped in front of the child's face. If you think your child would cope better with an injection, it is reasonable to ask the anesthesiologist if this is possible. Again, you must accept the anesthesiologist's professional judgment—if your child does not have very prominent veins, for example, repeated attempts to insert the needle could cause more distress. Many hospitals use a local anesthetic cream, such as Emla, to prevent the insertion of the needle into the vein from hurting.

Before your child has her operation she will see other children putting on operating gowns and being wheeled off on gurneys, so she will have some idea of what to expect. Hopefully she will not have seen other children crying, because such a reaction can be highly contagious. If she does see another child crying, and if she is old enough, you might try to counter this by telling her the other child is crying because that child does not understand what is happening—unlike your own child, of course. A number of children hate taking their own clothes off and putting on the hospital gown; some hospitals insist on paper pants, too. Other hospitals are changing this routine and allow children to wear their own pajama bottoms or loose-fitting nightgown and allow parents or nurses to carry them to the operating room instead of using a gurney. You can ask the surgeon about this. If your child does have to wear a gown but objects, try suggesting it is like the doctor's white coat, or like the ones the bigger children in the hospital wear, or is like putting a sheet on, or whatever you think might convince her to cooperate. Children probably get upset at this point because it signals the start of events leading to the operation and because they feel vulnerable and worried out of their own clothes and in something so strange. It may help if you can have an informative book to offer to read to her once she has changed—it can distract her and reassure her that she is not about to be whisked away.

While waiting for the premedication to take effect, do whatever you can to help your child settle down and relax—this may mean reading her something soothing and familiar, singing to her (if you have the confidence in busy surroundings!), or patting her head. If she does begin to doze off, do not leave her until you have seen her safely onto the gurney. If your child does get upset, only you can decide whether it is better for you to let the nursing staff take over or to stay. One mother described what happened to her daughter:

> I was dreading the moment when they came to take my daughter to the operating room. She was dozing lightly but opened her eyes if I let go of her hand. When the gurney did arrive she fulfilled all my worst fears by springing up and wrapping her arms in a tight grip around my neck and crying. The nurses said I'd better go, and as I honestly didn't have a hope of calming her, I went into the nurses' office, where I watched through the window. The minute I left, she lay down on the gurney and stopped crying. I think she was just panicking over the moment of parting. She was wheeled past me sucking her thumb with her eyes closed and clutching her blanket.

It is usually a good idea to send a favorite toy, blanket, or other comforter down on the gurney, if possible labeled with your last name. Usually the nursing staff will send the toys back with the appropriate bandages to match the owner's!

While Your Child Is in the Operating Room

The nurses will be able to tell you roughly how long your child will be in the operating room. Afterward the child will also spend some time in the recovery room, where her condition will be carefully monitored. It is a good idea to get away from the ward for a cup of coffee or a walk even if you find it hard to think of anything else, because there will be many hours ahead when you need to sit by your child's bedside. Make sure, though, that you let the ward or floor staff know where you are. When your child comes back to her room or the ward, hold her hand and tell her it is over and you are staying with her. She may be in pain or feeling sick, and the nurses may tell you how to help. Often just soothing and reassuring her that it will get better, or stroking or holding her hand, is the most important job and the kind that only a parent can do.

Who's Who in the Hospital

Doctors

- *Attending physician or pediatrician.* This doctor will be in charge of your child's care while she is hospitalized. The attending physician may be a pediatric surgeon or a pediatric medical physician. Attending physicians have their own teams of doctors working under them. They generally set the practice and tone of that team. Each is medically responsible for the patients under his or her care.

- *A fellow.*   A physician who has completed a residency and is being trained in a subspecialty such as endocrinology or oncology.

- *Chief resident.*   Supervises the residents.

- *Senior resident.*   This doctor supervises the care of all of the patients on the team and is responsible for the education of the house officers (i.e., interns, residents, and fellows) of that team.

- *Resident.*   Very likely to see your child in the ward or in her room and to supervise the care of your child with the attending physicians, who will perform the operation.

- *Intern or first year resident.*   Does most of the routine medical work in a hospital. These are doctors who are usually attached to a team for various periods before they specialize in specific areas of medicine or become family practitioners.

- *Medical students.*   Will be found throughout a teaching hospital, caring for inpatients as well as ambulatory ones in the clinic.

Often you will probably be dealing with the intern and possibly the resident. If you miss seeing the attending physician you can ask the nurse in charge of your child to arrange to see the attending physician. Do not be shy to ask if you do not understand exactly what your child is having done and why. Often the nursing staff, who may have more time and appear less intimidating, can help. When doctors or nurses ask your child questions, do not answer for her. They actually do this to make friends with your child as well as to get information.

Nurses

Some hospitals, particularly teaching or pediatric institutions, have their own nursing structures, but generally hospitals use models similar to the one that follows. Also, many hospitals use the primary nurse, one nurse who will be responsible for your child.

- *Vice president or director of nursing services.*   In charge of all nurses in one particular hospital.

- *Senior nurse/nurse manager.*   Responsible for a number of units, wards, or floors.

- *Charge nurse.*   In charge of that particular ward or floor.

- *Staff nurse.*   Next in line.

- *Student nurse.*   Studying to be a nurse.

- *Licensed practical nurse.*   Works under the supervision of a registered nurse.

- *Nurse's aide.* Involved in a variety of routine day-to-day nursing duties under supervision.

Some hospitals employ clinical nurse specialists and advanced practice nurse specialists to work with physicians in specific disciplines.

Nurses can be of tremendous help and support to families who have children in the hospital, and very many do well beyond what might be expected. Most of the nurses working with children will have had specialized training in pediatric nursing.

- *Social workers.* The bridge between the hospital's patients and community organizations and liaison between the family members to help them cope with their child's illness.

These days, most children's wards have a play specialist, known as a child life professional, educated in primary education or child development. The child life professional will work with you to find out through play how your child is coping with being in a hospital, to keep your child occupied, to help with understanding and overcoming her anxieties, and to contribute to her development while she is in the hospital. Make sure you meet this person, state what your child likes doing, and convey any worries about how she is going to settle in the hospital. For older children who are well enough to benefit, the hospital schoolteacher, if available, will provide further stimulation.

There are a number of other people who may play a very important part in diagnosing what is wrong with your child and helping her to get better. These include speech therapists, physical therapists, and psychologists. Try to be there when they come to see your child at least for the first time, so you can answer questions and help them with their investigations and treatment.

Common Hospital Procedures

- **Admission.** Except for an emergency, it is wise to check with your health care insurance carrier, privately held or through the state (funded by Medicaid and the state; rules vary from company to company and state to state), beforehand to make sure your child's hospital stay will be covered. Your physician's office staff will know the procedure. Health care plans and HMOs vary. The admission procedure usually involves a doctor taking a history of your child's health plus details about family history. Your child will get a name tag with a hospital number and the name of her physician, be weighed and measured, and may be asked for a urine sample. Children having operations usually, but not always, have a blood test. Pulse and temperature taking happen regularly.

- **X rays.** Parents are usually allowed into the X-ray rooms of hospitals, but women who think they may be pregnant should not stay because of the risk that X rays may harm the fetus. If you are asked to hold your child in a particular position, then hold her firmly. When the X-ray technician moves the X-ray tube into position you can reassure your child that it will not come near her because X rays are taken from a distance of three feet or more, except for dental X rays. There is no radiation in the room except at the moment the exposure button is pressed. X-ray rooms can often look somewhat intimidating with all their equipment, but tell your child this is just to take a special kind of photograph and will not hurt.

Special Radiologic Procedures

In the past decade several new radiologic techniques have been developed, which for the most part are not painful or invasive to the child. Important and useful information is derived from these procedures, and the diagnosis and treatment of many diseases has been enhanced and improved.

The ultrasound procedure is based on the reflection of sound waves that are transmitted by the use of a microphone-type instrument. This procedure is similar to that used prenatally to examine the fetus while in utero or the shape and structure of the heart as with an echocardiogram. The instrument is especially useful in examining structures in the chest, abdomen, and pelvis.

The CT (Computerized Tomography) scan uses X rays, which pass through body structures, and produces pictures that outline organs with different densities such as bone, fat, liver, lung, or air. In this procedure the part of the body to be examined is placed in a short circular tube. The child must remain still while the procedure is undertaken, and younger children and infants at times will be given mild sedatives to allow them to sleep through the procedure and thus remain still. At times, contrast material (a safe dye) is injected into the veins in order to outline some of the structures more definitively.

Magnetic Resonance Imaging (MRI) is the most sophisticated of all of these techniques and, similar to the CT scan, will differentiate different densities of the various structures to be examined but with greater definition. Hence, more information can be obtained with this procedure. While no X ray exposure occurs with this procedure, there are drawbacks. The entire body of the individual to be examined must be placed in a long narrow tube for up to 45 minutes, and must remain perfectly still. This procedure is also very noisy, so that ear plugs are inserted. The driving force of the procedure is a very large magnet. Because of this, nothing metal can be worn on the body. Infants and younger children usually must be sedated for this test, and usually contrast material has to be injected intravenously in order to better outline specific structures and organs.

- **Painful procedures.**   Having dressings changed or applied, stitches inserted, injections, and blood tests are all examples of things that happen frequently in wards, in patients' rooms, or in emergency units. Young children usually have to be held, but there is no reason why the holder should not be the parent unless the parent would be upset. A small child who is already hurt and is taken away from her parents is likely to get upset even before anything more happens. You can hug and speak to her at the same time as keeping a firm grip. Try to realize that if your child cannot be calmed or needs something urgently, it is better to get it over with quickly rather than prolong the agony. Often, to make sure children keep still, they are wrapped in a blanket to hold their limbs still, but again, you can ask to be the one who holds your child.

- **Plaster of Paris.** This is usually applied under anesthesia when a fractured limb is fixed in position, but children can be frightened of the tiny saw used to take the plaster off when the fracture is healed. Try to distract your child while this is happening.

Staying or Visiting?

Staying with Your Child in the Hospital

Try imagining a stay or a visit the hospital through the eyes of a young child. Being left with people she does not know in unfamiliar surroundings is quite an experience for a child who may never have stayed at someone else's house or spent a day at school. Then add routine hospital procedures such as temperature taking—even this can be alarming to a child too young to understand what is happening. She needs Mom or Dad on hand to comfort, explain, and reassure. Fortunately, most hospitals do not have restrictions about parents staying or visiting. Often the parents are advised to stay with their child and participate in her care by feeding her, bathing her, etc. Sometimes parents are still excluded from wards or their child's room during doctors' rounds. If your child's visit to the hospital is planned, then ask your physician who makes the decision about hospital treatment at the time of the consultation.

If your child is admitted through an emergency room, then obviously there is no opportunity to select a hospital. If you want to stay with your child, tell the doctor who makes the decision to admit your child. In general it is best to make such requests to the most senior member of staff involved or through the admissions department. As with most requests, you will be more likely to succeed if you can be polite and reasonable while remaining confident and determined. This is not necessarily easy if you are feeling upset and anxious because your child has been injured or taken ill suddenly. But if you are in a very emotional state it may sometimes appear to the hospital staff that they will have two patients to deal with instead of one.

Most hospitals try to arrange beds for one parent who plans to stay overnight. Otherwise they may be happy for you to stay in a chair beside your child's bed. Some hospitals have space for parents but away from their child's ward or room—in other wards or rooms, in houses, and so on. This can be very valuable for the families of children who are staying in hospital for some time or who have traveled from far away. There are about 200 McDonald Houses across North America. Of these, 175 are in the United States. If you are far away from your home, and near a McDonald House, you may be able to have a room at a modest cost in one of these facilities, which provide a home away from home for a modest fee. In hospitals not renowned for their relaxed attitude, parents have met doctors and nurses who go out of their way to help.

Rarely, children may be admitted to adult wards or adult sections of the hospital. This is more likely if they are in an area where children's hospitals are not close or convenient. It is important that you check to be sure your child is allowed a time and a place to play, and that the hospital allows free access for parents. If this is not the case, remember that you can ask for your child to be moved to a children's hospital instead. Ask your physician to make the referral. Give the insurance or HMO information to his office so that your eligibility for such a move can be checked.

If You Cannot Stay with Your Child

Quite apart from the hospital's policy, there may be many reasons why you may find it hard to stay with your child in the hospital all the time. You may feel torn between the child in the hospital and the demands of other young children at home. Generally, your priority should be for the child in the hospital, at least for the first few days; children at home may miss you, but their life is continuing along reasonably familiar lines, and they are not having to cope with medical procedures or feeling ill. A child in the hospital has a great deal to cope with, and separation from you should be kept to a minimum. If you do not have a partner who can take time off to be with other children at home, would a relative or a friend help? The social worker at the hospital may be able to help with backup services or details of home helpers, family care workers, day nurseries, child minders, and after-school centers. If you really cannot stay or visit very much, ask a relative or a friend who knows your child well enough to take your place to spend time with your hospitalized child. Many hospitals can offer help with the cost of public transportation or might be able to arrange rides to the hospital if your child is to be hospitalized for a prolonged time—the hospital social worker should be able to assist you.

Visiting

Be honest about when you are next coming to see your child. You may dread to see her crying if you cannot come as soon as you would like, but it is far worse for her to wait all day and be disappointed and upset when you do not arrive when expected. If you are delayed or do not know exactly what time you will arrive, do not promise an exact time—for example, to be there before lunch, or by the time a certain TV program comes on. Tell the primary nurse when you are next coming so your child's questions can be answered, and if your plans change or you are delayed, then call and tell her. If you are going to be at work or out of touch, leave the number of a friend or a relative who would go to the hospital if your child is upset. Explain to your child that you have arranged for this person to be called until you can get there if she needs someone.

When it is time for you to leave after a visit, do not try to sneak out without your child's noticing, in an attempt to avoid her getting upset. She may then spend your whole next visit worrying that you are suddenly going to disappear. Tell one of the nurses when you have to go and, if necessary, hand the child over to her, saying when you will be back. It is better to have the nurse comfort and distract her than to leave a crying child alone in her bed.

You may be upset yourself if you get a mixed reaction when you visit—instead of seeming pleased to see a parent, children often burst into tears. This just shows that your child has probably been making an effort not to cry, and breaks down with relief upon seeing you. It is better for her to be able to show her feelings, so comfort and reassure her and try not to feel guilty or think that your visit is making things worse. It is also quite common for children to ignore their parents when they first arrive. This is their way of showing they are angry or hurt that you have been away. Even if you feel rejected, continue to be loving and come as often as you possibly can so she does not feel forgotten or abandoned.

Breast-fed Babies

It is not always easy to continue breast-feeding a baby who is hospitalized because of the lack of privacy and the difficulties that might be imposed by the child's illness, but you will be giving her the best sort of comfort as well as food if you can make arrangements to breast-feed. Mothers have even been able to feed small babies who are immobilized in traction because of fractures or bones that need to be corrected, by lying down on the bed beside them. You should enlist the help and support of the primary nurse, but even if you cannot pick up your baby, your physical presence will be very important to her.

If you have an older child in the hospital and are breast-feeding a baby it may be possible to bring the baby into the hospital as well. If that is not possible, try to arrange to bring a friend with you during the day so he or she can look after the baby in a waiting area while you give the sick child your attention. Alternatively, you could express your milk for your baby to be fed at home. Most hospitals that care for children have a special area where you can express your milk with a breast pump. You can store the milk in a refrigerator and take it home with you later.

Sometimes mothers of breast-fed babies have to go into the hospital themselves—do not stop feeding unless you plan to or are too sick to continue. Instead you can ask your hospital to arrange for your baby to come in with you, though individual arrangements within hospitals will vary regarding this. Again, breast pumps should be available so you can collect the milk and send it home to be used by your baby.

How Parents Can Help

- DO care for and entertain your child, freeing nurses for more skilled work.

- DO NOT let your child or your visiting children run unchecked all over the ward, room, or halls; expect nurses to exercise disciplinary control.

- DO continue to exercise authority and discipline over your child or visiting children.

- DO NOT give your child treats, food, and drinks when she is not allowed them and without checking with staff. Also, do not leave treats, food, and drinks on the side table for your child to help herself or to share with other children.

- DO check with the nursing staff whether it is all right to give anything to eat or drink, and keep foodstuffs, including treats, out of young children's reach.

- DO NOT put your own child, and any others on hand, into a state of anxiety by being emotionally out of control, talking loudly about medical disasters you have known, or showing panic at every medical procedure.

- DO stay calm, positive, and optimistic, and put this across to your child.

- DO NOT walk away from cribs and beds leaving the side down, which could allow your child to fall or roll onto the floor.

- DO find out about your child's condition and how best you can care for her. Also find out the routine rules of the ward or floor, such as mealtimes.

- DO NOT bring valuables to the ward or room. If you do, recognize that you are responsible for keeping an eye on them.

- DO understand that if your child cannot be pacified or if something needs to be done urgently, it is better to hold the child or let the nurses hold her and get whatever it is over as quickly as possible. Often the anticipation can be worse than the actual procedure for a child.

- DO NOT disappear from the ward or room without alerting the nurses that they need to look after your child or without telling them when you are planning to return.

- DO take care of your own needs so you are strong for your child and so the staff does not have to end up taking care of you.

- DO NOT ignore your child and spend all your time chatting with other parents.

How Much Can You Do for Your Child?

The principles of nursing care are changing very rapidly. In addition to carrying out nursing procedures themselves, nurses are often teaching and supervising parents to do things for their own children—for example, giving medicine. In training there is more emphasis on the psychological aspect of nursing in working with children. But obviously these are relatively new ideas and not everyone in the nursing profession agrees with them; when it comes to nursing care, you'll need to accept the practices of the institution.

However much you are able to do in practical terms for your child, there is an additional, powerful way in which you can help to minimize the stress of a hospital visit—and that is in your own attitude toward hospitals, illness, and medical staff. "Calmness" and "optimism" are the key words. Your positive attitude will help your child deal with her illness and treatment and be confident she will recover. Children are very sensitive to emotional messages. Of course, the more seriously ill a child is, the harder it is to be optimistic. Parents of children likely to be left disabled, seriously sick children, and those who are known to be dying need very special support and counseling. But all children unconsciously look to their parents to set the right tone, so help them by trying to make sure it is a positive one.

A Long Hospital Stay

The longer your child is in the hospital, the greater the strain it places on the family, and the harder it is for a parent to stay all the time. Ask friends and relatives to share with visiting. Many children who spend several weeks in the hospital are in casts or traction because of fractures. The child life specialist and, for older children, the hospital schoolteacher will both try to make sure your child is well stimulated, but they will not always be around. Amusing a young child who cannot move around is very difficult indeed. There have been cases of children in traction being cared for at home, so it is worth asking if this can be arranged, though you need to be sure you could cope with changing your home routine, getting a hospital bed, etc. You can usually entertain an older child (aged three to five) for at least some of the time by reading stories to her, watching television or videos, doing puzzles, and listening to story tapes. For all ages, mirrors fixed at different angles give different views to look at and vary the scene; and so does moving the child's bed around if possible. For young children, many parents are endlessly inventive, making intriguing things to hang around the bed. Mobiles that make noises, glitter, or can be touched can be made out of all sorts of materials.

Isolation

A child with a contagious illness may be isolated in an infectious diseases unit or a single-bed room so others will not get the disease. A child without much resistance to infection, perhaps because she is being treated with drugs that make the immune system less effective, may be protected by reverse isolation. In this case families have to wear gowns and masks. Items cannot be freely taken in or out.

Children in isolation need a parent to stay with them even more than those in an open ward because they are more likely to get lonely or bored. Staying with a child in isolation is also more stressful than life in an ordinary ward. It is unnatural for parent and child to spend such a lot of time alone together in confined circumstances, and both of you are likely to get irritable, so you need other relatives or friends to give you both a break. Because nurses need to be able to watch children, the room or cubicle will likely have windows at least along one side so there is no privacy, which is another strain. You need to come in armed to the hilt with books, amusements, diversions, and supplies for yourself and your child because you and she cannot just wander in and out. The best support for parents in this position tends to be other parents who understand. Many hospitals have a parents' room where you can go to have refreshments and let off steam.

Taking Care of Yourself

All through this chapter we have stressed the importance of staying with your child, whether during a relatively short procedure in an accident and emergency unit, or for a longer period if your child has to stay in the hospital for several weeks. But actually staying with a child in the hospital is emotionally draining, physically exhausting, and very demanding. Being marooned by a bedside and cut off from the outside world can be a disorienting experience. It is very important that you try to arrange for other people to visit so you can get a break, if possible to leave the hospital and go home for a while. This will help you to be more supportive to your child in the long run. Do not try to attempt the impossible and manage without sleep for so long that you end up being a liability yourself.

It may be difficult for you to leave your child for the first day or so while she is in the hospital, or during the period after an operation when she will need you by her most of all. This means being well prepared with supplies for yourself because the hospital cafeteria can be a long way away, and food and drinks brought to the room are intended for the patients, not their visitors. Some hospitals will provide meals at a minimal cost for the parents. Ask the primary nurse to make these arrangements. It is a good idea to bring some food and beverages for yourself, plus a good supply of undemanding reading material. Even if you are not planning to stay the night, a change of clothes is often a good idea in case you end up being there longer than you imagined, or if your child spills something over you or vomits. Lots of change for phone calls is also very useful.

Having a child in the hospital can be a big financial burden. If you think you might be entitled to any financial help, ask the social worker, who will advise you. Do not be afraid to do this—you will be able to give more attention to your child's feelings if you yourself are less worried about making ends meet, so you should claim any benefits to which you may be entitled. The hospital finance department or the social worker can be helpful. You should also ask to see a social worker if you feel it would be helpful to talk about family problems or your own feelings with someone other than family, friends, and nursing staff. Social workers are trained to help in these situations and may be able to provide counseling themselves or put you in touch with someone else who can do this. If your child has a long-standing problem they may also be able to put you in touch with an organization for parents of children with similar conditions.

Coming Home

However many friends you have made, however nice the physicians and nursing staff are, and however short your stay, you will still both be counting the hours until your child's release. Anyone who has ever been a patient herself or has stayed with a child knows just how disorienting being in the hospital, even for a short time, can become. The real world seems to retreat. Children need time to readjust, just as adults do, and at first may find ordinary life extra-tiring. Even if you stayed with your child in the hospital all the time it is very common to find that her behavior is different to begin with when she first comes home. She may be extra-clingy, wakeful at night, regress to more babyish habits, or just be generally unsettled. Just being able to be in your own home with so many more things to amuse your child, and able to get drinks and food for her when and as you like, seem like wonderful treats, so take life as it comes and enjoy it to the fullest.

Of course, some children will still need considerable nursing when they come out of the hospital. It is important that you understand just what you need to do, which may mean writing down times to give medicine and amounts to give. The good news is that even long hospital stays are unlikely to permanently affect children emotionally. The best you can do for your child is to be honest and explain things, stay as much as possible, and give her extra love and comfort.

Appendix: Resources

Following are the names, addresses, and phone numbers of some organizations that may provide additional information. Many have local branches or chapters; your phone book will list them. Most groups provide literature. E-mail addresses are shown where available.

American Academy of Pediatrics
141 Northwest Point Boulevard
Elk Grove Village, IL 60007-1098
847-228-5005
Fax: 847-228-5097

American Red Cross Association
8111 Gatehouse Road
Falls Church, VA 22042
703-206-6000
E-mail: internet@usa.redcross.org

Association for the Care of Children's
 Health
19 Mantua Road
Mount Royal, NJ 08061
609-224-1742
Fax: 609-423-3420
E-mail: amkent@smarthub.com

Auto Safety Hotline
888-DASH-2-DOT

Head Start Programs
Mailing address:
 ACYF/Head Start Bureau
 P.O. Box 1182
 Washington, DC 20013

Office location:
 Mary E. Switzer Building
 330 C Street, SW, Room 2050
 Washington, DC 20201

La Leche League International
1400 North Meacham Road
P.O. Box 4079
Schaumburg, IL 60168-4079
847-519-7730
1-800-LALECHE

March of Dimes
1275 Mamaroneck Avenue
White Plains, NY 10605
888-663-4637
E-mail: resourcecenter@modimes.org

National Association of Children's
 Hospitals and Related Institutions,
 Inc.
401 Wythe Street
Alexandria, VA 22314
703-684-1355
Fax: 703-684-1589

National Education Association
1201 16th Street, NW
Washington, DC 20036
202-833-4000

National Healthy Mothers/Healthy
Babies Coalition
121 North Washington Street,
Suite 300
Alexandria, VA 22314
703-836-6110
Fax: 703-836-3470

National Institute of Emergency Care
P.O. Box 11176
Philadelphia, PA 19136
215-624-4500

National Safe Kids Campaign
1301 Pennsylvania Avenue, NW,
Suite 1000
Washington, DC 20004-1707
202-662-0600
Fax: 202-393-2072
E-mail: info@safekids.org

The National Perinatal Association
3500 East Fletcher Avenue, Suite 209
Tampa, FL 33613-4712
813-971-1008
Fax: 813-971-9306
E-mail: npaonline@aol.com

Poison control center—see phone
book or call your local hospital.

Toys to Grow On
P.O. Box 17
Long Beach, CA 90801
1-800-542-8338; in Los Angeles,
310-603-8890
Fax: 310-537-5403

U.S. Consumer Products Safety
Commission (CPSC)
Office of Information and Public
Affairs
Washington, DC 20207
1-800-638-2772 (consumer product
safety hot line)

Special Conditions

If your child has special needs, you may receive help by calling the national
headquarters of the following organizations. E-mail addresses are shown where
available.

About Face U.S.A.
P.O. Box 93
Limekiln, PA 19535
1-800-225-FACE
Fax: 610-689-4479
E-mail: abtface@aol.com

American Academy of Allergy,
Asthma, and Immunology
Online Communications Department
611 East Wells Street
Milwaukee, WI 53202
414-272-6071

American Academy of Child and
   Adolescent Psychiatry
3615 Wisconsin Avenue, NW
Washington, DC 20016-3007
202-966-7300

American Brain Tumor Association
2720 River Road, Suite 146
Des Plaines, IL 60018-4110
847-827-9910
1-800-886-2282 (patient and family
   line)
E-mail: info@abta.org

American Cancer Society
1599 Clifton Road, NW
Atlanta, GA 30329
800-ACS-2345

American Cleft Palate–Craniofacial
   Association (ACPA) and Cleft
   Palate Foundation (CPF)
1829 East Franklin Street, Suite 1022
Chapel Hill, NC 27514
919-933-9044
Fax: 919-933-9604

American Diabetes Association
1660 Duke Street
Alexandria, VA 22314
1-800-DIABETES (diabetes information and action line)

American Psychiatric Association
Division of Public Affairs
1400 K Street, NW
Washington, DC 20005
202-682-6325
E-mail: mbennett@psych.org

American Psychological Association
750 First Avenue, NE
Washington, DC 20002-4242
202-336-5500
E-mail: atstrauma@aol.com

The American Society for Deaf
   Children (ASDC)
1820 Tribute Road, Suite A
Sacramento, CA 95815
916-641-6084
1-800-942-ASDC (parent hotline)

American Sudden Infant Death
   Syndrome (SIDS) Institute
6065 Roswell Road, Suite 876
Atlanta, GA 30328
404-843-1030
Fax: 404-843-0577
E-mail: prevent@sids.org

American Trauma Society
8903 Presidential Parkway, Suite 512
Upper Marlboro, MD 20772
301-420-4189
1-800-556-7890
E-mail: atstrauma@aol.com

Association for the Care of Children's
   Health
19 Mantua Road
Mount Royal, NJ 08061
609-224-1742
Internet: acch.org

Asthma and Allergy Foundation of
   America
1125 15th Street, NW
Washington, DC 20005
202-466-7643
1-800-7-ASTHMA

Attention-Deficit Disorders
   Association (ADDA)
P.O. Box 972
Mentor, OH 44061
216-350-9595
1-800-487-2282 (voice mail to request
   information packet)

The Candlelighters Childhood Cancer
   Foundation
7910 Woodmont Avenue, Suite 460
Bethesda, MD 20814-3015
301-657-8401
Toll-free information line:
   1-800-366-2223
Fax: 301-718-2686
E-mail: info@candlelighters.org

Children and Adults with Attention
   Deficit Disorders (CHADD)
499 Northwest 70th Avenue, Suite
   101
Plantation, FL 33317
954-587-3700

Cooley's Anemia Foundation, Inc.
129-09 26th Avenue, Suite 203
Flushing, NY 11354-1131
718-321-2873
800-522-7222
E-mail: ncaf@aol.com

Coordinating Council for
   Handicapped Children
220 South State Street, Room 412
Chicago, IL 60604
312-939-3513

Cystic Fibrosis Foundation
6931 Arlington Road
Bethesda, MD 20814
301-951-4422
800-FIGHT-CF
Fax: 301-951-6378
E-mail: info@ccf.org

Depression Awareness, Recognition,
   and Treatment (D/ART)
National Institute of Mental Health
5600 Fishers Lane, Room 10C-03
Rockville, MD 20857
800-421-4211

Epilepsy Foundation
4351 Garden City Drive
Landover, MD 20785-2267
1-800-EFA-1000; 301-459-3700
Fax: 301-577-2684

Federal Emergency Management
   Agency (FEMA)
500 C Street, SW
Washington, DC 20472
202-566-1600

Federation of Families for Children's
   Mental Health
1021 Prince Street
Alexandria, VA 22314-2971
703-684-7710
Fax: 703-836-1040

Help-Line Crisis Center
3 West 29th Street
New York, NY 10001
212-532-2400

Institute for Family-Centered Care
7900 Wisconsin Avenue, Suite 405
Bethesda, MD 20814
301-652-0281
Fax: 301-652-0186
E-mail: IFCC@aol.com

Kids' Camps
5455 North Federal Highway, Suite O
Boca Raton, FL 33487
561-989-9330, extension 2
Fax: 561-989-9331

Learning Disabilities Association
(LDA)
(formerly the Association for
Children and Adults with Learning
Disabilities)
4156 Library Road
Pittsburgh, PA 15234-1349
412-341-1515
E-mail: ldanatl@usaor.net

Leukemia Society of America
600 Third Avenue
New York, NY 10016
212-573-8484
800-955-4LSA (information resource
center)

Make-A-Wish Foundation of America
100 West Clarendon, Suite 2200
Phoenix, AZ 85013
1-800-722-9474

Muscular Dystrophy Association
3300 East Sunrise Drive
Tucson, AZ 85718
800-572-1717
mda@mdausa.org

National Association for Down
Syndrome
P.O. Box 4542
Oak Brook, IL 60522-4542
630-325-9112

National Association for Sickle Cell
Disease, Inc.
3345 Wilshire Boulevard
Los Angeles, CA 90010-1880
1-800-421-8453
Fax: 213-736-5211

National Brain Tumor Foundation
785 Market Street, Suite 1600
San Francisco, CA 94103
415-284-0208
1-800-934-CURE
Fax: (415) 284-0209

National Cancer Institute
Building 31, Room 10A24
9000 Rockville Pike
Bethesda, MD 20892
1-800-4-CANCER (for specific inquiries about cancer or NCI programs)
301-402-5874 to call the CancerFax
computer

National Center for Learning
Disabilities (NCLD)
(formerly the Foundation for Children
with Learning Disabilities)
381 Park Avenue, Suite 1401
New York, NY 10016
212-545-7510
1-888-575-7373 (toll-free information
and referral number)

National Depressive and Manic-
Depressive Association (NDMDA)
730 North Franklin Street, Suite 501
Chicago, IL 60654
312-642-0049
1-800-826-3632

National Down Syndrome Society
666 Broadway
New York, NY 10012-2317
1-800-221-4602
212-460-9330
E-mail: mmadnick@ndss.org

The National Federation of the Blind
1800 Johnson Street
Baltimore, MD 21230
410-659-9314

National Heart, Lung, and Blood
Institute
NHLBI Information Center
Attention: web site
P.O. Box 30105
Bethesda, MD 20824-0105
301-496-4000
Fax: 301-251-1223

National Hemophilia Foundation
116 West 32nd Street, 11th Floor
New York, NY 10001
212-328-3700
Fax: 212-328-3777
Email: info@hemophilia.org

National Institute of Allergy and
Infectious Diseases
NIAID Office of Communications
31 Center Drive, MSC 2520
Bethesda, MD 20892-2520
301-496-4000

National Kidney Foundation
30 East 33rd Street
New York, NY 10016
1-800-622-9010

National Marrow Donor Program
3433 Broadway Street, NE, Suite 400
Minneapolis, MN 55413
1-800-MARROW-2 (1-800-627-7692)

Orton Dyslexia Society
8600 LaSalle Road
Chester Building, Suite 382
Baltimore, MD 21286-2044
Phone: 1-800-ABCD-123
Fax: 410-296-0232

Ronald McDonald Houses
Golin/Harris Communications, Inc.
111 East Wacker Drive
Chicago, IL 60601
312-729-4000

Sickle Cell Disease Association of
America, Inc.
200 Corporate Point, #495
Culver City, CA 90230-7633
1-800-421-8453 or 310-216-6363

Spina Bifida Association of America
4590 MacArthur Boulevard, NW,
Suite 250
Washington, DC 20007
1-800-621-3141 or 202-944-3285
Fax: 202-944-3295
E-mail: spinabifda@aol.com

Index